T0180289

Lecture Notes in Computer Science 593

Edited by G. Goos and J. Hartmanis

Advisory Board: W. Brauer   D. Gries   J. Stoer

P. Loucopoulos (Ed.)

Advanced Information Systems Engineering

4th International Conference CAiSE '92
Manchester, UK, May 12-15, 1992
Proceedings

Springer-Verlag

Berlin Heidelberg New York
London Paris Tokyo
Hong Kong Barcelona
Budapest

Series Editors

Gerhard Goos
Universität Karlsruhe
Postfach 69 80
Vincenz-Priessnitz-Straße 1
W-7500 Karlsruhe, FRG

Juris Hartmanis
Department of Computer Science
Cornell University
5148 Upson Hall
Ithaca, NY 14853, USA

Volume Editor

Pericles Loucopoulos
Univ. of Manchester, Inst. of Science and Technology, Dept. of Computation
P. O. Box 88, Sackville Street, Manchester, M6O IQD, UK

CR Subject Classification (1991): D.2.1-2, D.2.10, H.2

ISBN 3-540-55481-5 Springer-Verlag Berlin Heidelberg New York
ISBN 0-387-55481-5 Springer-Verlag New York Berlin Heidelberg

Typesetting: Camera ready by author
Printing and binding: Druckhaus Beltz, Hemsbach/Bergstr.
45/3140-543210 - Printed on acid-free paper

Preface

The CAiSE•92 Conference at UMIST in Manchester, is the fourth in a series of Conferences on Advanced Information Systems Engineering.

The growing demand for information systems of ever-increasing size, scope, and complexity has highlighted the benefits that may be accrued from approaches which recognise the interrelationships between different technological strands in the field of information systems. Typical examples of these areas include: system development methods, CASE, requirements engineering, database design, re-use. The CAiSE series of conferences provides the forum for the exchange of results and ideas within these different technological spheres from a single perspective namely, that of information systems development and management. This year's conference is no exception in continuing with this tradition.

The call for papers for CAiSE•92 was given a wide international distribution. I would like to express my gratitude to all the members of the Programme Committee and regional coordinators for their help in this matter and to the following scientific journals for their support in providing publicity space: Communications of the ACM (ACM), Information Systems (Pergamon Press), Journal of Information Systems (Blackwell Scientific Publications), SIGMOD (ACM), SIGSOFT (ACM), Data and Knowledge Engineering (North-Holland). There were over 85 papers submitted from 22 countries.

The accepted papers, assembled in this volume, represent authors from 16 countries and cover a wide range of topics within the context of this conference. These topics include: object-oriented analysis and design methods, development process and product support, requirements engineering, reuse, design approaches, and deductive approaches. I would like to acknowledge the efforts of the authors in making an excellent scientific contribution to the field and of the Programme Committee members and additional referees who carried out the reviewing process in a most thorough manner under a very tight schedule.

The CAiSE•92 programme would not have been possible without the assistance of many people. I am particularly indebted to Janet Houshmand for dealing with so many diverse administrative matters and to Babis Theodoulidis for his help in all publicity aspects and his help in the organisation of the progamme.

March 1992

Pericles Loucopoulos
Programme Chair

CAiSE·92 Conference Organisation

General Chair

Dennis Tsichritzis
University of Geneva, Geneva, Switzerland

Organising Chair

Keith Jeffery
Rutherford Appleton Laboratory, Oxford, UK

Programme Chair

Pericles Loucopoulos
UMIST, Manchester, UK

Programme Committee

Ahlsen Matts, SISU, Sweden
Andersen Rudolf, NTH, Trondheim, Norway
Avison David, University of Aston, UK
Baldock Robert, Andersen Consulting, UK
Barker Richard, ORACLE, UK
Bouzeghoub Mokrane, Infosys, France
Bubenko Janis, SISU, Sweden
Calow Hilary, FI Group, UK
Ceri Stefano, Politecnico di Milano, Italy
Dadam Peter, University of Ulm, Germany
Dittrich Claus, University of Zurich, CH
Falkenberg Eckhard, University of Nijmegen, Holland
Fiadeiro Jose, INESC, Portugal
Fickas Steven, University of Oregon, USA
Finkelstein Antony, Imperial College, London, UK
Flory Andre, University of Jean-Moulin, Lyon, France
Folkmanis Janis, European Commission
Furtado Antonio, IBM, Brazil
Gardarin George, INRIA, France
Gray Alec, University of Wales, UK
Habrias Henri, University of Nantes, France
Holden Tony, University of Cambridge, UK
Jarke Mathias, University of Passau, Germany
Kambayashi Yahiko, University of Kyushu, Japan
Kangassalo Hannu, University of Tampere, Finland
Layzell Paul, UMIST, UK
Lindencrona Eva, Swedish Telecom, Sweden
Lochovsky Fred, University of Toronto, Canada

Lockeman Peter, University of Karlsruhe, Germany
Looney Michael, ARE Portsdown, UK
Lundberg Bengt, University of Stockholm, Sweden
Mannino Michael, University of Texas, USA
Mylopoulos John, University of Toronto, Canada
Nilsson Bjorn, SISU, Sweden
Okkonen Ari, VTT/TKO, Finland
Olivé Antoni, University Polyt. Catalunya, Spain
Parkinson John, Arthur Young International, UK
Pernici Barbara, University of Udine, Italy
Pirotte Alain, Philips Research Lab, Belgium
Rolland Colette, University of Paris I, France
Ryan Kevin, University of Limerick, Ireland
Sernadas Amilcar, INESC, Portugal
Sølvberg Arne, NTH Trondheim, Norway
Spaccapietra Stefano, Polyt. of Lausanne, CH
Steinholtz Bo, University of Stockholm, Sweden
Stocker Peter, University of East Anglia, UK
Sutcliffe Alistair, City University, UK
Thanos Constantino, IEI-CNR, Italy
Theodoulidis Babis, UMIST, UK
van Assche Frans, JMA, Belgium
van de Riet, Vrije Universiteit Amsterdam, Holland
van Rijsbergen Keith, University of Glasgow, UK
Vassiliou Yannis, FORTH, Crete, Greece
Vasey Phil, LPA, UK
Wangler Benkt, SISU, Sweden
Zicari Roberto, Politechnico di Milano, Italy

Additional Referees

Anderson, J.	Durney, B.	Métais, E.	Pulli, P.
Aver, A.	Helm, B.R.	Meunier, J.-N.	Reid, I.
Badarinath, N.	Hofstede, A.H.	Moreno, M.	Robinson, W.N.
Berild, S.	Irving, R.W.	Nagui-Raiss, N.	Rosengren, P.
Brajnik, G.	Johannesson, P.	Nellborn, C.	Schmitt, J.-R.
Brinkkemper, S.	Katsouli, E.	Norrie, M.C.	Souveyet, C.
Brunet, J.	Koistinen, J.	Oei, J.L.H.	Tari, Z.
Cauvet, C.	Kosher, C.H.A.	Oelmann, A.	Thomas, P.
Colignon, P.	Leon, R.	Ohlund, S.-E.	Walker, A.
Crestani, F.	Levassuer, P.	Papastamatiou, G.	Welland, R.C.
Dittrich, A. K.	Levreau, G.	Petrounias, I.	Wohed, R.
Dupont, Y.			Yang, J.J.

Regional Coordinators

Rudolf Andersen, Norway
Rogerio Carapuca, Portugal
J. Fong, Hong Kong
Jane B Grimson, Ireland
Martin Kersten, Netherlands
Ke-Chang Lee, Taiwan
Michel Léonard, Switzerland
Bengt Lundberg, Sweden
Shojiro Nishio, Japan

Maria Orlowska, Australia
Alain Pirotte, Belgium
Shixuan, Sa, China
Felix Saltor, Spain
Gunter Schlageter, Germany
Chee Kiow Tan, Singapore
Constantino Thanos, Italy
Luiz Tucherman, Brazil
Yannis Vassiliou, Greece

Conference Supporters

COMMISSION OF THE EUROPEAN COMMUNITIES

computing

UMIST

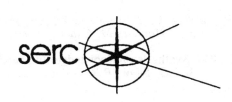

serc

Table of Contents

Requirements Engineering - I

Reuse

Requirements Engineering - II

Design Approaches

Requirements Engineering - III

CASE-I

CASE- II

Deductive Approach

How Objective is Object-Oriented Analysis?

Simon McGinnes

School of Information Systems, Queensland University of Technology
PO Box 2434, Brisbane QLD 4001, Australia
email: mcginnes @snow.fit.qut.edu.au

Abstract. There are many techniques for information systems analysis. Some techniques are complementary to one another, while others address similar issues in different ways; typically, methods concentrate on a subset of the total systems development process, or embody a particular way of viewing information systems. Recently, a number of object-oriented analysis techniques have been published; this paper briefly considers where these techniques fit in the overall spectrum of methods, and asks to what extent they can be judged to be 'complete' analysis methods in the context of business information systems development. A simple set of requirements for useful information systems analysis methodologies is outlined and is used as a framework for discussion of object-oriented analysis methods generally. Finally, some suggestions are made for further work to help evaluate and improve the effectiveness of object-oriented analysis methods for business information systems analysis.

1 Introduction

A recent survey of information systems analysis approaches [26] highlighted the wide diversity of both information systems methodologies and comparative frameworks for the evaluation of methodologies. There are many conflicting views on what constitutes an acceptable approach to systems analysis. In this paper, some very high-level but important requirements are given in an attempt to establish what makes analysis methods useful. These requirements are based on the needs of the main participants in the systems development process.

The structure of the paper is as follows: first, we briefly review current thinking on information systems analysis; in section 2 a number of requirements for analysis methods are outlined; in section 3 object-oriented analysis methods are reviewed in the light of the requirements; in section 4 some observations of a general nature are made about the methods reviewed; and in section 5 a summary of the main points is given.

1.1 Limited Views of Systems Analysis

To a large extent, thinking by information systems professionals about analysis methods has been rather compartmentalised. Practicing analysts tend to stick to the small number of techniques they know best [22]. This is one reason why

CASE tools have not been taken up as rapidly as predicted, since moving to a CASE tool often means adopting new techniques. In view of the high stakes involved in business software development, and of the risks inherent in adopting new and possibly unproven techniques, this conservatism is not surprising.

A compartmentalised view is also evident in the research efforts devoted to information systems analysis. Typically, research can be classified under one of a number of headings: *formal methods* (e.g. [4]), *strategic information planning* (e.g. [3]), *human factors* (e.g. [6]) and so on. Someone with a business analysis bias is likely to view the process of systems analysis rather differently from someone with a software engineering background, and both will disagree with the view put forward by a formal methods specialist. There is nothing inherently wrong in having such a multiplicity of views; the huge range of computer applications today means that no one technique can possibly be the best under all circumstances. What is undesirable is for practitioners and researchers to be unaware of alternative viewpoints put forward in disciplines related to their own. For an interesting discussion of these issues, see [36].

1.2 Methodology as Reaction

Of the wide range of information systems methodologies available, many can be seen as reactions against perceived situations. For instance, structured analysis and design [44] can be seen as a reaction against a perceived lack of formality in systems development. Formal methods go even further in the same direction. Socio-technical approaches [32] can be seen as a reaction against the failure of systems designers to take into account the impact of information systems on people. Systems approaches [41] can be seen as a reaction against systems developers' inability to question their own assumptions about solving problems. Prototyping (and variations) [27] can be seen as a reaction against the institutionalised delays created by the 'traditional' life cycle approach and against the inability of users to deal with requirements when expressed in abstract ways. JAD [43] can be seen as a reaction to the common 'paralysis by analysis' syndrome and to the political manoeuvering which often bogs down systems development projects.

1.3 Effect of Narrow View

In fact, it seems that the authors of almost every methodology all have at least one axe to grind. Methodologies which concentrate in this way on a limited view of the systems development problem run the risk of failing to address important issues. Of course, this does not mean that systems developments using these methods will necessarily fail, although a large number of systems developments do [12]. One reason is that an experienced analyst will tend to take into account everything which seems relevant when formulating requirements, regardless of what methodology is in use [39].

Perhaps, then, it is useful to view a methodology, not as a prescription for effective analysis, design and so on, but as a way of representing and justifying a mental view of the requirements which the analyst has already assembled. That is, the methodology is used for post hoc *rationalisation* (for example, see [31]).

From my own experience of using and teaching analysis techniques such as data modelling, this view seems valid: novice data modellers often produce poor results, not because they fail to grasp the technique's rules, but because they do not have a view of the end result in their minds' eye before they start!

1.4 Systems Analysis as an Intuitive Process

This paper is not the place for a thorough discussion of the mental processes involved in systems analysis. Suffice to say that thinking by successful analysts may be more intuitive (i.e. right-brain) and less consciously analytical (i.e. left-brain) than previously thought. Therefore, an important question we should ask about each methodology is: how useful is it for documenting an intuitively-created model? If an analyst has built up a rather holistic mental model of a particular problem situation, it would be desirable to have a reasonably neutral, or objective, medium in which to express this view. Natural language is one such medium, which has been used extensively for the expression of specifications in the past. Unfortunately, natural language is perfectly capable of representing poorly structured or unstructured specifications as well as structured ones. Instead, we need techniques which allow structure to be built into a specification, but which do not impose any particular structure. That is, we need *objective* methods.

Objectivity is not the only desirable attribute of analysis methods. In the following section, several additional requirements are identified.

2 What Should an Analysis Technique Be?

Many frameworks for the evaluation and comparison of information systems methodologies have been published. Each emphasises particular aspects of the systems development process. Examples include [9], [15], [16], [17], [19], [24], [25], [30], [34] and [38], ranging from simple comparisons of methodologies to comprehensive checklists which are so all-encompassing as to approach methodology specifications themselves. In this paper, I present only a very simple and high-level view of the requirements for useful analysis methods, in an attempt to keep the discussion clear. My approach is based on the needs of the key participants: the clients and the developers.

2.1 Clients' Needs

Multiple Views of Problem Situation. Typically, requirements for information systems are gathered through consultation with a number of clients (or users). Each client is likely to hold a slightly different view of the problem situation and of its potential solutions. It is up to the analyst to use suitable techniques to elicit the different clients' views of the situation. Since there is often insufficient time or money to model each individual's own view of the world separately, a compromise view may be developed (for instance, a corporate data model). Despite this, the analysis technique must be able to capture at least the most important variations between the different user groups, otherwise the compromise may satisfy nobody at all.

For example, it is common for different sets of users in the same organisation to view specific parts of the corporate data model in different ways. One set might have a simpler view of the data than another. The database structure must accommodate the more complex of the two views in order to avoid losing information. But the users with the simpler conception of the data can still be helped, if they are given ways of accessing the data which hide complexity (such as SQL views). This can only be done if the two views of the data structure have been described independently during analysis.

Easily Understood Method. Because this compromise model must be seen and used by a variety of people, with differing levels of knowledge and differing requirements, it must be expressed in a way which is easily understood without the need for extensive explanation. Ideally, the technique will allow the clients to participate fully in the production of the models. This means making the technique as simple as possible: perhaps simpler than many systems developers would like.

Often, graphical techniques are offered in an attempt to satisfy these needs, and there is evidence that they can help a great deal [1]. However, the mere fact that a technique involves the drawing of diagrams is no guarantee that it is any more understandable or practical.

Relating Views at Different Levels. For similar reasons, it must be possible to represent chosen key aspects of the model in a way which avoids confusion, which means that the technique must support *abstraction* or *information hiding*. It must be possible to gather high-level requirements as well as low-level ones, and where low-level requirements refine higher-level ones, the connection should be clear.

For example, the higher levels of management often have a wide-ranging but simplified view of the operations in their organisation. Their view can be very useful in helping to define a global architecture for the organisation's information systems. The high-level model can then be refined by through consultation with people who have a more detailed view of specific areas. Relating these high- and low-level views is an important advantage of abstraction.

Since there are many ways of achieving these aims, we say only that a methodology must provide useful abstraction mechanisms, and that these mechanisms must apply to every type of model, whether it be data, process or behaviour (or anything else). This does not preclude the use of object classes in analysis, but says something about how they can be used to provide abstract views of the model.

Richness. The technique must be powerful and rich enough that it can represent a reasonable amount of information in a succinct manner. The requirements for an *easily understood method* and for *richness*, are in some ways contradictory, although they are not necessarily mutually exclusive. The temptation is to load the techniques with as many information-holding features as possible. But adding more information into a diagram can overload a user. This is another reason for having an abstraction mechanism: diagrams can be made simple by hiding certain information. In other words, only certain facts need be captured initially, details being filled in later. This is one reason why techniques which support a single level of abstraction are at a considerable disadvantage to those which allow many levels.

The kinds of information a client is interested in having recorded could differ from the information the systems developer is interested in recording. The analyst may focus directly on the information required to construct a database and programs, without explicitly considering other important issues such as politics, ergonomics, job design and so on (see 'technical content', below). There is much debate about what issues should be addressed by information systems methodologies (refer to the frameworks mentioned earlier). While that debate is important, this paper avoids discussion of particular content issues by attempting to identify more general principles of methodology use.

Recognisable Terminology. Finally, it is imperative that any model produced during analysis is firmly rooted in the clients' own terminology. The mark of an ineffective analyst is the sight of clients translating words used in a model into their own terminology. This failure of communication may sometimes be so subtle as to go unrecognised, with both parties believing they are speaking the others' language. The model must express concepts familiar to the clients, in their own terms.

2.2 Developers' Needs

The information systems professionals concerned with producing and maintaining automated information systems have needs which are distinct from those of their clients and which are, in some ways, at odds with them.

Technical Content. In view of their primary product, computerised information systems, developers require detailed and accurate specification of data and processes (whether expressed separately, as in conventional database-program architectures, or combined, as in the object-oriented approach). In general, the more formal the representation of this information, the better, since any ambiguity needs to be resolved before the information can be used to design workable systems. In an ideal world, developers would be presented with a complete statement of requirements before they embark on each development. This is rarely the case in practice, and developments where the requirements do not undergo substantial modification are even rarer.

Objectivity. If we accept the view of an analysis technique as rationalisation (discussed in the introduction), then we must ask how well each method is suited to documenting, without inherent bias, an intuitively arrived-at model. Another way of asking the same question is to see how free the technique is of implementation-specific constructs.

For example, the use of algorithms to specify processes is heavily implementation-specific, since it determines not only the effect of the processes, but also their implementations. Using pre- and post-conditions is one way of avoiding this bias.

Minimal Solution. From a practical point of view, the fewer techniques the client, analyst and designer have to learn and use the better. This is especially the case where analysis proceeds from an initial identification of requirements through to a detailed requirements statement. If it is possible to use a single technique for expression of the requirements at all stages, several benefits accrue: (a) work is saved because using more than one technique would almost inevitably lead to a degree of overlap; (b) it is easier to see the relationship between initially expressed requirements and detailed requirements.

Being able to relate high-level requirements to detailed ones can be crucial. For instance, a software house developing software on behalf of a client has to be very aware of any requirements which were not originally contracted for, and the client will be careful to ensure that all requirements originally contracted for have been addressed. Therefore, methodologies should offer, at least, excellent integration between the tools used at different stages.

Self-Checking Method. The advent of widespread use of CASE tools has led to an improvement in the internal consistency of analysis models. The laborious cross-checking required in paper-based methods was often simply not done. CASE tools can now automate much of this task. Methods should take advantage of this capability to produce better quality models.

For example, a common form of checking now performed routinely by CASE tools which support E-R and DFDs is to determine whether each data entity is used in at least one process, and whether each data entity has a complete life cycle (birth, life, death). Manually carrying out these checks in large systems can be very tedious.

2.3 Summary of Requirements

Table 1 summarises the requirements identified in section 2.

Clients' Needs	Developers' Needs
Multiple views of problem situation	Technical content
Easily understood method	Objectivity
Relating views at different levels	Minimal solution
Richness	Self-checking method
Recognisable terminology	

Table 1   Requirements for analysis methods

3   Object-Oriented Analysis Techniques

Several books have been published recently, detailing comprehensive approaches to object-oriented systems analysis (and, in some cases, to design and implementation). It is not the purpose of this paper to describe those methods in any detail. Instead, the methods reviewed are briefly mentioned below and then observations are made, based on the set of requirements identified in the previous section.

3.1 Methods

Coad and Yourdon [7] present a method which is firmly based in data modelling and which includes a technique similar to program flowcharts as a process modelling tool. Odell and Martin's method [29] uses event and activity schemata, to model behavioural and procedural aspects, together with a data modelling technique. Shlaer and Mellor [35] offer a method primarily based in entity-relationship modelling, but which also suggests the use of state transition and data flow diagrams. Weiss and Page-Jones' [40] method is an attempt to combine object-orientation with the best features of structured analysis. Rumbaugh et al's [33] method is a comprehensive approach which covers analysis, design and implementation in a well-integrated way. The approach by Wirfs-Brock et al [42] is remarkable in that it uses novel concepts, in particular focusing on the responsibilities of objects rather than simply examining their behaviour.

Other approaches are too numerous to describe, but include those of Jacobson [21], Bailin [2], Henderson-Sellers and Edwards [20], Kurtz et al [23], Colbert [8] and Gibson [18].

3.2 Discussion of Methods

When the object-oriented techniques discussed above are viewed in the light of the simple set of requirements for analysis techniques presented in the previous section, a number of general observations can be made. The points below are given in the same order as those in section 2. As before, we start with the clients' needs.

Multiple Views of Problem Situation. Few, if any, of the methods provide explicit support for modelling several views of the same situation. (It would, of course, be possible to build support for multiple views into most of the methods). Like structured analysis, object-oriented analysis tends to assume that things in the world have objective existence, and doesn't concern itself too much with the fact that different users may prefer to see things in different ways.

Easily Understood Method. Are the techniques useful when it comes to communication between analyst and client? The argument on this is likely to continue for some time, and the only real proof will be experience. At this stage, it appears that most of the diagrammatic techniques proposed in the major methods work reasonably well, provided that some licence is allowed in their use, especially in the representation of simplified or abstracted views of the models. Those techniques which do not use diagrams, such as several of the formal methods, are probably at a disadvantage in this respect.

For instance, Figure 1 shows three different means of specifying models. It is clear that some would require more explanation than others.

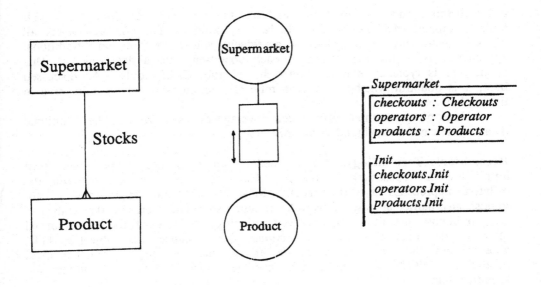

Fig. 1 Models (a) E-R (b) NIAM (c) Object-Z

Relating Views at Different Levels. Few of the methods offer much in the way of a 'big picture' view of a system. Those object-oriented analysis methods which offer a top-down approach to processes generally do it through data flow diagrams or similar constructs. Whether this is the best way is the subject of some debate [13]. Top-down functional decomposition, used with care, can be a useful tool for expressing, at a high level and in terms familiar to the clients, the business functions which a system will implement. This does not mean that a system need be viewed entirely as if it consisted of a single top function, split into lower-level functions and so on: it means simply that the concept of top-down decomposition can be a useful abstraction mechanism and ought to be available so that it can be used when appropriate. In fact, imposing a *rigid* top-down view of functions is often difficult and unnatural, so it is wise to make the use of this capability optional.

It seems that alternative ways of expressing operations at high and low levels are needed. Wirfs-Brock et al take a promising approach, using *contracts* and *subsystems* to group operations and objects. Presumably, these concepts could be extended to allow further levels of abstraction as required in larger systems. Aggregation also shows promise as a possible abstraction mechanism for object modelling.

Richness. Most of the techniques offer diagrammatic notations which are of a similar level of richness to (and in many cases are very similar to) commonly-used existing methods, such as E-R and data flow diagrams. The information captured when using object-oriented analysis is practically the same as when using methods such as structured analysis: the repository structure for CASE tools to support each approach would be very similar. The one area where all of the object-oriented methods are in agreement, and differ from more traditional approaches, is in the association of each operation with a data object. This connection is typically not maintained by existing CASE tools. As discussed later, it is doubtful whether it always reflects a relationship which holds true in the application domain.

None of the methods offer much coverage of issues beyond the traditional data, process and behavioural perspectives.

Recognisable Terminology. Do the methods allow the use of the clients' own terminology in constructing models? There is some variation between the different approaches in this respect. Most of the major approaches do not impose any particular way of wording requirements, and therefore the analyst is free to choose the most appropriate terminology. Some of the more formal methods do impose certain restrictions: for instance, in Object-Z [14], abbreviations and short names are *de rigueur* and the use of a mathematical notation is likely to reduce the average client's ability to understand specifications.

Having discussed the clients' needs, we now consider those of the developers.

Technical Content. As observed above ('Richness'), object-oriented analysis methods do not differ markedly from structured analysis in their technical content.

Objectivity. The object-oriented approach is often described as 'natural' and 'intuitive', because it attempts to represent the application domain more closely than conventional ways of structuring information systems. This sounds ideal, but glosses over the fact that the object-oriented 'model' is simply another way of abstracting from reality. In fact, it is a rather implementation-specific way of modelling, since it assumes particular constructs (object classes, operations, messages and so on) which are stronger than those in other common modelling approaches.

For example, no-one seriously believes that the entity types depicted on ER diagrams necessarily exist in reality. Entities, like words, are simply a convenient way of capturing meaning. In contrast, objects in an object-oriented model are often equated with objects in the world.

Objects in an information system are distinct from objects in the real world, and can never be more than a representation or model of the real thing. If we make no distinction between analysis and design, as is proposed in a number of the methods, and instead view the process as one of progressive refinement, then we are stuck with the idea that the objects in the system are equivalent to those in the world. In fact this is not the case: it is often necessary to 'bend' reality to fit the object model.

For instance, the initial identification of object classes is often tricky. Is a *purchase* a class, an operation or an event? In the real world it is all of these things. Similarly, the choice of 'owner' for each operation may be difficult - some operations are not naturally the responsibility of any single object.

This lack of a conceptual model - the failure to distinguish between system objects and real world objects - is very much in evidence in the object-oriented literature.

Minimal Solution. Most of the object-oriented analysis techniques presume that analysis is preceded by a requirements definition activity, the output of which is usually assumed to be a narrative requirements specification. This activity is similar to the well-known idea of *business analysis*. Some authors, such as de Champeaux [13], refer to this process as 'domain analysis'.

However, the trend in recent years has been away from narrative specifications and towards more structured ways of representing requirements. It is generally agreed that this is desirable (for an example, see [22]). It is not immediately clear why a reversal of this trend is being proposed, unless, perhaps, the new techniques are seen as unsuited to high-level requirements analysis.

Self-Checking Methods. One of the chief distinguishing features of the object-oriented approach is that the process and data models are closely combined, in contrast with the separate models used in other approaches (such as structured analysis). However, the availability of appropriate CASE technology makes this distinction far less meaningful: CASE tools can now routinely be used to integrate the three perspectives at a very detailed level, so that there is essentially little difference between the 'integrated' (object-oriented) and the 'unintegrated' (non-object-oriented) approaches in this respect.

4 Discussion

In evaluating the object-oriented analysis methods against the set of requirements outlined in section 2, several issues of a more general nature raised themselves. These are discussed below.

Prototyping Approach. The systems development life cycle proposed for most of the methods is less rigid than the traditional 'waterfall' model. The consensus on the most appropriate life cycle for object-oriented development appears to be that either a weak life cycle, or no life cycle at all, should be used. Instead, a form of prototyping is recommended [27].

What distinguishes this approach from more conventional prototyping methods is that, in the object-oriented approach, both data and processes are developed concurrently, whereas in conventionally organised systems it is typically only the processes which are prototyped, the data structures being arrived at through some initial modelling process. It seems likely that the sort of risks inherent in allowing a database structure to be prototyped would also be present in the object-oriented equivalent: consider the great importance attached to data modelling and to the activities of data administrators and database administrators in most large organisations. This is not to say that the 'gestalt round-trip design' approach [5] is infeasible, but rather that we already know just how hard, and how risky, it is on large projects.

What Does Reuse Mean in Analysis? In the context of systems analysis, reuse means picking suitable existing classes in order to construct models. Reuse of existing models is widely cited as a possible means of reducing the effort required in analysis and design. Generally, abstraction is seen as the primary mechanism to enable reuse: if we make our classes abstract enough, they are sufficiently general to be reusable in other situations. However, as Sutcliffe [37] demonstrates, inappropriate use of abstraction can limit the potential for reuse, not increase it.

An organisation of any reasonable size may have hundreds of classes, if existing corporate data models are anything to go by. In this situation, it will be hard to know if an existing class is what is required, without looking in detail at its specification (for instance, what the effect of its operations are) and then comparing them to a well-researched requirement. In other words, you have to do some analysis *anyway*: matching the requirements to existing classes is then an additional task.

For instance, the meaning of the class *customer* in the context of a stock control application may be very different from the meaning of the class *customer* in the same organisation's credit checking system. Since it is impractical to analyse an entire organisation in one go, classes are only ever valid for the systems analysed so far.

The assumption made in the literature seems to be largely that the problem of selecting existing classes for reuse is simply one of finding an appropriate technological solution (such as class browsers, and so on). This misses the point that a detailed knowledge of the required class is necessary before a suitable existing class can be selected. The idea that there is only one way of seeing the application domain, and that it follows that any class which has already been 'discovered' will be as is required for new applications, is far too simplistic.

For these reasons, it is likely that the benefits of reuse in analysis will only be apparent in the 'core' classes of an organisation (i.e. the ones that are likely to occur repetitively). For the rest, it may well be quicker to define the classes from scratch.

Analysis or Design? If there is a general criticism in the area of terminology, it is that most of the methods require a certain 'recasting' of reality before they can represent it effectively. This really means that an element of design is allowed to creep in to what ought to be purely analysis. For example, in most of the methods, the principle of encapsulation ensures that every class contains the operations which apply to it. However, in some of the methods, the reverse is also true: every operation must be attributed to a given object class. While the first rule is useful from the point of view of analysis, the second can be very awkward: it is not difficult to think of business functions in which several 'objects' participate but which no one object owns. Some methods suggest constructing a pseudo-class to own this operation, simply so that the model does not break the rules. Others suggest breaking the operation down into smaller operations which can then be distributed amongst the existing classes. Both alternatives require some tailoring of reality to fit the model.

A second example concerns the modelling of continuous processes. In most methods, the representation of constantly-evolving processes needs to be reduced to a succession of events, each one associated with a state change for one or more objects (sometimes referred to as ticks of an imaginary clock). While this captures the effect of the process, it is a nevertheless a distinctly artificial construction required only because the method contains no better alternative.

An analysis method which is not implementation-neutral forces the analyst to alter the world to fit the model, rather than vice-versa. The need for this mental conversion process reduces the value of the analysis model as a representation of reality. It means that, to understand the model, one has to be aware of the preconceptions embodied in it. Compare this with techniques such as NIAM [28] and (to a lesser extent) E-R, which strive to represent the world in an objective and unbiased way.

Convergence of Methods. Some of the methods mentioned above suggest the use of techniques for modelling the three information systems perspectives (data, process and behaviour). For instance, several authors propose the use of an ER-like technique for data modelling, a state transition diagram-based approach for behaviour modelling and data flow diagrams for process modelling (e.g. [33], [35]). The techniques are not necessarily used in a well-integrated way. Whether or not these techniques are ideal is the subject of some debate, which at this stage is unresolved.

However, there is nothing particularly new about this particular juxtaposition of techniques. For instance, the very popular methodology SSADM [11] has for some time recommended the use of exactly this combination. Even structured analysis [44] now includes similar data- and behaviour-modelling capabilities (although the behaviour-modelling technique is recommended only for real-time systems). This point is important when we consider the large investments in existing methods. For an organisation using a given systems analysis method, allowing a method to evolve over time is generally preferable to discarding it in favour of a new one.

5 Conclusion

It is one of the aims of this paper to move the debate away from technical issues and towards more real-world concerns such as the needs of client and analyst discussed in the preceding sections. There is by no means universal acceptance amongst the object-oriented fraternity of the need for analysis as a distinct activity. For instance, a prevalent view is that objects 'are there for the picking'. Therefore, the emergence of methods specifically for object-oriented analysis is welcome. However, some work will be necessary before these methods can be said to be suitable for general use. In summary:

• The content of some of the methods is not as revolutionary as we might be led to believe, and therefore most organisations now using structured analysis or data modelling would have little difficulty in using them.
• Further investigation is needed to see if the reuse of analysis models will save effort when applied in large organisations.

- It would be wise to adopt only those aspects of the methods which actually improve the resulting information system. This means taking a pragmatic approach to choosing techniques, and not using techniques simply because they are 'object-oriented'.
- The confusion between objects in the system and objects in the world, and the lack of an intermediate conceptual model, are cause for concern. The idea that object-oriented systems are a 'natural' representation of the world is a seductive but dangerous over-simplification. In reality, the fact that the object model seems so close to reality makes it far easier to misuse it than other modelling techniques which do not purport to represent the world so directly.
- The methods will not become widely accepted if they cannot be used from the earliest stages of analysis. The concept of a prior narrative requirements specification needs to be viewed with some caution.
- Some simplification and standardisation of the diagrammatic techniques will probably be necessary to ensure their usefulness as a vehicle for communication between analyst and client.
- Explicit support for high-level views of an application domain must be present in any method which is to have wide applicability. How this is to be achieved in object-oriented analysis is open to question and is the subject of current research efforts.
- If we recognise that the sum total of all objects owned by an organisation is effectively equivalent to the corporate database together with all applications which use the database, then the risks inherent in taking a prototyping-style approach to both data and processes, as recommended in several major methods, need to be carefully considered.
- The object-oriented methods are similar in content to structured analysis methods. To be useful in the earliest stages of analysis, and to capture more application domain knowledge, they might well benefit from augmentation with other methods.

Object-oriented analysis methods are new and relatively untested. It is important that the different methods are now critically evaluated by being put into use. Applying them in a variety of practical situations will allow their practicality to be investigated and will help their effectiveness to be improved.

References

1. Avery G, Baker E (1990) *Psychology at Work*, Prentice Hall.

2. Bailin S C (1989) 'An object-oriented requirements specification method', *Communications of the ACM*, **32**, 5, 608-623.

3. Battaglia G (1991) 'Strategic information planning: a corporate necessity', *Journal of Systems Management*, Feb. 1991, 23-26.

4. Bjorner D, Hoare C A R, Langmaack H (eds) (1990) *VDM and Z: Formal Methods in Software Development: Proceedings of the Third International*

Symposium of VDM Europe, Kiel, FRG, April 17-21 1990, Springer-Verlag.

5. Booch G (1991) *Object-Oriented Design*, Benjamin Cummings.

6. Carey J M (1988) *Human Factors in Management Information Systems*, Ablex Publishing Corp.

7. Coad P, Yourdon E (1991) *Object-Oriented Analysis*, Yourdon Press.

8. Colbert E (1989) 'The object-oriented software development method: a practical approach to object-oriented development', *TRI-Ada '89 Proceedings*, Oct. 1989.

9. Colter M (1984) 'A comparative analysis of systems analysis techniques', *MIS Quarterly*, **8**, (1), 51-66.

10. Cooper R B, Swanson E B (1979) 'Management information requirements assessment: the state of the art', *Data Base*, **11** (2), Fall 1979, 5-16.

11. Cutts G (1987) *Structured Systems Analysis and Design Methodology*, Paradigm.

12. Davies L J (1991) 'Assessing the business impact of information systems failures: a risk analysis methodology', *Computer Control Quarterly*, **9** (4), Oct. 1991.

13. de Champeaux D (1991) *A Comparative Study of Object-Oriented Analysis Models (Technical Report HPL-01-41)*, Hewlett Packard Laboratories, Palo Alto CA.

14. Duke R, King P, Rose G, Smith G (1991) *The Object-Z Specification Language, Version 1*, Technical Report 91-1, Software Verification Research Centre, University of Queensland.

15. Essink L J B (1988) 'A conceptual framework for information systems development methodologies', *Information Technology for Organisational Systems*, H J Bullinger et al (eds), North-Holland.

16. Eurinfo '89 (1989) *A Conceptual Framework for Information Systems Development Methodologies*, Eurinfo 89, 354-362, North-Holland.

17. Floyd C (1986) 'A comparative evaluation of system development methods', *Information Systems Design Methodologies: Improving the Practice*, Olle T W et al (eds), North-Holland 1986.

18. Gibson E (1990) 'Objects - Born and Bred', *Byte*, Oct. 1990, pp 245-254.

19. Hackathorn R D, Karimi J (1988) 'A framework for comparing information engineering methods', *MIS Quarterly*, June 1988, 203-220.

20. Henderson-Sellers B, Edwards J M (1990) 'The object-oriented systems life cycle', *Communications of the ACM*, **33**, 9 Sep. 1990.

21. Jacobson I (1987) 'Object-oriented development in an industrial environment', *OOPSLA '86 Proceedings*, ACM.

22. Kay S (1990) 'Demand up for experts in information engineering', *Computerworld*, Sep. 21 1990, p 53.

23. Kurtz B D et al (1991) *Object-Oriented Systems Analysis and Specification: A Model-Driven Approach*, Prentice-Hall.

24. Lyytinen, K (1987) 'A taxonomic perspective of information systems development: theoretical constructs and recommendations', *Critical Issues in Information Systems Research*, Boland R J, Hirschheim R A (eds.), Wiley 1987.

25. Maddison R N et al (1984) 'A feature analysis of five information system methodologies', *Beyond Productivity: Information Systems for Organisational Effectiveness*, Bemelmans T H (ed.), North-Holland 1984.

26. McGinnes S (1991) *A Framework for the Comparison of Requirements Analysis Methods*, internal report available from School of Information Systems, Queensland University of Technology.

27. Mullin M (1990) *Rapid Prototyping for Object-Oriented Systems*, Addison-Wesley.

28. Nijssen G M, Halpin T A (1989) *Conceptual Schema and Relational Database Design: a Fact Oriented Approach*, Prentice Hall.

29. Odell J J (1991) *Object-Oriented Analysis*, IFIP Working Conference on the Object-Oriented Approach in Information Systems.

30. Olle T W (1988) *Information Systems Development Methodologies: A Framework for Understanding*, North-Holland.

31. Parnas D, Clements P (1986) 'A rational design process: how and why to fake it', *IEEE Transactions on Software Engineering*, Feb. 1986.

32. Pasmore W A (1988) *Designing Effective Organisations: the Sociotechnical Systems Perspective*, Wiley.

33. Rumbaugh J et al (1991) *Object-Oriented Modelling and Design*, Prentice-Hall.

34. Seligmann P S, Sol, Wijers (1989) 'Analysing the structure of information systems methodologies: an alternative approach', *Proc. 1st Dutch Conf. on IS, Amsterdam Neths*, Nov 1-2 1989.

35. Shlaer S, Mellor S (1988) *Object-Oriented Systems Analysis*, Prentice Hall/Eaglewood Cliffs.

36. Sutcliffe A (1990) 'Human factors in information systems: a research agenda and some experience', *Human Factors in Information Systems Analysis and Design*, A. Finkelstein et al (eds), North-Holland.

37. Sutcliffe A (1991) 'Object-oriented systems analysis: the abstract question', *Object-Oriented Approach in Information Systems*, F. Van Assche et al (eds), North-Holland.

38. Teng J T C, Sethi V (1990) 'A comparison of information requirements analysis methods: an experimental study', *Data Base*, Winter 1990, 27-39.

39. Vitalari N P (1984) 'Critical assessment of structured analysis methods: a psychological perspective', *Beyond Productivity: Information Systems for Organisational Effectiveness*, Bemelmans T H (ed.), North-Holland 1984.

40. Weiss S, Page-Jones M (1991) *Synthesis: An Object-Oriented Analysis and Design Method*, Macmillan.

41. Wilson B (1984) *System Concepts: Methodologies and Applications*, John Wiley.

42. Wirfs-Brock R J, Wilkerson B, Wiener L (1990) *Designing Object-Oriented Software*, Prentice-Hall.

43. Wood J, Silver D (1989) *Joint Applications Design: How to Design Quality Systems in 40% Less Time*, Wiley.

44. Yourdon E (1989) *Modern Structured Analysis*, Prentice-Hall.

Integrating Object and Agent Worlds

Thomas Rose	Carlos Maltzahn	Matthias Jarke
Dept. of Computer Science	Universität Passau	RWTH Aachen
University of Toronto	Innstr. 33	Ahornstr. 55
Toronto, M5S 1A4	D-8390 Passau	D-5100 Aachen
Canada	Germany	Germany

Abstract: Repositories provide the information system's support to layer software environments. Initially, repository technology has been dominated by object representation issues. Teams are not part of the ball game. In this paper, we propose the concept of sharing processes which supports distribution and sharing of objects and tasks by teams. Sharing processes are formally specified as classes of non-deterministic finite automata connected to each other by deduction rules. They are intended to coordinate object access and communication for task distribution in large development projects. In particular, we show how interactions between both sharings improve object management.

Keywords: software repositories, team support, access and task coordination

1   Introduction

In today's software development environments object repositories play a key role. While early repositories merely provide the service to manage evolving objects, more recent approaches—AD/Cycle, CDDplus/Cohesion and PCTE—deploy repository technology to integrate environments layered around an object management system. Maintaining the consistency of software and software-related objects emerges as a crucial challenge requiring contributions from distinct perspectives.

Each object management system embodies a distinctive *meta model* of software objects and software processes. This meta model, even if not often explicit, describes the structures and mechanisms [18] the object repository is designed to support. Traditionally, environments are tailored towards *information processing* [8, 22]. Software and project databases account for complex structured systems which exist in several versions. Their underlying meta models focus on the products of software processes. Their goal is to capture the *world of objects*. Configurations and versions are necessary concepts since they provide a pattern to organize systems and components.

Yet, software systems are built by human designers. The increasing size and limited time of software projects place a growing importance on *group processes*. The size and

This work was supported in part by the Deutsche Forschungsgemeinschaft under Grant Ja-445/1-2. Work of the first author is funded by the Federal Networks of Excellence programme through the Institute of Robotics and Intelligent Systems (IRIS).

distribution of development teams result in the necessity to support *collaboration* and *communication* in the **world of agents**. Collaboration refers to the access and maintenance of objects evolving across a network of agents, and communication refers to the exchange of messages related to the access and change of objects.

What then are reasonable meta models which embody group processes and are feasible to relate group and information processing? In terms of conceptions, one may distinguish connectivity, interoperability and cooperation. *Connectivity* refers to the facility to exchange data physically, possibly across world-wide networks. The ability to exchange semantically meaningful information emerges as *interoperability*. Connectivity and interoperability provide the technological infra-structure for cooperation which is about to enhance individual work by contributing to a common task. Yet, the larger the corporation the more *coordination* of collaboration and communication becomes necessary [8].

For the most part, cooperation support in current environments is fixed to one *protocol*, which is hard-coded into the system. Such technological protocols structure group processes by prescribing patterns of consistent communication and collaboration. But, one distinctive feature of group processes is that groups establish *social protocols* and dynamically adjust them. Thus, fixed technological protocols may be overly constraining. Unstructured communication and collaboration might work well for small groups, but likely cause information overloading and untraceability of development processes in large teams. However, merely focusing on "neat" communication and collaboration patterns will likely result in approaches neglecting the world of objects.

This paper presents the concept of a **sharing process** as a model for integrating object and agent worlds. A sharing process describes consistent participation of agents in group processes through classes of non-deterministic finite automata related to each other by deduction rules. Instances of sharing processes govern the distribution of objects across networks of workplaces—called *object sharing*—as well as the delegation of tasks among agents—called *task sharing*. Different instances may adhere to distinct protocols which are formally represented in a knowledge representation language. Since sharing processes are part of our meta model, we are in the position to formally:

- represent distinct object sharings and workspace structures, e.g. optimistic and pessimistic approaches, and
- establish interactions among different instances of sharings, e.g. the admissibility of object modifications with respect to assigned tasks.

This paper is organized as follows. Section 2 draws the development world and reviews proposals to capture the world of objects and agents. Section 3 introduces the concept of a sharing process. Subsequent sections present the formal representation of object and task management and reasonable interaction among them. A prototype implementation *ConceptTalk* is presented in section 7.

2   State-of-the-Art

When people think about humans and group processes in software environments, they think about shared access to repositories, electronic mail communication for notification services, monitoring of task assignments, or collaboration among development processes.

Transaction management is the traditional database technology that provides reliable shared access to repositories. In the *reserve-deposit* paradigm, objects are shared in a serialized way which makes the coordination formally sound but factors out cooperation. Nested transactions just refine this idea [2]. They cluster groups of designers with respect to common, closely-related objects, or vice versa. Making users aware of important changes to their work is outside the scope of the transactional approach. Designer productivity is lowered because of limited parallelism and superficial conflict avoidance [4].

The *copy-merge* paradigm [1] allows parallel changes to one object possibly due to distinct tasks. Parallel changes may cause conflicts which could be resolved by merging. Copying and merging allows closer collaboration, but for the price of additional coordination. The repository should monitor object distribution as well as changes.

In both cases, collaboration can be improved by *notification services* triggered at the time objects are changed by, or transferred between, designers. However, notification services must be structured to avoid information overloading. In [13], content and routing of messages are determined by object relationships. Agents are notified about those changes affecting their own modules. But the problem is merely viewed from the angle of object management.

Workspace hierarchies have been introduced to structure group processes. Objects and changes are allocated to hierarchies of workspaces tailored to the architecture of systems [14]. Highly interrelated objects, e.g. due to module relationships, are allocated to sibling workspaces. Changes are merged from sibling to parent workspaces which likely require the most intensive collaboration because of their tight interrelationships. Structures along this line are intended to minimize necessary collaboration and to impose an organizational pattern on group processes. Although these structures are motivated by quality assurance experiences, they impose a fixed structure on communication and collaboration. Hence, system structures pose fixed limitations on group processes, even though there is strong evidence that group structures and processes have a major impact on system architectures [7]. When upgrading to a new operating system version, for instance, task force groups cross fire walls of workspace hierarchies and therefore might face serious problems. Thus, limiting communication and collaboration to workspace structures determined by system architectures is overly constraining. However, workspace structures are a feasible context mechanism to monitor object distribution and evolution, if they could provide more flexibility. We shall refer to this object management within groups as *object sharing*.

A recent survey concludes that transaction concepts need more *semantics* for further improvement, and that these semantics can only come from information about the *tasks* to be performed by the team [3]. Where does this task information come from ?

Ideas originating from *distributed problem solving* [23] and *office information systems* emphasize social structures and procedures in teamwork. The outcomes are still the objects, but they are considered side-effects of communication activities. Systems influenced by research in speech act theory manage communicating agents rather than resulting actions and objects. Such systems include discussion tools to figure out design decisions, as in gIBIS [6], and to record the justification of design decisions [19]. Others account for assigning and monitoring contract-based working activities, like Coordinator

[25]. They view agents and their activities as parts of group processes which share tasks to be processed. Conversation structures describe consistent participation of agents in communication processes. This shows a different kind of integration. Agents articulate their contributions at different workplaces. Then, how do these articulations fit together ?

However, systems like gIBIS or Coordinator do not formally relate to the object world. We shall refer to this object-independent management of tasks within and by groups as *task sharing*.

To conclude, there have been two lines of management approaches, one for *object evolution* and the other for *tasks affecting objects*. The challenge addressed by the *sharing process approach* is to integrate both, object management and group process aspects. To capture both worlds, sharing processes have to feature:

- different kinds of agents, like human agents performing tasks or technical agents managing objects,
- different kinds of interaction between agents, like emailing—e.g. where agents are used to communicate to each other—and object tracing—e.g. where technical agents are used for object management, and
- a synchronization facility which allows the specification of consistent patterns of interactions among human and technical agents in a flexible and adoptable kind.

3   Sharing Processes

The sharing process concept allows agents to share objects and tasks within an environment which is comprised of a set of workplaces connected to a network. Formally, a sharing process can be defined as a triple $< E, N, S >$ consisting of events E, a NFA N (non-deterministic finite automaton) and a state S determined by the history of events. Many sharing processes can have the same NFA structure and many events can be associated to a single process.

A *sharing process* documents and structures *events* (fig. 1). Conversely, events drive the evolution of a sharing process. An event is caused by an *agent* at any place in the network. Agents can be human designers who might communicate to other designers to assign a task, as well as technical agents, for instance, workspaces which acquire objects from other workspaces.

NFAs provide synchronization by specifying the consistent evolution of sharing processes in terms of states and transitions. A process has one start state and possibly several final states. Transitions describe state changes and represent the progress of a process with respect to selected final states, the goal states. An event may non-deterministically cause different transitions depending on the state of the sharing process and the agent that delivered the event. In addition, events can trigger notifications to agents.

Conversely, rules can be associated with transitions that trigger consequent events in parallel-running processes of a specified type. In the following, we often use the terms event and transition interchangeably where no confusion can arise; note, however, that transition is a formal concept, used in a limited modeling framework for understanding a wide variety of real-world phenomena, the events. It could well be that events happen that do not really fit the automaton schemata, and we want to be able to record such "exceptions" in our model, hence the separation in fig. 1.

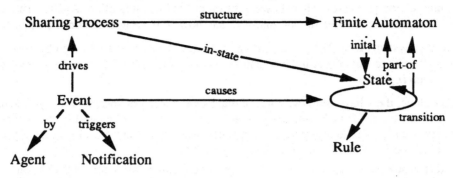

Fig. 1: Sharing processes

Sharing processes are intended to embed object evolution into the more general context of a development project. Each project initially appears like a task and comprises a possibly ordered set of sub-tasks. The state of a project is represented by the tasks completed at a given moment. A project reaches its final state when each sub-task has been completed. The input and results of tasks are managed by *workspaces* which are assigned to groups and single agents respectively. The top-level workspace contains fully integrated "final" project results, whereas lower levels in a workspace hierarchy contain more private and less integrated objects [2, 14]. Due to the conceptual similarity of work organization and work environment, we can associate workspaces with hierarchically organized projects that view objects. Hence, task responsibility assignment and object visibility by certain groups of agents must go together. This does not mean that both have to be identical, but they have to adhere to some kind of well-formed patterns.

In subsequent sections, we show how to utilize sharing processes to *define visibility by object sharing and modifiability by task sharing* in terms of classes of sharing processes. These classes represent schemas for sharing inside a specific environment. Specific objects, specific tasks and changes to specific objects are instances of these classes. Consistency of individual sharings is controlled by instantiation of the classes.

4   Task Sharing

One instance of sharing processes is the sharing of tasks. Task sharing processes handle the execution of tasks which has to adhere to certain protocols. The definition of these protocols depends on the work setting; a particular group may be in different settings at different times or may even adapt standard protocols to their specific needs dynamically. We can abstract from such options by looking at a broader phase structure for task sharing, consisting of the four phases of *orientation*, *assignment*, *realization*, and *inspection*.

During *orientation*, agents identify a problem in one way or another and may come up with the definition of a set of tasks to be executed (cf. [9]). After a task has been identified, it enters the ball game which is about realizing the task. If the task consists of sub-tasks, then the task's sharing process forks into sub-processes, one for each sub-task.

Realization and *inspection* can be tackled within different work structures [4]. An *integrative work structure* involves the whole group; this would be an application domain for real-time collaboration tools that increase group awareness and intensify cooperation [8]. A *delegative work structure* is more formal. It usually separates the realization and inspection phase even though it may iterate through intermediate reviews and similar techniques.

While early workflow protocols were based on the assumption that events would just happen "on command", current conversation-based approaches typically begin with a negotiation phase followed by an asynchronous work mode. The *assignment* could follow an *electronic market protocol* with group members or external agents "bidding" for tasks [23], or a bilateral haggling according to *conversation-for-action protocols* with message types such as request, offer and counter-offer, promise and renege [25].

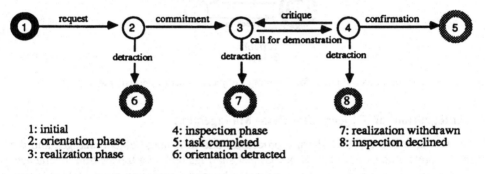

1: initial
2: orientation phase
3: realization phase
4: inspection phase
5: task completed
6: orientation detracted
7: realization withdrawn
8: inspection declined

Fig. 2: A phase structure for delegative task sharing

Fig. 2 abstracts from individual protocols by defining an event type called *commitment* which defines the transition from the task definition to the realization phase where the task is worked on in a subordinate workspace. Some time later, a *call for demonstration* initiates an inspection phase in which members of the task sharing process evaluate the results. In practice, these results are often called beta versions; they are distributed to all agents who have influenced the task definition. Usually, errors and weaknesses are detected and lead to events of type *critique* which have the task sharing subprocess return to its realization phase. If, however, the group is satisfied with the results, the subprocess goes into the successful final state by transition of type *confirm*. Further, processes can terminate at any phase unsuccessfully.

To reiterate, fig. 2 shows an abstracted schema for delegative work structures. This schema can be specialized with particular market or bilateral conversational protocols. For example, the ConceptTalk prototype adopts a Coordinator-like protocol [25] for bilateral task sharings but allows users to augment and alter it dynamically.

5   Object Sharing

A second instance of sharing processes is the sharing of objects among workspaces in the network. In the sequel, we assume that each workspace constitutes the workplace of a human designer but may be shared with other workplaces. The generalization to the case

where each workplace consists of multiple workspaces—the designer´s working environment—does not pose major problems in our model but may of course be an interface organization problem [10].

If copies of objects are distributed across workspaces, parallel accesses within different workspaces create multiple variants of an object. Object sharing processes conceive workspaces as technical agents, which manage objects and communicate to coordinate object accesses and changes. To support distributed object management, object sharing processes should feature:

- creating and maintaining *availability* of objects in workspaces, possibly with different access rights,
- maintaining *relationships* among workspaces—e.g., hierarchies—and controlling adherence of availability with respect to these relationships,
- managing *version histories* of objects within and across workspaces, and
- monitoring and controlling *concurrent access* to objects to detect and notify conflicts.

Each object sharing process handles the sharing of one object across two workspaces. Both workspaces contain a copy of the object. A object sharing is initiated between workspaces $work_1$ and $work_2$ when $work_2$ acquires an object from $work_1$ for the first time. It terminates when the object is removed from $work_2$ or $work_1$. The workspace, an object originates from, is called its public workspace. The acquiring workspace is considered a private workspace relative to the public one. The state of an object sharing represents how the private version relates to the public version. The state evolves due to changes to the object in one or both workspaces and transfers of the object among both workspaces. Thus, the process structure specifies concurrent access to shared objects.

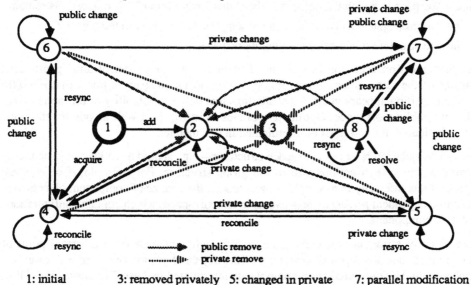

Fig. 3: Structure of object sharing for "copying" objects (copy-merge paradigm)

One possible instance of concurrency control specified as a object sharing process shows fig. 3. It adheres to the copy-merge paradigm offered by SUN´s Network Software Environment NSE [1]. Such a object sharing protocol supports an integrative work structure and may thus lead to a better overall group result than the usual reserve-deposit paradigm, provided sufficiently dense group collaboration can be achieved [4].

Using the same general approach, one can define different versions of concurrency control depending on the project requirements; in particular, for larger groups, the familiar check-in/check-out locking mechanisms can be used to provide more control (cf. fig. 4 for its fairly simple protocol). But we have to be careful with the concurrent existence of different protocols [24]. This problem is part of the more general issue of how to define the interaction of multiple sharing processes, to be discussed next.

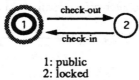

1: public
2: locked

Fig. 4: Structure of object sharing for "moving" objects (reserve-deposit paradigm)

6   Integration of Object and Task Management

So far, we have two types of sharing processes, one to manage object changes and the other to monitor the evolution of tasks. Object sharings realize a transaction mechanism in its own right [1]. Yet object sharings go a step beyond transaction concepts, since they incorporate a novel feature into the nature of a transaction, the *change.*

Transaction concepts process a change in terms of its pre- and post-transaction value. Integrity constraints may place more restrictions on the change. Yet, transactions neither consider the agent who is doing the change, nor possible relationships to other transactions and their intended change. Even the nature of involved objects is not considered. Take a bug-fix in a component of a large software system. Two kinds of information can be utilized: the character of the component and the experience of the programmer. Both have impacts on the change, i.e., the transaction to replace the buggy version by the fixed version. If it is a fringe component, any programmer is qualified to make the change. If it is a central component of the system heavily used by other components, access should be limited to experienced programmers, preferably those having a record of this component. Both kinds of information are not captured by a transaction—i.e. the concept is invariant with respect to objects, callers, and intended modifications—but are relevant to a change in the context of group work.

Object sharing is intended to utilize different sources of information. Some information might originate from a recording of design processes [12, 20] or others from a reverse engineering tool that measures structure [16]. On the other hand, programmer profiles can

---

[1]   [BK 91] surveys the virtues and limitations of transaction concepts originating from both communities, databases and software development environments.

be obtained from recorded task sharings (success rates, in-time ratios, etc.). Some features could merely be designed for describing admissible object sharings, such as "no acquisition of a vulnerable component by an agent with a low profile".

Object sharings and task sharings are also a valuable source for determining the consistency of an object change. *Possible conflicts* arise, when two agents acquire the same object for modifications. They may become an *actual conflict*, when both agents modify and reconcile the object into a common parent workspace. Thus, we have to interface different object sharings.

Furthermore, object sharings have to adhere to some project discipline. It is fine when someone acquires an object to make some quality improvements, but it is bad policy to allow agents to reconcile arbitrary objects and changes into public workspaces. Thus, the eligibility of object changes depends on assigned tasks. This does not imply that only those changes to objects are eligible which have been agreed on; but, the agent who is responsible for the public workspace must be contacted before reconciliation.

6.1 Coordinating Object Changes across Workspaces

A workspace manages objects: objects are available in workspaces and a workspace "stores" the version history of objects. Hence, a workspace appears like a local library which is accessible by owners of the workspace.

An object sharing establishes a communication line between two workspaces $work_1$ and $work_2$ at the time $work_2$ acquires an object from $work_1$ with respect to a specific object obj. However, it only defines the availability of obj in $work_2$, the private workspace. Availability in $work_1$, the public workspace, is defined in a further object sharing that has the public workspace $work_1$ as its private workspace, and so forth up to some workspace in which the object has the status "only private". Two questions remain:

- how to propagate changes to related workspaces with respect to the object ?
- how to structure relationships among workspaces ?

The first question accounts for the problem of concurrency control among different sharings of the same object. For example, the product's integrity requires that a *public change* transition appears in all object sharings that define availability of the same object with this public workspace. Optimistic policies as in fig. 3 as well as pessimistic policies as indicated in fig. 4 must be coordinated in this manner.

The second question refers to workspace structures—e.g., should a workspace structure be tailored to the system architecture or the group structure. For example, if objects are organized hierarchically in a complex object model, the change of component objects may also cause dependent *private change* events in all workspaces which contain configurations with this component.

Both objectives may appear orthogonal at first sight—at least from a formal point of view. In fact, they are dependent, because of the objects they are governing. For example, a system may be configured from components interrelated by "uses" relationships. Thus, a change interferes with appearances of the same object in other workspaces and it might possibly affect other objects, which are related because of the system structure. Thus, coordination of object changes has to consider multiple objectives. Hence, flexible couplings of object sharings are necessary; yet workspace structures should adhere to some empirical policies [4, 14]. The sharing process approach, especially the rule-based coupling of sharing process protocols, provides a flexible environment in which such policies can be defined and maintained.

6.2 Controlling Object Changes from a Task Perspective

Whenever a subprocess of a task sharing enters its realization phase, an object sharing is initiated that makes the required objects available (by physical copy or by access rights) to the workspace of the server agent of the subprocess. Since the results based on these objects may have to be re-integrated later on, the workspace is subordinated to the workspace where the objects come from. Briefly, the *commitment* in the task sharing causes a *copy* in the object sharing.

Conversely, if an agent attempts to integrate a private object into another workspace in the object sharing protocol, this may have consequences in corresponding task sharing protocols. If the agent is already involved in a commitment for this task, the attempt to *integrate* would cause a *call for demonstration* in the task sharing.

Several kinds of *conflict* may occur. *Differences of opinion* are recorded in idea sharing protocols, as rationales for design decisions [19]. *Differences of interest* can be worked out in the negotiation loops of the task sharing protocols. *Technical conflicts* due to parallel work on the same objects are resolved either formally, under consideration of the task structures, or by introducing an integrative work setting where changes are merged. Thus, our approach accepts the existence of such conflicts and provides ways to make them productive, rather than suppressing them like transactions do. We give two examples that highlight the integration of object and teamwork management.

Creativity in design teams may be enhanced by encouraging unsolicited contributions. When a user *acquires* an object on which another user already works due to a contract, a notification is sent to set up direct communication among the two users. They may then choose to (1) collaborate in an integrative work structure without concurrency control, (2) define notification services which inform one user when the other has completed certain critical subactivities after which parallel work is meaningful, or (3) work in parallel and resolve conflicts by merging results.

The *reconcile* transition of the object sharing protocol triggers two checks. With respect to other object sharings, reconcile may lead to a *conflict* state; in this case, it is aborted and conflict resolution (*resolve*) must precede a new attempt to *reconcile*. With respect to task sharing, it must be evaluated if there is a task sharing between the owners of both workspaces which is in the realization phase for the objects in question. Otherwise, a notification is sent to the originator of the *reconcile* command to start such a task sharing.

6.3 Managing Ideograms Evolving in a Network

To exemplify the different possibilities for couplings, imagine a project and a distribution of objects as shown in fig. 5. Among others, there are three designers—*Mike, John* and *Christian*—working on one project developing ideograms. Their private workspaces and the public workspace are connected to a network, a local or an organization-wide one. The public workspace manages entirely configured ideograms as well as parts of ideograms, some of them having revisions and variants. Versions are related by horizontal lines. As of now, there exists one configured version of the ideogram in the public workspace, the "girl" shown at the left-hand side. So far, the setting mimics object management systems.

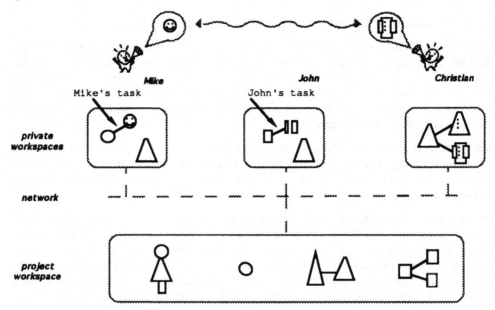

Fig. 5: Ideogram management in a network

Mike's task is to refine the head component to produce a more appealing version of the current ideogram as managed by the workspace of the project. A task sharing between Mike and its client establishes this task. Mike's client is the ideogram manager who administers the project's product. Mike acquires the latest version of the head because of his task, which results in an object sharing between both workspaces. Acquisition might be done automatically at the time Mike has committed to the task—e.g. determined from structured emails—or manually by a designer and his workspace respectively any time after his commitment.

In the meantime, John is working on his task to refine the bottom part. To check compatibility with respect to the central part, John also requires access to the middle part. Mike and John have decided to get a copy of the middle part, since both require a stable context, i.e., changes to that component should not corrupt their work. If a new version comes along in the project workspace, they will receive an email notification and then decide whether to re-synchronize their private version. The latter is again a specific coupling tailored to their needs.

In our setting so far, there are two task sharing and four object sharing processes alive, plus additional object sharings between the public workspace and its client workspace(s) which govern the objects residing in the public workspace.

- The two task sharing processes concern the assignments of the tasks *improve-head* to Mike and *refine-base* to John. The client in both task sharings is the ideogram manager.
- Two object sharing processes are initiated between the public and Mike's workspace, and between the public and John's workspace. They concern the head and the bottom part respectively. Both object sharings start in state *identical* and enter state *changed-in-private* after some modifications have been done in the private workspace (cf. fig. 3). Both changes are associated to a task. The other two object sharings concern the body part. They are still in state *identical*, since nothing happened to the body in both, the private and the public workspace.

After some time, the third designer *Christian* acquires the body part. A third object sharing for the body part starts. In contrast to Mike and John, Christian starts changing the body part significantly yet there is no agreement on this job, i.e., no task sharing has been established. Although Mike acquired the object first, he has not gained the right to prohibit Christian from changing the body. That is a matter of the protocol used. However, Mike and John may want to get a notification. The actual sharings are related by the object, of the project workspace, which they share as common source. Hence, parties to be notified will be derived by deduction rules.

The purpose of their acquisition was a stable context, since they have to interface their parts with the body. Contrary, the acquisition of the head part by Mike is intended to be more exclusive. Suppose, Christian wants to check how his new body versions fit the head and bottom part. When acquiring the head part for instance, he gets a note that this object is in change. Christian can contact Mike to get an intermediate version—Mike may reconcile his current version to the public workspace—or wait until Mike finishes his task and commits the change.

A conflict arises when Mike or John have to adapt their copy of the body part in order to make the body fit to their parts. Then, a conflict occurs and changes have to be merged by Mike and John. Their progress cannot be rolled-back due to a shared componet that requires minor adaptations—like transaction concepts usually do. Further, Christian's change has to be considered too. Christian, Mike and John may communicate to agree on the party responsible for merging their changes.

Since object sharings tolerate conflicts, inconsistency matures as a matter of management, in contrast to the reserve-deposit paradigm. Object sharing protocols manage inconsistency, since they detect conflicts, notify about conflicts and monitor conflict resolution. At first thought, tightly interfacing object and task sharing appears to better designer comfort and enforce stronger policies on object modifications. Interfacing allows the system to provide necessary objects automatically and ensures that no object modification happens without task permission. But, at second thought, a tight and rigid coupling could come in the way of designer productivity and momentum. One may want to develop different conflict notification and resolution protocols. Such a diversity should consider the kind of object and its role inside the system, the kind of change—viewed from an angle of content as well as project deadlines—and the profile of the party responsible for the change.

The examples show just a few of the many possible couplings among sharing processes. Which of these are actually realized, is a management decision. Despite all the flexibility of the sharing process approach, each coupling determines yet another technological protocol that impacts workflow and habits in design teams. The need for formal couplings should therefore be carefully considered in each case. Tools are needed by which the group can re-define the terms of their interaction, without having to go to some systems specialist. Otherwise, we see little chance of acceptance for systems based on these models—or any other models, for that matter.

7   ConceptTalk

Another prerequisite for successful organizational implementation is that the introduction of team support should be unobtrusive. Existing work practices for communication, collaboration, and coordination should be altered as little as possible [21]. The design of the ConceptTalk prototype [15] has tried to follow these premises as far as possible, firstly by using meta-modeling techniques instead of hardcoding of protocols, secondly by building upon standard software environments rather than starting from scratch.

The UNIX world was chosen as an example of a standard development platform. For our experiments, we assume that one is familiar with the following kinds of UNIX tools:

- an object management system (NSE [1]) which offers workspaces as well as simple version and configuration management (based on SCCS and MAKE),
- standard electronic mail, and
- the basic command set of Unix (or a fancier user interface on top of it).

ConceptTalk itself is a small C program that integrates such tools, based on protocol, state, and rule information obtained from a background knowledge server, *ConceptBase* [11]. ConceptBase uses the conceptual modeling language Telos [17] for the formal representation of sharing processes and its instances. Besides the abstraction facilities of object-oriented data models, Telos contributes two important features to our approach: assertional facilities and metaclasses. The assertional facilities come along as integrity constraints and deductive rules. Constraints and rules are heavily used in the coupling of sharing processes. Metaclasses are a natural way to integrate distinct protocol and object models. One instance of a metaclass is the concept of a sharing process which introduces the concept of *agents*. The classes of designers as well as workspaces in the network are represented as instances of agents. In [20], the use of metamodeling for integrating group models, as proposed here, with specific object models is demonstrated.

Communication via *mail* and collaboration via NSE is coordinated by Telos models. As a specific task sharing protocol, we use a slightly modified version of the one proposed in [25]. Since this protocol is not real-time, each of its message types is directly associated with a state transition; the overall structure elaborates the phase model shown in fig. 2 by various negotiation loops. ConceptBase offers a choice of graphical and textual editing tools for changing protocols interactively, even while conversations under these protocols are going on. Flexibility in sharing processes is also provided by the option of moving up and down in generalization (*isA*) hierarchies of existing protocols; the top of such a hierarchy could be the simple *send-respond* pattern of standard email. Finally, the environment also offers a few specialized shared-window tools for real-time collaboration on common workspaces, including a specialized graphical editor and a public domain conferencing software for informal chatting over low-bandwidth channels.

For cases where no graphical interface is available, a simple command interface allows the use of ConceptTalk in standard Unix environments. *Confer* is an extended *mail* that offers the available message types at any moment in time and records the exchange of typed messages; the user can review the state of the task sharings in which he is involved as a customer resp. contractor. *Note* allows each user to define personalized notification services which "observe" either an individual process or some class of processes with respect to particular events. The events are specified either by a general class of events or by some structure element of the NFA, e.g., an edge; the available classes of processes and the already existing notification services can be shown. Finally, *pose* structures workspaces as project processes by associating scheduling information (e.g., problems, tasks, and dependencies among them). This information can be either completely informal (e.g., text, drawings), or represented in Telos.

In line with our philosophy of changing the existing work environment as little as possible, object sharing directly uses the NSE commands *acquire, resync, resolve*, and *reconcile* [1] to denote the corresponding state transitions in the protocol automaton shown in fig. 3. However, in ConceptTalk, these commands to not work autonomously but are controlled in ConceptBase with respect to their feasibility and consequences, especially in terms of coupling with other result and task sharing processes according to the defined rules. Several built-in notification services are provided for notification of conflicts due to concurrency control problems or missing tasks.

8 Conclusions

Information systems technology is expected—even stronger, is demanded—to play a key role in future software environments [5]. There is a strong request for *object management* technology going beyond file servers and that is the very nature of information systems. Yet, at least two requirements of engineering domains are not adequately covered by information systems technology: *group support* and *change management*. The approach presented in this paper is a step towards these objectives.

From the viewpoint of *group support*, the sharing process approach brings the consideration of the objects back into formalisms underlying conversation-oriented models. Sharing processes provide a schema to describe the consistent access of agents to tasks and objects. Suitable agents are human designers as well workspaces; participation covers contribution of designers to task executions in terms of semi-structured messages, as well as object transfers and change tracking in workspaces. *Task sharing* structures communication while *object sharing* defines the structure for collaboration. Both of them are brought together in a common framework by defining rules that associate dependent events in object sharing protocols with events in task sharing protocols, and vice versa.

From the viewpoint of *change management*, we have not only taken a different view of advanced transaction concepts (object sharing), but have also provided formal means to associate it with group-oriented extensions to software process modeling (expressed as task sharing protocols). Together with the use of a knowledge representation language, the sharing process model allows a more flexible definition and control of change types and their interrelationships than fixed "red-book" rule collections or pre-defined Petri nets. As an example, we mentioned the idea that the group could define different protocols for the change of central and of fringe components. This can be a starting point for improving process-oriented consistency and data quality in repositories.

On the other hand, experience in office automation has shown that formal consistency and enforcement of bureaucratic procedures is not everything. Conflicts are a valuable source of diversity and better long-term product quality—*inconsistency* must be managed with equal emphasis as *consistency*. The copy-merge paradigm adopted in ConceptTalk is intended to intensify collaboration in smaller subgroups. Instead of superficially avoiding conflicts by exclusive access rights, it emphasizes conflict recognition and explicit conflict resolution. To prevent lost work due to communication-less optimistic parallel work, very large groups should embed this protocol in a stricter global protocol.

The ConceptTalk prototype is only a first step in evaluating the potential of the sharing process approach for change management. As already shown in usage experiences with extensible tool kits such as NSE, the definition and enactment of specific change types, and their integration into coherent management policies for group-intensive work structures is a major challenge which will probably also require extensions of the underlying reasoning mechanisms and protocol compilation techniques to be computationally effective. Ongoing application experiments with the ConceptTalk prototype in software engineering, hypertext co-authoring, and industrial engineering contexts are further revealing a large number of practical requirements.

References

1. E.W. Adams, M. Honda, T.C. Miller (1989). Object Management in a CASE Environment. *Proc. 11th Intl. Conf. Software Engineering*, Pittsburgh, Pa, 154-163.
2. F. Bancilhon, W. Kim, H.F. Korth (1985). A Model for CAD Transactions. *Proc. 11th Intl. Conf. Very Large Data Bases*, Stockholm, Schweden, 25-33.
3. N.S. Barghouti, G.E. Kaiser (1991). Concurrency Control in Advanced Database Applications. *ACM Computing Surveys 23*, 3, 269-317.
4. S. Bendifallah, W. Scacchi (1989). Work Structures and Shifts: An Empirical Analysis of Software Specification Teamwork. *Proc. 11th Intl. Conf. Software Engineering*, Pittsburgh, Pa, 260-270.
5. P.A. Bernstein (1987). Database System Support for Software Engineering - An Extended Abstract. *Proc. 9th Intl. Conf. Software Engineering*, Monterey,Ca., 166-178.
6. J. Conklin, M.L. Begeman (1988). A Hypertext Tool for Exploratory Policy Discussions. *ACM Transactions Office Information Systems 6*, 4, 303-331.
7. M.E. Conway (1968). How do Committees Invent. *Datamation 14*, 4, 28-31.
8. C.A. Ellis, S.J. Gibbs, G.L. Rein (1991). Groupware—Some Issues and Experience. *Communications of the ACM 34*, 1, 39-58.

9. U. Hahn, M. Jarke, T. Rose (1990). Group Work in Software Projects - Integrated Conceptual Models and Collaboration Tools. *Proc. IFIP WG 8.4 Conf. Multi-User Interfaces and Applications*, Iraklion, Greece, 83-101.

10. B. Hartfield, M. Graves (1991). Issue-Centered Design for Collaborative Work. *Proc. IFIP TC8 Working Conference on Collaborative Work, Social Communications, and Information Systems*, Helsinki, Finland, 295-310.

11. M. Jarke, ed. (1991). *ConceptBase V3.0 User Manual*. Report MIP-9106, Universität Passau, Germany.

12. M. Jarke, J. Mylopoulos, J.W. Schmidt, Y. Vassiliou (1990). Information Systems Development as Knowledge Engineering: A Review of the DAIDA Project. *Programirovanie 17*, 1, Report MIP-9011, Universität Passau, Germany.

13. G.E. Kaiser, S.M. Kaplan, J. Micallef (1987). Multiuser, Distributed Language-based Environments. *IEEE Software 4*, 11, 58-67.

14. G.E. Kaiser, D.E. Perry (1987). Workspaces and Experimental Databases: Automated Support for Software Maintenance and Evolution. *Proc. of the 1987 Conf. on Software Maintenance*, 108-114.

15. C. Maltzahn (1990). An Environment for Cooperative Development. Diploma thesis, Universität Passau, Germany (in German).

16. H. Müller, J.S. Uhl (1990). Composing Subsystem Structures Using (k,2)-Partite Graphs. *Proc. Conf. Software Maintenance*, San Diego, Ca, 12-19.

17. J. Mylopoulos, A. Borgida, M. Jarke, M. Koubarakis (1990). Telos: A Language for Representing Knowledge about Information Systems. *ACM Transaction on Information Systems 8*, 4, 325-362.

18. D. Perry, G. Kaiser (1991). Models of Software Development Environments. *IEEE Transactions Software Engineering 17*, 3, 283-295.

19. C. Potts, G. Bruns (1988). Recording the Reasons for Design Decisions. *Proc. 10th Intl. Conf. Software Engineering*, Singapore, 418-427.

20. T. Rose, M. Jarke, M. Gocek, C. Maltzahn, H. Nissen (1991). A Decision-Based Configuration Process Environment. *Software Engineering Journal 6*, 3 (Special Issue on Software Process and its Support), 332-346.

21. W. Sasso (1991). Motivating Adoption of KBSA: Issues, Arguments, and Strategies. *Proc. 6th Knowledge-Based Software Engineering Conf.*, Syracuse, N.Y., 143-154.

22. I. Shy, R. Taylor, L. Osterweil (1990). A Metaphor and a Conceptual Architecture for Software Development Environments. *Proc. Intl. Workshop on Software Environments*, Chinon, France, LNCS 467, Springer-Verlag, 77-97.

23. R.G. Smith, R. Davis (1981). Frameworks for Cooperation in Distributed Problem Solving. *IEEE Transactions Systems, Man, and Cybernetics 11*, 1, 61-70.

24. R. Unland (1991). TOPAZ: A Toolkit for the Construction of Application-Specific Transaction Managers. Report MIP-9113, Universität Passau, Germany.

25. T. Winograd, F. Flores (1986). *Understanding Computers and Cognition*. Norwood, NJ: Ablex.

A Fully Integrated Programming Environment for an Object-Oriented Database

Patrick Borras †
O_2 Technology
7 rue du Parc de Clagny
78000 Versailles (France)
Anne Doucet †
LRI - Bat 490
Université Paris Sud
91405 Orsay Cedex (France)
e-mail : anne@lri.lri.fr

Patrick Pfeffer †‡
Alcatel Alsthom Recherche
Route de Nozay
91460 Marcoussis (France)
patrick@aar.alcatel-alsthom.fr

Abstract

This paper describes the design and the implementation of OOPE, the graphical programming environment of the prototype version of O_2, an object-oriented database system. One of the distinguishing features of this environment is that it mixes the functionalities of programming environments, of both databases and programming languages. Thus, it facilitates and fastens not only the schema design, but also the development of application programs. Another interesting characteristic is that it is being developed using as much as possible the functionalities provided by the O_2 system, namely the programming language, the database and the graphics functionalities.

Keywords: Object-Oriented Database Management Systems, Programming Environment

1 Introduction

O_2 is an object-oriented database system developed at Altaïr, and presently distributed by O_2 Technology. Such a system provides the functionalities of a DBMS, of a programming language and of a programming environment. In this paper, we describe the design and the implementation of OOPE, the programming environment of the O_2 prototype. As a large amount of time while developing a database application is spent in programming activity, a big effort has been made in designing the programming environment.

---

†This research was developed while the authors were working for GIP Altaïr.   †This research was developed while the authors were working for GIP Altaïr.

‡The views and conclusions contained in this article are those of the author and should not be interpreted as representing the officials policies, either expressed or implied of Alcatel Alsthom Recherche

Database programming presents two main aspects: the first one consists in building and manipulating the schema, while the second, consisting in writing application programs, is very close to conventional programming. Traditional database system, with the fourth generation languages, favoured the former. They provide facilities for schema manipulations, reports and forms edition, and user interface generation. Application programs are generally written in a host language. The programmer uses then the programming tools provided by the programming environment of the host language. In O_2, there is a unique language for schema design and manipulation and for programming. Therefore, we integrated features specific to schema design (database manipulations) and traditional programming tools in the same environment.

In order to provide ease of use and user-friendliness, OOPE makes an important use of graphics. All information is graphically displayed on the screen, and user interaction is always done via direct manipulation.

The implementation of OOPE fully uses the functionalities provided by the O_2 system. Modelization and implementation are respectively done in O_2 and CO_2, one of the languages developed by Altaïr, the database is used to store and manage the information used by OOPE, and the graphical interface has been built by LOOKS, the interface generator provided by Altaïr.

The paper is organized as follows. After a quick description of the main features of the O_2 system in Section 2, we present in Section 3 the design of OOPE, its functionalities and tools. Section 4 concerns the implementation choices of OOPE. The next section (Section 5) compares OOPE to other database programming environments. Implementation aspects are discussed. Lastly, we conclude in Section 6.

2 Overview of the O_2 Programming System

While designing the O_2 system, a major concern was to increase the power of the language without having to write a completely new language. Therefore, O_2 is an object-oriented layer which is added on top of existing languages (C and Basic). This layer, the O_2 data model, fully described in [LRV88], is used to design the application schema. For the time being, the O_2 system provides two languages, CO_2 and BasicO_2 with which the programmer can implement the behavioral part of the application. In this section, we briefly present the O_2 features proposed to build a database schema, and we give the example of a method. More details on the O_2 system can be found in [LR89],[VDB89]and [Da90].

O_2 is object-oriented, which means that information is organized as objects, which encapsulate data and behavior. Objects are instances of classes, which describe the common structure and the common behavior of a set of objects. The structure of a class is defined by a type. O_2 provides atomic types (integer, real, float, char, string, boolean, ...) and three constructors, which are the tuple constructor, the list constructor and the set constructor.

Examples of types are:

        tuple(name: string, age: integer);
        set(string);
        list(integer);
        list(tuple(name: string, city: string)).

```
       add class City
               type tuple (name : string,
                           map : bitmap,
                           hotels : set (Hotel))
       method Compute_stars(maxprice: integer, minstar: integer)
```

Figure 1: Definition of the class *City*

```
(1)     body Compute_stars(maxprice: integer, minstar: integer) in class City
(2)     co2
(3)     {
(4)     o2 set(name: string, star: integer, price: integer) result;
(5)     o2 Hotel h;
(6)     result=list();
(7)     for (h in self →hotels)
(8)            {
(9)            int p;
(10)           if ((h →stars > minstar) || ((p=[h price]) > maxprice))
(11)              {
(12)              result += set(tuple(name:h→name,
(13)                                  star:h→stars,
(14)                                  price:p));
(15)              }
(16)           }
(17)    display(result);
(18)    }
```

Figure 2: Body of the *Compute_stars* method.

The behavior of a class is represented by a set of methods. Their definition is done in O_2 while their body can be written using any of the existing programming languages accepted by O_2. Figure 1 gives an example of a class definition, and Figure 2 shows the body of a method written in CO_2. The O_2 keywords are displayed in bold font. O_2 variables definitions are preceded by the O_2 keyword (lines 4 and 5), while other variables are declared using the C syntax (line 9). The message passing syntax is delimited by "[ ]" brackets, as shown line 10. The purpose of this method is to build and display an O_2 set, named *result*, in which are collected the name, the number of stars, and the night price of all the hotels of the city for which the number of stars is superior to *minstar* and the night price superior to *maxprice*.

O_2 supports multiple inheritance, and classes are organized into a hierarchy. The inheritance mechanism is based on subtyping. A class, always defined as a subclass of another class, inherits from its superclass(es) the structure and the behavior.

A database application in O_2 consists of programs which represent the different tasks supported by the application. As for methods, the body of a program can be written in any of the O_2 languages. However, the body of a program differs from the body of a method in that it manages transactions. Furthermore, programs contain calls to methods, but not to other programs, and a program cannot be shared between several applications.

3   Design

Programming environments are essential both for programming languages and for database systems. Their functionalities are however slightly different. Programming environments for database systems, generally called fourth generation languages, arose later. They mostly provide tools for building the schema in a non-procedural way, for creating menus and query forms automatically. Programming environments for traditional programming languages often offer syntax directed editors with many editing and browsing facilities, program verifiers, debugging tools and source code control systems. The main difference between these two approaches comes from the separation of data manipulation and programming languages which exists in database systems. The O_2 system provides a single language for programming and for data manipulation. Its programming environment, OOPE, merges the functionalities of the two approaches in a uniform framework.

The design of OOPE was inspired by the programming environment of Smalltalk-80 [Gol83]. It makes an intensive use of graphics, and has an "all-object" design philosophy. All information is represented by an object, and every action is performed by sending a message to an object.

The care of simplicity led us to represent the information used by the programming environment the same way they are represented in the system, where all information is stored as objects, for bootstraping reasons [VDB89]: the data in the database, the classes, the methods, the applications and the programs. In OOPE, the programmer manipulates all this information as database objects.

This design presents many advantages. First of all, it uses the database functionalities of the O_2 system to store the information managed by OOPE, providing a fast access to it. Secondly, it provides uniformity: the programmer only deals with objects, and every action is performed the same way. The use of a generic display and edition mechanism allows a uniform representation of the objects and of the message passing mechanism. Another advantage concerns the learning time. If everything is represented and manipulated the same way, the only thing the user needs to learn to use OOPE is how to manipulate objects and how to send messages to these objects, which considerably reduces the learning time. Having an object-oriented design, OOPE is easily extensible. A new functionality can be added by defining a new method, or a new object with a method. Finally, this design provides a good integration between the various tools and functionalities: information can be copied, cut and pasted from any object to any other object.

Following the same idea, all the tools (the *Journal*, the *Browser*, the *O_2-shell*, the *Workspace*, the *Debugger*, the *Queries*, and the *Applications*) provided in OOPE are designed with the same philosophy. They all consist of objects stored in the database.

In the sequel, in Sections 3.1 and 3.2, we explain how to build an application (i.e we present the functionalities provided by database programming environments) by showing how to create a class, how to define a method and its body for that class, and how to create an application and its programs. Then we present some tools (which are commonly provided by programming environments for languages) intended to help the programmer and to ease his/her work. A more detailed description of OOPE and of its usage is given in [BDPT90] and in [OOP90].

3.1   Programming a Database Application

Creating an application involves the following three steps:

- First, the programmer generates the schema, which consists of classes. A class in
  OOPE is represented by a tuple structured object, as shown in Fig. 3. This tuple specifies the name of the class, its type (the internal structure of the objects
  of this class), its position in the hierarchy (its superclasses and subclasses), and
  the set of its private and public methods. It also indicates whether the structure of the class is private or public. The *Infos* field contains some additional
  information, such as the documentation.

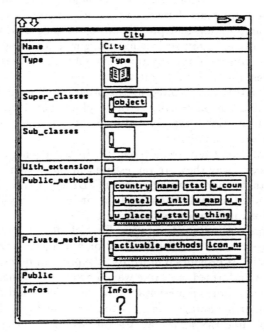

Figure 3: The City class

  To be definitively defined, a class must be compiled. This compilation checks if
  the structural part of the class and the signatures of its methods are correct.

- The next step is the implementation of the methods. A method in OOPE is also
  represented by a tuple structured object (Fig. 4). It contains the signature of the
  method, namely its name, its parameters, its result, and the class of its receiver.
  As the body of a method can be written in any of the O_2 languages, a field
  indicates which language has been used. Other information (documentation,
  compiling errors, a compiled or not compiled flag) are gathered in the *Infos*
  field.

- Finally, once the schema is defined and implemented, the programmer defines
  and implements the application and its programs. Again, applications and
  programs are represented as objects of type tuple.

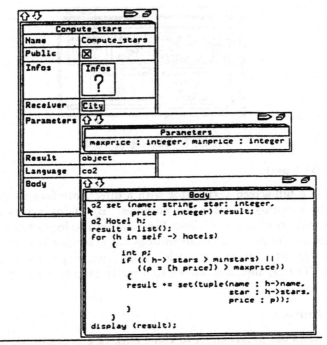

Figure 4: Template for the method *Compute_stars*

These four classes are sufficient to build an entire application. Methods attached to these objects allow to perform the basic functionalities provided by programming environments (compilation, creation of new objects of these classes and deletion of existing instances). It is also possible to run an application, a program or a method.

3.2 Software Development Tools

In this section, we present the different programming tools of OOPE. We do not present a sketch of the programming activity with the use of the OOPE, some examples of this use can be found in [BDPT90] and [OOP90]. They are gathered in an object of type set, which is displayed from the beginning to the end of a session. The programmer has thus access to any of these tools, at any time during the programming session. This object, named *Tools*, is shown in Fig. 5.

3.2.1 The Browser

The *Browser* is generally the first tool used by a programmer, when he/she starts a session. Indeed, it allows to navigate through the database, and to access the objects it contains. The name of these objects are displayed on user demand. The programmer only selects a name and the display command to access an object.

The browser also gives the possibility to display the whole hierarchy of the classes, with the class *object* as a root, as shown in Fig. 6.

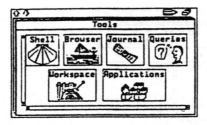

Figure 5: The set of Tools

3.2.2 The O$_2$-Shell

The O$_2$-shell is a full screen text editor with a direct interface to the O$_2$ command interpreter. It is mainly used for two purposes. By giving access to the Unix file system, it allows to read and write Unix files, and thus to import or export new data. The programmer can thus store the definitions of the schema he/she is developing, or bodies used to test parts of the application, in an Unix file, and load them in order to execute them. The O$_2$-shell also allows to directly execute O$_2$ instructions in order to test them.

3.2.3 The Journal

The journal allows the programmer to come back to a previous version of an object he/she has modified during the session. This point is important: the journal does not replace a complete versioning system. It is only a simple and fast way to retrieve versions of objects that have just been modified. The journal records critical operations made on OOPE objects, namely classes, methods, programs, applications and named objects. Each time an object is successfully compiled, its version is automatically saved in the journal, with the date. At any time, the programmer can consult the journal, get back a version of an object and restore it. Restoration is manual, and only under user control. The journal only keeps versions of objects during a session. It is initialized to an empty set at the beginning of each session.

3.2.4 The Workspaces

When a programmer builds an application, he/she needs very often to access objects of the database. This is generally done by the browser, as explained above. But, in order to save time, the programmer can store in a workspace all the objects he/she needs, from a session to another. As the workspaces are persistent, the programmer can retrieve at once all the objects he/she was working on during the previous session, avoiding a sometimes tedious navigation through the database. The workspaces, displayed in the *Tools* window, are immediately accessible and can be seen as entry points to the browsing and programming activities. Being a set of objects, the workspace can contain any kind of objects. A programmer can have as many workspaces as he/she wants.

3.2.5 The Debugger

Every programmer knows that programming without bug is utopian. A programming environment providing no debugger is not complete. The O$_2$ debugger follows the

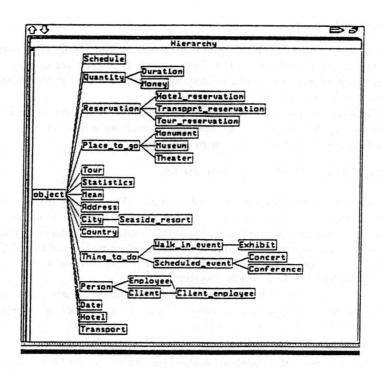

Figure 6: The class hierarchy

object-oriented principles of the OOPE. The debugger paradigm is the following: a program under the control of the debugger is aware of this control and will modify its internal behavior in consequence. The program itself constructs a database of O_2 objects that reflects its internal state at each step of the computation. Composed of four O_2 objects, the O_2 debugger is fully integrated in OOPE. It behaves as any other tool and does not necessitate the learning of a new command language. The four objects of the debugger are (i) an editor to display the source of the programs or methods, (ii) symbol tables, containing information about a method (types and values of the variables, for example), (iii) an execution stack, composed of the symbol tables of the methods called during the execution of a program, and (iv) an execution manager providing a set of commands the user can perform. The execution manager is the tool used to control the execution of a program.

If the programmer detects an abnormal behavior of a program he may execute it under the control of the O_2 debugger, which provides the programmer an interactive control on the program execution and on the message passing, the possibility to edit the values of variables and to execute methods and functions external to the program. To be used in a efficient way, the O_2 debugger supports late binding. The interested reader can find further information in [DP89] and [DP90].

3.2.6 Miscellaneous

In addition to these tools, OOPE gives an access to the O_2 Query language. The *Queries* object, which belongs to the *Tools* object, is of type set(query). It contains a set of existing queries which can be displayed and executed. It also allows the user to create and edit new queries.

The *Tools* also contain an icon called *Applications*, which contains all the applications known by the system. The user can launch an application by opening the corresponding icon and sending a *run* message to it.

4   Implementation Aspects

Programming environments handle a lot of data. The idea of using a database to store and manage these data is common now [Ber87], because of all the services to manage a large amount of data (such as data sharing and integrity, fast access to the data, protection against failure) it provides, comparing to traditional file systems. Our choice of an object-oriented design for OOPE was obviously influenced by the perspective of using the O_2 database system.

In this section, we describe how we implemented OOPE, using the various functionalities (not only the database functionalities, but also those of the language and the interface) provided by the O_2 system.

- The database functionalities

  The main feature of a database is the capacity to store a large amount of data, and to provide a fast and convenient access to it. OOPE manipulates a lot of data, which amount is potentially increasing. All the objects needed to build an application, namely the classes, the methods, the applications and the programs, are stored in the database, as well as the objects they are composed of (the *information* object, the *documentation*, the *errors*), and all the objects composing the different tools. This architecture allows a noticeable performance gain. For instance, retrieving the source of a method is done in a constant time, whatever the number of methods stored in the database (which is not always the case in relational systems where the retrieving time is generally proportional to the size of the relations).

  Using a database to store the programming objects also allows a convenient retrieval: it can be done either by navigation through the objects in the database or by using the query language, which provides high level retrieval operations.

  Another important facility offered by database systems is data sharing, which is not provided by traditional file systems. In programming environments, where objects are often shared among others, this functionality avoids important redundancy and management of this redundancy. For example, a software component can be shared by requirements, documentation, product, milestone.

  Furthermore, database systems offer data integrity, which guarantees a consistent database, and protection against system failures. A good recovery mechanism is of primary importance, because it prevents the programmer from loosing his/her data due to system failures.

  Data independence is also an interesting feature of databases. It allows the tools to remain independent from each other, and to view only the part of the database they need.

The different tools of OOPE make an intensive use of the database, increasing their performance. The journal and the workspace for instance, which are both of type set, take advantage of the efficient set management provided by O_2. But, the debugger is probably the tool which takes the most benefits from the database. The implementation of the debugger and its advantages are fully described in [DP90]. We only mention here the main features of its design and their benefits. Instead of having one unique symbol table for a whole program, the debugger stores its information in several small symbol tables, represented by objects, one per method. This allows a considerable performance gain, by decreasing the access time to the symbol information, as well as a space gain: the process size of the O_2 debugger is much smaller than process sizes of other traditional debuggers, such as GDB [Sta86] or DBX [AM86]. Other functionalities of the debugger also improved their performance: breakpoints are gathered in a list structured object, and detecting if a breakpoint has been set on a given line is equivalent to the access time of an object in main memory. It is clear that the use of the database has been very positive for the implementation of the debugger.

- The use of the O_2 language

The use of the O_2 database induces the use of the O_2 languages, to define the schema and to write the methods.

Programming with O_2 provides all the advantages of the object-oriented programming.

First of all, the modelization power of the language allowed a very simple and easy specification of our objects. The possibility, for instance, to define sets of heterogeneous objects was very useful for the workspaces. Indeed, workspaces can contain any kind of objects. It is not possible to know in advance which objects the user wants to keep. The object *Workspace* must be able to contain any kind of classes. Using a set of objects to modelize it, the programming of this tool became very simple and fast, while it could have been quite complex in a relational database.

An important feature of the O_2 system is extensibility. The addition of a new tool or of a new functionality to an object does not require modifications of existing tools, which avoids tedious recompilations. For instance, the last tool added to OOPE was the Journal. Its development was made independently of the other components of OOPE. Its integration in OOPE has been done without any modification of the other tools. Likewise, it is possible to remove one of the tools without modifying the other tools. Adding a new functionality to a tool can be done by simply writing a new method for this tool, and does not affect at all any other tool. Object-oriented programming allows a complete integration of the tools in the programming environment. Their behavior is similar, all interactions are done through selection of items in menus, and by editing objects. There is no special command language because of this uniform interaction way.

Object-oriented languages are well suited for reusability. In order to avoid frequent rewriting of pieces of code already written, O_2 provides a tool box containing a predefined set of classes, objects and values that the programmer can use. For example, the tool box contains all classes and methods used to handle dates and currency. It also provides all functionalities to implement dialogs in an application. For more details, the reader can read [Ara90], which fully describes this tool box.

- The use of LOOKS

The user interface of OOPE is entirely written using LOOKS [LOO89]. LOOKS is a user interface generator supporting the graphic and interactive manipulation of O_2 values and objects. It provides a set of 14 primitives which allow to create, remove, edit and save, maintain the consistency of the presentations of any O_2 value or object.

Using LOOKS to build a user interface simplifies a lot the programming activity. The complete management of a user interface is done in a very simple way using the set of primitives it offers. For instance, only two primitives are needed to display a presentation of an object on the screen, as shown in the following example:

class Address
        type tuple (number : **integer**,
                 street : **string**,
                 city : City,
                 zip_code : **string**,
                 country : Country)

An object o, belonging to the class *City* is displayed, in a generic fashion, with the primitives **present** and **map** of LOOKS as follows:

        p = **present** (o, EDIT, LEVEL_ONE, NESTED_WINDOW);
        map (p, SCREEN, COORDINATE, NO_PERSIST, 10, 10);

present creates a presentation for the object *o* and **map** displays this presentation as shown in Figure 7.

The parameters of **present** and **map** control the amount of information displayed, its editability and its placement on the screen.

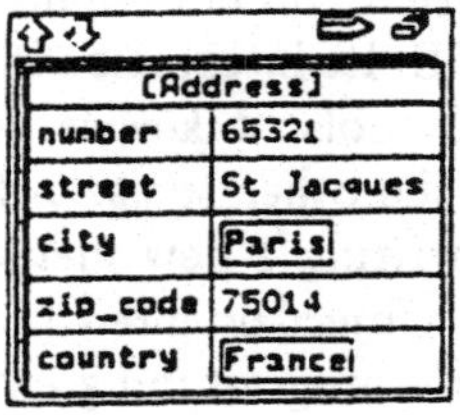

Figure 7: The class *Address*

Moreover, LOOKS offers a generic display and editing mechanism which allows a uniform representation of the objects and the message passing mechanism. This standardization of the object behavior reduces the learning time of OOPE and its tools.

The source code of OOPE is composed of 15000 lines of CO_2 code. It consists for the given time of 75 classes and 320 methods (excluding the inherited methods). OOPE is a quite complex O_2 application. Its success in terms of functionalities and performance validates our implementation choices. Indeed, the use of the O_2 system to implement the programming environment was very positive, for all the reasons previously given. In addition to the services provided by the database, it allowed a gain in performance, a gain in development time, and the use of a generic display and edition mechanism. Furthermore the use of CO_2 provided much flexibility in the design of the schema.

5 Related Work

In this paper, two aspects were considered: the design and the implementation of OOPE. We first compare the design of OOPE with other related work, and then discuss our implementation choices.

For the time being, not much work has been done on programming environments for OODBMS (Object-oriented database management systems), mostly because they are still recent. Among the existing systems (Orion [KBC+88], Ontos [TAD90], Gemstone [MS87], Iris [FBC+87]), only Gemstone uses a programming environment (which is the Smalltalk-80 [Gol83] programming environment) comparable to OOPE. Smalltalk-80 has a very powerful and complete programming environment, emphasing visual accesses to objects. As in O_2, commands are mostly performed through menus. The Smalltalk-80 browser is a sophisticated and efficient tool, but does not allow a graphical display of the class hierarchy, as it is done in O_2.

Being more related to programming environments for languages than for databases, OOPE is mostly to be compared with programming environments for languages. Languages such as C++ or Objective-C provide efficient and complete programming environments inherited from C. But they do not reflect the object-oriented aspects of the language. Moreover, the tools they provide, particularly browsers and debuggers, have poor performance, principally because they are based on Unix files scanning.

Previous approaches for implementing software engineering or programming environments tended to use conventional file system to store their data. To manage it efficiently, additional management components had to be developed. These tools usually are built to deal with particular problems and do not always fit well together or with all the other requirements. In principle, database systems can help to manage this data, by offering functionalities to efficiently store and manage a large amount of data. Indeed, several attempts [Pen86] have been done to use a database, mostly using the relational or the entity-relationship model. But these experiences were not completely satisfying, partly because of the absence of some functionalities (such as versioning, long and nested transactions), but also because of the lack of a good data model. Software development applications involve large and complex objects, which are often related by various relationships, and which need to be manipulated by special operators (able for instance to operate on syntax trees, flow graphs,...) which are usually not provided by DBMS.

The object-oriented model is best suited to represent complex data, but up to now, experiences in using object-oriented database systems to handle the data manipulated by software development systems are quite rare, because available products appeared only recently.

Another approach, taken by Damokles [DGL86] and Cactis [HK88], consists to extend database systems to support the data management needs of software engineering. They provide features such as complex objects representation, software versions, long transactions. These two interesting experiences are intended to support large software engineering environments rather than database application development environments as done by OOPE, which does not address the "programming in the large" issues.

6 Conclusion

In this paper, we described OOPE, the interactive programming environment of O_2. It provides both the functionalities of database and of languages programming environments, and is one of the few existing programming environment for object-oriented database system. Due to its homogeneity, OOPE is easy to use and to understand. It has a nice interface, which allows simple manipulations of objects on the screen and avoids to learn a new command language.

OOPE is a quite complex O_2 application. It has been developed using as much as possible the various possibilities provided by the O_2 system, namely, the database to store the objects it manipulates, the language to implement the functionalities, and the interface generator to build the interface. OOPE is used inside the Altaïr group and is in Beta-test in several French industries and universities. Its success, in terms of performance and of functionalities validates our design and implementation choices.

OOPE was designed for a prototype version of O_2. O_2 is a now a product, commercialised by O_2 Technology. Its programming environment, named O_2 Tools is an improved and completed version of OOPE. It integrates new functionalities, such as schema update functions, transactions and multi-base functionalities. The user interface is more convenient and provides customization facilities. The browser is divided into five specialized sub-browsers and will provide a much faster and convenient access to the classes, methods, named objects, applications and programs. Other services, such as a test generation tool, a versioning system for the objects, the classes and the methods, and a complete documentation tool are planned to be added to the programming environment.

7 Authorship and Acknowledgements

OOPE was designed by the authors with the collaboration of Jean-Claude Mamou. Didier Tallot and Jean-Claude Mamou helped in the implementation of OOPE. This paper benefits from the careful reading of our colleagues from Altaïr, in particular Gilles Barbedette and Didier Plateau.

References

[AM86]   E. Adams and S. S. Muchnick. Dbxtool: A Window-Based Symbolic Debugger for Sun Workstations. *Software, Practice and Experience*, 16 (7), July 1986.

[Ara90]   G. Arango. Self-Explained Toolboxes: a Practical Approach to Reusability. In *TOOLS 90*, Paris, France, June 1990.

[BDPT90] P. Borras, A. Doucet, P. Pfeffer, and D. Tallot. OOPE : The O_2 Programming Environment. In *Proceedings of the 6th PRC BD3* , Montpellier, FRANCE, September 26-28 1990.

[Ber87] Philip A. Bernstein. Database System Support for Software Engineering - An Extended Abstract - . In *Proceedings of the 9 th International Conference on Software Engineering*, pages 166 –178, Monterey, California, March 1987.

[Da90] O. Deux and al. The Story of O_2. *Special Issue of IEEE Transactions on Knowledge and Data Engineering*, March 1990.

[DGL86] K. R. Dittrich, W. Gotthard, and P. C. Lockemann. DAMOKLES - A Database System for Software Engineering Environments. In *Proceedings of the IFIP Workshop on Advanced Programming Environments*, June 1986.

[DP89] A. Doucet and P. Pfeffer. A Debugger for O_2, an Object-Oriented Database Language. In *Proceedings of the First International Conference on Technology of Object-Oriented Languages and Systems*, pages 559 – 571, CNIT Paris - La Défense - France, November 1989.

[DP90] A. Doucet and P. Pfeffer. Using a Database to Implement a Debugger. In *IFIP : Conference on Database Semantics*. North-Holland Elsevier, July 1990.

[FBC+87] D. H. Fishman, D. Beech, H. P. Cate, E. C. Chow, T. Connors, J. W. Davis, N. Derrett, C. G. Hoch, W. Kent, P. Lyngbaek, B. Mahbod, M. A. Neimat, T. A. Ryan, and M. C. Shan. Iris: An Object-Oriented Database Management System . *ACM Transactions on Office Information Systems*, 5(1), 1987.

[Gol83] A. Goldberg. *Smalltalk-80 : The Interactive Programming Environment*. Addison-Wesley, 1983.

[HK88] Scott E. Hudson and Roger King. The Cactis Project: Database Support for Software Environments . *IEEE Transactions on Software Engineering* , 14(6):709 – 719, June 1988.

[KBC+88] W. Kim, J. Banerjee, H. T. Chou, J. F. Garza, and D. Woelk. Composite Object Support in an Object-Oriented Database System . In *Proceedings of the ACM SIGMOD Int. Conf.*, Chicago, USA, May 1988.

[LOO89] Gip Altair, BP 105, 78153 Le Chesnay. *LOOKS users manual*, 1989.

[LR89] C. Lécluse and P. Richard. The O_2 Database Programming Language. In *Int. Conf. on Very Large Databases*, The Nederlands, August 1989. ACM.

[LRV88] C. Lécluse, P. Richard, and F. Vélez. O_2, an Object-Oriented Data Model. In *ACM SIGMOD*, pages 424 – 434, 1988.

[MS87]   D. Maier and J. Stein. Development and Implementation of an Object-Oriented DBMS . In B. Shriver and P. Wegner, editors, *Research Directions in Object-Oriented Programming* , pages 355 – 392. MIT Press, Cambridge, MA, 1987.

[OOP90]   *OOPE: The Object-Oriented Programming Environment.* Gip Altair, BP105, 78153 LE CHESNAY Cedex, FRANCE, Version 1.0, Released 15 December 1989. Printing revision 1.1 edition, 9 January 1990.

[Pen86]   Maria H. Penedo. Prototyping a Project Master Data Base for Software Engineering Environment. In *Proceedings of the ACM SIGSOFT/SIGPLAN Software Engineering Symposium on Practical Software Development Environments*, pages 1 – 11, December 1986.

[Sta86]   R. Stallman. The Gnu Debugger . Technical report, Free Software Foundation, Inc., 675 Mass. Avenue, Cambridge, MA, 02139, USA, 1986.

[TAD90]   C. Harris T. Andrews and J. Duhl. The Ontos Object Database. Technical report, Ontologic Inc, Burlington MA, 01803, 1990.

[VDB89]   Fernando Vélez, Vineeta Darnis, and Guy Bernard. The O_2 Object Manager, an Overview. In *Int. Conf. on Very Large Databases*, The Nederlands, August 1989. ACM.

Automatic Generation of Documentation for Information Systems

Lurdes Jesus
Rogério Carapuça

IST/INESC
Rua Alves Redol, 9, 1000 Lisboa, Portugal
Phone: +351.1.3100326 - Fax: +351.1.525843 - Email: mlp@eniac.inesc.pt

Abstract. Documentation plays a central role in Information Systems (IS) development and use. Software tools must be built to allow its automatic generation. In the same way as the need of prototyping for IS construction is generally accepted, so must be the need for "Documentation Prototyping". In this paper a paradigm for the generation of documentation is proposed. It can be adapted to any IS development approach. In order to illustrate the proposed ideas, the Infolog approach was chosen in this paper.

On-line documentation is, in most cases, preferable to off-line one (the traditional paper manuals). The paradigm for generation of documentation herein proposed can be used to obtain both on-line and off-line documentation. Moreover, it is obtained in hypertext form for better browsing. The linearization of the hypertext network is also possible in order to produce the often required linear form (for example to obtain paper manuals).

The main contributions of this work are the generation paradigm, which uses the semantics of the modelling primitives in order to obtain natural language text fragments describing the specified models, and the generation of the "User Manual", the more critical of the documents to be produced.

1 Introduction

Documentation plays a central role in Information Systems (IS) development and use. Software tools for IS development must facilitate the production of documentation based on the specification models for requirements and design. That way it is possible to keep up-to-date the documents as changes are made to the objects described [6].

Manual elaboration of documentation is fastidious and time consuming. In the current state of computational tools for IS development, if automatic documentation generation is not supported, there is a big disparity between the time consumed to produce a version of the IS ready to use and the time to build the corresponding documentation.

Hence we want to see fast "documentation prototyping" going at a same pace as the already common notion of IS prototyping.

Automatic generation is possible when the requirements for documentation are described and the necessary information is available. The generation should (must) be possible either using documentation templates supplied with the tool or user defined templates. This work recognizes a set of requirements and proposes a set of templates for IS documentation. A method to automatically produce the defined documents from stored specifications is also defined.

The structure of the documentation could be the traditional linear or in hypertext form [6]. In the work reported in this paper, the hypertext structure was adopted in order to support both kinds of presentation (the linear form can be obtained from the hypertext one). Furthermore, the structured nature of the stored information and the requirements on how to browse through it, suggest naturally the hypertext presentation form.

Currently it can still be said that most of the documentation produced to support applications is essentially linear [6], presented either in paper manuals or on-line context documentation. On-line context documentation is, for many users, preferable to paper manuals. Specially if they are able to use sophisticated browsing capabilities in hypertext form instead of linear text.

IS development can generally be divided into the traditional analysis, design, construction and use/maintenance phases. According with each particular methodology, a sequence of models (Universe of Discourse interpretations) is obtained during the execution of these phases. The set of concepts (or primitives) used to build each interpretation is a Concept Structure. In order to present the ideas of this work any Concept Structure could be adopted. In this paper the one of Infolog [7,8] was chosen. It has the advantage of being rich enough so as to allow the derivation of good descriptions due to its underlying semantics. In section 2.1 the Infolog approach is briefly presented.

Specifications resulting from analysis and design normally include:
- diagrams;
- sentences in some specification language;
- unstructured (natural language) text fragments.

Using the semantics of the underlying Concept Structure it is possible to derive descriptions for the specified models. The richer the Concept Structure, the more precise and adapted to the UoD, the derived descriptions are. Furthermore, from the stored definitions of the Human-Machine Interfaces (HMIs) it is also possible to derive the User Manual. The non-automatic construction of a User Manual is, in fact, a rather complex, repetitive and time consuming operation. So, to automate its production means to considerably simplify the documentation production task. The use of the semantics of the underlying Concept Structure to produce descriptions for the specified models and the generation of the User Manual are the two fundamental contributions of this work.

It should also be noted that according to [1] HMI default definitions can also be produced automatically. This process can be coupled with that of producing the default User Manual.

There are several documents to be considered, according to the objects described and the expected reader. As referred in [9], two kinds of requirements descriptions are usually suggested in the Software Engineering field: the <u>Requirements Definition</u> stating, in natural language, what user services the system is expected to provide, and the <u>Requirements Specification</u> stating, in a formal notation, the system services in a more detailed way. The requirements definition must be understandable by non-specialist staff, like management people and potential system users. As mentioned in [9], the requirements specification "must be couched in such terms that is understandable to technical staff from both procurers and developers, and it is reasonable to assume some understanding of the software engineering process on the part of the procurer" .

The proposed documents to be generated are: the <u>Requirements Definition Document</u> and the <u>Requirements Specification Document</u>, both resulting from the Requirements Analysis phase, the <u>Design Specification Document</u>, that results from Design phase and the <u>User Manual</u> used in the Operation/maintenance phase (note that this manual does not result from the Operation/maintenance phase, instead it is used in that phase).

In the next section a brief overview of the Infolog approach and some hypertext concepts are presented. In section 3 the proposed paradigm for generation of documentation is described. Some rules used to derive the natural language description of an Infolog schema are included. An example of its application is given in section 4 where fragments of the Requirements Definition Document and of the User Manual automatically generated are shown. In section 5 the computational tool that is being developed applying the proposed ideas and its integration in an workbench for IS prototyping are referred. Some conclusions are made in section 6.

2 Basic Concepts

The objective of this section is to give an overview of the background concepts. In section 2.1 the Concept Structure of the Infolog static model is described. In section 2.2 some hypertext concepts are focused.

2.1 The underlying approach for IS development

In this section the Concept Structure of the Infolog static model is briefly presented. The basic Infolog abstractions are described along with their graphical definitions. Illustrations are presented using a fragment of the already "famous" IFIP Conference example. The Infolog schema for that UoD is presented in fig. 1.

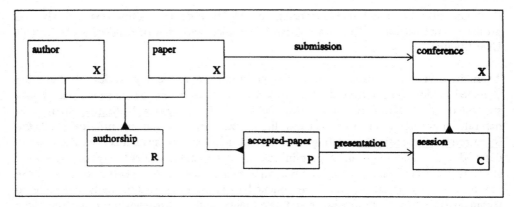

Fig.1. Infolog Conceptual Schema for the Conferences UoD (X - surrogate; R - relation; P - specialization; C - characteristic)

For a better understanding of the Infolog primitives, in the next figure the corresponding ER schema is depicted.

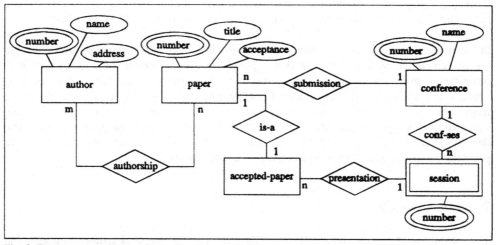

Fig. 2. ER Conceptual Schema for the Conferences UoD

The basic Infolog abstraction at the static level is the archetype. An archetype sort is a class of similar objects which are called archetype instances. An archetype instance aggregates the information about some real-world entity or association between entities. For example, *paper* is an archetype representing an entity and *authorship* is an archetype representing an association between *paper* and *author*. The word archetype is often used in this text to designate both the type and the instances. For each particular case, the reader will distinguish from context if a reference is made to a type or to an instance.

In the archetype, the information is structured in attributes. An attribute is a mathematical function whose domain is an archetype. Attributes can be either properties or designators. The codomain of a property is a data type whereas the codomain of a designator is an archetype. For example, *title* is a property of *paper* whose codomain is the *string* data type and *submission* is a designator of *paper* whose codomain is the *conference* archetype. By means of the *submission* designator a *conference* (instance) is associated to each *paper* (instance) - the conference where the paper has been submitted. Designators correspond to a one to many relationship in the ER approach [3].

There are several categories of archetype. Each of the archetype categories have a different key mechanism (identification mechanism for the instances) and corresponds to a different real world abstraction. In this paper only the surrogate, relation, characteristic and specialization categories of archetype are described, the ones that appear in the Conference schema. For more details on the Infolog approach see [7] and [8].

A surrogate archetype represents an entity whose existence and identification mechanism does not depend of the rest of the UoD entities. The corresponding ER semantic primitive is the entity type whose instance naming and existence are independent of other entities. In the case of the Conference UoD, *paper* is a surrogate archetype sort. Each paper is uniquely identified by a number that does not depend of any other object of the Conference UoD. *number* is the key property of *paper*.

All other categories represent entities or associations that depend for definition on other - the arguments. A relation archetype represents a many to many association between the argument archetypes. The corresponding ER approach primitive is the M:N relationship (with arity equal to the number of archetype arguments).

In the case of the Conference UoD, *authorship* is a relation archetype sort. In fact, each author may contribute to more than one paper whereas, on the other hand, one paper may be authored by more than one author. So it corresponds to a M:N relationship between entities *author* and *paper*.

A characteristic archetype sort is an archetype whose instances are dependent for existence and naming on other archetype instances. In particular, a unary characteristic archetype corresponds to an ER 1:N relationship between two entities A and B where the B entity (the one with the N multiplicity in the relationship) is a week entity - the relationship between A and B is necessary to identify its instances. For example *session* is a unary characteristic of *conference*. That means that for each conference there are many sessions and that a session is related to only one conference. Moreover, to identify a session the related conference is needed. Note that the identification of a conference is not enough to identify a particular session, since there are several sessions for each conference. So a partial key mechanism must be defined in order to distinguish the sessions related to each conference. The definition of a characteristic sort includes a partial key property. Instances of that sort related to the same argument instances can not have repeated values for the partial key property. In the Conference example, *session* as a partial key property *number*. All sessions of the same conference must have different numbers. Sessions of different conferences may have equal numbers.

A specialization archetype sort denotes a sub-class of some other class (its argument archetype). Whenever a specialization is defined, a discriminant property must be introduced in the corresponding argument. The value associated through this property with each argument instance indicates if a specialization instance must or not be defined as well.

In the case of the Conference UoD, a paper may or not be accepted. In the archetype *paper* a property *acceptance* is defined to discriminate between accepted papers and non-accepted ones. If a paper is accepted then its *acceptance* property has the value "acc" and an instance of *accepted-paper* must be defined.

2.2 Hypertext

Hypertext, in opposition to traditional text, has not implicit a sequential reading order. Traditional text has a single linear sequence defining the order in which the text is to be read (page 1 -> page 2 -> ...). By contrast, in hypertext there is no single order that determines the sequence in which the text is to be read [5]. Hypertext has a network structure associated (fig. 3). Each node of that network has a text fragment[1] with a certain subject. Links are used to establish associations between subjects: each node has links for the nodes with related subjects.

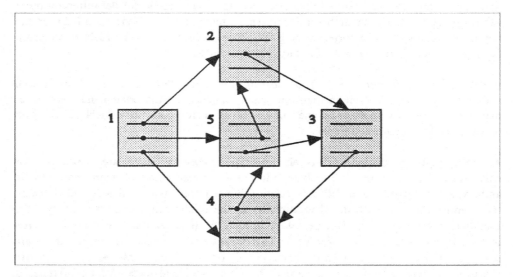

Fig. 3. Hypertext has a network structure

---

[1] Sometimes when the information in one node is expressed in non-textual form (usually graphics, video images or sound), the term hypermedia is used. Nevertheless, some authors (Jackob Nielsen [Niel90], for instance) use indistinctly the term hypertext defending that there is no need to reserve a special term for text-only systems.

An hypertext system offers an interactive presentation form of documentation highly adaptable to the user needs (interest level, understanding and other individual factors). Hypertext reading is made by navigation through the network (using the defined links), according to the user interest. For instance, in fig. 3 from node 1 the reader can go to node 2 or 5 or 4. As mentioned in [5], hypertext links are frequently associated with specific parts of the departure nodes (as depicted in fig. 3, where links are anchored at specific locations in the departure node). A typical application of this feature, that will be used in this paper, is to have the definition of a link anchored at a certain word in the departure node. That word can be presented, for instance, in reverse video, a different color or simply underlined to denote the link. In this paper underlined words represent the links, as exemplified in fig. 4.

Infolog

Infolog is a data oriented modelling approach.Nevertheless, not only the statical aspects of the UoD may be captured, but also the dynamical aspects. ...

Approach

An approach is formed by a Concept Structure and a methodology. ER, Infolog and Relational are examples of approaches.

UoD

Universe of Discourse - real word fragment that we want to represent.

Fig. 4. An hypertext fragment where links are denoted by underlined words

3 The proposed paradigm

The paradigm herein proposed for documentation generation is based on a set of rules that, applied to the models obtained as result of the analysis and design phases, gives an hypertext network describing those models. Moreover, and most important, there are rules that applied to the interface specifications, generate the user manual.

Several groups of rules are defined, according to the Concept Structure used and the derived types of description. Namely, there are rules to generate from Infolog schemas not only its formal descriptions, but also descriptions in a fragment of natural language. This two kinds of descriptions are also derived from the specifications of dynamic aspects. From relational schemas only technical descriptions are derived. From HMIs definitions two kinds of descriptions are generated: a technical description and a description of its presentation and expected interactions (user manual). In this paper only the natural language description of Infolog schemas and the user manual will be focused. In [4] the complete work underlying this paper was reported.

Each set of rules describes how the nodes and links of the hypertext network for each schema are defined. In the rules the (schema-)text of the nodes is defined. Underlined words correspond to links. Like in BNF, words between ' < ' and ' > ' must be replaced, text between '[' and ']' is optional and '|' means alternative. By convention, generated text appears between '«' and '»'.

3.1 Natural language description of an Infolog schema

There is a node of the hypertext network for each archetype. That node contains text describing the archetype. The text depends on the archetype category, its attributes and its relationships. Hypertext links result from links between archetypes (either from archetype categories or designators). If in a node N, associated to an archetype A, an archetype B, with associated node M, is mentioned then there is a link from node N to node M.

The text of each node results from the concatenation of several fragments of text obtained from the application of different rules. To obtain the text of the node associated to a given archetype the application of the rules is done by the following order: first the rule that corresponds to the archetype category, next the rule for the attributes and finally the rules that corresponds to the categories of the associations from which the archetype is argument.

As an example, the next rule gives the description for surrogate archetypes. A surrogate archetype has a naming mechanism of its occurrences which is independent of those of other entities. Each instance of a surrogate archetype is uniquely identified by the value of its key property.

Rule 1:
If <A> is a surrogate archetype with key property <kp>

```
┌─────────────────────────────────────────────────────────┐
│                                                           │
│                    ┌──────────────────────┐               │
│                    │ A                    │               │
│                    │                    X │               │
│                    └──────────────────────┘               │
│                                                           │
└─────────────────────────────────────────────────────────┘
```

then the node of <A> begins with the following text:
«A <A> is uniquely identified by its <kp>.»
◻

An example of application of this rule:
«A author is uniquely identified by its number.».

Note in the example that an 'An' should be used instead of 'A'. This and other "linguistic features" are not introduced in the current version of this work.

A typical relationship is the one-to-many relationship were a weak entity is involved. That corresponds to the unary characteristic in Infolog. In the next rule there is a one-to-many relationship between B and A and to identify an instance of A the related B instance is needed.

Rule 2:
If < A > is an unary characteristic of < B >

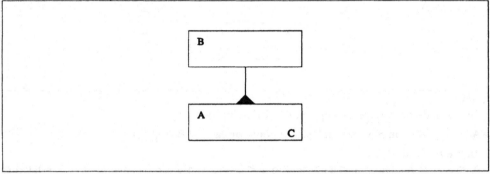

then
- In the node of < B > :
«A < B > has several <u>< A ></u> related.»
- In the node of < A > :
«There are several < A > for each <u>< B ></u>. Each < A > is identified by the related <u>< B ></u> in conjunction with the < pkp > of < A >.».
  ¤

To illustrate the application of this rule lets see how we would begin the description of *session*, since it is a characteristic of *conference* (see all the example of section 2.1):
«There are several session for each <u>conference</u>. Each session is identified by the related <u>conference</u> in conjunction with the number of session.».

This relationship between session and conference generates also a piece of text in the description of conference:
«A conference has several <u>session</u> related.».

That text in the node of conference establishes the link to the node of session.

Note here again the lack of concordance in 'several session' due to the yet limited linguistic features.

Another common relationship is the many-to-many relationship. The next rule establishes the description to be generated in the case that A is a many-to-many relationship between entities B1 and B2.

Rule 3:
If $<A>$ is a binary relation of $<B_1>$ and $<B_2>$

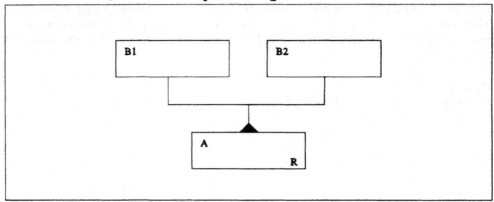

then
- In the node of $<B_{1(2)}>$ appears the following text:
«A $<B_{1(2)}>$ can have several $\underline{<A>}$, one for each $\underline{<B_{2(1)}>}$.»;
- In the node of $<A>$:
«A $<A>$ is related to a $\underline{<B_1>}$ and to a $\underline{<B_2>}$. There can be several $<A>$ related to each $\underline{<B_1>}$, one for each $\underline{<B_2>}$. In the same way, there can be several $<A>$ related to each $\underline{<B_2>}$, one for each $\underline{<B_1>}$.».
□

In the case of the Conference example, *authorship* is a binary relation of *author* and *paper*. Applying the previous rule it results:
- in the description of *authorship*:
        «A author can have several authorship, one for each paper.»;
- in the description of *paper*:
        «A paper can have several authorship, one for each author.»;
- and the description of *authorship* begins with the text:
        «A authorship is related to a author and a paper. There can be several authorship related to each author, one for each paper. In the same way, there can be several authorship related to each paper, one for each author.».

The is-a relationship is defined in Infolog by means of the specialization category of archetype. In the next rule "each A_i is a B" and a B can only be of one kind (A_1 or A_2 ... or A_n). The discriminant property of B indicates for each instance if it is an A_1 or an A_2 ... or an A_n.

Rule 4:

If $<A_1>$, ..., $<A_n>$ are specializations of $<B>$ with discriminant property $<dp>$

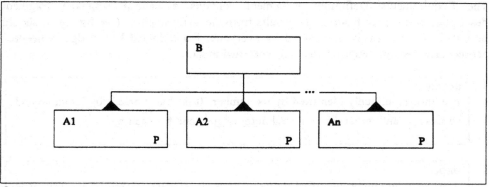

then

- In the node of $<B>$:

«A $<B>$ can be a $\underline{<A_1>}$ or a $\underline{<A_2>}$, ... or $\underline{<A_n>}$, depending on its $<dp>$.»;

- In the node of $<A_i>$:

«A $<A_i>$ is a $\underline{<B>}$.».

¤

Applying this last rule to the specialization of *paper*, *accepted-paper*, **and being** acceptance the discriminant property, results:

- in the description of *paper*

«A paper can be a accepted-paper, depending on its acceptance.»;

- and the description of *accepted-paper* begins with the text:

«A accepted-paper is a paper.».

Note that similar rules could be defined for the ER approach. If roles are attached to the arguments of the defined associations, the generated descriptions can be well adapted to the UoD.

4 Applying the paradigm

In this section a fragment of the generated hypertext network for the Conference example is presented. In section 4.1 the natural language fragment included in the Requirements Definition Document is represented. In section 4.2 the problem of generation of the User Manual is discussed and illustrated.

To represent the hypertext network without drawing the links, the nodes have been labeled with a number. Whenever there is a link from a word in a certain node to a node n, that same word is underlined and indexed by n. For instance "authorship[3]" indicates a link to node number 3 associated to "authorship".

4.1 Requirements Definition Document

The Requirements Definition Document contains a natural language fragment description of the specification that results from the analysis phase (see fig. 5). It should be noted that it is easily understood by everyone. No technical knowledge is needed. Moreover it can be used to validate the specified model.

---

1 | **author**
A author is uniquely identified by its number. It is characterized by its name and address. A author can have several authorship[3], one for each paper[2].

---

2 | **paper**
A paper is uniquely identified by its number. It is characterized by its title. It is also characterized by its submission which is a conference[5]. A paper can have several authorship[3], one for each author[1]. A paper can be a accepted-paper[4], depending on its acceptance.

---

3 | **authorship**
A authorship is related to a author[1] and a paper[2]. There can be several authorship related to each author[1], one for each paper[2]. In the same way, there can be several authorship related to each paper[2], one for each author[1].

---

4 | **accepted-paper**
A accepted-paper is a paper[2]. It is also characterized by its presentation which is a session[6].

---

5 | **conference**
A conference is uniquely identified by its number. It is characterized by its name. A conference has several session[6] related.

---

6 | **session**
There are several session for each conference[5]. Each session is identified by the related conference[5] in conjunction with the number of session.

Fig. 5. Natural language fragment of the Requirements Definition Document

4.2 User Manual

The User Manual is produced from the HMI specifications. Those specifications are in a format described in [2]. In order to shorten this presentation neither the HMI specification format nor the rules to obtain the HMI descriptions from its definitions are presented. In [4] both aspects are extensively reported.

The objective of this section is to exemplify the format of the User Manual by presenting a fragment of the automatically generated description. That description consists on a list of the interfaces that appear to the user on the different situations to which he may go (see fig. 7 as an example).

One of the basic building blocks of the HMI specifications is the Card (the "Card" designation follows the one of the HyperCard objects). An example of a Card Widget is shown in fig. 7 where the card associated with archetype *paper* is presented.

Each HMI has the following structure: it has a Main Menu and several cards, where each card is an image of an object of the UoD. The Main Menu has several buttons, each one giving access to a Card (see fig. 6).

In fig. 6 the automatically generated description for the Main Menu of a HMI for the Conferences example is presented.

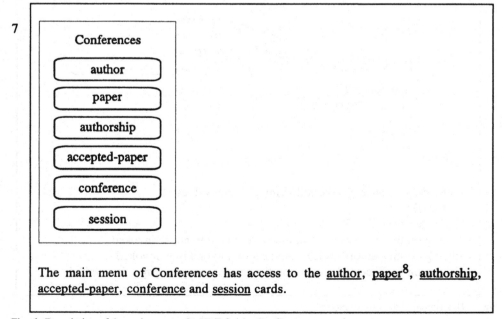

The main menu of Conferences has access to the author, paper[8], authorship, accepted-paper, conference and session cards.

Fig. 6. Description of the main menu of a HMI for the Conferences example

A card has four components: title, properties zone, icons zone and messages device. The title is a text expression that informs the user about the archetype represented by the card ("paper" in the case of the card of fig. 7). The properties zone contains an entry for each property of the archetype. It includes either key and non-key attributes. The icons zone includes a set of navigation points, each one leading to another card. This is the case of buttons *submission*, *authorship* and *accepted-paper* in the card of *paper* depicted in fig. 7. Activating an icon, the user invokes a new card through which he can access instances related with the data reported in the present card. For example, the icon *submission*, when set, maps an instance of the card corresponding to the archetype *conference*. The messages device is used for visualizing error, warning or information messages.

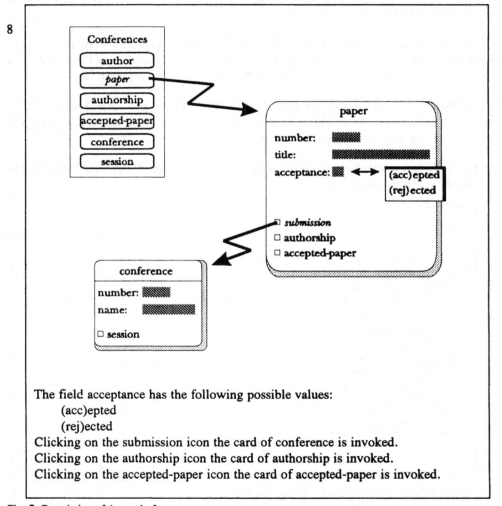

The field acceptance has the following possible values:
    (acc)epted
    (rej)ected
Clicking on the submission icon the card of conference is invoked.
Clicking on the authorship icon the card of authorship is invoked.
Clicking on the accepted-paper icon the card of accepted-paper is invoked.

Fig. 7. Description of the card of *paper*

5 Documentation Generation Support System

IS prototyping is widely accepted and increasingly used. The Caravela workbench [1] was developed with that purpose. In this paper "Documentation prototyping" is proposed. The computational tool that is being developed applying the proposed ideas will be integrated in the Caravela workbench, as depicted in fig. 8 where the global architecture of the Caravela workbench is presented. The tool proposed in this work is shadowed.

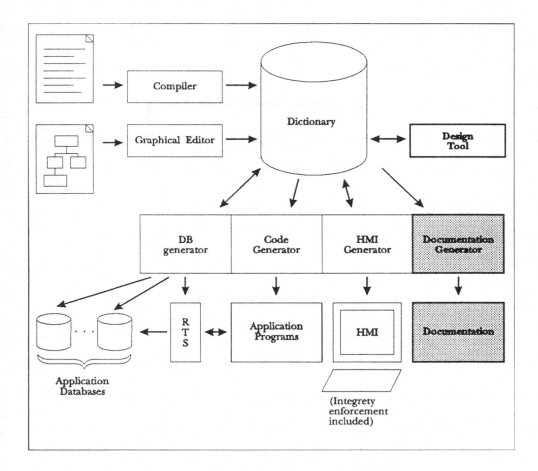

Fig. 8. Global architecture of the Caravela Workbench - adapted from [2]

In an abbreviated form it may be said that the input specifications, either in graphical or textual form, are stored in the dictionary. From this specifications, several 'products' are generated: relational schemas for each local database, default HMI, application code and documentation.

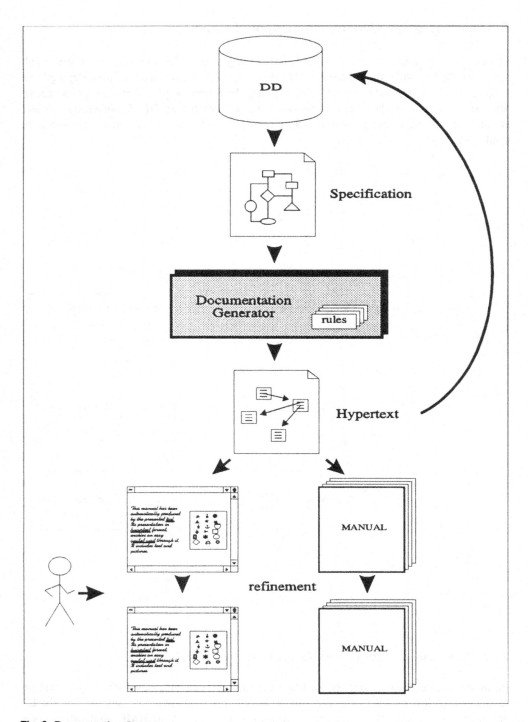

Fig. 9. Documentation Generator

In fig. 9 the Documentation Generator is depicted. From the stored specifications and using a set of rules (like the exemplified in 3.1), the Documentation Generator produces a representation, in hypertext format, of the documents. From this representation, several forms of presenting the documents can be produced. In particular, the hypertext one and paper supported (paper manuals).

6 Conclusions

The simplification of the task of documentation production requires the inclusion of the automatic generation of documentation in CASE tools for IS development. In this paper, a paradigm for the generation of documentation was proposed.

A demonstrator of the proposed ideas is being developed. It will be integrated in the Caravela CASE Workbench [1].

The exhaustive experiment of the generated User Manual is needed. The resulting feedback will serve to improve the present ideas. In fact, only with a great deal of experience it is possible to come up with ideas to improve this manual. Also the introduction of linguistic features in all the generated fragments of text is a foreseen future work.

References

1. R. Carapuça, L. Andrade and A. Sernadas, "A Database Design and Construction Workbench", in Computerized Assistance During the Information Systems Life Cycle, T.W. Olle, A.A. Verrijn-Stuart, L. Bhabuta (Eds), Elsevier Science Publishers B.V. (North-Holland), IFIP 1988
2. R. Carapuça et all., "Computer-Aided Database Development Tools: Extending the Caravela workbench", ESPRIT project report, IACIS, April 1991
3. P. Chen, "The Entity-Relationship Model: Toward an Unified View of Data", ACM TODS, 1:1, pp9-36, 1976
4. L. Jesus, "Geração Automática de Documentação para Sistemas de Informação", MsC thesis, IST, October 1991
5. J. Nielsen, "Hypertext & Hypermedia", Academic Press, Inc., 1990
6. J. Parkinson, "CASE - An Introduction, IBC Financial Books, 1989
7. A. Sernadas and C. Sernadas, "Infolog: An Integrated Model of Data and Processes", IFIP WG8.1 Meeting, York, July 1983
8. A. Sernadas e C. Sernadas, "Infolog 86", (in Portuguese) Revista de Informática, Vol. 5 Núm. 10, 1986
9. I. Sommerville, "Software Engineering", Addison-Wesley Publishing Company, 1989

A Framework for
Performance Engineering during
Information System Development

Andreas L. Opdahl* and Arne Sølvberg†
The University of Trondheim
andreaso@ifi.unit.no, asolvber@idt.unit.no

Abstract

Software performance engineering aims at predicting and improving the
performance of applications during development and in production. This paper
presents a framework for performance engineering of information systems with
emphasis on parameter estimation support.

The need for performance engineering of information systems is discussed.
Views of information system and performance modelling are presented. It is
shown how application specifcations can be extended with performance annotations. The resulting framework is applied to predict and improve the
performance of projected applications during development. Sensitivity analysis is supported to point out performance bottlenecks in the application and
suggest which parameters to estimate with most care. Target platform modelling is provided to relieve the information system developer from assessing
the performance of the target platform and operating system software. The
framework is realised in terms of the PrM language for software specification.
Finally, some conclusions are offered.

Introduction

Software performance engineering [Smi90, AWS91] aims at predicting and improving the performance of software during development and in production. Efficient
utilisation of information technology has become a decisive competition factor in
industry and business. Although the price of computers is steadily decreasing, the
total hardware expenses are *increasing* along with the demand for computing power.

*Department of Informatics, Faculty of Nature Sciences, College of Arts and Sciences
†Information Systems Group, Department of Electrical Engineering and Computer Science,
The Norwegian Institute of Technology

As a result, hardware expenses have become visible at the organisation level, and therefore a limited resource. At the same time, the price of unacceptable performance has grown due to tightened market competition. New methods must be applied to utilise the organisation's computer resources more efficiently.

This paper will present a framework for performance engineering of information systems. The framework focuses on predicting the performance of projected applications during development. It has been developed with the goals of 1) integrating the state of the art of information system development and performance engineering [OS92]; 2) supporting performance parameter estimation [Opd91b]; 3) interacting with the capacity management process [Vet91], and 4) supporting database design [OS81]. In addition, simplicity and generality has been emphasised. This paper will focus on parameter estimation support in particular.

Although the framework is presented in a theoretical form, it has been developed as a result of practical considerations and experience. A realisation of the framework has been made in connection with the experimental integrated CASE tool environment PPP [GLW91]. A graphical interface for annotating PPP specifications with performance parameters has been implemented, together with the basic associated analysis techniques [Opd92b]. The tool has been developed as part of the IMSE[1] project, which provides state-of-the-art performance modelling tools at the computer system level [HP89]. A case study has been undertaken, using the framework and tool to monitor the development of a commercial information system [BOVS91].

Views of information system and performance modelling are presented in sec. 1, and application specifcations are annotated with performance parameters. The resulting framework is applied to predict and improve the performance of projected applications during development in sec. 2. Sensitivity analysis is supported to point out performance bottlenecks in the application and suggest which parameters to estimate with most care in sec. 3. Target platform modelling is provided to relieve the information system developer from assessing the performance of the target platform and operating system software in sec. 4 The framework is realised in terms of the PrM language for software specification in sec. 5. Finally, some conclusions are offered.

In the remainder of this paper, important terms are **bold-faced** when introduced.

1   The basic framework

The basic framework for performance engineering during information system development is based on general views of information system and performance modelling, as well as on annotating application specifications with performance parameters.

---

[1]The IMSE project was a collaborative research project supported by the CEC as ESPRIT project no 2143. It was carried out by the following organisations :- BNR Europe STL, Thomson CSF, Simulog A.S., University of Edinburgh, INRIA, IPK (Berlin), University of Dortmund, University of Pavia, SINTEF (University of Trondheim), University of Turin and University of Milan.

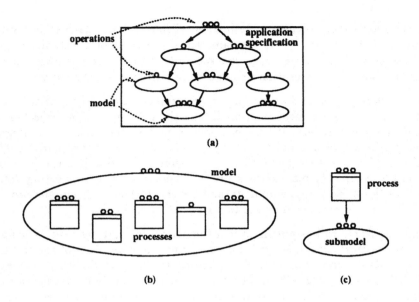

Figure 1: An application specification contains a DAG of models (a). A model contains a set of processes (b). A non-primitive process has a submodel (c).

The three are treated in separate.

1.1   Information system modelling

Fundamental to the basic framework is the view of *information system modelling* presented in [OS92]. According to this view, an **application specification** S represents the **projected application** during development. No assumption is made about the manner in which this specification is established, only that it exists in a consistent state every time a **performance prediction** is to be made. An application specification provides **operations** o resembling how the projected application will provide **functions** to the organisation using it. Since the projected application is likely to be complex, the specification is hierarchical, comprising a DAG (directed acyclic graph) of *models* (fig. 1a).[2]

A **model** m is a composite, dynamic, partial view of an application. A model provides a set of operations, just like an application specification. It is composite because it contains a set of *processes* (fig. 1b).[3] Models may have **submodels**, and models which are not submodels of any other models are **top-level models**. The set

---

[2]The framework has been developed in the context of dataflow diagram modelling, in which *cycles* in submodel graphs are uncommon. Allowing cycles is a possible future extension of this work.

[3]Of course, most models will contain constructs other than "processes," e.g. "stores" and "flows" in the dataflow based class of languages. However, these constructs are not relevant

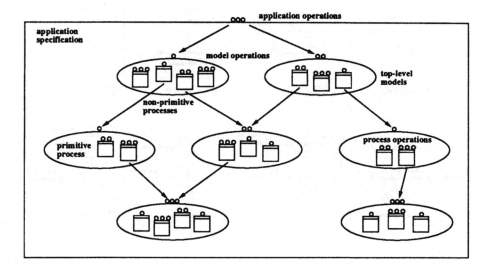

Figure 2: Overall picture of the information system view.

of operations provided by an application specification corresponds to the operations provided by its top-level models.

A **process** p is an atomic, dynamic, partial view of an application. A process provides a set of operations, just like an application specification or a model. A process is atomic because it is not a composition of something else in the way models are.[4] Note that the only difference between the definitions of model and process is that the former is composite while the latter is atomic. This means that a process at one level in the decomposition graph may correspond to a model at the next (fig. 1c). Such a model is the **submodel** of the process. Processes with no submodels associated with them (yet) are **primitive**. Other processes are **non-primitive**.

The operations provided by a model are the **external operations** of that model. The operations provided by the processes contained in a model are its **internal operations**.

Fig. 2 shows an overall picture of the information system view of this section.

1.2 Performance modelling

Complementary to the information system view of sec. 1.1 is the view of *performance modelling* also presented in [OS92]. According to this view, a **performance model** M abstracts a computer system. A performance model provides **service centers** s to

within the framework, which considers only the *dynamics* of the application specification.
[4]However, processes may have submodels containing other processes *associated with* them.

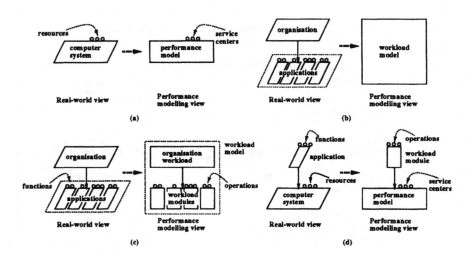

Figure 3: Performance modelling views of performance model (a), workload model (b), organisation workload (c), and workload module (c-d).

resemble how the computer system provides **resources** to the applications running on it (fig. 3a). Examples of such resources are CPU's, disks, communication channels, and other hardware devices. The aim of performance modelling is to obtain a **performance prediction** through analysis of a performance model under a *workload model*, just like the computer system exhibits a certain **performance** under some **workload**.

A **workload model** W abstracts the projected and existing applications that (will) run on a computer system and the organisation which uses (will use) them (fig. 3b). A workload model consists of an *organisation workload* and a set of *workload modules* (fig. 3c).

An **organisation workload** O abstracts how often an organisation uses the functions provided by the available applications. An organisation workload is a set of **operation intensities**, which abstract how often an organisation uses a specific function provided by an application. An operation intensity is either *transaction, interactive,* or *batch* [LZGS84]. The set of operation intensities contained in the organisation workload corresponds to the set of functions provided by the applications and used by the organisation.

A **workload module** w abstracts how the functions provided by a projected or existing application use the resources provided by the computer system (fig. 3d). A workload module provides operations to the organisation workload and uses the service centers of the performance model. The set of operations provided by a workload module corresponds to the set of functions provided by the application it abstracts, just as for application specifications. The workload module of an application specification S is represented as a **module demand matrix** $\mathbf{D}^{ws}$ of average service center uses. Each row of this matrix represents an operation provided by the workload module, and each row element represents a number of uses of a service centre of the performance model.

1.3 Annotating application specifications

To interface information system with performance modelling, the information system view of sec. 1.1 must be extended so that a *workload module* $\mathbf{D}^{ws}$ can be derived from an application specification S. For this purpose, three kinds of performance annotations are needed [OS92]. These are the *initiation descriptions* and the *execution descriptions* for models, and the *demand descriptions* for primitive processes. Each such description corresponds to annotations that must be added to the application specification prior to performance analysis.

Initiation and execution descriptions together specify how many uses of each internal operation of some model that correspond to one use of each of its external operations. First, the initiation description specifies on average which internal operations are used initially when each external operation is used. Then, the execution description specifies on average which internal operations are used next when each internal operation itself is used.

An **initiation description** abstracts how each external operation on some model initiates uses of its internal operations (fig. 4a). This defines the initial state of the model for each of the operations it provides. The initiation description of a model m is represented as an **initiation matrix** $\mathbf{I}^m$ of average initial internal operation uses. Each row of this matrix represents an external operation of the model, and each row element represents an initial number of uses of an internal operation. The framework requires initiation descriptions for all models in the application specification.

An **execution description** abstracts how each internal operation of some model next lead to uses of other of its internal operations (fig. 4b). This defines the state transitions of the model. The execution description of a model m is represented as an **execution matrix**[5] $\mathbf{A}^m$ of average next internal operation uses. Each row of this matrix represents an internal operation of the model, and each row element represents a number of subsequent uses of an internal operation of the model. The framework requires execution descriptions for all models in the application specification. This means that creating both initiation and execution descriptions must be simple for a realisation of the framework to be successful.

In addition to relating internal and external operations of models to one another, a relation is needed between the operations of primitive processes and the service centers of the performance model. A **demand description** abstracts how each operation of a process or model requires uses of the service centers of the performance model (fig. 4c). At this stage, we are only interested in the demand descriptions of primitive processes.

---

[5]Note that this execution matrix is *not* a Markov matrix (or transition probability matrix) [TK84], as its elements abstract transitions between *processes* rather than between *states*.

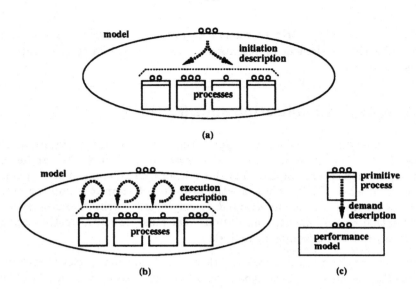

Figure 4: The initiation description relates uses of external operations to the internal operations used initially (a), the execution description relates uses of internal operations to the internal operations used next (b), and the demand description relates uses of operations of primitive processes to uses of performance model service centers (c).

The demand description of a primitive process p is represented as a **primitive demand matrix** $\mathbf{D}_p^m$ of average service center uses, where m is the model containing p. Each row of this matrix represents an operation provided by the process, and each row element represents a number of uses of a service centre of the performance model. The framework requires demand descriptions for all primitive processes in the application specification. This means that demand descriptions will be created for close to every process of the application specification, since every process is primitive at some point of application development. Therefore, creating demand descriptions must also be easy for a realisation of the framework to be successful.

2   Performance prediction

The goal of the basic framework is to predict the performance of projected applications during development. This section demonstrates how a workload module can be derived from an annotated application specification, before considering *performance analysis* and the *performance measures* it produces.

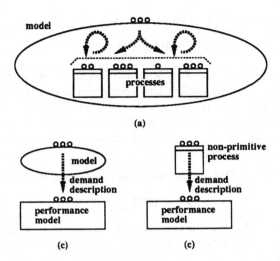

model

processes

(a)

model

demand
description

performance
model

(c)

non-primitive
process

demand
description

performance
model

(c)

Figure 5: The operation count relates uses of external operations to uses of internal operations (a), while the demand descriptions also relates uses of operations of models (b) and non-primitive processes (c) to uses of performance model service centers.

2.1 Workload module derivation

The three kinds of performance annotations presented in sec. 1.3 facilitate automatically deriving a workload module from an annotated application specification S. *Workload module derivation* proceeds through bottom-up collapsing of its decomposition graph, starting with the lowest level of models. When all the submodels of model m have been collapsed, an **operation demand matrix** $\mathbf{D}^m_{\mathcal{O}_m}$ is derived by stacking all its **process demand matrices** on top of one another in the appropriate order,

$$\mathbf{D}^m_{\mathcal{O}_m} = \begin{array}{c} \overline{\mathbf{D}^m_{p_1},} \\ \vdots, \\ \underline{\mathbf{D}^m_{p_n}} \end{array}, \tag{1}$$

since each internal operation of model m (represented by a row of $\mathbf{D}^m_{\mathcal{O}_m}$) corresponds to an operation provided by some process p_i (represented by a row of $\mathbf{D}^m_{p_i}$). An **operation count matrix** $\mathbf{C}^m$ for model m specifies how many times each internal operation is used when each of its external operations are being used. It is derived as (fig. 5a) [Low73, OS81]

$$\mathbf{C}^m = \mathbf{I}^m(\mathbf{1} - \mathbf{A}^m)^{-1}, \tag{2}$$

where $\mathbf{1}$ is the identity matrix, since the total number of internal operations used (represented by $\mathbf{C}^m$) equals the sum of operations used initially (represented by $\mathbf{I}^m$)

and subsequently (represented by $\mathbf{C}^m \mathbf{A}^m$) so that

$$\mathbf{C}^m = \mathbf{I}^m + \mathbf{C}^m \mathbf{A}^m.$$

For the sensitivity analysis of sec. 3 we also define a **process count matrix** $\mathbf{C}_p^m$ for process p of model m, which specifies how many times each internal operation of model m provided by process p is used when each of its external operations are used. It is directly derived as the corresponding subset of columns of the operation count matrix, since each column of $\mathbf{C}^m$ corresponds to an internal operation provided by one of its processes.

A **model demand matrix** $\mathbf{D}^m$ for the model is then calculated as (fig. 5b)

$$\mathbf{D}^m = \mathbf{C}^m \mathbf{D}_{\mathcal{O}_m}^m, \tag{3}$$

since the total number of service centre uses $\mathbf{D}^m$ is determined by 1) the number of service centre uses of its internal operations (represented by the rows of $\mathbf{D}_{\mathcal{O}_m}^m$) and 2) how many times each internal operation is used (represented by the columns of $\mathbf{C}^m$). If m is the submodel of process p of model m', its **non-primitive process demand matrix** $\mathbf{D}_p^{m'}$ is derived as (fig. 5c)

$$\mathbf{D}_p^{m'} = \mathbf{D}^m,$$

since the operations provided process p corresponds to the external operations of its submodel m (both represented by the rows of $\mathbf{D}_p^{m'}$ and $\mathbf{D}^m$). This prepares for collapsing of model m' at the next-higher level of decomposition. When all the top-level models of application specification S have been collapsed in this way, its **module demand matrix** $\mathbf{D}^{ws}$ can be derived by stacking all its top-level **model demand matrices** on top of one another in the appropriate order,

$$\mathbf{D}^{ws} = \begin{array}{c} \overline{\mathbf{D}^{m_1},} \\ \vdots \\ \mathbf{D}^{m_n}. \end{array}$$

again since each operation provided by the specification (represented by the rows of $\mathbf{D}^{ws}$) corresponds to an operation provided by a top-level model of the specification (represented by the rows of $\mathbf{D}^{m_i}$).

Unless the computer system will be dedicated to the projected application, additional workload modules must be created for each existing application running on the computer system. Workload modules representing existing applications are similar to those representing projected ones. All these additional workload modules, as well as the corresponding organisation specifications, must be established by conventional means [LZGS84, Fer78].

2.2 Performance analysis

A **performance analysis** of the computerised information system can be undertaken as soon as all the workload modules necessary have been derived or established. The performance model used in this analysis must be created by conventional means. In some cases, the performance model will already have been created for capacity management purposes, or as a result of previous performance engineering efforts. In a wider sense, performance models may be queueing networks, Petri-net models, or written in special- or general-purpose simulation languages. Within the basic framework, however, mean-value analysis (MVA) [LZGS84] of separable queueing network models has been assumed for simplicity. Each operation provided by the workload modules is represented as a *customer class* in this analysis. The corresponding row of the module demand matrix, together with its operation intensity, becomes a customer description of the class.

2.3   Performance measures

[LZGS84] identifies two groups of **performance measures** output from this analysis: 1) **responsiveness measures**, for the provided and existing applications which are either a) response times $r^{o,S}$ for terminal operations, b) throughputs $x^{o,S}$ for batch operations, or c) residence times $r^{o,S}$ for transaction operations o of application specification S, and 2) **service centre measures**, for the computer system which are either a) utilisations $u^{s,M}$ or b) sojourn times $z^{s,M}$ for service centre s of performance model M.

In this manner, performance predictions are obtained for the computerised information system *before* the projected application is in production. The responsiveness measures for the projected application indicate whether it will perform clearly acceptable or clearly unacceptable, or if further analyses based on refined application specifications are needed. These measures may also be used to compare the performance of alternative designs. The responsiveness measures for the existing applications predict to what extent their performance will be degraded by the projected one. If the performance of some projected or existing application is unacceptable, precautions can be taken before the projected application in put in production. Service centre utilisations for the performance model indicate where bottlenecks will be located. This information is useful if the computer system must be upgraded, or in case some application must be optimised. In the latter case, its module demand matrix predicts which resources it will use most heavily.

A service centre **sojourn time** predicts how much time *a single use* of the corresponding computer system resource will take on average. The **sojourn time vector** Z^M for performance model M is defined as

$$Z^M = \langle z^{1,M}, \ldots, z^{S_M,M} \rangle. \tag{4}$$

These sojourn times will become important in sec. 3.

Performance analyses should be carried out several times throughout application development. The workload module representing the projected application must be derived anew every time the application specification has been changed. However, the operation intensities, workload modules for existing applications, as well as the performance model, can be reused. This considerably reduces the effort involved.

3 Sensitivity analysis

The basic framework of sec. 1 requires numerous parameters. Secs. 3 and 4 will extend the framework to support *estimation* of performance parameters.

Sensitivity analysis on the residence times of a model is useful for determining: 1) which parameters that are most crucial to performance, thus focusing design and code optimising effort, and 2) which parameters that must be estimated with most care and which parameters are less important, thus focusing parameter capture effort accordingly. Sensitivity analysis is either: 1) *local*, deriving the sensitivity of a model residence time on parameters of that model, or 2) *global*, deriving the sensitivity of a model residence time on parameters of its direct or indirect submodels. We will treat the two in separate, after introducing the concept of residence times of models. This section applies methods developed in [OS81], and extends them to cover hierarchical modelling.

3.1 Residence times

A **residence time vector** R^m for model m specifies how much time is spent when each of its external operations are being used. It is derived as

$$R^m = \mathbf{D}^m Z^M, \tag{5}$$

since each row of $\mathbf{D}^m$ represents the number of times each performance model service centre is used by model m when each of its external operations are used, and each element of Z^M represents *how much time* is spent per service centre use. By insertion of eqs. 3 and 2 into eq. 5, we arrive at

$$R^m \;=\; \mathbf{I}^m(1 - \mathbf{A}^m)^{-1}\mathbf{D}^m_{\mathcal{O}_m} Z^M, \text{ and} \tag{6}$$

$$r^{o,m} \;=\; (I^{o,m})^T(1 - \mathbf{A}^m)^{-1}\mathbf{D}^m_{\mathcal{O}_m} Z^M, \tag{7}$$

for the residence time $r^{o,m}$ of operation o on model m, where $I^{o,m}$ is the o'th row vector of $\mathbf{I}^m$ and $r^{o,m}$ is the o'th element of R^m. These equations define the residence times of a model in terms of its initiation and execution descriptions, and in terms of the demand descriptions of its processes.

3.2 Local sensitivity analysis

The sensitivities of the residence time of operation o on model m can now be determined by differentiation of eq. 7. The sensitivities of residence time $r^{o,m}$ on initiation row vector $I^{o,m}$, on execution matrix $\mathbf{A}^m$, and on operation demand matrix $\mathbf{D}^m_{\mathcal{O}_m}$ become

$$\frac{\partial r^{o,m}}{\partial I^{o,m}} \;=\; (1 - \mathbf{A}^m)^{-1}\mathbf{D}^m_{\mathcal{O}_m} Z^M, \tag{8}$$

$$\frac{\partial r^{o,m}}{\partial \mathbf{A}^m} \;=\; [(1 - \mathbf{A}^m)^{-1}]^T I^{o,m}(Z^M)^T(\mathbf{D}^m_{\mathcal{O}_m})^T[(1 - \mathbf{A}^m)^{-1}]^T, \text{ and} \tag{9}$$

$$\frac{\partial r^{o,m}}{\partial \mathbf{D}_{\mathcal{O}_m}^m} = [(1 - \mathbf{A}^m)^{-1}]^T I^{o,m} (Z^M)^T, \tag{10}$$

where the non-trivial derivation of $\frac{\partial r^{o,m}}{\partial \mathbf{A}^m}$ is outlined in appendix A. Appendix B accordingly defines (trivial) *vector forms* of eqs. 8–10 which are necessary in sec. 3.3.

These vector equations provide all local parameter sensitivities on $r^{o,m}$ with a minimum of calculation. A local sensitivity analysis for model m implies calculating the sensitivities of all its parameters and sorting the results. Top parameters in the sorted list are most important to the model residence time, while middle and lower rank parameters can be regarded as unimportant. In this way, sensitivity analysis not only suggests which parameters to estimate with most care, but also points out *where* design and code optimisations will have the most impact, as already mentioned.

3.3 Global sensitivity analysis

The equations of sec. 3.2 defined the sensitivities of the residence times r^{o,m_1} for model m_1 on all its parameters. However, these residence times may also depend on parameters of the direct and indirect submodels m_n of model m_1. This case calls for *global* sensitivity analysis, as opposed to local.

Let r^{o,m_1} be the residence time for operation o on model m_1 and let x^{m_n} be a scalar parameter of one of its direct or indirect submodels m_n. Assuming that the decomposition graph of the application specification is a *tree*[6], the sensitivity of residence time vector $R^{m_1} = \langle r^{o_1,m_1}, \ldots, r^{o_n,m_1} \rangle$ on x^{m_n} is derived as [Opd91b]

$$\frac{\partial R^{m_1}}{\partial x^{m_n}} = C_{p_1}^{m_1} C_{p_2}^{m_2} \cdots C_{p_{n-1}}^{m_{n-1}} \frac{\partial R^{m_n}}{\partial x^{m_n}}, \tag{11}$$

where $\frac{\partial R^{m_n}}{\partial x^{m_n}}$ is one of the vector forms[7] of eqs. 8, 9, and 10 defined in appendix B, and the process count matrices $\mathbf{C}_{p_i}^{m_i}$ were defined in sec. 2.1, and model m_{i+1} decomposes process p_i of model m_i, $i = 1 \ldots n - 1$.

An exhaustive global sensitivity analysis for model m implies calculating the sensitivities of all its parameters, as well as all the parameters of its direct and indirect submodels, and sorting the results. Again, top parameters in this list are most important to the model residence times, while middle and lower rank parameters can be regarded as unimportant.

An important special case of global sensitivity analysis is the **overall sensitivity analysis**, which is an exhaustive global sensitivity analysis for all the top-level models of an application specification. Although the equations of this section have been designed to be computationally efficient, the cost of performing an exhaustive sensitivity analysis may become prohibitive due to the possibly large number of parameters involved. Methods to reduce the search space should be sought for.

---

[6][Opd91b] also considers the more general case where the decomposition graph is a DAG.

[7] ...depending on whether x^{m_n} is an initiation, execution, or demand matrix element.

The simplest approach is of course to restrict the scope of a global sensitivity analysis to 1) certain kinds of parameters or 2) certain levels of decomposition only. [Opd91b] also extends the framework with *residence time analysis* to provide some of the sensitivity analysis support at lower computational cost.

3.4 Performance model sensitivity analysis

A single parameter of the annotated application specification is not likely to have major impact on the overall workload generated by the application. Therefore, the performance model sojourn time vector Z^M of eq. 4 can be regarded as constant during sensitivity analysis. However, if this assumption does not hold, the Z^M vector will vary slightly when application specification parameters are changed. In particular, this may be the case for initiation and execution matrices of higher-level models in the specification. A forthcoming paper [Opd92a] will address this topic in detail, providing *exact* sensitivity analysis for combined software and hardware performance models. Hence, it must be kept in mind that the sensitivities calculated from eqs. 8–11 are only *approximations* in such cases.

4 Target platform modelling

Sec. 3 introduced sensitivity analysis to support performance parameter estimation, based on the assumption that some parameters *already* had been estimated. This section makes parameter estimation easier in the first place by extending the basic framework with *target platforms*.

So far, we have annotated application specifications with resource demand estimates in terms of computer system resources. This creates two main problems:

- Today there is a tendency to build software by putting together existing **components** [Søl90, Vet91]. Common examples of such components are high-level languages (HLL's), database management systems (DBMS's), and screen handlers constituting the **target platform software** of the projected application. This means that an application is specified in terms of target platform functions rather than in terms of resources at the computer system level.

  This makes the framework difficult to apply because: 1) application developers are not used to think in terms of computer system resources, and it is difficult for them to annotate application specifications in terms of such low-level concepts, and 2) assessing the performance of the target platform software, e.g. an optimised relational database management system, is a very specialised task.

- Every application running on a computer system induces operating system overhead on that computer system. Common examples of such overhead are the workloads of virtual memory managers, dispatchers, and interrupt handlers constituting the **operating system software** of the computer system.

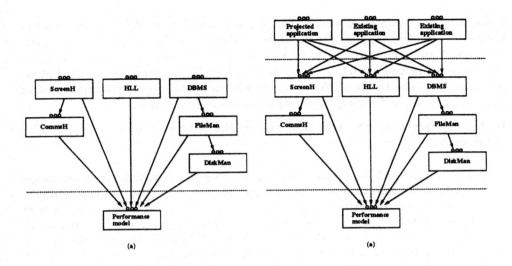

Figure 6: A target platform model (a), and composite workload model (b).

This means that the resource annotations of an application specification must include estimates of the induced operating system overhead for the derived workload module to be correct.

Again, this makes the framework difficult to apply because: 1) application developers are not used to take the performance of the operating system software into consideration when designing applications, and 2) the operating system overhead of an application is not fixed for that application, but a function of the *total* workload on the computer system. This workload is produced both by the projected application *and* by other, already existing applications.

All the above difficulties conflict the aim of making performance engineering closely integrated with information system development.

4.1 The target platform model

The framework therefore introduces *target platform modelling* to avoid the above problems. A **target platform model** P abstracts the target platform and operating system software of a computer installation. A target platform model provides operations, just like application specifications, models, and processes. Since the target platform and operating system software is likely to be complex, the target platform model is again hierarchical, comprising a DAG of workload modules (fig. 6a).[8]

As in the basic framework, we derive a workload module from the annotated application specification, and establish additional workload modules for each existing

---

[8]This view of workload modelling is based on Hughes' *sp* approach [Hug88].

application by conventional means. The resulting workload model therefore consists both of 1) top-level application workload modules and 2) lower-level target platform workload modules (fig. 6b). In contrast to the workload models of sec. 1.2, a **composite workload model** W thus comprises a DAG (as opposed to a *set*) of workload modules. The target platform model (without workload modules representing applications), is itself a composite workload model in this sense.

In this way, target platform modelling resolves the problems stated at the beginning of this section:

- The higher-level target platform workload modules correspond to the target platform software components that the projected application will be implemented upon, typically a high-level language (HLL), a database management system (DBMS), and a screen handler. Each top-level target platform module provides operations that the application workload modules use. Thus instead of annotating the primitive processes of the application specification in terms of performance model service centre uses, we supply them with demand descriptions in terms of target platform operations.

- The lower-level target platform workload modules correspond to the operating system software components of the computer system, such as the virtual memory manager, the dispatcher, and the interrupt handler. Thus instead of having to include estimates of the induced system software workload in the demand descriptions, the overhead is automatically calculated during the *workload model analysis* of sec. 4.2.

4.2 Workload model analysis

The composite workload model resulting from target platform modelling must be analysed prior to performance analysis. Analysis proceeds through bottom-up collapsing of its module graph with repeated matrix multiplications, much as in the workload derivation of sec. 2.1. The outcome is a collapsed **module demand matrix** $\mathbf{D}^w$ for each application workload module w of the workload model. These matrices constitute the workload modules representing the projected and existing applications. The workload modules are applicable for performance analysis according to sec. 2.2.

4.3 Interface with sensitivity analysis

Apart from the additional workload model analysis prior to performance analysis, target platform modelling does not require modifications of the basic framework. However, to combine the sensitivity analysis technique of sec. 3 with target platform modelling, we need to redefine the concept of residence times of operations on models. Sec. 3.1 defined these times in terms of service centre sojourn times. Since target platform modelling replaces the concept of performance model service centres with target platform operations, we need to introduce the new concept of platform estimates $z^{o,P}$ representing the sojourn time of operation o provided by target platform P. Again, a target platform operation sojourn time predicts how much time *a single use* of the corresponding target platform function will take on average.

To provide such platform estimates we first need perform a *target platform analysis*. Target platform analysis proceeds exactly like the workload model analysis of sec. 4.2, with the top-level application workload modules removed. The outcome is a **platform demand matrix** $\mathbf{D}^P$ for target platform P.

We now define the **platform estimate vector** $Z^P = \langle z^{1,P}, \ldots, z^{O_P,P} \rangle$ for target platform P as

$$Z^P = \mathbf{D}^P Z^M, \tag{12}$$

since 1) each row of $\mathbf{D}^P$ represents the number of times each performance model service centre is used when each target platform operation is used, and 2) each element of Z^M represents *how much time* is spent per service centre use.

Sensitivity analysis now proceeds with platform estimates $z^{o,P}$ and Z^P replacing the computer system resource sojourn times $z^{s,M}$ and Z^M. This substitution, however convenient for the purpose of sensitivity analysis, is not obvious. [Opd91b] presents two alternative techniques for validating this *platform estimate assumption*.

4.4 Database optimisation

The critical point in establishing a target platform model, is representing the optimised database management system (DBMS) as a workload module. [BO91, BOVS91] discusses alternative parameter capture strategies for an SQL-type DBMS in the context of a practical case study. Wieland [Wie91] has established and validated a workload module specification for simple queries on the INGRES relational database system. This is a topic for further research.

5 A realisation of the framework

This paper has presented a framework for performance engineering during information system development based only on a minimal set of requirements about the development methodology and modelling language used. Isolating the framework in a linear algebra representation, as has been done, ensures its *generality*. In principle, it can be interfaced with any operationally oriented and hierarchic methodology for information system development, and with any performance evaluation method. To demonstrate the *practicalness* of the approach, a realisation of the framework has been made in connection with the IMSE environment for performance evaluation and the experimental integrated CASE tool PPP.

The IMSE is an *integrated modelling support* environment for performance evaluation. It focuses on 1) *availability* of state-of-the-art performance evaluation meth-

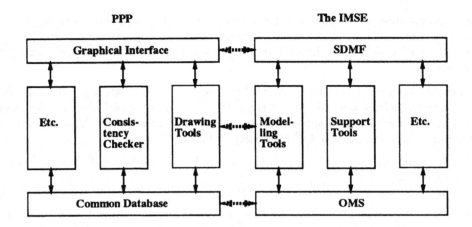

Figure 7: The performance modelling and analysis support provided by the IMSE made available to the PrM tool user.

ods through easy-to-use graphical interfaces, and 2) *integrating* and *supporting* the performance evaluation methods through a common set of utilities. The IMSE builds on existing performance evaluation tools for workload derivation [CS85], workload modelling [Hug86], queueing networks [Pot85], Petri-net models [BC89], and special-purpose simulation [PB88]. In addition, the IMSE provides a set of environmental tools supporting execution of static and dynamic performance models, animation of model executions, automated support for planning and performing experiments, and generation of reports from experiments. The IMSE tools share a *support environment* containing a graphical user interface system and a common object management system.

PPP (*p*rocesses, *p*henomena, and *p*rograms) is an experimental integrated CASE tool for information system development [GLW91]. It focuses on 1) *formality* to facilitate early verification and validation as well as automated model-to-model translation and code-generation, and 2) *integration* between the modelling tools used, and between different phases of development.[9] PPP builds on well-known approaches to information system development, such as top-down design and the DFD and ER paradigms.

In particular, the *PrM language* [BCSA86] of PPP is a formalised extension of dataflow diagrams, avoiding several of their imprecisenesses by introducing 1) *flow of control* as well as data flow; 2) *triggering* and *termination* to define process dynamics; 3) *port connectives* to define what is consumed and produced by each process per execution, and 4) *operations* to distinguish between different ways of triggering a process or a model. A *PrM tool* has been implemented as a realisation of the framework of this paper. Fig. 7 depicts how the IMSE and PPP environments

---

[9]And between the problem analysis and design phases in particular.

can be integrated through the PrM tool, which lets PrM specifications be annotated with performance parameters. The tool automatically generates IMSE workload models from annotated application specifications, using the algorithm of sec. 2.1.

Conclusions

The need for performance engineering of information systems was discussed. Views of information system and performance modelling were presented in sec. 1, and application specifcations were extended with performance annotations. The resulting framework was applied to predict and improve the performance of projected applications during development in sec. 2. Sensitivity analysis was supported to point out performance bottlenecks in the application and suggest which parameters to estimate with most care in sec. 3. Target platform modelling was provided to relieve the information system developer from assessing the performance of the target platform and operating system software in sec. 4 The framework was realised in terms of the PrM language for software specification in sec. 5.

In the introduction, the goals of the framework were stated as 1) integrating the state of the art of information system development and performance engineering; 2) supporting performance parameter estimation; 3) interacting with the capacity management process, and 4) supporting database design.

Concerning the first one, [OS92] has presented a conceptual integration of information system and performance modelling. This paper has focused on meeting the second of the goals. Furthermore, [Opd91b] extends the framework with additional techniques for a) *residence time analysis* which suggests which parts of the application to annotate; b) *bounds analysis* as an alternative to average analysis early in the design, and c) *parametric analysis* in case obtaining one or a few parameters is infeasible. The third goal of relating capacity management to the framework is discussed in [Vet91, BOVS91], while database design has been treated in [OS81]. Thus while work remains on the latter two, two of the goals have been met so far. Furthermore, a tool has been implemented to support the framework [Opd92b], and has been applied in a practical case study [BO91].

Composite workload models for the organisation's software systems can be used to balance workload between the available computers while controlling application response times. Alternative hardware configurations can be evaluated and compared. Workload modules for projected applications can be combined with models of the existing ones, and the hardware resources can be extended at the right moment. The performance of the projected application is continuously monitored throughout development. Good resource utilisation is ensured and it is made clear where the design and code may be improved.

The framework is an advancement on contemporary approaches to performance engineering of information systems in the areas focused on. The framework gains on its simplicity, generality, and emphasis on parameter estimation support. The most important advancement, however, is integrating the information system and performance modelling fields at the conceptual level and at the tool level. This facilitates bringing together recent advances in performance modelling with integrated CASE tools for information system development.

The complexity of contemporary information systems will continue to increase along with the organisation's dependency on them. Controlled, tool-supported management of the computer resources will therefore give the organisation an increasing competitive edge in the future.

Acknowledgement

We would like to thank the edp-personnel at The Regional Hospital in Trondheim, Tandem Computers in Trondheim and Oslo, and Twinco in Oslo for their continuing support and supply of information throughout this work.

References

[AWS91] Reda A. Ammar, J. Wang, and H. A. Sholl. Graphic modelling technique for software execution time estimation. *Information and Software Technology, Vol. 33, No. 2, Butterworth-Heinemann Ltd.*, March, 1991.

[BC89] Gianfranco Balbo and Giovanni Chiola. Stochastic Petri net simulation. Technical report, University of Turin, 1989.

[BCSA86] S. Berdal, S. Carlsen, A. Sølvberg, and R. Andersen. Information system behaviour expressed through process port analysis. Technical report, Division of Computer Science, The Norwegian Institute of Technology, 1986.

[Ber84] Margaret E. Berry. The best of both worlds: An integrated approach to capacity planning and software performance engineering. *Proc. Computer Measurement Group Conference XV, San Fransisco*, pages 462–466, Dec. 1984.

[BO91] Gunnar Brataas and Andreas L. Opdahl. Deriving workload models of projected software: A case study. Technical report, IMSE Project Report R6.6 – 9, Version 1, The Norwegian Institute of Technology, October 23, 1991.

[BOVS91] Gunnar Brataas, Andreas L. Opdahl, Vidar Vetland, and Arne Sølvberg. Information systems: Final evaluation of the IMSE. Technical report, IMSE Project deliverable D6.6 – 2, Version 1, SINTEF (Unversity of Trondheim), December, 1991.

[CS85] M. Calzarossa and G. Serazzi. A software tool for the workload analysis. *Proceedings from 'Modelling Techniques for Performance Analysis'*, 1985.

[Fer78]   Domenico Ferrari. *Computer Systems Performance Evaluation*. Prentice-Hall, Inc., Englewood Cliffs, New Jersey 07632, 1978.

[GLW91]   Jon Atle Gulla, Odd Ivar Lindland, and Geir Willumsen. PPP — An integrated CASE environment. *Proceedings of "CAiSE91, Trondheim, Norway"*, May 1991.

[HP89]   Peter H. Hughes and Dominique Potier. The integrated modelling support environment (ref. r1.2-3 ver. 1). *Presented at the ESPRIT-Week, Brüssels*, 1989.

[Hug83]   Peter H. Hughes. A structural analysis of information processing systems (with applications to the sizing problem). Technical report, no. 28/83, Division of Computer Science, The Norwegian Institute of Technology, June, 1983.

[Hug86]   Peter H. Hughes. Notes on system structure and performance specification. Technical report, The Norwegian Institute of Technology, April, 1986.

[Hug88]   Peter Hughes. *sp* principles. Technical report, STC Technology Ltd. o59/ICL226/0, July 1988.

[LOS88]   Odd Ivar Lindland, Andreas L. Opdahl, and Guttorm Sindre. PPM — The process & phenomenon model. *Proc' Infotech '88, Oslo*, 1988.

[Low73]   T. C. Lowe. Analysis of an information system model with transfer penalties. *IEEE Trans. Comput. C-22, pp. 469-480*, 1973.

[LZGS84]   Edward D. Lazowska, John Zahorjan, G. Scott Graham, and Kenneth C. Sevcik. *Quantitative System Performance: Computer System Analysis Using Queueing Network Models*. Prentice-Hall, Inc., Englewood Cliffs, New Jersey, 07632, 1984.

[Opd91a]   Andreas L. Opdahl. Deriving workload models of projected software: Basic framework. Technical report, IMSE Project Report R6.6 – 8, Version 2, The Norwegian Institute of Technology, October 23, 1991.

[Opd91b]   Andreas L. Opdahl. Deriving workload models of projected software: Parameter estimation support. Technical report, IMSE Project Report R6.6 – 10, Version 1, The Norwegian Institute of Technology, October 23, 1991.

[Opd92a]   Andreas L. Opdahl. Sensitivity analysis of combined software and hardware performance models. Not yet published, 1992.

[Opd92b]   Andreas L. Opdahl. A CASE tool for performance engineering during software design. *Proceedings of "The Fifth Nordic Workshop on Programming Environment Research", Tampere/Finland*, 8–10 January, 1992.

[OS81]   Harald Oftedahl and Arne Sølvberg. Data base design constrained by traffic load estimates. *Information Systems, Vol. 6, No. 4, pp. 267-282*, 1981.

[OS92]   Andreas L. Opdahl and Arne Sølvberg. Conceptual integration of information system and performance modelling. *Proceedings of IFIP WG 8.1 Working Conference on: "Information Systems Concepts: Improving the Understanding", Alexandria/Egypt*, 13–15 April, 1992.

[PB88]   R. J. Pooley and M. W. Brown. A diagramming paradigm for hierarchical process oriented discrete event simulation (ref. csr-254-88). Technical report, University of Edinburgh, January 1988.

[Pot85] Dominique Potier. New users introduction to QNAP2. Technical report, Rapport technique 40, INRIA, 1985.

[San77] John Winston Sanguinetti. Performance prediction in an operating system design methodology. Technical report, Ph.D. Thesis, University of Michigan, 1977.

[SB75]   Howard A. Sholl and Taylor L. Booth. Software performance modelling using computation structures. *IEEE Transactions on Software Engineering, Vol. SE-1, No. 4, December*, 1975.

[Smi80] Connie U. Smith. The prediction and evaluation of the performance of software from extended design specifications. Technical report, Ph. D. dissertation, Department of Computer Sciences, The University of Texas at Austin, August, 1980.

[Smi90] Connie U. Smith. *Performance Engineering of Software Systems.* Addison-Wesley Publishing Company, 1990.

[Søl90] Arne Sølvberg. Integrated modelling and support environments for information systems. *Paper presented at the 23rd Newcastle-upon-Tyne International Seminar on the Teaching of Computing Science at University Level*, 1990.

[TK84]   Howard M. Taylor and Samuel Karlin. *An Introduction to Stochastic Modeling.* Academic Press, Inc., 1984.

[Vet91] Vidar Vetland. Deriving composite workload models of existing software. Technical report, IMSE Project Report R6.6 – 7, Version 1, The Norwegian Institute of Technology, 1991.

[Wie91] Peter Wieland. Performance modelling and performance measurements of a relational dtabase management system. Technical report, Diploma Thesis, The Norwegian Institute of Technology, The University of Trondheim, 1991.

A Deriving execution matrix derivates

The sensitivity of $r^{o,m}$ on execution matrix $\mathbf{A}^m$ becomes

$$\frac{\partial r^{o,m}(\mathbf{A}^m)}{\partial \mathbf{A}^m} = \frac{r^{o,m}(\mathbf{A}^m + \mathbf{dA}^m) - r^{o,m}(\mathbf{A}^m)}{\mathbf{dA}^m}.$$

We have [OS81]

$$
\begin{aligned}
r^{o,m}(\mathbf{A}^m + \mathbf{dA}^m) &= (I^{o,m})^T (1 - \mathbf{A}^m - \mathbf{dA}^m)^{-1} \mathbf{D}^m_{\mathcal{O}_m} Z^M \\
&= (I^{o,m})^T [(1 - \mathbf{A}^m)(1 - (1 - \mathbf{A}^m)^{-1}\mathbf{dA}^m)]^{-1} \mathbf{D}^m_{\mathcal{O}_m} Z^M \\
&= (I^{o,m})^T (1 - (1 - \mathbf{A}^m)^{-1}\mathbf{dA}^m)^{-1}(1 - \mathbf{A}^m)^{-1} \mathbf{D}^m_{\mathcal{O}_m} Z^M.
\end{aligned}
$$

We set

$$\mathbf{Q}^m = (1 - \mathbf{A}^m)^{-1}$$

and get

$$
\begin{aligned}
r^{o,m}(\mathbf{A}^m + \mathbf{dA}^m) &= (I^{o,m})^T (1 - \mathbf{Q}^m\mathbf{dA}^m)^{-1}\mathbf{Q}^m \mathbf{D}^m_{\mathcal{O}_m} Z^M \\
&= (I^{o,m})^T [\sum_{i=0}^{\infty}(\mathbf{Q}^m\mathbf{dA}^m)^i]\mathbf{Q}^m \mathbf{D}^m_{\mathcal{O}_m} Z^M \\
&= (I^{o,m})^T [1 + \mathbf{Q}^m\mathbf{dA}^m + (\mathbf{Q}^m\mathbf{dA}^m)^2 + \cdots]\mathbf{Q}^m \mathbf{D}^m_{\mathcal{O}_m} Z^M \\
&= (I^{o,m})^T \mathbf{Q}^m \mathbf{D}^m_{\mathcal{O}_m} Z^M + (I^{o,m})^T \mathbf{Q}^m\mathbf{dA}^m\mathbf{Q}^m \mathbf{D}^m_{\mathcal{O}_m} Z^M \\
&= (I^{o,m})^T (1 - \mathbf{A}^m)^{-1} \mathbf{D}^m_{\mathcal{O}_m} Z^M + (I^{o,m})^T \mathbf{Q}^m\mathbf{dA}^m\mathbf{Q}^m \mathbf{D}^m_{\mathcal{O}_m} Z^M \\
&= r^{o,m}(\mathbf{A}^m) + (I^{o,m})^T \mathbf{Q}^m\mathbf{dA}^m\mathbf{Q}^m \mathbf{D}^m_{\mathcal{O}_m} Z^M.
\end{aligned}
$$

This means that

$$
\begin{aligned}
\frac{\partial r^{o,m}(\mathbf{A}^m)}{\partial \mathbf{A}^m} &= \frac{r^{o,m}(\mathbf{A}^m + \mathbf{dA}^m) - r^{o,m}(\mathbf{A}^m)}{\mathbf{dA}^m} \\
&= \frac{(I^{o,m})^T \mathbf{Q}^m\mathbf{dA}^m\mathbf{Q}^m \mathbf{D}^m_{\mathcal{O}_m} Z^M}{\mathbf{dA}^m} \\
&= [(I^{o,m})^T \mathbf{Q}^m]^T [\mathbf{Q}^m \mathbf{D}^m_{\mathcal{O}_m} Z^M]^T \\
&= (\mathbf{Q}^m)^T I^{o,m} (Z^M)^T (\mathbf{D}^m_{\mathcal{O}_m})^T (\mathbf{Q}^m)^T \\
&= [(1 - \mathbf{A}^m)^{-1}]^T I^{o,m} (Z^M)^T (\mathbf{D}^m_{\mathcal{O}_m})^T [(1 - \mathbf{A}^m)^{-1}]^T.
\end{aligned}
$$

Q.E.D.

B   The vector forms of eqs. 8–10

The vector forms of eqs. 8–10 are defined as

$$
\frac{\partial R^m}{\partial i_{o'',p''}^{o',m'}} = \langle \frac{\partial r^{1,m}}{\partial i_{o'',p''}^{o',m'}}, \ldots, \frac{\partial r^{o,m}}{\partial i_{o'',p''}^{o',m'}}, \ldots, \frac{\partial r^{O_m,m}}{\partial i_{o'',p''}^{o',m'}} \rangle,
$$

$$
\frac{\partial R^m}{\partial a_{(o',p'),(o'',p'')}^{m'}} = \langle \frac{\partial r^{1,m}}{\partial a_{(o',p'),(o'',p'')}^{m'}}, \ldots, \frac{\partial r^{o,m}}{\partial a_{(o',p'),(o'',p'')}^{m'}}, \ldots, \frac{\partial r^{O_m,m}}{\partial a_{(o',p'),(o'',p'')}^{m'}} \rangle, \text{ and}
$$

$$
\frac{\partial R^m}{\partial d_{s,M}^{o',p'}} = \langle \frac{\partial r^{1,m}}{\partial d_{s,M}^{o',p'}}, \ldots, \frac{\partial r^{o,m}}{\partial d_{s,M}^{o',p'}}, \ldots, \frac{\partial r^{O_m,m}}{\partial d_{s,M}^{o',p'}} \rangle,
$$

where

$$
\frac{\partial r^{o,m}}{\partial i_{o'',p''}^{o',m'}}
$$

is element (o'', p'') of vector $\frac{\partial r^{o,m}}{\partial I^{o,m}}$ defined in eq. 8;

$$
\frac{\partial r^{o,m}}{\partial a_{(o',p'),(o'',p'')}^{m'}}
$$

is element $[(o', p'), (o'', p'')]$ of the matrix $\frac{\partial r^{o,m}}{\partial \mathbf{A}^m}$ defined in eq. 9, and

$$
\frac{\partial r^{o,m}}{\partial d_{s,M}^{o',p'}}
$$

is element $[(o', p'), (s, M)]$ of the matrix $\frac{\partial r^{o,m}}{\partial \mathbf{D}_{O_m}^m}$ defined in eq. 10.

A Framework for Software Maintenance

Chiang-Choon Danny POO

Department of Information Systems and Computer Science
National University of Singapore, Kent Ridge Road,
Singapore 0511

Abstract.   In describing a software system, there are three elements that are always considered : objects, functional requirements and business policies. In the traditional approach to software development, these elements are often mixed with one another in a system's definition in such a way that their meanings are embedded into the software, making their identification very difficult. This has the knock-on effect of making maintenance, and hence evolution, difficult.

This paper suggests a framework for addressing software maintenance and it calls for a clearer separation between the business policies, functional requirements and object models.

1. System Evolution is Inevitable

Software investment cost has been recognised by many as expensive. The high cost incurred is attributed not to the complexity of creating systems but to the maintenance efforts required to accommodate changes in inflexibly-designed systems [11,13].

The design of an information system often changes throughout its lifecycle; this has been attributed to changing users' requirements. These changes have been recognised to be intrinsic to software, often unpredictable and cannot be accommodated without iteration in the definition and development phases. Thus, the key to successful systems development, lies not in designing systems that satisfy the initial users' requirements but in the continuous provision for system evolution, particularly in the area of accommodating changes due to users' requests [1, 2,11].

2. The Object-Oriented Approach

The functional approach to information systems development has been the primary approach used for the past two decades. This approach is characterised by data flow and operations upon them. The structure of systems produced is based mainly on system functional activities. This approach has two major problems. First, system functionalities are highly volatile elements, and will inevitably lead to more frequent changes in system structure, which in turn translates to increased maintenance efforts. Second, systems produced using the functional approach have an architecture whose structure is characterised by a string of sequential functional operations. Any changes to these functionalities will create a chain reaction and the effect will be propagated throughout the system. Thus, the complexity involved in making such changes is usually not proportional to the requirements.

In recent years, there has been a shift in the way systems are designed: from a function-oriented to an object-oriented approach. The latter focuses on the objects that describe the problem domain and their mutual interactions. Unlike the functional approach, the primary design issue of the object-oriented approach is no longer *what functionalities* the system does, but what *object* it does it to.

The primary motivation for adopting the object-oriented approach is the stable model of reference upon which a problem space can be examined. Objects in a problem domain are comparatively more stable than functional requirements [10]. For instance, the objects in a library or order processing environment today will probably be the same as the objects in such an environment a few years from now. Thus books and library users, and customers and orders will continue to be the principal objects in library and order processing environments, respectively, even though the functionalities of the applications may have changed over the years.

The object-oriented approach has several advantages over the traditional functional approach in terms of the *correctness, robustness, extensibility, reusability,* and *compatibility* of the final delivered system [12]. These key aspects of software quality are especially important because of the difficulties experienced with present-day systems development practices -- that is, programs often do not do what they are supposed to do; they are not equipped enough to deal with abnormal situations; they are not amenable to change; their construction does not rely on previous efforts; and they do not combine well with each other.

3. Object-oriented Software Structure

The advantages of adopting an object-oriented approach in software system definition have been well documented elsewhere [e.g. 3, 12, 23]. The structure of a system developed using the object-oriented approach is different from that produced using a function-oriented approach. How then should we model our problem domain in terms of objects? and How are functional requirements which are part and parcel of an information system description be considered in the modelling activity? The next few sub-sections will elaborate on these two issues.

3.1. Characteristics of an Object Model

Actions
Since objects in the real world participate in a set of events, their actions in the events would indicate what can happen to them. For example, a Customer in a banking environment participates in events such as Deposit money, Withdraw money, Open an account and Close an account, the actions that are relevant to a customer in such a situation would be those actions relating to the opening and closing of accounts, and depositing and withdrawing of money from the account. Nevertheless, a Customer in an order-processing environment would participate in events[1] that are different from those in the banking environment, thus his actions would be completely different from customers in the banking application. In other words, the meaning of a customer, and hence objects in a problem domain, is defined by the actions that it performs or the events with which it undertakes. That is, object actions characterise the behaviour of the object.

Ordering of Actions
It is obvious that an object does not conduct its actions in the real world randomly. There is a pattern by which the sequence of actions follows. For example, when a user wishes to borrow some items from the library, he first has to register himself as a member

---

[1] The events are Order, Cancel, MakePayment, etc.

of the library. Only when he has become a member of the library, may he performs other actions like borrow a book, renew a book and return a book. He may also repeatedly renew other books which he has initially borrowed, etc. He continues to perform these actions until such time when he decides to terminate his membership with the library, during such time he executes a Terminate action which formally ends his membership. Thus, we see a pattern of actions for a library member i.e. Register, Borrow, Renew, Return, (and repeated Borrow, Renew and Return) and Terminate. This pattern of actions describes the life history or dynamic behaviour of the member. Modelling the dynamic behaviour of an object provides us with a more accurate representation of an object since events in the real world are constraint by a certain time ordering.

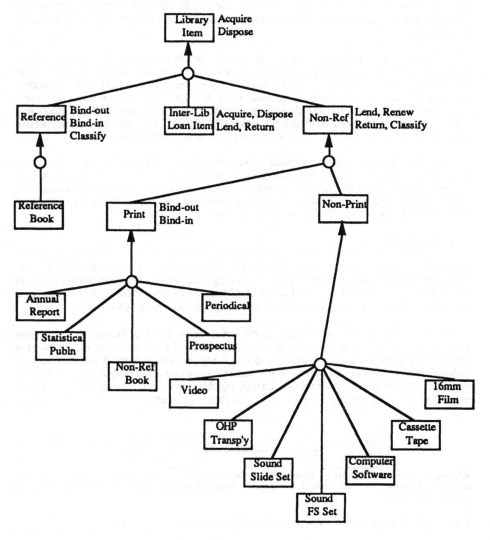

Figure 3.1 : Object Classification Diagram for Library Items

Attributes

In addition to actions, an object is also characterised by a set of properties known as attributes. The latter describes the state of an object. An example of attributes for a library member might be : Name, address, age, and loan-limit.

Classification

Objects in the real world are usually classified. For instance, books, periodicals, annual reports, prospectus and statistical publication may be classified as print items in a library environment; and these items may either be of reference or non-reference materials. A reference item may only be used in the library premises and unlike non-reference items may not be loaned out to any library users. The computational model representing similar informations of objects in the real world should thus include the concept of classification in its description.

An object is classified by factoring common properties of similar objects into a class. The class then specifies the behaviour of all instances. Classes can be partitioned into subclasses, in which case the superclass is known as a *generalisation* [24] of the subclasses (and the subclasses are termed *specialisations* of the superclass). Figure 3.1 is an *Object Classification Diagram (OCD)* illustrating a classification hierarchy of library items in a library circulation application. Notice the action Classify has been defined in the respective subclasses; this is because Classify does not apply to Inter-Library Loan Item.

From the figure, we see that actions Acquire and Dispose have been repeated in Inter-Library Loan Item; the reason is due to different semantic requirements of these actions on the part of Inter-Library Loan Item from the others. For instance, we need to know the source library from which the inter-library loan item is acquired but this piece of information is not relevant to the other library items.

Relationships

Besides the *vertical relationship* of objects through classification, there is another form of relationship known as *horizontal relationship*. This kind of relationship describes the affiliation between two or more objects. Modelling relationships between objects provides us with an overview of the affiliation of objects with one another. For instance, a relationship between a borrowing member and a non-reference book is Borrow[1].

We can further impose upon a relationship a static restriction that dictates the cardinality of participation of object instances in the relationship. If the cardinality of the Borrow relationship between a borrowing member and non-reference book is one-to-many, it indicates that a member can borrow many non-reference books but only one non-reference book can be borrowed by one member. Expressing this form of relationship can be achieved with an *Object Relationship Diagram (ORD)* as shown in figure 3.2.

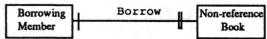

Rectangles represent objects; a line connecting the two objects indicates a relationship (in this example, Borrow). Double vertical bar denotes multiple relationship and single bar indicates single relationship.

Figure 3.2 : Relationship between Member and Non-reference Book (1:M)

---

[1] Borrow or Lend could be used depending on the direction in which the relationship is specified.

3.2. A Proposed Object Model

In summary, we can define objects as having five characteristics :
1. Objects have actions that describe their behaviour.
2. The actions of objects are time-ordered.
3. Objects have attributes that describe their states at a particular point in time.
4. The definition of objects can be organised into a class-instance relationship in a classification hierarchy.
5. Objects are affiliated to one another through relationships.

Figure 3.3 summarises this object model.

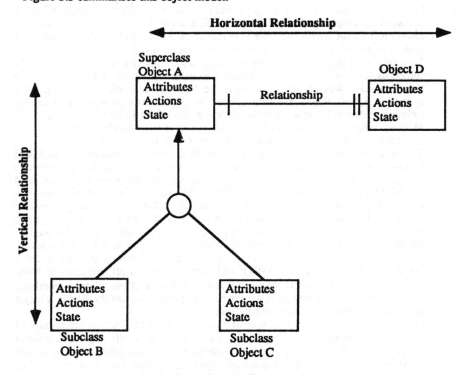

Figure 3.3 : Characteristics of Objects in an Object Model

4. Functional Requirement Modelling

Functional requirements are those input, output and processing requirements; they are part and parcel of any information systems description. They are specified in order to satisfy users' functional requirements. An example of a functional requirement in a library circulation application might be : *On request, lists all books currently on loan to staff member A.* This functional requirement is related to two objects : *Non-reference Book* and *Staff Member*. Contemporary object-oriented modelling approaches suggest the encapsulation of this functional requirement as an operation of a model object, i.e., define it as an operation of either Non-Reference Book or Staff Member. While this solution is plausible, it is not favourable for the following reasons:

1. It violates the essence of the definition of *object*. An operation defined for an object should be applicable to the object, the whole object and nothing but the object [3]. Since a functional requirement is a statement which is related to more than one object *(in this case, Non-Reference Book and Staff Member)*, we cannot categorically say that a functional requirement belongs to a particular object. Hence, functional requirements should not be defined as operations of objects in the object model.

2. It weakens the visibility of functional requirements, making changes to functional requirements difficult. For instance, in which of the two objects in the above example *(Non-Reference Book and Staff Member)* is the functional requirement represented, since representation of the requirement in both objects is possible.

3. Functional requirements are highly volatile elements. The principle of good software development practice [16, 17, 25] advocates the separation of volatile elements from the stable ones; this is to reduce the effect of change in one part of a system to another (possibly not related to the change at all).

4. To model functional requirements as operations of model objects has effectively forced us to consider the way a system is to be designed and implemented since there are many ways in which a requirement can be satisfied in the design of a system at a later stage. For instance, the functional requirement above can be satisfied in design by defining an operation in either Non-Reference Book or Staff Member, alternatively, we can define it as an operation of another third object that interact with Non-Reference and Staff Member to fulfill what is required.

5. This solution will lead to maintenance complexity in future changes to functional requirements. To illustrate, let us assume that the above functional requirement is encapsulated as an operation in one of the objects, say Non-Reference Book, and consider how a symmetric problem such as : *On request, lists all books currently on loan to staff members who have joined the library between 1 January 1990 and 1 January 1991* would affect the definition of the model. If this problem were to be satisfied as before, it would require a separate service module. The service module would have to interact with all instances of Staff Member to select the relevant instances (i.e. satisfying the constraint that he joined the library between the 1 January 1990 and 1 January 1991); and then looking up all instances of Non-Reference Book[1] and selecting those that are on loan to those relevant members. We note that a simple change in the functional requirement has resulted in a major change in the way the problem is resolved.

6. Finally, to insist on the definition of functional requirements as operations of model objects would go against the way a user would generally express functional requirements. They view functional requirements in a functional way and do not consider them as being part of a model object (i.e. it should not be considered as operation of either Non-Reference Book or Staff Member).

Hence, in conclusion, we state that it is necessary to separate the definitions of the object model from its functional requirements. If objects have been correctly modelled they are likely to change infrequently, if at all. Modification of objects should only be effected by major changes to the basic meaning of the system and generally reflects a change in the business environment.

---

[1] We may define an object keeping a record of the books that the member has borrowed; this is certainly much better than searching through all instances of books to derive the answer. But this is more of a design issue of describing how the solution could be achieved, and is not suitable in the analysis phase where we aim to understand what the solution is.

5. A Partial Framework for System Evolution

The discussion so far suggests that a system's framework consists of two layers as shown in figure 5.1. At the kernel of the diagram is the object model.

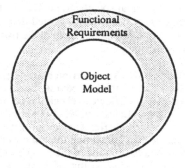

Figure 5.1 : Object Model and Functional Requirements

6. Business Policies

Consider the entries of Table 1. The latter contains a business policy pertaining to the loan quota for each class of member in a typical library environment (refer also to figure 3.1).

Member Class	Restrictions	Loan quota
Staff (Producer)	All items	4 print and 5 non-print items
Staff (Non-Producer)	All items except 16mm films	4 print and 5 non-print items
External Individual	All items except 16mm films	4 print and 5 non-print items
External Institutional	All items except 16mm films	10 print and 10 non-print items
Approved Training Centres	All items except 16mm films	10 print and 10 non-print items
Reader	Use library facilities only	0 item

Table 1 : Loan quota business policy

For instance, in Table 1, a staff member (Producer) may borrow all types of library items subject to a maximum of 4 print items and 5 non-print items. For Readers, they may only use the library facilities (such as using the library for reference work) but may not borrow any library items.

Consider the following policies : A borrowed item is said to be overdue when it is not returned to the library a day after the due date. Also, any overdue item is subjected to a fine of 50 cents per day per item. These policies read :

FineMember IF BorrowedItemIsOverdue.
BorrowedItemIsOverdue IF TotalFine > 0.

The total fine is governed by a computational policy indicated by the following formulae :

TotalFine = TotalDaysOverdue * 50 (cents)
TotalDaysOverdue = NumberOfDaysBorrowed - 1(day grace period) - TotalSundays
- TotalPublicHolidays.

NumberOfDaysBorrowed = ReturnDate - LendDate[1].

These high-level declarative business policy statements are what a user would generally define in their context and are what they would view them as; unfortunately, they are usually not represented as they are. Instead, they are commonly transformed into low-level computational representation in its final specification. That is, the set of business policies, with which the definition of a system depends, is buried deep within the system program code, totally obscured from the users who define them in the first place and who are the ones that will request for changes in the future.

This mode of representation suffers from a number of problems. Firstly, programs become complex because the order of the procedural statements determines much of the logic of the program. Secondly, it is difficult to check the correctness of a program as few people with the knowledge of the policies will be able to understand the implementation. Finally, maintenance of programs is difficult, since programs describe a procedure of carrying out these policies rather than containing the policies themselves. Any changes to the business policy would require a re-ordering of the program logic and this could be costly [7]. In other words, procedural representation of business policies requires the pre-determination of the order of execution (of the program logic), whereas if they have been represented declaratively, then it is the environment that chooses the policy to be applied whenever the situation arises.

6.1. Taking a Synergistic Approach to Structuring a System

Based on the above, we can conclude that business policies of a system specification should be explicitly specified in software development and identifiably maintained throughout the development process and subsequent evolution, so as to permit immediate and flexible response to changes in users' requirements. Hence, in addition to separating object model from its functionalities, we also need to explicitly represent business policies such that the definition of the policies and their corresponding operational application are separated. Thus, in addition to the two layers, we have a third layer, the business policy layer as shown in figure 6.1.

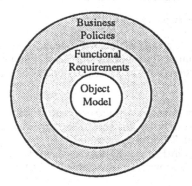

Figure 6.1 : The three layers of a system structure

---

1   ReturnDate and LendDate are attributes of library items; they record the date upon which the item is returned and borrowed respectively.

This synergistic approach to structuring a system can potentially alleviate the deficiencies of present-day systems development methods, with particular emphasis on software maintenance.

7. Explicit Representation of Business Policies

To explicitly represent a business policy is to raise the level of representation of the business policy. As business policies are declarative statements about objects, their attributes and their actions, we thus expect them to be represented in the same manner. Let us now examine the areas in which business policies can be explicitly represented given the framework as illustrated in figure 6.1.

There are 4 areas in which explicit representation of business policies is applicable :
1.   Object action
2.   Object attribute
3.   Condition derivatives
4.   Computation derivatives.

7.1. Object Action

An action denotes a participation on the part of an object in an event. The execution of an action changes the state of an object. For instance, a Non-reference book issue is an event participated by two objects - Non-reference Book and Member. The action is a common action between the two objects (let's call the action 'Lend'), and when this event occurs, the Lend actions of the two objects are executed. The completion of the actions update the states of the two objects (i.e. the data values of the relevant attributes such as loanCount and currentBorrower will be updated).

7.1.1. Pre-Action Constraint and Post-Action Triggering Policies

However, before any actions can be executed, certain conditions may have to be satisfied. For example, before a book can be loaned to a member, it must first be available for loan; also, that the member has not exceeded his loan quota. For a book renewal, the book must not be initially reserved by another member, etc.

The above constraints are related to the point in time before the execution of an action. This is known as *pre-action conditional constraint*. There are also cases where upon the completion of an action, certain functionalities must follow. For instance, when a book which has been initially reserved by a member is returned, a notification card must be printed, to be sent to the reserving member. The action concerned is "Renew[1]", and the functionality is "Print a notification card".

In other words, for each action, there are pre-action condition and post-action triggering business policies associated with it. The pre-action condition business policies serve as a gate to the execution of an action; opening only when the conditions are satisfied and barring any execution if the situations are not consistent with the constraints. The post-action triggering business policies are links that connect actions to other functionalities which are regularly performed upon the completion of an event.

---

[1]   Renew is a common action of library item and member.

The pre-action condition business policies for the Lend action (Staff Member object) could be expressed as :
        BEFORE Lend CONDITION PrintloanCount < PrintloanQuota.

For the action Renew, the pre-action condition business policy may be specified as :
        BEFORE Renew CONDITION noPriorReservation
    (where noPriorReservation is a functional module that returns a boolean value)

The post-action trigger business policy "When a book which has been initially reserved by a member is returned, print a notification card" can be expressed as follows :
    AFTER Return AND ResvnCount > 0 CALL PrintNotificationCard(BookId).

This policy brings together the three related elements : Action (Return), attributes (ResvnCount) and functionality (PrintNotificationCard).

Explicit representation thus makes clear the policies relating to pre-action constraints and post-action functionality triggers.

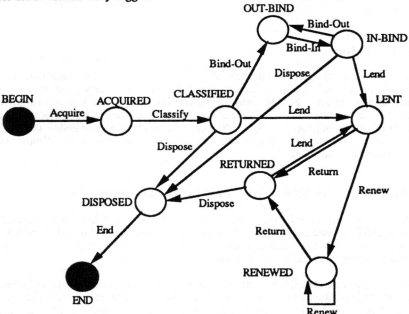

A circle denotes a state. A darkened circle indicates the beginning and ending states of an object; they are special states applicable to all objects. A line connection indicates an action; the activation of the action moves the object from a state to another. For example, if the object is currently at CLASSIFIED state, it may accept actions Bind-Out (which will lead it to the OUT-BIND state) or Lend (which will lead it to the LENT state). The diagram also indicates the set of actions that the object may accept at a given state. In other words, the Non-Reference Book can only accept Bind-Out or Lend (and nothing else), if it is at the CLASSIFIED state.

Figure 7.1 : State-transitions of Non-Reference Book

7.1.2. Action Sequencing Policies

We saw in the earlier sections that an action is time-ordered. An object changes its state upon the completion of an action. The state transition is represented in the object by a change in attributes' values. State-transitions can be depicted graphically using the standard state-transition diagram as in figure 7.1, or textually, in the following form :

FROM source-state   WHEN action   TO destination-state

For the object Non-reference Book, we may tabulate its state-transitions (or temporal constraints) as in Table 2. The FROM column consists of all source states. Given the set of respective actions in the WHEN column, the TO column defines the set of corresponding destination states. Since a state denotes the point in time when an action event has taken place, we use past-tense verb phrase to denote state. For example, the state for action Lend is LENT and for actions Renew, RENEWED, and Return, RETURNED etc.

Table 3 is another example but it is for *Reference* Book. The difference between tables 2 and 3 is that there are no state-transitions entries for the loan of book in the case of the Reference Book.

FROM	WHEN	TO
BEGIN	Acquire	ACQUIRED
ACQUIRED	Classify	CLASSIFIED
CLASSIFIED	Lend	LENT
CLASSIFIED	Bind-Out	OUT-BIND
CLASSIFIED	Dispose	DISPOSED
LENT	Renew	RENEWED
LENT	Return	RETURNED
RENEWED	Renew	RENEWED
RENEWED	Return	RETURNED
RETURNED	Lend	LENT
RETURNED	Dispose	DISPOSED
DISPOSED	End	END
OUT-BIND	Bind-In	IN-BIND
IN-BIND	Dispose	DISPOSED
IN-BIND	Lend	LENT

Table 2 : Temporal constraints for Non-reference Book

FROM	WHEN	TO
BEGIN	Acquire	ACQUIRED
ACQUIRED	Classify	CLASSIFIED
CLASSIFIED	Bind-Out	OUT-BIND
CLASSIFIED	Dispose	DISPOSED
DISPOSED	End	END
OUT-BIND	Bind-In	IN-BIND
IN-BIND	Dispose	DISPOSED

Table 3 : Temporal constraints for Reference Book

Action calls in the WHEN part of the expression correspond to action modules of objects. These modules are independent modules performing the tasks required of the objects in fulfilling the events. These tasks include the following kinds of operations :

1. attributes updates operations
2. value verification operations and
3. derivative operations where the derivation is based on other attributes.

Combining the state-transition expressions and action modules, we derive a situation as illustrated in figure 7.2 where action modules and their temporal constraints are loosely coupled and shared through the inheritance hierarchy as and where applicable[1]. Thus, the above suggests that temporal constraint policies *(business policy definition)* of actions and their corresponding action modules *(mechanism)* should be separately defined, so that changes in the temporal constraints[2] (state-transitions) are confined to changes in the set of state-transition expressions as tabled above. For instance, if for some reasons, the renewing policy for library items has changed as follows :

All items which are available for loans are renewable
except Non-Reference Books which must be returned when due.

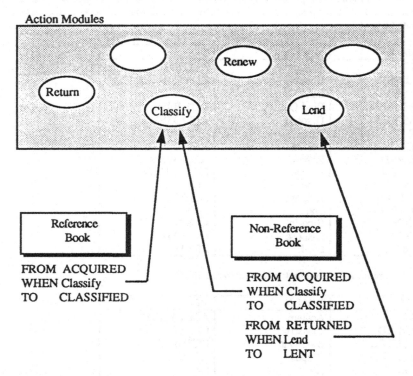

Figure 7.2 : Loosely coupling Action modules and their temporal constraints

This is a case of a change in the temporal constraints on actions and in this case, it applies to a Non-Reference Book. What is required to fulfill the change in the policy is to amend the set of state-transition expressions. In this instance, it entails the deletion of the followings from the set (see Table 2), all others remaining the same.

FROM	RENEWED	WHEN	Renew	TO	RENEWED
FROM	LENT	WHEN	Renew	TO	RENEWED

---

[1] where an action is a specialised action then it has to be specifically defined in the specialisation class where it applies.

[2] denoting a change in the life-history of an object.

Hence, explicitly representing the temporal constraints and separating their definitions from the action modules would thus provide a platform upon which changes in business policies could be made.

7.2. Object Attributes

An object has attributes and attributes affect one another in two ways. First, an attribute may only take a certain value depending on the object class. For instance, the loanQuota attribute of each member class is based on the following policies :

IF Producer	THEN	PrintLoanQuota = 4 and NonPrintLoanQuota = 5
IF NonProducer	THEN	PrintLoanQuota = 4 and NonPrintLoanQuota = 5
IF ExtIndivlMember	THEN	PrintLoanQuota = 4 and NonPrintLoanQuota = 5
IF ExtInstitnMember	THEN	PrintLoanQuota = 10 and NonPrintLoanQuota = 10
IF MemberATC	THEN	PrintLoanQuota = 10 and NonPrintLoanQuota = 10
IF Reader	THEN	PrintLoanQuota = 0 and NonPrintLoanQuota = 0

Second, the value of an attribute may be constrained by another attribute. For example, the attributes DisposedDate and ReturnDate of the Non-Reference Book are constrained in the following manner :

$$DisposedDate \; >= \; ReturnDate.$$

This means that a book cannot be disposed unless it has been returned earlier. Also, loan quota and loan count are similarly constrained in the following manner :

$$PrintLoanCount <= PrintLoanQuota$$
$$NonPrintLoanCount <= NonPrintLoanQuota$$

The above are constraint policies pertaining to object attributes; these policies do change. The meaning of these policies is usually encoded into low-level computational statements often obscured by the complexity of program code. Of course, constant parameters could be used; in which case, PrintLoanQuota and NonPrintLoanQuota could be stored in a parameter table and changed as and when the quota value for each of the member category changes. This solution is feasible but limited. For instance, the second kind of constraint which is also related to the first constraint cannot be represented using a parameter table. In fact, the second constraint has to be encoded within program logic, obscuring the definitions. Hence, to reduce the maintenance effort, we also need to consider the explicit representation of attribute value constraints as discussed above.

7.3. Condition Derivatives

Another area of concern is in the factoring of derivatives of condition policies. For example, the condition BorrowedItemIsOverdue was first expressed as :

$$BorrowedItemIsOverdue \; IF \quad TotalFine > 0$$

Alternatively, we may express BorrowedItemIsOverdue as :

$$BorrowedItemIsOverdue \; IF \quad (ReturnDate - DueDate) > 1$$

That is, if an item is returned more than a day after the due date then the item is considered as overdue. The digit "1" on the right-hand side of the expression indicates a one-day grace period for the member.

This policy (BorrowedItemIsOverdue) may be applied in various part of the system and possibly hidden in the complexity of the system, leading to difficulty in making changes to the policy when the need arises. However, if the definition of the policy is abstracted and explicitly represented in a specification, then changes to the policy applies only at the policy definition rather than at *where* the policy occurs.

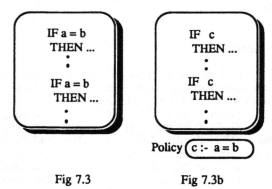

Fig 7.3   Fig 7.3b

Figure 7.3 illustrates the advantage of explicitly representing this type of condition derivative policies. In figure 7.3a, we have a policy (c IF a=b) which occurs at various parts of a system being represented as it is (a=b) in the system. Changing this policy would require the search for their occurrences and then making the required changes. However, in figure 7.3b, abstracting and explicitly representing the policy would confine the change only to the definition of the policy without affecting the entire system. Certainly, the latter approach is much better.

Explicit representation of condition derivative policies is particularly useful in system simulations where the change in conditions, representing different situations, could be facilitated easily. It is also useful for the monitoring of systems particularly when the system is implemented in a new environment. For instance, the above OVERDUE policy may include the one-day grace period for the initial two months of implementation but would have to be removed once the period is over. In this case, since the change is a policy change, then only the meaning of the policy should be changed from

BorrowedItemIsOverdue IF (ReturnDate - DueDate) > 1

to

BorrowedItemIsOverdue IF (ReturnDate - DueDate) > 0

and the others should remain the same as before.

7.4. Computational Derivatives

A condition derivative policy is related to another kind of policy known as *computational* policy. The term *computational* indicates that the policy has an arithmetical flavour. Indeed, the policy connects object attributes and other computational policies via an arithmetical formula. While the condition derivative policy suggests that a certain condition is true, it is the computational policy that stipulates how the value is to be calculated. For instance, we could tell if a Non-Reference Book is overdue via the condition derivative policy but we need a computational policy to indicate the total fine due. The formula for the calculation is stated in a computational policy as follows :

TotalFine   = TotalDaysOverdue * 50.
TotalDaysOverdue   = ReturnDate - DueDate - 1 - TotalSundays - TotalPublicHolidays.

ReturnDate and DueDate are attributes of the object Non-Reference Book; TotalSundays and TotalPublicHolidays could be pre-defined functions that return integer values relating to total Sundays and public holidays during the overdue period respectively.

The above computational policy not only makes clear the meaning of the formula but also brings together all related components associated with the computation. Since users generally express computational policies in such a declarative manner, representing them in a computer system in similar form would greatly enhance the maintenance effort.

Consider, for instance, the formula for the calculation of fine :

TotalFine   = TotalDaysOverdue * 50.
TotalDaysOverdue   = ReturnDate - DueDate - 1 - TotalSundays - TotalPublicHolidays.

These formulae may be used in various parts of a system. Hence, when there is a change in the definition of the formulae, there is a need to first locate where they have been used and change them accordingly. To alleviate this problem, one may package the calculation within a single module so that changes to the formula could be limited to the module. Although this solution is possible, it falls short of making the definition explicit. What this solution has achieved is to transform the meaning of the policy into a set of low-level program logic, albeit in a single module; often making the policies unrecognisable.

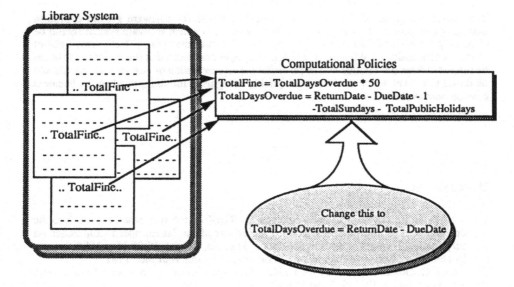

Figure 7.4 : Explicit Representation of Computational Policies

To illustrate, let's consider the previous computational policies on TotalFine. The TotalFine policy takes into consideration the fact that the library is not open on Sunday and Public holidays; that is why the calculation of the total fine amount does not include these days. Also, there is a one-day grace period given to the member for returning items that are due. Let's assume now that the library is open to members on Sundays[1], then the policy has to be amended to :

TotalDaysOverdue = ReturnDate - DueDate - 1 - TotalPublicHolidays.

Furthermore, grace period may be revoked and if such a situation occurs, the policy will have to be changed to :

TotalDaysOverdue = ReturnDate - DueDate - TotalPublicHolidays.

---

[1] Highly possible in Singapore.

and if need be, the policy may be reduced to :

$$TotalDaysOverdue = ReturnDate - DueDate.$$

Even the rate of fine may be changed from 50 cents to say $1 to encourage members to return the items on time.

Although the changes may seem trivial, the efforts required to make the change may not be so using the conventional approach; and certainly the efforts would not be proportionate to the complexity of change if the policy is not represented explicitly as in figure 7.4.

Based on the above, we can conclude that there is a need to factor out the derivation of condition and computational policies from the environment in which they are used. In so doing, we aim to enhance the maintenance of the policies when the need arises.

8. Conclusion

This paper recognises the need to continuously provide for software system evolution throughout its entirety. It also suggests a framework upon which software system should be structured for easier maintenance. The framework is characterised by 3 elements : object model, functionalities and business policies. The paper concludes that these elements should be separated from one another and in particular the representation of business policies should be raised to a level where they can be explicitly recognised for changes when the business environment evolves.

References

1. vanAssche F., Layzell P.J. and Anderson M. RUBRIC : A rule-based approach to the development of information systems, Proceedings of the 1st European Conference on Information Technology for Organisational Systems, Athens, 16-20 May 1988.
2. Boehm B.W., Software Engineering Economics, Prentice Hall Inc., 1981
3. Booch G. Object-oriented Development, IEEE Transactions on Software Engineering, Vol SE-2, No. 2, Feb 1986, pp 211-221.
4. Cameron J.R. An overview of JSD, IEEE transactions on Software Engineering Vol SE-12, No 2, Feb 1986   pp 222-240.
5. Cox, B.J., Object Oriented Programming: An Evolutionary Approach, Addison-Wesley Publishing Co., August 1986
6. Davis R. and Buchanan B. Production rules as a representation for a knowledge-based consultation, Artificial Intelligence 8, 1977 pp 15-45.
7. Fjeldstad R.K et al, Application program maintenance in [15], pp 13-27.
8. Gustafsson M.L., Karlsson T. and Bubenko J.A. A declarative approach to conceptual information modelling   in [14].
9. Hayes-Roth F. Rule Based Systems,   Communications of the Association of Computing Machinery, Vol 28, No. 9, Sept 1985, pp 921-932.
10. Jackson M.A. System Development, London : Prentice Hall International Inc., 1983.
11. Lientz B.P. & Swanson B. Problems in Application Software Maintenance, Comm. ACM, Vol 24, No. 11, pp 763-769, 1981.
12. Meyer B. Object-oriented Software Construction, Prentice-Hall, 1988.
13. Morris E.P. Strengths and Weaknesses in Current large scale data processing systems, Alvey/BCS SGES workshop, Jan 1985.

14. Olle T.W. et al (eds). CRIS1 - Information System Design Methodologies : A Comparative Review Amsterdam : North-Holland, 1982.
15. Parikh G. and Zvegintzov N. Tutorial on Software Engineering, IEEE, 1983.
16. Parnas D.L. On the criteria to be used in decomposing systems into modules Communications of Association of Computing Machinery, Vol 15 No 12, 1972 pp 1053-1058.
17. Parnas D.L. Designing software for ease of extension and contraction IEEE Transactions on Software Engineering SE-5, March 1979, pp 128-138.
18. Poo Chiang-Choon Danny. The integration of Rules into the Object-oriented Paradigm to facilitate Software Maintenance Ph D thesis, Dept of Computation, UMIST, Manchester, May 1988.
19. Poo Chiang-Choon Danny et al. Information Systems Development - A new direction, Proceedings of SEARCC 90, Dec 1990, Manila (Philippines).
20. Poo Chiang-Choon Danny. Adapting and using JSD modelling technique as a front-end to object-oriented systems development, Journal of Information and Software Technology, Vol.33, No. 7, Sept 1991, pp 466-476.
21. Poo Chiang-Choon Danny. An Object-oriented Software Requirements Analysis Method, (accepted for publication in International Journal on Software Engineering and Knowledge Engineering in June 1992).
22. Poo Chiang-Choon Danny. TarTan : An object-oriented System Modelling Method for MIS applications, Technical report, Dept of Information Systems and Computer Science, National University of Singapore (same as author's correpondence address).
23. Rumbaugh James et al. Object-oriented Modelling and Design, Prentice-Hall, 1991.
24. Smith J. and Smith D. Database Abstractions : Aggregation and Generalisation, ACM Transactions on Database Systems, Vol 2, No. 2, 1977, pp 105-133.
25 Yourdon E. and Constantine L., Structured Design : Fundamentals of a discipline of computer program and systems design, Yourdon Press, 1979.

THE SOL OBJECT-ORIENTED DATABASE LANGUAGE

**R. Zicari, F. Cacace, C. Capelli, A. Galipo', A. Pirovano,
A. Romboli**

Politecnico di Milano
Dipartimento di Elettronica
Piazza Leonardo da Vinci, 32
20123 Milano, Italy

G. Lamperti

TxT Ingegneria Informatica
via Socrate, 41
20128 Milano, Italy

- Work supported by EEC under the ESPRIT-II project 2443 "Stretch"-

Abstract. SOL is a language for databases with tuples, sets, lists, object-identity and multiple inheritance. Other features of SOL are: The existence of a generic type which allows the definition of the schema by step-wise refinements, and the use of null values to express incomplete information in objects. A uniform way of coding both methods and programs is provided through an algebra for objects . The algebra is used both for querying and updating a SOL database. SOL has been defined and implemented as part of the Esprit-II project 2443 "*Stretch*".

1 INTRODUCTION

This paper presents an overview of SOL (Stretch Object-Oriented database Language). The main features of SOL are summarized as follows:

• The SOL data model is a typical object-oriented data model, with *inheritance* hierarchies and object sharing. A novel feature of the SOL data model is existence of a *generic* type which allows the definition of a SOL schema by *step-wise refinements*.

• *Null values* are used to express incomplete information for objects.

• An algebra for objects, called *EREMO*, is used both for coding methods and programs. *EREMO* is used both for expressing SOL queries and updates. In this way, in contrast to other object-oriented database languages, for example the one of O2 [Lecluse et al89], and ORION [Kim89], there is no need to distinguish between the language for implementing methods (in most cases an imperative language) and the language for expressing non-procedural queries (in most cases an SQL-like set-oriented language). The SOL approach solves the "impedance mismatch" problem which still exists, despite all, in many of the proposed object-oriented database languages [BCD89], [CDLR89], [Kim89], [OOP88]. The *EREMO* algebra respects the encapsulation principle and takes advantage of *inheritance* hierarchies and object identifiers.

SOL has been implemented on top of the ALGRES advanced nested-relational system. ALGRES is a powerful rapid prototyping platform which offers an   extended nested relational data-model and a language for data definition and manipulation based on an extended algebra for nested relations [Ceri et al.88], [CCLLZ90].

This paper presents the main features of SOL: The data model in Section 2, and the algebra for objects in Section 3. Each of the two sections also includes a comparison with recent similar proposals. The conclusions are reported in section 4. In Appendix we show a simplified version of an application implemented in SOL in the context of the *STRETCH* project.

2. THE SOL MODEL

The SOL data model is similar to that of IQL [Abiteboul90], [Abiteboul Kanellakis 89], LOGRES [Cacace et al 90], and O_2 [Lecluse et al. 89], but with some differences as described in subsections 2.2.4 and 2.5.

2.1 OBJECTS, TYPES, VALUES and CLASSES

SOL entities are **objects** and **values** as in IQL [Abiteboul 90], LOGRES [Cacace et al. 90], and O_2 [Lecluse et al.89]. A SOL entity has a **type**. A type expression is built starting from **elementary types**, and using one of the following **type constructors**: tuple, set, multiset (i.e. a set with duplicates) and list.

Every object is uniquely identified by an object identifier (**oid** in the following). To each oid is associated the value of the object.
A function v maps each oid into a value: $v: O \to V$
where O is the set of oids and V the set of all values, which will be defined in Section 2.1.2.

The function v defines the SOL instance (Section 2.2.2).

A type in SOL is associated to a *class* . A class defines the structure of a set of objects with the same type. A SOL class declaration contains the class name and its type. These concepts are defined more formally in the rest of this section.

2.1.1 Types

SOL elementary types, denoted as D, are:

$$D = \text{integer I real I string I boolean I text}$$

Let C be the set of class names, L be the set of labels used to name types, O the set of oids.
The type constructors are:

$$
\begin{array}{ll}
(\ ): & \text{tuple} \\
\{\ \}: & \text{set} \\
[\ ]: & \text{multiset} \\
<\ >: & \text{list}
\end{array}
$$

A **type expression** (or simply type) τ is:

$$\tau \to \emptyset \mid D \mid C \mid (L_1:\tau,....,L_k:\tau) \mid \{\tau\} \mid [\tau] \mid <\tau>$$

where $\emptyset$ denotes the empty type, $D \in D$, $C \in C$ and $L_i \in L$. A **type definition** is defined as $L: \tau$, where $L \in L$.

Each type expression defines a set of values which are compatible with the defined type as follows:

comp $(\emptyset) = \emptyset$
comp (integer) $= I$
comp (real) $= R$
comp (string) $= S$
comp (boolean) $= \{$ true, false $\}$
comp (text) $= T$
comp (C) $= O$
comp ($(L_1:\tau,....,L_k:\tau)$) $= \{ (v_1,...,v_k) \mid v_i \in$ comp $(\tau_i) \}$
comp ($\{\tau\}$) $= \{ \{ v_i \} \mid \forall i > 0, v_i \in$ comp $(\tau) \}$
comp ($[\tau]$) $= \{ [v_i ,n_i] \mid \forall i > 0, n_i > 0, v_i \in$ comp $(\tau) \}$
comp ($<\tau>$) $= \{$ w I w is a finite sequence of elements v_i, v_i comp$(\tau) \}$

where I is the set of integers, R the set of reals, O the set of oids, etc. Note that the value of a multiset includes the number n_i of occurrences of each element.
A tuple (or set, multiset, list) constructor allows introducing internal labels into the type definitions; for instance if we want the tuple (t_1,t_2) to be labelled N, we write $T = N(t_1,t_2)$. Such a label is not mandatory though. This is explained in the following example.

Example:

The type :
                  (first_name: string,
                   family_name: string,
                   age: integer,
                   date_of_birth: string,
                   place_of_birth: string)

is equivalent to:

    personal_data : (first_name: string,
                       family_name: string,
                       age: integer,
                       date_of_birth: string,
                       place_of_birth: string)

Example. The following is a class declaration:

  class PERSON is
             struct (first_name: string,
                   family_name: string,
                   age: integer,
                   date_of_birth: string,
                   place_of_birth: string)
  end PERSON

An object is created with an explicit operator, *new*, which takes a class name as parameter and gives as a result an oid of an object which is included in the class.

Each class has associated the set of oids of the objects of the class. Such a set is called the *class extension* (a more formal definition of a class extension is given in section 2.1.5).

Example We create an object of class PERSON with the following declaration:

                #p=new(PERSON)

where #p is a label which contains the oid of the newly created object.

We now define a *subtyping* relationship between two types. *Subtyping* is a feature of the typing discipline [Cardelli 84] [Balsters,Fokkinga 89].

We speak of subtyping when [Balsters Fokkinga89]:

• a partial order exists on types, and from types σ and τ, with $\sigma \leq \tau$ there exists a ("conversion") operation $cv_{\sigma \leq \tau}$ that behaves like a function mapping arguments of type σ into results of type τ .

• an expression e of type σ is allowed to occur at a position where something of type τ is required, provided that $\sigma \leq \tau$ and that the operation $cv_{\sigma \leq \tau}$ is applied (implicitly) to the value of e. We call τ the *supertype* of σ, and σ the *subtype* of τ.

We have extended Cardelli's notion of sybtyping between tuple-types [Cardelli88] to any SOL type, as follows:

We say that τ_1 is a subtype of τ_2, denoted $\tau_1 \leq \tau_2$, if and only if one of the following conditions holds (see also [Lecluse et al. 89]):

1- $\tau_1 \in D \cup C \cup \emptyset$ and $\tau_2 = \tau_1$.
2- $\tau_1, \tau_2 \in C$ and *struct* $(\tau_1) \leq$ *struct* (τ_2).
3- τ_1 is $(L_i: \tau_i)$, $1 \leq i \leq p$, τ_2 is $(L_k: \tau_k)$, $1 \leq k \leq q$, $q \leq p$, $\forall k \; \exists ! \; i: L_i = L_k, \tau_i \leq \tau_k$.
4- τ_1 is $\{\tau_1'\}$, τ_2 is $\{\tau_2'\}$ and $\tau_1' \leq \tau_2'$.
5- τ_1 is $[\tau_1']$, τ_2 is $[\tau_2']$ and $\tau_1' \leq \tau_2'$.

6- τ_1 is $<\tau_1'>$, τ_2 is $<\tau_2'>$ and $\tau_1' \leq \tau_2'$.

where *struct* is a mapping from C to the set of type expressions; *struct* is induced by v, as explained in the following (Section 2.3.2).

2.1.2 Values

In classical object-oriented languages such as Smalltalk [Goldberg Robson 83], the value encapsulated in an object is always an atom or a tuple of other objects. In object-oriented database systems this value is a tuple or a set of objects. Following the approach of O_2 [Lecluse et al. 89] , SOL beside objects provides *values*.

Values are recursively built starting from domains of elementary types using type constructors, as follows:

1- each element of I, R, S, T, O, {true, false} is a value;
2- $\emptyset$ is a value;
3- if $v_1,...,v_k$ are values, $k \geq 0$,
   $(v_1,...,v_k)$, $\{v_1,...,v_k\}$, $[(v_1,n_1),...,(v_k,n_k)]$, $<v_1,...,v_k>$ are values;

4- *unk*, *dne*, *open* are values.

The set of all values which can be built in the SOL language is denoted by V.

Example: Consider the following two classes:

class PERSON is
struct (first_name: string,
         family_name: string,
         age: integer,
         date_of_birth: string,
         place_of_birth: string,
         address: ADDRESS)
end PERSON

class ADDRESS is
struct (city: string,
         street: string,
         number: integer)

Suppose we have defined two objects of class PERSON and ADDRESS respectively (object identifiers are written using a #):

#1 : ("John", "Smith", 30, "12-04-60", "London", #2)

#2 : ("Manchester", "Parker", 34)

If one does not want to model ADDRESS as an object, it is possible in SOL to define the class PERSON in a different way, using a so-called *complex attribute*, as follows:

class PERSON is
struct (first_name: string,
         family_name: string,
         age: integer,
         date_of_birth: string,
         place_of_birth: string,
         address:: (city: string,
                     street: string,
                     number: integer)
end PERSON

Now we have only one object:

#1 : ("John", "Smith", 30, "12-04-60", "London", ("Manchester", "Parker", 34))

A complex attribute , *address* in the example, has a *structured value*. Structured values can be used every time there is no need to define an independent object.

Among the values allowed for SOL basic attributes, *null* values are permitted. We follow the approach proposed in [Gottlob Zicari88] and define the following types of null values for attributes of basic type: unknown (*unk*), does not exist (*dne*), and *open* . The semantics of such null values is given in [Gottlob Zicari88]. The domain of SOL basic types therefore includes null values (section 2.1.2). Null values are used to express incomplete information for objects [Zicari 90] as the following example shows.

Example: Consider the two class declarations:

class LESSON is
struct (name: string,
        sublessons: < sublesson: LESSON_TREE >,
        lesson_text_list: < page: text >,
        question_list: < question: QUESTION >)
end LESSON_TREE

Class QUESTION is
struct < (question: text ,
        possible_answers: < (answer: string, score: integer) >)   >
end QUESTION

and the following objects:

#p1: ("User Interface", { } , <"This is a lesson on the user interface....">, <#q1,#q2>)

#q1: <   ("How do you invoke the user interface?",   < ("By clicking the user icon", **unk**), ("Using shut-down", 0) >) , ("How do you return to the main menu?", < ("PF1 key", **unk**) >)   >

In the example we have :

- object lesson #p1 does not have sublessons (the corresponding value is the empty set);
- object question #q1 has two unknown scores.

2.1.3 Generic type

SOL allows the definition of a class with a *generic* type [Zicari 90]associated. A *generic* type corresponds to the empty type Ø. The value of an object of type *generic* is*not* defined, and is denoted with ⊥. This corresponds to saying that the value function v is a partial function.A generic type is useful in defining a SOL schema by step-wise refinements, as the following example shows:

Example   We create a class DEAN with type generic:

class DEAN is
 struct *generic*
end DEAN

Objects for such class do not have values (we write v (#oid) to denote the value of the object):

#d1 = new(DEAN)
v (#d1) = ⊥

We can refer to a generic class within another class:

```
class UNIVERSITY is
  struct (name: string,
          dean: DEAN )
end UNIVERSITY
```

```
#u1 = new(UNIVERSITY)
v (#u1) = ("Politecnico di  Milano", #d1)
```

Because the generic type does not have value associated, it respects the inclusion semantics for subtyping. In particular we have $\emptyset \leq \emptyset$, and $\emptyset \leq \tau_i$, for each type in the system. It does *not* hold $\tau_i \leq \emptyset$, if $\tau_i \neq \emptyset$. Therefore, we can have a generic class in an inheritance hierarchy as a subclass of a class with type non generic, but not vice-versa.

Example:

```
class  PERSON is
struct ( first_name: string,
         family_name: string,
         age: integer,
         date_of_birth: string,
         place_of_birth: string )
end PERSON
```

```
class STUDENT inherits PERSON  is
  struct generic
end STUDENT
```

When a generic class is updated to a different type τ then objects of that class get a default value.

2.1.4 Object sharing

Object sharing is used whenever an attribute A in a class C is of type C_1 where C_1 is an element of *C*. The value of the attribute A is the oid of an object of class C_1. An object may be contained into one or more objects, as illustrated by the following example.

Example:

In the following declaration each object of class SYSTEM refers to objects of other classes, namely MATERIAL, CONNECTOR, PROCEDURE and to objects of the same class SYSTEM.

```
class SYSTEM is
struct ( name:string,
         part#: integer,
         serial#: integer,
         date_of_making: string,
         T_min: real,
         T_max:real,
         made_of: { ( material: MATERIAL, quantity: real ) },
         connected_to:  { ( system: SYSTEM, connectors: { link: CONNECTOR  } ) },
         brand: string,
         model: string,
         subsystems: { system: SYSTEM   },
         procedures:  { procedure: PROCEDURE  } )
end SYSTEM
```

2.1.5 Inheritance

The SOL data model is based on the inheritance relationships among classes.The semantics of inheritance is given using the *subtyping* relationship as follows:

A *class hierarchy* is a triple $(C, struct, \angle)$, where C is the finite set of class names, *struct* is a mapping from C to types, and $\angle$ is a strict partial ordering on C.

Inheritance (isa relationship) between two classes C_1 and C_2 is expressed in the language by adding the statement C_1 *inherits* C_2. This means that each object of the class C_1 also belongs to the class C_2. C_1 is called a *subclass* of C_2. Conversely C_2 is called a *superclass* of C_1.

An inheritance hierarchy $(C, struct, \angle)$ is consistent if for any two classes C, C' of C, where C' is a subclass of C, we have $struct$ (C') $\leq struct$(C).

For example, a consistent inheritance hierarchy is defined as in the following example.

Example:

```
class PERSON is
struct ( name: string,
         salary : integer,
         friends: {friend: PERSON } )
end PERSON

class MANAGER inherits PERSON is
struct ( name: string,
         salary: integer,
         friends : { friend: STUDENT   } )
end MANAGER

class STUDENT inherits PERSON is
struct ( company: string,
         role: string,
         lessons_attended : < ( lesson: LESSON,  score: integer ) >,
         total_score: integer,
         additional_info: text )
end STUDENT
```

Note that inherited attributes from a superclass need not to be repeated in the subclass (unless the associated type is different).

So for example, one could re-write class MANAGER in the following equivalent way:

```
class MANAGER inherits PERSON is
 struct ( friends: { friend: STUDENT } )
end MANAGER
```

At the instance level, we model is-a hierarchies by inserting the oid's of sub-classes within the oid's of the superclasses.

The type associated to the class MANAGER is:

τ: (name: string, salary: integer, friends: {friend: STUDENT })

The type associated to the class STUDENT is:
τ': (name:string,
         salary: integer,
         friends:{ friend:PERSON },
         company: string,
         role: string,
         lessons_attended < (lesson: LESSON, score: integer) >,
         total_score: integer, additional_info: text)

To each class is associated the set of oids of the objects of the class, which is called **class extension**.

A class extension can be defined more precisely as follows[Abiteboul90] :

We define a function π which maps each name in C to a finite set of oid's such that $C \neq C'$ implies $\pi(C) \cap \pi(C')$ = Ø (where C,C'∈ C). We call the set $\pi(C)$ the *local extension* of the class C. If C is an inheritance hierarchy, then we define a *class extension* as the set
$\pi_{in}(C) : \pi_{in}(C) = \cup\{ \pi(C') \mid C'\in C, C' \leq C\}$ (for each C).

Example:

Consider the class PERSON , its subclass STUDENT, and objects:

#p1, #p2, #p3 of class PERSON
#s1, #s2, #s3, #s4 of class STUDENT

we have:

local extension of PERSON ={#p1, #p2, #p3 }
extension of PERSON ={ #p1, #p2, #p3, #s1, #s2, #s3, #s4 }
local extension of STUDENT = { #s1, #s2, #s3, #s4 }
extension of STUDENT = { #s1, #s2, #s3, #s4 }

We assume that STUDENT does not have subclasses.

2.1.6 Multiple Inheritance

In SOL multiple inheritance is allowed, namely, the possibility of declaring a class as a subclass of two or more classes.A special class called OBJECT (see 2.2.3) is always a common ancestor class for each class in the schema. In the language multiple inheritance between a class C_3 (with type τ_3) and two direct superclasses C_1 (with type τ_1) and C_2 (with type τ_2) is expressed as follows: class C_3 *inherits* C_1, C_2
The above is a consistent declaration iff $(\tau_3 \leq \tau_1)$ and $(\tau_3 \leq \tau_2)$.

In the definition of multiple inheritance, name conflicts may occur.For solving name conflicts in multiple inheritance we use the special keyword *from* to rename the label of an attribute.

Example:
class PERSON is
struct (name: string,......)

class FISH is
struct (name: string,....)

Suppose we define a class MERMAID which inherits from PERSON and FISH. We write:

(i)   class MERMAID inherits PERSON, FISH is
        struct (name from PERSON.name)

or in alternative, the following are other possible legal definitions :

(ii)   class MERMAID inherits PERSON, FISH is
         struct (name from FISH.name)

(iii)   class MERMAID inherits PERSON, FISH is
          struct (p_name from PERSON.name,
                  f_name from FISH.name)

Note that in declaration (iii) both attributes labelled *name* in classes *Person* and*Fish* are inherited in class *Mermaid* by changing their names.

2.2 SOL DATABASE

A SOL database is composed of a schema and an instance.

2.2.1 SOL Schema

A SOL database is fully described by the v function, defined in Section 2.1, which associates a value to each oid. Classes are themselves considered as objects, they are defined by the v function as well, as described in Section 2.2.3.

Given an oid o, we will indicate its value as $v(o)$; if the value is a tuple, we will use a dot notation $v(o).attr$ to denote the value of a particular attribute. Note that each class has its own oid; if o is the oid of a class, $v(o)$ contains (Section 2.2) the class name (denoted $v(o).name$), its type ($v(o).struct$), its extension ($v(o).ext$), and the associated methods (see Section 2.2.3).

A SOL *schema* is a set of classes related to each other by *inheritance* relationships and object sharing. In order to describe a correct SOL database, the v function must satisfy a number of constraints. These constraints can be divided into *schema constraints* and *instance constraints.*.

Schema constraints are the following:

1- the *inheritance* relationship must be a-cyclic;
2- types associated by v to each $C \in C$ must be correct SOL types, according to the definition of Section 2.2.1;
3- class methods must have correct types (see section 2.4);
4- if $C_1 isa\ C_2$ then it must be $\tau_{C1} \le \tau_{C2}$;
5- for any pair of oids (o1,o2) corresponding to classes, $v(o_1).name \ne v(o_2).name$;
6- for any class C different from OBJECT , its type τ_C is not τ_0 (cfr. Section 2.2.3).

2.2.2 SOL instance

A SOL instance defines the objects in the system. Objects belongs to classes. There are some constraints on the SOL instance.

In particular, *instance constraints* for the function v are the following (we write $v(C)$ for $v(o)$, meaning that o is the oid of the class C; $v(C).ext$ to denote the extension of the class C, $v(C).struct$ to denote the type of the class C):

1- if $C_1\ isa\ C_2$, then $v(C_2).ext \supseteq v(C_1).ext$;

2- if $v(C_1).ext \cap v(C_2).ext \ne \emptyset$, then ($C_1\ isa^+ C_2$) or ($C_2\ isa^+ C_1$), where isa^+ is the transitive closure of the is-a relationship.

3-type compatibility: if $o_1 \in v(C_2).ext$, $v(o_1)$ must be in $comp(\tau_3)$, where τ_3 is a subtype of $v(C_2).struct$;

4- referential integrity: if C1 occurs in $v(C_2).struct$, then for any $o' \in v(C_2).ext$, $projection_{C1} (v(o'))\in v(C_1).ext$; where projection is the usual relational projection operator.

- Condition 1. says that the extension of a subclass is contained in the extension of the superclass;
- Condition 2. says that subclasses of the same class have disjoint extensions in the SOL model, unless they have a common descendant;
- Condition 3. says that the type of an object in a class extension must be subtype of the type of the class;
- Condition 4 defines object sharing.

2.2.3 Metaclasses

SOL is a reflexive language, i.e. each information describing the database (usually called meta-information, or data dictionary) is defined and manipulated within the language. This is obtained with the introduction in the language of a particular type of classes called *meta-classes*.

Meta-classes have been introduced first in object-oriented languages, such as CLOS[Clos87], and in the Smalltalk system [Goldberg Robson 80].

SOL defines eight metaclasses: *OBJECT, CLASS, CLASS_IN_ISA, CLASS_SHARED_BY, CONNECTED_CLASS, METHOD, STRUCTURE, SCHEMA.*

The top of every SOL schema is the system class *OBJECT* with associated type τ_0. The class *OBJECT* is the superclass of each class in the schema. By definition we have $\tau_i \leq \tau_0$, for each type τ_i defined in the schema. The type τ_0 cannot be used to build user-defined types; by definition we have comp(τ_0)=V, where V is the set of all values which can be built in SOL.

In SOL, a class is considered as an object of the special meta-class **Class**. The **value** of an object of the class *CLASS* is the meta-information corresponding to a class instance, i.e. its name, type, methods (see Section 2.3), the set of classes from which it inherits, its extension (Section 2.3.1).

In particular, the correspondence between the oid of a class and its name is bijective. This is exploited in the EREMO algebra (section 3.) by using class names instead of oids.

2.2.4 Comparison with related approaches

The SOL data model is rather similar to the data models provided by other object-oriented database systems such as IQL [Abiteboul90],O_2 [Lecluse et al.89], Encore [ShawZdonik89] to name a few, but with some differences.

In particular, the data model of IQL allows union and intersection of types while in SOL the equivalent to the union of types is defined only for the top class OBJECT. No intersection of types is provided. IQL and LOGRES both define associations beside classes. SOL does not provide associations. In IQL multiple inheritance is not provided. SOL and LOGRES provide multiple inheritance. However, LOGRES does not have an OBJECT class and therefore constraints multiple inheritance on the existence of a common ancestor class. In SOL no constraints on multiple inheritance are given. Essential features of the SOL data model are the generic type and the possibility of expressing null values, both features are missing in IQL, LOGRES, O_2 and Encore.

Another distinct feature of SOL is the possibility to express the data dictionary in the model through meta-classes. IQL, LOGRES, O_2 and Encore do not support meta-classes.

2.3 METHODS

In SOL object values are manipulated only by methods. A method is just a function which has some typing constraints. A method has a *signature* which defines the type of its input parameter and the type of the output parameter (if any). In SOL, methods are attached to classes and therefore are part of the schema. The definition of a method is done in two steps: first the method signature is given, then its body. The name of the class to which the method is associated can be omitted from the method signature.In such a case, it is implicitly considered when the signature of a method is analyzed.

Example:

```
class PERSON is
  struct (....)
has
  method Get_name () → string is
end PERSON
```

This is equivalent to the following signature:

Get_name (p:PERSON) → string is

Methods are coded using the EREMO algebra (see section 3.). The body of the method is delimited by *begin end*:

```
method body Get_name () → string is
  begin name end
```

Method can be associated to *generic* classes as well.

Example:

class MONUMENT is
  struct *generic*
has
  method Number_of_visitors() → integer
end MONUMENT
method body Number_of_visitors() → integer
  {return a default integer}

A class with a generic type may be used in a method signature:

Example: method X (m: MONUMENT)

2.3.1 Method inheritance.

Methods are inherited as well. If a method is associated to a class p, it is inherited by all classes p', such that p' is a (direct or indirect) subclass of p.

2.3.2 Name conflicts

Multiple inheritance may cause name conflicts for methods. We decided to treat method name conflicts in the same way as for name of attributes using a *from* clause (see section 2.2.) as the following example shows:

Example:

Consider the following classes:

Class C is struct (...) has method m ( )

Class C1 is struct (...) has method m( )

Class C3 inherits C, C1

There are three possible legal ways to inherit a method m in C3:

    (i)   C3 has method m() from C.m ( )   ; (C inherits method m from C).

    (ii)   C3 has method m() from C1.m ( ) ; (C inherits method m from C1)

    (iii)   C3 has method m1() from C1.m(), m2() from C.m( ) ;

               (C inherits both methods labelled m from C and C1 by re-defining their names).

2.3.3 Method Overloading (rules for consistency)

SOL allows method overloading. It is therefore possible to re-define a method (with same name) in an *is-a* hierarchy. The re-definition of the method must respect a compatibility rule with respect to its signature.

We use the following rule of subtyping among functional types [Cardelli88]:

σ' and σ are types,   if σ'≤ σ and τ≤τ' then σ→ τ ≤ σ'→ τ'

Example

The following declarations define a consistent overloading of a method m in an *is-a* hierarchy :

Class C is struct (...)
has method m(c: C)→ (p:C')

Class C' inherits C is struct(...)
has method m(x:C')→(y: C)

SOL methods (and functions see section 2.4) use late binding.

Because methods are associated to classes, we have that a *class declaration* also contains for each class C :

- the set of **methods** which can be applied to the objects of the class (this set contains both methods defined locally in C and inherited from the superclasses of C).

2.4 Functions

SOL beside methods allows a set-oriented manipulation of objects by using *functions*. Functions are not attached to classes as methods. They have a signature which defines the domain and codomain of the function; domain and codomain are typed. Objects referred to in a function parameter can only be accessed by using appropriate methods.

Functions are polymorphic with respect to the input parameters; polymorphism is based on the notion of **weak** subtyping as defined in Section 3.2.2.

Functions body are written, as for methods using the EREMO algebra for objects.

Example These are examples of two function declarations:

function **Get_system_component** (Systems: { system: SYSTEM}) → { name: string }

function **Find_material** (materials: {MATERIAL}, m_name: string, m_code: string) → boolean

2.5 Comparison with related approaches

IQL and its extension do not have covariance for method overloading and do not attach methods to classes. The latter is equivalent to SOL functions. O_2 attaches methods to classes. It also imposes a covariance covariance on method overloading and specifies only one method when a name conflict in multiple inheritance occurs. LOGRES does not have methods. A distinct feature of SOL is the existence both of methods and functions. Functions allow the manipulation of class extensions, thus allowing a set-oriented manipulation for objects within the language (see section 3).

3. SOL DATA MANIPULATION LANGUAGE

3.1 EREMO: An algebra for objects

In this section we informally introduce the algebra for objects EREMO. EREMO (Extending Relational Environment for Manipulating Objects) allows the manipulation of objects using a *set-oriented* algebraic approach.

The EREMO algebra respects encapsulation. We use EREMO to write SOL methods, functions and programs. It is however conceptually possible to use a non-encapsulated version of EREMO to write some special type of applications. In the non-encapsulated version of EREMO, attributes of a class structure are seen as particular methods which give the value of the corresponding element of the structure.

In this paper we only consider the algebra which respects the encapsulation.

In particular, EREMO can be used to:

- write method bodies;
- write function bodies;
- write SOL programs;
- perform object and schema updates [Zicari 91];
- write queries .

3.2 EREMO operators

EREMO consists of a complete set of algebraic operators to handle complex values, grouped as follows:

- comparison and membership operators
- set operators
- projection
- selection
- join
- re-structuring operators
- aggregate operators
- conditional operator
- fixpoint operator
- assignment

Algebraic operators consider oids as a particular type of elementary *values* for which special operators are defined
.

Operators can be combined to form an algebraic expression, with the usual meaning.

The use of EREMO algebraic operators makes possible to manipulate set of objects at the time, thus allowing a more declarative style of programming than in most conventional object-oriented database systems [Lecluse et al89].

3.2.1 Comparison and membership operators

Comparison operators are the following: $=, >, \geq, <, \leq, \neq$, for basic and structured values and **in** for structured values. There is an overloading in the definition of these operators.

Object identity is obtained as equality of oids. The **in** operator tests the membership of a value to a collection of values of the corresponding type. $>, \geq, <, \leq$, are used in the case of collection to express set inclusion, with the appropriate semantics.

3.2.2 Set operators

Set operators are the following: UNION, DIFFERENCE, INTERSECTION. Their semantics is different in case of sets ,multisets, lists. Set operators exploit a type of polymorphism based on the so called *weak subtyping* defined as follows:
We say that $\tau1$ is a *weak subtype* of $\tau2$ (written $\tau1 << \tau2$) if one of the following conditions holds:

1- $\tau_1 \in D \cup C \cup \emptyset$ and $\tau_2 = \tau_1$.
2- $\tau_1, \tau_2 \in C$, there exists a τ_3 such that: $\tau_1 \textit{ is-a } \tau_3$, and $\tau_2 \textit{ is-a } \tau_3$.
3- τ_1 is $(L_i: \tau_i)$, $1 \leq i \leq p$, τ_2 is $(L_k: \tau_k)$, $1 \leq k \leq q$, $q \leq p$, $\forall k \; \exists! \; i: L_i = L_k, \tau_i << \tau_k$.
4- τ_1 is $\{\tau_1'\}$, τ_2 is $\{\tau_2'\}$ and $\tau_1' << \tau_2'$.
5- τ_1 is $[\tau_1']$, τ_2 is $[\tau_2']$ and $\tau_1' << \tau_2'$.
6- τ_1 is $<\tau_1'>$, τ_2 is $<\tau_2'>$ and $\tau_1' << \tau_2'$.

Note that the definition of weak subtyping is similar to that of subtyping except for condition (2). Condition (2) says that in case of a set , the operation can be performed between two classes whose type is compatible with that of a common superclass. The result of such operation is a class with the type of the common superclass.

3.2.3 Projection

Projection is the usual operator. The result of a projection is in general a collection having as attributes the specified ones. Projection can be done for attributes which are locally defined in a class, and not indirectly for inherited attributes (if any).

3.2.4 Selection

Selection has the usual meaning.The structure of the result is identical to the structure of the operand.The predicate of a selection may contain an EXIST operator which returns a true value iff there exists at least one element of the collection which satisfies the predicate.
It may also contains an ALL operator which returns true iff for each element the predicate is verified. The quantification level of the select predicate can be nested in case the operand (a collection) contains complex elements.

Example. "Select those students having L5 as next lesson":

SELECT [Next_lesson() = L5] STUDENT.ext()

3.2.5 Join operator

Join is a binary operation defined in the usual way on two collections of the same category :set, multiset, list.

3.2.6 Re-structuring operators

They inlude the usual NEST, UNNEST operators of the nested relations model.

3.2.7 Aggregate operators

Aggregate operators are applied to collections and return a value corresponding to the specified operation.They are:

min, max, average, count.

The general form of an aggregate operator is:

operation [expr] V

where *operation* belongs to one of the above lists, expr is an expression of type compatible with *operation* and V is the operand value (a collection).

Example. "Find the average age of a set of persons":

average [oid.age()] PERSON.ext()

3.2.8 Conditional operator

The conditional operator returns a value depending on the predicates evaluation inside its specification part. The general form is:

COND [if p_1 then $expr_1$
       elsif p_2 then $expr_2$
       ...
       elsif p_{n-1} then $expr_{n-1}$
       otherwise $expr_n$]

where p_i and $expr_i$, i = 1..n, are respectively a predicate and an expression. The list of predicates is evaluated and if a predicate is true, then the corresponding expression is returned as computed value else if none of the predicates is verified, the last expression (corresponding to otherwise) is the result. The otherwise branch can be omitted. In this case, the result is the *unknown* values when all predicates are false.

3.2.9 Fixpoint operator

The unary fixpoint operator allows the definition of recursive algebraic expressions.
We show the use of this operator to compute the classical "bill_of_material" problem referred to our ITS example.

Example. "Find all components of a set of systems":

FIXPOINT [subcomponents ←[UNION [system.subsystems()],
JOIN [system = oid]
systems SYSTEM.ext(),
subcomponents <= systems,
UNION systems subcomponents] systems

3.2.10 Assignment operator

The assignment operator associates the result of an expression to a value in the following form:

V ← expr

where V is the name of a value while *expr* is a generic algebraic expression. If the value has been declared with a structure definition, the type of *expr* must be compatible with the one of V, otherwise the structure of V is automatically inferred by the one of *expr*. As a particular case, if *expr* returns an object of type class C then V contains the oid of the object. A value V can be assigned many times. This implies that, in case of oids, the association between V and the oid can change.

3.3 SOL Programs

A SOL program consists of three separate units:

- A schema unit:
- An implementation unit
- A query/update unit

The *schema unit* contains the declarations of the schema, i.e. the definitions of the structure of the classes, and the signature of the methods associated to classes and of functions.

The unit is composed of two subsections: one for classes and one for functions.

Schema <Schema_name> is
 Class section:
   <class definitions>

 Function section:
   <function definition>

<class definition> : = <class structure>, { <method signature>}

<function definition> : = <function signature>

The *implementation unit* contains the body (implementation) of all methods and functions in the schema. It is composed of two sections: A class section, which indicates for each class its associated methods, and a function section. The signature of both methods and functions is also repeated here together with their implementation. The body of both methods and functions is written using EREMO algebraic expressions.

Schema <Schema_name> body is
Class section:
  <methods body>
Function section:
  <functions body>

<method body> := <method signature>, <method code>

<function body> := <function signature> , <function code>

The *quey/update unit* corresponds to a set of SOL statements. A SOL statement is an invocation of a method or is an EREMO algebraic expression. A method call may contain as a parameter another method call. In SOL there is no distinction between the language for the implementation of methods (functions) and the language for querying and updating of the database . The unifying language is provided by the EREMO algebra.

The following is an example of a query unit .

Example:

Query unit is:

```
def value SeniorStudent is
      [ (student:STUDENT,
            name: string,
            age: integer      ) ]

SeniorStudent <-  PROJECT [name( ), age( )] self
                  IN (Student.older(21)) and (Student.given_exams("Software Engineering")

DISPLAY [ ] SeniorStudent
```

The result of an EREMO expression can be associated to an identifier (section 3.3.10). This creates a *temporary value*. (SeniorStudent in the example). Differently from classes, values are not encapsulated, they are used for storing results of SOL computation and relationships between objects.

Examples of SOL programs are described in [Zic91b].

4. CONCLUSIONS

We have presented the SOL object-oriented database programming language. The various features of SOL have been described by examples. The SOL language has been implemented on top of the Algres system. The implementation of SOL on Algres meant as a rapid prototype gave us useful insight into the SOL features and provided an important validation to some of the language design decisions. SOL now constitutes one of two languages which compose the multi-paradigm language interface [Zicari Ceri Tanca 91] implemented on top of ALGRES, being the other one a rule-based database programming language called LOGRES [Cacace et al 90].

Acknowledgments

Rolf De By, Herman Balsters, Stefano Ceri, Stefano Crespi-Reghizzi, and Letizia Tanca provided useful comments on earlier drafts of this paper.

REFERENCES

[Abiteboul90] Abiteboul S., "Towards a Deductive Object-Oriented Database Language", Journal of Data and Knowldege Engineering, to appear.

[Abiteboul Kanellakis 89] Abiteboul S., Kanellakis P.C., "Object Identity as a Query Language Primitive", Proc. ACM-SIGMOD, Portland, Oregon, June 1989.

[Balsters Fokkinga 89] Balsters H., Fokkinga M., "Subtyping can have a Simple Semantics", Theoretical Computer Science, to appear.

[Bertino et al. 89] Bertino E., Negri M., Pelagatti G., Sbattella L., "Object-Oriented Query Languages" The Notion and the Issues", Politecnico di Milano, Report no. 89.054, October 1989.

[BCD89] Bancilhon F., Cluet S., Delobel C., "A Query Language for an Object-Oriented Database System", proc. Second Workshop on Database Programming Languages, Salishan, Oregon, June 1989, Morgan Kaufman.

[Cacace 90] Cacace F., "Implementing an Object-Oriented Data Model in Extended Relational Alagebra: Choices and Complexity", Politecnico di Milano, Report no. 90.009, 1990

[Cacace et al 90] Cacace F., S. Ceri, S. Crespi-Reghizzi, L. Tanca, R. Zicari, "Integrating Object-Oriented Data Modeling with a Rule-Based Programming Paradigm", Proc. ACM-SIGMOD, Atlantic City, May 1990.

[Cardelli88] Cardelli L., "A Semantics of Multiple Inheritance", Information and Computation 76, Academic Press, 138-164, 1988.

[Ceri et al 88] Ceri S. et. al, "The ALGRES Project", proc. EDBT 88, Venice, 1988. Springer Verlag, Lecture Notes in Computer Science, no., 1988.

[Zicari Ceri Tanca 91] Zicari R. , Ceri S., Tanca L., "Interoperability between a Rule-based Language and an Object-Oriented Database Language", First Int. Workshop on Interoperability in Multidatabse Systems, Kyoto, April, 1991.

[CCLLZ90] Ceri, S., S. Crespi-Reghizzi, G. Lamperti, L.Lavazza, R. Zicari, "ALGRES: A System for the Specification and Prototyping of Complex Applications", IEEE SOFTWARE, July 1990.

[CDLR89] Cluet S., Delobel C., Lecluse C., Richard P., "Reloop, an Algebra Based Query Language for an Object-Oriented Database System", proc. First International Conference on Deductive and Object-Oriented Databases, Kyoto, Japan, December 1989.

[Clos87] Bobrow et al., "Common Lisp Object System Specifications", X3 87-002, February 1987.

[Goldberg Robson 80] Goldberg A., D. Robson, "Smalltalk80: The Language and its Implementation", Addison Wesley, 1983.

[Gottlob Zicari 88] Gottlob,G., Zicari R., "Closed World Databases Opened through Null Values", proc. VLDB, August 1988, Los Angeles.

[ITS ISIDE] "The User Interface of the ITS ", ISIDE 1133, doc-as-csp-swd-008, May 1989.

[Lecluse et al. 89] Lecluse C., Richard P., Velez F., "O_2, an Object-Oriented Data Model", Proc. ACM-SIGMOD, Chicago,June 1988.

[Kim89] Kim W., "A Model of Queries for Object-Oriented Databases", proc. 15th VLDB, Amsterdam, August, 1989.

[OOP88] Conferencce on Object-Oriented Programming Systems, Languages and Applications", SIGMOD RECORD, (J.Joseph, C. Thomposon, D. Wells eds.), vol.18, no.3, September 1989.

[Shaw Zdonik89]Shaw G.M., Zdonik S.B., "An Object-Oriented Query Algebra", IEEE Data Engineering, September 1989, vol.12, no. 3.

[Zicari 90] Zicari R., "Incomplete Information in Object-Oriented Databases", proc. IFIP Working Conference on Database Semantics(DS-4), July 1990, Windermere.

[Zicari 91] Zicari R., "A Framework for Schema Updates in an Object-oriented Database System", in Proc. IEEE Data Engineering Conf., Japan, 1991.

[Zic91b] Zicari. R, Cacace F., C. Capelli, A. Galipo`, A. Pirovano, A. Romboli, G. Lamperti, The SOL Object-Oriented Database Language, Politecniuco di Milano, Report 91.053, November 1991.

APPENDIX SOL ITS Application

We describe a simplified version of an application developed and implemented in SOL within the ESPRIT-II project *STRETCH* .

A.1 Intelligent Training System : description

We consider a subset of the *STRETCH* Intelligent Training System (ITS) application which involves managing data-components of the hydraulic system of an helicopter. The goal of the ITS application was to define an "intelligent" system which helps a student in learning the various maintenance procedures for specific helicopter components. We use here a considerable smaller subset of such an application.

The schema of the simplified ITS application consists of ten classes, as reported in figure 1. The SOL schema can be logically partitioned in two parts: the first one which stores the description of the various components of the hydraulic sub-system of the helicopter (called *technical database* in the rest) and the second one which stores the structure of the lessons and the student personal data (called *didactic database* in the rest). The technical database is composed of six classes:SYSTEM, MATERIAL, CONNECTOR, PROCEDURE, TROUBLE-SHOOTING, MAINTENANCE. The didactic database is composed of four classes: LESSON_TREE, PERSON, STUDENT, and QUESTION. (We indicate class names with capital letters).

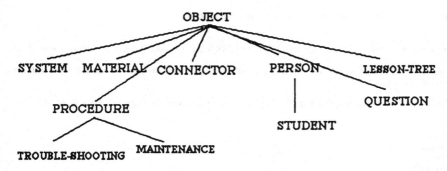

Fig. 1 ITS Schema

A.2 ITS SOL DEFINITION

A SOL program is composed of three units: A schema unit, an Implementation unit, and a Query/Update unit [SOL90]. We present the SOL schema definition for the ITS.

SCHEMA UNIT

We first define the technical database schema.

A class SYSTEM describes the structure of a generic "component" of the hydraulic sub-system. Its associated type is a tuple with twelve attributes. Each attribute is either single-valued or multi-valued. (We recall that types in SOL are either basic types, such as integer, real, or complex types built with the type constructors tuple, set, multiset, and list denoted ( ), { }, [ ], < > respectively, and class names). The attributes of the SYSTEM class are: the system name(*name*), a system part number (*part#*), a serial number (*serial#*), the date in which the component has been produced (*date_of_making*), min. and max. running temperatures of the system (*t_min*, *t_max*), the materials which constitute the system together with their quantity (*made_of*), the set of other subsystems (*subsystems*) which are connected to the one described through some type of connectors (*connected_to*), the set of procedures which are associated with the described system, the brand (*brand*) and model of the system (*model*). The attribute *made_of* is a set of tuple of two attributes: material of class MATERIAL and quantity. The attribute *connected_to* is a set of tuples of two attributes: *system* of class SYSTEM, and *connectors* which is a set of *link*, where *link* is of class CONNECTOR. The attribute *subsystem* is a set of tuples of one attribute: *system* of class SYSTEM (this is a recursive definition) , and the attribute *procedures* which is a set of tuple of *procedure* of class PROCEDURE. Classes MATERIAL, CONNECTOR and PROCEDURE are in *part_of* relationships with the class SYSTEM.

The corresponding SOL declaration is as follows:

Class SYSTEM is
struct (name: string,
     part#: integer,
     serial#: integer,
     date_of_making: string,
     T_min: real,
     T_max: real,
     made_of: { (material: MATERIAL, quantity: real) },
     connected_to: { (system:SYSTEM, connectors: { link: CONNECTOR }) },
     brand: string,
     model: string,
     subsystems: {system: SYSTEM},
     procedures: {procedure: PROCEDURE})

end SYSTEM

Two functions **Get_system_components** and **Select_by_material** are defined:

function **Get_system_components** (systems: { system: SYSTEM }) → { name: string }

The function, given a set of systems, computes all its subsystem components .

function **Select_by_material** (systems: { system: SYSTEM }, name_of_material: string)   → {name: string}

The function, given the set of systems and the name of a specific material, finds the name of the systems which are made of the indicated material .

A class MATERIAL contains all the different materials which constitute the hydraulic system. It has a tuple type with three attributes:

Class MATERIAL is
struct (name: string,
     code: string,
     manufacter: string)

end MATERIAL

Another function is defined:

function **Find_material** (materials: {MATERIAL}, name: string, code: string) → boolean

This function, given a set of materials and the name and code of a specific material , verifies if the given material is listed. It returns a boolean.

A class CONNECTOR contains all different types of connectors used to link together the subsystems composing the hydraulic system. It has a tuple type with three attributes. The type of one of the attributes is text, as it is used to store text.
The various part of the system are associated to procedures for their ordinary maintenance or when a fault is detected. The class PROCEDURE factors out the common characteristics of a procedure. Classes TROUBLE_SHOOTING and MAINTENANCE both describes special procedures, one invoked when a fault is detected and the other one used for normal maintenance. TROUBLE_SHOOTING and MAINTENANCE are subclasses of the superclass PROCEDURE and inherit the attributes and methods of class PROCEDURE.

class CONNECTOR is
struct (connector_code: string,
     brand : string,
     properties: text)

Class PROCEDURE is
struct (name: string,
     tools: {tool: string},
     time_required: real,
     ref_manual: text)
 has

method **Procedure_time()** → real (This method returns the time required to perform a procedure) .

end PROCEDURE

Class TROUBLE_SHOOTING inherits PROCEDURE is
struct (cause: text,
　　　description: text ,
　　　remedy: text)

Class MAINTENANCE inherits PROCEDURE is
struct (case_of_application: text,
　　　description: text)

The didactic database schema is composed of the following classes: Class PERSON factors out the common characteristics of a person: it has a tuple type with five attributes, all of which are simple. Class STUDENT is a subclass of PERSON and describes the information associated to an ITS student. It has a tuple type of five attributes. In particular the attribute "lessons_attended" is a list of tuples, where each tuple contains two attributes: lesson of type class LESSON_TREE and score obtained in that lesson. The *part_of* relationships here is cyclic. Class LESSON_TREE defines the set of lessons for the application with a tree-structure. Class LESSON_TREE has four attributes, the name of the lesson, the set of sublessons composing the lesson, the list of pages containing the text of the lesson, and a question_list. Each element of the question_list is of class QUESTION. Class QUESTION is a list of tuples, each of which has two attributes: a question formulated to the student, and a list of possible answers each one with an associated score. The SOL declarations are as follows:

Class PERSON is
struct (first_name: string,
　　　family_name: string,
　　　age: integer,
　　　date_of_birth: string,
　　　place_of_birth: string)
end PERSON

Class STUDENT inherits PERSON is
struct (company: string,
　　　role: string,
　　　course: LESSON_TREE,
　　　lessons_attended : < (lesson: LESSON_TREE, score: integer) >,
　　　total_score: integer,
　　　additional_info: text)
　has

　　method **Assign_total_score** (score: integer)   (This method assigns a given score to the
　　　　　　　　　　　　　　　　　　attribute *total_score*)

　　method **Last_lesson** () --> lesson_name: string (This method returns the name of the last
　　　　　　　　　　　　　　　　　　lesson attended by the student)

　　method **Next_lesson** () --> string (This is a method which, given a student and the name
　　　　　　　　　　　　　　　　　of its last lesson attended, computes the next lesson
　　　　　　　　　　　　　　　　　the student should attend.)
end STUDENT

Class LESSON_TREE is
struct (name: string;
　　　sublessons: < sublesson: LESSON_TREE >,
　　　lesson_text_list: < page: text >,
　　　question_list: < question: QUESTION >)

　has

Method **Lesson_name** () --> string (This method returns the name of the lesson).

end LESSON_TREE

Class QUESTION is
struct < (question: text,
    possible_answers: < (answer: string, score: integer) >) >

 has

Method **Average_score ( )**

(This is an aggregate method which computes the average of the answers given by the student for each question, and stores the result in the attribute *total score* of the object of class STUDENT) .

end QUESTION

We now define the body of methods and functions defined in the schema. *EREMO* is used to code both bodies of methods and of functions.The same algebra is also used to code SOL programs, as described later.

A.2.2 IMPLEMENTATION UNIT

function body **Get_system_components** (systems: {system: SYSTEM})→{name: string}
begin
  PROJECT [system.name()]
  FIXPOINT [subsys := AGGREGATE [UNION / system.subsystems()]
        JOIN [system= oid]
        systems SYSTEM.ext(),
      subsys <= systems,
      UNION systems subsys] systems
end

This function computes the classical bill-of-material problem. It uses a fixpoint operator.

function body
Select_by_material (systems: {system: SYSTEM}, name_of_material: string)
  → {name: string}
  begin
  PROJECT [system.name()]
  SELECT [EXIST [material.name() = name_of_material] made_of] systems
  end

function body
Find_material (materials: {MATERIAL} , m_name: string, m_code: string)
→ boolean
  begin EXIST [m_name = name AND mcode = code] materials end

method body **Procedure_time** () → real
  begin time_required end

method body **Assign_total_score** (score: integer)
  begin total_score <- score end

method body **Last_lesson** () → string
  begin LAST (lessons_attended).lesson.Lesson_name() end

method body **Next_lesson** () → string
  begin
  COND [if total_score < DISCRIMINATOR then
     COND [if Last_lesson().Child_lesson() = *dne* then
       COND [if Last_lesson().Father_lesson().Left_brother() = *dne* then
        "failure"
       otherwise
        Last_lesson().Father_lesson().Left_brother()

```
                    otherwise
                         Last_lesson().Child_lesson() ]
              otherwise
                  COND [ if Last_lesson().Right_brother() = dne then
                             COND [ if Father_lesson().Right_brother() = dne then
                                        "end of lesson tree"
                                     otherwise
                                         Father_lesson().Right_brother() ]
                      otherwise
                         Last_lesson().Right_brother() ] ]
    end
```

method body **Lesson_name** () → string
 begin   name end

method body **Average_score** ( )
  begin   Assign_total_score(AGGREGATE [average / score] lessons_attended) end

SOL PROGRAMS

We report now two examples of SOL programs working on the ITS schema.

Program 1

The following program "check if a given material (name and code) is used in the helicopter. It then find all systems which use such a material and display them". The program does the following:

- Declare a tuple value corresponding to name and code of a material
- Read the material instance
- Control if material is included into the extension of class MATERIAL and assign the boolean result to the variable
  is_*material* (whose structure is defined implicitly by the right part of the assignment) .
- The result of the COND factor depends on the specified predicate. If true (not a material) then the result is the empty
  set, else it is the returned value of the Select_by_material method.
- Declare a string value corresponding to the name of a system
- Read the instance of the value
- Select the systems corresponding to the system_name
- Display all the system subcomponents for the found systems

SOL Program 1

value material is (name: string, code: string)

READ [material]

is_material <- Find_material (MATERIAL.ext(), material.name, material.code)

user_systems <- COND [**if** not is_material then {}
                            otherwise
                                Select_by_material (SYSTEM.ext(), comp.name, comp.code)]

DISPLAY user_systems

value system_name **is** string

READ [system_name]

systems <- Find_systems_by_name(SYSTEM.ext(), system_name)

DISPLAY Get_system_components (systems)

END SOL Program 1

SOL PROGRAM 2

The following program reads the name of a student, then selects all students with the given name. For each of such students, it computes the next lesson the student must attend and display it.

** Declare a string value corresponding to a student name **

value student_name **is** string

** Read the instance of the value **

READ [student_name]

** Select all students with the specified name and assign the result to a new value **

students <- Find_students_by_name(STUDENT.ext(), student_name)

** Display the last and next lesson for each found student **

DISPLAY PROJECT [Last_lesson(), Next_Lesson()] student

Interactive Design of Object Oriented Databases

E. ANDONOFF - C. SALLABERRY - G. ZURFLUH

Laboratoire I.R.I.T. - Pôle S.I.G., Université Paul Sabatier
118 Route de Narbonne, 31062 TOULOUSE Cedex (FRANCE)

Abstract. This paper describes a method for designing object-oriented databases and a tool to implement it.
The method provides the designer a set of rules which allows the design of an object-oriented database from specifications taken out from the problem specification. It has two steps. In the first step, the designer formally describes the semantic of the problem to model through a set of functional and multivalued dependencies between elementary properties taken out from the specifications. Then, he simplifies this set of dependencies by reducing redundancy. He also expresses constraints which traduce integrity constraints of the problem to model. In the second step, the designer derives from the reduced dependencies, a set of classes, nested classes and methods. Then, he organizes these classes into an inheritance hierarchy. He finally deduces the corresponding object-oriented schema.
The tool is an interface which automatizes the two steps of the method ; it assists the designer in defining object-oriented databases schemas.

1   Introduction

During the past several years, the object-oriented paradigm has been particularly developed in the field of programming languages [14,20]. Various experiences have shown that it improves programmers' productivity and modularity of programs.

In the databases field, it is widely accepted that the relational model does not fit to describe and to handle data of new applications [19]. To compensate for these weakness, various models have been proposed. Some of them emphasize the behavioural aspects of objects they handle ; they are based on some concepts copied on the object-oriented programming and are said to be object-oriented. Systems which implement those models are called object-oriented DBMS. Among the most famous ones, we can quote GEMSTONE[13], ORION[4], O2[23], ONTOS[2], ... But the proposed models and the corresponding systems do not provide a methodology for designing object-oriented databases schemas.

In this paper, we describe a method for designing object-oriented databases. This method provides the designer a set of rules which allows the design of object-oriented schemas from specifications taken out from the problem specification. It takes its inspiration from the design algorithms of the relational model (decomposition [6,17] or synthesis [7]) which provide, from a set of functional dependencies, a relational schema where redundancy is reduced. It takes also inspiration from algorithms of decomposition in normal form for nested relations which compute, from a set of multivalued dependencies, schemas of nested relations where redundancy is reduced [24]. It is based on an object-oriented data model [1].

We also describe the interface which implements the method. It is a tool which automatizes the two steps of the method ; it helps the designer in making object-oriented databases schemas.

This paper is organised as follows. Section 2 locates our studies in the field of design methodologies for object-oriented databases. Section 3 presents the main features of the object-oriented model used. An example is given in section 4. The design methodology is described in section 5. It is illustrated by the example and presented through the associated interface. Section 6 is the conclusion.

2 The Design Methodologies for Object-Oriented Databases

When speaking about design methodologies for object-oriented databases, it is useful to differentiate two approaches [18] :

- the first one is traditional ; it consists in translating a classic conceptual schema (e.g. Entity-Relationship) into a logical schema described with an object-oriented model without calling into question the design methodology,
- the other one is new ; the object-oriented concepts are used to directly result in the corresponding object-oriented schema.

The studies devoted to the first approach provide procedures which describe how to translate the conceptual model into the logical model. The conceptual schema is described by a semantic data model having concepts of abstraction as powerful as those proposed by the classic object-oriented models. The logical schema is described by an object-oriented data model. The used methodology is the semantic model one. We can quote the studies of Bouzeghoub [8] which allow the translation of a conceptual schema MORSE into an object-oriented schema O2. We can also quote the works of Briand [9] allowing the translation of a conceptual Entity-Relationship schema into an object-oriented schema O2. Such an approach has an undeniable advantage ; it allows the migration of applications intended for relational DBMS to object-oriented DBMS. But, it does not suit well the object-oriented paradigm where static and dynamic aspects are regrouped [27].

In the studies devoted to the second approach, object-oriented concepts are introduced in the design methodology. It is the case of O* [11] or OOERM [16] methods. For example, O* is based on an object-oriented model which integrates the main features of the object-oriented paradigm [10] and the notions of dynamic we can find in some of the design methods for information systems (e.g. REMORA [26]). The database is described using static and dynamic objects. The design is organised in three stages : identification, structuration and refinement of objects ; those stages are successively applied to the static and dynamic objects.

Our proposal falls into this category of methods. It allows the design of an object-oriented schema ; it is based on a model which integrates the main features of the object-oriented programming. It is different from other proposals for the following reasons :

- the designer expresses a set of functional and multivalued dependencies which describe, *at the same time*, the static and dynamic properties of objects,
- this set of dependencies is reduced to *minimize* redundancy in the database,

• the designer identifies *nested classes* which modelize complex objects.

3   The Object-Oriented Model

We only describe here the useful concepts for presenting the design method.

3.1   Objects and Classes

An *object* is a collection of structured components ; it is identified by a unique reference [19]. It has a state and a behaviour and is consulted through its *interface*.
The structure of an object is described by a collection of *attributes*. Its state is a pair (identifier, value). The identifier is unique ; it is, at the conceptual level, an attribute of an object [27], and, at the phisical level, the *object identity* [22]. The value of the object corresponds to the values of its attributes. Constraints are sometimes expressed on the attributes of the object : they restrict the value associated to the attributes.
The behaviour of an object is defined by a set of operations called *methods*. They manipulate and return the state of the object.
The interface of an object is composed by the methods the object offers to the other objects. Those methods correspond to the *attribute-methods*, defined for each attribute of the object (in order to respect the notion of encapsulation), and to the *operatory-methods* defined to manipulate the object. These ones are characterized by their signature i.e. their name, parameters and the result they provide.

The objects described by the same structure, the same constraints and the same behaviour are grouped together into the same conceptual entity, the *class*. A class is designated by a name and has an *intension* and an *extension*.
The intension describes the common properties (attribute- and operatory-methods, constraints) of its objects. Its interface is composed by the methods described in the object interfaces. The extension is the set of *instances* of the class. An instance corresponds to the state of an object at a given moment.
The model provides atomic classes (Integer, Real, String, Picture and Text). It also provides the structural classes Set, List and Tuple which are used as constructors [19].

3.2 Inheritance and Inheritance Hierarchy

Inheritance comes from the concept of generalization in semantic models [21]. The generalization allows a hierarchical organization of classes. It gathers the common properties of several classes (called subclasses) in a more general class (called superclass).
Inheritance expresses a IS-A relationship between classes. It corresponds to the mechanism which allows the transmission of properties from a class to a subclass. The intension of a subclass is described by the set of properties owned and inherited. It is defined by adding new attribute- or operatory- methods or new constraints or by overriding one of the inherited properties. Its interface is described by the set of attribute- and operatory-methods, owned and inherited.

3.3 Domain

Each attribute-method of a class is defined on a class called *domain* of the method. The value of a method is an object owned by its domain or by one of the subclasses of the domain. This value is the the value of the object itself if the domain is atomic, else it is the class of the method and the definition class of the method. This association can be monovalued or multivalued (if the Set or List constructors are used). The class definition of the method can be :

- a predefined class or a class defined in the object-oriented database,
- a class defined using the Tuple constructor and other classes ; such a class is only owned by the class in which it is defined and cannot be shared by other classes.

Example: Let be the classes Student and Diploma which describe students who prepare diplomas.

class	Student		**class**	Diploma
methods	name	: string;	**methods**	title_diploma : string;
	address	: [street : string, city : string];		...
	prepare	: Diploma		

In this example, the domains of the attributes *name* and *prepare* are respectively defined on the classes String and Diploma, which correspond to a predefined class and a user-defined class of the object-oriented database. On the other hand, the domain of the attribute *address* is built with the Tuple constructor. It is a domain which is owned by the class Student, i.e. a specific class whose default name is #Address#, and which is nested in the class Student. Such a class is called a *nested class*. It allows the definition of complex objects ; it corresponds to the notion of complex value of O2 [23], or to the notion of nested relation [24], or to the notion of NF2 relation of [25].
We quote that such classes are invisibles whereas the other ones (e.g. Student) are visibles.

4   THE EXAMPLE

We present in this section the example which will be used in the following part of the paper. In this example, we are interested in the design of a database University. The informal description of the problem to model is the following :

A student is described by a number, a name, a first-name, an age, an address (street and city) and the diploma he prepares. Each diploma proposed by the university has a title, several units to obtain and a manager ; this last one is a teacher (professor) who intervenes at least in one of the units of the diploma. The teachers are characterized by a name, a first-name, an age, an address, and the historic of the grades (assistant, professor) and wages they obtain. The units are described by a title, an intervenor which is a teacher, and a list of books which constitutes the bibliography of the units. Those books are characterized by a title, a list of key words, and a list of authors who are teachers. Moreover, those books are composed of chapters which have a title and a set of sections for each chapter.

5   The Design Method

The design method proposed here enables the designer to transform a set of informal specifications into an object-oriented schema. It has two steps : a *formal specification step* and a *design step*.

The formal specification step is based on the informal specifications. Indeed, the designer determinates a set of functional (FD) and multivalued (MD) dependencies between *elementary properties* taken out from the specifications. This set is then reduced : redundancy is frayed. Finally, the designer reuses the informal specifications to express constraints and associate them to the related properties.

In the design step, the designer applies a set of rules to the reduced set of dependencies to identify classes, nested classes and methods associated. Then, he organizes these classes in an inheritance hierarchy. He finally deduces the corresponding object-oriented schema.

We present the design method through the associated interface ; this interface is a tool which implements the method. At the beginning, the designer indicates the name of the database performing the *Connect* method (Fig. 1). Then, he performs the *Specify* method for the formal specification step and the *Design* method for the design step. The user can start again the specification step if he does not agree with the object-oriented schema obtained.

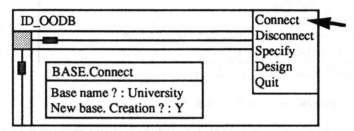

Fig. 1. Connexion to the University database

5.1 The specification step

5.1.1 Expression of the FD and MD

The designer traduces the semantic of the problem to model with these dependencies. The notions of FD and MD are well known in the database field [15]. Let U be a finite set of properties and X,Y and Z sub-sets of U. FD and MD are defined as follows :

FD : There is a FD between X and Y, noted X --> Y, if for each value of X corresponds one value of Y at the most.

MD : There is a MD between X and Y, noted X -->> Y, if for each value of X corresponds one or several values of Y, independent of the values of Z.

FD are a particular case of MD ; indeed, if X --> Y then X -->> Y.

The notation - indicates a dependency which can be either functional or multivalued. Dependency X - Y/Z correspond to the factorisation of the dependencies X - Y and X - Z. Moreover, the notation XYA represents the set $X \cup Y \cup \{A\}$, where X and Y are set of properties and A is a property.

The designer performs the *Initial_dependencies* method to key in dependencies he determined during analysis of informal specifications (Fig. 2).

Every property has different names ; if properties which have the same name intervene in several dependencies (e.g. name, first name), then they are the same.

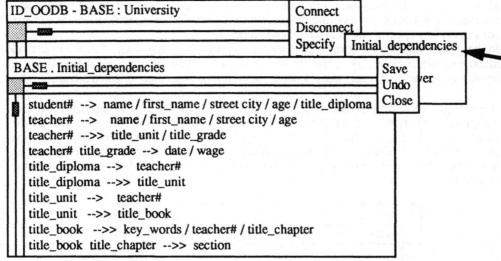

Fig. 2. Specification of initial dependencies

5.1.2 Reduction of the FD and MD

The designer determines the transitive closure and the minimal cover of the set of FD and MD to reduce redundancy. To do that, he uses a set of axioms proposed in literature [15]. This set is closed and complete for FD and MD [6] :

[A1] Reflexivity   :   if $Y \subseteq X$ then $X \dashrightarrow Y$,

[A2] Augmentation   :   if $X \dashrightarrow Y$ and $V \subseteq W$ then $XW \dashrightarrow YV$,

[A3] Transitivity   :   if $X \dashrightarrow Y$ and $Y \dashrightarrow Z$ then $X \dashrightarrow Z$,

[A4] Trivial   :   if $Y \subseteq X$ then $X \dashrightarrow\!\!> Y$ (reflexivity) and $X \dashrightarrow\!\!> \varnothing$,

[A5] Complementation   :   if $X \dashrightarrow\!\!> Y$ then $X \dashrightarrow\!\!> U - XY$,

[A6] Augmentation   :   if $X \dashrightarrow\!\!> Y$ and $V \subseteq W$ then $XW \dashrightarrow\!\!> YV$,

[A7] Transitivity   :   if $X \dashrightarrow\!\!> Y$ and $Y \dashrightarrow\!\!> Z$ with $Y \cap Z = \varnothing$ then $X \dashrightarrow\!\!> Z$

                                            moreover, if $Y \cap Z \neq \varnothing$ then $X \dashrightarrow\!\!> Z - Y$,

[A8] FD particular case of MD   :   if $X \dashrightarrow Y$ then $X \dashrightarrow\!\!> Y$

[A9] Projectability   :   if $X \dashrightarrow\!\!> Y$ and $Z \dashrightarrow W$ with $Y \cap Z = \varnothing$ et $W \subseteq Y$
                                  then $X \dashrightarrow W$.

Let D be the set of FD and MD, D^+ the transitive closure of D and D^- its minimal cover. D^+ is the set of FD and MD deduced from D using the previous axioms. D^- is the set of FD and MD of minimum cardinality such as $(D^-)^+ = D^+$. To obtain D^-, the designer performs the following algorithm :

$D^- = \varnothing$

For each dependency d in D **Do**

    If d is a redundant dependency i.e. such as $D^+ = (D - d)^+$ **Then**

        Let be d1, ..., dn, n > 1 such as $\forall\ i \in [1,..,n]$, di $\in$ D
        dependencies which allow deducing d from D-d using axioms [A1]...[A9].
        If the semantic of d is not the same as the semantic of d1...dn **Then**

            -- d is kept in D^-
            $D^- = D^- + \{\ d\ \}$
        Endif
    Else
        -- d is kept in D^-
        $D^- = D^- + \{\ d\ \}$
    Endif
Endfor

The designer associates a semantic meaning to the FD and MD ; so, several different relationships between classes can be modelized through dependencies. We can quote that algorithms to compute the set of d such as $D^+ = (D - d)^+$ where D is a set of dependencies have been proposed in the literature [15].

In the proposed example, the dependency d : title_diploma -->> title_unit is redundant. Indeed,

- title_diploma --> teacher# ==>[A8] title_diploma -->> teacher# (1),
- teacher# -->> title_unit (2) and
- (1)+(2) ==>[A7] title_diploma -->> title_unit.

Therefore $D^+ = (D - d)^+$. But the semantic of d is *"a diploma is described by several units to obtain"*. The one of d1 : title_diploma --> teacher# is *"the manager of a diploma is a teacher"* and the one of d2 : teacher# -->> title_unit is *"a teacher intervenes in several units"*. The semantic of d is now different from the one of d1 and d2. Therefore, d is kept in D^-.

The minimal cover is automatically computed by the interface. The designer only notifies in an interactive way, for each redundant dependency d in D, if the semantic of d is the same as the semantic of d1, ..., dn where d1, ..., dn are such as d in $\{d1, ..., dn\}^+$ (Fig. 3).

Then, the designer can consult the result performing the *Minimal_cover* method (Fig. 4).

5.1.3   Expression of constraints

These constraints correspond to the integrity constraints described in the informal specifications of the problem to model. They are expressed between properties which appear in functional or multivalued dependencies.

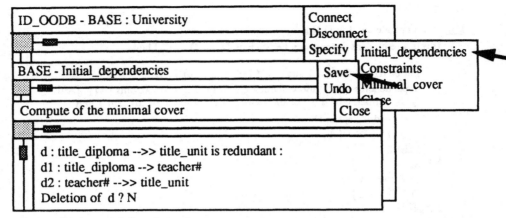

Fig. 3. Compute of the minimal cover

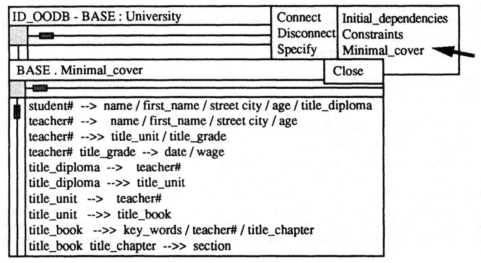

Fig. 4. Consultation of the minimal cover

The designer distinguishes constraints on one property from those on several properties. The first one, called *valorization constraints*, concern the value of a property ; this value can be fixed or chosen among a finite set of values or yet can own particular characteristics. The second ones are of two kinds. We distinguish :

- the *comparison constraints* which express rules (equality, difference, ...) between the values of properties taken out from distinct dependencies.
- the *reciprocity constraints* which traduce the semantic of two properties ; the designer here indicates if a property is reciprocal to another one. The term reciprocal must be interpreted in the mathematical sense : a property is a function which returns a value.

In the following, each property belongs to a class. The constraints related to each property are bound to the class they belong to ; they are applied to every object of the class.

The designer performs the *Constraint* method to key in the constraints he determinates during analysis of informal specifications (Fig. 5).

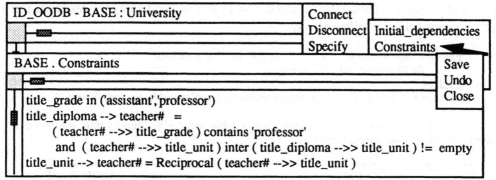

Fig. 5. Specificaton of constraints

5.2 The design step

The designer identifies classes, nested classes and methods associated from FD and MD of D⁻ and organizes them in an inheritance hierarchy. To do that, he applies rules which lead him to formulate again D⁻. The result is a new set of FD and MD, called (D⁻)' ; left- and right- hands of these dependencies are classes and/or methods.

The designer performs the *Conception* method to completely realize this step. The result is the University object-oriented schema (Fig. 12). The designer can meanwhile consult (D⁻)' after the determination of classes and associated methods (Fig. 7) ; he can also consult (D⁻)' after the determination of nested classes and associated methods (Fig. 9) and after the organization of classes in an inheritance hierarchy (Fig. 11).

5.2.1   Determination of classes and associated methods

Rule 1 : Determination of classes
Each property A which appears alone in left-hand of a FD or MD, d : A - X, identifies a class : it corresponds to the identifier of the conceptual level. The designer states the name of that class : Ca. (D⁻)' is computed in the following way :

$(D^-)' = D^-$
For each dependency d : A - X1 /.../ Xn, d in (D⁻)' **Do**
    Replace d with d1 : Ca --> A et d2 : Ca - X1 /.../ Xn
        For each dependency d' : XAY - Z1 /.../ Zn such as X or Y are not empty **Do**
            Replace d' with d3 : XCaY - Z1 /.../ Zn
    Endfor
        For each dependency d" : X - Y1 /.../ Yn / YAZ / Z1/.../ Zn **Do**
            Replace d" with d4 : X - Y1 /.../ Yn / YCaZ / Z1 /.../ Zn
    Endfor
Endfor

The identified classes are the visible classes of the object-oriented schema.

Rule 2 : Determination of methods

Each property which is not a class is a method. Moreover, each dependency between any left-hand and a class expresses the existence of a relationship between sets of properties. This relationship is expressed by a method whose name is specified by the designer : ma. $(D^-)'$ is computed in the following way :

> **For** each dependency d : X - Y, d in $(D^-)'$ where Y is a class **do**
> > Replace d with d1 : X - Y (ma)
>
> **Endfor**
> where ma is the name of the method expressing the relationship between X and Y

The designer intervenes in an interactive way during the design step to state the name of identified classes and methods (Fig. 6).

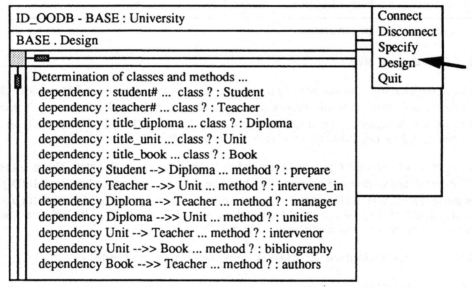

Fig. 6. Determination of classes and methods

The new set of dependencies $(D^-)'$ obtained is described in Fig. 7.

5.2.2 Determination of nested classes and associated methods

The designer tries now to identify nested classes and associated methods : those classes correspond to the invisible classes of the object-oriented schema. This identification is realised in two stages ; the designer applies a set of rules during those stages.

Stage 1 : The designer considers dependencies X Y - Z where X, Y and Z are sets of classes and/or methods. He applies the rule 3 to them .

We can note that such dependencies indicate that classes and/or methods X and Y determines, in a functional or multivalued way, a set of classes and/or methods Z.

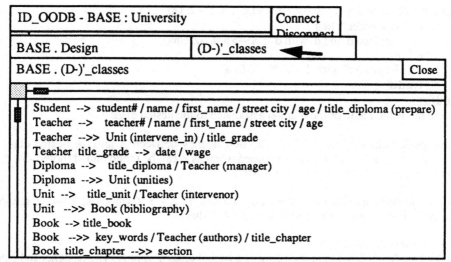

ID_OODB - BASE : University		Connect
		Disconnect

BASE . Design | (D-)'_classes

BASE . (D-)'_classes | Close

Student --> student# / name / first_name / street city / age / title_diploma (prepare)
Teacher --> teacher# / name / first_name / street city / age
Teacher -->> Unit (intervene_in) / title_grade
Teacher title_grade --> date / wage
Diploma --> title_diploma / Teacher (manager)
Diploma -->> Unit (unities)
Unit --> title_unit / Teacher (intervenor)
Unit -->> Book (bibliography)
Book --> title_book
Book -->> key_words / Teacher (authors) / title_chapter
Book title_chapter -->> section

Fig. 7. (D-)' after identification of classes and methods

Rule 3: Dependencies X Y - Z

Rule 3.1
The designer begins arranging these dependencies in decreasing order. The order of a dependency is the number of properties (class or methods) which appear left-hand. The designer then performs the following algorithm :

For each dependency, arranged in decreasing order **Do**
    Research in D^+ X -->> Y or Y -->> X
    If none of these dependencies belongs to D^+ **Then**
        Create a new class Cxy
        (D⁻)' = (D⁻)' + { Cxy --> X Y, Cxy - Z } - { T - U X Y V } + { T - U Cxy V }
                where T, U and V are sets of classes and/or methods
        Give a name to the methods which express the relationship between Cxy and X
        or Y if X or Y are classes
    Else
        If one of these dependencies belongs to D^+ **Then**
            Perform rule 3.2 with this dependency and X Y - Z
        Else
            Choose one of the two dependencies
            Perform rule 3.2 with this dependency and X Y - Z
        Endif
    Endif
Endfor

Rule 3.2
Let X be a class and Y, Z two sets of classes and/or methods. If dependencies X -->> Y and X Y - Z exist, then Y Z is a nested class. Then, the designer indicates the name of the method associated to Y Z. (D⁻)' is computed in the following way :

For each dependency d : X -->> Y and d' : X Y - Z **Do**
    If d is 1-order **Then**
        Replace d and d' with d'' : X -->> Y, -Z (ma)
    Else
        Replace d' with d'' : X Y - Z (ma)
    Endif
Endfor
where ma is the name of the method associated to the nested class Y Z

The new nested class is noted Y, -Z. The dependency between X and the nested class is always multivalued. Y is always monovalued whereas Z can be monovalued (noted -> ; d' is a FD) or multivalued (noted ->> ; d' is a MD).

Stage 2 : The designer considers now dependencies d : X - Y Z where X, Y and Z are sets of classes and/or methods. He applies the rule 4 to them .

Rule 4 : Dependencies X - Y Z
Dependencies X - Y Z indicate the being of a nested class Y Z in X. The designer indicates the name of the method associated to Y Z. (D⁻)' is computed in the following way :

For each dependency d : X - Y Z **Do**
    Replace d with d' : X - Y Z (ma)
Endfor
where ma is the name of the method associated to the nested class Y Z

The designer intervenes in an interactive way during the design step to state the name of the identified methods (Fig. 8).

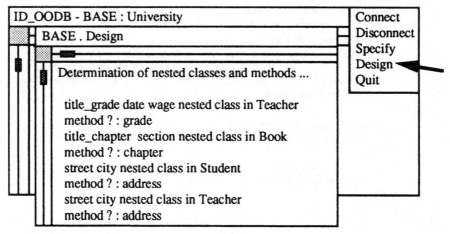

Fig. 8. Determination of nested classes and methods

The new set of dependencies (D⁻)' obtained is described in Fig. 9.

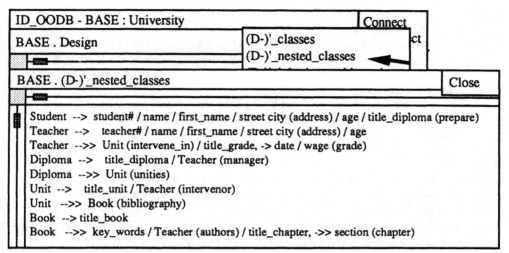

Fig. 9. (D-)' after identification of nested classes and methods

5.2.3 Organization of classes in an inheritance hierarchy

The designer now tries to organize classes in an inheritance hierarchy. To do this, he successively applies rules 5.1 and 5.2 which lead him to formulate again (D⁻)' introducing inheritance dependencies (ID) between classes. ID are defined as follows :

ID : There is an ID between X and Y, noted X ==> Y, if X is a sub-class of Y.

Rule 5 : Inheritance hierarchy between classes

Rule 5.1
Let be two classes X and Y and U,V,W three sets of classes and/or methods such as :

X --> A / U and X - V   or   X -->> A / U and X - V
Y --> B / U and Y - W   Y -->> B / U and Y - W

with A and B which are methods issued from left-hand dependencies of (D⁻)' (applying rule 1 & 2) such as A ≠ B, and with U ≠ ∅, U ∩ V = ∅, U ∩ W = ∅, V ∩ W = ∅.

The designer applies the following algorithms :

Algo 1 :
    If V = ∅ et W ≠ ∅ **Then**
        Y is a sub-class of X and B a redefinition of A
        (D⁻)' = (D⁻)' - {Y - B/U, Y - W} + {Y ==> X, Y - B, Y - W}
    Else   **If** V ≠ ∅ et W = ∅ **Then**
                X is a sub-class of Y and A a redefinition of B
                (D⁻)' = (D⁻)' - {X - A/U, X - V} + {X ==> Y, X - A, X - V}
            Else
                apply algo 2
           Endif
    Endif

Algo 2 :

   If $V \neq \emptyset$ et $W \neq \emptyset$ **Then**

        Create Z super-class of X and Y ; Z gathers the common properties of X and Y

        $(D^-)' = (D^-)' - \{X - A/U, X - V, Y - B/U, Y - W\} + \{X \Longrightarrow Z, Y \Longrightarrow Z, Z - U, X - A,$
                                                                    $X - V, Y - B, Y - W\}$

   Else $\{V = \emptyset$ et $W = \emptyset\}$

        Create Z super-class of X and Y ; Z gathers the common properties of X and Y

        $(D^-)' = (D^-)' - \{X - A/U, Y - B/U\} + \{X \Longrightarrow Z, Y \Longrightarrow Z, Z - U, X - A, Y - B\}$

   Endif

Rule 5.2

Let be two classes X and Y and U,V,W three sets of classes and/or methods such as :

$X \longrightarrow A / U$ and $X - V$ **or** $X \longrightarrow\!\!\!> A / U$ and $X - V$

$Y \longrightarrow B / U$ and $Y - W$ $Y \longrightarrow\!\!\!> B / U$ and $Y - W$

with A and B which are methods issued from left-hand dependencies of $(D^-)'$ (applying rule 1 & 2) such as $A \neq B$, and with $U \neq \emptyset$, $U \cap V = \emptyset$, $U \cap W = \emptyset$, $V \cap W = \emptyset$.

The designer must distinguish, for coherence reasons, U associated to X from U associated to Y changing the name of any of U.

The designer intervenes in an interactive way during the design step to state the name of the identified super-classes (Fig. 10).

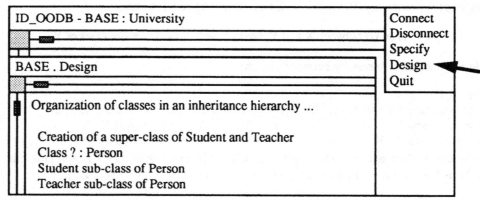

Fig. 10. Organisation of classes in an inheritance hierarchy

$(D^-)'$ is, after this stage, described in Fig. 11.

We can note that $(D^-)'$ is always a minimal cover. Indeed, when the designer adds an ID dependency, he simplifies existing dependencies concerned with inheritance gathering some of their methods into a more hierarchical class level. Moreover, when he adds the dependency $Z - U$, Z is a new class which does not belong to $((D^-)' - \{Z - U\})^+$.

We can also note that each method is now associated to only one class. For example, name is only a method of Person.

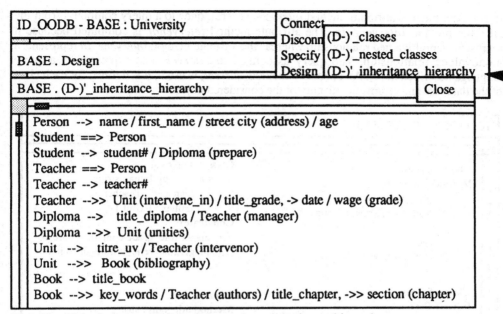

ID_OODB - BASE : University		Connect

BASE . Design

BASE . (D-)'_inheritance_hierarchy

Discon (D-)'_classes
Specify (D-)'_nested_classes
Design (D-)' inheritance hierarchy

Close

Person --> name / first_name / street city (address) / age
Student ==> Person
Student --> student# / Diploma (prepare)
Teacher ==> Person
Teacher --> teacher#
Teacher -->> Unit (intervene_in) / title_grade, -> date / wage (grade)
Diploma --> title_diploma / Teacher (manager)
Diploma -->> Unit (unities)
Unit --> titre_uv / Teacher (intervenor)
Unit -->> Book (bibliography)
Book --> title_book
Book -->> key_words / Teacher (authors) / title_chapter, ->> section (chapter)

Fig. 11. (D-) after organisation of classes in an inheritance hierarchy

5.2.4 Determination of the object-oriented schema

The object-oriented schema is deduced from (D⁻)'. It corresponds to a description of (D⁻)' in words of classes, methods and inheritance. It also describes the various constraints recorded during the specification step. The object-oriented schema is presented in Fig 12.

The designer indicates which the attribute-methods are and which the operatory-methods are. Attribute-methods can be defined on predefined classes or on classes defined in the database. Structural classes Set or List can be used ; then, the attribute-method is multivalued and it expresses a MD of (D⁻)'. Else, the attribute-method is monovalued ; it expresses a FD of (D⁻)'. In the example, methods *title_diploma* and *responsible* are monovalued whereas method *unities* is multivalued.
Attribute-methods can also be defined using the Tuple constructor and other classes. Then, domains of those attribute-methods are nested classes of the database. In the example, attribute-methods *address*, *grade* and *chapter* correspond to nested classes of the database.
Operatory-methods are characterised by their signature and by a set of conditions which must be true before and after the execution of the method. Their body are specified by the programmer when he implements them.

Valorization and comparison constraints are explicitly defined in classes as assertions associated to methods. Reciprocity constraints are described by attribute-methods. Meanwhile, those attribute-methods are not both stored ; the first one is stored, the other one is computed by a query from the first one. The designer stores the one whom cardinality is minimum. The idea to compute attribute-methods is also found in POSTGRES [28] ; it avoids useless redundancy in the database and inconsistency in relationships of the database.

In the example, the attribute-method *intervenor* corresponds to a query computed from the attribute-method *intervene_in*. The attribute-method *intervenor* is computed because it represents a multivalued relationship whereas the attribute method *intervene_in* represents a monovalued relationship. The query associated to *intervenor* is expressed in a query language described in [1]. An operatory-method, *current*, is used ; it is defined for each class of the database and returns the identity of the considered object.

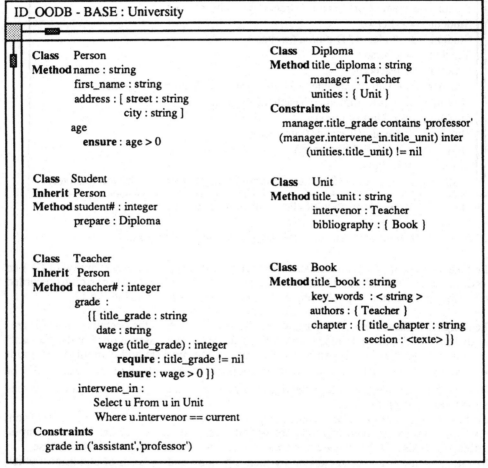

Fig. 12. Object-Oriented schema for the University database

6 Conclusion

We have proposed a design methodology for object-oriented databases and presented it through the interface which implements it.

The designer formally specifies the problem to model by a set of functional and multivalued dependencies between elementary properties. Our method helps him to progressively go from these formal specifications to the corresponding object-oriented schema. We can note that the determination of functional and multivalued dependencies requires some expert appeasements in the database field and a complete knowledge of the problem to model ; this sight is not considered in this paper.

Our method takes up a new approach which can be found in some studies of literature [11,16]. It is based on an object-oriented model. It takes its inspiration from the design methodology of relational databases [6,17] and from the algorithms of decomposition in normal form for nested relations [24].

Our method is composed of two steps. In the first step, the designer expresses functional and multivalued dependencies to describe formally the problem to model. This set D of FD and MD is then reduced by computing a minimal cover D^-. Finally, the designer expresses constraints which are associated to properties appearing in those dependencies. In the second step, D^- is derived into a set $(D^-)'$ of dependencies between classes, nested classes and methods. Classes are then organized in an inheritance hierarchy and the object-oriented schema is deduced.

The interface automatizes the two steps of the method. It is a tool which helps the user to design object-oriented databases schemas ; it implements the method.

The interface is being developed at the Toulouse Research Institute of Informatics (I.R.I.T.). It is implemented with the object-oriented DBMS O2 [23]. A class, named Design, gathers all the methods allowing the design of an object-oriented database. Those methods are known outside the class and are performed by the interface.

References

1. E. Andonoff, M. Canillac : Requêtes et transmission de messages dans une base de données orientée objet. Proceedings of the Inforsid Conference, Paris, May 1991

2. T. Andrew, C. Harris, J. Duhl : The ONTOS Object-Oriented Database. Ontologic Incorporation, February 1990

3. M. Atkinson, F. Bancilhon, D. DeWitt, K. Dittrich, D. Maier, S. Zdonik : The Object- Oriented Database System Manifesto. Proceedings of the 1st DOOD International Conference, Kyoto, December 1989

4. J. Banerjee,H.T. Chou, J. Garza, H.J. Kim, W. Kim, D. Woelk, N. Ballou : Data Model Issues for Object-Oriented Applications. Proceedings of the ACM TOIS, Vol 5, n°1, 1987

5. J. Banerjee, W. Kim, K.C. Kim: Queries in Object-Oriented Databases. Proceedings of the 4th International Conference on Data Engineering, Los Angeles, 1988

6. C. Beeri, R. Fagin, T.H. Howard : A complete axiomatization for functional and multivaled dependencies in relational databases. Proceedings of ACM SIGMOD, Toronto, August 1977

7. P.A. Berstein : Synthetizing Third Normal Form Relations from Functional Dependencies. Proceedings of the ACM TODS, Vol 2, n°3, 1976

8. M. Bouzeghoub, E. Métais : Transformation d'un modèle sémantique en un modèle objet. Proceedings of the 5th Advanced Databases Conference, Genève, September 1989

9. H. Briand, D. Ravelet : Transformation d'un schéma Entité-Association en base de données orientée objet. Proceedings of the EC2 Conference,Toulouse, December 1990

10. C. Cauvet, C. Rolland : O* : un modèle pour la conception de bases de données orientées objet. Proceedings of the Inforsid Conference, Nancy, May 1989

11. C. Cauvet, C. Proix : La conception de bases de données orientées objet : modèle et méthode, Proceedings of the 5th Advanced Databases Conference, Genève, September 1989

12. E.F. Codd : A Relational Model of Data for Large Shared Data Banks. Proceedings of the ACM TODS - Vol 13 - n° 6 - 1970

13. G. Copeland, D. Maier : Making Smalltalk a Database System. Proceedings of the ACM SIGMOD, June 1984

14. B. Cox, Objective-C : Object-Oriented Programming, an evolutionary approach". Addison-Wesley Publishing Compagny, 1986

15. C. Delobel, M. Adiba : Bases de données et systèmes relationnels. Eyrolles Publishing Compagny, 1982

16. F. Mac Fadden : Conceptual design of object-oriented databases. Proceedings of the JOOP, September 1991

17. R. Fagin, Multivalued Dependencies and a New Normal Form for Relational Databases. Proceedings of the ACM TODS, Vol 2, n° 3, 1977

18. A. Flory, C. Rolland : La conception de systèmes d'information : état de l'art et nouvelles perpectives. Proceedings of the Inforsid Conference, Eyrolles Publishing Compagny, Biarritz, May 1990

19. G. Gardarin, P. Valduriez : SGBD Avancées : bases de données objets, déductives et réparties, Eyrolles Publishing Compagny, 1990

20. A. Goldberg, R. Robson : Smalltalk-80 : the language and its implementation. Addison-Wesley Publishing Compagny, 1983

21. R. Hull, R. King : Semantic Database Modeling : Survey, Applications, and Research Issues. Proceedings of the ACM Computing Surveys, Vol 13, n° 3,1987

22. S. Khoshafian, G. Copeland : Object-Identify. Proceedings of the 1st OOPSLA International Conference, Portland, September 1986

23. C. Lécluse, P. Richard, F. Velez : O2, an Object-Oriented Data Model. Proceedings of the ACM SIGMOD, Chicago, May 1988

24. Z. M. Ozoyoglu, L.Y. Yuan : A New Normal Form for Nested Relations. Proceedings of the ACM TODS, Vol. 12, n°1, March 1987

25. P. Pistor, F. Andersen : Designing a generalized NF2 model with an SQL-type language interface. Proceedings of the International Conference on VLDB, Kyoto, August 1986

26. C. Rolland, O. Foucaut, G. Benci : Conception de systèmes d'information : la méthode REMORA. Eyrolles Publishing Compagny, 1988

27. C. Rolland, C. Cauvet : Modélisation Conceptuelle Orientée Objet. Proceedings of the 7th Advanced Databases Conference, Lyon, September 1991

28. L. Rowe, M. Stonebraker : The Postgress Data model. Proceedings of the 13th International Conference on VLDB, Brigton, 1987

Conceptual Graphs as a Framework for Deductive Object-Oriented Databases

Bikash C. Ghosh and Vilas Wuwongse

Division of Computer Science, Asian Institute of Technology
G.P.O. Box 2754, Bangkok 10501, Thailand
Fax: (66-2) 5245721, e-mail: vw@ait.th

Abstract. The idea of deductive object-oriented databases (DOODBs) is to combine the concepts of deductive databases (DDBs) and object-oriented databases (OODBs) into a single database system in order to gain the advantages offered by each of them. This kind of databases is suitable for knowledge bases and many advanced database applications. The formalism of conceptual graphs (CGs), a knowledge representation scheme in AI, is equipped with some useful constructs that are suitable for the requirements of DOODBs. A groundwork for DOODBs based on conceptual graphs has been carried out in this research. The DOODBs are characterized by data abstraction through objects, object identifiers, object types, type hierarchy, property inheritance, methods and message passing and a logical formalism with a sound inference system. Some restrictions and extensions are proposed for the general conceptual graphs so that they can be used to represent the DOODB concepts. These extended conceptual graphs are called deductive object-oriented conceptual graphs (DOOCGs). The object types, individual objects and object identifiers of DOODBs map into concept types, individual CGs and individual referents, respectively. Methods are defined using conceptual schema graphs with bound actors and interpreted in a success/failure paradigm. A set of extended derived rules of inference has been formulated for DOOCGs which are proved to be sound.

1 Introduction

Most of the currently popular "record-oriented" database systems have limited representational abilities that are considered particularly essential for some advanced application areas like CAD/CAM databases, VLSI design databases, office automation, engineering design and CASE databases [16], and knowledge bases. A detailed description of the major limitations of record-oriented data models can be found in [10]. The two of the major areas of extensions over the conventional databases are: i) capturing more semantics in the represention of data [3], and ii) storing intensional rules and performing reasoning over the database states [11]. The first extension leads to the research on *object-oriented database* (OODBs) systems [16], while the second one is handled by the *deductive databases* (DDBs) [12, 16].

Deductive databases integrate ideas from logic programming and relational databases [11] while object-oriented databases emerge from the integration of database concepts with object-oriented programming paradigm. Since each of the DDBs and ODDBs offers some advantages over conventional databases, there have been efforts to merge the two approaches to obtain the advantages of both the systems, and these efforts represent a challenge [1]. The notion of *deductive object-oriented database* (DOODBs) comes from some of these efforts. DOODBs can also serve as a starting point for a future *knowledge based management system* (KBMS) that integrates the ideas of artificial intelligence and databases [2].

The formalism of *conceptual graphs* (CGs), introduced by SOWA [13], offers some useful constructs which make it a likely platform for an integration of ideas from DDBs and OODBs. It is a powerful knowledge representation language in AI with a well-defined theoretical basis and a close mapping to both natural language and first-order logic [9, 13, 15]. The objective of this work is to develop a notion of a deductive object-oriented database system based on the formalism of CGs. Some restrictions and extensions to CG formalism are introduced and a theoretical basis for a DOODB system based on the extended CG formalism is developed.

2 Deductive Object-Oriented Database Systems

Two general approaches towards research in DOODBs have been mentioned in [17], namely DOODBs as an extension of DDBs and DOODBs as an extension of ODDBs. We propose a third approach which is to integrate the concepts of DDBs and OODBs and map them into a third framework. In this work, the formalism of CGs is used to represent the features of DOODB systems whose characteristics are outlined as follows.

(a)   *Objects and object properties*: A DOODB should allow all conceptual entities to be uniformly modeled as objects. Objects should be the unit of access and control. An object has properties which could be static or dynamic. Static properties represent states (or structures) of the object. Dynamic properties (called behaviors) are represented by a set of methods. A DOODB system should provide mechanisms for generating and maintaining unique object identifiers for individual objects.

(b)   *Types (or classes), type hierarchy and property inheritance*: Objects are instances of types. A type describes the structure and behavior of all of its instances. Types should form a type hierarchy based on the subtype/supertype relationships. Objects of one type inherit properties from the type and its supertypes. A DOODB system should have mechanisms for:

(i)   resolving the problem of multiple inheritance, and
(ii)   handling exceptions to property inheritance.

In general, the definition of an object type in a DOODB should include:

·   ·Specification of the structure of the objects that are instances of this type,
·   Specification of the position of the type in the type hierarchy,
·   Specification of the set of methods that are applicable to the instances or states of the instances of that type.

(c)   A DOODB system should have a logical formalism to represent objects, methods, intensional rules or (deductive) laws, integrity constraints and queries, with a well-defined semantics of all of these components as well as answers to queries. The logical system should have a sound (deductive) inference mechanism.

(d)   Some of the other desirable properties are : declarative expressions for databases, queries and answers to queries, and single language for expressing databases, queries and integrity constraints.

3 Conceptual Graphs

The primitives of the conceptual graph (CG) theory are : *concept instances* or *referents* and *conceptual relations*. A *conceptual graph* is formally defined [13] as a finite, connected, bipartite graph where the two kinds of nodes are concepts and conceptual relations. Every conceptual relation has one or more arcs, each of which must be linked to some concept. A single concept by itself may form a conceptual graph, but every conceptual relation must be linked to some concept. There are two forms of *display* for conceptual graphs: *graphical form* (Fig. 3.1(a)) and *linear form* (Fig. 3.1(b)).

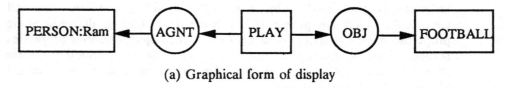

(a) Graphical form of display

[PERSON:Ram]<--(AGNT)<--[PLAY]-->(OBJ)-->[FOOTBALL]
(b) Linear form of display

Fig. 3.1 Two forms of display for a conceptual graph that may be read as "The person Ram plays football"

The set of type labels T forms a lattice, called type *type lattice* based on the partial order relation $\leq_T$. The top ($\top$) element is called UNIV and the bottom ($\bot$) element is called ABSURD. There is a predefined set I = {#1,#2,#3,...} whose elements are called *individual markers*. The function *referent* maps a concept c into I∪{*}, where * is called the generic marker. Every conceptual graph makes an assertion. An operator ϕ has been defined that maps conceptual graphs into formulas of first-order predicate calculus. For example, the graph in Fig. 3.1 makes the following assertion,

$\exists x, \exists y$ (PERSON(Ram)∧AGNT(x,Ram)∧PLAY(x)∧OBJ(x,y)∧FOOTBALL(y))

A *canonical graph* is a CG that specifies the constraints on the pattern of concepts and

A *canonical graph* is a CG that specifies the constraints on the pattern of concepts and relations that may be linked to a concept and relation type. There are some primitive concept types and conceptual relation types which have no explicit definitions. New concept types and relation types are defined using lambda abstractions adapted to CGs. There are four *canonical formation rules* for deriving new CGs from existing CGs: *copy, restrict, join* and *simplify*. A *maximal join* operation [13] is defined on CGs and can be considered as a generalization of unification under suitable mapping [9]. If a CG u is *canonically derivable* from another CG v, then u is called a *specialization* of v and v is called a *generalization* of u. Generalization defines a partial ordering ($\leq_G$) of conceptual graphs called the generalization hierarchy. For any conceptual graphs u and v, if u$\leq_G$v, then $\emptyset u \supset \emptyset v$ and there exists a mapping π:v→u, where πv, a subgraph of u is called *projection of v in u*.

Procedural information can be attached to CGs using *actors*. An actor is described as a process that responds to messages by performing some services and then generating messages that it passes to other actors. Actors are attached to CGs by input and output concepts linked to it. A *dataflow* graph consists of actors and concept nodes. It is defined as a finite, connected, bipartite graph with one set of nodes called actors and another set of nodes called concepts.

SOWA [13] developed a set of *first-order rules of inference* for CGs represented in terms of nested negative contexts and coreference links. A context is a special type of concept node with a type label called PROPOSITION and a set of CGs as referent. A negative context is a context with a monadic relation (NEG) attached to it. The coreference link is used to connect identical concepts and it is shown using a dotted line in the graphic form and using the same concept variables in the linear form. A game-theoretic semantics of CGs is given in [13] and the first-order rules are proved to be sound and complete. A set of derived rules of inference are also defined which are essentially sound and complete. Details about general CG formalism can be found in [13].

4 Deductive Object-Oriented Databases Using Conceptual Graphs

The features of DOODBs are to be represented by the *deductive object-oriented conceptual graphs* (DOOCGs) [7]. The major features of DOOCGs are explained in this section. More details about DOOCGs can be found in [7].

4.1 Primitives of Deductive Object-Oriented Conceptual Graphs

Object types in DOODBs are represented by concept types in CGs, *individual objects* of a type are represented by individual CGs of the corresponding concept type. For example, an object type STUDENT can be defined as a subtype of PERSON as shown in Fig. 4.1, where all other concept types and conceptual relations are assumed to be defined already. An individual object of type STUDENT is shown in Fig. 4.2. The object type hierarchy is represented by the concept type hierarchy that is a complete lattice based on the subsumption relation $\leq_T$. The type definition specifies the position of the newly defined type in the hierarchy. Individual referents for the concepts that are parameters of the type definitions are used as *object identifiers*. For example, the individual referent #112 in Fig. 4.2 is an object identifier. Note that the individual referents include the individual markers as well as other externally communicable objects like strings and numbers.

```
STUDENT = (λ x)
        [PERSON:*x] -
                (CHRC)-->[ID]
                (OBJ)<--[ENROLLMENT] -
                        (PTIM)-->[DATE]
                        (CHRC)-->[DEG]
                        (LOC)-->[DIVISION],
                (ADVISOR)-->[FACULTY].
```

Fig. 4.1 Definition of STUDENT type as a subtype of PERSON

```
STUDENT(#112) =
        [PERSON:#112] -
                (CHRC)-->[ID:3421]
                (OBJ)<--[ENROLLMENT:#321] -
                        (PTIM)-->[DATE:01/01/1990]
                        (CHRC)-->[DEGREE:"M Engg."]
                        (LOC)-->[DIVISION:"CS"],
                (ADVISOR)-->[FACULTY:#311].
```

Fig. 4.2 An individual object of type STUDENT

Formulation of *methods* and *message passing* is one of the important problems in merging OODB and DDB concepts. For our representation, the major requirements are as follows:

- a mechanism for defining methods and associating the method definitions for a type with the corresponding type definition,
- a format for method calling or message passing,
- a backtrackable method evaluation mechanism (so that all possible values are returned) with a success/failure interpretation [6] of method evaluation,
- a mechanism that allows individual objects of one type to share the methods defined for its supertypes.

A method is defined using a *conceptual schema graph* [13] with bound actors. A method call or message is represented by a *message graph*, that is a simple CG with an appropriate actor bound to it. An example method definition for the age of a person is shown in Fig. 4.3, where <TODAY> and <DIFF_DT> are two actors. The actor <TODAY> is a system defined actor that asserts the current date in the referent field of its output concept. The actor <DIFF_DT> is a primitive actor (or can be defined by a functional dataflow graph) that asserts the difference of two of its input dates into the referent field of its output concept. An example message graph is shown in Fig. 4.4, where the type label in the actor box before the name of the actor specifies the receiving object type. The graph in Fig. 4.5 is the same as that in Fig. 4.4 except that the output concept of the actor <PERSON:DIFF_DT> contain a request mark ("?") which signifies the triggering of the execution of the corresponding method. In general, if m is a message graph then ?m is used to denote the corresponding method call. Note that the projection of a message graph is defined as the projection of the CG obtained from the message graph by erasing the actor bound to it.

A new CG operation is necessary in formulating the rules for method execution. The main purpose of this operation is to find out the *maximal common overlap (modulo restrictions)* between two CGs.

Definition 4.1 Let two CGs u_1 and u_2 have a common generalization v with *maximally extended compatible projections* [13] $\pi_1:v \to u_1$ and $\pi_2:v \to u_2$. A join of the two graphs $\pi_1 v$ and $\pi_2 v$ on these maximally extended compatible projections is called a *constrained join*.

Example 4.1 Suppose we have two CGs u_1 and u_2 as shown in Fig. 4.6. The graph v is a common generalization of the two graphs u_1 and u_2 with two maximally extended compatible projections π_1 and π_2, where π_1 = {([PERSON],[STUDENT]),(AGNT,AGNT),([PLAY])} and π_2 = {([PERSON],[PERSON:Sam]),(AGNT,AGNT),([PLAY],[PLAY])}. The graph $\pi_1 v$ is a subgraph of u_1 and $\pi_2 v$ is a subgraph of u_2. A join of $\pi_1 v$ and $\pi_2 v$ (on the projections π_1 and π_2) yields the graph w. The operation is called the *constrained join* and the graph w is the graph obtained by constrained join of u_1 and u_2.

Rules for method execution

Let S be a set of CGs and m be a message graph which contains an actor e. the message is "passed" to the type t, i.e., the method call ?m is issued. Steps taken in executing the method with respect to S are as follows:

1)   Search for a definition of method corresponding to the message starts at the schematic cluster [13] of type t. If a schema is not found for the type t, then the search proceeds upwards along the hierarchy according to the rules of method inheritance. The search stops with one of the following conditions:

-        An appropriate method definition is found and a schema graph is selected. Suppose that the schema graph u is selected. The method evaluation proceeds.
-        The topmost concept in the hierarchy has been reached but no

SCHEMA for PERSON = (λ x)

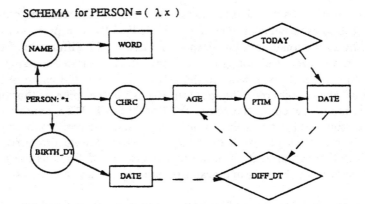

Figure 4.3: An example of method definition for the type PERSON

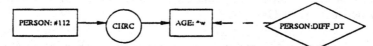

Figure 4.4: An example message graph

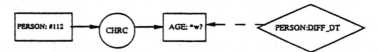

Figure 4.5: The message of Fig. 4.4 is being "passed"

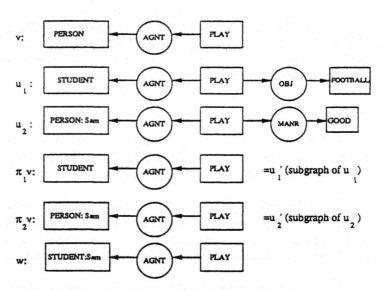

Figure 4.6: An example of constrained join - the graph w is obtained by constrained join of u_1 and u_2

appropriate method definition has been found. In this case, the method evaluation stops and the original method call fails.

2) The message graph ?m is joined with the selected schema graph u. Let u' be the resulting graph after joining m with u. After the join, the output concept in u' of the actor e will be marked with request ("?") marker. This will trigger a goal directed computation. For all input concept i, with referent (i) = *, mark (i) is set to "?" [13].

3) The next action will depend on the nature of the input concept nodes that are marked with "?" marker. According to the rules for method definition [7], each of the input concept of the actor e is either an output concept of another actor or a message to another type, or an "independent property" that is a part of the type defining graph.

- For each input concept that is an output concept of a message to another type, the message is passed to the corresponding type. If the evaluation of any of such message fails, then the actor e is blocked [13] and the original method call (?m) fails.
- For each input concept that is an output concept of another actor, the "?" maker is propagated in the backward direction.

The system would search for an individual graph to evaluate those concepts that represent independent property and are marked with request marker. This search can be performed in the following way:

- Suppose the corresponding type has been defined with an abstraction of the form $\lambda x v$. The graph v is joined with u' using the constrained join. Let v' be the resulting graph. If v' does not contain all those concepts that are marked with "?" marker but are not output concepts of any actor or message, then the search stops and the original method call fails. Otherwise, the graph v' is to be projected on the set of individual CGs in S. Two possible cases are:

  (i) The graph v' has no projection on the set of individual CGs in S. The original message call fails.
  (ii) The graph v' has a projection π' on the set of individual CGs in S.

- If the previous step succeeds, then the graph $\pi'v'$ is joined (using maximal join) with u' yielding w for each projection π' of v' on the individual graphs in S. As a result of this, individual referents would be asserted into some or all the concept nodes that were marked with "?" marker.

4) If all previous steps succeed, then the actor e in w must be enabled and fired.

This firing would assert a referent in the output concept of the actor. Let w' be the final working graph after the actor has fired. The original method call succeeds with the answer <true,π> where π:m→w'. In general, there may be more than one return value depending on the number of distinct projections of v' on the set of individual graphs in S. Suppose m' is the CG obtained from m by erasing actor(s) bound to it. Then πm' is also true, i.e., the assertion made by the message graph m is true.

Success and failure of a method call

The value of the method execution ?m will be <false,{}> only if the method evaluation fails. The method evaluation fails if any of the following is true:

- The search for an appropriate schema fails in the first step, i.e., their no method definition corresponding to the message.
- The firing of the actor is blocked in step 4 for any reason whatsoever.

If the method does not fail, then it succeeds with the answer <true,π> where π:m→w', where w' is the final working graph. Suppose m' is the conceptual graph obtained from m by erasing actor bound to it. Then πm' also makes a true assertion.

Property inheritance

In CG notations, a branch of the type defining graph consisting of a conceptual relation and a concept type label corresponds to an attribute in the DOODB concepts and an individual referent in the concept node of that branch is the value of that attribute. The inheritance of properties and the exception rules are "naturally" handled by the *type expansion* [13] operation of CGs that use the maximal join and replaces a single concept node with the graph that defines that concept type. Methods defined for a particular type are also inherited by its subtypes. The search for a method definition starts at the type that is specified in the actor box with the actor name. If a method is called with the type label t, then the search starts at the schematic cluster of type t. If the method definition is not found, then it is searched in the set of method definitions for each of its direct supertypes. The search proceeds upward along the chains of the hierarchy until an appropriate method definition is not found, then it is searched in the set of method definitions for each of its direct supertypes. The search proceeds upward along the chains of the hierarchy until an appropriate method is found or the topmost type UNIV is reached. The first method encountered in the search is the one that is executed.

4.2 Conceptual Basis

The meanings of conceptual graphs in CG formalism are implicitly related to some basic CG constructs. These are collectively referred to as a conceptual basis, which is defined as follows.

Definition 4.2 A conceptual basis is defined as

$CB = <(R,\leq_R), (T,\leq_T), D, SC, P, A >$, where

CB	:	Conceptual basis,
R	:	A set of conceptual relation labels,
$\leq_R$	:	Subsumption relation between conceptual relation labels,
$(R,\leq_R)$	:	Conceptual relation hierarchy,
T	:	A set of concept type labels,
$\leq_T$	:	Subsumption relation between concept type labels,
$(T,\leq_T)$	:	Concept type hierarchy - the type lattice,
D	:	A set of concept type definitions for types in T,
SC	:	A set of conceptual schema graphs for types in T,
P	:	A set of prototype graphs for types in T,
A	:	A set of actor definitions.

4.3 Deductive Object-Oriented Conceptual Graphs (DOOCGs)

Before defining DOOCGs, we define atomic conceptual graphs and compound graphs as follows.

Definition 4.3 An atomic conceptual graph (ACG) [4] is a conceptual graph that contains no logical connective and no quantifier other than the implicit existential quantifiers. An atomic conceptual graph containing only individual referents in all the concept nodes is termed as a ground atomic conceptual graph.

Definition 4.4 An conceptual graph is called a compound graph if any or all of the following conditions hold: (a) to contain contexts of depth [13] higher than 0, (b) it contains ACGs connected by coreference links.

Example 4.2 An example of atomic conceptual graphs and ground atomic conceptual graphs is shown in Fig. 4.7(a) and Fig. 4.7(b) respectively. A compound conceptual graph represented by nested negative contexts is shown in Fig. 4.7(c).

Now we define DOOCGs.

Definition 4.5 The deductive object-oriented conceptual graphs (DOOCGs) include the following graphs:

(a)   Atomic conceptual graphs.
(b)   Message graphs.
(c)   Compound graphs; represented in nested negative contexts with the following constraints:
-      The graphs consist of only two levels of nesting.
-      The context at depth 1 contains one or more atomic conceptual graphs and/or message graphs in addition to one negative context.
-      The context at depth 2 contains exactly one atomic conceptual graph.

[PERSON]<--(AGNT)<--[SIT]-->(LOC)-->[PLACE]
(a) An atomic conceptual graph

[PERSON:Sam]<--(AGNT)<--[SIT:#543]-->(LOC)-->[PLACE:Cafeteria]
(b) A ground atomic conceptual graph -
all concept nodes contain individual referents

¬
    [STUDENT]<--(AGENT)<--[ENROLLMENT]-->(DIV)-->[DIVISION:CS]

        ¬ [PERSON]<--(AGNT)<--[PLAY]-->(BENF)-->[DIVISION:CS]

(c) A compound graph that says "If a person is a student of CS division
then he/she can play for CS division"

Fig. 4.7 Three conceptual graph examples

There may be coreference links among concepts of the conceptual
graphs at various contexts.

These graphs have the general form: ¬[v_1 ... v_n ¬[w]] where, v_i (i=1,...,n) is an atomic
conceptual graph or message graph, w is an atomic conceptual graph. If n=0, the
above graph becomes ¬[¬[w]] or simply w that represents a single atomic conceptual
graph w in the outermost context.

4.4 Deductive Object-oriented Conceptual Graph Language (DOCL)

Definition 4.6 A *deductive object-oriented conceptual graph language* (DOCL) consists
of the following:

(a)   a *concept universe* consisting of,
   i)   a conceptual basis CB,
   ii)   a non-empty set of individual referents I_r that consists of the
            individual markers {#1,2,#3,...} as well as other externally
            communicable objects like strings, numbers and times,
   iii)   the conformity relation :: that relates types in T to individual markers
            in I_r, the function ltype that relates concepts and conceptual relations
            to type labels in T and R respectively and the function referent that
            relates concepts to the elements of $I_r \cup \{*\}$, where * denote the
            generic marker,
   iv)   the set of canonical formation rules together with the maximal join
            operation and the constrained join operation,

v)   the rules for actors and dataflow graph definitions [7, 13],

vi)   the rules for method definition, method call and method execution [7],

vii)   a canonical basis B which is a finite set of conceptual graphs with all types in T and all referents either * or individuals in I_r, and

(b)   a set of conceptual graphs formed from the concept universe.

Now we define some terms related to a DOCL.

Definition 4.7 A *conceptual program* CP is a finite set of deductive object-oriented conceptual graphs.

Definition 4.8 The *degree* of DOOCGs is a mapping from a set of DOOCGs into the set of integers. For a DOOCG C, the degree of C, denoted by DEG(C) is the number of conceptual graphs in the context at depth 1. For a DOOCG of the general form $C = \neg[v_1\ v_2\ ...\ v_n\ \neg[u]]$, DEC(C) = n. For an atomic CG or message graph u in the outermost context, DEC(u) = 0.

Definition 4.9 A *query graph* is either an atomic conceptual graph or a message graph.

Definition 4.10 A *query* consists of a single query graph or a number of query graphs in conjunction.

Thee may be coreference links among concepts of the query graphs in a query. For example $Q = q_1...q_n$ is a query where each of q_i is either an ACG or a message graph.

Definition 4.11 A *goal graph* is either an atomic conceptual graph or a message graph.

Definition 4.12 A *goal* consists of a set of goal graphs in conjunction. There may be coreference links among concepts of the goal graphs in a goal.

Definition 4.13 The goal G corresponding to a query $Q = q_1...q_n$ is represented as $\{q_1,...,q_n\}$, which is the assertion made by the query graph $q_1,...,q_n$ in conjunction (together with the coreference links of Q).

Definition 4.14 Let u and v be two conceptual graphs. The graph u is a referent-specialization of v if u is a specialization of v with the following property: u is the same as v except that zero or more generic concepts in v are specialized to individual concepts in u. Let π be a projection of v. The referent-specialization operator (rso) ρ for the projection π consists of a set of pairs of the form (c,c"), which is obtained from π in the following way:

a)   initially ρ is set equal to { },

b)   for each pair (c,c') such that $\pi c = c'$ where referent(c) = * and referent(c') ≠ *, a pair (c,c") is added to ρ, where type(c") = type(c) and referent(c") =

referent(c').

Note that, ρ = {} represents the identity referent-specialization.

Theorem 4.1 [7] Let v be a conceptual graph, π be a projection of v and ρ be the referent-specialization operator for the projection π. Then, $\pi v \leq_G \rho v \leq_G v$.

Definition 4.15 Let CP be a conceptual program and G = $\{g_1,...,g_n\}$ be a goal. An answer for G from CP is G' = $\{g'_1,...,g'_n\}$, where each g'_i, called an answer graph for the goal graph g_i is a referent-specifialization of g_i. It is to be noted that if G contains only individual concepts then the only possible answer is obtained by the identity referent-specialization.

4.5 Extended Rules of Inference for DOOCGs

The propositional rules of inference or alpha rules, the first-order rules of inference or beta rules and a set of derived rules or delta rules are presented in [13]. Two fundamental properties of DOOCGs are stated in the form of rules (α0) and δ0). Let S be a set of DOOCGs.

(α0)   Let u$\in$S and v be any atomic conceptual graph. If u is a specialization of v, (i.e., v is a generalization of u), then the assertion made by v is true if the assertion made by u is true. That means, if u$\leq_G$v, then $\phi u \supset \phi v$ where ϕ is the formula operator defined in [13].

(δ0)   Suppose m is message graph and the method call ?m succeeds with respect to S with a projection π. Let m' be the graph obtained by erasing the actors from the graph πm. The graph m' makes a true assertion in the outermost context.

Now a special case of the rule (α0) is stated here as (Δ0) as follows.

(Δ0)   Suppose, u and v are two atomic conceptual graphs, and the graph u makes a true assertion. Then the assertion made by v must be true if any of the following statements holds:

(1)   Subgraph: v is a subgraph of u.
(2)   Subtypes: u is identical to v except that one or more type labels of v are restricted to subtypes of the corresponding concept types in u.
(3)   Individuals: u is identical to v except that one or more generic concepts of v are restricted to individual concepts of the same type in u.

The extended derived rules of inference are formulated as follows.

Theorem 4.2 Let S be a set of DOOCGs and u and v be any conceptual graphs where $u \leq_G v$ with a projection $\pi : v \rightarrow u$. Let m be a message graph, and the method call ?m succeeds with respect to S with a projection π_m. Any graph derived from S by the following *extended derived rules of inference* is said to be provable from S.

($\Delta 1$)   In an oddly enclosed context, v may be replaced with πv where each coreference link to a concept c of v is transferred to the corresponding concept πc in πv. In an oddly enclosed context, m may be replaced with $\pi_m m$ and actors bound to $\pi_m m$ may be erased, where each coreference link to a concept c of m is transferred to the corresponding concept $\pi_m c$ in $\pi_m m$.

($\Delta 2$)   Let P be a graph $\neg[u \ \neg[v]]$. Then P itself is a theorem, and P with coreference links $<\pi c, c>$ for any c in v is also a theorem. The graph $\neg[\pi v \ \neg[v]]$, and $\neg[\pi v \ \neg[v]]$ with coreference links $<\pi c, c>$ for any c in v are also theorems.

($\Delta 3$)   In an evenly enclosed context, u may be replaced with v where each coreference link to a concept πc of u is transferred to the corresponding concept c of v and the other coreference links attached to u are erased.

($\Delta 4$)   Generalized modus ponents: If the outer context contains the graph u as well as a graph of the form $\neg[v \ \neg[w]]$, possibly with some coreference links from v to w, then the graph w may be derived with each coreference link attached to a concept c in v reattached to the corresponding concept πc in u. If the outer context contains the graph $\neg[m \ \neg[w]]$, possibly with some coreference links from m to w, then the graph w may be derived with each coreference link attached to a concept c in m reattached to the corresponding concept $\pi_m c$ in $\pi_m m$.

The following theorem holds [7].

Theorem 4.3 The extended derived rules of inference are sound.

As in linear logic, the notions of interpretations, models and logical consequence have been defined for DOOCGs [7]. Actors are interpreted as conceptual functions. Each conceptual function maps the referents of the input concepts of the corresponding actor into the set of referents of its output concept. The game theoretic semantics for general CGs with respect to a closed world [13] has been extended for the DOOCGs. A model-theoretic semantics and a fixpoint semantics of DOOCGs have been defined and they are proved to be equivalent for a conceptual program. A proof procedure, called direct derivation proof has been formulated for DOOCGs and it is proved to be sound and complete. Details about the semantics of DOOCGs and the proof procedure can be found in [7]. A notion of a DOOCG theory has been developed, and a DOODB is formally represented as a special DOOCG theory.

Definition 4.16 A DOOCG theory T_G consists of a DOCL L, a set of axioms and a set of inference rules,

- Logical axiom : { }, the empty set.
- Proper axioms : A set of DOOCGs.
- Set of inference rules : the set of first-order rules and the set of extended derived rule.
- Proof procedure : The direct derivation proof procedure [7].

Definition 4.17 A *deductive object-oriented database*, DOODB is a DOOCG theory whose proper axioms are:

- A conceptual program CP that consists of:
  - a set O of elementary facts or individual objects which are ground atomic conceptual graphs.
  - a set S that consists of deductive laws, which are compound DOOCGs and message graphs.
- A set of integrity constraints IC, which are DOOCGs.

5 Conclusions

A subset of general conceptual graphs has been extended to form deductive object-oriented conceptual graphs that includes simple graphs, message graphs and compound graphs with only two levels of nesting and exactly one simple graph in the context at depth 2.

The approach taken for this work towards representing DOODBs is fundamental in the sense that most of the other known approaches are either to extend DDBs to incorporate some of the constructs of OODBs or to extend OODBs with some of the features of DDBs [17]. Being a relatively new area of research, there is no generally accepted notion of DOODBs yet. A more concrete notion of DOODBs has been specified in this work in terms of characteristics of DOODBs. The use of conceptual graphs allows a large amount of "knowledge" to be statistically captured in the representation itself through the use of type definition, type hierarchy and property inheritance.

One of the major problems of integrating ideas of DDBs and OODBs is the representation and interpretation of methods [6]. The solution to this problem has been formulated with restrictive use of conceptual schema graphs, actors and dataflow graphs of conceptual graph formalism. This offers several advantages:

- Methods can be easily shared among different objects along a chain of type hierarchy without need for any additional cost, because conceptual schema graphs are associated to the type labels in the type hierarchy in the CG formalism by their definitions.

- The use of actors and dataflow graphs offers a natural means to merge the "procedural" notion of methods in OODBs with the declarative paradigm of DDBs, because actor and dataflow graphs in Cg formalism can be used declaratively when treated as a descriptions and procedurally when they are executed [13].

- The mechanism of method evaluation is formulated in a success/failure paradigm which is considered as one of the requirements for merging object-oriented concepts with deductive database concepts [6].

This work created a basis for a database system that would be useful for knowledge representation as well as many advanced database applications. However, much work has to be done over the basis founded by the results of this work to make it evolve into a complete operational database system.

References

1. S. Abiteboul, S. Grumbach: A Rule-Based Language with Functions and Sets, ACM Transactions on Database Systms, Vol. 16, No. 1, pp. 1-30, March 1991.
2. M.L. Brodie, J. Mylopoulos, eds,: On Knowledge Base Management Systems-Integrating Artificial Intelligence and Database Technologies, Springer-Verlag, 1986.
3. K.R. Dittrich: Object-Oriented Database Systems: The Notion and the Issues, Proceeding of International Workshop on Object-Oriented Database Systems, Dittrich, K.R. & Dayal, U. (eds.), IEEE Company Society Press, pp. 2-4, 1986.
4. G. Ellis: Compiled Hierarchical Retrieval, Proceeding of the Sixth Annual Workshop on Comceptual Structures, pp. 187-207, July 1991.
5. J. Fargues, Marie-Claude Landau, A. Dugourd, L. Catach: Conceptual Graphs for Semantic and Knowledge Processing, IBM Journal of Research and Development, Vol. 30, No. 1, pp. 70-79, January 1986.
6. H. Gallaire: Merging Objects and Logic Programming: Relational Semantics, Proceeding of Fifth National Conference on Artificial Intelligence, AAAI-85, Vol. 2, pp. 754-758, 1986.
7. B.C. Ghosh: Towards Deductive Object-Oriented Databases Based on Conceptual GRaphs, Masters Thesis, Division of Computer Science, Asian Institute of Technology, 1991.
8. T.R. Hines, J.C. Oh, M.L.A. Hines: Object-Oriented Conceptual Graphs, Proceeding of the Fifth Annual Workshop on Conceptual Structures, pp. 81-89, July 1990.
9. M. Jackman, C. Pavelin: Conceptual Graphs, Approaches to Knowledge Representation: An Introduction, Ringland, G.A. & Duce, d.A. (eds.), John-Wiley & Sons Inc., pp. 161-174, 1988.
10. W. Kent: Limitations of Record-Based Information Models, Readings in Artificial Intelligence and Databases, Mylopoulos, J. & Brodie, M.L., (eds.),

Morgan Kaufmann Publishers, Inc., pp. 85-97, 1989.

11. J.W. Lloyd: An Introduction to Deductive Database Systems, The Australian Computer Journal, Vol. 15, No. 2, pp. 52-57, May 1983.

12. J.W. Lloyd: Foundations of Logic Programming, Second Extended Edition, Springer-Verlag, 1987.

13. J.F. Sowa: Conceptual Structures: Information Processing in Mind and Machine, Addison-Wesley Publishing Company, Inc., 1984.

14. J.F. Sowa, E. Way: Implementing a Semantic Interpreter using Conceptual Graphs, IBM Journal of Research and Development, Vol. 30, No. 1, pp. 57-69, January 1986.

15. J.F. Sowa: Knowledge Representation in Databases, Expert Systems and Natural Language, Artificial intelligence in Databases and Expert System, Meersman, R.A., Shi, Zh. & Kung, C.H. (eds.), North-Holland Publishing Co., Amsterdam, pp. 17-50, 1990.

16. J.D. Ullman: Principles of Database and Knowledgebase Systems, Vol. 1, Computer Science Press, 1988.

17. K. Yokota: Outline of a Deductive and Object-Oriented Language: Juan. SIGDB No. 78, July 1990.

A Knowledge Based Technique for the Process Modelling of Information Systems: the Object Life Cycle Diagram

Saimond Ip and Tony Holden

Information Engineering Division
Department of Engineering, University of Cambridge
Trumpington Street, Cambridge CB2 1PZ, United Kingdom

Abstract. This paper presents a new technique for IS process/behavioural modelling. Object Life Cycle is proposed as an extension of the conventional entity life history diagram with a Petri-Net based formalism and an Event-Precondition-Action process representation. A normalization approach for IS process modelling is suggested and several OLC norms discussed. Generalization and aggregation of OLCs are explored along with the concepts of a substate and a component event. Coordination of the objects via event raising is visualized by the Inter-Object Communication Model. Finally, we discuss how OLCs relate with RUBRIC rules and data flow diagrams.

1 Introduction

As part of an ongoing project to develop a new generation of knowledge based IS Methodology, a set of new techniques is developed for conceptual modelling, one of which is the Object Life Cycle Diagram (OLC) for behavioural/process modelling. We examine several major existing techniques and try to find out what constitutes a good process model. The result is presented in section 2. With these discoveries as our guide, OLC is developed and its basic constructs are presented in section 3. Two important methodological features are also developed alongside OLC. Firstly, a normalization approach is adopted in process modelling and several OLC normal forms are discussed in section 4. Secondly, two abstraction principles, namely, generalization and aggregation, are employed extensively in OLC diagrams and detailed discussions of how they are used can be found in sections 5 and 6. A major advantage of OLCs is that, at a certain normal form, they can be easily implemented and executed in a knowledge based systems environment. The last section briefly examines this issue.

2 Towards an Integrated Extension of Existing Techniques

Roughly speaking, IS Engineering involves three different parties: the end-user, the programmer, and the modeller [7], with the last (who constructs the conceptual model) acting as the bridge between the first two. First and foremost, a conceptual model must be *user-oriented*, that is, it should be readily understood by an end-user and conform to his way of thinking about the problem. It would also be advantageous if the same techniques can be extended to model more implementational details for the programmer. The ideal solution is therefore a technique which can offer a *continuous* spectrum of forms, ranging from user-oriented high level models to programmer-oriented implementational models. Last but not least, a good model would lead itself to different *abstraction* principles.

What makes structured analysis techniques ([11] [15]) such as data flow diagrams so widely used? It appears that data flow is a very natural way for end-users to visualise a system and the diagrammatic representations are simple but very powerful. The important abstraction principle of functional decomposition is also naturally built into data flow diagrams and is often employed extensively. But their high level descriptions cannot be readily extended to provide more implementation details. Yet structured techniques is now so well established and popular that it is both unwise (since it is proven to be a useful approach) and impractical (since so many professionals are trained and so many specifications already written) to abandon them altogether. Any new technique should be complementary to structured analysis and integrate seamlessly with it.

Two other techniques have been applied fruitfully to IS analysis. First, there are interesting attempts to utilize different kinds of Petri Nets (eg. [13] [26] [32] [34] [36] [44]), most notably its successful integration with data flow and process models [13]. The main attraction of Petri Net is its ability to provide a continuous spectrum of forms covering both highly abstract user-oriented models and actually executable models with formal properties and implementation details. Several abstraction principles based on net refinements (which usually amounts to functional decomposition) have also been employed in IS analysis and design.[1] Second, the RUBRIC project[29] has demonstrated that business rule is a very useful paradigm for IS Engineering. It recognises the explicit separation of organizational policy from implementational details and is therefore geared towards the organization's way of thinking. On the other hand, sufficiently well defined rules can be readily analysed and are executable and, therefore, has a high degree of continuity. A rule is also a completely independent unit and free from considerations of procedural control flows.

It is observed that the only abstraction principle used in data flow diagrams and Petri Nets is functional decomposition. Generalization and aggregation, often in the form of "object-orientation", are now widely acknowledged as important and useful abstraction principles and are employed extensively in programming languages[42] [28] and databases[2]; but their use in ISE are so far confined to data modelling[45] [20]. Their extensive use becomes a major motivation behind the development of our new process model. The idea of an object is particularly appealing because it entails the concept of encapsulation[28] which tends to give more modular and re-usable designs. Entity Life History/Cycle (ELH/C) Diagram is a well-integrated

---

[1]Examples of net refinement principles are refinement of surroundings[26], refinement by S- and T-Sets[36], and refinement by primitives[13].

part of traditional structured methodologies, such as SSADM[16], and our approach is to extend it by giving it a new formalism and new concepts to become the Object Life Cycle (OLC) Diagram. The final representation chosen is Petri-Net based with additional rule-based constructs. This is made possible by the remarkable similarity between an event-condition-action rule ([29] [10]; the Remora IS methodology also employs similar constructs[35]) and a transition in a predicate/transition net with its input predicates represented by the conditions and output predicates determined by the rule's actions. The event of the rule is a special input predicate that will be consumed by another "garbage-collection" transition if it is not instantaneously used by the original transition. Finally, the integration of the OLC and data flow diagrams (section 8) is facilitated by the distinction between the two different ways which a process can involve any object, either to change its state (object flow) or simply to read and use some of its information (data flow) [32] [44].

3   The Object Life Cycle Diagram (OLC)

An OLC is constructed for every object class defined in Object Relationship Model (ORM) [20]. Figs. 1 & 2 give examples of different OLCs. Every object in a class must be in a certain *state*.[2] The possible states of an object class are shown as circles in an OLC. Every object class in ORM must also have "state" as one of its attributes. There are two special states that are universal to all OLCs: never-exist and cease-to-exist. A complete OLC must begin with the former and end with the latter. An object can be transformed from one state to another by a *process* (shown as a round-cornered box). A process may have more than one input and output states. An input and an output state of a process can be the same. If they have to be the same, a double-arrowed link is used. A double-lined and double-arrowed link next to a process means that it can operate on an object at any state (except never-exist and cease-to-exist) without changing the state.

The full definition of a process contains three distinct parts: event, precondition, and action. When an *event* (shown as a box with darkened left edge) is raised to an object at one of the input states of a corresponding process, the conditions are checked. If all the conditions are met, the actions will be performed and the object transformed to the output state of the process. A process can be triggered by more than one event and several processes may have the same triggering event (although once an event have triggered a particular process, it is retracted and cannot trigger further processes). For example, in fig. 1, if ?pub (an instance of Publication) is at the state borrowed or overdue and ?b (an instance of Borrower) at the state registered, the process Return-Publication will be triggered by the event Pub-Returned to check whether (?pub is-borrowed-by ?b). If the condition is met, the process will delete all the facts related to ?pub being borrowed by ?b and assert that a publication has been put back into the location ?loc. The state of ?pub will be changed to on-shelf.

---

[2]Similar to our approach, the Lifecycle diagram proposed by Shlaer[38] also uses events and states. However, Schlaer includes all the dynamic responses to incoming events in the concept of a state and does not put them in separate processes.

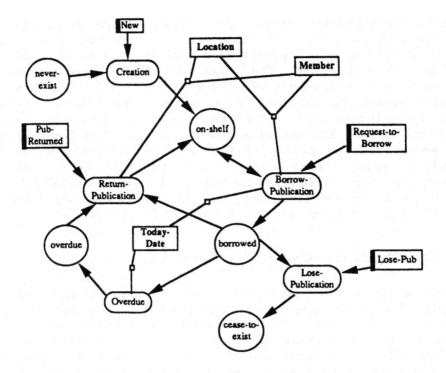

Fig. 1(a) OLC for Publciation

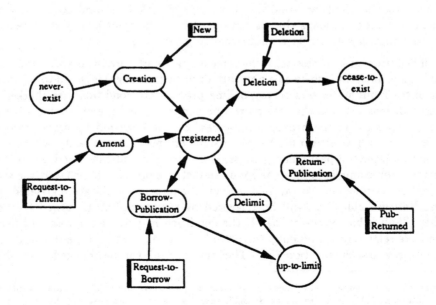

Fig. 1(b) OLC for Borrower

External object classes are simply shown as boxes. If a process belongs to more than one object, then, in the context of the OLC of any one of the objects, it can be linked to the appropriate external objects (shown as a link with a small box). For example, in fig. 1(a), the process Return-Publication involves objects of classes Publication (the class of the OLC itself), Member, and Location. If a process simply need to read-access the information about an external object, a simple link is used. The information required from an external object and an event can be (optionally) written on the link. For example, in fig. 2(a) the process Borrow-Publication needs the information about the identity of the publication to be borrowed (?pub) from the triggering event Request-to-Borrow, the state and the location of ?pub from Publication, and the accessibility of the location of ?pub from Location.

The events that trigger processes to create an object from the state never-exist (defaulted to be New) and to delete it into the state cease-to-exist are really raised to the class of the object instead of the instance itself. For example, in fig. 1(b) the event New tells the object class Borrower to create an instance of itself with certain parameters.

Where do events come from? Some are external events (eg. Request-to-Borrow in fig. 1) while others are internal ones (eg. Pub-Borrowed in fig. 2(c)) and are generated by the action of a process. Hence, an external event might trigger off a chain of events. But as far as an OLC is concerned, the source of an event is completely irrelevant. This independence is clearly an advantage since the boundary of a system often changes enormously. A process may also raise an event to the external environment. Such events to and from the external forms the sole interface between the process model and its environment.

Occasionally, a process has to be automatically triggered when all its preconditions are met. For example, in fig. 2(c) the process Overdue should be triggered to warn of an overdue whenever the due-date of the publication is today. This amounts to a process with a triggering event permanently and repeatedly raised (shown simply as a "TRUE" event). The process would simply be reduced to a normal forward chaining rule, that is, the actions would be performed if all the preconditions *become* true. The process would therefore only be triggered by some change in the system and not repeatedly by the preconditions remaining true.

4 A Normalization Approach to Conceptual Modelling

A *norm* (or a normal form) of any model is a particular form with some predefined desirable properties. But a normalization approach is more than just using norms in modelling. It is the provision of a spectrum of successively more restrictive norms. It is argued in section 2 that the ability of a modelling technique to provide such a spectrum (what we call the technique's continuity) is clearly advantageous.[3]

---

[3]The success of the normalization approach in the design of relational database [9] is at least a good indication of its potential in process modelling. In fact, relational normal forms (in particular, up to the third normal form) are so successful that normalization becomes almost synonymous with relational analysis.

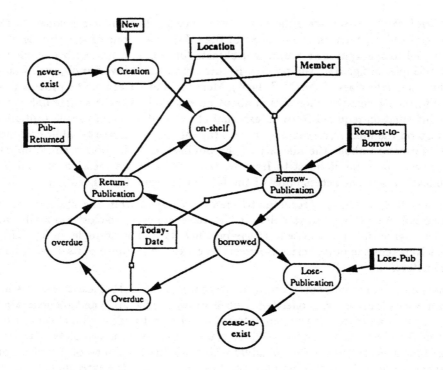

Fig. 1(a) OLC for Publciation

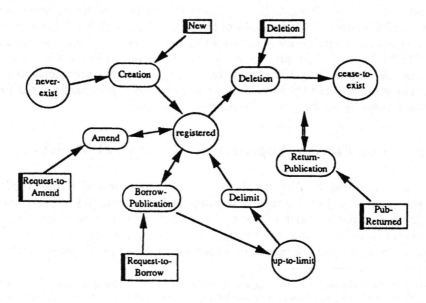

Fig. 1(b) OLC for Borrower

A normalization approach is appropriate for process modelling because of the different benefits offered by the models at the two ends of the spectrum. Relatively unnormalized forms are more abstract (easier to understand and to construct as a kind of "first draft"), less formal (requires less technical knowledge to use), and usually conform better to the end-users' way of thinking. On the other hand, successively more normalized forms contain more detailed information (valuable for implementation and possibly automatic code-generation) and is more formal (allow more formal analyses) and more similar to the way the IS is eventually implemented. Norms can also act as a template to standardize a model by enforcing specific arrangements of some model information. The beauty of the normalization approach is that no one is forced to go through a rigid set of norms. Experienced analysts (or even end-users) might skip the "early" unnormalized forms and increasingly model directly in more normalized forms. Modellers might not want to "go all the way" and use all the norms. They might find some norms too detailed to be used for conceptual modelling and others with properties unnecessary for their circumstances. Everyone just uses the norms they find useful and convenient.

The five norms of OLC are given in table 1. The encapsulation norm is based on the classification norm (ie. a model in the encapsulation norm must also be in the classification norm) and all the other three norms are based on the encapsulation norm. These last three norms are basically independent of each other. The list is not meant to be exhaustive and new norms might be developed as the need arises. It should also be pointed out that the encapsulation norm is regarded as the corner stone of our process model and any OLC should eventually be transformed into this norm while the last three norms are relatively optional and are useful only for specific reasons.

Table 1 Norms of OLC

The Classification Norm

Definition: An OLC is in the *Classification Norm* if and only if each process and each event belongs to one and only one object class.

Example: OLCs in fig. 1 are unnormalized since Borrow-Publication and Return-Publication belongs to two object classes but fig. 2 contains OLCs in the classification norm. Return-Publication of Borrower in fig. 2(a) and Return-Publication of Publication in fig. 2(c) are now two different processes.

Rationale: This norm forces the modeller to assign each process (and hence its triggering events) to an object class and hence makes all processes subordinate to objects and the abstraction of classification uniformly endorsed. Unnormalized forms allow assignment decisions to be delayed and recorded explicitly (possibly for future revisions).

The Encapsulation Norm

Definition: An OLC is in the *Encapsulation Norm* if and only if each process can only modify the object instance to which its triggering event is raised.

Example: Borrow-Publication in fig. 1 is broken into Borrow-Publication of Borrower, Borrow-Publication of Pub, and Remove-Pub of Location (not shown) in fig. 2 (all OLCs in encapsulation norm).

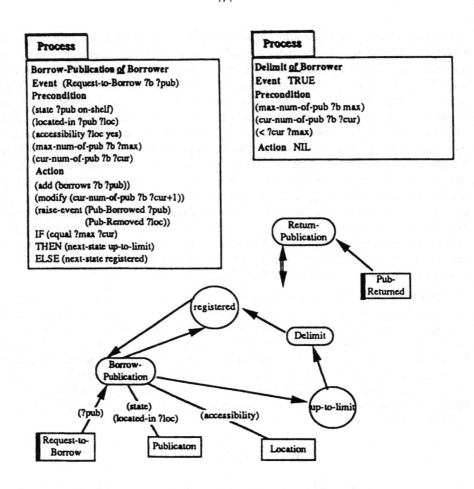

Process

Borrow-Publication of Borrower
Event (Request-to-Borrow ?b ?pub)
Precondition
(state ?pub on-shelf)
(located-in ?pub ?loc)
(accessibility ?loc yes)
(max-num-of-pub ?b ?max)
(cur-num-of-pub ?b ?cur)
Action
(add (borrows ?b ?pub))
(modify (cur-num-of-pub ?b ?cur+1))
(raise-event (Pub-Borrowed ?pub)
          (Pub-Removed ?loc))
IF (equal ?max ?cur)
THEN (next-state up-to-limit)
ELSE (next-state registered)

Process

Delimit of Borrower
Event TRUE
Precondition
(max-num-of-pub ?b max)
(cur-num-of-pub ?b ?cur)
(< ?cur ?max)
Action NIL

Fig. 2(a) The Processes Borrow-Publication & Delimit of Borrower
in Classification and Encapsulation Norm

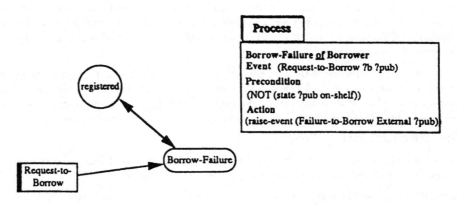

Process

Borrow-Failure of Borrower
Event (Request-to-Borrow ?b ?pub)
Precondition
(NOT (state ?pub on-shelf))
Action
(raise-event (Failure-to-Borrow External ?pub)

Fig. 2(b) The event Request-to-Borrow triggering an alternative Process

Rationale: Modular style of representation enforced by encapsulation or information hiding [28] [42]. A process can only modify another object by raising events to it; hence the triggering events to an object form its only interface with the rest of the system. The process model becomes a set of independent objects communicating via events.

The Weak and The Strong ORM Norms

Definitions: An OLC of an object class A is in the *Weak ORM Norm* if and only if an object to which one of its processes can raise an event must be: 1) an instance of an object class (or the object class itself) directly related to A in the ORM or 2) given to the process as an argument of its triggering event. The OLC will be in *Strong ORM Norm* if and only if it is in the weak ORM norm and each process can only read-access objects of the above two categories[27].

Examples: Let us assume that in the ORM Borrower is only related to Publication which is also related to Location. Borrow-Publication of Borrower in fig. 2(a) wants to raise an event Pub-Removed to Location and, in the weak ORM norm of fig. 3, this job is delegated to Borrow-Publication of Publication. Fig. 4 shows how strong ORM norm causes additional events to be raised for accessing an indirectly related object (note the final event Loc-info raised at the other end of the access path to pass back the information to the original enquiring object Borrower).

Rationale: Further enhance information hiding and decoupling of control by narrowing the accessibility of an object to its related objects in the ORM, cf. the inter-object communication model in section 7. If any process (or data structure) of an object class A is modified, one needs only to consider its effect on related objects in the ORM and objects taking A as an event argument. Standardization in the decomposition of event chains is also enforced along a path on the ORM. The strong ORM might hinder readability due to the large number of events being raised.

The Discrete Time Norm

Definition: An OLC is in the *Discrete Time Norm* if and only if each of its processes has no duration at all.

Example: Fig. 7 shows how part of an OLC can be transformed into the discrete time norm. Any non-discrete time elements are pushed into the states of the OLC and/or to other objects (in this case the state potentially-deleted and External).

Rationale: This norm ensures the independence of a process and its sole access to the relevant information. It tackles the problem of I/O uncohesiveness [1] and forces all complicated (and asynchronous) interactions among processes to be be modelled explicitly. It also makes an OLC executable (section 9).

The Explicit-Condition Norm

Definition: An OLC is in the *Explicit-Condition Norm* if and only if each of its processes has a unique output state.

Example: The Explicit-Condition norm of Borrow-Publication in fig. 2(a) is given in fig. 5.

Rationale: To explicitly model the conditions for choosing the output states as the preconditions of the process.

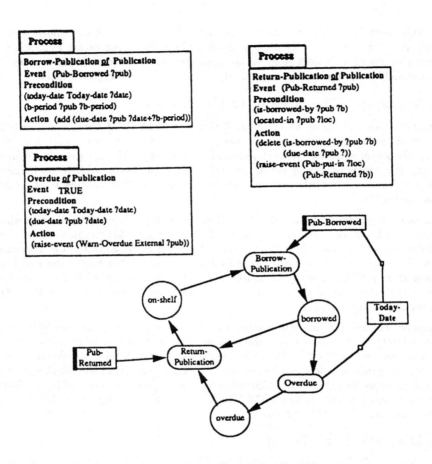

Process

Borrow-Publication of Publication
Event (Pub-Borrowed ?pub)
Precondition
(today-date Today-date ?date)
(b-period ?pub ?b-period)
Action (add (due-date ?pub ?date+?b-period))

Process

Return-Publication of Publication
Event (Pub-Returned ?pub)
Precondition
(is-borrowed-by ?pub ?b)
(located-in ?pub ?loc)
Action
(delete (is-borrowed-by ?pub ?b)
         (due-date ?pub ?))
(raise-event (Pub-put-in ?loc)
              (Pub-Returned ?b))

Process

Overdue of Publication
Event   TRUE
Precondition
(today-date Today-date ?date)
(due-date ?pub ?date)

Action
 (raise-event (Warn-Overdue External ?pub))

Fig. 2(c) Part of the OLC of Publication in the
Encapsulation (& Classification) Norm

Process

Borrow-Publication of Borrower
Event (Request-to-Borrow ?b ?pub)
Precondition
(state ?pub on-shelf)
(located-in ?pub ?loc)
(accessibility ?loc yes)
(max-num-of-pub ?b ?max)
(cur-num-of-pub ?b ?cur)
 Action
(add (borrows ?b ?pub))
(modify (cur-num-of-pub ?b ?cur+1))
(raise-event (Pub-Borrowed ?pub))
IF (equal ?max ?cur)
THEN (next-state up-to-limit)
ELSE (next-state registered)

(a) Modified part of OLC of Borrower

Process

Borrow-Publication of Publication
Event (Pub-Borrowed ?pub)
Precondition
(today-date Today-date ?date)
(b-period ?pub ?b-period)
Action
(add (due-date ?pub ?date+?b-period))
(raise-event (Pub-Removed ?loc))

(b) Modified part of OLC of Publication

Fig. 3 Borrower and Publication in Weak ORM Norm

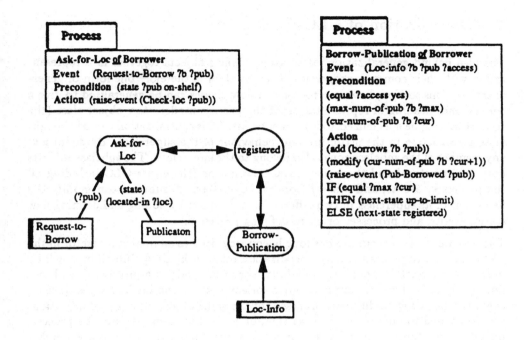

(a) Modified Part of OLC of Borrower

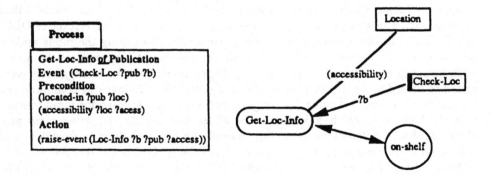

(b) Modified Part of OLC of Publication

Fig. 4 OLCs in Strong ORM Norm

5   Generalization of OLCs

The idea behind generalization[4] is to group similar objects together in a representation with their common properties. Classification is therefore one form of generalization. This section, however, focuses on how classes can be generalized to give a concise and meaningful representation of the process model. Any object class (the superclass) can be specialized to form a subclass. This specialization can be thought of as a *restriction* in the structure and behaviour of the superclass. By definition, any member of the subclass must also belong to the superclass. The subclass inherits both the structural and the behavioural information (the entire OLC including all the processes, events, and states) from its superclass. A subclass can modify the behaviour of its superclass in two different ways[5]: either by adding and defining new states, events, and processes or by re-defining processes.

The *granularity of inheritance* has long been recognized as an important factor in the usefulness of any generalisation/specialization relationships[42]. Inheritance will be much more powerful if incremental additions can be made to a process. OLC has a finer granularity than conventional object-oriented programming languages since an event can be raised to different processes of the same object and any modifications can be limited to only some of these (and only the necessary parts of the process, including i/o states, preconditions, or actions, are changed). There are a number of attempts in object oriented languages to provide incremental specialization of functions[42], most notably the declarative method combination (eg. the division of a method into before/after/main parts in Flavors) and the use of commands like "Super" in Loops which invokes the method of a superclass in a local method that re-defines it. The separation of processes and states allows specialization of OLCs to effectively subsume these two schemes. Firstly, by re-defining the input and/or output states of a "main" process, an arbitrary number of processes can be added both before or after it (or in any other topology) ,possibly with the triggering event raised to preceding processes instead. Secondly, the "Super" invoking command can be achieved by simply having the original process intact (except for input/output states). Any additional behaviour can be added on with the triggering event possibly raised to a different process. For example, in fig. 9(d) the process deletion of privileged borrower is inherited unchanged from the OLC of borrower. But an additional condition (check-address) is checked (with a new state mid-check added) and an extra action (send-farewell-letter) performed (with another state to-send-farewell introduced).

Multiple inheritance is so useful that most object oriented systems incorporate it in various degrees. OLC is rather flexible and can be associated with many different strategies of conflict resolution. For demonstration purpose, we have chosen a scheme that gives precedence to subclasses over superclasses and to different superclasses

---

[4] [22] gives a more detailed discussion of abstraction principles, including the concepts of a mixin and non-excluding-subclass norm in generalization, the concept of a perspective in aggregation, and examples of functional decomposition, as applied to OLCs.

[5] A third type of modification that excludes the processes or states of a superclass is discussed in [22].

176

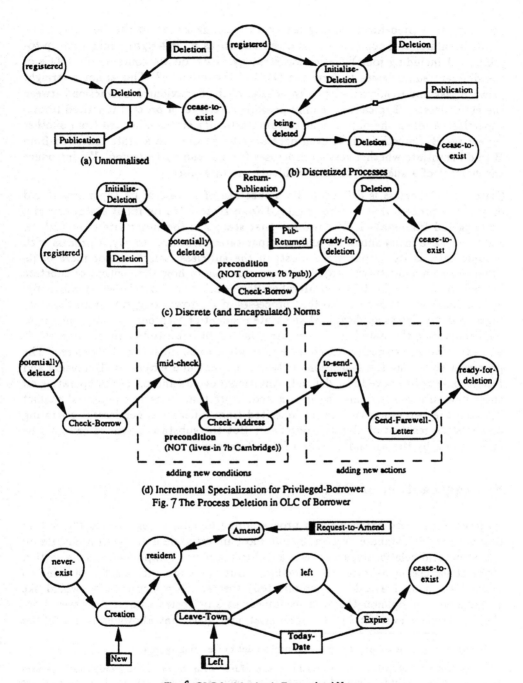

(a) Unnormalised

(b) Discretized Processes

(c) Discrete (and Encapsulated) Norms

(d) Incremental Specialization for Privileged-Borrower
Fig. 7 The Process Deletion in OLC of Borrower

Fig. 8 OLC for Member in Encapsulated Norm

according to a predefined priority list (with warning issued to the designer). The result is similar to Loops[42] and is often known as a "left-right depth first up-to-joint (and including joint)[6]" selection strategy. How do we combine the OLCs of the different superclasses to form the OLC of the subclass? This is not a straight forward task and requires in-depth knowledge of the behavioural interaction between the superclasses. Typically it is only possible to trigger a process inherited from a superclass A when the object is at certain particular states inherited from another superclass B. Sometimes it is even necessary to decompose a state inherited from B to differentiate whether certain processes from A can be triggered. We introduce the concept of a *substate*[7] to deal with such circumstances.

State-1 of a subclass is defined to be a substate of state-2 of its superclass if and only if any process that can be triggered from state-2 (as its input state) can also be triggered from state-1. We also say that state-2 is the superstate of state-1. A state can have many substates and/or superstates. Needless to say, a process with a superstate as its output state must, in the subclass, select one or more of its substates as a substitute[8]. Fig. 9 gives an example of how the concept of substate is used to combine the OLCs of Member-Borrower's two superclasses Member (fig. 8) and Borrower. It is observed that processes of Borrower triggered from the state registered are always applicable at the state resident of Member but only sometimes applicable from the state left. The solution is to split left into two substates just-left and extended and to declare extended and resident to be substates of registered. The processes governing the transitions between just-left and extended (Extension and Extension-Expire) have to be defined. Additional events and processes operating on these new substates can also be introduced. Note that there is a potential conflict between the two processes Amend inherited from different superclasses[9] operating on the state resident of Member-Borrower. But the substate extended can only be operated on by the Amend inherited from Borrower.

6 Aggregation of OLCs

Aggregation is used extensively in programming languages (eg. Loops[42]) and in object oriented database systems[2] but most investigations so far concentrate on the structural relationships between an object and its components. This section looks at its use in behavioural modelling. But what are the benefits of using so many (and, some may add, so complicated) abstraction principles? We would like to reiterate our opinion that the usefulness of any abstraction can be seen from three different views[20]: 1) the representational view that allows us to model the

---

[6]Loops' strategy is left-right depth first up-to-joint but excluding joint.

[7]This "substate of specialization" must not be confused with the more commonly used substates and subprocesses in the functional decomposition of a process. Another very useful concept to tackle these problems is "perspective"[22].

[8]A process of the superclass may always leave a superstate unchanged in which case an instance of the subclass will also remain unchanged at whichever substate it happens to be at.

[9]If the two processes are triggered by events of different names, they can co-exist. But in this case, they are triggered by events of the same name and a choice has to be made between the two.

178

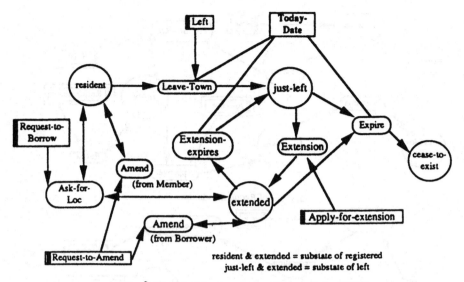

Fig. 9 Multiple Inheritance using Substate in the OLC for
Member-Borrower (subclass of Member and Borrower)

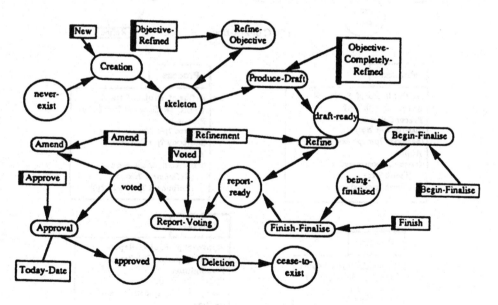

Fig. 10   OLC of Project-Report

179

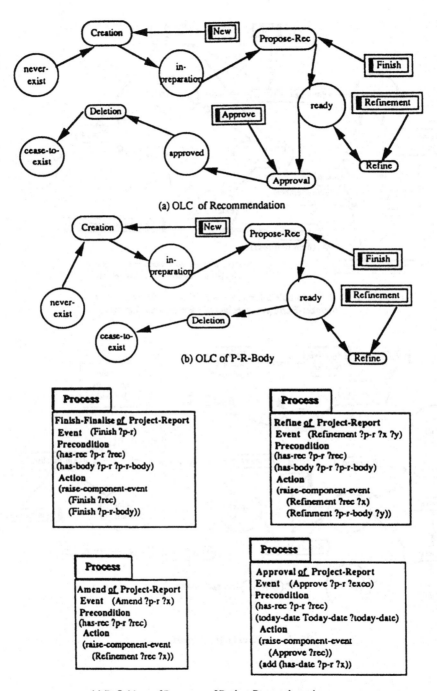

(a) OLC of Recommendation

(b) OLC of P-R-Body

Process

Finish-Finalise of Project-Report
Event (Finish ?p-r)
Precondition
(has-rec ?p-r ?rec)
(has-body ?p-r ?p-r-body)
Action
(raise-component-event
  (Finish ?rec)
  (Finish ?p-r-body))

Process

Refine of Project-Report
Event (Refinement ?p-r ?x ?y)
Precondition
(has-rec ?p-r ?rec)
(has-body ?p-r ?p-r-body)
Action
(raise-component-event
  (Refinement ?rec ?x)
  (Refinment ?p-r-body ?y))

Process

Amend of Project-Report
Event (Amend ?p-r ?x)
Precondition
(has-rec ?p-r ?rec)
Action
(raise-component-event
  (Refinement ?rec ?x))

Process

Approval of Project-Report
Event (Approve ?p-r ?exco)
Precondition
(has-rec ?p-r ?rec)
(today-date Today-date ?today-date)
Action
(raise-component-event
  (Approve ?rec))
(add (has-date ?p-r ?x))

(c) Definitions of Processes of Project-Report that raises component
events (to Recommendation and P-R-Body)

Fig. 11 OLCs of Recommendation and P-R-Body as Components of Project-Report

real world more closely and naturally; 2) the methodological view which sees an aggregate as a temporary "abbreviation" for further detailed expansion; and 3) the documentational view that presents relevant information of various degrees of details to users with different needs.

The use of complex objects in our data model ORM is reported in [20]. For our present purpose, it is suffice to know that a complex object class may contain many component object classes which may relate with each other. The example used here is the complex object class Project Report which has-rec an instance of Recommendation class and has-body an instance of P-R-Body which in turn may has-section one or many P-R-Section. As far as OLCs are concerned, a complex object is a sort of "supersystem" governing the behaviour of its subsystems, ie. its component objects. The current state of a complex object should indicate the availability of certain processes both of the complex object itself and of some of its components. Hence, when a process is performed on the complex object (and thereby attempting to change its state), some of the states of its components have to be changed simultaneously. Moreover, a process of the complex object often requires several simultaneous subprocesses of its components to achieve the desired effects. We propose the concept of a *component event* as the means to accomodate these characteristics.

The independent rule-like characteristic of an OLC process means that, under normal circumstances, after the process has raised an event, it would simply proceed to finish other actions and finally the object instance would be transformed to the output state[10]. But if a complex object raises component events to its component objects, the complex object instance can only proceed to the output state of the process when all the component events are "completely consumed". A component event is completely consumed when either 1) it does not trigger any process at all and is therefore deleted or 2) the component object instance is transformed to the output state of the process it triggers. Therefore, when a complex object reach the output state of a process, we can be certain that all the appropriate "subprocesses" are finished and corresponding state changes achieved. A complex object can, however, raise "ordinary" events to any of its components if the desired effect of component events is not needed. It is also noted that, in the weak ORM norm, a complex object can only raise component events to its direct components.

A rather detailed example of how the OLCs of the complex object Project-Report interact with the OLCs of its components (and with each other) is given in figs. 10 and 11. For instance, when the external event Finish is raised to a Project-Report (when it is at the being-finalised state), it triggers the process Finish-Finalise which raises two component events (both called Finish too!) to the Project-Report's Rec (Recommendation) and P-R-Body. The Project-Report can only proceed to the state report-ready when the processes triggered by the two Finish events are completed and both its Rec and P-R-Body have proceeded to their own ready states. It is interesting to observe that some of the processes of Project-Report, for example, Refine-Objective and Begin-Finalise, do not involve any of its components at all.

---

[10] This contrast sharply with the idea of a "method" in conventional object oriented programming language like Smalltalk-80. When a method send a message, it has to wait for an object to be returned before it can proceed.

These can be thought of as part of the *emergent* behaviour of a complex object.

7 The Inter-Object Communication Model (IOCM)

The OLC of an object class is the formalization of the typical behaviour of instances in the class. All instances (of all object classes) are assumed to operate independently, concurrently, and asynchronously and any coordinations and synchronizations should be modelled explicitly through the event raising mechanism. In order to help us to visualize these interactions, an *inter-object communication model* (IOCM) can be constructed[38]. It is simply a diagram with all the object classes joined by directional links labelled with the events raised. Fig. 12 shows part of the IOCM for the examples discussed in this paper. All specialization relationships should also be included in the IOCM because all events raised by/to a superclass are also raised by/to its subclasses. Component events raised by a complex object to its components is specially marked as such (in this case with dotted links). Following [38], we think it is sometimes useful to organize the large number of object classes (possibly dozens) into layers to facilitate the understanding of a IOCM. A set of very rough and informal guidelines is used. Examples include: an object usually receives guidance, requests, and coordinations from the objects above it (with complex objects always above their components), objects of a higher layer have more interaction with the "External", and the lowest layer consists of completely passive and unintelligent objects.

8 OLC and Related Process Modelling Techniques

This section will examine how OLC relates with other process modelling techniques, in particular, the RUBRIC project and conventional structured analysis. The dynamic rules of the process model of RUBRIC[29] is basically equivalent to a process in OLC with the same division into trigger (= OLC's event), precondition, and message (= action). In fact, OLC can be seen as an attempt to organize the vast amount of rules in a process model along the concept of an encapsulated object and to use a Net-based formalism to visualize their interactions. Some static RUBRIC rules are captured in our data model ORM while others are modelled as an OLC process with a "TRUE" event as explained in section 3 (eg. a constraint rule can be represented by such a "TRUE" event rule with warning actions).

OLC is seen as complementary to the use of data flow diagrams (DFD)[11] with the latter either developed in parallel with or act as the source specifications for the former. Most constructs in DFD can be represented accurately in OLC. A process in DFD can initially be modelled as an OLC process belonging to many different object classes in unnormalized forms and eventually be classified and attached to one specific object class (often one of its input data flow)[11]. An input data flow

---

[11] A data store is an object class with all its roles and attributes in ORM. All external entities are grouped into the "External" in OLC; though it might of course be broken up if necessary.

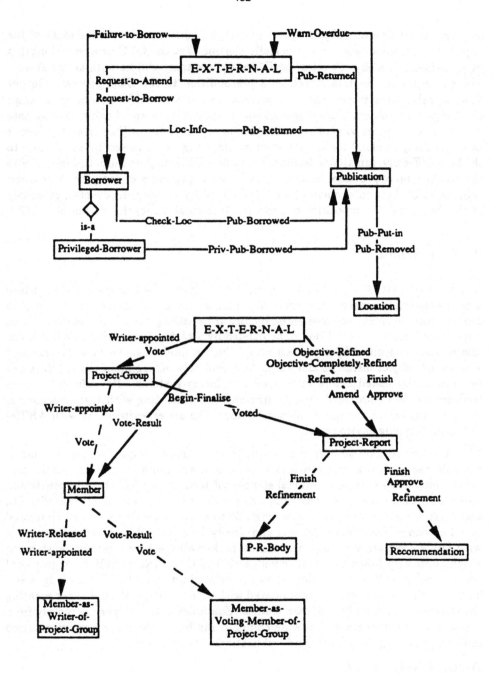

Fig. 12. Inter-Object Communication Model for Parts of the Case Study

to a process can be an "object flow", that is, a transformation of the state of the object if it is from a data store (especially the one that the OLC process belongs), a modification of the object's roles/attributes (where there will be both an input from and an output to the data store), or a precondition to the OLC process. Output flows to other data stores (that the process does not attach) signifies an attempt to change other object classes and should be normalized and broken up. A data flow from one process to another can either be a precondition (involving the former associated object class) for the latter or a triggering event raised by the former to the latter. Finally, functional decomposition of a DFD may be modelled in OLCs as the breaking up of processes in their normalization, processes of complex objects and subprocess of their component objects (triggered by component events), or simply as the functional decomposition of processes into small subcycles within an OLC[12].

9 Conclusion

It is believed that OLC can facilitate rapid prototyping by being transformed into a semi-executable conceptual model. With heavy designer interaction, an OLC in discrete-time norm can be represented by forward-chaining rules (with an event being a special left hand side condition to be deleted by a garbage-collection rule if it is not immediately consumed by a process rule). Such a model can be directly executed with sample object instances and data. As completely independent units, OLCs can be individually tested before integrated into larger systems. Powerful interactive facilities should be provided for browsing and experimenting with various scenarios to detect any errors and unintended behaviour. We are experimenting with ART[8] as the prototyping environment.

We set out to develop an user-oriented behavioural modelling technique that facilitates the use of abstraction, provides a continuous spectrum to different parties and is fully integrated with conventional structured techniques. We then demonstrated how a normalization approach for OLC can provide the spectrum, how generalization and aggregation can be applied meaningfully to OLCs, how OLCs can be simulated in a knowledge based environment, and finally how data flow diagrams integrate with OLCs. We are working on a prototype knowledge based support system on a Symbolics Lisp Machine for the construction of OLCs (and ORMs). A graphical editor is being built using Maxim[17] and translated into an ART[8] knowledge base. These are then validated and consolidated with other models. We are experimenting the techniques on a number of case studies. Examples in this paper are mainly from a case study involving a nation wide campaigning body which runs an information centre and has regular reports and publications.

Acknowledgement

We are grateful to Prof P. Loucopoulos and his colleagues at the Information Systems Group, Department of Computation, UMIST, UK, for discussions and the exchange of research information.

---

[12] We do not pay much attention to this important aspect of OLC modelling because there have already been a lot of investigations, especially as related to Petri Net-based models [13] [36] [26].

References

[1] ALABISO, B. "Transformation of Data Flow Analysis Models to Object Oriented Design". *OOPSLA '88 Proceedings*, pp.335–353, Sept 1988.

[2] BANERJEE, J. et al. "Data Model Issues for Object-Oriented Applications". *ACM Transactions on Office Information Systems*, 5(1):3–26, Jan 1987.

[3] BOBROW, D. G. et al. "CommonLoops: Merging Lisp and Object-Oriented Programming". *OOPSLA '86 Proceedings*, pp.17–29, Sept 1986.

[4] BOOCH, G. "Object-Oriented Development". *IEEE Transactions on Software Engineering*, SE-12(2):211–221, Feb 1986.

[5] BRUNO, G. and BALSAMO, A. "Petri Net-Based Object-Oriented Modelling of Distributed Systems". *OOPSLA '86 Proceedings*, pp.284–293, Sept 1986.

[6] CAUVET, C., PROIX, C. and ROLLAND, C. "Information Systems Design: An Expert System Approach". In MEERSMAN, R. A., (eds), *Artificial Intelligence in Databases and Information Systems (DS-3)*, North-Holland, 1990.

[7] CHEUNG, L., IP, S. and HOLDEN, T. "A Survey of AI Impacts on Information Systems Engineering". *Information and Software Technology*, To be Published.

[8] CLAYTON, B. D. *Inference ART: Programmers' Tutorial*, Inference Corporation, 1987.

[9] CODD, E. F. "A Relational Model of Data for Large Shared Data Banks". *Communications of ACM*, 13, 1970.

[10] DAYAL, U. et al. "Rules are Objects Too: A Knowledge Model for an Active Object-Oriented Database System". *Lecture Notes in Computer Science*, 334:129–143, Springer-Verlag, 1988.

[11] DE MARCO, T. *Structured Analysis and System Specification*, Yourdon Press, New York, 1978.

[12] ESSINK, L. J. B. and ERHART, W. J. "Object Modelling and System Dynamics in the Conceptualization Stages of Information Systems Development". *Object Oriented Approach in Information Systems*, pp.89–116, Holland, 1991.

[13] FALQUET, G. et al. "Concept Integration as an Approach to Information Systems Design". In OLLE T. W. et al., (eds), *Computerized Assistance During the Information Systems Life Cycle*, North-Holland, 1988.

[14] FRANCE, R. B. and DOCKER, T. W. G. "Formal Specification using Structured Systems Analysis". *Lecture Notes in Computer Science*, 387:293–310, Springer-Verlag, 1989.

[15] GANE, C. and SARSON, T. *Structured Systems Analysis: Tools and Techniques*, Prentice-Hall, Englewood Cliffs, NJ, 1986.

[16] HARES, J. S. *SSADM for the Advanced Practitioner*, Wiley, 1990.

[17] HOLDEN, T., WILHELMIJ, P. W. and APPLEBY, K. A. "Object-Oriented Design of Visual Software Using MAXIM". *European Conference on the Practical Applications of Lisp*, 1989.

[18] HOLDEN, T., CHEUNG, L. and IP, S. "Intelligent Support for the Information System Design Process". *European ART User-group Conference, Rome*, 1990.

[19] HULL, M. E. et al. "Object-Oriented Design, Jackson System Development (JSD) Specifications and Concurrency". *Software Engineering Journal*, pp.79–86, March 1989.

[20] IP, S., CHEUNG, L. and HOLDEN, T. "Complex Objects in Knowledge Based Requirement Engineering". *6th Knowledge-Based Software Engineering Conference, Syracuse, New York*, Sep 1991.

[21] IP, S., CHEUNG, L. and HOLDEN, T. "A Knowledge Based Requirement Engineering Assistant". *BCS CASE on Trial II Conference, Cambridge*, Mar 1992.

[22] IP, S. and HOLDEN, T. "Abstraction and Object Life Cycles in Process Modelling". submitted to *Journal of Information Systems*.

[23] IP, S. and HOLDEN, T. "A Knowledge Assistant for the Design of Information Systems". In DEEN, S. M. and THOMAS, G. P., editors, *Data and Knowledge Base Integration, Proceedings of the Working Conference on Data and Knowledge Base Integration held at the University of Keele, England on October 4–5, 1989*, Pitman, 1990.

[24] JACOBSON, I. "Object Oriented Development in an Industrial Environment". *OOPSLA '87 Proceedings*, pp.183–191, Oct 1987.

[25] KARAKOSTAS, V. "Modelling and Maintenance Software Systems at the Teleological Level". *Software Maintenance: Research and Practice*, 2:47–59, 1990.

[26] LAUSEN, G. "Conceptual Modelling Based On Net Refinements". *Database Semantics (DS-1)*, pp.41–57, North Holland, 1986.

[27] LIEBERHERR, K. et al. "Object-Oriented Programming: An Objective Sense of Style". *OOPSLA '88 Proceedings*, pp.323–334, Sept 1988.

[28] LOCKEMANN, P. C. "Object-Oriented Information Management". *Decision Support Systems*, 5:79–102, 1989.

[29] LOUCOPOULOS, P. "Improving Information System Development and Evolution Using a Rule-Based Paradigm". *Software Engineering Journal*, pp.259–267, Sept 1989.

[30] LOUCOPOULOS, P. "The Process Model of TEMPORA". UMIST, U.K., 1991.

[31] MANFREDI, F. et al. "An Object-Oriented Approach to the System Analysis". *Lecture Notes in Computer Science*, 387:395–410, Springer-Verlag, 1989.

[32] OBERQUELLE, H. "Human-Machine Interaction and Role/Function/Action-Nets". *Lecture Notes in Computer Science*, 255:171–190, Springer-Verlag, 1986.

[33] PALASKAS, Z. and LOUCOPOULOS, P. "AMORE: The RUBRIC Implementation Environment". UMIST, U.K., 1989.

[34] RICHTER, G. and DURCHHOLZ, R. "IML-Inscribed High-Level Petri Nets". *Information Systems Design Methodologies: A Comparative Review*, pp.335–368, North Holland, 1982.

[35] ROLLAND, C. and RICHARD, C. "The REMORA Methodology for Information Systems Design and Management". *Information Systems Design Methodologies: A Comparative Review*, pp.335–368, North Holland, 1982.

[36] REISIG, W. "Petri Nets in Software Engineering". *Lecture Notes in Computer Science*, 255:63–95, Springer-Verlag, 1986.

[37] SERNADAS, C. et al. "In-the-large Object-Oriented Design of Information Systems". *Object Oriented Approach in Information Systems*, pp.209–232, Holland, 1991.

[38] SHLAER, S. and MELLOR, S. J. "An Object-Oriented Approach to Domain Analysis". *ACM SIGSOFT Software Engineering Notes*, 14(5):66–77, Jul 1989.

[39] SIBERTIN-BLANC, C. "Co-operative Objects for the Conceptual Modelling of Organizational Information Systems". *Object Oriented Approach in Information Systems*, pp.297–321, Holland, 1991.

[40] SMITH, J. M. and SMITH, D. C. P. "Database Abstractions: Aggregation and Generalization". *ACM Transactions on Database Systems*, 2(2):105–133, Jun 1977.

[41] SNYDER, A. "Encapsulation and Inheritance in Object-Oriented Programming Languages". OOPSLA '86 Proceedings, pp.38–45, Sept 1986.

[42] STEFIK, M. and BOBROW, D. G. "Object-Oriented Programming: Themes and Variations". *The AI Magazine*, Winter 1986.

[43] STROUSTRUP, B. "What is Object-Oriented Programming?"

[44] STUDER, R. and HORNDASCH, A. "Modelling Static and Dynamic Aspects of Information Systems". *Database Semantics (DS-1)*, pp.13–26, North Holland, 1986.

[45] THEODOULIDIS, C., WANGLER, B. and LOUCOPOULOS, P. "Requirements Specification in TEMPORA". *Presented at Conference CAiSE'90, Stockholm*, May 1990.

[46] VOSS, K. "Nets in Office Automation". *Lecture Notes in Computer Science*, 255:234–257, Springer-Verlag, 1986.

DATABASE CASE TOOL ARCHITECTURE :
PRINCIPLES FOR FLEXIBLE DESIGN STRATEGIES

J-L Hainaut, M. Cadelli, B. Decuyper, O. Marchand

Institut d'Informatique - University of Namur
rue Grandgagnage, 21 - B-5000 Namur (Belgium)
jlh@info.fundp.ac.be

Abstract. The paper describes the architectural principles of a database CASE tool that allows more flexible design strategies than those of traditional tools that propose oversimplistic *draw-and-generate* approaches. Providing this flexibility is based on four basic principles, namely a *unique generic specification model* that allows the definition of a large variety of specific design products, *transformational functions* as major database design tools, a *toolbox architecture*, allowing a maximal independence between functions, and *multiple model definition* through parametrization of the unique generic model. These architectural characteristics themselves derive from two fundamental paradigms, namely the *process-product-requirements* approach to model design behaviours, and the *transformational approach* to system design.

Keywords : design modeling, system design, database design, transformational approach, CASE tools.

1. INTRODUCTION

Most current database CASE tools provide four major families of functions for their users, namely conceptual specification entry, conceptual specification validation, reporting and executable code generation. They concentrate mainly on conceptual specification acquisition, leaving the problem of producing efficient physical schemas practically unsolved. They are based on simple and rigid strategies that give the illusion that database design is a straighforward and deterministic process once the conceptual schema has been developed. Indeed, many CASE tools propose a *draw-and-generate* strategy that leads to poor and sometimes unreadable DBMS schemas. More sophisticated strategies that would allow the integration of more realistic requirements (time efficiency, space efficiency, distribution, privacy, modularity, hardware constraints, etc) are impossible. That leads designers to two unacceptable practices : integrating these requirements into the conceptual schema, or modifying the generated DDL text with a text processor.

TRAMIS is an experimental CASE tool that proposes a different approach through which both novice and skilled designers can produce database schemas according to their own strategies, ranging from draw-and-generate to fine-tuning. In particular, it offers its users both a high degree of flexibility, and the possibility to restrict it when needed.

The paper describes the architectural principles of TRAMIS. It describes the four basic principles that give it this flexibility, namely a *unique generic specification model* that allows the definition of a large variety of specific design products, *transformational functions* as major database design tools, a *toolbox architecture*, allowing maximal independence between functions, and *multiple model definition* through parametrization of the unique generic model. These architectural characteristics derive from two fundamental paradigms, namely the *process-product-requirements* model of design behaviour, and the *transformational approach* to system design.

However, the paper will not concentrate on database design methods in particular, nor on the detailed description of a specific CASE tool.

The paper is organized as follows. Section 2 develops the concept of design modeling, i.e. the description of how designers behave or should behave. Section 3 analyzes some important aspects of the transformational approach applied to database design. The other sections develop the four architectural principles of TRAMIS, namely the unique specification model (section 4), the transformation functions (section 5), the functions and architecture of the CASE tool (section 6), and the model specialization as a tool to define the skeleton of specific strategies (section 7).

2. MODELING THE DESIGN ACTIVITY

The design of any technical system is a complex task that is broken down into smaller design activities in such a way that each of them can be dedicated to solving specific design problems or satisfying specific requirements. The nature of these activities, the requirements that are taken into account and the way these activities can be carried out (partly) define *a design method* (SSADM, JSD, YOURDON, MERISE, NIAM are examples of software engineering design methods). We are dealing with the general properties that several design methods share, i.e. with some kind of *generic design model*. In the realm of software systems, and more specifically databases, two kinds of generic design models can be put forward, namely the *multilevel approach* and the more flexible *process-product-requirements model*. These models try to state how designers must behave (forward engineering), or even to describe how designers behave in practice (reverse engineering [6]).

The **multilevel approach** relies on a fixed hierarchy of levels of specification description, characterized mainly by their degree of independence according to the implementation tools. Each level is defined by a set of target documents, and by the design activities that produce these documents. Most current practical database design approaches offer three levels, namely the conceptual, logical and physical levels [16] [15].

The **process-product-requirements model** proposes a more flexible approach according to which a design is carried out by design processes that transform products in order to make them satisfy requirements (Figure 1). A *product* is any standard specification set that is considered as significant in the design method in concern. A *process* is an activity that is aimed at producing a set of products from another set of products[1]. Any process is goal-oriented, that is it must give the output products properties that the input products don't satisfy. In most cases, the objective is meeting specific *requirements* such as normalisation, readableness, space efficiency, time efficiency, DBMS compliance, organizational constraints, hardware limitation, parallelism, user's skill, etc [2].

The way a process is carried out is defined by a design *strategy*, that can be based on formal rules or on heuristics. Applying the strategy generally implies carrying out other, lower-level processes. The latter are in turn design processes, and therefore produce output products from input products according to strategies as well, and so on (Figure 2). The output products of these low-level processes satisfy requirements that are either the requirements of the higher-level process, or specialization thereof (e.g. time efficiency requirements can be translated (as suggested by T_{km} in Fig. 2) into maximum paging rate requirements in some physical design processes).

---

[1] Note that a product can be seen as a specific state of another product as well : an un-normalized schema and a normalized schema can be seen either as two products, or as two states of the same product; in the scope of this paper, both views are considered as equivalent.

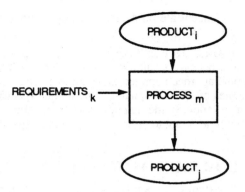

$$PRODUCT_j = PROCESS_m(PRODUCT_i, REQUIREMENTS_k)$$

Fig. 1. The process-product-requirements design model.

A strategy may use internal products that are not known at the higher level. Note that the multilevel approach can be seen as a specialization of this framework.

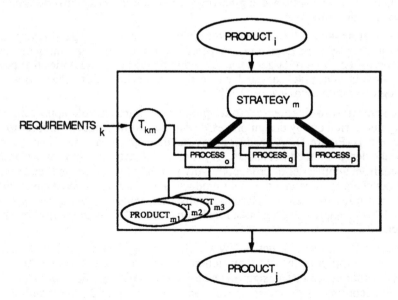

Fig. 2. A design process is defined by a strategy that describes how to produce $PRODUCT_j$ from $PRODUCT_i$. The strategy may use lower-level design processes, internal products and specialization of requirements.

3. THE TRANSFORMATIONAL APPROACH TO DATABASE DESIGN

3.1 Schema transformation

Modeling software design as the systematic transformation of formal specifications into efficient programs (and building CASE tools that support it) has long been considered as one of the ultimate goal of the research in software engineering [12]. Some important research programmes are dedicated to this approach (e.g. PROSPECTRA [10]). According to the former reference cited, *a transformation is a relation between two program schemes P and P' (a program scheme is the* [parametrized] *representation of a class of related programs*; a program of this class *is obtained by instantiating the scheme parameters). It is said to be correct if a certain semantic relation holds between P and P'.* These definitions still hold for database schemas, that are special kinds of abstract program schemes. The concept of transformation is particularly attractive in this realm, though it has not often been made explicit (for instance as a user tool) in current CASE tools. A (schema) transformation is most generally considered as an operator by which a data structure S1 is replaced by another structure S2 which has some sort of equivalence with S1. Schema transformation is a ubiquitous concept in database design. Proving the equivalence of schemas [9], refining a conceptual schema, integrating two partial schemas [1], producing a DBMS-compliant schema from a conceptual schema [13], restructuring a physical schema, DB reverse engineering [6], are basic design activities that can be carried out by carefully chosen schema transformations .

Though developing this concept and its formalization is beyond the scope of this paper (see [7] for a more formal treatment), we shall sketch the main definitions and properties that will be important from the methodological viewpoint.

A **transformation T** is an operator that replaces a source construct C in schema S by another construct C'; C' is the target of C through T, and is noted   C' = T(C)
A transformation T is defined by , (1) a precondition P that any construct C must satisfy in order to be transformed by T, (2) a maximal postcondition[1] Q that T(C) satisfies. T can therefore be written T = <P,Q> as well. P and Q are pattern-matching predicates that identify the components and the properties of C and T(C), and more specifically :
• the components of C that are preserved in T(C),
• the components of C that are discarded from T(C),
• the components of T(C) that didn't exist in C.

As an alternative to this predicative specification, [12]) proposes procedural rules that define the removing, inserting, renaming operations that produce the target schema when applied to the source schema. In the TRAMIS tool, the predicative specifications have been translated into procedural rules. In some cases, (i.e. when the graphical language is powerful enough), it is possible to give a more readable representation of a transformation by expressing C and T(C) graphically (Figures 3 and 4). A transformation T1 = <P,Q> is *reversible[2]*, or *semantics-preserving, iff* there exists a transformation T2 such that, for any schema S,

---

[1] The terms pre- and postcondition must not be confused with those used in programming theory (by Hoare and Dijkstra for instance). In the present context, predicates P and Q includes applicability preconditions but also terms that identify all the objects directly or undirectly implied in the transformation. This latter part is not relevant in programming theory.
[2] In fact, the issue is a bit more complex, since a transformation must be defined not only by a mapping T between schemas but also by a mapping t between data populations (instances) of the schemas. Two kind of semantics preservation can be defined, namely *reversibility* and *symmetrical reversibility* [7]. T1 is reversible iff, *for any instance s of schema S such that P(S), s = t2(t1(s))*; T1 is

$$P(S) \quad \Rightarrow \quad T2(T1(S)) = S$$

T2 is the reverse of T1, and conversely. We have the following property : T2 = <Q,P>

3.2 Generic *vs* specific transformation

Let's consider one of the most popular reversible transformations that replaces a many-to-many relationship type by a simpler construct based on two one-to-many relationship types. Figure 3 gives both a graphical representation and the predicative representation of this transformation[1].

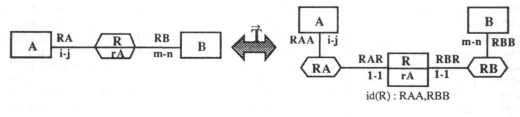

```
P = entity-type(A) & entity-type(B) & rel-type(R)
    & role(R,RA,A,[i,j]) & role(R,RB,B,[m,n]) & att(R,[aR])
Q = entity-type(A) & entity-type(B) & entity-type(R)
    & rel-type(RA) & rel-type(RB)
    & role(RA,RAA,A,[i,j]) & role(RA,RAR,R,[1,1])
    & role(RB,RBB,B,[m,n]) & role(RB,RBR,R,[1,1])
    & att(R,[aR]) & id(R,[RAA,RBB])
```

Fig. 3. Graphical and logic-based expression of a generic transformation. In the logic-based expression, predicate **entity-type**(X) means that X is the name of an entity type, predicate **role**(R,X,E,[i,j]) means that relationship type R has a role X, taken by entity type E, and with cardinality constraint [i,j], predicate **att**(R,[X,Y,..]) means that entity/relationship type R has attributes X,Y,..., and predicate **id**(X,[A,B,..]) means that entity/relationship type X has an identifier made up of {A,B,..}.

The transformation is defined for objects the names of which are generic (R, A, B, RAA, etc); therefore, it defines a *class of transformations* (a sort of *program scheme* according to [12]). Replacing these names by actual names gives a *specific transformation* (see Figure 4).

Schema transformation is a ubiquitous concept in database design, and appears explicitly or implicitly in many modeling and design activities (e.g. top-down design, reverse engineering, view integration, multibases). However, it has not been often studied as an design process of its own. Let's only mention [3], [9], [11], [14], [7] as some proposals in this direction.

3.3 Transformations in design processses

Schema transformations are not really design processes by themselves, but rather basic tools that can be used to carry out such processes.

---

symmetrically reversible iff both T1 and T2 are reversible, i.e., in addition to the property mentioned above, *for any instance s' of S' such that Q(S'), s' = t1(t2(s'))*. For simplicity, we shall ignore this distinction in this paper.

[1] To be quite precise, some parts are missing in predicate Q. In particular, R cannot have a role in other relationship types than RA and RB. Without these parts T is not reversible. See [7] for more details.

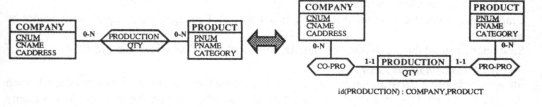

id(PRODUCTION) : COMPANY,PRODUCT

```
P =   entity-type(COMPANY) & entity-type(PRODUCT) & rel-type(PRODUCTION)
      & role(PRODUCTION,COMPANY,COMPANY,[0,N])
      & role(PRODUCTION,PRODUCT,PRODUCT,[0,N])
      & att(PRODUCTION,[QTY])
Q =   entity-type(COMPANY) & entity-type(PRODUCT)
      & entity-type(PRODUCTION) & rel-type(CO-PRO) & rel-type(PRO-PRO)
      & role(CO-PRO,COMPANY,COMPANY,[0,N])
      & role(CO-PRO,PRODUCTION,PRODUCTION,[1,1])
      & role(PRO-PRO,PRODUCT,PRODUCT,[0,N])
      & role(PRO-PRO,PRODUCTION,PRODUCTION,[1,1])
      & att(PRODUCTION,[QTY]) & id(PRODUCTION,[COMPANY,PRODUCT])
```

Fig. 4. Graphical and logic-based expression of a specific transformation. It has been obtained by substituting actual data type names for the generic ones.

Studying the problem of design strategies in some details is beyond the scope of this paper, however the role of transformations in a design process can be grossly sketched as follows :

Let   R be the set of requirements (expressed as a set of predicates or rules) of process P,
        S the input schema of the process,
        C a construct of schema S,
        r a rule of R such that : $\neg\, r(C)$
        T the set of available transformations.

C is a construct of schema S that does not satisfy requirements R, and that must be transformed.

An obvious elementary strategy is as follows :
    (1) select a transformation T of T such that $P_T(C)$ & $(Q_T \Rightarrow r)$
    (2) replace C by T(C) in S

Potential problems may arise that require more sophisticated strategies. Let's examine some of them.

P1 : Construct C may violate more than one rule.
Strategy : Let R' be the set of rules that C doesn't satisfy. Choose a rule r in R' such that there exists a transformation T in T such that : T(C) violates as few rules of R as possible. This strategy may generate a set of solutions[1].

P2 : More than one transformation satisfies : P(C) & (Q ⇒ r)
Strategy : the selection of T can be done either arbitrarily, or according to other rules. In the latter case, P generates a set of solutions. The final selection will be done according to other kinds of requirements, i.e. in another design process.

---

[1] In all generality, there will be a tree of solutions, since more than one design process may encounter this problem.

P3 : No transformations satisfy P(C)
Diagnostic : either the transformation set $\mathbb{T}$ is not powerful enough or the requirement cannot be satisfied.
Strategies : extend the set of transformations, keep construct C as it is or discard C.

P4 : No transformations satisfy : $Q \Rightarrow r$
Strategy : choose a transformation T such that $P_T(C)$, then select another transformation T' such that : $(Q_T \Rightarrow P_{T'})$ & $(Q_{T'} \Rightarrow r)$; if the latter cannot be satisfied, iterate the process. This strategy may generate a set of solutions.

P5 : T(C) violates a rule that C satisfied
This problem can be local, i.e. it concerns the termination of P, or it can be global, such as when P may destroy the effect (i.e. the satisfaction of a set of requirements) of a former process. Though it has been solved in TRAMIS with adhoc strategies, this problem still has no general solution and is currently under investigation.

These problems may induce the production of a large solution space. In such a situation, the concept of *output products* (PRODUCTj in Figure 1) must be replaced by that of *set of equivalent output products* that must be explored according to other criteria. A higher-level strategy must be defined to manage this space and reduce it to one solution.

4. THE UNIQUE SPECIFICATION MODEL OF TRAMIS

According to the generic design model developed in section 2, designing a database is decomposed into several processes, starting from, say, requirements collection, and ending with DDL schema generation[1]. These processes define a set of standard products, such as the validated conceptual schema or the executable DDL schema. This set of products can also be perceived as a set of states of the database schema. According to this view, designing a database consists in applying the design processes to a source schema (general a conceptual schema) in order to transform it into an executable database schema that satisfies a given set of requirements such as semantic correctness, readableness, efficiency and executability.

TRAMIS is based on a *unique generic model* to express database structures in any of its possible states. This unique model allows a neutral definition of the design processes, as well as a high flexibility in the design strategies used by the designers. For instance, a conceptual transformation can be used on a physical schema as well. The TRAMIS model is an extension of the Entity-Relationship model that can express both conceptual and technical structures. Its formalization can be found in [5]; however, we will follow a more intuitive approach in this section.

In addition, the design activities need richer specifications than mere structural description of the data. For instance, statistical information is needed for choosing adequate physical parameters, or for evaluating the volume and the response time of the database. Descriptive textual information and annotations are essential to define the semantics of the data objects, and to document the design process itself.

The *TRAMIS specification model* is made up of six generic objects classified into high-level objects that define macrostructures (schema, entity type, relationship type and space) and the

---

[1] In all generality, the database life-cycle is broader than suggested. For instance, phases such as schema reverse engineering, or schema and data maintenance according to changes in the requirements must be taken into account as well. It has been proved that the paradigms that underly TRAMIS and that are presented is this paper are well suited to support these phases [6].

low-level objects that define microstructures (attribute and group). Some objects (relationship type and group) can be given additional characteristics specifically aimed at describing technical or physical structures.

Schema : represents a description of a data base. Any number of entity types, relationship types and spaces can be associated with a schema. Schemas may be linked to other schemas according to specific relationships : *is the normalized version of, is a view of, is the ORACLE version of, is a space-efficient version of, is integrated into*, etc.

Entity type : represents any information unit that can be perceived or manipulated as a whole, at any level of the design process. It can be used to model both conceptual entities and technical objects (such as record types, tables, segment types, etc).

Relationship type : represents any significant aggregate of at least two entity types. Each position in the aggregate is called a role that is played by one or several entity types. The cardinality constraint of a role is a couple of integers specifying in how many (min-max) relationships an entity must and can play that role (N stands for ∞). It can be used to model both conceptual relationships and technical constructs (such as tuple linkage, CODASYL sets, parent/child relationships, file coupling, etc).

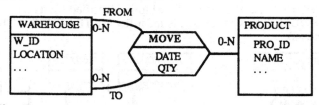

Fig. 5. Example of a relationship type of degree 3 with attributes

At a technical or programming level, a relationship can be perceived not only as a logical association between entities, but also as an access mechanism to navigate through (technical) entities; therefore, a binary relationship type can support zero, one or two *access paths*, each defined from the *origin* role toward the *target* role. This concept can be seen as an abstraction of CODASYL set types, IMS parent/child relationship, TOTAL paths, ADABAS file coupling, etc.

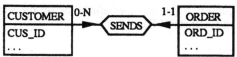

Fig. 6. A relationship type supporting two access paths

Space : is a collection of entities, possibly of different types. At the technical level, a space can model objects such as files, dbspaces, tablespaces, areas and datasets.

Attribute : is associated with a parent object, i.e. an entity type, a relationship type or a compound attribute. An attribute can be atomic or compound. It is qualified by a cardinality constraint expressed as a couple of integers stating how many (min-max) values can and must be associated with the parent object. Any number of attributes (including zero) can be associated with an entity type or a relationship type.

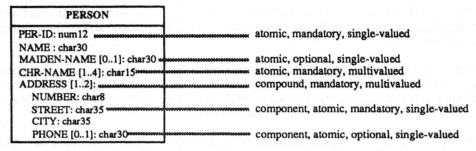

Fig. 7. Various types of attributes

Group : the group is a simple and powerful construct with which one can model entity and relationship identifiers, referential integrity, intra- and inter-entity attribute redundancy, logical access, statistical support, etc. A group is a collection of attributes and/or roles and is associated with an entity type or a relationship type. A group can have some specific functions regarding its parent entity or relationship type :

• it can be an **identifier** (in the example below, an EMPLOYEE is identified by its EMP-ID and its origin SUBSIDIARY, a MOVE relationship is identified by its date and its source and destination WAREHOUSES, a SCHEDULE is identified by TEACHER + TIME values and by TIME + PLACE values). . .

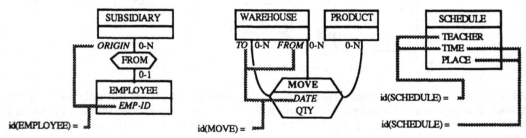

Fig. 8. Representation of identifiers as groups of attributes/roles

• **a reference** (inclusion, equality, copy) to other attributes (in the example below, SUBS-ID + EMPL-ID is a *foreign key* to EMPLOYEE) . . .

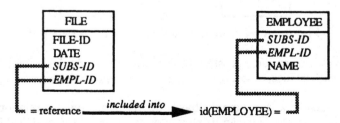

Fig. 9. Representation of an inclusion constraint (here a referential constraint) as the inclusion of a group into another one.

• or, at the technical level, an access mechanism called **access key** (the abstraction of index, calc keys, hash organization, etc). In the example below, FILE-ID is both an identifier and an access key to FILE; DATE and the EMPLOYEE entity it is coming FROM constitute an access key to FILE (i.e. given an EMPLOYEE entity and a DATE value, one can gain a quick and selective access to the concerned FILE entities).

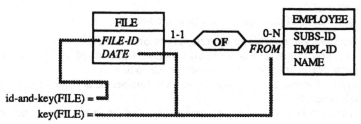

Fig. 10. Representation of an access key as a group of attributes/roles. This example is typical of CODASYL (indexed set types) and IMS structures.

Besides its intrinsic properties, a TRAMIS object can be characterized according to four facets : naming, structural, statistical, informal specification.

The *naming facet* names an object with up to four names[1].
- the *natural name* : the name that was first given when the object was defined;
- the *short name* : an abbreviated name for the object; can be used to build default names in some transformations;
- the *origin* : the natural name of the object from which the current object is derived;
- the *technical name* : a synonym that satisfies DBMS or programming language naming syntax and that will be used to generate executable descriptions (DDL schema); by default, the technical name is the natural name.

The *structural facet* defines the relationships between an object and its neighbor objects.
- a *schema* : comprises entity types and relationship types; is linked to other schemas;
- *entity type* : is in a schema, plays roles in relationship types, has attributes, has groups, is in spaces;
- a *relationship type* : is in a schema, has roles, has attributes, has groups;
- a *role* : is defined in a relationship type, is played by entity types, is in groups;
- an *attribute* : is attached to an entity or relationship type, is in a group;
- a *group* : comprises attributes and/or roles; is attached to an entity/relationship type; is linked with another group (included into, equals, copy of);
- a *space* : contains entity types.

The *statistical facet* defines static and dynamic quantification of the data.

Static statistics :
- entity type : average population size (N in schema 11);
- relationship type : average population size (derived: = μ of a role x N of its entity type));

---

[1] The notion of synonyms for a concept is considered another way. Indeed, when a problem is reasonably formalized, a consistent set of names is associated with a collection of objects in a given context, such as in a service. Therefore, it is better to represent the context in which a name is given to an object, rather than all the names under which this object is known. We have chosen to represent a context by a view, which in turn is represented by a schema. So, an object can have an arbitrary number of names, but each of them is defined in one of the contexts in which it is known, i.e. in a schema that includes this object.

- attribute : average length (μL), average number of values per entity/relationship (μN);
- role : average number of times an entity plays that role (μ);
- group : average number of distinct values (N), average number of entities with which a group value is associated (μ);
- space : average number of entities of each type it contains.

Dynamic statistics (average number of operations per time unit) :
- entity type : creation (add), deletion (delete), update (update) of entities; average number of sequential accesses (x average number of entities for each access);
- relationship type : for each access path, average number of accesses (x average number of entities for each access);
- group (with role *access key*): average number of accesses (x average number of entities for each access);

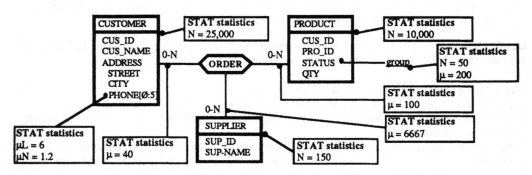

Fig. 11. Example of static statistics

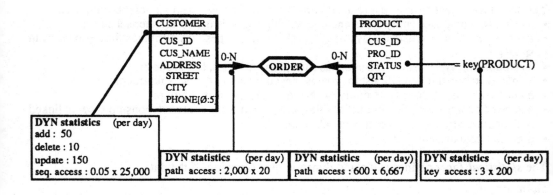

Fig. 12. Example of dynamic statistics

Through the *informal specification facet* textual information is added to objects.
- *Description* : gives an object its *interpretation* according to the real world concepts it denotes. This description gives the semantics of the object.
- *Technical notes* : annotation that gives justification concerning design choices or gives the future programmers and administrators useful informations and advices to maintain integrity of the DB. It is managed by both the designer and TRAMIS. Generally concerns lower-level schemas.

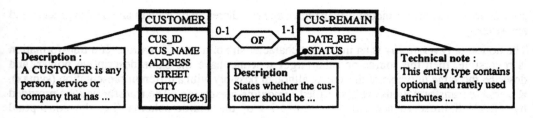

Fig. 13. Example of informal specifications of objects

The generic specification model of TRAMIS can be **specialized** into a great variety of **submodels**, for instance according to the design levels or design product classes of a standard or user-defined multilevel design method, or according to the target DBMS. The following schemas are typical examples of a consistent set of specification models describing standard design products. Each schema must include all the specifications of the previous one (i.e. the information must be either the same, or transformed through specification-preserving operations). Such products can be used by strategies such as that of Fig. 22.

- a *conceptual schema* comprises a schema, entity types, relationship types, attributes, identifier groups, static statistics.
- In an *interpreted conceptual schema* all objects have been given a semantic textual description;
- a *quantified conceptual schema* is a conceptual schema with static statistics;
- a *logical access schema* is a binary schema in which the logical access constructs (access key groups and access paths) needed by the applications have been defined;
- a *quantified access schema* is a logical access schema with dynamic statistics;
- an *optimized access schema* is a logical access schema in which performance-oriented transformations have been carried out (and justified in a technical note);
- a *DBMS-compliant schema* is a logical access schema that has been transformed in order to make it compliant with the specific model of a DBMS.

Specializing the generic model into a specific submodel can be done by the set of rules the schema must satisfy. These rules formalize a specific category of requirements as defined in 3.3.

Example : an ORACLE-compliant schema is a TRAMIS schema in which,

- there are no relationship types;
- there is from one to 254 attributes per entity type;
- the attributes are single-valued and atomic;
- a group must be an access key (i.e. an index);
- an entity type cannot be in more than one space.
- a name is made up of 1 to 30 characters, the 1st being a letter, and the other ones being letters, figures, '_', '$' or '#';
- a name cannot belong to the ORACLE reserved-word list ('create', 'index', etc);
- the total length of the attributes that make a group cannot exceed 240 char.

In these constraints an entity type is to be interpreted as a *table*, an attribute as a *column*, a space as an ORACLE *space*.

5. THE TRANSFORMATIONAL APPROACH IN TRAMIS

Specifications transformation is a basic paradigm of recent CASE tools such as KBSA [8]. In this perspective, TRAMIS generalizes the concept of schema transformation by providing a large set of transformations that can be used at any level of the design process. They are in no way goal-oriented (except for model-driven ones), and can therefore be used in any design process and any strategy.

The notion of *reversibility* is an important characteristic of a transformation. If a transformation is reversible, then the source and the target schemas have the same descriptive power, and describe the same universe of discourse, although possibly with a different presentation (syntax). Reversible transformations are also called *semantics-preserving*. The transformations provided by TRAMIS preserve not only the semantics of the source schema (i.e. the conceptual structures), but the other aspects of the specifications as well : technical structures, names, statistical and informal information. For instance, the access structures (access keys and access paths) in S1 are transformed into different, but functionally equivalent access structures in S2; statistics in S1 are recomputed according to the new structures in S2; informal specifications of objects that disappear from S1 are transferred, possibly with some adaptations, to the new objects in S2. TRAMIS transformations are not only semantics-preserving but also *specification-preserving*[1].

5.1 The transformation toolset

TRAMIS proposes a three-level transformation toolset[2] that can be used freely, according to the skill of the user, the desirable efficiency of the executable schema and the time allowed for producing that schema :

- **elementary transformations** : one transformation is applied to one object; with these tools, the user keeps full control on the schema transformation since similar situations can be solved by different transformations; e.g. a multivalued attribute can be transformed in four ways;
  Formally : given construct C in schema S and transformation T, both selected by the user, C is replaced by T(C) if $P_T(C)$.

- **global transformations** : one transformation is applied to all the relevant objects of a schema.
  Formally : given transformation T and a class of constructs CC, both selected by the user, for each C in CC such that $P_T(C)$, replace C by T(C). Examples : replace all one-to-many relationship types by foreign keys + referential constraints; replace all multivalued attributes by entity types + many-to-one relationship types.

- **model-driven transformations** : all the constructs of a schema that do not comply with the rules a given model are transformed; these transformations require virtually no control from the user; the resulting schema is correct, complies with, say, the relational or CODASYL model, but has few refinements as far as efficiency is concerned[3].

---

[1] To be quite precise, all the transformations of TRAMIS are specification-preserving, but some of them are not semantics preserving. For instance, transformation Tr-A3 is specification augmenting, since ordering and identity properties, lacking in the source schema, are given to the instantiated attributes. On the contrary, transformation Tr-A4 is clearly semantics-degrading.

[2] A schema transformation should not be confused with a design process, although the latter is said to *transform* a product into another one. Indeed, a design process that preserves the specifications need not be reversible (an unfortunate fact as far as reverse engineering is concerned). For example, adding an entity type to a schema transforms it into a richer schema that preserves the previous specifications, while the reverse process (deleting the entity type) doesn't preserve the specifications that are in the second schema.

[3] This is the only schema production function that is provided by many current database CASE tools.

This process is based on a complex strategy driven by two sets of requirements, namely compliance to the selected data model, and time efficiency[1]. According to the analysis presented in section 3, problem P1 is solved by rule priority (the rule with the highest priority among those that C violates triggers first), problem P2 is solved by defining a default transformation for each rule (a more sophisticated strategy is planned), problem P3 is solved by discarding the construct and by writing its description as an annotation in the informal specification, problem P4 uses a monotonicity property of some transformations that can be informally interpreted as follows : given a construct C that violates rule r, transformation T such that $\neg$ $P_T(C)$ can be applied provided T(C) "*is a less difficult problem according to r*" or T(C) induces "*a less severe violation of r*" or T(C) is "*closer to a satisfying construct than C*"[2]. Problem P5 is solved by adhoc ordering of rules to be checked.

Here follows a list of some **elementary transformations** proposed by TRAMIS. For conciseness, only conceptual structure transformations will be considered and given a short explanation; the transformation of the other facets will be evoked later. A formal description and the proof of the reversibility of most transformations that introduce/remove an entity type (TR-E1, TR-E2, TR-R1, TR-A1, TR-A2) can be found in [7].

5.2 Transformation of entity types

- Tr-E1 : Decomposes an entity type E into two entity types E1 and E2, and distributes the attributes, the roles and the groups of E among E1 and E2.
- Tr-E2 : Integrates an entity type E2 into an entity type E1. Reverse of Tr-E1.

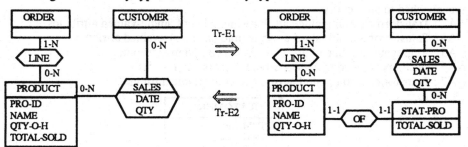

Fig. 14. Decomposition of PRODUCT into two entity types by extracting one attribute and a role.

5.3 Transformation of relationship types

- Tr-R1 : Replaces a relationship type R with an entity type and as many one-to-many relationship types as R had roles.
- Tr-R2 : Replaces a one-to-many relationship type R between E1 and E2 by attributes of E2 that are a copy of the identifying attributes of E1 + referential integrity constraint.

---

[1] In the current version, the efficiency requirements are satisfied by very simple rules. More advanced optimisation rules will be used in the future. The rationale is that, at least at present time, high efficiency can mainly be ensured by human expertise.

[2] This concept depends on the set of transformation that is available. For instance, according to the transformations set that has been chosen in TRAMIS, a one-to-many relationship type is not as far from relational structures as a many-to-many relationship type is. Another approach to this problem could have been to define new transformations as the composition of simpler ones [12].

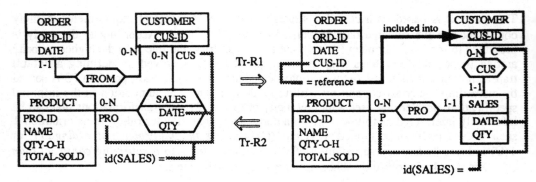

Fig. 15. Transformation of relationship type FROM into reference attributes (foreign key), and transformation of relationship type SALES into an entity type.

5.4 Transformation of attributes

- Tr-A1 : Transforms an attribute A of entity type E into an entity type EA and a many-to-many relationship type RA between E and EA. Each EA entity represents a distinct value of A.
- Tr-A2 : Transforms an attribute A of entity type E into an entity type EA and a one-to-many relationship type RA between E and EA. Each EA entity represents an occurrence of an A value attached to an E entity.
- Tr-A3 : Transforms a multivalued attribute into a list of single-valued attributes.
- Tr-A4 : Transforms a multivalued attribute into one single-valued attribute.
- Tr-A5 : Aggregates a group of attributes into a compound attribute.
- Tr-A6 : Decomposes a compound attribute. Reverse of Tr-A5.
- Tr-A7 : Transforms a compound attribute into an atomic attribute.

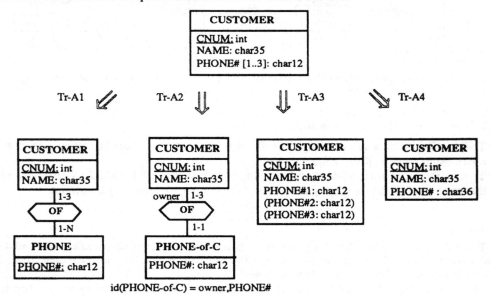

Fig. 16. Four possible transformations to get rid of a multivalued attribute.

5.5 Transformation of groups

- Tr-G1 : Separates two overlapping groups by duplicating common attributes (e.g. for COBOL data structures).
- Tr-G2 : Replaces a role component by the identifier of the entity type playing that role (e.g. for CODASYL schemas as in the schema below).
- Tr-G3 : Adds a singular relationship type role to a group (e.g. for CODASYL schemas).

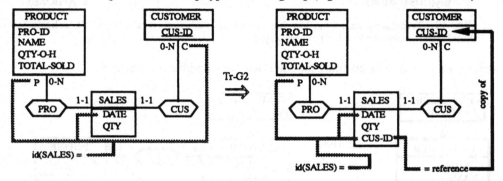

Fig. 17. Replacing role C in the identier of SALES by the identifier of CUSTOMER (the CODASYL data model doesn't accept more than one role in a unique constraint).

5.6 Transformation of names

- Tr-N1 : Substring substitution.
- Tr-N2 : Name prefixing.

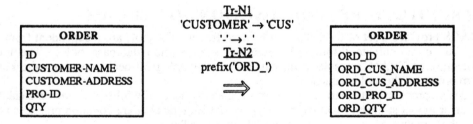

Fig. 18. Translation and prefixing operations.

5.7 *Transformation of the non-conceptual facets*

As already specified, the transformations concern all facets of the objects. For instance, transformation Tr-A1 processes the access structures ...

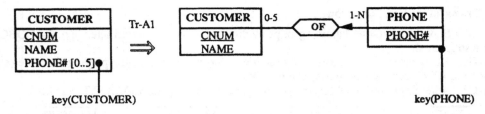

Fig. 19. Translating an access key into an access path (e.g. in a CODASYL schema that doesn't accept multivalued access keys).

as well as the statistical facets (only the static statistics are illustrated below), ...

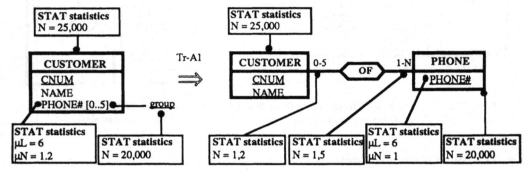

Fig. 20. Conversion of static statistics in a structural transformation.

6. ARCHITECTURE AND FUNCTIONS OF TRAMIS

TRAMIS provides a set of tools that can be used freely. The tools are independent from each other and communicate through the common specification database only. The toolset architecture of TRAMIS results primarily from methodological decisions about the kind of design processes the tool is aimed at.

- A design process, particularly in software engineering, generally follows an incremental, trial-&-error global strategy, in which prototyping and backtracking are common practices and in which more than one activity can be carried out in parallel;
- Both skilled and novice (or hurried) designers must find their way easily. In other terms, some users need fine-tuning tools on which they have full control, while other users need simple and automated tools for quick production of executable descriptions.
- Database schema specifications can be evaluated and processed even if they are incomplete and non consistent. Therefore, the tools must be *robust*.
- If the conceptual design step is recognized as a major activity, the technical design step must also receive sufficient attention. In most case, an automatic translation of the conceptual schema into a DBMS-DDL produces no more than an incomplete, prototype, database schema that must be further processed by hand. A database CASE tool must provide its users with a large set of tools for the evaluation and production of efficient executable solutions.
- The behaviour of the tool, and more specifically the specification model and the user interface, must be non-obtrusive for the different classes of users. The user must not be aware of concepts and tools he wants to ignore.

The toolkit organization of TRAMIS, together with the three-level architecture of the transformation toolset, provides an adequate basis for such a flexible database design approach.

TRAMIS is organized as an extensible collection of toolsets working on a common specification database (or repository). The specification database contains the current state of the project database schemas under development. The toolsets are accessed through a common dialog manager providing a WIMP-based user-interface.

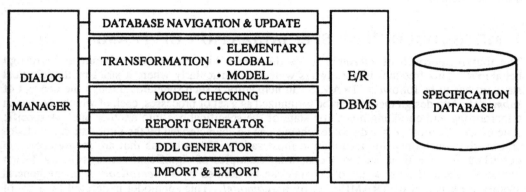

Fig. 21. Gross architecture of the TRAMIS CASE tool.

NAVIGATION and UPDATE : allows the browsing of the current state of the specification database, object selection by name or in a list of objects and the navigation from object to associated objects. Allows the consultation and updating of the different facets of the current object, together with the creation and deletion of objects.

SCHEMA TRANSFORMATION : allows the application of one elementary transformation on the current object, the application of one transformation on all the objects of the schema, and the application of all the necessary transformations on the objects of the schema in order to transform it into a new schema that complies with a selected model. All the facets of the transformed objects are recomputed in order to preserve their information contents (a typical elementary transformation requires from 10 to more than 100 elementary updates, a performance that cannot be done by hand).

MODEL CHECKING : at any moment, the user can validate its specifications against a selected submodel. TRAMIS compiles the rules defining the submodel and analyzes the current specifications according to these rules. TRAMIS generates diagnostics that will be examined by the user. A submodel is defined in an ASCII text consisting of a list of statements expressed in a specific rule language. The user can build any number of submodels. TRAMIS includes four predefined, general-purpose submodels (standard E/R, relational, CODASYL, COBOL files).

REPORT GENERATION : production of a detailed report , for all objects or for one object, a statistical report (with volumes and operations), a dictionary report (concise structured list of object names with *natural/technical* names translation or conversely).

DDL GENERATION : translation of a TRAMIS schema into executable descriptions according to a selected DBMS. The generation is twofold : production of a **DDL text** and generation of **an additional document** that reports all the integrity constraints that have not been translated in the DDL text together with validation procedures for these constraints. This report, aimed at the programmer and the DBA, includes the technical notes as well.

IMPORT / EXPORT : TRAMIS has been given an external specification language (Information System Specification Language, or ISL) in which any specification can be expressed. This language allows communication between tools, selective backup or even data input. Through the *export function*, a selected part (what objects and what facets) of the specification database contents can be generated in ISL. Through the import function, the contents of an ISL text can be integrated to the specification database. This function allows an incremental integration of different schemata.

7. METHODOLOGICAL SPECIALIZATION OF TRAMIS

The toolkit approach of TRAMIS gives the user a high degree of freedom in its design behaviour. This freedom is not always welcome, particularly where a strict methodological standard has to be followed. TRAMIS can help enforce such standards through the concept of *submodel*. Any design method can be formalized as a set of processes, each of which consists in transforming and enriching a specific state of the specifications into another one. A specific state of specifications, e.g. a database schema, can be characterized by the information it includes and by the constraints this information must satisfy. The schemas that are mentionned and described at the end of section 4 constitute examples of significant states in many design methods. Each of these kinds of schema can be defined by a *specialization* of the general specification model of TRAMIS, i.e. by a *submodel*. This submodel is defined by a set of restricting rules stating whether an arbitrary schema satisfies the submodel. Some general-purpose submodels are already built in TRAMIS : standard E/R, relational, CODASYL and standard file structures. More specific models are also proposed for actual DBMS (ORACLE, RDB, IDS-2, etc). However, TRAMIS provides the user with a **rule language** with which he can define his own submodels. In addition, the **model checking** function of TRAMIS can evaluate the current state of the specifications under development against a chosen set of rules, i.e. according to a given submodel, and reports all the violations[1].

It is therefore easy to implement a specific design method as follows :
• identify the main design processes;
• identify and define precisely the products, i.e. the specification states that are inputs and outputs for these processes;
• define these states by compliance with a submodel of TRAMIS and implement this submodel as a set of rules.
• each design process can be considered complete when its resulting schema satisfies the submodel concerned .

The following schema illustrates two typical design methods (processes and products) that can be implemented into TRAMIS through the definition of adhoc submodels. The left-hand approach defines a simple, three-phase process, particularly suited for prototyping. The right-hand approach proposes a detailed methodology for optimized schema production.

---

[1] In the current state of TRAMIS, the role of a submodel is basically passive. Indeed, the whole generic model is available to the users. The latter can only ask the tool to evaluate the current specifications against a selected submodel. An active role would be as follows : at any time, a submodel is current; all the operations on the specifications are monitored by the rules of the model. For instance, a submodel that defines the Bachman's model (Data Structure Diagrams) would prevent users from defining relationship types with a degree greater than two. Such a behaviour will not go without problems, since changing the current model (for example shifting from E-R to Bachman, or to SQL) would make the current state of the specifications partly invalid.

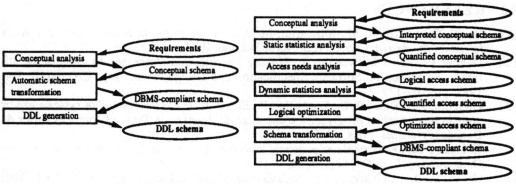

Fig. 22. Two typical strategies for database design.

8. CONCLUSIONS

TRAMIS is a database CASE tool that has been designed with two important hypotheses in mind. The first hypothesis is that designing a complex system can be perceived as carrying out design processes that produce design products from other design products, in such a way that the former satisfy requirements the latter don't satisfy. A tool must accept a great variety of design behaviour, and therefore, must support several standard or non-standard design strategies. The second hypothesis is that schema transformation is a major tool for database design, and that is can be the basis of many design processes. For instance, database schema design can be seen as a step-by-step transformation of some initial version of the conceptual schema.

These principles have lead to four important architectural decisions : the unique specification model whatever the design level, a toolset interface that includes transformational functions, and a facility for fefining design product classes through submodels. Indeed, the flexibility that must be provided to ensure maximum freedom in design processes and strategies makes it impossible to define a fixed set of models and standard design methods.

However, the two basic hypothesis have not been fully applied yet. Indeed, many design processes and strategies must be carried out by the designer himself, since the tool automates mainly low-level processes and strategies. The most complex process offered by TRAMIS is the automatic production of DBMS-compliant schemas. Beyond this function, defining and conducting sophisticated processes and strategies is up to the user, mainly helped by the submodel definition and the model checking function.

On the other hand, several additional schema transformations should be included in order to allow more sophisticated schema restructuring techniques. In particular, operators for manipulating generalization/specialization constructs, additional redundancy and denormalization transformations, and new reverse engineering transformations should be added.

TRAMIS has been developed by the University of Namur both as an educational tool and, later, as a component of an industrial design environment. It is written in C for MS-Windows workstations. A commercial version of TRAMIS is available under the name TRAMIS/Master[1]. It is complemented with TRAMIS/View, a graphical editor and integrator for MERISE-like database descriptions, and with TRAMIS/Flow, allowing the definition of data-flow diagrams.

---

[1] Distributed by CONCIS, 37bis, rue du Prébuard, 95100 Argenteuil, France.

10. REFERENCES

[1] Batini, C., Lenzerini, M., Moscarini, M., *View integration, in Methodology and tools for data base design*, Ceri, S., (Ed.)North-Holland, 1983

[2] Dubois, E., Van Lamsweerde, A., *Making Specification Processes*, in Proc. of the 4th Intern. Workshop on Software Specification and Design, Monterrey (CA), April, 3-4, 1987, pp. 169-177

[3] Giraudin, J-P., Delobel, C., Dardailler, P., *Eléments de construction d'un système expert pour la modélisation progressive d'une base de données*, in Proc. of Journées Bases de Données Avancées, Mars, 1985

[4] Hainaut, J-L., *Theoretical and practical tools for data base design*, in Proc. of Very Large Databases, pp. 216-224, September, 1981

[5] Hainaut, J.-L., *A Generic Entity-Relationship Model*, in Proc. of the IFIP WG 8.1 Conf. on *Information System Concepts: an in-depth analysis*, North-Holland, 1989.

[6] Hainaut, J-L, *Database Reverse Engineering, Models, Techniques and Strategies*, in Proc. of the 10th Conf. on Entity-Relationship Approach, San Mateo, 1991

[7] Hainaut, J-L., *Entity-generating Schema Transformation for Entity-Relationship Models*, in Proc. of the 10th Conf. on Entity-Relationship Approach, San Mateo, 1991

[8] Johnson,W., L., Cohen, D., Feather, M., Kogan, D., Myers, J., Yue, K., Balzer, R., *The Knowledge-Based Spesification Assistant*, Final Report, UCS/Information Sciences Institute, Marina del Tey, 19 Sept. 1988

[9] Kobayashi, I., *Losslessness and Semantic Correctness of Database Schema Transformation : another look of Schema Equivalence*, in Information Systems, Vol. 11, No 1, pp. 41-59, January, 1986

[10] Krieg-Brückner, B., *Algebraic Specification and Functionals for Transformational Program and Meta Program Development*, in Proc. of the TAPSOFT Conf. LNCS 352, Springer-Verlag, 1989

[11] Kozaczynsky, Lilien, *An extended Entity-Relationship (E2R) database specification and its automatic verification and transformation*, in Proc. of Entity-Relationship Approach, 1987

[12] Partsch, H., Steinbrüggen, R., *Program Transformation Systems*, Computing Surveys, Vol. 15, No. 3, 1983

[13] Reiner, D., Brown, G., Friedell, M., Lehman, J., McKee, R., Rheingans, P., Rosenthal, A., *A Database Designer's Worbench*, in Proc. of Entity-Relationship Approach, 1986

[14] Rosenthal, A., Reiner, D., *Theoretically sound transformations for practical database design*, in Proc. of Entity-Relationship Approach, 1988

[15] Teorey, T. J., *Database design*, Prentice-Hall, 1989

[16] Tardieu, H., Rochfeld, Coletti, *La méthode Merise*, Les Editions d'Organisation, 1983

The Synthesis of Knowledge Engineering and Software Engineering

Mildred L G Shaw & Brian R Gaines

Knowledge Science Institute
University of Calgary
Calgary, Alberta, Canada T2N 1N4.

Abstract: The term 'knowledge engineering' was coined in the 1980s to reference the processes whereby knowledge was elicited from human experts in order to develop knowledge-based systems. It was seen as reflecting an alternative paradigm for system engineering in which, for systems which were difficult to analyze in themselves but were subject to human activities, one modeled the human operators' skills rather than the system itself. In the 1980s, expert systems development appeared radically different from conventional systems development, but in the 1990s it is time to re-evaluate the reality and significance of the differences. The growth of expert systems development coincided with that of high-performance workstations, improvements in the efficiency of symbolic programming languages, and the development of graphic user interfaces. Much of what has been attributed to 'expert systems' may be seen as a halo effect of these other technologies. More fundamentally, the knowledge acquisition community has moved from an 'expertise transfer' to a 'knowledge modeling' perspective, in which knowledge is seen as not so much transferred from the expert as built in conjunction with the expert as a means of emulating his or her skill. This paper develops a modeling framework for systems engineering that encompasses systems modeling, task modeling, and knowledge modeling, and allows knowledge engineering and software engineering to be seen as part of a unified developmental process. This framework is used to evaluate what novel contributions the 'knowledge engineering' paradigm has made, and how these impact software engineering.

1 Introduction

Expert systems were seen originally as a development arising out of artificial intelligence research that offered new possibilities for implementing intelligent, knowledge-based systems emulating human expertise. They are still presented as a new information technology that has a major economic role to play in industrial organizations (Feigenbaum, McCorduck and Nii 1988). However, a major market place for expert system shells has not materialized, several of the companies offering specialist platforms and tools have ceased to operate, attendance at artificial intelligence and expert systems conferences is declining, and the number of expert system products is decreasing. In addition, deeply reasoned books have appeared arguing that there are significant aspects of human expertise that cannot be emulated by computers (Dreyfus and Dreyfus 1986). What is happening? Have expert systems been a dead-end in the evolution of information systems? Is the expert systems paradigm of any long-term significance?

This paper provides a framework for knowledge engineering and software engineering that views them as components of an overall systems engineering methodology for information systems development. Knowledge engineering for expert system development is shown to involve a definite paradigm shift, but one that has become embedded in many other trends in the 1980s that are part of the evolution of information systems in general rather than expert systems in particular. Our overall answer to the questions above is that the experience gained and techniques created in developing expert systems is becoming absorbed into modern information systems design, and that the term 'knowledge-based system' is not the name of a new technology but rather an appropriate term for the current and coming states of modern advanced information systems.

2 The Expert Systems Paradigm

What was presented originally as the distinguishing feature of expert systems is that they model the expertise of human experts as practical reasoners achieving objectives by actions in some domain. This can be seen as a significant alternative paradigm for system development when, for some reason, a usable model of the domain is not available (Gaines and Shaw 1985). We can then model the control strategy of the human expert.

Figure 1 illustrates this in more detail. The classical approach in decision and control system design is the instrumentation, data collection, modeling and optimization sequence shown on the left:

• Knowledge of past case histories is used to select a class of system models
• The information required to discriminate within this class determines how the system should be instrumented for data acquisition
• Data is collected from the system through the instrumentation
• A model is identified from the model class which best fits the data
• This model is used to design a decision or control system for optimal performance

This approach to system design underlies the methodologies of the physical sciences and technologies based on them. It has the merit that it has been extremely successful in engineering much of the technological infrastructure of our current society including our manufacturing industries. However, this approach is successful only to the extent that the systems under consideration are amenable to instrumentation and modeling. Its greatest successes have been where this amenability can be achieved normatively, that is in cases where the system to be controlled is itself a human artifact.

The expert systems paradigm may be seen to be particularly applicable when it is not possible to model the system but there is an alternative source of data available because human operators are able to performance the decision or control task. The right hand column shows the use of knowledge sources in the expert system design paradigm:

• Structured interviewing may be used to acquire knowledge directly from the operators
• Behavior modeling may be used to identify the operators' strategies even if they are unaware of them or give incorrect ones in interviews
• Text analysis may be used with instructional material such as the operators' manuals
• Reasoning by analogy may be used based on the case histories without the data collection of the classical system design paradigm

Note that the classical and expert system design paradigms, and the various acquisition techniques for expert systems, need not be regarded as competitive. They may all be used in the system design, and it may be that a collection of heterogeneous subsystems is necessary because there is no overall algorithm that can be applied.

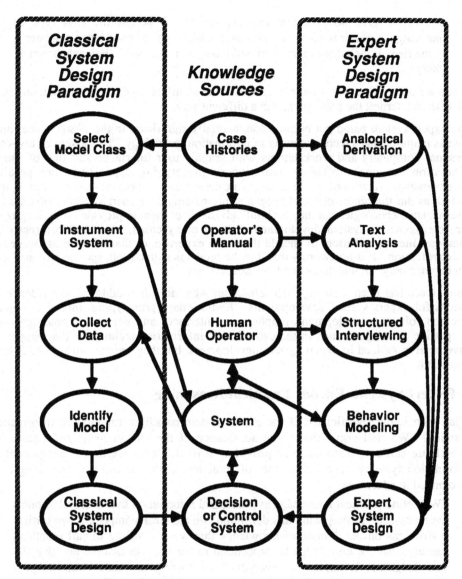

Fig.1. Classical and expert system design paradigms

There has been a tendency in recent literature to downplay the human expert as a source of knowledge for expert system design. The use of expert system shells for incremental system development, and the use of the shells themselves as rapid prototyping tools are seen as equally important:

"Currently there appear to be two types of knowledge engineers. The first type designs and implements reasoning systems that closely mimic the cognitive behavior of the experts. The second, new class of knowledge engineers organizes and encodes knowledge in forms dictated by expert system shells. They generally no not have an academic background in artificial intelligence;

they often have no programming experience. Whereas the first type of knowledge engineer is not very common, the latter type of knowledge engineer is on the rise. It includes experts who build their own systems." (Feigenbaum et al. 1988)

While we do not disagree with this remark or the significance of the phenomenon cited, we wish to interpret the phenomenon in a different way.

The expert system paradigm became commercially significant in the 1980s at the same time as major changes were occurring in information technology. The advent of low-cost personal computers and workstations with graphic user interfaces and that of fourth generation languages offering evolutionary prototyping capabilities are parallel developments. Networked access to corporate databases also became common during this period, as did the object-oriented programming paradigm. Expert system shells did not invent such technologies but they took full advantage of them to provide visual languages for heterogeneous system development that, in many cases, were usable directly by computer literate end-users to encode their own expertise, or that of close associates in their profession. It is noteworthy that it is the products with closed, specialized 'artificial intelligence only' architectures that have not survived.

Thus, there has been a strong 'halo effect' in what are often adduced as evidence of successful expert system developments. Evolutionary prototyping, modular, object-oriented software development, graphic user interfaces and networked heterogeneous integration are major trends in the evolution of information technology that happen to have been mobilized in expert system development, but they are not intrinsic to it, or a result of it.

3 Expert Systems Encode Practical Reasoning

What then is the significance of the expert system paradigm for modern information systems? We will argue that it the acceptance of the human *practical reasoning* underlying skilled performance as providing a model for a legitimate component of information systems. The significance of "practical modes of knowing" has long been recognized in education:

"We define practical knowledge as procedural information that is useful in one's everyday life. In proposing this definition, we are clearly imposing two critical restrictions on the domain of knowledge that we are willing to call practical, namely, that the knowledge be procedural rather than declarative and that the knowledge be relevant to one's everyday life. We require practical knowledge to be procedural because of our view that practical knowledge is of and for use. We view practical knowledge as stored in the form of productions, or condition-action sequences that implement actions when certain preconditions are met." (Sternberg and Caruso 1985)

The spirit of what is being said exactly captures that of the origins of expert system development. We go to experts when we do not have overt domain and problem solving models, precisely because they are the relevant practical reasoners in the domain, using their practical knowledge as part of their everyday professional life to achieve the practical objectives of interest in system development.

The emphasis of practicality is a classification of the mode of reasoning involved, not the domain. A skilled mathematician is a problem solver in a domain that may be highly theoretical but where his or her problem-solving skills are examples of the practical reasoning described above. The mathematician's everyday life as a mathematician is lived in the world of mathematics and he or she develops skilled behavior to navigate and manipulate that world. Even though we may have highly overt models of the domain they do not automatically provide us with overt knowledge of the practical problem-solving skills in that domain.

The reason why a deep model may be of little use in some domains is that restricted information flows about a particular situation may make it difficult to estimate the parameters required to use a deep model effectively. In such situations two types of practical knowledge arise: the first associated with avoiding catastrophic states such as those that prevent the goals being achieved; and the other with increasing the chances of the goals being achieved through actions that, due to uncertainties, may not be successful. Such knowledge tends to appear as a set of isolated and discontinuous condition-action rules that have little overall coherence in themselves, although they will be consistent with more coherent overall models of the domain.

It is interesting historically that further rationalizations of production rules were proposed other than that they are a natural effective representation of skilled behavior. Production rules were promoted as offering the advantage over normal programming that they were modular and hence more easily developed and modified. The fact that quite the contrary is true seems to have taken a long time to disseminate—papers are still appearing warning of the software engineering problems of system development based on production rules (Li 1991).

The expert systems paradigm is not to be preferred to classical system design in general. It is a price we have to pay when more principled design based on deep knowledge is not possible. Thus, we should not use it unnecessarily. It is to be expected as the expert systems approach becomes better integrated with conventional system development that major components of the 'knowledge base' become based on structured models rather than unstructured production rules. However, we should not assume that this will be universally possible.

4 Processes in Knowledge Engineering

What these arguments suggest is that we need an overall framework for advanced information system development that provides for the different roles of different approaches, and their integration, and shows the relation between knowledge engineering and software engineering. This is developed in the following section. We first examine knowledge engineering processes from a modeling perspective.

In the knowledge acquisition community the development of tools for eliciting knowledge from experts has come to be seen as a 'knowledge modeling' exercise in which human practical knowledge is modeled within the computer (Gaines, Shaw and Woodward 1992). It has been suggested that a common factor underlying all expert systems is that they contain qualitative world models, and that we can gain insights into the structure of knowledge bases and knowledge engineering by classifying the types of models involved

(Clancey 1989). These considerations suggest that a classification of the sources and types of models developed in system engineering may be used to provide a framework within which knowledge engineering and software engineering methodologies and tools can be analyzed and compared.

One might view the replication of human expertise in a knowledge-based system as involving the elicitation of the *mental models* of the human experts involved (Gentner and Stevens 1983). However, we do not have direct access to these models, and must create *conceptual models* of them through communication with the expert (Norman 1983). The representations made by the knowledge engineer are not isomorphic to structures in the mind of the expert (Compton and Jansen 1990). Within this framework, one can view knowledge engineers, or automated knowledge acquisition systems interacting with the expert, as accessing and developing the expert's conceptual models. Some parts of these models may be pre-existent, particularly if the expert has a teaching role, but other parts will come into being as a result of the knowledge acquisition process.

The distinction that Norman introduces between mental models and conceptual models, and the dubious status of mental models in themselves, suggests that a useful framework for the analysis of knowledge engineering may be developed through the analysis of the sources and types of conceptual model available to the knowledge engineer rather than focusing only on the mental processes underlying expertise. The situation of the introspective expert who can communicate his or her 'knowledge' well, may be treated as one where the 'knowledge engineering' and 'expert' roles are operating effectively together within the same person. The situation of the expert from whom knowledge is being 'elicited' actually building a new model on the basis of his or her skills through the process of elicitation may be treated as one where the conceptual model is developed as part of the process of knowledge engineering. In adopting the conceptual modeling perspective we do not exclude previous viewpoints, but rather supplement them with complementary perspectives.

In the early days of expert systems development, it was assumed that the direct communication of knowledge between expert and knowledge engineer was the preferred method. A classic experiment, showed that this was not necessarily so and inductive behavior modeling, in which the expert is observed in action and his or her activities modeled, may lead to a better knowledge-based system (Michalski and Chilausky 1980). This is an example of the expert systems paradigm above, of modeling the expert as opposed to modeling the system. However, it is rarely a purely behavioral paradigm since the knowledge engineer may not be able to discriminate the inputs that the expert is using and will normally rely on verbal reporting by the expert for a description of the inputs and outputs.

It is customary in expert system development, to assume that the expert has already constructed such models or may be in a privileged position to do so through self-observation and introspection, and these may be elicited by direct communication between knowledge engineer and expert. Additionally, the knowledge engineer may derive models from other experts, from the literature, and from the application of principles allowing performance skills to be derived from deep knowledge. The final knowledge-based system development involves the synthesis of these many models and the encoding of them to become an operational knowledge-based systems emulating the desired expertise.

Thus, the knowledge engineer, or knowledge engineering team and tools, has access to multiple sources of data through various channels and uses these to develop a variety of conceptual models. Figure 2 shows the major conceptual models that may be developed in knowledge engineering, distinguished by their sources, and indicating some of the knowledge engineering processes and skills involved. This figure attempts to be comprehensive, showing knowledge sources not only in association with the expert and his or her behavior, but also knowledge derived from others, the literature and through the application of laws and principles.

Figure 2 is an accurate representation of what is typically involved in knowledge engineering for a knowledge based system development nowadays. It uses any source of knowledge that is available for system development, not just the practical reasoning of the expert, and hence exemplifies the "second type" of knowledge engineering cited above (Feigenbaum et al. 1988). However, it still has a major, and irreducible component of the first type representing the central expert systems paradigm. What is significant is the way in which the two approaches are synthesized, and also the way in which many components of the "second type" of activity are already part of modern systems and software engineering. This is the basis of a much wider synthesis than that between two forms of knowledge engineering.

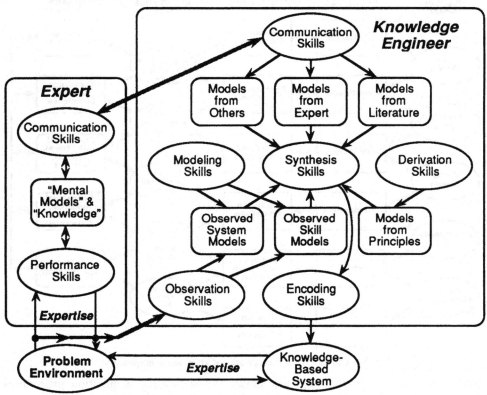

Fig. 2. Modeling processes in knowledge engineering

5 A Modeling Framework for Information System Development

The discussion of the preceding sections and the range of modeling processes shown in Figure 2 provide an overall framework for systems engineering in terms of the sources and types of models involved. Within such a framework it should become only a matter of internal classification and terminology that a method is part of a 'knowledge engineering' or a 'software engineering' approach, rather than a resultant system classification.

Figure 3 presents a modeling framework for knowledge acquisition methodologies, techniques and tools based on the distinctions already discussed and the incorporation of system analysis and software engineering procedures. In the leftmost column are the knowledge sources in terms of systems and modeling schema already discussed with the addition, at the top, of 'objective models' as a term for the formally specified operational models. In the column to the right of this are the processes giving access to these models. These processes are shown as mediating between the systems and models involved, deriving from and generating, the hierarchical relation between the systems and models in the leftmost column.

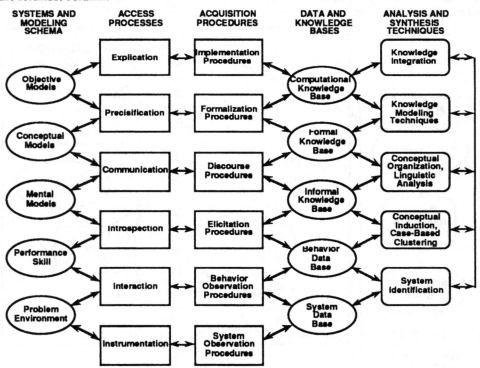

Fig. 3. A hierarchical framework for knowledge acquisition

In the next column on the right are shown the knowledge acquisition procedures appropriate to each of the access processes. These generate data and knowledge bases as shown to their right, which are in one-to-one correspondence with the original systems and models in the leftmost column. In the rightmost column are shown analysis and synthesis techniques that draw on these databases to generate the computational knowledge base, and also mediate between them generating one form of data or knowledge from another. These combine with synthesis techniques that integrate the results of analysis and of derivations from various knowledge sources to synthesize a computational knowledge base.

Thus the overall schema consists of five types of component:

1. *Systems and modeling schema*: the problem environment, performance skill to be emulated, expert's mental models, knowledge engineer's conceptual models, and, possibly, objective models.

2. *Access processes:* instrumentation of the target system, the expert's interaction with it, his or her introspection about the skill, communication about it, and its expression in formal terms as objective knowledge.

3. *Knowledge acquisition procedures*: observation of the target system, observation of the expert's behavior, elicitation procedures, discourse procedures, formalization procedures, and implementation procedures.

4. *Data and knowledge bases:* database of system data; database of behavioral data; informal knowledge base; formal knowledge base; computational knowledge base; objective models.

5. *Analysis and synthesis procedures*: classical system identification can be used to build system models from observation data; empirical induction and case-based clustering can be used to build skill models from behavioral data; conceptual organization and linguistic analysis techniques can be used to build a formal, or structured, knowledge base from an informal, or intermediate, one; knowledge modeling techniques can be used to represent the formal knowledge base in computational form; and logical deduction from laws and principles may be used to provide some knowledge about a system and this, together with the results of data analyses from various sources needs to be integrated to form a computational knowledge base.

All the earlier stages of analysis are shown as normally creating data at the next level but also as potentially creating computational systems in their own right.

Figure 3 illustrates the way in which knowledge engineering as a system design methodology is sandwiched between two classical approaches to system engineering. At the bottom of the figure is the path to system design through instrumentation, data collection and system identification. At the top of the figure is the path to system design through existing objective knowledge of the physical world allowing explication of particular requirements to lead directly to implementation. The middle layers represent the enrichment of the design process when we draw on human skills as exemplars of the system to be designed. Such a process has been common informally in engineering design, and knowledge engineering may be seen as formalizing it now that computer technology makes it feasible to develop knowledge-based systems operationalizing human expertise.

6 Knowledge Acquisition Issues in Terms of the Framework

This section focuses on some of the major classes of knowledge engineering methods now in use, and discusses them within the framework developed.

It is clear that a catchall term such as 'interviewing' does not designate a monolithic technique in terms of the framework of Figure 3. When we interview an expert we may be operating at any level of the hierarchy and may be supporting any one of the many processes shown. All that we can say about interviewing in general is that a flow of linguistic information is involved—it is the content of that flow that determines the type of knowledge engineering involved. The expert may provide observations of the system, observations of his or her own problem solving behavior, introspection about aspects of his or her mental models, statements about his or her conceptual models of any aspect of the situation, and statements of formal or even computational models relating to the situation.

Specific knowledge acquisition techniques are characterized by their vertical and horizontal locations within the framework. For example, protocol analysis involves data collection for the behavior data base through observation of interaction at one level or elicitation of introspection at the next. The behavior database is then subject to statistical system identification or to conceptual induction and clustering. The data collection methodology in protocol analysis may easily slip into the elicitation of not just a protocol but also an explanatory commentary which belongs in the informal knowledge base and is subject to linguistic analysis. Thus, applications of protocol analysis may involve multiple levels and activities that are confusing unless seen as organized within the framework.

Analytical tools such as induction and clustering algorithms have a well-defined location in the framework as analysis techniques providing a model creation technology. Their differentiation comes from what level, or levels, they can accept data, and at what level, or levels, they create data. A major focus in machine learning research for several years has been to create models at the knowledge level, conceptual structures rather than rules. To the extent that all the analytic techniques involved do this, the problem becomes one of integration of conceptual structures. However, it is more usual to find that the analytic tools create data or knowledge at different levels and further processing is required before integration is possible.

Methodologies such as KADS (Akkermans, Harmelen, Shreiber and Wielinga 1992) that provide a structured software engineering approach to knowledge engineering are focused at the penultimate level of applying formalization procedures to derive a formal knowledge base through making conceptual models precise. KADS focuses on the detailed structure of a formal problem solving architecture within which to operationalize the results of knowledge acquisition rather than on the processes of knowledge acquisition themselves. It may be seen as providing a formally specified 'virtual machine' well-suited to the range of system developments that have come to be classified under the heading of 'knowledge-based systems.' Less formally, one can say that it provides a 'high-level language' in contrast to the 'machine languages' provided by expert system shells.

Knowledge acquisition methodologies such as those stemming from personal construct psychology (Shaw 1980) that are based on a cognitive model of intelligent agents are focused on the middle levels in Figure 3, modeling the way in which mental models mediate between conceptual models and performance skills. Clearly any well-founded cognitive psychology has a potential role to play in knowledge acquisition that is strictly within the 'expert systems' paradigm of modeling the expert rather than the system. However, to be useful the psychology must result in operational models on the one hand and support methodologies giving access to its hidden variables on the other. Personal construct psychology has been particularly attractive in these respects because, even though it is a constructivist model, it takes a positivist, axiomatic approach based on a few well-defined primitives that correspond to a formal intensional logic (Gaines and Shaw

1992), and is well-supported by practical tools (Boose and Bradshaw 1987; Shaw and Gaines 1987; Shaw and Gaines 1989).

The interface between cognition and formalization for people is mediated through language and knowledge acquisition support is required for the communication and discourse procedures and analysis level in Figure 3. Current knowledge acquisition tools addressing this level range from those focusing on the inter-translation of restricted natural language and knowledge representation frames such as SNOWY (Gomez and Segami 1990), to those providing support for human classification of natural language components in terms of knowledge level primitives such as Cognosys (Woodward 1990). Improved natural language processing must have a very high priority in the support of the complete range of knowledge acquisition processes in the framework of Figure 3.

Classical system analysis focuses on the collection and analysis of system and behavior data at the lower levels of Figure 3. In complex system development the other levels play their part, but the basic assumption has been that the final system design is grounded in accurate models of the environment in which the system is to operate and in precise 'requirements specifications' corresponding to the top level goals of the human agents involved. The implementation is quite separate from the system analysis and design because conventional programming languages do not provide knowledge-level constructs supporting human understanding of their operation. In this respect, the framework of Figure 3 may be seen as an extension to classical system analysis appropriate to knowledge-based systems where very high level languages at the 'knowledge level' are being used for the implementation to provide this support of human understanding.

7 Conclusions

A complete account of system engineering acquisition for modern advanced information systems requires the integration of classical system analysis, cognitive modeling of intelligent agents, linguistic analysis of text and discourse, and a rich formal language at the knowledge level. This integration would provide us with a system development methodology adequate to cope with the increased expectations of those specifying requirements for knowledge-based systems.

However, note that the knowledge level language alone is only a target for specification. On the one hand it needs to be made operational as computational knowledge. On the other it needs to maintain an effective ongoing relation with the knowledge processes that drive it, many of which are those of active human agents forming an essential component of the ongoing system operation. Knowledge acquisition should not be seen as part of the system design process only. Knowledge is dynamic and changing, and acquisition, maintenance and upgrading must merge into one process that is fully supported as an ongoing system operation. In particular, the cognitive aspects of much of the knowledge must continue to be recognized and supported in the ongoing system operation. Formalization cannot be at the expense of human understanding. On the contrary, effective formalization should lead to enhanced human understanding. This is the greatest challenge in the development of an effective knowledge-based systems technology. The objective is not just emulation of isolated human peak performance, but rather the emulation of the total human ability to develop, adapt and maintain that performance in a dynamic and uncertain environment.

Acknowledgements

Financial assistance for this work has been made available by the Natural Sciences and Engineering Research Council of Canada. We are particularly grateful to Bill Clancey, Brian Woodward and other colleagues at the Knowledge Acquisition Workshops for discussions and critical comments that have improved the framework presented in this paper.

References

Akkermans, H., Harmelen, F.v., Shreiber, G. and Wielinga, B. (1992). "A formalisation of knowledge-level models for knowledge acquisition." International Journal of Intelligent Systems : to appear.

Boose, J.H. and Bradshaw, J.M. (1987). "Expertise transfer and complex problems: using AQUINAS as a knowledge acquisition workbench for knowledge-based systems." International Journal of Man-Machine Studies 26: 3-28.

Clancey, W.J. (1989). "Viewing knowledge bases as qualitative models." IEEE Expert 4(2): 9-23.

Compton, P. and Jansen, R. (1990). "A philosophical basis for knowledge acquisition." Knowledge Acquisition 2(3): 241-258.

Dreyfus, H.L. and Dreyfus, S.E. (1986). Mind over Machine: The Power of Human Intuition and Expertise in the Era of the Computer. New York, Free Press.

Feigenbaum, E., McCorduck, P. and Nii, H.P. (1988). The Rise of the Expert Company. New York, Times Books.

Gaines, B.R. and Shaw, M.L.G. (1985). "From fuzzy sets to expert systems." Fuzzy Sets and Systems 36(1-2): 5-16.

Gaines, B.R. and Shaw, M.L.G. (1992). "Basing knowledge acquisition tools in personal construct psychology." Knowledge Engineering Review : to appear.

Gaines, B.R., Shaw, M.L.G. and Woodward, J.B. (1992). "Modeling as a framework for knowledge acquisition methodologies and tools." International Journal of Intelligent Systems : to appear.

Gentner, D. and Stevens, A., Ed. (1983). Mental Models. Hillsdale, New Jersey, Erlbaum.

Gomez, F. and Segami, C. (1990). "Knowledge acquisition from natural language for expert systems based on classification problem-solving methods." Knowledge Acquisition 2(2): 107-128.

Li, X. (1991). "What's so bad about rule-based programming?" IEEE Software : 103-105.

Michalski, R.S. and Chilausky, R.L. (1980). "Knowledge acquisition by encoding expert rules versus computer induction from examples—A case study involving soyabean pathology." International Journal of Man-Machine Studies 12: 63-87.

Norman, D.A. (1983). Some observations on mental models. Mental Models. Hillsdale, New Jersey, Erlbaum. 7-14.

Shaw, M.L.G. (1980). On Becoming A Personal Scientist: Interactive Computer Elicitation of Personal Models Of The World. London, Academic Press.

Shaw, M.L.G. and Gaines, B.R. (1987). "KITTEN: Knowledge initiation & transfer tools for experts and novices." International Journal of Man-Machine Studies 27(3): 251-280.

Shaw, M.L.G. and Gaines, B.R. (1989). "A methodology for recognizing conflict, correspondence, consensus and contrast in a knowledge acquisition system." Knowledge Acquisition 1(4): 341-363.

Sternberg, R.J. and Caruso, D.R. (1985). Practical modes of knowing. Learning and Teaching the Ways of Knowing. Chicago, Illinois, University of Chicago Press. 133-158.

Woodward, B. (1990). "Knowledge engineering at the front-end: defining the domain." Knowledge Acquisition 2(1): 73-94.

Reconciling Operational and Declarative Specifications

J. Hagelstein and D. Roelants
{hagelstc,roelants}@sema.be

Sema Group Belgium
5, Place du Champ de Mars
B-1050 Brussels, Belgium

Abstract. There are two broad approaches to the specification of the dynamics of information systems, namely the operational and the declarative one. The declarative approach has advantages in terms of abstractness and of locality of information. Its main drawback is the so called frame problem, i.e. the need to explicitly forbid unwanted changes. We propose an extension of the declarative approach which incorporates some aspects of the operational one, thereby eliminating the frame problem. The technique is illustrated on an example, and the resulting specification is compared with the corresponding operational and declarative ones.

1 Introduction

The requirements engineering of information systems includes an identification of the structure of the relevant information, and of its evolution over time, or dynamics. There are two broad approaches to the description of these dynamics, namely the *operational* one and the *declarative* one, of which the *deductive* approach is a variant.

The declarative, or logic-based, approach uses logical formulas to constrain the evolution of information. It is supported by such languages as CIAM [GKB82], RML [GBM86], Infolog [FS86], or ERAE [Hag88]. This approach generalises the concept of integrity constraint to the temporal dimension: the same language is used to characterise valid states ('all salaries are greater than 5000') as well as valid changes ('salaries may only grow'). This is illustrated below using a function *salary* from types *Person* and *Time* to *Salary*. The logic used is first order logic.

$$salary(Person, Time) : Salary$$

% all salaries are greater than 5000
$$\forall p \, \forall t \, (salary(p,t) > 5000)$$

% salaries may only grow
$$\forall p \, \forall t_1 \, \forall t_2 \, (t_1 > t_2 \Rightarrow salary(p,t_1) \geq salary(p,t_2))$$

This work was partly funded by the Commission of the European Communities under the ESPRIT project ICARUS.

A variant of first order logic called *temporal logic* is used by some authors [Hag88] [DHR90] [FS86] to avoid the explicit reference to time. The formal semantics of temporal logic are recalled in Section 3.1, but their intuitive meaning is the following. Temporal logic formulas are interpreted in sequences of successive states, the valid sequences being those where formulas hold in every state. Most functions and predicates, like *salary*, are state-dependent, i.e. they may have different interpretations in different states. Temporal logic formulas may contain special operators ($\circ$, $\bullet$, $\diamond$, etc) which cause the subsequent sub-formula or term to be evaluated in a different state. For instance, the term '$\bullet \tau$' denotes the value of τ in the previous state. The temporal logic version of the specification above can be written:

$salary(Person) : Salary$

$\forall p\ (salary(p) > 5000)$

$\forall p\ (salary(p) \geq \bullet\ salary(p))$

The effect of an event is among the dynamic constraints that declarative languages can express. An event is modelled by a predicate which holds whenever the event occurs. The example above may be extended to express that an event *promotion* induces a salary increase:

$promotion(Person) : Event$

$\forall p\ (promotion(p) \Rightarrow salary(p) = 1.1\ *\ \bullet\ salary(p))$

The declarative approach has many advantages in terms of abstractness and locality of information [Oli86]. It suffers however from a drawback known as the *frame problem* [Min74]: it is not sufficient to require the needed changes; one must also exclude the undesired ones. The last formula above forces the salary to vary in case of promotion, but does not prevent it to change freely at other moments. To this end, we must add the following formula:

$\forall p\ (salary(p) \neq \bullet\ salary(p) \Rightarrow promotion(p))$

The deductive approach [Oli86] is a variant of the declarative approach which suffers however from the same drawback. It will be discussed in Section 4.

The operational approach controls the evolution of information in a program-like style. Typically, events trigger the execution of routines explicitly modifying the information. This approach avoids the frame problem through the implicit assumption that no change takes place, except if an operation explicitly requires it. However, it suffers from other drawbacks, the first one being a lack of abstractness. A property like 'salaries never decrease' cannot be directly expressed; it can only be deduced from a careful analysis of all routines. Its other weaknesses will be discussed in Section 4.

In face of this situation where the declarative and operational approaches have good qualities and drawbacks, we propose to extend the former in a way that circumvents the frame problem. The suggested technique is introduced in Section 2, and illustrated on a simple language called MINI-FOL. This language is given formal semantics in Section 3. It is compared to the operational, purely declarative, and deductive approaches in Section 4. Further extensions are proposed in the conclusion.

2 The MINI-FOL language

2.1 Active and Reactive Happenings

The difference between the declarative and operational approaches may be synthesised in the following two principles, as far as the specification of dynamics is concerned :

Declarativeness principle : any change is allowed, except those forbidden by the specification.

Operationality principle : any change is forbidden, except those imposed by the specification.

When specifying an information system, one seems to need the two principles in turn. There are indeed two categories of happenings that the specification is concerned with : the *active* ones and the *reactive* ones.

- An active happening is one that the planned information system will not control, typically an action of the user. Some authors call these happenings *external events*. The specification can express hypotheses that limit their occurrences, but it cannot force them to happen. The declarativeness principle suits their description optimally.

- A reactive happening is one that the information system will control. It happens in reaction (hence 'reactive') to an active happening and should only take place if requested. The specification will impose its occurrence in strictly limited circumstances. The operationality principle is better suited to describe this second category of phenomena.

As an example, consider an information system maintaining information about projects, and departments responsible for them. The start of a project in a department, and the end of a project are active events. The specification may not force them to happen; it may just prevent them from happening in certain circumstances. The record of which projects are running at any moment is reactive. The specification will force it to change when start or end events occur.

2.2 Description of MINI-FOL

The contradiction between the optimal handling of active and reactive happenings is resolved in the language MINI-FOL. This language is not meant as a complete specification language, but rather as a toy language illustrating a certain extension of the declarative approach. This extension is applicable to any practical declarative specification language.

Let us start from the example above, which can be modelled in temporal logic by means of the components below. (From now on, we use *component* to denote a function or predicate.

> $Start(Project, Department) : Event$
> $End(Project) : Event$
> $running(Project) : Boolean$

An attempt at specifying the value of $running$ may lead to the following formulas:

> $\forall p \forall d \, (Start(p,d) \Rightarrow running(p))$
> $\forall p \, (End(p) \Rightarrow \neg running(p))$

By convention, the universal quantifications at the outermost of formulas may be omitted. These formulas can thus be rewritten as follows.

> $Start(p,d) \Rightarrow running(p)$
> $End(p) \Rightarrow \neg running(p)$

In a purely declarative approach, these formulas are not sufficient: they only constrain the value of $running$ when the events $Start$ and End occur, and at no other moment. The formulas do not express that $running$ holds from a $Start$ to the subsequent End. The correct formulas are substantially more complex.

Still, these naive formulas are appealing and they would be correct if we could add that $running$ is reactive, in the sense of Section 2.1, and only changes if required. MINI-FOL allows it through the following extensions:

- Functions and predicates are partitioned into active and reactive ones.

- Formulas are similarly partitioned into *action restrictions* and *reaction conditions*.

Active and reactive components are declared in two separate sections introduced by the keywords active and reactive, respectively:

> **active**
> > $Start(Project, Department) : Event$
> > $End(Project) : Event$
>
> **reactive**
> > $running(Project) : Boolean$

The reaction conditions are given in a section introduced by the keywords **reaction condition**. This section associates each reactive component with a set of formulas controlling its changes:

> **reaction condition**
> > $running : Start(p,d) \Rightarrow running(p)$
> > $\qquad\qquad End(p) \Rightarrow \neg running(p)$

There may be two other sections in a MINI-FOL specification. One, introduced by the keywords **action restriction**, lists the action restrictions. In the example above, we could require that only running projects be ended:

> **action restriction**
> $End(p) \Rightarrow \bullet\, running(p)$

This formula cannot cause the event *End* to occur, nor does it cause **running** to change. It is only meant to prevent *End* from occurring.

Finally, a section introduced by the keyword **initially** lists conditions that must hold in the initial state, in addition to the other formulas. For example, that there is initially no running project:

> **initially**
> $\neg running(p)$

We postulate that all events are false in the initial state. The specification is thus interpreted as if the initially section implicitly contained the formula expressing this fact. In the example,

$$\neg Start(p, d) \wedge \neg End(p).$$

The semantics of MINI-FOL ensure that the declarativeness principle holds for the active components and the operationality principle holds for the reactive ones. A MINI-FOL specification admits a subset of the models obtained with the standard temporal logic interpretation, namely those that minimise the changes from state to state (hence its name which stands for MINImalised First Order Logic). These minimally changing models are those whose state transitions can be obtained as follows: first, the active components are changed within the limits of the action restrictions; after this, the reactive components may change, but only for the elements of their domain invalidating the reaction condition. In the example, *running* will only change for a project p if either $Start(p, d)$ occurs while p is not running, or $End(p)$ occurs while p is running.

In general, however, the situation is slightly more complex than suggested by this simple example. Let us introduce a second reactive component, the function *dept* giving the department that is responsible for a project:

> **reactive**
> $dept(Project) : Department$

This department is the one in which the project was started, or is *none* if the project is not running. The reaction conditions for *dept* are the following ones:

> **reaction condition**
> $dept : Start(p, d) \Rightarrow dept(p) = d$
> $\neg running(p) \Rightarrow dept(p) = none$

One observes that the reaction conditions of *dept* mention the reactive predicate *running*, which induces a dependency between the two reactive components. Therefore, a state transition generally consists in changes to the active components, followed by a *reaction chain* during which the reactive components are changed in sequence. If a component x depends on another y, then x must be changed after y in the chain. The reactive components must therefore be ordered by the specifier in the reactive section:

> **reactive**
>> $running(Project) : Boolean$
>> $dept(Project) : Department$
>
>> $running \prec dept$

In the context of this ordering, the models of a MINI-FOL specification are the temporal logic models whose state transitions can be obtained as follows:

- active components are first changed within the limits permitted by the action restrictions;

- after this, the reactive functions and predicates are considered in any order compatible with their partial ordering; each of them is changed minimally to restore the associated reaction conditions; 'changed minimally' means that the value of the function or predicate is changed for as few elements in its domain as possible.

Section 3 formalises these semantics.

The order $\prec$ may be partial, because independent components need not be ordered. The following well-formedness rules ensure that this ordering is consistent with its intended purpose.

- First, $\prec$ must indeed define a partial order, i.e. its transitive closure may not contain any loop.

- If a component c is constrained by a statement ϕ, then ϕ may only refer to another component c' if this component is guaranteed to be updated before c. This is however not necessary if c' occurs within the scope of $\bullet$, in which case no dependency is induced.

This rule has the following implications:

  - reactive components may not occur in action restrictions, except in the scope of $\bullet$;

  - a reactive component x occurring in the reaction condition of a different component y must verify $x \prec^* y$ (where $\prec^*$ is the transitive closure of $\prec$), except if x occurs within the scope of $\bullet$;

  - in any of its reaction conditions, a reactive predicate or function x must have its arguments bound to the same variables in all its occurrences not within the scope of $\bullet$; this is to avoid dependencies between the values of a predicate or function for different elements of its domain.

In practice, these rules are easily obeyed, provided the dependencies between components are well identified.

Although it is not critical, it often simplifies the specifications to assume that only one event occurs, or only one other active component changes from one state to the next. This property is taken into account by the following implicit formula, required to hold in all but the initial state:

$$\bigvee_{i=1}^{n'} (\exists! p_i \; x_i(p_i) \wedge \bigwedge_{j=1,j \neq i}^{n'} \forall p_j \; \neg x_j(p_j) \wedge \bigwedge_{j=n'+1}^{n} \forall p_j \; x_j(p_j) = \bullet \; x_j(p_j))$$
$$\vee$$
$$\bigvee_{i=n'+1}^{n} (\exists! p_i \; x_i(p_i) \neq \bullet \; x_i(p_i) \wedge \bigwedge_{j=n'+1,j \neq i}^{n} \forall p_j \; x_j(p_j) = \bullet \; x_j(p_j) \wedge \bigwedge_{j=1}^{n'} \forall p_j \; \neg x_j(p_j)$$

where '$\exists!$' means 'there exists exactly one', $x_1, \ldots, x_{n'}$ are all active events and $x_{n'+1}, \ldots, x_n$ are the other active components, and where, for $i \in \{1, \ldots, n\}$, p_i is a tuple of variables on the domain of x_i.

2.3 A Larger Example

In this section, we give the complete MINI-FOL specification of an extension of the example used in the previous sections.

> The planned information system maintains information about projects running in departments and programmers assigned to these projects. Projects can be started in a department and ended; programmers can be assigned to or removed from a project; departments can receive the responsibility for a project or lose it.
>
> The information system must record which projects are running, which programmer works for which project, which department is responsible for which project, and which programmer has ever worked for which department.
>
> It must prevent the ending of non running projects, the start of a running project, and the removing of a programmer from a project to which he or she is not assigned.

The corresponding MINI-FOL specification is the following:

active

    $Start(Project, Department)$: $Event$
    $End(Project)$: $Event$
    $Assign(Programmer, Project)$: $Event$
    $Remove(Programmer, Project)$: $Event$

reactive

    $running(Project)$: $Boolean$
    $dept(Project)$: $Department$

$$assigned(Programmer, Project) : Boolean$$
$$has\text{-}worked(Programmer, Dept) : Boolean$$

$$running \prec assigned \prec dept \prec has\text{-}worked$$

initially

$$\neg running(p)$$
$$\neg has\text{-}worked(pg, d)$$

action restriction

$$End(p) \Rightarrow \bullet\, running(p)$$
$$Start(p, d) \Rightarrow \bullet\, \neg running(p)$$
$$Remove(pg, p) \Rightarrow \bullet\, assigned(pg, p)$$

reaction condition

$running$: $\quad Start(p, d) \Rightarrow running(p)$
$\quad\quad\quad\quad End(p) \Rightarrow \neg running(p)$

$dept$: $\quad Start(p, d) \Rightarrow dept(p) = d$
$\quad\quad\quad\quad \neg running(p) \Rightarrow dept(p) = none$

$assigned$: $\quad Assign(pg, p) \Rightarrow assigned(pg, p)$
$\quad\quad\quad\quad Remove(pg, p) \Rightarrow \neg assigned(pg, p)$
$\quad\quad\quad\quad \neg(\neg running(p) \wedge assigned(pg, p))$

$has\text{-}worked$: $assigned(pg, p) \wedge dept(p) = d \Rightarrow has\text{-}worked(pg, d)$

It can be verified that the various formulas comply to the well-formedness conditions. In this case, the declared ordering of reactive components is slightly stronger than needed, as *assigned* and *dept* are actually independent of each other. This strengthening does no harm.

Notice that the usual temporal logic deductions are still valid, as all action restrictions and reaction conditions hold in all states. In particular, we can conclude from the **initially** section that no project is initially assigned to any department

$$dept(p) = none$$

and that no programmer is initially assigned to any project

$$\neg assigned(pg, p).$$

3 Formal semantics of MINI-FOL

This section presents two equivalent formal semantics for MINI-FOL. The first one is constructive and specifies the elaboration of a model state by state. This semantics is probably the most intuitive. The other is a rewrite semantics, specifying the formulas that must be added to a MINI-FOL specification to reduce it to a classical temporal logic specification. This clearly identifies the expressive power of MINI-FOL and guarantees that it is amenable to deduction and theorem proving. The proof of the equivalence of the two semantics is in appendix.

3.1 Temporal Logic

MINI-FOL is an extension of a linear temporal logic which is first defined in this section. Its models are right-infinite sequences of states of the form $\Sigma = (\sigma_m : m \in N)$. As in first order logic, a state is a valuation function for variable, function and predicate symbols. The valuation of variables is identical in all states of a sequence.

A formula holds in a model Σ if its value is true with respect to every state of this model. The value of the formula ϕ with respect to the ith state of a model Σ is noted '$val(\Sigma, i, \phi)$' The value of a term τ is noted '$val(\Sigma, i, \tau)$'. The function val is defined recursively as follows (p, f, and x denote respectively a predicate symbol, a function symbol, and a variable):

$$val(\Sigma, i, x) = \sigma_i(x)$$

$$val(\Sigma, i, f(\tau_1, \ldots, \tau_n)) = \sigma_i(f)(val(\Sigma, i, \tau_1), \ldots, val(\Sigma, i, \tau_n))$$

$$val(\Sigma, i, p(\tau_1, \ldots, \tau_n)) = \sigma_i(p)(val(\Sigma, i, \tau_1), \ldots, val(\Sigma, i, \tau_n))$$

$$val(\Sigma, i, \neg\phi) = \text{true} \quad \text{iff} \quad val(\Sigma, i, \phi) = \text{false}$$

$$val(\Sigma, i, \phi_1 \wedge \phi_2) = \text{true} \quad \text{iff} \quad val(\Sigma, i, \phi_1) = \text{true and } val(\Sigma, i, \phi_2) = \text{true}$$

$$val(\Sigma, i, \forall x \phi) = \text{true} \quad \text{iff} \quad val(\Sigma', i, \phi) = \text{true for all } \Sigma' \text{ differing from } \Sigma \text{ at most by the value assigned to } x \text{ in all states}$$

$$val(\Sigma, i, \bullet \tau) = \text{if } i > 0 \text{ then } val(\Sigma, i-1, \tau) \text{ else } val(\Sigma, 0, \tau)$$

$$val(\Sigma, i, \bullet \Phi) = \text{if } i > 0 \text{ then } val(\Sigma, i-1, \Phi) \text{ else } val(\Sigma, 0, \Phi)$$

Additional operators ($\exists$, $\vee$) can be defined in terms of these. We also need the predefined predicate $initially$ which holds only in the first state of a sequence. Its semantics is given by the following property:

$$\sigma_i(initially) = \text{true} \quad \text{iff} \quad i = 0.$$

3.2 Constructive Semantics

Let S be a MINI-FOL specification, where the implicit formulas restricting the simultaneous changes have been added to the action restriction section (prefixed by '$\neg\ initially \Rightarrow \ldots$'):

active $\quad x_1 \ldots x_n$
reactive $\quad u_1 \ldots u_k$
initially $\quad \Gamma$
action restriction $\quad \Psi$
reaction condition $\quad u_i : \forall p_i\ \Phi_i(p_i) \quad (1 \leq i \leq k)$

For each $i \in \{1, \ldots, k\}$, p_i is a tuple of variables on the domain of u_i. We assume that the partial order between reactive components is such that if $u_i \prec u_j$ then $i < j$. The specification is well-formed, which implies that

- any u_i in Ψ is under the scope of $\bullet$;

- any u_j $(j > i)$ and any $u_i(p_i')$ $(p_i' \neq p_i)$ in $\Phi_i(p_i)$ is under the scope of $\bullet$.

The constructive semantics reflects the following intuition. A model of a specification is a sequence of states, where every next state is obtained in two steps. First some arbitrarily chosen active components are changed without invalidating the action restrictions. Then, the reactive components are checked and updated if necessary, starting with the smallest one.

Formally, a sequence of states $(\sigma_i : i \in \mathbf{N})$ is a model for the specification S if σ_0 satisfies

$$\Gamma \wedge \Psi \wedge \bigwedge_{i=1}^{k} \forall p_i \ \Phi_i(p_i)$$

and if the following conditions hold for any two successive states σ and σ':

- there is an intermediate state ρ_0 which is obtained from σ by changing the values assigned to the active components in a way that preserves Ψ;

- there is a sequence of intermediate states $\rho_1, \ldots, \rho_k$, where $\rho_k = \sigma'$, verifying the following properties:

  - ρ_i $(i > 0)$ differs from ρ_{i-1} at most by the value assigned to u_i;
  - consider the p_i in the domain of u_i in any order; if the formula $\Phi_i(p_i)$ evaluates to true in state ρ_{i-1}[1], then $\rho_i(u_i(p_i)) = \rho_{i-1}(u_i(p_i))$, else $\rho_i(u_i(p_i))$ is any value such that $\Phi_i(p_i)$ is true at state ρ_i.

This semantics may only be called constructive if the domains of all reactive components are finite. This restriction is quite natural in the field of information systems specification.

To distinguish σ and σ' from the states ρ_i which do not belong to the model of the specification, we call the former *observable* states and the latter *intermediate* states. It is proven in appendix that all action restrictions and reaction conditions hold in all observable states.

3.3 Rewrite Semantics

The purpose of these second semantics is to identify the formulas that must be added to a MINI-FOL specification, to reduce it to a specification in the temporal logic of Section 3.1. We will need the following notation:

---

[1] The evaluation is according to the rules of temporal logic as defined in Section 3.1, with ρ_{i-1} considered the successor of σ.

$\Phi[y : c]$ means that each occurrence of y which is not under the scope of $\bullet$ in the formula Φ is replaced by c; $\Phi[y_1 : c_1, y_2 : c_2] = (\Phi[y_1 : c_1])[y_2 : c_2]$.

The initial state should satisfy the initially section, the action restrictions, and the reaction conditions:

$$initially \Rightarrow \Gamma \wedge \Psi \wedge \bigwedge_{i=1}^{k} \forall p_i \ \Phi_i(p_i)$$

In each other state, an active component is chosen and its value may be changed without invalidating the action restrictions. We therefore have:

$$\neg initially \Rightarrow \Psi$$

During the subsequent reaction chain, all reaction conditions must be satisfied, and a reactive component u_i should only change if its associated formula is invalidated.

$$\neg initially \Rightarrow \bigwedge_{i=1}^{k} \forall p_i \ (\Phi_i(p_i) \wedge (\Phi_i(p_i)[u_i(p_i) : \bullet u_i(p_i)] \Rightarrow u_i(p_i) = \bullet u_i(p_i)))$$

We can simplify these formulas into the four following ones:

$$initially \Rightarrow \Gamma$$
$$\Psi$$
$$\bigwedge_{i=1}^{k} \forall p_i \ \Phi_i(p_i)$$
$$\bigwedge_{i=1}^{k} \forall p_i \ (\Phi_i(p_i)[u_i(p_i) : \bullet u_i(p_i)] \Rightarrow u_i(p_i) = \bullet u_i(p_i))$$

The reduction of a MINI-FOL specification to temporal logic therefore consists in converting the initially section into its obvious counterpart, in taking the action restrictions and reaction conditions, and in adding the formula

$$\bigwedge_{i=1}^{k} \forall p_i \ (\Phi_i(p_i)[u_i(p_i) : \bullet u_i(p_i)] \Rightarrow u_i(p_i) = \bullet u_i(p_i))$$

which expresses the minimisation of changes in the reactive components.

As an example, the formula that corresponds to the predicate *has-worked* is the following (p_i is (pg, d) for this predicate):

$$\forall pg \ \forall d \ (\forall p \ (assigned(pg, p) \wedge dept(p) = d \Rightarrow \bullet \ has\text{-}worked(pg, d))$$
$$\Rightarrow has\text{-}worked(pg, d) = \bullet \ has\text{-}worked(pg, d))$$

4 Comparison

This section uses the example of Section 2.3 to highlight the differences between MINI-FOL and the operational approach, the purely declarative one, and the deductive one.

4.1 The Operational Approach

In an operational approach, external (active) happenings trigger routines which modify the internal (reactive) variables. For example, the routine triggered by the event $End(p)$ may be written as follows:

```
if running(p)
then running(p) := false
     dept(p) := none
     foreach pg
     do assigned(pg, p) := false
```

A first difference between this specification and the MINI-FOL one is that the routine associated to End must consider all possible consequences of this event, be they direct (stopping a project) or indirect (setting the project department to *none* and unassigning all programmers). In comparison, the MINI-FOL approach cuts reaction chains into pieces handled by separate formulas: one saying that $End(p)$ sets $running(p)$ to false; another to say that a stopped project has *none* as department; etc.

The need to consider all consequences at once reduces the readability of operational specifications: for example, the conditions under which *assigned* changes must be gathered from the routines triggered by the events End, $Assign$ and $Remove$. The maintainability is reduced as well: if the definition of *assigned* changes, the operational specification must be adapted in all these places. These drawbacks are of course amplified when the size of the specification grows.

Besides, the operational style suffers from its inherent inability to directly state crucial properties like 'a project which is not running has no assigned programmer'. Such properties can only be deduced from a careful analysis of the specification.

Note that the advantages of MINI-FOL over the operational style are shared by the other non-operational approaches, i.e. the declarative and deductive ones.

4.2 The Declarative Approach

A purely declarative specification written in first order or temporal logic contains the same formulas as the MINI-FOL one, plus those required to explicitly circumvent the frame problem. These formulas, which must prevent the undesired change of reactive variables, could be the following ones:

$$\neg Start(p, d) \wedge \neg End(p) \Rightarrow (running(p) \Leftrightarrow \bullet\, running(p))$$
$$\neg Start(p, d) \wedge (running(p) \Leftrightarrow \bullet\, running(p)) \Rightarrow dept(p) = \bullet\, dept(p)$$
$$\neg Assign(pg, p) \wedge \neg Remove(pg, p) \wedge running(p)$$
$$\Rightarrow (assigned(pg, p) \Leftrightarrow \bullet\, assigned(pg, p))$$
$$has\text{-}worked(pg, d) \Leftrightarrow (\bullet\, has\text{-}worked(pg, d) \vee \exists p\, (assigned(pg, p) \wedge dept(p) = d))$$

Each formula is devoted to a specific reactive component, and states that it may not change outside of the conditions known to require a change. For example, the first formula prevents any change of *running*, if there is no *Start* or *End* event.

These formulas can be proven equivalent to those automatically generated by the rewrite semantics of MINI-FOL. Leaving these formulas implicit has several benefits. Of course, it rids the user of finding them, which is often not too easy. It also reduces the total size of the specification, which is always a win. Finally, it improves the maintainability of the specification, i.e. its ability to be easily changed. Suppose we add the possibility to change the department responsible for a project:

active
> $ChangeDept(Project, Department) : Event$

action restriction
> $ChangeDept(p, d) \Rightarrow \bullet running(p)$

reaction condition
> $dept : ChangeDept(p, d) \Rightarrow dept(p) = d$

In the first-order logic approach, the mere adjunction of the last formula simply prevents any *ChangeDept* to occur, because this would contradict the second frame formula above, namely:

$$\neg Start(p, d) \wedge (running(p) \Leftrightarrow \bullet running(p)) \Rightarrow dept(p) = \bullet dept(p).$$

This axiom must also be changed, and replaced by:

$$\neg Start(p, d) \wedge \neg ChangeDept(p, d) \wedge (running(p) \Leftrightarrow \bullet running(p))$$
$$\Rightarrow dept(p) = \bullet dept(p)$$

The need to change the frame axioms makes any modification more delicate, especially if the specification is large.

4.3   The Deductive Approach

The deductive approach [Oli89] is a variant of the declarative approach. External events are modelled by adding or removing *base* predicates, corresponding to the MINI-FOL active predicates. Active functions have no counterpart. These changes are constrained by *integrity constraints*, similar to the MINI-FOL action restrictions. Information that must be maintained by the information system is represented by *derived* predicates, corresponding to the MINI-FOL reactive predicates. Reactive functions have no counterpart.

The main difference is in the expression of reaction conditions which are called *deduction rules* in the deductive approach. There is no assumption that reactive components change minimally; there is another assumption, sometimes called the *closed world assumption*, implying that the predicates are false in all states where they are not said to be true. For example, the derived predicate $assigned(pg, p)$ can be specified by the following deduction rules (notations in [Oli89] are adapted to temporal logic):

$$Assign(pg, p) \Rightarrow assigned(pg, p)$$
$$running(p) \wedge \neg Remove(pg, p) \wedge \bullet \, assigned(pg, p) \Rightarrow assigned(pg, p).$$

The closed world assumption implicitly adds

$$assigned(pg, p) \Rightarrow Assign(pg, p)$$
$$\vee \, (running(p) \wedge \neg Remove(pg, p) \wedge \bullet \, assigned(pg, p))$$

The deductive approach allows some saving in writing, compared to the declarative approach, but it does not help avoiding the frame problem : a specifier still has to specify when a predicate does not change, as in the second formula above. As a consequence, a MINI-FOL specification is usually easier to write, more compact and more readable than a deductive specification.

Besides, the deductive approach does not allow the use of functions and restricts the forms of rules to ensure their efficient automatic interpretation. This limited form may obscure simple properties, or require to introduce intermediate predicates.

5 Conclusion

A declarative (logic-based) specification has advantages over an operational (assignment-based) one, in terms of modularity and expressiveness. The former suffers, however, from a drawback known as the *frame problem*, i.e. the need to explicitly state what may not change in addition to saying what must change. Actually, each approach is best suited to specify part of the dynamics of information systems. The declarative approach assumes that all changes are possible, except those explicitly excluded. This is optimal for specifying the events which are external to the information system, and constitute its input. The operational approach assumes that no change is allowed, except the explicitly required ones. This avoids the frame problem and is optimal for specifying the reactions of the information system.

We have proposed a technique that reconciles the two approaches. It extends the declarative approach by distinguishing two kinds of application-dependent functions and predicates, the active and reactive ones. The former are treated in the classical declarative style; they may change freely, except if constrained by formulas called action restrictions. The reactive functions and predicates may not change, except if forced to do so to maintain the truth of associated formulas called reaction conditions. This technique is illustrated in a simple language called MINI-FOL, which has been given formal semantics. The specification of a simple case study allows to compare this approach with the operational one, the purely declarative one, and a variant called the deductive approach.

We are currently working on several extensions of MINI-FOL. The first one consists in suppressing the requirement to order reactive components. This not only frees the specifier from some work, but also allows to treat the special cases where these components cannot be ordered, because of mutual dependencies. The second extension in sight is the inclusion of more temporal operators than just $\bullet$. Introducing other temporal operators referring to the past is almost straightforward. More delicate is the introduction of temporal operators referring to the future, like $\circ$, $\diamond$, or $\square$.

References

[DHR90] E. Dubois, J. Hagelstein, and A. Rifaut. *ERAE : A Formal Language for Expressing and Structuring Real-time Requirements.* Manuscript M 353, Philips Research Laboratory Belgium, 1990.

[FS86] J. Fiadeiro and A. Sernadas. The Infolog linear tense propositional logic of events and transactions. *Information Systems*, 11(1), 1986.

[GBM86] S.J. Greenspan, A. Borgida, and J. Mylopoulos. A declarative approach to conceptual information modeling. *Information Systems*, 11(1):9–23, 1986.

[GKB82] M.R. Gustafsson, T. Karlsson, and J.A. Bubenko. A declarative approach to conceptual information modeling. In T.W. Olle, H.G. Sol, and A.A. Verrijn-Stuart, editors, *Information System Design Methodologies : A Comparative Review*, pages 93–142, North-Holland, 1982.

[Hag88] J. Hagelstein. Declarative approach to information systems requirements. *Knowledge Based Systems*, 1(4):211–220, 1988.

[Min74] M. Minsky. *A Framework for Representing Knowledge.* Artificial Intelligence Memo 306, MIT, 1974.

[Oli86] A. Olivé. A comparison of the operational and deductive approaches to conceptual information systems modeling. In *IFIP'86*, pages 91–96, North-Holland, 1986.

[Oli89] A. Olivé. On the design and implementation of information systems from deductive conceptual models. In Peter Apers and Gio Wiederhold, editors, *Proc. 15th International Conference on Very Large Databases*, pages 3–11, Amsterdam, The Netherlands, August 1989.

Appendix : Equivalence of rewrite and constructive semantics

Let S be the MINI-FOL specification of Section 3. Let $\Sigma = (\sigma_m : m \in N)$ be a temporal logic model. For practical reasons, we use the following notation to denote the truth of a formula Υ in Σ with respect to the mth state :

$$\Sigma, m \models \Upsilon.$$

This notation is equivalent to '$val(\Sigma, m, \Upsilon)$ is true'.

Theorem

Each constructive model of S corresponds to a temporal logic model of the specification obtained from S by the rewrite semantics.

Proof : Let $\Sigma = (\sigma_m : m \in N)$ be a constructive model of S.

1. By definition of a constructive model, we have

$$\Sigma, 0 \models \Gamma \wedge \Psi \wedge \bigwedge_{i=1}^{k} \forall p_i \; \Phi_i(p_i)$$

and hence the following formula is true in Σ :

$$initially \Rightarrow \Gamma \wedge \Psi \wedge \bigwedge_{i=1}^{k} \forall p_i \; \Phi_i(p_i).$$

2. We have to prove $\Sigma, m \models \Psi$, for any $m > 0$.

By definition of a constructive model, there exists a state ρ_0 obtained from σ_{m-1} by changing only the values assigned to active components, and such that ρ_0 satisfies Ψ (according to the rules of temporal logic as given in Section 3.1, with ρ_0 considered the successor of σ_{m-1}).

Since the values assigned to $x_1, \dots, x_n$ in σ_m are the same as in ρ_0 and since none of $u_1, \dots, u_k$ occurs outside the scope of $\bullet$ in Ψ, Ψ cannot be invalidated by the subsequent changes of reactive components. Hence, $\Sigma, m \models \Psi$.

3. We prove that, for any $m > 0$, for any i $(1 \leq i \leq k)$,

$$\Sigma, m \models \forall p_i \; (\Phi_i(p_i) \wedge (\Phi_i(p_i)|u_i(p_i) : \bullet \, u_i(p_i)] \Rightarrow u_i(p_i) = \bullet \, u_i(p_i))).$$

By definition of a constructive model, there exists a sequence of states $(\rho_1, \dots, \rho_k)$ such that ρ_i differs from ρ_{i-1} at most in the value assigned to u_i, and such that $\sigma_m = \rho_k$.

As a consequence, for any i $(1 \leq i \leq k)$,

$$\begin{aligned} \rho_i(u_g) &= \sigma_m(u_g) & 1 \leq g \leq i \\ \rho_i(u_g) &= \sigma_{m-1}(u_g) & i+1 \leq g \leq k \end{aligned} \tag{1}$$

and hence, if ρ_i satisfies Υ, then

$$\Sigma, m \models \Upsilon|u_{i+1} : \bullet \, u_{i+1}, \dots, u_k : \bullet \, u_k]. \tag{2}$$

Let p_i be in the domain of u_i. According to the constructive semantics, the value of $u_i(p_i)$ in state ρ_i is obtained differently, depending the case :

(a) In the first case, $\Phi_i(p_i)$ is satisfied in ρ_{i-1}. By the definition of a constructive model, we then have $\rho_i(u_i(p_i)) = \rho_{i-1}(u_i(p_i))$, and, hence,

$$\Phi_i(p_i)|u_i(p_i) : \bullet \, u_i(p_i)] \Rightarrow u_i(p_i) = \bullet \, u_i(p_i))$$

holds trivially in ρ_i. From (1), and since $u_i(p_i')$ $(p_i' \neq p_i)$ occurs only under the scope of $\bullet$ in $\Phi_i(p_i)$, $\Phi(p_i)$ cannot be invalidated by changes to $u_i(p_i')$ $(p_i' \neq p_i)$, hence $\Phi_i(p_i)$ holds in ρ_i.

(b) In the second case, ρ_{i-1} does not satisfy $\Phi_i(p_i)$. Then, since $u_i(p_i')$ $(p_i' \neq p_i)$ occurs only under the scope of $\bullet$ in $\Phi_i(p_i)$, ρ_i does not satisfy $\Phi_i(p_i)[u_i(p_i) : \bullet \, u_i(p_i)]$, and, hence,

$$\Phi_i(p_i)[u_i(p_i) : \bullet \, u_i(p_i)] \Rightarrow u_i(p_i) = \bullet \, u_i(p_i)$$

holds in ρ_i. Moreover, $\Phi_i(p_i)$ holds in ρ_i by definition in a constructive model.

Hence, for any p_i,

$$\Phi_i(p_i) \wedge (\Phi_i(p_i)[u_i(p_i) : \bullet \, u_i(p_i)] \Rightarrow u_i(p_i) = \bullet \, u_i(p_i))$$

holds in ρ_i. By (2), and since $u_{i+1}, \ldots, u_k$ occur only under the scope of $\bullet$ in $\Phi_i(p_i)$, it follows that

$$\Sigma, m \models \forall p_i \, (\Phi_i(p_i) \wedge (\Phi_i(p_i)[u_i(p_i) : \bullet \, u_i(p_i)] \Rightarrow u_i(p_i) = \bullet \, u_i(p_i))).$$

Theorem

Each temporal logic model of the specification obtained from the specification S by the rewrite semantics is a constructive model of S.

Proof : Let $\Sigma = (\sigma_m : m \in N)$ be a temporal logic model for the specification obtained from S by the rewrite semantics.

- As we have 'initially $\Rightarrow \Gamma \wedge \Psi \wedge \bigwedge_{i=1}^{k} \forall p_i \, \Phi_i(p_i)$', it is clear that

$$\Sigma, 0 \models \Gamma \wedge \Psi \wedge \bigwedge_{i=1}^{k} \forall p_i \, \Phi_i(p_i).$$

- We prove that for each $m > 0$, σ_m can be obtained from σ_{m-1} as described in the constructive semantics.

  – We have to find a state ρ_0 which can be obtained from σ_{m-1} by changing only the values assigned to active components, and such that ρ_0 satisfies Ψ.
  Let ρ_0 be obtained from σ_{m-1} by setting x_i to $\sigma_m(x_i)$ for $1 \leq i \leq n$. Since $\Sigma, m \models \Psi$ and since $u_1, \ldots, u_k$ occur only under the scope of $\bullet$ in Ψ, it follows that ρ_0 satisfies Ψ.

  – We have to find a sequence of states $(\rho_1, \ldots, \rho_k)$ with the properties mentioned in the constructive semantics.
  Let $(\rho_1, \ldots, \rho_k)$ be the states such that ρ_i is obtained from ρ_{i-1} by setting the value of u_i to $\sigma_m(u_i)$. In other words, for $1 \leq i \leq k$,

$$\begin{aligned} \rho_i(u_g) &= \sigma_m(u_g) \text{ for } 1 \leq g \leq i \\ \rho_i(u_g) &= \sigma_{m-1}(u_g) \text{ for } i+1 \leq g \leq k \end{aligned} \tag{3}$$

  Note that it follows that $\rho_k = \sigma_m$.
  We prove that ρ_i can be obtained from ρ_{i-1} as described in the constructive semantics. Let p_i be in the domain of u_i.

(a) Suppose $\Phi_i(p_i)$ is satisfied in ρ_{i-1}. Then, since $u_i(p_i')$ $(p_i' \neq p_i)$ occurs only under the scope of $\bullet$ in $\Phi_i(p_i)$, $\Sigma, m \models \Phi_i(p_i)[u_i(p_i) : \bullet \, u_i(p_i)]$ and hence, $\Sigma, m \models u_i(p_i) = \bullet \, u_i(p_i)$.

Consequently, $\sigma_m(u_i(p_i)) = \sigma_{m-1}(u_i(p_i))$ and, by (3), $\rho_i(u_i(p_i)) = \rho_{i-1}(u_i(p_i))$.

(b) Suppose $\Phi_i(p_i)$ is not satisfied in ρ_{i-1}. Since $\Sigma, m \models \Phi_i(p_i)$ and since $u_{i+1}, \ldots, u_k$ occur only under the scope of $\bullet$ in $\Phi(p_i)$, by (3), it follows that $\Phi_i(p_i)$ is satisfied in ρ_i.

NelleN: a Framework for Literate Data Modelling

Michel Léonard
Ian Prince

Centre Universitaire d'Informatique
Université de Genève
1207 Genève
Switzerland

leonard@cui.unige.ch
prince@cui.unige.ch

Abstract

The literate data modelling paradigm provides a basis for structuring, justifying, and documenting the data modelling process. The paradigm is based on deliberation schemas consisting of issues, positions, and arguments. Deliberation schemas provide both a default argumentation space for decision-taking and a structure for recording the rationale once a decision is taken. An extendable class-based implementation framework, NelleN, provides a foundation for complementing a CASE-tool data dictionary with deliberation schemas. The framework consists of algorithm, deliberation schema and deliberation triggering classes. A subclassing mechanism is used for extending the framework. A small prototype demonstrates the type of CASE-tool that may be implemented using the framework.

1 Introduction

Traditional information system design methodologies such as DATAID-1 [4], Information Engineering [11], and Remora [19] have arisen from the need to manage the development of increasingly larger and more complex applications. These methodologies concentrate on the quality of the information system by promoting a strict sequence of refinement steps and formalisms and imposing validity rules on the specifications produced. Productivity of the development process is usually provided for by CASE tools (IEF [11], for example, supports the Information Engineering methodology).

A number of assumptions prevail behind most of the current information system design methodologies. One assumption is that systems are designed from scratch. Methodologies provide an analysis phase that prescribes an objective examination of the problem domain but most do not, however, provide methods for integrating the existing system with the new system to be developed. Instead, most methodologies concentrate only the creation of the new system. Methodologies also frequently assume that the requirements of the application domain are stable. This assumption fixes the problem statement at the beginning of the development process and excludes problem statement redefinition during the development process. Fixing the problem statement at the beginning of the development process assumes that the application domain's requirements can actually be described completely and correctly during the analysis phase. This presumes that complete and correct information is available during the analysis phase. The most important assumption — and the one that results from those previously mentioned — is the assumption that the development process is essentially linear. A linear development process, for example, prohibits the re-analysis of the application domain once the analysis phase has been completed. This assumption is reflected by methodologies frequently being based on the waterfall [14] model of development.

The consequence of the assumptions outlined above is that most methodologies and their supporting CASE-tool's stress *what* is produced by the method (the design products) and neglect *how* the design products are analyzed, refined and documented (the design process). This bias has lead to the following shortcomings:

- maintenance of the design product is rarely considered as an integral part of the design process because most methodologies only consider constructing a new system.

- design alternatives may not be easily explored because of the linear approach to the development process.

- undocumented assumptions must be made during the design process, severely hindering maintenance, because the methodology does not provide for the decision process.

- the design process is hindered by excessively pessimistic computer assistance because completeness and consistency of the design products is stressed.

- CASE-tools provide little support besides facilities for consistency checking, diagrams and documentation in the form of reports [2].

Design is essentially a complex iterative process that can not be determined *a priori*. Yet current information system methodologies and tools — because of the assumptions they are based upon — do not support this complex cognitive process. The most popular — and controversial — process model used for information system design is the waterfall model. The waterfall model, because it prescribes a linear process, has come under considerable criticism because in real-world design it is not practical — even possible — to anticipate all design issues during the early phases of the development process. Other models for the design process have been proposed to overcome the waterfall model's limitations: the spiral model of Boehm and models based on prototyping are just two. The focus, however, is still on supporting *what* is designed and not on *how* it is designed.

What are the elements of the design process and how may they be supported by computer-based tools?

Decision Making Any design process involves making decisions. Decisions may be rationale but can also be irrational. Decision making involves evaluating arguments for and against a solution to a problem. Tools can support decision making by providing solutions and justifications for the designer to confirm or choose between.

Decision Recording Decisions recording is the documentation of the design process. It is a separate activity from decision making. When, for example, a decision is taken but not recorded the decision becomes an assumption. Assumptions, of course, are undesirable because implicit design decisions hinder maintenance. Documenting the design process with explicit decisions taken provides an essential record for when the design needs to be modified because design decisions might have to be reviewed in light of the modifications at hand. In this respect tools should facilitate documenting the decisions *at the time* they are made and before the rationale behind them is lost.

Exploration Exploration is the process of examining alternatives to a design problem. Design problems are often 'solved' with the first satisficing solution found because of their sheer complexity [13, p. 36]. What must be stressed here is that the design process should be concerned with the effectiveness of a solution and not with its efficiency: the designer should not be concerned with finding *the* solution but analyzing a range of solutions. Design tools should allow the designer to backtrack in his, or her, design process and therefore permit the designer to freely explore alternative solutions to a problem without the cognitive overhead of remembering a found satisficing solution.

Construction Construction is act of 'doing' design and progressing from specifications to solutions. Construction is rarely an argumented activity and therefore is difficult to record. Design tools can provide the 'building blocks' for a given design domain.

Argumentation Argumentation is the counterpart to construction [12]. Argumentation is the act of deliberating about the state of a design and correcting any perceived undesirable elements. Tools can provide elements of a design to analyze by applying rules and heuristics to a design and detecting anomalies.

Iteration Design is an iterative process between construction and argumentation (Morch [12] proposes the term *reflection in action* and Simon [21] the term *generator-test cycle*). Both construction and argumentation are interleaved and tool support should reflect this cyclic nature.

2 The Literate Data Modelling Paradigm

Literate programming is an approach to programming proposed by D.E. Knuth [7,1] that promotes interleaving, in the same document, both the source code of a program and a full account of the rationale that went into constructing the program. Literate programs should be as readable, and interesting, as a piece of literature.

Database modelling is not the same activity as programming but both are design activities and share common characteristics such as choosing between alternatives, exploration of possible representations and testing whether the result of the design activity corresponds (or satisfies) the given requirements.

The literate data modelling paradigm which we present here, as with literate programming, considers the documentation of the design process (using deliberation schemas) as important as the results of the process (the design products).

In this section we will first present some assumptions and limitations of our approach. We will briefly justify why an algorithmic approach is not always sufficient. We will then present deliberation schemas as a structure for the design process, first through an example, then in more detail.

2.1 Assumptions

We will be making certain assumptions about design products and the design process and limiting our approach to only certain aspects of both.

First, we will be limiting ourselves to examining only the data analysis and data modelling phases of the design process.[1]

We will also be assuming that the modelling process is undertaken using the relational data model.

We will be assuming that the modelling process is punctuated with remarkable situations (*cas remarquables* [9,10]). A remarkable situation reflects a specific state of the evolving design that necessitates the intervention of an analyst and/or designer. We will be using the term deliberation to describe this intervention.

2.2 Why not an algorithmic approach?

Relational data modelling (or logical data modelling) is usually seen as a task that can be aided with algorithms — for example by algorithm that decomposes a scheme into 3NF. However the algorithmic solution to the decomposition problem is not without its problems as we will show in the next few paragraphs.

The first is that complete and coherent data is necessary for the algorithms to give meaningful results. If the analysis phase specifies, for example, that the functional dependencies $a \rightarrow c$ and $ab \rightarrow c$ hold, then any algorithm will arbitrarily reject $ab \rightarrow c$ as not being elementary. Likewise, if the functional dependencies $a \rightarrow b$ and $b \rightarrow c$ are specified then any algorithm will generate $a \rightarrow c$. In the first case the algorithm retracts a dependency, in the second it asserts a dependency. Checking for incompleteness and incoherence could be tasks within the analysis phase but we believe that this is rarely possible or even desirable. We believe it is very difficult for analysts to acquire *all* the information necessary before the modelling phase starts. If the analysis phase is undertaken by separate groups then it is preferable not to try and reduce the viewpoints to a single one, if in fact the 'reality' is viewed differently. We believe that the study of the dependencies during the modelling phase reveals such cases of incompleteness and inconsistency. The designer — or the algorithm — should not arbitrarily decide on correcting any incoherence or inconsistency; instead the designer should consult with the analysts responsible for the analysis phase for clarification.

Another problem with the algorithmic approach is that, usually, only one result is given when in fact a number of equivalent results are possible. This is often true for algorithms that calculate decompositions that may return only one decomposition when in fact the are a number possible. The choice of decomposition should also be under the control of the designer and not arbitrarily chosen by an algorithm.

---

[1]we hope to show, however, that the paradigm could be applied to all phases and elements of design process

Algorithms are frequently simple functions and as such can be viewed as 'black-boxes' that given data for input will return a result as output. The problem here is that the designer using such an algorithm is not given any feedback or justification about the algorithm's result.

A final problem we will mention here is that, for some algorithmic problems, there exists no solution. For example, it is not always possible for a scheme to satisfy a lossless join and dependency-preserving BCNF, as we will see in Section 2.3.1.

2.3   Deliberation schemas

The literate data modelling paradigm prescribes using deliberation schemas as a structuring method for decision-taking and documentation.

Deliberation schemas provide a default argumentation structure about some aspect of the evolving design. They are based on Toulmin's work on argument patterns [23] and the IBIS method for structuring the design process as a conversation [8].

The principle elements of deliberation schemas are issues, positions, and arguments.

Issue Issues provide a focus of concern during the design process. Issues can arise from reviewing design artifacts with respect to certain criteria, rules, norms or heuristics. Issues can also be raised by the design process itself; for example, selecting a position to an issue might cause an issue to be raised.

Position A position is a candidate response to an issue. Positions will often be mutually exclusive (but is not necessary).

Argument Arguments are justifications that support and/or object to positions. Arguments establish claims [23] for and against positions. A single argument can support one position yet object to another.

2.3.1   An example deliberation schema

We will see — through a simple design scenario — how the structure of issues, positions and arguments can help structure the decisions a designer might be confronted with. Take the following database scheme[2] that has the functional dependency $city, street \rightarrow postalCode$ defined on it:

   $Addresses(city, streetpostalCode)$, *for all tuples of Addresses (c s p), city c has a building with street address s and p is the postal code of for that address in that city.*

The single key for the scheme is (city street) and the scheme is in Boyce-Codd Normal Form (BCNF) because all the elementary functional dependencies are those in which a key functionally determines one or more of the attributes.

Now imagine that the functional dependency $postalCode \rightarrow city$ also holds for *Addresses*. The set of keys for *Addresses* becomes (street city) and (street postalCode). The scheme *Addresses* is no longer in BCNF because the left-hand-side of $postalCode \rightarrow city$ is not a key of *Addresses*. *Addresses*, however is in 3NF because *city* is a prime attribute. Decomposing the scheme into BCNF

---

[2]adapted from [24]

StreetCodes(*street*, *postalCode*) and *CityCodes*(*postalCode*//*city*)[3] does not preserve dependencies because *city*, *street* → *postalCode* is not implied by the projected dependencies.

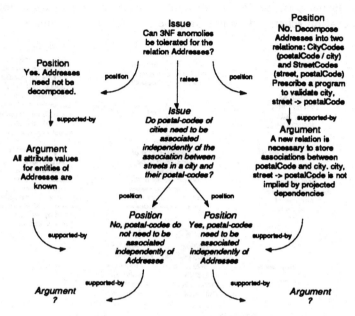

Figure 1: An initial deliberation schema

Figure 1 represents an initial deliberation schema for the designer and analyst.[4] Issue, positions and arguments are represented as nodes. The nodes in *italics* are those concerning the analyst, those in plain concern the designer. We will first examine the deliberation concerning the designer.

The designer's issue in this situation is whether the anomalies of 3NF can be tolerated for the relation *Addresses*. Two positions respond to the issue: the first tolerates the anomalies of 3NF and proposes to not decompose *Addresses*; the second position proposes decomposing *Addresses* into a non dependency-preserving BCNF and prescribing a validation method for *city*, *street* → *postalCode*. The position to accept 3NF anomalies is justified by the argument that all attribute values for entities of *Addresses* are known. The second position is justified by the argument that a new relation is necessary to store associations between *postalCode* and *city*.

Both arguments, however, are supported by positions that respond to an analysis issue, and as such the designer must suspend deciding on his/her position until s/he can get a confirmed position from the analyst on the issue of whether postal-codes need to be associated independently of addresses.

---

[3]non prime attributes, if the relation has any are written to the right of the double-slash (//), if the relation accepts more than one key then they are separated by a single-slash (/)

[4]by analyst we refer to a person (or group of people) that are responsible for communicating with end-users about application domain requirements and by designer as a person (or group of people) that are responsible for developing computer models and systems respecting specifications produced by analysts. Analyst and designer *could* be the same person or group of people

The analyst's issue is to elicit from end-uses whether or not postal-codes need to be associated independently of addresses. The two positions responding to this issue are simply the positive and negative responses. No formal *a priori* justifications can be given for either position (as these would concern the application domain) so the initial deliberation schema does not propose any default arguments.

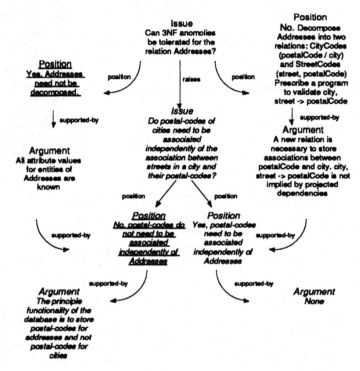

Figure 2: Deliberation in favour of not associating postal-codes and addresses independently

We will see how the deliberation, in this simple example, can go one of two ways. First, let's imagine that the analysts elicit from the end-users that: *The principle functionality of the database is to store postal-codes for addresses and not postal-codes for cities.* This is clearly support for the position that postal-codes do *not* need to be associated independently from addresses and is recorded within the deliberation schema as a supporting argument for this position. The analyst deliberates in favour of this position. The designers now has support for the argument in favour of not decomposing the *Addresses* relation and may deliberate in favour of this position. Figure 2 resumes this deliberation. Note the end-user argument and the selected (underlined) positions.

We can easily imagine a different argument the analysts might elicit from the end-users: *The data given by the Post Office concerns only postal-codes and cities.* This argument supports the position for that postal-codes need to be associated separately from addresses. Imagine that the analysts deliberates in favour of this position. The designer now has support for the argument in favour of decomposing the *Addresses* relation. Figure 3 resumes this deliberation. Note the end-user argument and the selected (underlined) positions.

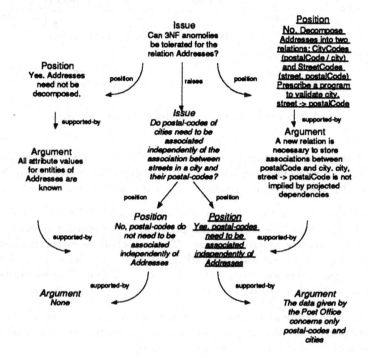

Figure 3: Deliberation in favour of independently associating postal-codes and addresses

2.4 A model for deliberation schemas

We will now propose a model for deliberation schemas. We will present their static aspects first, followed by definitions for their dynamic triggering.

2.4.1 Static aspects

Figure 4 illustrates the associations permitted between elements of deliberation schemas. Issues, positions and arguments are nodes and are associated with labeled arcs. A deliberation schema is therefore a directed graph consisting of typed nodes (issue, position or argument).

We will now examine the properties of each node-type:

Issue An issue has properties concerning its audience, expression, and resolution. The **audience** property indicates whether the issue is addressed at analysts or designers. The **expression** property indicates the focus of concern in natural language, usually in the form of a question. The **artifacts** property lists the

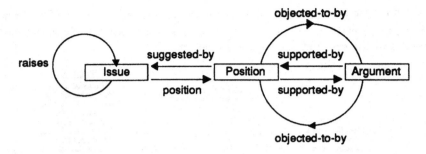

Figure 4: A model for deliberation schemas

set of artifacts the issue is concerned with. They provide the 'evidence' for the issue. The **resolved** property is initially given the value 'false' but is set to 'true' (by the analyst or designer) when the issue is considered resolved.

Position A position has three properties: its expression, whether or not it is selected and its audience. The **expression** property is the position expressed in natural language, usually as an assertion. The **selected** property indicates whether the position has been selected and is initially set to false but is set to true by the analyst or designer when the position in chosen. The **audience** property indicates whether the issue is addressed at analysts or designers.

Argument An argument has two properties: its expression and its audience. The **expression** indicates a justification and the **audience** indicates whether the argument is addressed at designers or analysts.

2.4.2 Dynamic aspects

Section 2.4.1 described a structure for storing deliberation schema in a CASE-tool dictionary. It did not, however, describe how, or when, a deliberation schema could automatically be created.

A deliberation schema need to be created whenever a certain state of evolving model reflects the need for designer and/or analyst intervention. This state can be specified as a condition. Let's call this condition the *triggering condition*. In the example presented in Section 2.3.1 the triggering condition would be a relation being in 3NF yet not decomposable into BCNF.

Normally, the triggering condition would have to be tested each time the evolving model is changed to ensure that the set of deliberation schemas created would be up-to-date. To reduce this costly operation a *triggering range* can define a set of modelling primitives that necessitate testing the triggering condition. We saw in Section 2.3.1 how adding a functional dependency could cause a triggering condition to be satisfied. This primitive would be an element of the deliberation schema's triggering range.

2.5 Advantages of deliberation schemas

Let's examine some of the advantages of using deliberation schemas during the design process:

1. All positions to an issue are explicit and the designer (or analyst) is encouraged to explore all the positions before choosing one over the other.

2. Arguments for choosing between positions are explicit and place the designer on clear ground for decision-making.

3. Rationale for position selection is clear. By choosing a position the designer (or analyst) is implicitly accepting its supporting arguments and refuting its objecting arguments. The decision *not* to choose a position implicitly means that its supporting arguments (if any) do not play an important enough role for its selection and/or its arguments objecting to it are important enough for its rejection.

4. Separation of responsibilities, since issues regarding analysis and design are separate. In the example the analyst's task is clear: elicit from the end-users whether city postal-codes need to be associated independently of addresses. The designer's issue is quite separate: whether or not to tolerate the *Addresses* relation in 3NF. Issues addressed to analysts concern aspects and requirements of the application domain whereas issues addressed to designers are more technical in nature and refer to properties of the evolving model. The responsibilities of analysts and designers are clearly distinguished. Designers can not make short-cuts by accepting a position without justification by analysts (if the deliberation schema requires it; i.e. a designer argument is supported by a analyst's position). In this case a deliberation schema can be seen as prompts for the designer to collaborate with analysts and obtain additional information from them before proceeding with the design.

5. Issue precedence is inherent in the schema. In the example the issue *Do postal-codes of cities need to be associated independently of the association between streets in a city and their postal codes?* needs to be resolved before the issue *can 3NF be tolerated for Addresses?* since the arguments to the second issue can not be supported before positions have been taken on the first.

6. Documentation becomes an integral part of the design process. The designers (and analysts) are facilitated and encouraged to structure their design process using the deliberation schemas. Documentation of information systems is rarely undertaken during the design process itself. Documentation is usually considered at the end of the process once a stable system is obtained. The problem with documenting 'after-the-fact' is that most of the rationale behind the decisions and trade-offs taken during the design is not available any more. Yet good documentation is critical to maintaining a system in response to changing requirements. Deliberation schemas facilitate documenting *during* the process of actually taking design decisions. This allows the design to be reliably associated with the complete rationale that went into its construction.

7. Design enrichment can be accommodated. In the example it is specified that a program must be written to ensure a functional dependency not validated by the decomposition. This information becomes part of the documentation of the modelling phase and a requirement for the implementation phase. This is an important because most design dictionaries do not allow this kind of supplementary information during the design phase. Note that the supplementary requirement will not only specify that such a program is necessary but will include the *justification* for such a program in terms of the application domain and modelling constraints.

8. Common documentation format. Deliberations schemas provide a common structure for recording rationale of decisions taken during the design process.

3 NelleN: an Implementation Framework

Most CASE-tools implement a data dictionary that stores the *results* of the development process. We propose augmenting the data dictionary with deliberation schemas that record the *process* of reaching those results. NelleN is a framework for implementing CASE-tools with such an augmented dictionary.

3.1 The NelleN Framework

Implementation frameworks are foundation architectures for building computer applications. They are based on two principles; the first that a class of programs can share a core set of code that should not be re-written each time a program of this class is written, the second that most code particular to a specific application can be written as subclasses of the core code. One such framework is the MacApp framework [20] for developing Apple Macintosh applications; another is the Model-View-Controller (MVC)[6] framework for implementing graphical user-interfaces.

Reflecting these two basic principles, the NelleN framework is divided into two parts. The first, the NelleN kernel, is a core set of abstract classes that supports deliberation schemas. The second part of the framework consists of a subclassing mechanism to extend the framework with concrete classes for specific types of deliberation schemas.

The NelleN framework has been implemented in Smalltalk. Smalltalk is an object-oriented programming language and its subclassing mechanism is ideally suited for implementing a framework. Smalltalk has already proved an ideal vehicle for the MVC framework — in fact its programming environment is written as an extension of the MVC framework. Smalltalk also has the advantage of a large and stable class library. The extensive collections class hierarchy, for example, is a valuable aid to implementing modelling algorithms that frequently need sets for their implementation.

3.1.1 The NelleN kernel

The NelleN kernel provides the general functionality for triggering and storing deliberation schemas.

The NelleN kernel is a set of Smalltalk class hierarchies. These class hierarchies are divided into three categories: the algorithm kernel, the deliberation schema kernel, and the deliberation triggering kernel.

Figure 5 represents the current structure and status of the NelleN kernel. Items in a typewriter typeface are classes. All links indicate the subclass relationship. The roots of each partial class hierarchy are part of the standard Smalltalk implementation.[5]

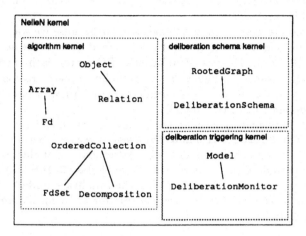

Figure 5: The NelleN kernel

The algorithm kernel

The algorithm kernel is a set of classes that implement the data structures necessary to store the data model and calculate its properties. Smalltalk classes are used to represent modelling entities. For example, the class FdSet is a subclass of the Smalltalk class OrderedCollection that accepts elements of class Fd. Methods implement algorithms that can be performed on modelling entities. For example, the class FdSet provides a method named minElementaryClosure that returns the minimal elementary closure of a set of functional dependencies.

The deliberation schema kernel

We saw in Figure 4 that deliberation schemas can be represented by directed graphs. The basic functionality of deliberation schemas is therefore implemented by an abstract class, DeliberationSchema, a subclass of RootedGraph. Being an abstract class, DeliberationSchema does not provide protocols for creating instances. Concrete subclasses of DeliberationSchema handle this task as we will see in Section 3.1.2.

---

[5]the RootedGraph class are not a standard part of the Smalltalk hierarchy. We have used the public domain graph classes developed by Mario Wolczko of the University of Manchester

The deliberation triggering kernel

The deliberation triggering kernel is roughly based on the Model-View-Controller mechanism (MVC). The MVC-triad allows the model (or application) to be developed (and maintained) independently of its interface (a common requirement for highly interactive applications). Views and controllers in MVC are dependent on their model. The model itself does not 'know' about the views that are dependent on it but simply broadcasts messages to them if an aspect of it changes. Views are updated using this mechanism.

The deliberation triggering mechanism is similar because we want the data model dictionary and the operations that can be performed on it to be separate from the triggering of deliberation schemas. The benefit of this approach is that deliberation schema triggering becomes configurable (any number of deliberation schema 'types' can be 'installed') just as in the MVC paradigm (any number of arbitrary views can be displayed, independent of the model).

The deliberation triggering mechanism is achieved by the abstract class **DeliberationMonitor**. The **DeliberationMonitor** class is responsible for 'registering' the instances of its subclasses as dependents of a data model. Subclasses of **DeliberationMonitor** are 'paired' with a concrete subclass of class **DeliberationSchema** (the class of deliberation schema it raises). Using the Smalltalk update mechanism subclasses of **DeliberationMonitor** are responsible for creating instances of issues to be stored in the dictionary.

3.1.2 Extending the NelleN framework: concrete subclasses

The NelleN kernel provides only the general functionality for creating and storing deliberation schemas. Deliberation schema types (corresponding to a remarkable situation type) are implemented by writing two concrete subclasses (somewhat like implementing a view-controller pair in the MVC framework): the first a concrete subclass of **DeliberationSchema**, the second a concrete subclass of **DeliberationMonitor**. Figure 6 shows where in the framework a deliberation schema pair (underlined in the figure) are placed. The first implements the structure of the issue, the second the conditions for creating an instance of that deliberation schema type.

Subclassing DeliberationMonitor

Concrete subclasses of **DeliberationMonitor** implement the triggering and range conditions for creating instances of a deliberation schema type.

Two methods need be implemented (the dependency methods are inherited from **DeliberationMonitor**). The first is an instance creation class method that creates an instance of its class and assigns itself as a dependent of a model. This method must respect the protocol **on: aModel** and typically contains only a few lines of code.

The second method is responsible for determining whether a certain state holds true for the data model and (if so) creating an instance of its 'paired' deliberation schema type. This method must have the selector **update: anAspect**. This is a typical Smalltalk keyword selector with the keyword **update** and the argument **anAspect**. This method implements the response necessary during the Smalltalk update mechanism. If, for example, a functional dependency is added to the data

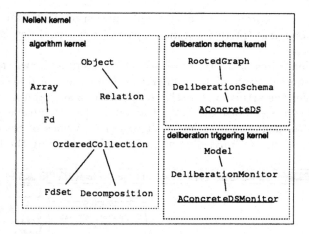

Figure 6: Extending the **NelleN** Framework

model, the method implementing this modelling primitive will contain a line of code **self update:#fdAdded**. This means that each dependent (in this case instances of subclasses of **DeliberationMonitor**) will receive the message **update:anAspect** 'broadcasted' by the data modelling primitive. The dependent receiving this message can determine whether it is concerned by this message by testing the **:anAspect** argument. If for example, the range of the deliberation schema we want to implement includes the **add functional dependency** primitive then the **update:anAspect** method would test if **:anAspect** equals the symbol:**#fdAdded** and then test to see if its condition holds. The condition is tested by asking the model (in this case the data model) for its elements. If the condition is found to hold true on the data model then the method creates the deliberation schema by sending an instance creation method to its 'paired' class and then sending a message to the model asking for the deliberation schema to be stored.

Subclassing DeliberationSchema

Subclasses of **DeliberationSchema** receive instance creation messages from its paired monitor class. They are responsible for creating a deliberation schema graphs similar to the example in Figure 1.

All the methods for actually constructing the deliberation schema graph, testing, accessing and displaying the graph are part of the **DeliberationSchema** class and do not need to be re-written for each subclass because of the code inheritance mechanism. Subclasses must specify the graph that represents its deliberation schema, according to the model outlined in Section 4.

3.2 A prototype using NelleN

We will now briefly present a simple example of the type of modelling tool that can be built with using the **NelleN** framework. It does not in any way pretend to be a complete tool but simply to demonstrate the feasibility of the framework.

The example we propose here uses only one simplified concrete deliberation schema class: one that queries whether a pair of functional dependencies are contradictory or not.

Figure 7 illustrates this prototype. [6] The example shown here displays the deliberation schema graph slightly differently from the one described in Figure 4. Here we consider the artifacts and selected properties as graph nodes.

The prototype uses both the MVC framework for its interface and the NelleN framework for its deliberation schema. Two hundred lines of Smalltalk code were necessary to build this (admittedly small) example, excluding the frameworks.

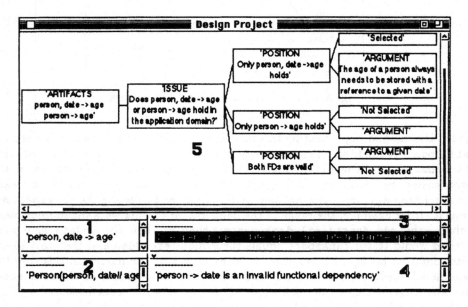

Figure 7: A example modelling tool using the NelleN Framework

The interface chosen for the prototype is one that is often used in Smalltalk applications: a browser interface. The browsing window consists of a number of views, or panes, which we will briefly examine in turn:

view 1: the list of functional dependencies

view 2: the list of relations forming the decomposition

view 3: the list of issues addressed to the analyst. If an item in the list is selected (like in Figure 7) the partial deliberation schema (corresponding to the subgraph that concerns the designer) is displayed in the larger view (5)

view 4: the list of issues addressed to the designer. If an issue in the list is selected it is displayed in the larger view (5).

---

[6] the windows panes have been numbered for demonstration purposes

view 5: this view graphically displays the last selected issue of views (3) and (4). The layout and display are automatic[7].

4   Related Work

We will briefly review other research work that is related to our approach.

The research closest to our approach is probably the work of Rolland [18,22,3]. Rolland proposes 'representation-triplets' consisting of a situation, a decision and an action to guide the designer in his, or her, work. The proposed situations are similar to deliberation schema triggering conditions because they both indicate a significant state of the evolving design. A 'decision' corresponds to a choice made by the designer and can easily be compared with the selecting of a position in our approach. An 'action' consists of the transformations performed resulting from a decision and resemble the modelling positions we propose. Rolland, however proposes a fully fledged CASE-tool (ALECSI) based on an expert system approach, while we propose an extendable framework for implementing CASE-tools.

Conklin and Begeman have demonstrated with gIBIS [5] the feasibility of an issue-based tool. gIBIS is a hypertext system for capturing the rationale behind early design decisions and has proved useful in the domain of CSCW (Computer Supported Cooperative Work).

Potts and Bruns [16,15] have worked on the importance of documenting the decision process in software engineering by proposing a generic model of deliberation. Their model is also based on Rittel's IBIS method.

Finally, Rätz, Lusti and Glaubauf [17] have designed and implemented an ITS (Intelligent Tutoring System) that tutors students on the task of data normalization. They propose 'psychologically valid' algorithms for data normalization that are closer to how designers actually reason about normalization. Their diagnostic model, for when errors are made, is similar to our approach of positions and arguments responding to issues.

5   Conclusions

We have proposed the literate data modelling paradigm that takes into account the iterative nature of the data modelling design process. We have argued that it can structure the complex design process by integrating deliberation and documentation.

We have also presented an extendable implementation framework, NelleN, that implements the abstract functionality of deliberation schemas. We have shown that the framework can easily be extended by using a subclassing mechanism. A prototype has been presented that uses the framework.

The research we have presented here is on-going. Research efforts currently being pursued are identifying and classifying the types of deliberation schemas that can be encountered during the modelling process and extending the NelleN framework

---

[7]the grapher classes developed by Mario Wolczko of the University of Manchester perform the automatic layout and displaying of the graph

with them. We are also considering implementing a meta-CASE-tool that would configure the NelleN framework to a given modelling method.

References

[1] BENTLEY, J. Literate programming. *Communications of the ACM 29*, 5 (May 1986), 364 – 369.

[2] BUBENKO, JR, J. A. Information system methodologies — a research view. In *Information Systems Design Methodologies: Improving the Practice* (Amsterdam, 1986), T. Olle, H. Sol, and A. Verijn-Stuart, Eds., IFIP, North-Holland, pp. 289 – 318.

[3] CAUVET, C., PROIX, C., AND ROLLAND, C. ALECSI: an expert system for requirements engineering. In *Advanced Information Systems Engineering, CAiSE'91* (1991), R. Anderson, J. Bubenko, and A. Sø lvberg, Eds., vol. 498 of *Lecture Notes in Computer Science*, Springer-Verlag, pp. 31–49.

[4] CERI, S. Methodology and tools for data base design. In *Methodology and Tools for Data Base Design*, S. Ceri, Ed. North-Holland, 1983, pp. 1 – 6.

[5] CONKLIN, J., AND BEGEMAN, M. gIBIS: a hypertext tool for exploratory policy discussion. *ACM Transactions on Office Information Systems 6*, 4 (1988), 303 – 331.

[6] GOLDBERG, A. *Smalltalk-80: the Interactive Programming Environment*. Addison-Wesley, 1984.

[7] KNUTH, D. E. Literate programming. *Computer Journal 27*, 2 (May 1984), 97 – 111.

[8] KUNZ, W., AND RITTEL, H. Issues as elements of information systems. Working Paper 131, Institute of Urban and Regional Development, University of California, 1970.

[9] LÉONARD, M. *Structure des Bases de Données*. Dunod, 1988.

[10] LÉONARD, M. *Database Structures*. Macmillan, 1992. In press.

[11] MACDONALD, I. Automating the information engineering methodology with the Information Engineering Facility. In *Computerized Assistance During the Information Systems Life Cycle* (1988), T. Olle, A. Verrijn-Stuart, and L. Bhabuta, Eds., North-Holland, pp. 337 – 373.

[12] MORCH, A. JANUS: Basic concepts and sample dialog. In *CHI'91, ACM Conference on Human Factors in Computing Systems — Reaching Through Technology* (1991), S. Robertson, G. Olson, and J. Olson, Eds., ACM, pp. 457–458.

[13] NEWELL, A., AND SIMON, H. *Human Problem Solving*. Prentice-Hall, 1972.

[14] PETERS, L. *Advanced Structured Analysis and Design.* Prentice-Hall, 1988.

[15] POTTS, C. A generic model for representing design methods. In *11th International Conference on Software Engineering* (1989), pp. 217 – 226.

[16] POTTS, C., AND BRUNS, G. Recording the reasons for design decisions. In *10th International Conference on Software Engineering* (1988), Computer Society Press, pp. 418 – 427.

[17] RÄTZ, T., LUSTI, M., AND GLAUBAUF, M. An intelligent tutoring system for database normalization. WWZ-discussion papers, Universität Basel, WWZ, 1991.

[18] ROLLAND, C., AND PROIX, C. Vers une automisation des processus de conception par les outils. In *Autour et à l'Entour de Merise. Les Méthodes de Conception en Perspective* (1991), CERAM, AFCET, pp. 271 – 286.

[19] ROLLAND, C., AND RICHARD, C. The Remora methodology for systems design and management. In *Information Systems Design Methodologies* (1982), T. Olle, H. Sol, and A. Verijn-Stuart, Eds., North-Holland, pp. 369 – 426.

[20] SCHMUCKER, K. *Object-Oriented Programming for the Macintosh.* Hayden, 1986.

[21] SIMON, H. *The Sciences of the Artificial,* 2 ed. MIT Press, 1981.

[22] SOUVEYET, C., AND ROLLAND, C. Correction of conceptual schemas. In *Advanced Information Systems Engineering, CAiSE'90* (1990), B. Steinholtz, A. Solvberg, and L. Bergman, Eds., Lecture Notes in Computer Science, Springer-Verlag, pp. 152 – 174.

[23] TOULMIN, S. *The Uses of Argument.* Cambridge University Press, 1958.

[24] ULLMAN, J. *Database Systems,* 2 ed. Computer Science Press, 1983.

A NATURAL LANGUAGE APPROACH FOR REQUIREMENTS ENGINEERING

C. ROLLAND[1] C. PROIX[2]

ABSTRACT : The term Requirements Engineering refers to this part of a database development cycle that involves investigating the problems and requirements of the users community and developing a conceptual specification of the future system.
Natural language plays an important role during this stage that has proved to be crucial in the development of computerized systems. The required acquisition of application domain knowledge is achieved either through documents and texts analysis or by means of interviews i.e through language manipulation. Similarly validation of the specification is made via oral discussions with users.
The paper proposes that Requirements Engineering (R.E) should be supported by a CASE tool based on a linguistic approach. It presents a R.E support environment that generates the conceptual specification from a description of the problem space provided through natural language statements. Complementary, validation is based on texts generation from the conceptual specification to natural language. The paper focuses on the linguistic approach, demonstrates its generality and overviews its implementation in a CASE tool.

KEY WORDS : Requirements engineering, Natural language analysis, conceptual schema, information system design, text generation

1. Introduction

The need for modelling techniques by which systems may be described in high level conceptual terms has been recognized in the earlier phases of Databases and Information Systems (DB/IS) development in industry, business and administration.

---

[1] Université de Paris 1, 17 rue de la Sorbonne, 75231 Paris cedex 05, France
[2] Société CRIL, 146 Boulevard de Valmy 92707 Colombes cedex, France

This has caused the introduction of various conceptual models that have proved to be extremely useful to build in a high level specification of the future system (the so called conceptual schema) before this system is developed. (see the survey presented by Hull and King [Hull 87] for example).

However, the task of constructing the conceptual schema remains problematical. The route to reach the conceptual schema e.g the conceptual modelling process has the purpose of abstracting and conceptualizing the relevant part of the application domain. This is guided by requirements. The term Requirements Engineering introduced by Dubois [Dubois 89] has been used for this part of the DB/IS development that involves investigating the problems and requirements of the users community and developing a specification of the future system. The succeeding phase, where this specification is realized in a working system which is verified against the specification may be called Design Engineering [Bubenko 90]. Figure 1.1 shows the organization of DB/IS development cycle based upon requirements and system engineering.

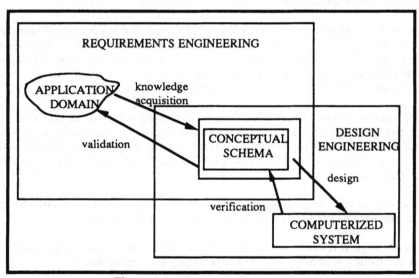

Figure 1.1 : DB/IS development cycle

Requirements Engineering consists of knowledge acquisition and validation.

The **acquisition task** falls into two areas, namely, analysis and modelling. The Requirements Engineering process starts with an observation of the real world, in order to identify pertinent real phenomena, their properties and constraints, and to classify similar phenomena into classes. Then the analyst represents and describes the classes, their properties and constraints through types of a specific conceptual model. Analysis leads to problem-statements, while modelling allows the description of elements of the conceptual schema.

The **validation task** has the objective of checking whether the conceptual schema is consistent and whether it correctly expresses the requirements informally stated by the users.

In many cases, analysts are able to correctly use concepts of a model but have difficulties to abstract reality in order to represent it through these concepts. This is similar to school students who are able to use simple equations but have many difficulties to build in equations from problem-statements. Similarly correcting a conceptual schema is easy while validating its adequacy to requirements is more difficult.

Analysis, modelling and validation are cognitive processes. However, analysis is based on domain-dependent knowledge, modelling requires model-dependent knowledge and validation requires both. More generally, Vitalari has shown, [Vitalari 83], [Vitalari 85], that experienced analysts use different categories of knowledge namely : organization specific knowledge, application domain knowledge, development methodology knowledge and functional domain knowledge.

It is the authors' belief that there is a need for CASE tools that support the Requirements Engineering process in a way that better reflects the problem solving behaviour of experienced analysts. This requires to identify, understand and formalize the cognitive mechanisms that allow the analyst to abstract reality and to represent it through concepts and to diagnose the specification from users points of view.

OICSI[1] (French acronym for intelligent tool for information system design) is a system prototype based on this premise. It exploits knowledge-based paradigms to provide an active aid to DB/IS analysts during the Requirements Engineering process. OICSI supports the analysts in the process of problem-statements acquisition, elicitation, modelling and validation.

In addition, the authors recognize that Requirements Engineering is mainly based on abstraction and have granted a privilege to a natural language approach.

Indeed, psychological research works dealing with the study of abstraction mechanisms show that abstraction is strongly interlocked with language manipulation.

Following this line, problem-statements in OICSI are expressed with the French natural language and automatically interpreted in terms of the OICSI conceptual model. Complementary, OICSI uses a text generation technique to feed back to the user information about the specification (i.e the conceptual schema).

This choice is enhanced by the fact that analysts do not proceed by direct observation of the real world but through a media which is the natural language. Indeed, the two most common ways for acquiring application domain knowledge are interviews and studies of existing documents (forms, legal documents...).

---

[1] OICSI is the name used in the academic area; in the industrial world this case tool is named ALECSI, it is developed by CRIL company.

According to the OICSI paradigm illustrated in figure 1.2, the analysis task refers to the description of the relevant real world phenomena using the French natural language, the modelling task refers to the mapping of problem-statements onto basic concepts of the OICSI underlying DB/IS development methodology and the validation task is based upon a paraphrased description of the conceptual schema in the French natural language.

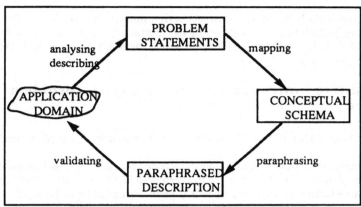

Figure 1.2 : Analysis and Modelling process.

Using OICSI, the conceptual schema is hidden to the future system users. The "system referential", they have to understand, comment upon and validate, is expressed using natural language. Even for the analysts the conceptual model and the conceptual schema are partially hidden since OICSI automatically supports modelling as well as text generation.

However, it must be mentioned that OICSI provides a graphical interface. Depending on their personal abilities to understand conceptual modelling, the analysts will use the most appropriate interface.

Similar approaches to solving Requirements Engineering from the description of the application domain uttered with natural language sentences have been followed for example in the AMADEUS project which aims at combining graphics and natural language [Black 87]. Others examples are SECSI [Bouzegoub 86] and ACME [Kersten 86] which are conceptual modelling expert systems.

Text generation has been used in different areas of databases : it is an important matter in natural language interfaces to databases; it also used for tutorial purposes in learning a query language and for generating readable error messages. Examples of prototype systems are EXPOUND [Chester 76] which translates formal proofs into English, CO-OP [McKeown 86] based upon a syntactic approach, PERFORM [Muckstein 85] and ELFS [Luk 86] which are knowledge based approaches for text generation from SQL to natural language, De Roeck paraphrasing of relational calculus [De Roeck 88] and Grishman paraphrasing of predicate logic [Grishman 79].
The remainder of this paper describes the natural language approach for Requirements Engineering and its implementation in OICSI. Section 2 presents the linguistic approach for requirements acquisition and elicitation. The paraphrasing mechanism for validation is presented in section 3. A brief overview of implementation aspects is given in section 4.

2. The linguistic approach

Conceptual modelling in OICSI is based on a linguistic approach that tries to formalize the linguistic mechanisms through which analysts are able to abstract observed phenomena onto concepts.

The problem-solving behaviour of analysts is first intuitively introduced. The "CASE for CASE" theory (which is the foundation of the formalization of the analyst behaviour) is thus recalled. Finally, our linguistic approach is detailed and the conceptual schema generation is presented.

2.1 Intuitive introduction to analysts problem solving behaviour

This section is an attempt to highlight the linguistic mechanisms used by analysts.

Let us imagine that our favourite analyst *Ado* is used to manipulate the Entity-Relationship (E-R) model [Chen 76]. This means that *Ado* will try, when observing the real world, to identify classes of real world phenomena that can be modelled as entity types, attributes or relationship types.

Thus, during an interview, if *Ado* hears the sentence:
"A subscriber has a name and an address."
He will probably introduces in the conceptual schema an entity type SUBSCRIBER with two attributes NAME and ADDRESS.
Now, in order to understand the analyst behaviour, let us ask the question :"How did *Ado* get this result?".

A first response could be that *Ado* knows the meaning of the words "*subscriber*", "*name*" and "*address*", and how they relate one with others. This means that *Ado* uses a kind of common-sense knowledge to match the sentence onto the E-R schema. This knowledge is based on couples (word, real object) which allow to relate a word to a well known object in the real world.

But assume now that the sentence is :
"The colydrena have a pedistylus and a folicul."
As *Ado* did, many analysts will make the hypothesis that the word "*colydrena*" is a non lexical object type that can be modelled by an entity type and that "*pedistylus*" and "*folicul*" are two attributes related to the entity type. *Ado* is not certain that he did the right interpretation of the sentence but the interpretation is plausible and he can, later, validate its truth discussing with domain specialists.

In this case, *Ado* did not use the same kind of common-sense knowledge as previously. He does not know the meaning of the words (they are imaginary), but, however without any understanding of the words he found a model of the described situation (which is, indeed, correct).

Ado's reasoning is based on the recognition of a particular sentence pattern which is colloquial to him. The knowledge which is used, is a linguistic knowledge related to language manipulation. It allows him to recognize and to interpret the following sentence pattern :

<Subject Group><Verb expressing ownership><Complement Group>

The pre-established interpretation of such pattern allows Ado to associate the subject group of the sentence to a real entity class as the owner of the attributes represented by the complement group's words.

The linguistic knowledge is certainly the most common knowledge within the analysts population. Analysts use it, sometimes explicitly, but most often in an implicit way. Our goal is to make explicit the different types of sentence patterns in order to formalize this kind of linguistic knowledge and to support the process of the problem-statements interpretation and modelling in a computerized way.

The linguistic approach implemented in OICSI is borrowed from the Fillmore's theory "Case for Case" [Fillmore 68].

Section 2.2 summarizes the main points of this theory. Its specialization for OICSI is presented in section 2.3.

2.2 The Fillmore's case system

The main concept of the Fillmore's theory is the notion of case introduced as follows: "*the case notions comprise a set of universal, presumably innate, concepts which identify certain types of judgement human beings are capable of making about the events which are going on around them...*".

Cases are types of relationships that groups of words have with the verb in any clause of a sentence. One of the basic Fillmore's assumption is that it exists a limited number of cases. Fillmore exhibits six major cases: AGENTIVE, INSTRUMENTAL, DATIVE, FACTITIVE, LOCATIVE and OBJECTIVE.

```
(1) John opens the door.
(2) The door is opened by John.
(3) The key opens the door.
(4) John opens the door by means of the key.
(5) John uses the key in order to open the door.
(6) John believes that he will win.
(7) John is ill.
```

Figure 2.1 : Examples of sentences

For example in sentences (1) and (2) of the figure 2.1 "*John*" is associated to the case AGENTIVE and "*door*" to the case OBJECTIVE; the word "*key*" in sentences (3), (4), (5) is associated to the INSTRUMENTAL case, while in sentences (6) and (7) "*John*" is associated to the DATIVE case.

Obviously, the same word can correspond to different cases in different sentences.

One complementary assumption of the Fillmore's theory is that the meaning of any clause is derivable from the meaning of the verb and the recognition of embedded cases. This leads to the identification of predefined patterns with associated derivable meanings.

For example, due to the fact that sentence (1) has a structure of the type:
<Verb expressing action, AGENTIVE, OBJECTIVE>
allows to infer that "*John*" is the agent who performs the action on the object "*door*".

Sentences (1) and (2) correspond to the previously mentioned structure; the structure of sentence (3) matches the type :
<Verb expressing action, INSTRUMENTAL, OBJECTIVE>
and finally, sentences (4) and (5) have the following pattern :
<Verb expressing action,OBJECTIVE, AGENTIVE, INSTRUMENTAL>.

The Fillmore's patterns allow to perform a classification of natural language sentences with regards to their structure and, thus, to infer their meaning according to the class they belong to.

2.3 Specialization of the Fillmore's case system

Experimentations of the Fillmore's theory convinced the authors that the theory was applicable and pertinent to support the DB/IS analysis and modelling process. However, we reach the conclusion that the cases might be adapted to the purpose of establishing problem-statements allowing the construction of an DB/IS conceptual schema. Indeed statements about real world phenomena fall into two categories: fact descriptions and rules.

Examples of fact descriptions (we consider a subscription library system) are as follows:

(1) In the library, a book is described by a unique reference number, the authors' names, the publisher name and the year and version of editing.
(2) Last and first names of the subscriber, his address, first year of subscription and last date of subscription fees payment are recorded.
(3) The status of each copy of a book is recorded in real time.

Our understanding of facts is similar to the Nijssen's approach [Nijssen 89].

The following are examples of rules:

(1) Subscription fees are paid every year.
(2) A subscriber, properly registered (i.e who paid the fees) is called an "active" subscriber.
(3) A subscriber cannot borrow more than three books at the same time.
(4) Books are only loaned to active subscribers.
(5) When a loan request cannot be satisfied it becomes a "waiting request".
(6) After 13 months without paying the subscription fees, the subscriber status becomes "inactive".
(7) "Waiting request" are treated in their chronological order.

As just exemplified, rules can express management rules independent or dependent of time, static constraint rules or dynamic constraint rules .

Sentences describing either facts or rules are the problem-statements that OICSI automatically interprets by performing a case approach.

2.3.1 The case classification

The case notion has been extended in two directions: cases are applicable to clauses and the classification of cases has been revised.

. According to the Fillmore's theory, cases relate to words in sentences. It is the authors' belief that the notion of case could be successfully applied not only to words but also to clauses in sentences. This allows to interpret a complex sentence in a top-down fashion. The case approach is first applied to subordinate clauses with regards to the verb of the main clause. Thus, the case approach is again applied to each of the subordinate clause.

. The classification of cases used by OICSI is as follows :
<OWNER, OWNED, ACTOR, TARGET, CONSTRAINED*, CONSTRAINT*, LOCALIZATION* , ACTION* , OBJECT>.

We exemplified the meaning of these cases on the following set of sentences.

(1) A subscriber is described by a name, an address and a number.
(2) A subscriber borrows books.
(3)When a subscriber makes a request of loan, the request is accepted, if a copy of the requested book is available, else the request is delayed.

In sentence (1), "*subscriber*" is associated to the OWNER case and "*name*", "*address*" and "*number*" are associated to the OWNED case.

In sentence (2), "*subscriber*" is associated to the ACTOR case and the OWNER case, while "*books*" is associated to the OWNED case; these two cases express that there is a relationship between "*subscriber*" and "*books*". The entire clause is associated to the ACTION case.

In sentence (3) :
- the clause "*When a subscriber requests for a loan*" is associated to the LOCALIZATION case,
- inside this clause, the phrase "*request of loan*" is associated to OBJECT case,
- the clause "*if a copy of the requested book is available*" is associated to the CONSTRAINT case,
- the clause "*the request is accepted*" is associated to the ACTION and the CONSTRAINED case,
- inside this clause, the word "*request*" is associated to the TARGET case.

---

* denotes cases that may be applied to clauses

Complementary, classes of verbs have been identified. The figure 2.2 shows both the hierarchy of classes and some examples of class instances.

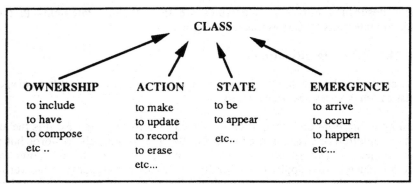

Figure 2.4 : Hierarchy and instances of classes of verbs

2.3.2 The linguistic patterns

A set of patterns that combine cases and classes of verbs previously introduced have been defined. These patterns are of two different types:
- elementary patterns allow to associate cases to syntactic units of a clause,
- sentence patterns allow to associate cases to clauses of a sentence.

Both are introduced and exemplified in turn.

Elementary patterns

They fall again into three different categories:
- structural pattern,
- behavioural pattern,
- constraint pattern.

SP1 and SP2 are examples of simple **structural patterns**.

SP1 : [Ng_subject](OWNER) [verbal form](ownership_subject)
[Ng_complement](OWNED)

SP2 : [Ng_subject](OWNED) [verbal form](ownership_complement)
[Ng_complement](OWNER).

The notation [syntactic unit](case) means that the "syntactic unit" is associated to the case "case". The following abbreviations Ng, Cl, Sub, Mn, are respectively used to refer to a Nominal group, a Clause, a Subordinate clause and a Main clause.

The clause : "*any subscriber has a name and an address*" matches the SP1 pattern and can be interpreted in the following way:
- the clause subject "*any subscriber*" plays the role of OWNER,
- "*has*" is the verb belonging to the ownership class,
- "*a name* " and "*an address*" are subject complements playing the role of OWNED.

It is obvious that patterns of the SP1 family are appropriated to fact sentences.

The sentence " *loan-requests are made by subscribers*" can be unified to pattern SP2.

BP1, BP2, BP3, and BP4 are four examples of **behavioural patterns**.

BP1 : [Ng_subject](ACTOR) [verbal form](action)
[Ng_complement](TARGET)

BP2 : [Conjunction](LOCALIZATION) [Ng_subject](ACTOR)
[verbal form](action) [Ng_complement](OBJECT)

BP3 : [preposition](LOCALIZATION) [Ng](OBJECT)

BP4 : [Ng](TARGET) [verbal form](action)

"*Subscribers borrow books*" is a clause that matches the BP1 pattern :
- "*subscribers*" as the subject of the clause plays the role of ACTOR,
- "*borrow*" is a verb belonging to the action class,
- "*books*" is the subject complement which plays the role of TARGET.

The clause : "*when a subscriber returns a book copy*" can be unified with BP2 pattern with the following interpretation:
- "*when*" is a conjunction that expresses the LOCALIZATION of the action,
- "*a subscriber*" is the subject that plays the role of ACTOR,
- "*returns*" is the verb that belongs to the action class,
- "*a book copy*" is the complement that plays the role of OBJECT of action.

BP3 is a pattern which deals with circumstantial complements and, for this reason, is not organized around the verb but around the preposition.

Within the clause: "*As soon as the receipt of a subscriber's subscription fees, the subscriber's status is updated*", the phrase "*As soon as the receipt of a subscriber's subscription fees*" matches the BP3 pattern with the following interpretation:
- "*As soon as*" is the preposition that describes the LOCALIZATION of action expresses by the clause,
- "*the receipt of a subscriber's subscription fees*" is the phrase that plays the role of OBJECT.

Finally the BP4 pattern allows to interpret a particular type of clauses which describe actions such as "*the loan is agreed upon*".

At last CP1 is an example of **constraint pattern**.

CP1 : [Ng_subject](CONSTRAINED) [verbal form](state)
[Ng_complement](CONSTRAINT)

The clause: *"the number of loans is equal or less than three"*, can be unified to the CP1 pattern in such a way that:
- *"the number of loans"* plays the role of CONSTRAINED, and
- *"equal or less than three"* is the predicate group associated to the CONSTRAINT case.

Sentence patterns

The sentence patterns define the cases of embedded clauses in a same sentence. They are constructed combining elementary patterns. Let us consider two examples:

SPT1 : [Main clause]

SPT2 : [Subordinate clause unifying a BP pattern](LOCALIZATION)
[Subordinate clause unifying a BP2 pattern](CONSTRAINT)
[main clause unifying a BP pattern with a verb expressing an action](ACTION + CONSTRAINED)

SPT1 corresponds to sentences composed with only one main clause. This clause must be able to match :
- either a structural pattern; the sentence *"A subscriber is described by his name and his address"* is an example of it,
- or a behavioural pattern with a verb expressing an action; *"Subscribers borrow copies of books"* matches this pattern. The ACTION case is thus affected to the sentence,
- or a constraint pattern; this corresponds to the sentence *"The number of loans is limited to three"*. This sentence is associated to the CONSTRAINT case.

The subordinate clause that can be unified to a behavioural pattern determines the spatio-temporal LOCALIZATION of the action described by the main clause.

The sentence: *"When there is a loan request, the loan is agreed only if the subscriber's status is "active" and if a copy of the requested book is available"* corresponds to the SPT2 pattern :
- the clause *"When there is a loan request"* matches the BP2 pattern and is associated to the LOCALIZATION case;
- the clauses *"only if the subscriber's status"* and *"if a copy of the requested book is available"* match the CP1 pattern and are associated to the CONSTRAINT case.
- the clause *"the loan is agreed"* matches the BP4 pattern and corresponds simultaneously to the ACTION and CONSTRAINED cases.

2.4 Conceptual schema generation

We assume that it is possible to simply link cases and concepts. Thus the conceptual schema generation is grounded upon rules that map cases onto concepts. These rules are dependant of the target conceptual model. Conversely the linguistic patterns are independent of a particular modelling technique and can be used within any design methodology.

Figure 2.3 gives a brief overview of the main mapping rules implemented in the OICSI environment. We recall that OICSI is based upon the REMORA methodology [Rolland 82] which identifies four basic concepts namely, objects, actions, events and constraints. A detailed description of this aspect can be found in [Rolland 87]. These are the four type of nodes of the semantic net used by OICSI to implement the conceptual schema under construction. Arcs of the net are of five types :

- rl : expresses a relationship between two objects nodes;
- md : expresses that an action modifies an object;
- tr : expresses that an event triggers an action;
- act : expresses that an object has a particular state change which is an event;
- ct : connect a constraint to the node (object, action or event) which is constrained.

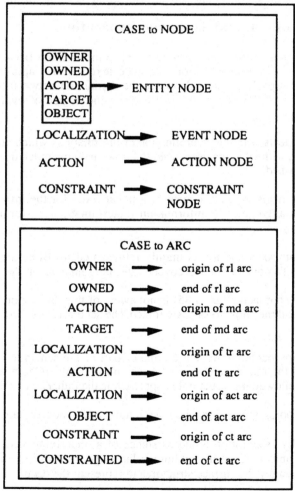

Figure 2.3 : Mapping rules

3. Conceptual schema validation and paraphrasing

The Requirements Engineering process includes also the validation cycle. In order to base the whole Requirements Engineering process on a natural language approach, we propose to feed back to the user information about the conceptual schema using again the French natural language.

The paraphrasing technique we have developed has the scope to generate natural language texts using the words and expressions of the users community and avoiding to describe the conceptual schema contents in technical terms.

We introduce first the main principles of the techniques used for text generation and then we present our solution to conceptual schema validation by paraphrasing.

3.1 Principle of natural language generation

A system for text generation must be able to select information from some knowledge base and to organize it into a natural language text. Several approaches have been proposed for this purpose. Most of them use the distinction between the "what to say" from the "how to say". However, they differ from the degree of overlap of these two aspects.

The "what to say" deals with the determination of informations which are relevant for the purpose of the text, with what the users need to know, and how much detailed an object or event must be described.

The "how to say" deals with the choice of a linear order for the information selected, specifying how to aggregate the information (determination top-form paragraphs and sentence boundaries).

The structuralist approach, which is mainly represented by Bloomfield [Mounin 72], [Harris 85], admits this distinction but concentrates the semantics in the "how to say".

The fonctionnalist approach [Harrys 85] is not aware of this distinction. In this approach the "what to say" and the "how to say" are mixed.The sentences are directly built from the knowledge base.

Finally the third approach admits that the major part of the semantic is included in the "what to say" and the minor part of it is in the "how to say" [Chomsky 57]. Chomsky who has initially followed the structuralist approach is the father of this third approach.

Among the set of possible solutions we have retained the Chomsky approach [Chomsky 65] .
The basic Chomsky assumption is the existence of a underlying structure, namely the deep structure, to any sentence in any human language. In addition, there is an infinite number of ways, namely the surface structures to represent the deep structure in different languages.

The deep structure expresses the semantics of a sentence by means of semantic elements and relationships among them. It corresponds to the "what to say".

Grouped all together, the deep structures corresponding to a knowledge base, allow us to reach a semantic understanding of its contents.

The surface structure represents each sentence of a text by means of a set of phrases. It corresponds to the "how to say". Many sets of surface structures may correspond to the same deep structure. In addition, it is possible to define a set of transformation rules (a generative grammar [Chomsky 69]) which allow to map a deep structure into an infinite set of surface structure.

Based upon this distinction the process of generating natural language texts is summarized in figure 3.1.

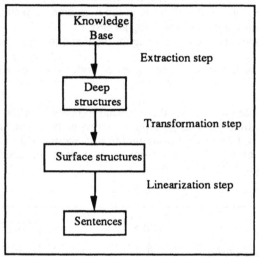

Figure 3.1 : process of generating natural language texts

It is assumed that the knowledge base provides the description of some application domain.

The first step consists of defining the appropriate deep structures for the knowledge base contents. Deep structures are often represented through semantic nets.

The second step maps the deep structure onto a surface structure. This step uses a generative grammar [Chomsky 69] which allows to produce skeletons of sentences in the target natural language. This surface structure includes all the phrases of the future sentence and its grammatical structure.

The last step, so called linearization step, uses the surface structure to produce a readable sentence. This step uses a lexical knowledge base in order to solve problem such as :
- determination of valid articles,
- tacking into account singular, plural, ...
- use of idiomatic forms,
- phonological short-cuts.

It is eventually possible to complete the process by a structuration step which aims at reorganizing the collection of sentences into chapters, sections and paragraphs.

3.2 The OICSI paraphrasing process

Following the Chomsky's guidelines we have organized the process for paraphrasing from the conceptual schema to a French text into a similar way which is shown in figure 3.1.

The knowledge base mentioned in figure 3.1 is the OICSI base of facts i.e. the semantic net which represents the conceptual schema under construction.

The deep structure definition consists of grouping nodes and arcs of the semantic net. As a matter of fact, two rules are used in order to group in a same deep structure :
- all the nodes and arcs describing an entity,
- all the nodes and arcs describing an event and its triggered operations.

We name a situation of the semantic net, a set of nodes and arcs which correspond to a deep structure.

This solution is motivated by the fact that we want to restitute to the users descriptions of their application domain as close as possible to the problem statements they have initially provided to the system. Following our assumption in section 2.3 , we consider that facts and management rules are the two easier entry points for users in the process of developing information systems.

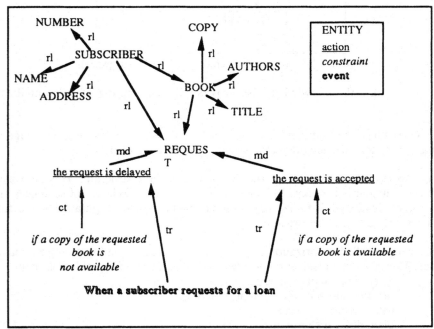

Figure 3.2 : The graphical representation of the conceptual schema

Thus the text generated by the system will describe :
- on one hand, the static aspects of the world through entities, their properties and relationships;
- on the other hand, the behavioural aspects through rules with the standard pattern "*when event, if condition then action*".

For example, from the conceptual schema presented in the figure 3.2, the system recognizes the two deep structures shown in the figure 3.3.

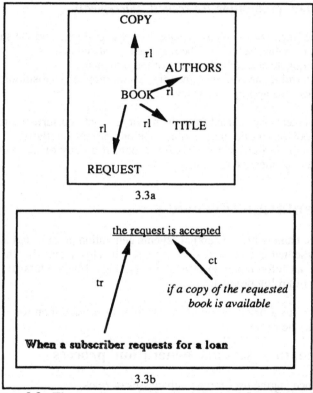

Figure 3.3 : The two deep structures recognized from figure 3.2

The 3.3a deep structure includes all informations about the entity BOOK, and the 3.3b deep structure includes all informations about the event "*a subscriber requests for a loan*".

The second step is the transformation of a deep structure into a surface structure. We make the hypothesis that the number of different types of situations in the conceptual schema is limited and that these situations are well defined. Therefore, the transformation step is based on a set of surface structure patterns which are associated to each type of situation.

For example, the 3.3a deep structure will be associated to the following surface structure:

sentence(verb(*to have*), **subject**(*book*), **complement**(*title, many copies, one or many authors, one or many requests*)).

The 3.3b deep structure corresponds to the following surface structure :

> **sentence(circumstantial proposition**(*a subscriber requests for a loan*),
> **conditional proposition** (*if a copy of the requested book is available*),
> **main proposition**(*the request is accepted*)).

The last step is the linearization phase. Using lexical knowledge and the surface structure this step produces readable sentences. The main tasks realized here is :
> - to conjugate correctly the verbs of the sentence;
> - to determine the conjunctions for the subordinate propositions;
> - to select the appropriate articles.

For example, the sentences produced from the previously defined surface structure are :
> - A book has a title, many copies and one or many authors.
> - When a subscriber requests for a loan, if a copy of the requested book is available then the request is accepted.

4. Implementation overview

The two processes, namely the conceptual schema generation process and the paraphrasing process are implemented in an expert system approach. This means that the two processes are performed by an inference engine which uses rules. For modularity and flexibility reasons the rules are Prolog production rules.

We limit ourselves to a brief overview of the two processes mentioning the different classes of rules and their role.

4.1 The conceptual schema generation process

The OICSI inference engine uses three main classes of rules :
> - lexical and syntactic rules,
> - linguistic rules,
> - mapping rules,

in order to progressively transform NL sentences onto nodes and arcs of the semantic net. The process is organized into three steps.

. During the **analysis step** the system builds an internal representation of the initial sentences by means of syntactic trees, with the purpose of decomposing each sentence into grammatical unit.
This part of the process is based on wellknown techniques developed for the general purpose of natural language recognition [Bruce 75], [Cordier 79] and [Kayser 81].

The role of lexical rules is to determine the grammatical nature of each word of any clause of a sentence and to classify the verb clause into the four classes: ownership, action, state, emergence. Lexical rules use a dictionary which contains information about the grammatical nature of words and about the meaning and the classification of verbs. Syntactic rules allow the system, on one hand, to verify that a sentence belongs to the authorized language, and, on the other hand, to build up the syntactic trees. These rules are based on the use of a generative grammar which corresponds to the system's grammatical knowledge.

. During the **linguistic step**, the system makes pattern matching in order to unify each syntactic tree with one of the sentence pattern defined in section 2, and to associate each syntactic unit with a case. Pattern matching and association of cases to the phrases of a sentence is performed simultaneously in the same rule. Basically any linguistic rule as the following form :

- the premise of the rule correspond to the conditions that allow to recognize the sentence (or clause) pattern,
- the conclusions of the rule associate cases to elements of the sentence (or clause).

Patterns recognition is based both on the class of the verb (as identified during step 1 and attached to it in the syntactic tree) and on the grammatical structure of the sentence (or clause). Generally, a pattern is implemented through a set of linguistic rules in order to take into account the variety of grammatical structures. As an illustration, rules RL1 and RL2 are two examples of rules necessary for implementing the pattern SP1.

> **RL1** :
> IF meaning(clause(verbal form)) = ownership_subject
> AND gram_structure(Ng_subject) = <article, noun_1>
> AND gram_structure(Ng_complement) = <article, noun_2>
> THEN case(noun_1) = OWNER
>   case(noun_2) = OWNED.

> **RL2** :
> IF meaning(clause(verbal form)) = ownership_subject
> AND gram_structure(Ng_subject) = <article, noun_1, predicate_1>
> AND gram_structure(Ng_complement) = <article, noun_2>
> AND gram_structure(predicate_1) = <preposition, article, noun_3>
> THEN case(noun_1) = OWNER(verb)* and OWNED(predicate)
>   case(noun_2) = OWNED.

* the notation OWNER(verb) and OWNED(predicate) mean that the role OWNER is played in regards to the verb and that the role OWNED is played in regards to the predicate. By default, the case meaning is in regards to the verb.

. Finally, the **mapping step** consists of building the semantic net. Each syntactic tree is mapped onto a set of nodes and arcs of the semantic net. Mapping rules implement the relationship summarized in figure 2.3 (see section 2). They allow to automatically build nodes and arcs of the semantic net from cases and patterns determined in the previous step.

4.2 The paraphrasing process

Similarly the OICSI inference engine uses three main classes of rules :
- extraction rules,
- transformation rules,
- linearization rules,

in order to perform the three steps of the paraphrasing process illustrated in figure 3.2.

. **Extraction rules** are used to cluster nodes and arcs related to either an entity or an event type and to construct the corresponding deep structure.

. **Transformation rules** allow to map the deep structures into surface structures. A pattern matching mechanism is used in order to associate to a deep structure the appropriate surface structure.

. **Linearization rules** are used in order to rewrite a surface structure into a readable sentence. They include rules for to conjugate the verbs, to select the article and so on. A major part of these rules use a dictionary which represents the lexical knowledge of the tool.

Obviously, the two processes (conceptual schema generation and paraphrasing) are performed in an interactive way. For example the user's aid may be solicitated during the analysis step to add a new verb in the dictionary. At any time the user can ask for explanation about the system deductions and this can lead to pattern transformation. At last the analyst/user is allowed to directly manipulate the semantic net through a graphical interface in order to add, delete or change any arc or node of the net. In addition, the two processes are fully integrated. This means that the user can ask for paraphrasing from the conceptual schema at any point of its generation process. This allow to constantly keep the equivalence between a set of natural sentences and the formalized conceptual schema. We believe that this is helpful to validate the conformance of the system specifications to the user requirements.

Similar considerations have been discussed as the premise of the RUBRIC [Van Assche 88] and TEMPORA [Loucopoulos 90] projects.

A more detailed description may be found in [Loucopoulos 92].

5. Conclusion

The paper has argued that the natural language plays an important role during the DB/IS development cycle. Therefore, the ideas that Requirements Engineering should be supported by a Case tool based on a linguistic approach and that validation of specifications must be performed by means of text generation technique have been presented.

In a first time, the work reported in this paper is based on the premise that Requirements engineering is strongly interrelated to language manipulation. It represents an attempt at improving problem-statements elicitation, interpretation and modelling through the use of a linguistic approach. It is proposed that the problem-statements for an information system development should be expressed via natural language sentences.

The work reported presents how a linguistic approach based on the Case notion can be used to automatically carry out the IS modelling. The paper details the linguistic approach and its implementation in the expert design system, known as OICSI. The thesis put forward in the paper is that the linguistic approach is general, in the double sense that it can be customized for different modelling techniques and, in addition, it can be applied in a wider sphere of problems. From this point of view the work reported relates to other research works such KOD [Vogel 88] or SECSI [Bouzeghoub86].

In a second time, the paper presents some solutions based on theorical linguistic works in order to validate the conceptual schema by paraphrasing from conceptual schema to natural language texts. This paraphrasing technique has the scope to generate natural language texts with words and expressions of the users community and avoiding description of the conceptual schema contents in technical terms.

References

[Bouzeghoub 86] M. Bouzeghoub and G. Gardarin : "SECSI : an expert system approach for data base design", in Proc. of IFIP world congress, Dublin, Sept 1986.

[Bruce 75] B. Bruce : "Case systems for natural language", Artificial Intelligence Nb 6, 1975.

[Black 87] WJ. Black: "Acquisition of Conceptual data models from natural language descriptions, 3rd Conf. of the European chapter of ACM, Danemark, 1987.

[Bubenko 90] J. Bubenko et all : Syslab/Decode research plan Syslab report 1990.

[Chen 76] P.P.S Chen : "The entity relationship model : toward a unified view" ACM Trans. on data base systems, Vol 1, Nb1, 1976.

[Chester 76] D. Chester : "The translation of formal proofs into English", Artificial Intelligence, vol 7, n°2, 1976.

[Chomsky 57] N. Chomsky : "Syntactic strutures", Mouton Ed, The Hague 1957.

[Chomsky 65] N. Chomsky : "Aspects of the theory of syntax", MIT Press Ed, Cambridge Mass, 1965.

[Chomsky 69] N. Chomsky : "Language and Mind", Payot ed, 1969.

[Cordier 79] M. Cordier: Connaissances sémantiques et pragmatiques en compréhension du langage naturel, 2Çme congrés AFCET-INRIA, Reconnaissances des formes et Intelligence Artificielle, Toulouse 1979.

[De Roeck 88] A.N.D Roeck, B.G.T. Lowden : "Generating English paraphrases from formal relational calculus expressions" Coling (Pub) 1988.

[Dubois 89] E. Dubois, J. Hagelstein, A. Rifaut : "Formal requirements engineering with ERAE", Philips journal of research, vol 43, N) 3/4 1989.

[Grishman 79] R. Grishman : "Response generation in question answering systems" in ACL 1979.

[Fillmore 68] CJ. Fillmore : "The Case for Case", in Universals in linguistics theory; Holt, Rinehart and Winston, Inc., E. Bach/R.T. Harms (eds) 1968.

[Harris 85] M. Dee Harris : "Introduction to Natural Language processing", Reston Publishing company, 1985.

[Hull 87] R. Hull and R. King : Semantic Database Modeling : Survey, Applications and Research issues", ACM computing Surveys, vol 19, n⁻3, 1987.

[Kayser 81] D. Kayser : "Les ATN sÇmantiques" 3Çme congräs AFCET-INRIA, Reconnaissances des formes et Intelligence Artificielle, 1981

[Kersten 86] M.L. Kersten, H. Weigand, F. Dignum, J; Proom: "A conceptual modelling expert system", 5th Int. Conf. ont the ER Approach S. Spaccapietra(ed), Dijon, 1986.

[Loucopoulos 90] P. Loucopoulos et all : "From software engineering to business engineering: Esprit projects in information systems engineering", in CAISE'90, Int. Conference on : "Advanced Information System Engineering ", Springer-Verlag, 1990.

[Loucopoulos 92] "Conceptual modelling databases and Case: an integrated view of information systems development", P. Loucopoulos (ed), Mac Grawhill (Pub) 1992 (to be published).

[Luk 86] W.S Luk, S. Kloster : "ELFS: English language from SQL", ACM Trans. on Databases systems, vol 11, n°4, 1986.

[Mc Keown 86] K. Mc Keown : "Paraphrasing questions using given and new information", Am. journal of computational linguistics, vol 9 n°1, 1986.

[Muckstein 87] E.M Muckstein, M.G. Datovsky :" Semantic interpretation of a database query language", Data and Knowledge engineering, vol 1, 1985.

[Maddison 83] R. Maddison : "Information System methodologies", Wiley-Heyden 1983.

[Mounin 72] G. Mounin : "La linguistique du 20ième siècle", Presses Universitaires de France Ed, 1972.

[Nijssen 89] G.M. Nijssen, T.A. Halpin : "Conceptual Schema and relational database design : a fact oriented approach", Prentice-Hall, Englewood Cliffs, New Jersey, 1989.

[Olle 82] T.W. Olle, H.G. Sol and A.A Verrijn Stuart :"Information System design methodologies : a comparative review", (IFIP WG 8.1 CRIS 1) North Holland, Amsterdam , NL, 1982.

[Rolland 82] C. Rolland and C. Richard : "The Remora methodology for information systems design and management" in [Oll 82].

[Rolland 87] C. Rolland, G. Benci and O. Foucault : "Conception des systèmes d'information : la méthode REMORA", Eyrolles (Pub) 1987.

[Van Assche 88] F. Van Assche, P.J. Layzell, P. Loucopoulos and G. Speltinex : "Information Systems development : a rule based approach", in Journal of knowledge based systems, 1988.

[Vit alari 83] N.P. Vitalari and G.W. Dickson : "Problem solving for effective systems analysis : an experimental exploration ", in Comm. ACM Vol 26 N⁻11, (November 1983).

[Vitalari 85] N.P. Vitalari : "Knowledge as a basis for expertise in systems analysis : an empirical study", MIS Q, (September 1985).

[Vogel 88] : C. Vogel : "Génie cognitif", Masson collection Sciences cognitives, 1988.

Building a Tool for Software Code Analysis
A Machine Learning Approach

Gilles Fouqué[1]
B 004
EDF-DER
1, av du Gal de Gaulle
92141 Clamart Cedex
Tel : (33) 1-47-65-57-03
e-mail : gfouque@csi.uottawa.ca

Christel Vrain[2]
LIFO
Université d'Orléans
Rue de Chartres
45067 Orleans Cedex
Tel : (33) 38-41-70-00
e-mail : cv@univorl.univ-orleans.fr

Abstract. This article presents the application of a machine learning technique to a software code analysis tool. This tool builds a base of elementary and relevant program structures, acquired from the analysis of a primitive set of programs of good programming style. These program structures are compared to new programs to determine the quality of the latter. In this paper we stress the framework of the tool and discuss the critical details of its modules.
The learning technique has been developed to use intensively a specific knowledge base in order to acquire the base of relevant program structures. We present problems that arise due to the necessity of using knowledge which is non-monotonic in nature.
Particular issues will be highlighted by the analysis of requests written in the SQL language.

1. Introduction

Software engineering has to provide tools and techniques to improve software quality. To this end, the automatization of the analysis and validation process is an important issue and several tools have been developed [4, 15]. Usually, these tools are classified in two groups : dynamic and static tools. The former concludes with a diagnosis of the quality of the code from observations of its execution. The latter is based on the study of the data flow and the control flow of the code to check if it satisfies a set of known rules for identifying good programming style code.

In our point of view, neither of these approaches concludes with a satisfactory diagnosis. In most cases, dynamic approaches are intractable and are used for very specific domains such as autonomous or safety systems. Static approaches use metrics to measure the quality of the analyzed code and they then compute an abstract view of this code which involves an important expertise step. Aware of these limitations, we kept in mind the behavior of a programmer during his analysis task, to specify our tool. The programmer compares the elementary program structures of new code to similar structures within his experience. He is thus able to give a precise semantic meaning to those structures. At the end of this review process the analyzed program is a mosaic of known and unknown structures. From a detailed understanding of the latter the programmer will have enriched

---

[1] G. Fouqué is currently pursuing post-doctoral studies at the University of Ottawa with the Ottawa Machine Learning Group

[2] a part of this research has been made in the Inference and Learning Group, LRI, Université Paris XI

his knowledge of elementary program structures or will have modified them. As the strategy of the programmer is adaptative we were interested in a machine learning approach which could resolve the problems previously presented.

The paper is organised as follows. The next section presents previous approaches for software code analysis. We then detail our approach and its advantages, and go on to describe each one of its modules. The last sections are devoted to the description of the developments to the learning technique and to the experiments performed on several kinds of data.

2. Previous static code analysis approaches

The main task of software engineering researchers deals with decreasing the weight of the maintenance step in the software life cycle. As this maintenance is related to the understanding of the code, the first approaches have been to standardize the program writing task using program standards and macros. These approaches are not commonly used because they are inflexible, difficult to perform and cannot be used to understand existing programs.

More elaborate approaches [10, 16] compare new programs with a fixed and hand-build base of structures called *clichés*. This comparison process is performed using a knowledge base including properties of the domain. These approaches have to face two problems : the acquisition of the clichés and their recognition. Firstly, there are too many clichés to generate a complete base of them. Secondly, construction of a complete and consistent knowledge base for manipulating these clichés is also intractable if we consider the extraordinary complexity of the domain.

Our tool uses a machine learning techniques in order to have an incremental acquisition of the program structures - the clichés - and a powerful matching process which uses intensively a knowledge base. Our approach allows us to build a tool having a dynamic form of management as the base of clichés grows during the analysis of new structures. Moreover, our specific approach does not need a complete knowledge base as we detail below. The idea to use machine learning for a software engineering task is not a new one [2]. Most research in this domain deals with using analogy [1, 5] often combined with an EBL approach [3]. These projects involve important research in both the fields of, software engineering - to specify a design language or to generate some code - and machine learning - most of this research uses a case-based reasoning approach and has to resolve indexing and retrieving problems. Here, we limit our approach to the analysis of final code using the grammar of the programming language as the main source of knowledge in the domain.

3. An adaptative acquisition of programming structures

3.1. A global schema

Our tool is composed of two modules, the acquisition and the recognition module. Figure 1 presents a global schema of the tool.

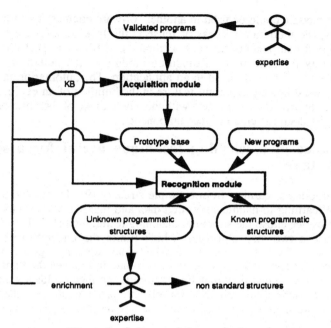

Figure 1 : Schema of the analysis tool

The acquisition module analyses a primitive set of validated programs and builds a base of program structures. A validated program is a program having certain standards of good programming style. These standards do not have to be explicit, they are concluded from a by-hand analysis of the programs. This module uses a two steps process. First, it defines the program structures for each program. Second, it builds a base of prototypes from these structures using its knowledge about the specific programming language. So, the primitive set of program structures is subsumed within the base of prototypes considered by the knowledge base.

The recognition module compares new programs to the base of prototypes. It specifies the program structures it is able to recognize and those it considers as new structures.

Most of our work deals with the acquisition module, the recognition one has not yet been implemented but should be based on the same learning techniques as the former in order to compare the prototypes to new structures.

The previous schema presents the use of our tool for a validation task. The base of prototypes is an extended representation of the rules of good programming style used to write the set of validated programs. The acquisition module removes the features of each implementation to keep the syntactic characteristics shared by several programs. Applied to a new application, the recognition module highlight new structures which do not contain these characteristics in order to help the programer understand this application. A similar approach could be used to look at bugs in a new application where the acquisition module would have to analyze programs with common bugs.

The acquisition module could be used in another software engineering task : the reuse of code. Currently, the moderate success of reuse is the lack of software libraries as the choice of the good components for such a library is difficult to perform [8, 11]. This choice is presently the task of the acquisition module which determines the program structures which are commonly used in an application. The automation in the choice of the components would be an important feature in the building of an evolutionary library. Nevertheless, our approach does not deal with the whole range of the reuse process such as the indexing or the documentation of the components.

3.2. The choice of a learning technique useful for a software engineering task

Our approach implies a learning from example strategy [9]. To resolve the problem of using inductive learning to handle structured data and make use of a knowledge base of domain properties, we chose the structural matching technique [6]. This technique has the advantage to use a two step algorithm which limits the uncertainty brought by an inductive approach. The first step uses intensively the domain properties according to a deductive process. The second step is an inductive one, it removes the remaining features of analyzed examples so that they match structurally and then builds a generalization for these structures. In our application, the examples are program structures and the domain properties are transformation rules used in order to get the analyzed structures more similar in a syntactic meaning.

So, the aim of the first step is to use a knowledge base to transform the program structures so that the second step is able to induce the most specific prototype considering this knowledge base. Expressed in formal terms, the structural matching definition is :

> Let $\{e_1, e_2, ... , e_n\}$ be a set of n examples. These examples
> match structurally iff there exists a formula F and n
> substitutions σ_i such that, for each i, $\sigma_i(F) = e_i$.

F is the recognition function or the generalization of the examples and its "quality" depends on the knowledge base. In our approach, an example is a program structure and a generalization is a prototype. The primitive structural matching technique needs several developments to be used for this specific application. These developments rely on improving the efficiency and the ability of this technique to handle structured data.

4. The Acquisition module

This section describes the acquisition module which includes : the data structure, the definition of the program structures, a clustering process based on syntactic features and a learning process to build the set of prototypes.

4.1. The data structure

Our tool uses a first order logic representation of the programs in order to easily manipulated them considering our knowledge based approach. This representation is based on the recognition of a finite set of sub-trees in the parse tree of each program. During a parsing, a specific predicate name is given to each sub-tree of the parsing tree and the arguments of this predicate are the values of the sub-tree nodes.

4.2. Definition of a program structure

We did not yet define what we mean by a program structure which is the elementary data structure used by our tool. Such structures must have a syntactic and semantic integrity in order to be manipulated independently of the rest of the program. A program structure has a syntactic integrity if it is composed of a set of contiguous instructions. Moreover, this structure has a semantic integrity if the variables of its instructions are independent of the instructions of the other structures. These specific structures are built using an analysis of the data flow of each program to define its connected components. This process is based on the work used in the LAURA system [7] for the analysis of PASCAL programs. The result of this analysis is a set of program structures defined as a block of instructions with specific properties. An important property is the possibility to perform transformations on the instructions of a block without looking at the other blocks. We will not describe this process further as most of our developments are dealing with the analysis of SQL requests. These requests have, by nature, this semantic and this semantic integrity because the way that each request performs its operations is independent of the other requests of the application.

4.3. The clustering process

The aim of this step is to cluster the program structures which are similar in a syntactic meaning. These clusters will be the inputs of the learning process which has to build a prototype for each of them.

We chose to include two processes in the acquisition module - clustering and learning - rather than to get a single classifier based on an inductive process or on a data analysis technique because :
- The application domain has a strong structure which allows efficient clustering using a standard data analysis process. Nevertheless, such an approach requires a posteriori analysis of its results as it deals with numeric criteria.
- The main purpose of the learning process was to use intensively a knowledge base specialized in the manipulation of derivation trees. Learning-based classifiers are inappropriate for this task.

Considering these characteristics, the aim of this combination of a numeric and a symbolic approach was to build first drafts of the program structures with the clustering process and then to refine them with the machine learning one.

We are using an ascending clustering process [12] to compare the syntactic derivation trees of several program structures. This process repeatedly clusters the two most similar structures using a distance function D. We defined D in order to perform a breadth first parse of the parse trees during its comparisons because the main features of the program structures are in the higher nodes of there trees. Considering two program trees Pk and Pl, represented as two ordered vectors of length n, the distance function we built is :

$$D(Pk, Pl) = \Sigma_{j=1,n} \; c_j \; |Pk_j - Pl_j| = \Sigma_j \; d_j(k,l)$$

where Pk_j and Pl_j are the jth elements of the Pk and Pl vectors and c_j is a decreasing factor expressing the decreasing meaning of the analyzed elements.

The choice of the clustering method and of the distance function factors has been made in order to cluster SQL requests. For another programming language, the factor c needs to be modified considering the link between the depth of the tree and the semantic meaning of its nodes. The results of this clustering for the SQL requests are, for example, to cluster select requests with monotable queries and a single condition, select requests with a single joint order, etc...

4.4. Learning recognition functions

Now, each class has to be analyzed in order to build a relevant prototype. We chose the system OGUST [14] based on the principle of structural matching and we developed it to deal with our specific application. OGUST learns a recognition function of a concept from a set of examples of this concept and knowledge about the application domain. According to the structural matching technique, OGUST's learning process is divided in two steps. The deductive step chooses a constant in each example, replaces all its occurrences by a generalization variable and tries to make all its discriminating occurrences disappear using the knowledge base, i.e. the aim of the learning process is to use the knowledge base in order to have the biggest set of constants sharing the same properties. Schematically, an occurrence of a variable x, argument of a predicate P, is a discriminating one if x is not an argument of the same predicate P in the other examples.

These operations are performed until no constant remains. The inductive step , then, builds a generalization of these examples keeping their common properties.

An example :: we present here the general learning process applied to 3 requests :

$S1$:   Select Name from person
            where not (date_exam is null) and age > 18 and age < 25 and status = 'student'
            order by no_d_inscription

$S2$:   Select Name from person
            where age > 30 and age < 45 and status = 'professor' and salary is not null
            order by no_order

$S3$:   Select Name from person P1
            where status = 'visiting professor' and age between 25 and 35
                and exists (select job from person P2
                                where P1.name = P2.name)
            order by no_order

If we consider the knowledge base :

$Rg1$: P1 and P2 $\Leftrightarrow$ P2 and P1
$Rg2$: P1 between B1 and B2 $\Leftrightarrow$ P1$\geq$ B1 and P1 $\leq$ B2
$Rg3$: P1 is not null $\Leftrightarrow$ not (P1 is null)
$Rg4$: Select R1 from T1 $\Leftrightarrow$ Select R1 from T1 C1
            where P1 is not null   where exists (select R2 from T1 C2
                                                            where C1.P1 = C2.P2)

During the deductive process :
the rule Rg3 is applied to S1 to transform : *not (date_exam is null)* into *date_exam is not null,*
the rule Rg1 is applied three times to S2 to transform : *age > 30 and age < 45 and status = 'professor' and salary is not null* into *salary is not null and age > 30 and age < 45 and status = 'professor'*
the rule Rg4 is applied to S3 to transform : *Select Name from person P1 where status = 'visiting professor' and age between 25 and 35 and exists (select job from person P2 where P1.name = P2.name)* into *Select Name from person where status = 'visiting professor' and age between 25 and 35 and name is not null*
then, the rule Rg2 and five times the rule Rg1 are applied to transform : *status = 'visiting professor' and age between 25 and 35 and name is not null* into *name is not null and age > 25 and age < 35 and status = 'visiting professor'*

Then the inductive process builds the generalization of the three examples keeping their common properties, using the "dropping conjunction rule" for the remaining discriminating variables :

G : Select Name from person
    where col1 is not null and age > n1 and age < n2 and status = ch1
        order by ch2

where n1, n2 are numbers, ch1, ch2 are strings and col1 is a column-name.

This example shows the strategy of the OGUST algorithm. One of the main problems of this algorithm is the choice of constants in predicates. Different choices led to several recognition functions which could be irrelevant or incomparable. For an effective application of this algorithm to software code analysis information specific to the domain must be applied, as will be described below.

5. The recognition module

In this section, we present our specifications of the recognition module which has not yet been implemented. The acquisition module produced a base of m prototypes from the set of n initial programs. Then, the recognition module compares a new program structure e to this base and concludes about its recognition or its non-recognition. e is recognized by a prototype G_i if G_i covers e :

Gi covers e iff *Gi* is more general than e
Gi is more general than e iff $\exists$ σ_i, a substitution and F_i a function such that :
$\sigma i(Fi) = e$ and, for the set X of F variables, $Fi(X) \Rightarrow Gi(X)$

There are three outputs of the recognition module :

- $\exists! \ G_i$: the program structure e has been recognized as a known prototype. It inherits of the properties which could have been linked to G_i.
- $\exists \ G_{i1}, ..., G_{ik}, k$ generalizations such that $\cup_{i=i1,...,ik}G_i = e$: e is a complex program structure composed of several concepts independently learned in several prototypes. e inherits of a combination of the properties linked to each prototype.

- *others* : the recognition module has not been able to recognize *e* and a programmer needs to diagnose about :
  - the validity of *e*,
  - the validity of the knowledge base,
  - the validity of the prototype base.

The explanations of the failures in matching help the programmer to choose between two possibilities. In the first case, *e* is not considered as valid and cannot be efficiently transformed to make it similar to a known prototype. In the other case, the concept described by the example has already been met but the knowledge base does not include the useful transformation rules. If these rules are easy to acquire the programmer completes the knowledge base, otherwise he completes the prototype base. The programmer does the latter choice too if *e* describes a new concept.

6. Developments of the learning technique

Previous sections described the core of the learning process. This section presents the developments of OGUST which enable it to analyze software code. These developments involve the program structures and the knowledge base.

6.1. Problems to be solved

Constants choice. A priori, the matching strategy of OGUST is a good one because it takes care of the big nodes of the parse trees, i.e. the nodes which have many sons. A skeleton of the prototype is quickly built. Nevertheless, as this strategy is a syntactic approach rather than a semantic one, some unimportant nodes can be chosen. Then the result of the matching process will be an useless set of disjoint sub-trees rather than a consistent parse tree. Another problem with the primitive strategy of OGUST is its exhaustive comparison of constants. To compare *n* examples with an average of *m* constants, the complexity formula is : $O(m^n)$. This complexity is intractable considering the amount of data to be analyzed in a software code analysis approach.

The use of the knowledge base. The rules Rg1, Rg2, Rg3 and Rg4 described for the analysis of SQL requests are non monotonic in nature. OGUST uses these rules to transform the derivation trees - to drop branches and to add new ones. Previously, OGUST used idempotency to apply its rules - taxonomies or implications - adding new predicates without dropping any information. Using non-monotonic rules - named equivalences - involves taking care of the long-range consequences of the transformations they perform on the program structures.

6.2. Solutions

Two kinds of solutions have been implemented : using biases to decrease the complexity formula and an improvement of the resolving process.

Using biases. The quality of the result of the matching process cannot be ensure because it performs syntactic feature comparisons. Thus, we introduced semantic features using biases [13] deduced from the grammar. These biases are ordering typed constants and incremental learning.

Each constant can be typed using the transition of the production it is derived from. The similarity is only computed between constants of the same type. Moreover, it is interesting to favour constants derived from the first steps of the syntactic analysis because they get the main semantic features. So we built a hierarchy of types according to the call graph of the program.

During the matching process, the constants of the higher type are analyzed followed by constants of the lower type, etc... This choice simulates a breadth first parse of the parse tree. This strategy has already been used during the clustering process to build ordered vectors. It is useful for the recognition module too as it speeds up the retrieval process and avoids an indexing step.

The previous biases on types change the factor m in the complexity formula, less constants are compared during an iteration of the OGUST algorithm. Nevertheless this formula is still an exponential one. To transform the factor n into a constant we use an incremental approach. In fact, we use two kinds of incrementality, a constant-based and an example-based incrementality :

- *constant-based incrementality* : as the primitive set of examples of the acquisition module is known and finite, it can be ordered according to the information that each example gets (this information is computed using the hierarchy of types). Then, we compare couples of vectors rather than to compare n vectors of constants.
Expressed in a formal way :

Rather than to look at a set $(C_{1i_1}, ... , C_{ni_n})$ such that :
$Sim (C_{1i_1}, ... , C_{ni_n}) = Max (Sim (c))$
$\forall c \in \mathfrak{C}$
Where $\mathfrak{C} = \{(C_{11}, ..., C_{1m_1}) \otimes ... \otimes (C_{n1}, ..., C_{nm_n})\}$
and $\otimes$ represents the cartesian product of two sets and C_{ij} is the jth constant of example i,

The constant-based incrementality strategy looked at $(C_{1i_1}, ... , C_{ni_n})$ such that :
$Sim(C_{1i_1}, C_{2i_2}) = Max (Sim(c1)), \forall c_1 \in \mathfrak{C}_1$
$Sim (C_{1i_1}, C_{2i_2}, C_{3i_3}) = Max (Sim (c_2)), \forall c_2 \in \mathfrak{C}_2$
...
$Sim (C_{1i_1}, ... , C_{ni_n}) = Max (Sim (c_{n-1})), \forall c_{n-1} \in \mathfrak{C}_{n-1}$
where
$\mathfrak{C}_1 = \{(C_{11}, ..., C_{1m_1}) \otimes (C_{21}, ..., C_{2m_1})\}$
$\mathfrak{C}_2 = \{(C_{1i_1}) \otimes (C_{2i_2}) \otimes (C_{31}, ..., C_{3m_3})\}$
...
$\mathfrak{C}_{n-1} = \{(C_{1i_1}) \otimes ... \otimes (C_{n-1i_{n-1}}) \otimes (C_{n1}, ..., C_{nm_n})\}$

- example-based incrementality : when the recognition module concludes that the new analyzed example e inherits of the properties of several prototypes, a new prototype is stored in the base of prototypes as the generalization of e and each prototype. To be able to build the most specific generalization we should have to compare e with the examples covered by each prototype because the sets of rules used to build a generalization can be different if we compare an example with an abstraction of several examples $(Gen(G, e))$

rather than with other examples (Gen(e_1, e_2,..., e_n, e)). For the software code analysis process, there is no gap of meaning between a generalization and an example because both are derivation trees expressing a consistent program structure. So, using previous biases we do not loose information if we directly generalize a new example with the generalization, so : Gen(G, e_{n+1}) = G(e_1, ..., e_{n+1})

Theorems using. The characteristics of the knowledge base used for software code analysis are : a finite set of predicate names, many rules and complex equivalence rules. OGUST uses a mixed resolution strategy which led to loops during the backward resolution. We do not describe here biases we used to manage the resolver but we detail the main bias developed to use efficiently the equivalence rules. This bias, called "spreading", allows looking at the long-range consequences of the application of an equivalence rule. Consider that we have to analyze two examples *E1* and *E2* and that we match *T* typed constants. For each constant *C* of type *T* of an example *E* we define its "surrounding" *S(C,E)* as the set of constants belonging to the same predicates than *C* but having a lower type than *C* type in the hierarchy of nodes. Then, to compute the similarity of two constants *Sim(C1, C2)* we compute the similarity between their "surroundings" *Sim(S(C1, E1), S(C2, E2))*. A forward saturation is performed to the predicate of the analyzed constants in order to take care of all their properties, explicit or implicit ones. This first saturation is an artificial one as it is used to find the best constants to be matched, then the primitive resolving process is applied. This spreading strategy improves the quality of the results and the efficiency of the tool too as OGUST does not match separate nodes but sub-trees.

7. Initial results

Several steps of our tool have been validated analyzing SQL requests used in real applications :

- *Clustering :* we used two sets of requests (70 and 54 requests) to define the distance function. The first set has been clustered by hand by a SQL programmer. This first clustering has been compared to several automatic clustering techniques to define the parameters of the distance function. These parameters have, then, been validated by an a posteriori analysis of the clustering of the second set. From the application of the same process to larger sets of requests we concluded that the number of classes with a functional meaning is stabilizing and that abnormal requests are the only element of their own class.

- *The acquisition of the recognition functions :* different kinds of examples have been used to check the knowledge base :
    * *Examples deduced from the rules :* we deduced artificial examples from the knowledge base building an example from the condition and an example from the conclusion of some rules. These examples were useful to test the "spreading" process. Currently, this process is statically limited in its depth and the user has to choose between several matching constants when the spreading process has not been able to do it.
    * *Real examples :* these examples does not need an intensive use of the knowledge base to be matched as they are well-formed and so have a regular structure. This approach was useful to test the incremental approach which

allows to analyze an important set of SQL requests (to 25 real requests) without using a knowledge base.

* *Toy-examples* : which need a complex use of the knowledge base. These examples have been useful to test the behavior of the motor engine at the limit, specifically to resolve the problems of loops during the backward chaining.

8. Conclusion

In this paper we have presented the advantages of adopting a strategy based on a static analysis of code in order to improve the maintenance of software. Then, we have described our approach based on the application of a complex machine learning technique. We have discussed the extensions needed to existing machine learning techniques in order to apply them to our specific software engineering task. These extensions used features of the domain to increase the quality of the results and the efficiency of the system. Currently our tool resolves most of the problems we have presented for specific requests, a couple of developments have to be done in order to merge all those solutions to deal with real requests. These developments included :

- to adapt the limits of the surrounding of constants during the spreading process, according to the amount of effort needs to compute the similarity between two constants,
- to reuse the saturation of the examples by the knowledge base during the spreading process to improve the resolving strategy of OGUST during the matching process,
- to be able to perform several generalizations rather than only one when several constant choices are possible,
- to improve the efficiency of the implementation of OGUST.

An interesting application of our tool will be to analyze classical programming languages. Tests have been performed with subsets of grammars such as declarations in FORTRAN programs or input/output orders of PASCAL programs. Nevertheless, the analysis of programs of these languages using their whole grammar is not a simple extension of the approach presented here as their grammars are bigger and more complex than the SQL one. Currently, we are interested to use data flow and control flow graphs of structured programs. Those graphs should be helpful to choose the productions of the grammar which are useful to build the data. Then, the traditional code optimization technics based on those graphs should be adapted in order to build the knowledge base.

References

1   Bailin, S.C. & Gattis, R.H. & Truszkowski, W. 1991. A learning software engineering environment. *6th knowledge-based software engineering conference.* pp 251-263.

2   Dershowitz, N. 1986. Programming by analogy. *Machine learning 2 : an artificial intelligence approach. Michalski R.S., Carbonel J.G., Mitchell T.M., Morgan Kaufmann eds*, pp 395-423.

3   Geldrez, C. & Matwin, S. & Morin, J. & Probert, R.L. 1990. An application of EBL to protocol conformance testing. *IEEE Expert.* October 1990. pp 45-60.

4   Halstead, M. 1978. Elements of software engineering. *Elsevier eds.*

5   Harandi, M.T. & Lee, H. 1991. Acquiring software design schemas : a machine learning perspective. *6th knowledge-based software engineering conference.* pp 239-250.

6   Kodratoff, Y. & Ganascia, J.G. 1986. Improving the generalization step in learning. *Machine learning 2 : an artificial intelligence approach. Michalski R.S., Carbonel J.G., Mitchell T.M., Morgan Kaufmann eds*, pp 215-244.

7   Laurent, J.P. & Fouet, J.M. 1982. Outillage de manipulation de programmes fondé sur une représentation arborescente. *Premier colloque de génie logiciel.* pp 105-118.

8   Maarek, Y.S. & Berry, D.M. & Kaiser, G.E. 1991. *An Information Retrieval Approach For Automatically Constructing Software Libraries.* IEEE Transactions on Software Engineering. Vol 17, N 8. pp 800-813.

9   Michalski, R.S. 1983. A theory and methodology of inductive learning. *Machine learning 1 : an artificial intelligence approach. Michalski R.S., Carbonel J.G., Mitchell T.M., Morgan Kaufmann eds*, pp 1-19.

10   Ning, J. & Harandi, M.J. 1989. An experiment in automatic program analysis. *Proc AAAI symp artificial intelligence and software engineering. AAAI Press eds.* pp 51-55.

11   Prieto-Diaz, R. 1991. *Implementing Faceted Classification for Software Reuse. Communication of the ACM.* Vol 34, N 5. pp 88-97.

12   Saporta, G. 1990. Probabilités, analyse des données et statistiques. *Editions technip.*

13   Utgoff, P.E. 1986. Shift of bias of inductive concept learning. *Machine learning 2 : an artificial intelligence approach. Michalski R.S., Carbonel J.G., Mitchell T.M., Morgan Kaufmann eds*, pp 107-148.

14   Vrain, C. 1990. OGUST : a system that learns using domain properties expressed as theorems. *Machine learning 3, an artificial intelligence approach. Kodratoff, Y. & Michalski, R.S. Morgan Kaufmann eds.* pp 360-382.

15   Webb, J. 1988. Static analysis : an introduction and example. *Journées Internationales : le génie logiciel et ses applications.* pp 523-539.

16   Wills, L.M. 1990. Automated program recognition : a feasibility demonstration. *Artificial intelligence N°45.* pp 113-171.

Supporting Component Matching for Software Reuse

Alistair Sutcliffe and Neil Maiden

Department of Business Computing,
City University,
Northampton Square,
London EC1V 0HB,
U.K.,
Phone: +44-71-253-4399 ext 3420,
E Mail: sf328@uk.ac.city.

Abstract

A mechanism is proposed for analogical matching of specifications for reuse. The process uses generic domain templates with matching heuristics to determine the fit between a source (existing and potentially reusable) specification and the description of the target domain. The design of supporting tools for the matching process is described, with evidence from experimental studies upon which the design was based. The prospects for analogically based software reuse and the requirements for tool support is discussed.

1. Introduction

One of the critical problem in software reuse is finding software components which are appropriate to a new application context and then ascertaining the goodness of fit between reusable components and their target application.

The potential of reusing existing specifications to develop new systems has been brought closer by the CASE tool revolution. It has been suggested that successful specification reuse can assist requirements analysts to develop more complete, consistent and clearly-defined specifications. Intelligent CASE tools require method and domain knowledge to assist the analytic process. For example Ryan [1] reports providing software engineers with method knowledge alone failed to enhance analytic performance. Exploiting the rich seam of domain knowledge captured in reusable specifications is one source of intelligent support which has so far received little attention. Reuse at the specification level offers a new paradigm for requirements engineering by exploiting existing knowledge about a domain in new application contexts. Analogy may be a powerful paradigm which enables matching and retrieval of components for specification reuse, however it has received little attention in the literature [2,3].

Whilst considerable research is currently focused on the development of knowledge-based CASE tools less attention has been directed to the practical problem of initially eliciting such knowledge. The dilemma is how to economically gather and then subsequently identify the appropriate domain knowledge. Deriving application knowledge through domain analysis can be difficult and time consuming [4,5]. One approach is to describe generic types of systems rather than specific applications. CASE tools endowed with abstract specifications as templates [6], cliches [7] or generalised application frames [8] might provide considerable assistance. However, selection of the most appropriate template is difficult especially as reuse repositories increase in size.

Searching and selecting is one part of the reuse problem; however, equally important is matching to determine the goodness of fit between reusable component(s) and a new application context. This paper reports the development of a tool for specification reuse by analogy which addresses one of the central problems of large scale reuse: the selection and matching of reusable components to a new application context. The paper is organised as follows: first the schema and models of domain abstractions are introduced and illustrated with an example. This is followed by description of the application of these models in a prototype tool for specification retrieval and matching. The structure of the tool and its use are briefly reviewed, followed by a discussion of related work.

2. The Analogical Matching Process

The perceived power of analogy is its potential to retrieve knowledge from one domain and apply it to a different domain [9]. This suggests that analogical reasoning may be able to support reuse across different problem domains, and has the potential to exploit CASE repositories populated with specifications representing a wide variety of applications. Many cognitive theories of analogical mapping exist [10]; however a common factor between the theories is the development of a abstract knowledge structure which represents an inter linked set of facts common to two or more domains. Analogical based reuse therefore aims to identify these abstractions, develop a matching process which can partially automate this task and then a retrieval process which can select appropriate reusable specifications from a CASE repository. The process is summarised in figure 1 which illustrates the concept of structural analogy and its application as a matching mechanism for reusable components. To demonstrate this potential an example of a software engineering analogy is presented.

Fig 1. Summary of the Process of Reuse by Analogy ˈ

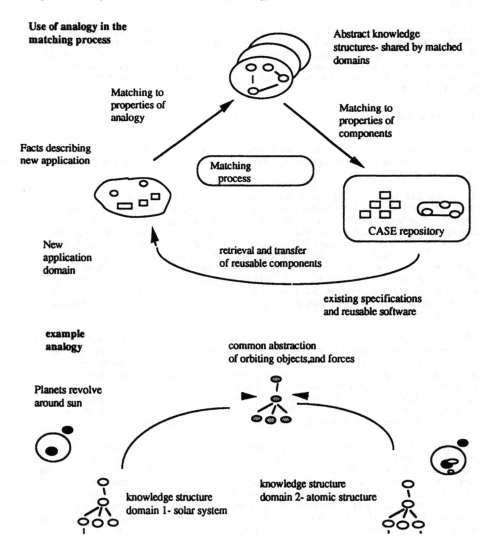

Theatre Reservation/Course Administration Example

The analogy is between a system for theatre seat reservations and a system supporting applications to a university course. The theatre reservation system allows theatregoers to reserve seats for any performance. They can reserve one or a block of seats, and seats vary in price. Theatre staff use the system to reply to enquiries and to manage reservations. A waiting list is created whenever a performance is over-booked, and theatregoers are transferred from the waiting list to seats when cancellations are made. The context diagram for this theatre reservation system is given in Figure 2(a).

A university course application system manages applications to a full-time and part-time MSc course. The course administrator uses the system to reply to enquiries on place availability and course requirements and to manage the take-up of course places. Candidate students are offered conditional places on either course, which both have an upper limit on total places in any academic year. A waiting list is used for additional students who cannot be offered places immediately. Students on the waiting list have first option on any places which become available due to cancellations. The diagram for this system is given in Figure 2(b).

Figure 2. Context diagrams for the Course Administation and Theatre booking Systems

Figure 2(a) Context diagram for the Theatre Reservation System

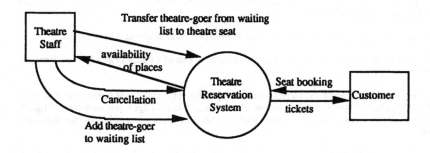

Figure 2(b) Context diagram for the Course Administration System

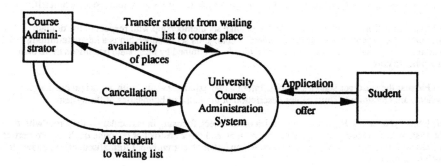

The two context diagrams (Figures 2(a) and 2(b)) demonstrate the potential reuse which can be exploited from this analogy. Reuse is also possible during more detailed analysis, between processes (e.g. reservation of theatre seat\course place), data stores (e.g. theatre seat\course place) and external agents (theatregoer\student). Although in different domains, the two systems share significant surface features (e.g. reservations, waiting lists, places) which assist analogical recognition and understanding. A common abstraction links the two domains, involving a resource (seats, places) being allocated to clients (theatregoers, student applicants).

Further analogies with the theatre reservation and course administration examples can be identified, for instance car rental and airline seat reservation share significant similarities which make specification reuse possible. Analogy enables mapping between domains, although to be effective a set of domain abstractions is required. Reuse of generic templates has been suggested by several authors [6,10], however templates have a limited reuse value because details have to be omitted whereas implemented specifications contain additional domain knowledge which can be reused. We therefore see analogy and domain abstractions are a mechanism for facilitating reuse of matching specifications rather than providing reusable components per se.

3. Schema and models of domain knowledge.

The analogy matching process utilises partial domain knowledge to reason about the links between applications. A set of domain abstractions have been devised to support this process. The set of abstractions, so far, has been targeted on information system rather than real time domains. The approach is based upon the following propositions:

(i) Application domains are organised into classes sharing general features. Each class level adds more specialised features to differentiate it.

(ii) Domain classes are distinguished by a small number of key determining features.

(iii) Most software engineering problems can be ascribed to one of a tractably small set of domain classes.

Domain knowledge is modelled as classes which are specialised by addition of further knowledge to achieve appropriate targeting in new domains. The schema of knowledge types, as shown in figure 3, is used to define a set of abstract domain models. Currently seven types of knowledge structure are used:

(a) The structure of the domain. This is knowledge of the objects within domains and the sets they naturally fall into. The prediction is that people will perceive sets which pertain to physical structures in the real world. Hence the term 'containment' may be a familiar cue for domain structure, e.g. stock objects are-contained-in warehouse; students are-contained-in a school.

The system structure describes the object sets implicated in input and output (i.e. changes in object status across the system boundary) and any major physical entity sets within the system itself.

(b) State transitions which cause objects to change set membership with respect to the domain structure. Any event which causes an object to change its set membership is a key determining feature. Inter-domain class differences are critically determined by these state transitions more than any other feature.

(c) Events: these trigger state transitions. Internal and external events (with an origin outside the system) are recognised. This enables description of the scope or boundaries of the system.

(d) Object properties. High level properties of an object, focusing in particular on their role within the system (e.g. resource, mechanism), movement, and other abstract or concrete qualities. Properties are essentially a type definition of objects, which although currently not formalised, are amenable to such treatment.

Figure 3. Meta-schema of knowledge types and their relationships

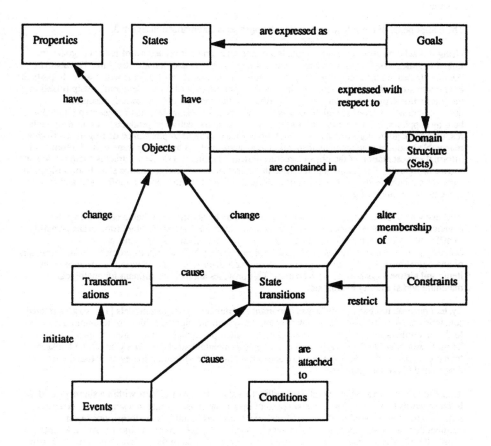

The schema is not intended to be a formal representation of domain knowledge, instead it represents the organisation of predicates which describe facts about a domain model.

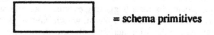

= schema primitives

= relationships between primitives, the arrow denotes the locus of effect.

(e) Purpose of the system: This is the goal or solution state that the system exists to achieve. Goals and statements of purpose are difficult to describe formally because they are expressed in natural language, differ between users and may be expressed at a variety of levels and with different degrees of precision. Consequently goals are expressed as the system state which must be achieve to satisfy a linguistically expressed goal.

(f) Constraints: These are 'negative rules' which define the object states which the system must prohibit or prevent from happening, i.e. future states which must not happen

(g) Conditions: Stative information or values held in attributes of an object and other non-object states (e.g. time, duration) which are evaluated before a state transition can occur.

(h) Transformations: Procedures and algorithms which cause a state change in the system. Transformations are triggered by events and may result in a state transition of an object in the domain structure.

The components of the schema and their relationships is summarised in figure 3.

Using this schema abstract domain models are defined as an inter-related set of facts, i.e. goals are linked to states, conditions to transitions, transitions to objects and domain structure. The abstract domain classes are differentiated by actions leading to state changes of objects with respect to parts of the system structure. System structure is a set theoretic concept of object-set membership linked to the transactional purpose of the system. To illustrate the concept, in a renewable resource management abstraction, of which stock control is a concrete example; sets of objects (products) are held by suppliers, in an inventory (stock) and with customers (delivered products). A non-renewable resource management abstraction, of which library loans is an example, can be distinguished from a renewable resource management abstraction (e.g. stock control) by the key transition of return. An informal representation of the object-structure-transition semantics of two abstract domain models is shown in figure 4. The return action causes the object (library book) to change state from on-loan to a resource-available state whereas return in the stock control abstraction is an infrequent and non mandatory action (see fig 4).

Within each abstract domain class specialisation occurs by addition of schema components. For instance non renewable resource management applications are specialised by further transformations to differentiate between booking and hiring systems. Other schema components are used to corroborate differences between sub classes. Object types, which have been promoted as determinants of analogical reuse by [6], are categorised according to their role in the domain, for instance stock items and airline seats both act as resources. This provides another determinant for analogical matching and similarity evaluation.

System purpose has been identified as important determinant of abstract models [11], so goal related semantics are defined in terms of states which the system attempts to achieve or maintain. Returning to the example domains, the stock control system attempts to maintain a minimum quantity of items-in-stock, while the library system attempts to maintain stock constancy so all the books-on-loan are returned. Activities (i.e. a set of actions, or algorithms) leading to key state transitions are determined by system purpose.

Transformations`are a set of operations leading to a state change of objects within a single procedure. In other words transformations are composed of operations must execute in a single uninterrupted sequence to change the object's state. Transformations may result in state transitions in set membership in the system structure; however, conceptually they alter an object's status. Events caused by the status change may then result in object transition in the system structure. To illustrate the concept, common transformations in information systems are, scheduling, allocation by constraint satisfaction, searching for objects, reservation, etc. These result in conceptual-stative changes to objects such as 'reserved, found, sorted, scheduled.' Transformations are similar to 'methods' in object oriented specifications or procedures in structured methods.

Other knowledge types (triggers, conditions) play a supplementary role in differentiating domain classes. Equivalent state transitions can be distinguished by their triggering events. Each transition is either triggered by the information system or by events beyond that system, which have important influences on the information system. For instance, an allocation action in the airline booking domain can be differentiated from allocation of stock to orders in a warehouse domain because the former allocation is triggered by the information system while the latter is not.

Users are predicted to recognise objects and purpose as the most 'natural' descriptors of domains, hence these features should be more easy to elicit [12]. However, given the ambiguity inherent in many teleological descriptions, system structure and state transitions are predicted to be the most reliable determinants of domain identity. A composite of system structure and related transitions could be taken as the domain/class 'key' in database terms. Matching rules and heuristics enable selection of the appropriate domain abstraction for a set of predicates describing a new application. Use of multiple heuristics and a rich schema for the knowledge base enables sophisticated search strategies to be generated thus avoiding the computational inefficient, and often intractable, approach of linear searching multi variate sets of properties, typified by faceted classification.

Fig 4 Abstract Domain Models: Object Allocation and Object Hiring Abstractions

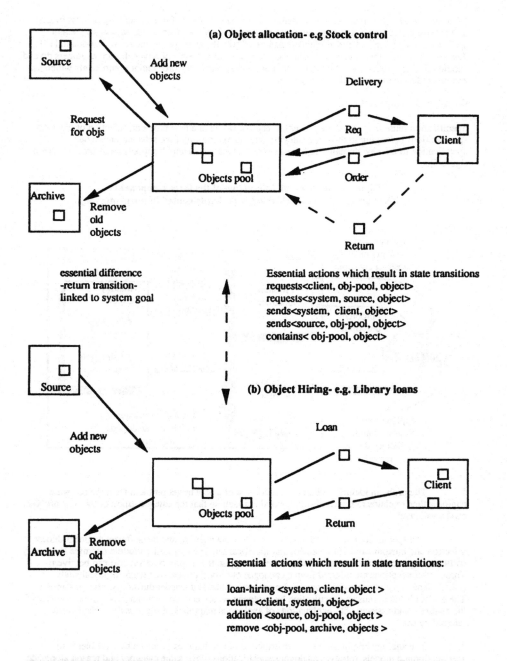

(a) Object allocation- e.g Stock control

Source

Add new objects

Delivery

Request for objs

Req

Client

Objects pool

Order

Archive

Remove old objects

Return

essential difference
-return transition-
linked to system goal

Essential actions which result in state transitions
requests<client, obj-pool, object>
requests<system, source, object>
sends<system, client, object>
sends<source, obj-pool, object>
contains< obj-pool, object>

Source

(b) Object Hiring- e.g. Library loans

Loan

Add new objects

Client

Objects pool

Return

Archive

Remove old objects

Essential actions which result in state transitions:

loan-hiring <system, client, object >
return <client, system, object>
addition <source, obj-pool, object >
remove <obj-pool, archive, objects >

The domain abstractions are represented semi-formally as sets of typed Prolog predicates. This enables semantic networks to be constructed to store each abstraction a composite knowledge structure of facts, as defined by the schema, and relationships between those facts. The matching engine then searches on the fact primitives in the models, their first order and second order relationships with powerful algorithms which utilise the syntactic and semantic properties of the models.

Effective specification reuse requires intelligent tool-based support for the matching process in large scale repositories. However successful reuse also requires an intelligent reuse advisor to prevent specification copying and enhance understanding of both the analogy and the reusable domain [13]. The intelligence of this advisor is based upon cognitive task models of how software engineers do and should reuse specifications. The intelligent reuse advisor (Ira) has three major components which are examined during the remainder of this paper.

4. The Reuse Advisor

Specification reuse involves three processes: categorisation of a new problem, selection of candidate specifications belonging to the same category and customisation of the selected analogous specification to the new domain. Ira has three main components which support these processes (see figure 5):

**Figure 5 - overview of interaction of the three components
which constitute Ira (darkened indicates implemented in the prototype)**

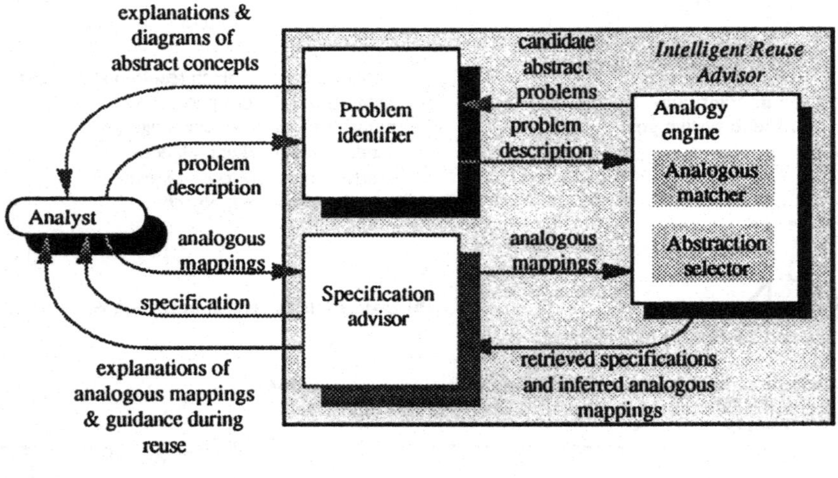

* The problem identifier obtains a description of a new target problem from the software engineer then explains retrieved abstract domain models so that the categorisation of the new problem can be validated.

* The specification advisor controls interaction between Ira and the software engineer during selection and customisation of an analogous specification. The diagnostic module attempts to identify software engineers' misconceptions about the analogy so that appropriate support can be given. These misconceptions are inferred from a catalogue of error types derived from empirical study [12,13]. The explanatory module acts as the analyst's guide and teacher during specification reuse. The analyst is led to reuse a specification by strategies which encourage understanding and transfer of the analogy, and assisted with explanations of analogous mappings of the reusable specification inferred by Ira.

* The analogy engine reasons with critical problem features to match new problems to abstract domain models, retrieves analogous specifications of the same category and reason alongside the software engineer during specification customisation. The role of the analogy engine is constrained by the domain knowledge available to it. There have been a number computational models of analogical and case-based reasoning [14,15,16,17], however they assume perfect and complete knowledge of the domains. The analogy engine can reason about many domains because it

is equipped with partial domain knowledge in an abstract form, although it is limited by the critical problem features represented in the abstract domain models which it possess (see section 3).

The problem identifier, specification advisor and analogy engine components are described in more detail to demonstrate how analogous specifications are retrieved and reused by Ira.

4.1 The Problem Identifier

The problem identifier supports elicitation of a new problem description and explanation of abstract domain models retrieved by the analogy engine. We view matching of new applications to domain abstractions as an iterative process of retrieval and understanding involving:

* elicitation of facts about the new problem,
* retrieval of abstract domain models to match those facts by the analogy engine, and
* explanation of the abstract domain models to the software engineer.

Initial interaction with the software engineer aims to elicit key problem features which map to critical features of abstract domains. The problem identifier provides a predefined set of predicates to model relationships between domain objects, so the software engineer is required to partially abstract their model of the domain during description. Descriptions, justifications and examples are used to explain retrieved abstractions so that the software engineer can select or reject them as representative of the new problem, as illustrated in fig 6 which shows a sample dialogue session. Explanation strategies help the software engineer understand and abstract concepts which critically determine an analogy, while the specification advisor explains analogous mappings between the new problem and the selected analogous specifications.

4.2 The Analogy Engine

Currently the analogy engine employs structure-matching [18] and heuristic-based reasoning to identify analogical matches between a problem description and a set of known domain abstractions [12]. Structure-matching identifies an interrelated network of analogical mappings [9] between a problem description and candidate domain abstractions using a structural coherence algorithm similar to the Structure-Mapping [18] and Analogical Constraint Matching Engines [19]. The analogical matcher maps semantically-equivalent predicates representing critical knowledge structures identified by our model of software engineering abstractions, including state transitions and object structural knowledge (see Figure 3). The outcome from this process is retrieval of one or more candidate abstract domains for the new problem.

The analogy engine also employs heuristics which discriminate between abstract domain models. Hierarchical structuring of the abstract domain models ensures that the analogy engine only attempts to match likely abstractions for a new problem. The fact acquisition dialogue requests fact-types motivated by the theory to help discriminate between domains, e.g. critical state transitions and object set membership. Search is thus driven by predicted attributes of superordinate classes in the abstract domain hierarchies and then refine down a selected hierarchy to match an appropriate domain model as further facts are acquired from the user. Each domain model in the hierarchy inherits all the features of its parent and specialises it to represent a sub-type of that software engineering problem. Practical experience with the analogy engine revealed that the similarities between abstract domain models at lower levels in the hierarchy indicated the need for a more finely-tuned retrieval mechanism. The abstraction selector differentiates between candidate abstractions using a set of heuristics which identify critical differences between abstract domain models at each sub-level in the hierarchy. The heuristics calculate the degree of difference between two abstract domains as a percentage of the total differences possible.

Successful categorisation of the target problem is followed by retrieval of reusable specifications belonging to the same domain abstraction using similar analogical matching techniques. The result of this matching process is the retrieval of one or many candidate reusable specifications ranked by their similarity with the target problem. Ranking is achieved by matching analogous features shared by the new and reusable domains, for example, similarities between the physical structure of both domains.

Figure 6 Explanation windows representing a retrieved abstract domain class for a stock control
system. The three windows, from top to bottom, represent: the critical abstraction for the analogy;
a likely physical application for the domain; an alternative, analogical example of the domain

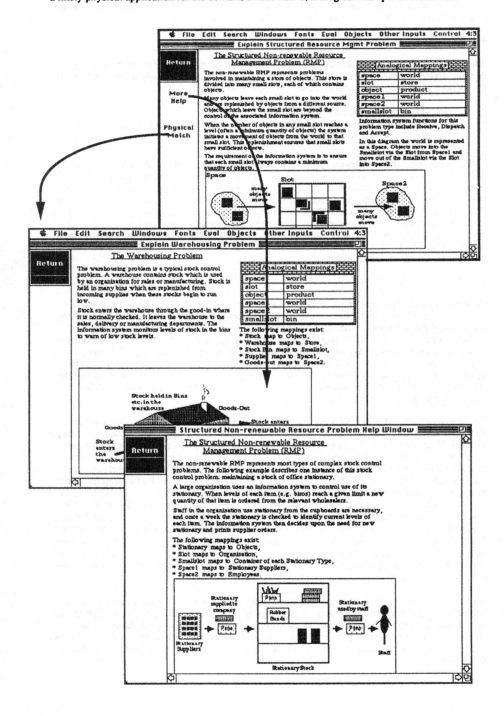

4.3 The Specification Advisor

This work is currently in the specification stage, so it is reported to give an overall picture about how the reuse assistant may function. Implementation may change some of the details. The specification advisor must support the software engineer during two tasks: (i) specification selection from several candidates, and (ii) specification customisation to fit the new domain. Both tasks require the software engineer to have a good understanding of the specifications, so the specification advisor will explain relevant analogies to the software engineer. In addition, during specification selection, the differences between candidate analogies will be described. Tutoring strategies to support the analyst during both tasks are being developed, although only strategies which support understanding and reuse of a single specification are described in this paper.

The specification advisor will explain and guide the software engineer during analogical comprehension and transfer using strategies derived from empirical studies of expert software engineers during successful reuse of analogous specifications [20,21]. The system employs plan-based, context-independent reuse strategies to ensure that it has control over its environment. A single, prescribed strategy guides inexperienced analysts to reuse specifications, while explanatory and error-correcting tactics support analyst's individual differences within each step of the reuse strategy.

Prior to specification reuse the software engineer will be encouraged to develop a basic analogical understanding necessary to enhance and maximise effective customisation of the specification. This analogical understanding concentrates attention on critical domain objects, functional goals and the boundaries of the problem, and builds on software engineer's understanding of the abstract domain developed during problem categorisation. The software engineer is assisted by explanatory dialogues and narrative descriptions of the reusable problem, and diagramming aids are provided to graphically represent the analogy. Software engineers mappings can be evaluated by using analogical mappings inferred by the analogy engine and the empirically-based error library [22]. Subsequent feedback from the tool can be used to generate a correct understanding of the analogy.

The specification advisor will control the software engineers' access to the specification to encourage further analogical understanding and inhibit mental laziness. Mental laziness is discouraged by consideration of all reusable components and by exposing only the relevant, analogous components in the specification. Learning of individual analogical components is iterative following other studies [23,24,25,26] which suggest an iterative approach promotes more effective problem understanding. Coupling the explanatory dialogue with gradual exposure of the specification seems to be the most effective strategy to encourage analogical understanding.

To summarise, the specification advisor attempts to guide and assist the software engineer by dialogues based on cognitive models of successful reuse behaviour. It employs intelligent tutoring techniques to assist software engineers to overcome the problem of understanding an unfamiliar specification, and uses context-independent strategies to lead the analyst through the complex transfer and testing stages.

5. Implementation of the Prototype Reuse Advisor

A partial prototype of Ira as shown in Figure 6 has been implemented in LPA Prolog on an Apple Macintosh FX. The problem identifier and analogy engine components were evaluated during several studies. The analogy engine was populated with 10 hierarchically-structured abstract domain models supported by approximately 30 heuristics identifying critical differences between them. It has proved effective at retrieving abstractions given only partial or ambiguous problem descriptions. User studies with the problem identifier revealed the need for visualising critical problem features, so the problem elicitation dialogue was modified to encourage more problem visualisation. Subsequent studies indicated that greater problem visualisation enhanced problem description and permitted Ira to retrieve the correct domain abstractions in 75% of trials.

6. Discussion

Specification level reuse can help to overcome the considerable difficulties experienced by inexperienced software engineers during the early stages of software development [27,28]. Formation of mental models is necessary to understand a domain, however as Young [29] and Sein [30] have reported, mental model formation can be error-prone and hard. In addition Sutcliffe and Maiden, [20] found that initial problem scoping was important in determining success for inexperienced software engineers. Reusable specifications could reduce the analyst's mental load during model formation. Evaluating candidate designs in new scenarios is a key element in successful software development [31,32], hence analogy may help development of alternative scenarios. Reusing specifications will inevitably encourage a more prototypical approach to requirements analysis, as suggested by Luqi [33] and Balzer et al. [34]. Prototyping in turn may encourage more and frequent evaluation of requirement specifications, implying more indirect benefits from specification reuse.

Successful reuse can also enrich the software engineer's own knowledge base, providing experience necessary to solve similar problems or explain further analogous reusable specifications. Viewing CASE environments as both problem solving and learning tools may ease the skills shortage, providing knowledge gained from experienced software developers to help less experienced software developers practice reuse and requirements engineering. However tool support for matching, retrieval and understanding is vital. Analogical based matching enables reuse to effected across domains at the problem level, whereas generic application frames [8] are restricted to evolutionary style reuse within a domain. It also enables active support for matching which can not be achieved by faceted classification schemes [35,36].

However a cautionary note should be sounded. Dependence on specification reuse could discourage innovation, and bring about the mental laziness which we are seeking to avoid. The reuse advisor tool is designed to discourage such practices, based on extensive empirical studies of software engineering's behaviour and reasoning during reuse [13,27]. These studies have proved invaluable in anticipating problems such as mental laziness, as well as providing models and strategies to encourage good design practice. Another open question is the effectiveness of transfer in analogically mediate, or other reuse. Our current system matches on structural knowledge combined with other attributes of what could be expected from the semantics of conceptual models in development methods (e.g. event, entity, relationship, etc. primitives). So far we can achieve matching and transfer of specifications which approximate to a medium sized entity relationship diagram. However transfer of the more dynamic aspects of systems is more problematic [37] so further investigation is required to support transfer of different types of knowledge contained within specifications. We intend to elaborate our model of domain abstraction to deal with matching at different levels of granularity and for different conceptual model components.

Future research directions are two-fold. First, the matching process is dependent on the set of domain abstractions. The completeness and validity of known abstract domain models must be evaluated through case studies of software engineering problems encountered in industrial organisations. Further validation will be achieved by formal representation of the models in a suitable language, e.g. Z [38] to test for isomorphism, consistency and redundancy. The coverage of the current set of 10 domain abstractions is being increased by study of new system types (e.g. real time, process control applications). Secondly, further evaluation of the problem identifier is necessary to assess its usability when eliciting complex application descriptions from inexperienced software engineers. Finally, the specification advisor must be implemented to assess the effectiveness of explanation tactics and reuse strategies described in this paper. Evaluation of such a prototype will provide an important feedback of a collaborative assistant approach to specification reuse, with implications for future research directions.

Acknowledgements

Neil Maiden is a SERC supported research student. The authors wish to thank students on the MSc in Business Systems Analysis and Design who helped evaluate the Reuse Advisor.

References

[1]. Ryan K., 1988, Capturing and classifying the software developers expertise, Proceeding of the International Workshop on Knowledge-based Systems in Software Engineering, UMIST, March 1988.

[2]. Finkelstein A., 1988, Re-use of formatted requirements specifications, Software Engineering Journal, September 1988, pp 186 - 197.

[3]. Karakostas V., 1989, Requirements for CASE tools in early software reuse, ACM SIGSOFT Software Engineering Notes, Vol 14, No 2, pp 39 - 41.

302

[4]. Arango G., 1987, 'Evaluation of a Reuse-based Software Construction Technology', internal document, Department of Information and Computer Science, University of California, Irvine.

[5]. Prieto-Diaz R. and Freeman P, 1987, Classifying software for reusability, IEEE Software, January 1987, pp 6 - 16.

[6]. Harandi M.T. and Lee M.Y., 1991, Acquiring Software Design Schema: A machine learning perspective. In Proceedings of 6th Conference on Knowledge Based Software Engineering, pp239-250, Syracuse, NY, Sept 1991.

[7]. Reubenstein H.B., 1990, 'Automated Acquisition of Evolving Informal Descriptions', Ph.D. Dissertation (A.I.T.R. No. 1205), Artificial Intelligence Laboratory, Massachusetts Institute of Technology.

[8]. Constantopoulos P., Jarke M., Mylopoulos J., Vassiliou Y. (1991) Software Information Base: A Server for Reuse. Submitted for Publication. Technical Report, FORTH Res Inst, Univ of Heraklion, Crete.

[9]. Gentner D., 1983, Structure-mapping: a theoretical framework for analogy, Cognitive Science 7, pp 155 - 170.

[10]. Russel S.,1988, Analogy By Similarity, Analogical Reasoning, Kluwer Academic Publishers, 1988

[11]. Maiden N.A.M., 1991, Analogy as a paradigm for specification reuse, Software Engineering Journal 6(1), pp 3 - 15.

[12]. Maiden N.A.M. & Sutcliffe A.G., in press, Analogous matching for specification reuse. To appear in CACM

[13]. Sutcliffe A.G. and Maiden N. (1990); Specification reusability: Why tutorial support is necessary. In Proceeding SE 90, BCS Conference on Software Engineering. Ed Hall P.A.V., pp 489-509, Cambridge Univ Press.

[14]. Alterman R., 1986, An adaptive planner, Proceedings of AAAI-86, 5th National Conference on Artificial Intelligence, Philadelphia, pp 65 - 69.

[15]. Hammond K.J., 1986, CHEF: A model of case-based planning, Proceedings of AAAI-86, 5th National Conference on Artificial Intelligence, Philadelphia, pp 267 - 271.

[16]. Hall R.P., 1989, Computational approaches to analogical reasoning: a comparative analysis, Artificial Intelligence 39, pp 39 - 120.

[17]. Schank R.C. and Leake D.B., 1989, Creativity and learning in a case-based explainer, Artificial Intelligence 40, pp 353 - 385.

[18]. Falkenheimer B., Forbus K.D. & Gentner D., 1989, The structure-mapping engine: algorithm and examples, TR No. UIUCDCS-R-87-1361, Dept Computer Science, University of Illinois at Champaign.

[19]. Holyoak K.J. & Thagard P., 1989, Analogical mapping by constraint satisfaction, Cognitive Science, pp 295 - 355.

[20]. Sutcliffe A.G. and Maiden N. (in press); Analysing the Analyst: Cognitive models in software engineering. To appear in International Journal of Man machine Studies.

[21]. Maiden N.A.M. & Sutcliffe A.G., manuscript in preparation(b), Cognitive models of expert software reusers.

[22]. Johnson W.L., 1990, Understanding and debugging novice programs, Artificial intelligence

42(1), pp 51 - 97.

[23] Lewis M.W. and Anderson J.R., 1985, Discrimination of operator schemata in problem solvers, Journal of Experimental Psychology: Learning, Memory and Cognition, Vol 8, No 5, pp 484 - 494.

[24]. Miyake N, 1986, Constructive interaction and the iterative process of understanding, Cognitive Science 10, pp 151 - 177.

[25]. Burstein M.H., 1988, Incremental learning from multiple analogies', in Analogica (Research Notes in Artificial Intelligence), edited by A.E. Prieditis, Pitman, London, pp 37 - 62.

[26]. Jansweiller W., Elshout J.J., and Wielinga B.J., 1989, On the multiplicity of learning to solve problems, in "Learning and Instruction. European Research in an International Context. Vol II & III", ed. by H. Mandel, E. de Corte, N. Bennet and H.F. Friedrich, Oxford: Pergamon.

[27]. Sutcliffe A.G. and Maiden N.A.M. (1991), Analogical software reuse: Empirical investigations of analogy based reuse and software engineering practices. Acta Psychologica 78(1-3), pp 173-197.

[28]. Maiden N.A.M and Sutcliffe A.G. (in press); Analogously based reusability, to appear in Behaviour and Information Technology.

[29]. Young R.M., 1983, Surrogates and Mappings: two kinds of conceptual mappings for interactive devices, in "Mental Models", ed. by D. Gentner and A.L. Stevens, Lawrence Erlbaum Associates, pp 35 - 52.

[30]. Sein M.W., 1988, Conceptual models in training novice users of computer systems: effectiveness of abstract vs analogical models and influence of individual differences, Ph. D. Thesis, School of Business, Indiana University, January 1988.

[31]. Abelson B. and Soloway E., 1985, The role of domain experience in software design, IEEE Transactions on Software Engineering, Vol SE-11, No 11, November 1985, pp 1351 1360.

[32]. Guindon R. & Curtis B., 1988, Control of cognitive processes during software design: What tools are needed ?, Proceedings of CHI '88 conference: Human Factors in Computer Systems, edited by E. Soloway, D. Frye and S.B. Sheppard, pp 263 - 269, ACM Press.

[33]. Luqi, 1989, Knowledge-based support for rapid software prototyping, IEEE Expert, Winter 1988, 9-18.

[34]. Balzer R., Cheatham T.E. and Green C., 1983, Software technology in the 1990s: using a new paradigm, IEEE Computer, November 1983, pp 39 - 45.

[35]. Boldyref, C., Elzer, P., Hall, P., Kabber, U., Keilman, J. and Witt J.,. 1990. 'PRACTITIONER: Pragmatic support for the reuse of concepts in existing software'. In Proceedings SE 90, BCS Conference on Software Engineering. Ed Hall P.A.V., pp 574-591, (Cambridge Univ Press. 1990)

[36]. Prieto-Diaz R., 1991, 'Implementing Faceted Classification for Software Reuse', Communications of the ACM 34(5), 88-97.

[37]. Sutcliffe A.G. (1991), Object oriented systems analysis: The abstract question. In proceedings of IFIP working group 8.1. Conference on Object oriented approaches in Information System Development. Eds Van Assche F., Moulin B., and Rolland C., pp 23-37, North Holland

[38]. Spivey, J.M.,1988, The Z notation: a Reference Manual. Prentice-Hall International, Englewood Cliffs, NJ

A Browser for Software Reuse

Panos Constantopoulos and Elena Pataki

Institute of Computer Science
Foundation of Research and Technology - Hellas
Heraklion, Crete, Greece
e-mail: {panos|pataki}@csi.forth.gr

Abstract

One important aspect of software reuse is the organization of collections of reusable software artifacts. The Software Information Base (SIB), developed within the ESPRIT project ITHACA, provides a directory to reusable software by storing information about software objects concerning the entire software life-cycle, namely requirements, design and implementation descriptions, as well as aggregate representations of complete systems and application domains. The SIB has an attributed graph structure. The selection of artifacts from the SIB, either directly or through other software development tools, is performed using a specialized Selection Tool (ST). In this paper we present the design and functionality of the Selection Tool. The main search mode supported by the Selection Tool is browsing. It is a flexible navigation process that takes full advantage of the knowledge representation mechanisms underlying the SIB semantic network, and provides local search of controllable size, direct access to specific areas or objects in the SIB, filtering mechanisms, and orientation aids. The information stored in the SIB and displayed by the Selection Tool is multimedia. The representational issues addressed by the SIB - ST system, as well as the relationship between the ST and hypertext systems are discussed.

1 Introduction

Software productivity is far from being considered satisfactory and several alternatives for improving it are being explored [1, 5, 21]. Reusing software components is a natural and very appealing idea, since the reuse of artifacts is encountered in all technical endeavours. Object-oriented programming, software libraries, AI-based design methods and organizational support are but some approaches to software reuse. On the other hand, it is commonly accepted that software reuse concerns not only code but the entire software development process, including requirements analysis, design, implementation and the development experiences gained in all stages. Thus source code is only one part of a reusable software object.

This paper presents the tool used for selecting software objects in connection with a software information base. The Software Information Base (SIB) is intended to store information about requirements, designs and implementations of software and supports selection of software through an associated Selection Tool (ST).

The whole system (SIB-ST) has been developed within the context of the ITHACA project, a large software engineering project sponsored by the European Communities through the ESPRIT programme, which aims at developing an integrated application development environment based on object-oriented techniques. The ITHACA environment includes an object-oriented programming language and database, application development and support tools, and an evolving software base [8, 9, 33].

As the name indicates, the Software Information Base (SIB) stores *information about* software components, not the components themselves. It is meant to serve as a directory to a collection of software components in order to facilitate their reuse. Information about the early stages of software construction (requirements analysis, design) is important because any necessary modification of an object is easier to identify at those stages. The representation language used in the SIB is Telos [22]. This is an E-R based language specifically designed for the development of information systems. The preference for Telos over other extended E-R models is due to its treatment of metaclasses and attributes. The organization of the SIB is based not only on the usual conceptual modeling principles of classification, generalization and aggregation, but also on principles addressing particular user and methodological needs, such as modularization, versioning, semantic similarity and others. Besides, the contents of the SIB actually are multimedia objects created and used by different development tools which require them to be presented in corresponding particular forms (e.g., E-R diagrams, data flow diagrams).

The Selection Tool (ST) is the main communication point between the SIB and the external world, i.e. users and other software development tools (e.g. the ITHACA Visual Scripting Tool [23]. Its task is to extract information from the SIB and to provide an interface for presenting this information in an appropriate way. The ST views the SIB as an abstract data type through the SIB Query Processor. The latter filters the SIB and passes the information to the ST for further processing.

The ST has two major functional parts. A querying mechanism filters the SIB to produce a subset of it possibly containing candidates for reuse. A browser allows viewing parts of the SIB at various levels of detail and navigating in a hypertext-like fashion through them. The filtering and browsing functions are actually interleaved in the operation of the ST.

Choosing a software component for reuse from the SIB is an ill-structured decision problem and there is no "best" solution to it that an automated procedure could find. There are subjective factors in judging the suitability of a software component for reuse, therefore the user will eventually have to examine a set of candidates in order to select the one that best fits his needs.

Browsing suggests itself as a natural mechanism not only for examining a query answer set containing potential candidates for reuse, but also for exploring a subset of the SIB in small steps. Indeed, browsing is a navigational search process that exploits the references established between objects by the SIB structuring principles. The structure of the SIB is designed to be rich enough to ensure the effectiveness of browsing which, in view of the uncertain nature of the software selection process, is the search mode of choice. As we shall see, the browser of the SIB has a substantial resemblance to a hypertext system. Consequently, the ST has the functional advantages of hypertext systems yet it also has to deal with their problems.

In section 2 we introduce the contents and structure of the SIB and the selection mechanisms. In section 3 we describe the functionality and current implementation of the

Selection Tool. In section 4 we discuss the relationship of the ST with hypertext systems and planned further development.

2 Description and Selection of Reusable Software

The SIB contains information about software objects in the form of a variety of descriptions of software objects and semantic relations that hold among them. Moreover, aggregations of descriptions pertaining to specific systems or even to entire application domains are defined as Application Frames. The notion of the Application Frame (AF) is central to the scenario for software reuse adopted in ITHACA [8, 33].

2.1 Structure of the SIB

The exposition in this subsection mostly follows [10]. The SIB is structured as an attributed directed graph the nodes and links of which represent *descriptions* of software objects and semantic relations respectively.

There are three kinds of descriptions:

- requirements descriptions (RD);
- design descriptions (DD); and
- implementation descriptions (ID).

These descriptions provide three corresponding views of a software object:

- an application view, according to a requirements specification model (e.g., SADT);
- a system view, according to a design specification model (e.g., data flow diagram); and
- an implementation view, according to an implementation model (e.g., set of C++ classes together with documentation).

Descriptions can be simple or composite, consisting of other descriptions. The term *descriptions* reflects the fact that these entities only describe software objects. The objects themselves reside outside the SIB. Descriptions are related to each other through a number of semantic relations listed below. In addition to the usual isA, instanceOf and attribute relations supported by object-oriented data models and knowledge representation schemes, several special attribute categories have been defined for the purposes of the SIB. The SIB is defined, as mentioned, in terms of the Telos knowledge representation language which supports creating an infinite instantiation hierarchy and treats attributes as objects in their own right (which, therefore, can also have attributes). These features of Telos are fully exploited in structuring the SIB.

The following relations are supported in the SIB (the link names are those appearing on the ST interface, see fig. 1):

(1) *Attribution*, represented by *attribute* links. This is a general, rather unconstrained representation of semantic relations, whereby the attributes of a description are defined to be instances of other descriptions. An attribute can have zero or more values.
Example:

```
Description SoftwareObject with
    attributes
```

```
author: Person
version: VersionNumber
```

Software Object has attributes author and version whose values are instances of Person and VersionNumber respectively.

(2) *Aggregation*, represented by *hasPart* links. This relates an object to its components which have to be objects of the same kind.
Example:

```
Description SoftwareObject with
    ...
    hasPart
        components: SoftwareObject
```

The components of an object have a distinct role in the function of the object and any possible changes to them affect the aggregate object as well (e.g., new version).

(3) *Classification*, represented by *instanceOf* links. Objects sharing common properties can be grouped into classes. An object can belong to more than one classes. Classes themselves are treated as generic objects which their members are instances of and which, in turn, can be instances of other, more generic objects. In fact, every SIB object has to be declared as an instance of at least one class. Thus, an infinite classification hierarchy is established starting with objects that have no instances of their own, called tokens. Multiple instantiation is allowed. Instantiation of a class involves instantiating all the associated semantic relations. Thus relations are treated as objects themselves.
Example:

```
Description BankIS instanceOf SoftwareObject with
    author
        : Panos
    version
        : 0.1
    components
        : CustomerAccounts, Credit, Investments
```

The attribute and hasPart links of BankIS are instances of the corresponding attribute and components links of SoftwareObject.

Classification is perhaps the most important modeling mechanism in the SIB ([34], and [25] give a detailed account of the construction of models and descriptions in the SIB).

(4) *Generalization*, represented by *isA* links. This allows multiple, strict inheritance of properties between classes leading to the creation of multiple generalization hierarchies. A class inherits all the attributes of its superclasses (one or more, multiple inheritance), however inherited properties can only be constrained, not overridden (strict inheritance).

(5) *Correspondence*, represented by *correspondsTo* links. A software object can have zero or more associated requirements, design and implementation descriptions. In fact, a

requirements specification may generate more than one alternative designs and a design may give rise to more than one implementations. Correspondence links denote such correspondences between requirements, design and implementation descriptions of a single software object.

Correspondence links define the internal structure of application frames. An *Application Frame* (AF) is a construct of coarse granularity in the SIB which represents a complete system or family of systems and comprises (*hasPart*) at least one implementation and optional design and requirements descriptions. Thus AF's encapsulate all the information pertaining to specific applications regardless of complexity (e.g., inventory monitoring or complete production planning and control system). In addition they support a natural organization of the SIB by application domain.

(6) *Similarity*, represented by *similarTo* links. The similarity relation is defined between objects of the same kind (i.e., RD, DD, ID, or AF) and has two attributes: a similarity criterion and a similarity measure. Two objects are said to be similar with respect to some criterion if they can substitute one another with regard to this criterion. The similarity criterion can be endogenous, defined in terms of relations already stored in the SIB, or exogenous, provided by the user who specifies a particular similarity link. Accordingly, similarity links can be computed or user-defined. The similarity measure expresses the degree to which the substitution of two similar objects, in either direction, is satisfactory and is a number in the range [0,1]. The similarity criterion is a mandatory attribute while the measure is optional.

Similarity links give rise to equivalence classes, possibly endowed with their own internal distance measures, which can support the application of analogical reasoning in software reuse and development.

(7) *Specificity*, represented by *specialCaseOf* links. This relation is defined only between application frames to denote that one application frame is less parameterized than another. E.g., a bank accounting and a hotel accounting application frame could both be derived from a more general, parametric accounting application frame.

2.2 Selection in the SIB

The SIB system offers a number of maintenance, selection and workspace management functions. Maintenance functions include insertion, deletion and update of information in the SIB and are supported by appropriate textual and graphical editors. Selection functions include querying and browsing the SIB for purposes of selecting reusable artifacts. And workspace management involves the dynamic definition and modification of workspaces to provide easier and more efficient interaction with the SIB [8].

The selection of software descriptions from the SIB is accomplished through the *Selection Tool* (ST) and it is an iterative process comprising alternate stages of retrieval and browsing. Browsing usually is the final and often the only stage of the process. The functional difference between the retrieval and the browsing mode is that the former supports the retrieval of an arbitrary subset of the SIB while the latter supports local exploratory searches withing a given subset of the SIB. Operationally, both selection modes address queries to the SIB.

Seen as operations on an abstract data type, the selection functions can be defined as follows [10]:

Retrieve: Query x Associations → SetOf (Descriptions , Weights)

Browse: Identifier x Links x Associations → Views

Associations can be seen as groupings of descriptions (see [10] for details). The SIB system is intended to support non-Boolean queries. Query conditions consist of logical combinations of predicates which are, in general, fuzzy. A real number between 0 and 1, called *weight* is associated with each predicate. Boolean predicates are simply special cases with weight 1 if the value of the predicate is 'yes' and 0 if the value is 'no'. The result of a query is a set ranked by weight. Weights of logical expressions are computed on the basis of the following rules:

Let p and q be predicates with weights $w(p)$ and $w(q)$ respectively. Then

$w(p\ OR\ q) = max\ \{w(p),\ w(q)\}$

$w(p\ AND\ q) = w(p) * w(q)$

$w(NOT\ p) = 1 - w(p)$

Alternative rules for the computation of weights exist (e.g., see [16, 29]), as well as alternative retrieval models altogether. An important feature of the present approach (though not unique to it) is the ability to express such notions as similarity or affinity [26] in terms of weights on fuzzy relations which give rise to fuzzy predicates. Boolean queries are merely a special case.

The *Retrieve* function takes as input an association and a (compound) non-Boolean query and returns a subset of the association with weights attached indicating the degree to which the descriptions in the answer set match the query. In the current implementation only Boolean queries are supported, yet the extension to non-Boolean is currently undertaken.

Browsing clearly is a special retrieval operation. It starts at a specified SIB description which is the focus of attention and is called *current object* and produces a view of a neighbourhood of interest of the current object within a given association. Since the SIB has a network structure, the neighbourhood of the current object (node) is defined in terms of the links of interest adjacent to it. As we shall later see, the size of the neighbourhood can also be controlled. Thus, the *Browse* function takes as input the identifier (name) of the current object, a list of names of link classes of interest and an association, and determines a local view centered around the current object. By calling *Browse* again with the identifier argument equal to the name of one of the objects contained in the browser's view, that object is made current and the view is updated. Effectively, the *Browse* function provides a moving window with controllable filters and size, which allows navigational search over subsets of the SIB network. The default association is the entire SIB.

The multimedia nature of SIB descriptions calls for the development of a hypermedia annotation mechanism that would gracefully complement the SIB semantic network. This is accomplished by establishing referential links between descriptions, treated as a special category of attribute links, thus completely integrated in the SIB network model. Hypermedia annotations include text, graphics, raster images and algorithm animations.

3 The Selection Tool of the SIB (ST)

Queries to the SIB can be classified as *explicit* or *implicit* and as *interactive* or *programmatic*. An *explicit* query involves an arbitrary predicate explicitly formulated in a query language or through an appropriate form interface. An *implicit* query, on the other hand, is one generated as a result of navigational commands in the browsing mode, or one of particular significance and frequent occurrence, "pre-canned" for ease of use and offered as a button or menu option. An *interactive* query is formulated through the user interface of the ST, while a *programmatic* one is submitted by another software development tool, such as the Visual Scripting Tool of ITHACA, through its own user interface.

The ST is designed to support all the relevant kinds of queries. In the current implementation, priority has been given to *implicit, interactive* queries. As already explained, these correspond to the browsing selection mode and are expected to take up the majority of the interaction with the ST. A form-based query interface, closely related to the data entry form of the SIB, as well as a query language are being developed to support *explicit, interactive* queries. Finally, *explicit, programmatic* queries are supported by the ST providing a programmatic interface to other tools, through which the primitive query operations of the Telos system underlying the SIB can be used.

In what follows we present the browsing functions of the ST.

3.1 Functionality of the Selection Tool

The ST user interface consists of the following windows (fig.1):

- a *Graphical Browser* which displays a part of the network of the SIB around a selected object (current object).

- a *Link Filter* with buttons, each corresponding to a link type, used for filtering the information displayed by the Graphical Browser.

- a *History List* which keeps a record of users' moves through the SIB network.

- an *Application Frames List* listing the contents of the entire SIB in terms of application frames.

- a *Main Form* which shows information about the current object.

- an *Auxiliary Form* which displays information about any other object, after a selection made by the user in a hypertext-like manner on the Main Form.

- a *Function Menu* which offers a variety of useful functions.

In what follows we describe the functionality of each component.

- *Graphical Browser:*

The Graphical Browser, built using the LABY graphical editor, displays a part of the SIB network around a selected object (*current object*). The structures currently displayed have the form of a star whose central node is the current object. The window of the Graphical Browser is semantically divided in two parts. From each node appearing in the lower part emanates at least one link pointing to the current node. Similarly, there is at least one link emanating from the current node and pointing to each node appearing in the upper part. The types of links are denoted by a colour code. For example the isA relation is shown with red links while the instanceOf relation with green links. The colour code is shown in the Link Filter. Nodes appearing in the graph of the browser are selectable with the mouse. When selected, a node becomes current, it is placed in the middle of the display and a move in the SIB network results. The links displayed include direct links from the current object to other objects and computed isA and instanceOf links.

The population of the display is controlled by means of the *Link Filter* (see below) and the *Instance Box*. The Instance Box appears in the display of the Graphical Browser when the instances of a certain active link class (i.e. selected by the Link Filter) adjacent to the current object are too many to be shown on the display. On selecting the Instance Box of a link class with the mouse, a list of objects related to the current one by that type of links appears (see fig.4). The objects on this list are selectable just as those displayed graphically.

- *Link Filter*:

The Link Filter provides buttons corresponding to link classes and is used for activating/deactivating links thus controlling the information displayed in the Graphical Browser. Each button acts as a filter on a certain relation. If the button is selected (on), the corresponding relation is displayed and vice versa. The isA and instanceOf buttons further offer the option of displaying computed in addition to direct isA and instanceOf links. All buttons show the colour code of the link classes and have a help facility. When moving from node to node in the Graphical Browser, the state of the Link Filter does not change unless the user does so explicitly.

- *History List*:

The History List is a navigation aid intended to prevent users from getting lost, a common problem in hypertext systems [6]. The History List is scrollable and contains the names of the objects selected as current during a session in chronological order, the most recent one shown at the bottom (as in the history command of Unix). All entries of the list are selectable. A selection made on the History List is functionally equivalent to one made on the Graphical Browser.

- *Application Frames List*:

The Application Frames List contains the names of the application frames, reflecting the overall structure and contents of the SIB. The purpose of the Application Frames List is to compensate for the limited scope of the Graphical Browser, which is a shortcoming if an extended area of interest is sought by navigation rather than by explicit querying. The application frames are displayed in an indented list representing the existing hierarchical structure. Each item on the list is selectable, which effectively allows big steps over the SIB network in the browsing mode.

Moreover, the Application Frames List serves as the initial entry point to the ST.

- *Main Form*:

The Main Form is the top right-most window of the ST and invariably displays information about the current object. It shows the abstracted definition of the object in a form layout. The information presented is generated by unparsing the SIB. The form can also contain multimedia annotations to the object, each one displayed in a separate window. At present, this annotation is textual and graphical (fig.5), but can be of any other type with no additional effort, provided that appropriate tools exist in the working environment.

- *Auxiliary Form*:

To get information about a displayed object, other than the current one, without changing the actual view in the Graphical Browser, the user can select the name of the desired object on the Main Form in a hypertext-like fashion (see fig.1). An Auxiliary Form will appear at the bottom right of the ST and display information about the selected object in the manner of the Main Form. To prevent user distraction, only one auxiliary form can be open at a time; also objects are not selectable on auxiliary forms. The auxiliary form is actually a preview mechanism and is offered as an orientation aid.

- *Function Menu*:

Through the Function Menu, several other windows for performing various useful functions can appear on demand. Currently these functions are:

- *GotoObject*: Allows direct access to invisible objects by name.
- *EnterData*: A Data Entry Form is offered for entering data into the SIB (fig. 6). The Query Form, currently under construction, will have a similar appearance.
- *KeepObject*: Keeps a retrieved object in a local workspace.
- *Iconify* and *Quit*: Closes and iconifies a window; and quits the ST respectively.

3.2 Usage Example

Suppose we would like to add in the SIB an application dealing with processing of letters, which will assist secretaries, managers, and others to write professional letters, check them, and, after final approval, mail them through post or electronic mail. Looking at the Application Frames List, we observe that there is already an Office Information System called WooRKS. The basic concepts in WooRKS are actors, roles and procedures.

Our starting point will be WooRKS, which we select through the Application Frames List. As we can read in the natural language comment attached to the corresponding Main Form, WooRKS is a work flow system for offices, which handles a variety of activities (see fig.1). So this might be one of the candidate places to search for a letter processing application. WooRKS has three attributes which are further explained in its Main Form. One of them, *reqDescr*, deals with WooRKS requirements descriptions and it will probably provide us with more information about what the WooRKS system actually does. Before making it current, we preview its contents on the Auxiliary Form, by selecting WooRKS1_RD_FORM from the Main Form, and we decide to visit it. In figure 2 WooRKS1_RD_FORM is current in the Graphical Browser window. We observe that it handles the following *classes* of activities: OrderProcessing, WarehousePro-cessing, and AccountProcessing. OrderProcessing sounds the most close to letter processing, since letter and order processing share some operations, such as checking and archiving. We decide to visit OrderProcessing to see if it includes what is needed for letter processing in general. After examination we conclude that this is not true. We return to WooRKS1_RD_FORM through the History List and decide to preview WarehouseProcessing and AccountProcessing to see if there is anything relevant there. By previewing these nodes we realize that none of them fulfills our needs. We further notice that they are all instances of FormProcessClass.

We take a closer look on FormProcessClass by moving to it through the GotoObject facility (fig.3). As FormProcessClass is a subclass of FormClass, it inherits its attributes. By previewing FormClass, we find out that it has two attributes, *roles* and *baseRole* (see fig.3) and decide to create a new instance of FormProcessClass, called LetterProcessing, whose *roles* will correspond to the initial requirements imposed on our letter processing application. In particular, the *baseRole* of LetterProcessing will be LP_base_role, and the *roles* will be LP_letterCompose, LP_letterCheck, LP_letterApprove, LP_letterSend, LP_letterReceive, and LP_letterArchive.

We have chosen this convention for naming the *roles* by analogy to the existing *roles* of the other activities. To see these names we first made FormRole current using the GotoObject facility (see fig.4). Since FormRole has too many instances to be displayed on the Graphical Browser, an Instance Box appears by clicking on the "MANY INSTANCES" box of the Browser.

At this point we start creating the *roles* and *baseRole* of LetterProcessing. Before creating LP_letterArchive, we visit OP_orderArchive by selecting it from the Instance Box (fig.4). This act is worthwhile because we find a *correspondsTo* link from OP_orderArchive to ArchiveAct, which is an instance of ADMActivity (see the Main Form in fig.5). Knowing that ADMActivity handles the design descriptions, we can further proceed by defining the ADMActivity corresponding to the new LP_letterArchive in a similar way, or even use the ArchiveAct as the ADMActivity of LP_letterArchive. Similarly, we may use CompileRefAct and/or EvaluationOrderAct which *correspondTo* OP_orderCheck as the ADMActivity of LP_letterCheck, etc.

Finally, we are in a position to define the new LetterProcessing node. We move to FormProcessClass using the GotoObject option and use the EnterData facility, which will make our task easy, even if we have no knowledge of the syntax of Telos. The Data Entry Form for LetterProcessing is shown in figure 6. In the same figure you can see the results of entering the information.

3.3 Implementation

The SIB system consists of the following major parts (Figure 7):

- The *SIB Interactive User Interface* generates and coordinates the other parts, including the interface tools of the Data Entry Forms and the Selection Tool, except for the Graphical Browser. It is implemented using the OSF/Motif toolkit.

- The *Graphical Browser* presents parts of the SIB network graphically and allows the user to browse through it by sending messages to the SIB Interactive User Interface in response to user actions. The Graphical Browser is a LABY graphical editor with only the working area present.

- The *Display Forms* are used to provide information about the current node or another selected node in a form layout. They are designed to support multimedia information (text, graphics, images, animation, etc.).

- A special *Data Entry Form* provides for entering data into the SIB through a form interface.

- The *Query Interface* handles queries about SIB objects, issued to it by the various components of the ST or by the Data Entry Form. As a result of processing a query it constructs a file suitable for display by the Graphical Browser or the Data Entry Form. In the current implementation a separate query interface (based on the client-server model) is used for programmatic queries. However, the two query interfaces will be integrated in the future.

LABY is a general purpose graphical editor developed in part within the ITHACA project [19]. The entire SIB-ST prototype system has been implemented in C++, including the underlying Telos system. The Telos implementation has particularly emphasized query performance and efficiency of memory usage (for more details see [8]). The system runs on Sun3, Sun4 series, SparcStations and 386 machines under Unix and requires the X window system and a colour monitor.

4 Discussion

[20] identifies the following three steps in reusing software: selection, specialization, and integration. Abstraction plays a central role in each of these steps. It makes artifacts easier to understand and to specialize, by chosing specific realizations, and allows information about their interface to be abstracted from the definitions. In the work reported here we are concerned with abstractions for supporting the process of selecting software for reuse.

The same steps of the reuse process are identified by Prieto-Diaz [27, 28], with an additional evaluation step, when there is no exact match with the imposed requirements. The candidates for reuse are ranked according to the adaptation and conversion effort they require before reuse can actually take place. In this approach, a faceted classification scheme supports both the retrieval process and the evaluation and adaptation of code segments. The terms in each facet are organized in a directed acyclic graph with weights indicating their conceptual closeness. The selection of the facets and terms (namely the faceted classification schedule) is a process that requires careful consideration in order for the classification scheme to be successful. The system allows for a flexible change of the classification schedule as implied by the specific application domain the library is supposed to cover. The query process allows the modification, generalization/specialization and expansion of queries while vocabulary control is assisted by a dictionary of synonyms. Despite the shortcomings of defining the conceptual distances, the classification scheme is promising, yet the query interface is suitable for expert users only. Browsing through the conceptual graph would be an easier and, in some cases, more efficient retrieval method.

User interface and functionality issues have, in fact, been so far one of the chief three problems that have hindered the acceptance of database technology in software engineering, the other two being the technical support (efficiency, safety) and the

Even elementary configuration management features, such as the re-configuration of objects as a result of component changes, are hardly supported by databases (an exception is CACTIS [18]).

[2] recognize the importance of good documentation for understanding the reusable components. Hypertext systems allow the attachment of various annotation elements interconnected with each other, to components, and provide instant access to this supporting information. The SIB allows the user to relate any kind of annotation to a description. Furthermore, our plans for a Hypermedia Annotation Mechanism, explained below, will greatly support the understanding of the reusable components.

The node and link model of the SIB resembles the hypertext model. In both, nodes and links are of equal importance, serving as units of information and as orientation cues. The type of link emanating from a given node conveys information about the target node. In addition, the name of a node usually reflects its content. This helps the user find a path to his destination. The question naturally arises of whether an existing hypertext system could provide a satisfactory interface to the SIB. It turns out that the full representational power of Telos, underlying the SIB, cannot be rendered by one of the currently available hypertext systems known to us, let alone efficiency issues arising from heterogeneity. The tools that compose the Selection Tool (e.g. the Graphical Browser and the Link filter, the Application Frames List, the Forms, etc.) take advantage of the underlying knowledge base in order to help the user locate and reuse the software modules. Moreover, given that the SIB will be highly populated, other features common in most hypertext systems (e.g. global browsers) or the ability to directly following links are not enough to prevent *disorientation* and *cognitive overhead* [6], which are inherent problems of hypertext systems. On the other hand, using Telos, we provide users with pre-defined views (e.g. Application Frames List), constructed by querying the SIB and updated dynamically reflecting changes in it. Such views reduce the cognitive overhead problem. The History List combined with the ability to preview the contents of a specific object on the Auxiliary Form before actually visiting it prevent disorientation.

Of a number of advanced hypertext systems, such as gIBIS [7], DIF [13, 14], Intermedia [15, 35], NoteCards [17, 32] and Neptune [3, 12], all of which have some of the desirable features for a selection tool of the SIB, DIF is designed to serve a purpose similar to the SIB-ST system, namely to support a software life-cycle with emphasis on reuse. However, the basic reusable constructs of DIF, *Basic Templates* and *Standardized forms*, have only one level of instantiation and the system relies upon the use of keywords to preserve the consistency of information. Structural information is kept in an Ingres database, which has to be queried or navigated through to locate reusable Basic Templates. Unfortunately, the searching process cannot use the actual information stored using software engineering tools for functional and architectural specifications and this limits the flexibility of the selection process.

The current version of the SIB prototype system, including the ST presented here, has been subjected to relatively extensive experimentation by users inside and outside the implementors' organization, indicating a high acceptance level. Nevertheless, no formal evaluation experiments have yet been conducted. A number of desirable improvements, on the other hand, have been identified [24], briefly listed below.

Several enhancements to the Graphical Browser are planned. First, the presentation of all direct links on the display, not only the ones adjacent to the current node, so as to show all the direct relations that exist between nodes in the local view. Second, the option to control the size of the displayed neighbourhood of the current node will be provided. In a graph-theoretic sense, the size of the neighbourhood currently is 1 : each path connecting the current node to another node in the neighbourhood contains exactly one link. This restricts the view to a small area and imposes a small step size during navigation. On the other hand, it also keeps the information in the browser's window from exploding. Control over the neighbourhood size will be granted by attaching *scope parameters* to the buttons of the Link Filter. The value of a scope parameter will determine the size of the neighbourhood with regard to the corresponding type of links. Third, the layout of the browser's display will be re-arranged so that the spatial distribution of links will be directed by their semantics.

The History mechanism will be enhanced to support the reuse of paths [36] once the *context* mechanism of Telos [8] is available.

Similarly, the context mechanism will enable the definition of context-specific Application Frames Lists. Highlighting the current view area in the Application Frames List is an obvious further orientation aid.

Given that *attribute* links can be specialized to represent user-defined relations, the question naturally arises of representing such relations in the Link Filter. A user-configurable Link Filter with the present one as a default is a possible solution. Furthermore, it has been noted that a sequence of changes of state in the Link Filter results in an unpleasant sequence of updates of the display. This can be avoided by committing all the changes at once at the user's command.

The free-text comments that appear in the Forms serve as a primitive annotation mechanism. We are currently exploring ways to provide an enhanced Hypermedia Annotation Mechanism by either incorporating in the SIB one of the existing hypertext models [4, 11, 30, 31] or developing a new one that will best serve our needs for flexibility and efficiency.

Finally, the Query Form, currently under development, will complete the Selection Tool. The Query Form will offer a form-based query interface similar to the Data Entry Form (fig. 4) and the option to formulate queries directly in a query language.

References

1. J. Bigelow, "Hypertext and CASE," *IEEE Software*, March 1988.

2. Ted Biggerstaff and C. Richter, "Reusability, Framework, Assessment & Directions," *IEEE Software*, vol. 4(2), March 1987.

3. Brad Campbell and Joseph M. Goodman, "HAM: A general purpose Hypertext Abstract Machine," *Communications of the ACM*, vol. 31(7), pp. 856-861, July 1988.

4. R. Caudillo and M. Mainguenaud, "A Hypertext - Like Multimedia Document Data Model," *Int'l Conf. on Multimedia Information Systems*, pp. 221-241, McGraw-Hill, 1991.

5. E. Chikofsky and Rubenstein B., "CASE: Reliability Engineering for Information Systems," *IEEE Software*, March 1988.

6. J. Conklin, "Hypertext: An Introduction and Survey," *IEEE Computer*, September 1987.

7. J. Conklin and M. Begeman, "gIBIS: A Hypertext Tool for Exploratory Policy Discussion," *ACM Tr. on Office Information Systems*, vol. 6(4), October 1988.

8. P. Constantopoulos, M. Doerr, E. Pataki, E. Petra, G. Spanoudakis, and Y. Vassiliou, *The Software Information Base-Selection Tool integrated prototype*, Institute of Computer Science, Foundation of Research and Technology - Hellas, Heraklicn, Crete, January 12 1991.

9. P. Constantopoulos, M. Jarke, J. Mylopoulos, B. Pernici, E. Petra, M. Theodoridou, and Y. Vassiliou, *The ITHACA Software Information Base : Requirements, Functions, and Structuring Concepts*, Institute of Computer Science, Foundation of Research and Technology - Hellas, Heraklio, Crete, May 1989.

10. P. Constantopoulos, M. Jarke, J. Mylopoulos, and Y. Vassiliou, *Software Information Base - A Server for Reuse*, Institute of Computer Science, Foundation of Research and Technology - Hellas, Heraklion, Crete, November 1991.

11. W.B. Croft and H. Turtle, "A Retrieval Model for Incorporating Hypertext Links," *Hypertext '89, Proc.*, pp. 213-224, Pittsburgh, Pennsylvania, November 5-8, 1989.

12. Norman M. Delisle and Mayer D. Schwartz, "Contexts - A Partitioning Concept for Hypertext," *ACM Tr. Office Information Systems*, vol. 5(2), pp. 168-186, April 1987.

13. P.K. Garg and W. Scacchi, "Composition of Hypertext Nodes," *Proceedings of the 12th Online Information Meeting*, London, December 6-8, 1988.

14. P.K. Garg and W. Scacchi, "A Hypertext System to Manage Software Life-Cycle Documents," *IEEE Software*, vol. 7(3), pp. 90-98, May 1990.

15. Garrett, Smith, and N.K. Meyrowitz, "Intermedia: Issues, Strategies and Tactics in the Design of a Hypermedia Document System," *Proc. Conf. on Computer-Supported Cooperative Work*, MCC Software Technical Program, Austin, Texas, 1986.

16. S. Gibbs, "Querying Large Class Collections," *Object Management (D. Tsichritzis, ed.)*, Centre Universitaire d' Informatique, Universite de Geneve, 1990.

17. F.G. Halasz, "Reflections on NoteCards: Seven Issues for the Next Generation of Hypermedia Systems," *Communications of the ACM*, vol. 31(7), pp. 836-852, July 1988.

18. S.E. Hudson and R. King, "Cactis: A Self-Adaptive, Concurrent Implementation of an Object-Oriented Database Management System," *ACM Trans. on Database Systems*, vol. 14(3), September 1989.

19. M. Katevenis, T. Sorilos, C. Georgis, and P. Kalogerakis, *LABY User's Manual*, Computer Science Institute, Foundation of Research and Technology, Heraklio, Crete, May 1990.

20. C.W. Krueger, *Models of Reuse in Software Engineering*, Carnegie Mellon, December 1989.

21. C. Martin, "Second Generation Case Tools: A Challenge to Vendors," *IEEE Software*, March 1988.

22. J. Mylopoulos and others, *TELOS: Representing Knowledge about Information Systems*, Institute of Computer Science, Foundation of Research and Technology - Hellas, Heraklion, Crete, August 1990.

23. O. Nierstrasz and others, "Objects + Scripts = Applications," *Esprit '91*, pp. 534-552, Commission of the European Communities, 1991.

24. E. Pataki and P. Constantopoulos, "The Selection Tool of the Software Information Base: A Hypertext Perspective," *Working Paper*, Institute of Computer Science, Foundation of Research and Technology - Hellas, Heraklion, Crete, November 1991.

25. E. Petra and C.V. Vezerides, *SIB Content's Manual*, Institute of Computer Science, Foundation of Research and Technology - Hellas, Heraklion, Crete, January 1991.

26. X. Pintado, "Selection and Exploration in an Object-Oriented Environment: The Affinity Browser," *Object Management (D. Tsichritzis, ed.)*, Centre Universitaire d' Informatique, Universite de Geneve, 1990.

27. Ruben Prieto-Diaz, "Implementing Faceted Classification for Software Reuse," *Communications of the ACM*, vol. 34(5), pp. 89-97, ACM, May 1991.

28. Ruben Prieto-Diaz and Peter Freeman, "Classifying Software for Reusability," *IEEE Software*, pp. 6-16, January 1987.

29. G. Salton, E.A. Fox, and H. Wu, "Extended Boolean Information Retrieval," *Communications of the ACM*, vol. 26, pp. 1022-1036, 1983.

30. M.A. Shepherd and C. Watters, "Virtual Structures for Hypertext," *Int'l Conf. on Multimedia Information Systems*, pp. 201-219, McGraw-Hill, 1991.

31. F.WM. Tompa, "A Data Model for Flexible Hypertext Database Systems," *ACM Tr. on Information Systems*, vol. 7(1), pp. 85-100, January 1989.

32. Randall H. Trigg and Lucy A. Suchman, "Collaborative Writing in NoteCards," *In: Ray McAleese (Ed.), Hypertext: theory into practice*, pp. 45-61, Intellect Inc., Oxford, 1989.

33. Y. Vassiliou, M. Jarke, E. Petra, T. Topaloglou, G. Spanoudakis, and C. Vezerides, *Technical Description of the SIB*, Institute of Computer Science, Foundation of Research and Technology - Hellas, Heraklio, Crete, January 1990.

34. C.V. Vezerides, "The organization of an SIB for software reuse by a programming community," *Master's Thesis*, University of Crete, 1991.

35. N. Yankelovich, B.J. Haan, N.K. Meyrowitz, and S.M. Drucker, "Intermedia: The Concept and Construction of a Seamless Information Environment," *IEEE*

Computer, pp. 81-96, January 1988.

36. P.T. Zellweger, "Scripted Documents: A Hypermedia Path Mechanism," *Hypertext '89 Proceedings*, 1989.

320

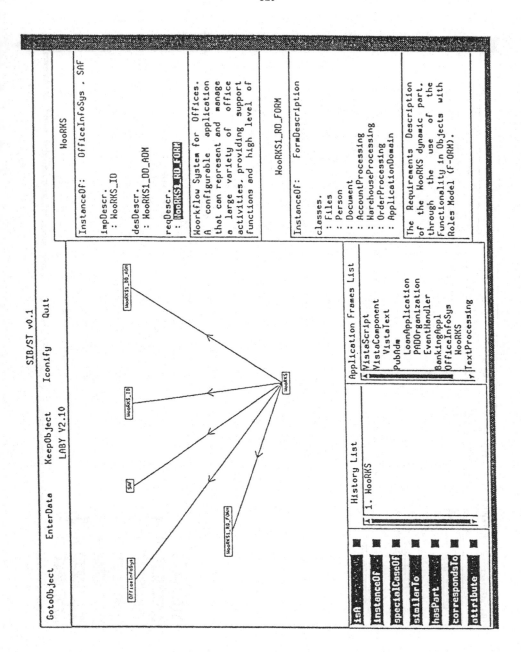

Figure 1. The Selection Tool of the Software Information Base. Current in the Graphical Browser is WooRKS, the starting point of the usage example.

321

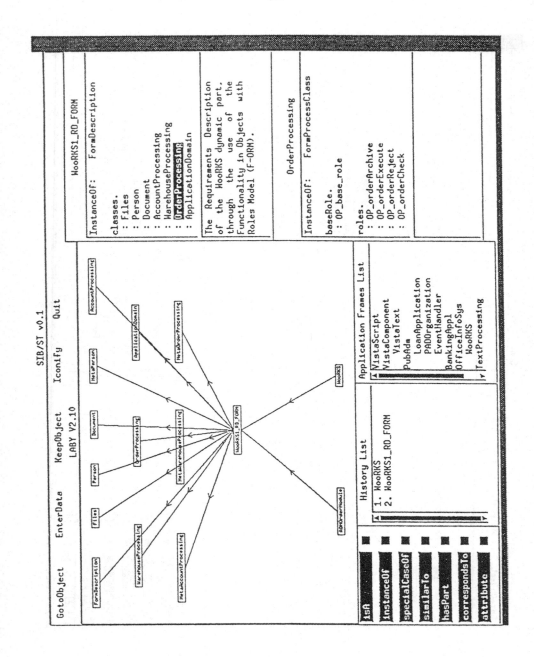

Figure 2. Inspecting the requirements descriptions of WooRKS and previewing OrderProcessing.

322

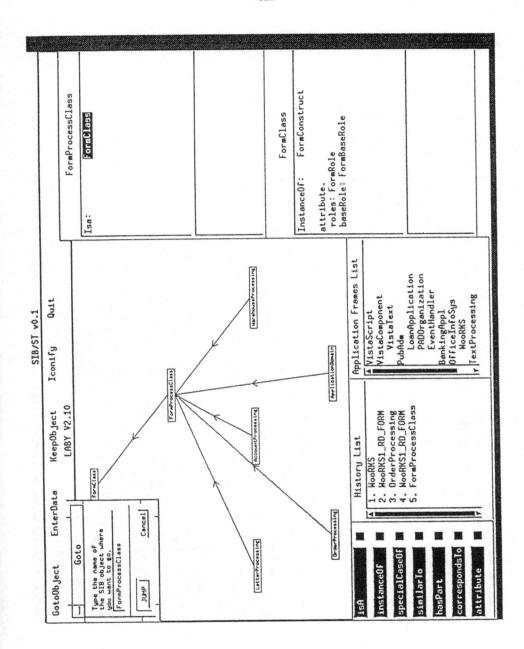

Figure 3. Visiting FormProcessClass and previewing its superclass, FormClass

323

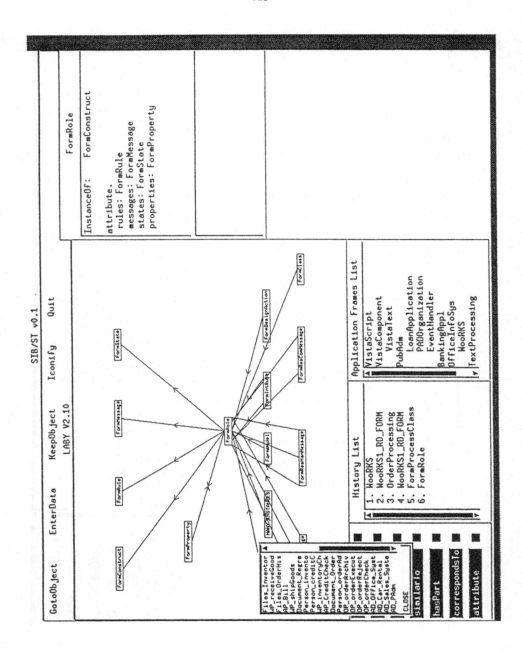

Figure 4. The Instance Box handles the instances of FormRole.

324

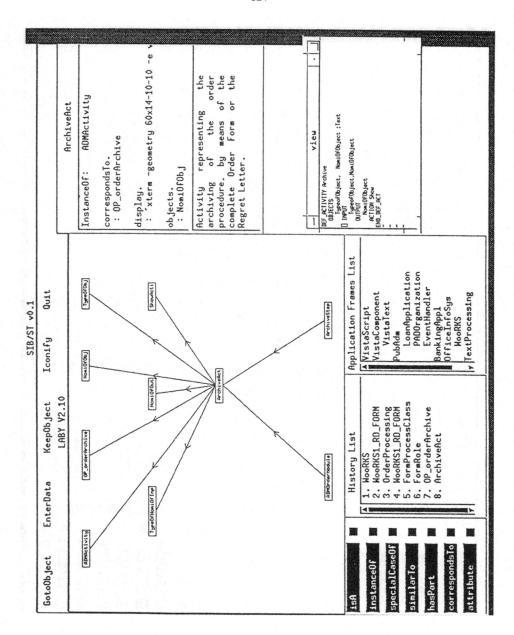

Figure 5. An annotation attached to ArchiveAct.

325

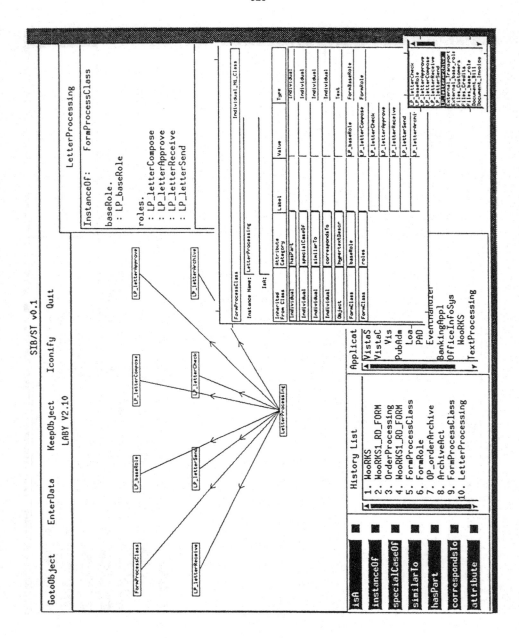

Figure 6. The EnterData facility used to insert LetterProcessing in the SIB.

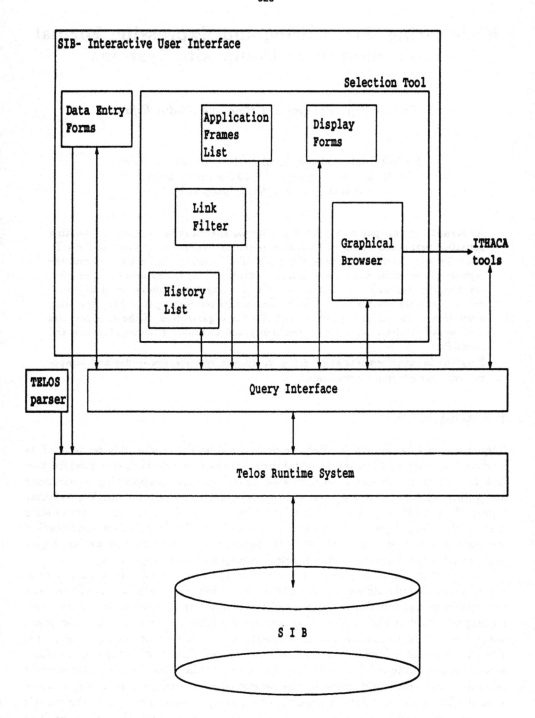

Figure 7. The architecture of the SIB-ST

Elaborating, Structuring and Expressing Formal Requirements of Composite Systems

Eric Dubois, Philippe Du Bois and André Rifaut

Institut d'Informatique, Facultés Universitaires de Namur
21 rue Grandgagnage, B-5000 Namur (Belgium)
E-mail: {edu,pdu}@info.fundp.ac.be

Abstract . In this paper, we propose a formal specification language supporting activities performed during the initial requirements engineering phase of the software lifecycle. During this phase, those activities include (i) the elicitation and the capture of the initial description of a given problem, (ii) the expression of requirements associated with a 'composite system' (i.e. a system including manual procedures, hardware devices and software components interacting together) providing a solution to the original problem and (iii) the organization of the requirements document in order to enhance its readibility and to promote its maintenance and reusability.

Keywords : requirements engineering, composite systems, first-order and temporal logic, structuring mechanisms.

1 Introduction

Requirements Engineering (or Requirements Analysis) is now widely recognized as a critical activity in the context of information systems development. Despite this fact, only a few methods and tools, providing a real guidance, supporting verifications and validations, are emerging and used in an industrial environment. We feel that a part of this difficulty is due to the lack of adequacy of the current requirements specification languages. In this paper, we present and illustrate a new specification language based on some recent ideas investigated within the framework of an Esprit II project (called *Icarus*) entirely devoted to Requirements Engineering.

We feel that the first quality of a requirements specification language is its *expressiveness*. One should keep in mind that requirements should not only address the description of the functional behavior of the computerized system but should also encompass the description of a *composite system* (like, e.g., requirements on manual procedures to be installed or on a specific hardware and/or device to be used). Thereby, a suitable language should support the expression of computer artefacts as well as the "natural" (i.e. without any computer bias) description of statements related to the real-world entities. The language, presented in this paper, devotes a particular attention to the expression of *accuracy* requirements (like "the stock's quantities recorded on the computer should reflect the real-world stock's quantities with some delta"), and *real-time* requirements (like "this report has to be issued by the computer within 5 seconds"). On top of its expressiveness, we plead that a requirements specification language should be *formal* enough so that a number of analysis activities (not only restricted to syntactic checks) can be supported by the availability of (i) rigorous *rules of interpretation* defining precisely the language constructs and (ii) a set of *deductive rules* allowing to reason about pieces of specifications. In Sect. 2, we present the basic features of our language with respect to its expressiveness and its associated formal framework. In Sect. 3, we illustrate them on an excerpt of a library case study.

The requirements engineering activity is a complex activity which starts from incompletely defined wishes expressed by several customers about a desired complex composite system. One could imagine that this activity consists only in the transcription of the customers' wishes in a requirements document. This is far from true because those wishes are in most cases imprecise, incomplete, ill-structured and even inconsistent. Thereby, it is essential to have some methodological guidance in the *progressive* elaboration of the requirements document (see e.g. [Fin89] [Fea89]). For some years, we are experimenting an incremental development strategy (i) starting from a simple specification of the desired external behavior exhibited by the system to be developed and (ii) gradually moving towards a more complex specification of the internal behavior of the system considered as a *composite* one, viz considering the responsibilities associated with the different components as well as the nature of the interfaces existing between them [Dub88b] [Dub90]. In Sect. 4, we illustrate the capability of our language for supporting this incremental elaboration of requirements for composite systems. In particular, we will suggest how the global specification associated with the library case-study can be refined in a more detailed specification where two library's components are identified.

Usually, an important part of the work performed by the requirements analysts relies on the organization of the whole requirements document. This is particularly true for complex descriptions including several thousands of requirements statements. Thereby, we feel essential that the requirements specification language be equipped with *structuring mechanisms* making possible the requirements document be organized into specification units with well-defined inter-units relationships. Structuring mechanisms available in the language are introduced in Sect. 2 and their use illustrated in the other sections. In particular, in Sect. 5, we suggest how the use of the parameterization mechanism may support a requirements elaboration mechanism [Reu89] [Pro89] based on the identification of generic concepts for a given *problem domain* and on their tailoring to the needs of the requirements expressed for a *specific application*. In this section, the approach is illustrated by considering the requirements expressed about one of the library components in terms of basic concepts related to a *resource allocation* problem domain.

Finally, after a short comparison of our language with some other existing approaches, Sect. 6 concludes this paper with some directions for future work.

2 Overview of the Language

As we pointed out in the Introduction, a suitable language for the Requirements Engineering activity should be a general customizable language supporting an incremental elaboration and analysis of the requirements document. To this end, the language that we have developed has been designed according to three essential features : expressiveness, structuring mechanisms and formality.

2.1 Expressiveness

The language must be sufficiently rich to support some "natural" mapping between all kinds of things of interest and the various language concepts being available. In other words, requirements specification should remain a problem definition activity, not a coding task. In particular :

- The language supports the use of different and possibly mixed styles of specification. At the Requirements Engineering level, we have experimented that there are numerous properties which are not of an *algorithmic* nature, i.e. cannot be expressed in terms of successive transformations applied on arguments to produce results. This is why a more *declarative* style is also supported in the language.
- Immutable values, such as numbers or strings, are not rich enough for modelling 'real-world' dynamic systems. Observations associated with *the state of such systems are intrinsically time-varying*. Thereby, in the language, an important distinction is introduced between *data type* (i.e. immutable values) and *type clusters* (used for recording time-varying states observations).
- With respect to clusters, the language does not only support the expression of constraints on admissible states or on the transition between two successive states (the usual *pre/post*) but also on the *ordering of states*. These constraints make possible to refer future states (like e.g. 'if this property holds in this state, then it holds in all future ones') as well as previous states. Furthermore, *real-time constraints* like 'this property is true during 3 minutes' can also be expressed.
- During the incremental elaboration of a requirements specification, it is usual to deal with *incomplete requirements* (viz. requirements which are in an intermediate – non-finished – stage). The language permits to retain this information so that it may direct the acquisition of further requirements. Furthermore, the semantics of the language supports the handling of incomplete requirements.

2.2 Structuring Mechanisms

In most cases, the specification of requirements results in large documents where complex interactions exist between different pieces of descriptions. Such documents should be *organized* into separate units which can be combined in a controllable way to yield the complete specification. Moreover, structuring mechanisms are also essential to support the *reuse* of specification's components and the *maintenance* of the requirements document. In our language, we have identified four structuring mechanisms :

- A natural part of the specification process includes the identification of various things of interest sharing some common characteristics (like, e.g., the set of admissible values for an account number or the set of admissible behaviors (states) for a library system). In the language, this activity is modelled by the introduction of *types* which follow the Object-Oriented paradigm [Fia91] [Jun91] by packaging a set of properties together. The language also includes a set of built-in predefined types associated with usual data types (integers, strings, booleans, etc) and with combinators (cartesian product, sequence, set, bag and table) for putting together data specifications.

- The language supports the introduction of *parameterized* type clusters and data types allowing to factor out common properties shared by individual elements (playing the role of instantiated units) at different locations of the requirements document, thus ensuring a better readability of the document. It should be also noted that parameterization is one of the most useful structuring mechanism with respect to reusability.

- Two *inheritance* mechanisms are available in the language. The first one (corresponding to the usual mechanism referred in the literature) is based on the introduction of *sub-types* (like, e.g., 'Employee is a Person'). The second mechanism is less classical and is more syntactic in the sense that it is based on a *cut and paste* of an existing specification piece (like, e.g. 'Properties of an Airbus are a copy of the properties of a Boeing'). The inheritance mechanism supports the definition of a new specification by inheriting another specification and by extending and/or restricting it.

- The 'scoping' mechanism controls the visibility of names in a large document. This is particularly helpful when multiple specifiers have to integrate their specifications into a coherent document. This mechanism is not illustrated in the rest of this paper because no name clashes occur in the small case study considered here.

2.3 Formality

A formal language depends on the availability of rigorous *rules of interpretation* which guarantee the absence of ambiguity. Besides, rules of deductive inference are needed to make possible the derivation of new sentences from given ones. The deductive power supports the analysis, the validation (e.g. with the generation of a prototype) of formal specifications but also gives a handle for a rigorous investigation of the requirements engineering process (see e.g. [Joh88] [Dub91c]).

The choice of a adequate formal framework for our language has been influenced by two conclusions following the study of existing formal specification languages:

- At the expressiveness level, the use of a first-order *logic* framework seems to be a reasonable basis because of the variety and the naturalness of constraints that can be expressed. Moreover, some specific *modal* extensions are interesting because of the availability of specific deductive rules which makes possible to reason on specific concepts and the conciseness reached in the expression of constraints. Examples are Infolog [Ser80] and Erae [Dub88] based on a 'temporal logic' (i.e. a logic dealing with histories) and Mal [Fin87] and [Dub91c] based on a 'deontic logic' (i.e. a logic dealing with actions and agents).

- At the structuring mechanisms level, only a few syntactical structuring mechanisms are available for *first-order logical* frameworks but it appears that, within the *algebraic* framework, a number of semantic relationships can be envisaged (e.g. parameterization, inheritance, etc). However, in most cases, these mechanisms have been investigated within the framework of an 'equational' logic (i.e. a subset of first order logic), not sufficiently expressive for our requirements modelling purposes.

For our language, the conclusion of these experiences led to the choice of the so-called *loose semantics* formal framework [Ehr90] [Ore89] based on an algebraic framework (with the usual structuring relationships) but where the properties can be expressed in terms of a set of typed first-order formulas.

3 Writing and Structuring Expressive Formal Requirements

The objective of this section is to illustrate the expressiveness and the formality of our language sketched in Sect. 2. To this end and all along the rest of this paper, we will refer to a simplified version of a library problem. The informal description of this case study is the following one :

> We consider a library where users may issue requests for books belonging to the library and become borrowers of these books. The following rules are:
> - the set of books owned by the library and the set of library's users are considered fixed in time. Books can be either available on shelves or borrowed by users. Users are identified by their name and surname;
> - requests are issued by users for books and remained pending up to their satisfaction that should occur without unecessary delay;
> - books can be borrowed by users for a period of maximum 30 days. The borrowing of a book by a user is possible only if this user has issued a request for this book.

3.1 A First Specification

To help in the elicitation and the understanding of a problem, we have found useful to express it in terms of an ERA diagram complemented with constraints (this approach was inspired by some previous experiences made by the authors using the ERAE language [Dub88] [Dub91a]).

Figure 1 proposes a graphical ERA diagram associated with the library case study where :

- Books and Users are considered as sets of entities,
- Requests and Borrowings are relationship between users and books,
- Name and Surname are attributes identifying users.

LIBRARY

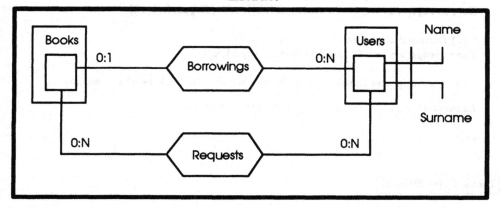

Fig. 1

Hereafter, in Fig. 2, the formal specification of the requirements associated with the library case study is presented.

Type Cluster LIBRARY

State inspection operations

Fixed $Books : BOOK$
$Users : USER$

Varying $Borrowings : BOOK \times USER$
$Requests : BOOK \times USER$

Constraints

* Constraints (1), (2), (3) are connectivity constraints derived from the ERA diagram

* (1) Borrowings are restricted to books and users of the library
$Borrowings(b, u) \Rightarrow Books(b) \wedge Users(u)$
* (2) Requests are restricted to books and users of the library
$Requests(b, u) \Rightarrow Books(b) \wedge Users(u)$
* (3) A book may be borrowed by at most one user
$Borrowings(b, u1) \wedge Borrowings(b, u2) \Rightarrow u1 = u2$

* (4) A user cannot issue a request for book he/she borrows
$Requests(b, u) \Rightarrow \neg Borrowings(b, u)$

* (5) Books available on shelves and for which requests are pending are allocated without unecessary delay
$(\not\exists u : Borrowings(b, u)) \wedge (\exists u' : Requests(b, u')) \Rightarrow \bigcirc (\exists u'' : Borrowings(b, u''))$
* It should be noted that no particular assumption is taken about which pending request is served first

* (6) A book can only be allocated to a waiting user
$Borrowings(b, u) \wedge \ominus (\neg Borrowings(b, u)) \Rightarrow \ominus (Requests(b, u))$

* (7) Borrowed books are returned within 30 days
$Borrowings(b, u) \Rightarrow \diamond _{\leq 30 days}(\neg Borrowings(b, u))$

* (8) A waiting user is waiting until he/she borrows the book he/she is waiting for
$Requests(b, u) \Rightarrow \bigcirc (Requests(b, u) \vee Borrowings(b, u))$

•••

Data Type BOOK

Data Type USER

is $CP[Name : STRING, Surname : STRING]$

Fig. 2

The following features should be noted:

− In the specification, properties are grouped in *type definitions*, respectively associated with the specification of the library *cluster* and with the specification of *data* values.

Data types are associated with the definition of immutable values, i.e. values which are not supposed to change with time. In our example, data types are associated with BOOK and USER. In the case of USER, the use of the cartesian product (CP) combinator precises that a user is identified with two string values (respectively associated with the name and the surname of a user).

By contrast, if we consider the set of users belonging to the library case study, data are not sufficient for modelling it since this set will typically vary with time. This is why the library is described as a *type cluster*. In our example, the type cluster is used to characterize the set of possible histories modelling all the admissible behaviors of the library. A history is a discrete sequence of states, each labeled by a time value which increases all along the history. The state can be inspected through a set of so-called *state inspection operations* which are used to return all relevant informations about the system at that moment. These inspections are modelled in terms of data values. In the above example, there are four inspection operations (*Books, Users, Borrowings, Requests*) for the different library state components. It should be noted that these components can be denoted state *varying* (e.g. *Borrowings*) or *fixed* (e.g. *Books*).

- In the specification, there are data types (e.g. STRING) and combinators (e.g. cartesian product) which are built-in in the language. Using these types makes possible to inherit from their predefined associated operations. For example, one may write "Name(u)" to access the name of a user.
- The purpose of first order constraints is to identify the set of admissible histories. Constraints are written according to the usual rules of strongly typed first order logic. In particular, they are formed by means of logical connectives ¬ (not), ∧ (and), ∨ (or), ⇒ (implies), ⇔ (if and only if), ∀ (for all), ∃ (exists). Moreover, it should be noted that the outermost universal quantification of formulas can be omitted. The rule is that any variable, which is not in the scope of a quantifier, is universally quantified outside of the formula. There are different kinds of constraints.

    1. There are constraints which act as *invariants*, i.e. which are true in all states of the system. This is the case in our example for constraints (1) to (4).
    2. There are constraints on the evolution of the system. Writing these constraints require to be able to refer more than one state at a time. This is done in our language by using additional temporal connectives which are prefixing statements to be interpreted in different states. The following table introduces these operators (inspired from temporal logic, see e.g. [Ser80] [Dub91a]) and their intuitive meaning (ϕ and ψ are statements):

        $\bigcirc \phi$ $\quad \phi$ is true in the next state
        $\ominus \phi$ $\quad \phi$ is true in the previous state
        $\Diamond \phi$ $\quad \phi$ is true sometimes in the future (including the present)
        $\diamondsuit \phi$ $\quad \phi$ is true sometimes in the past (including the present)
        $\Box \phi$ $\quad \phi$ is always true in the future (including the present)
        $\boxminus \phi$ $\quad \phi$ is always true in the past (including the present)
        $\phi \, \mathcal{U} \, \psi$ $\quad \phi$ is true from the present until ψ is true (strict)
        $\phi \, \mathcal{S} \, \psi$ $\quad \phi$ is true back from the present since ψ was true (strict)

        Constraints can involve two successive states (like in constraints (5), (6) and (8)) or states which are further apart (like in constraint (7))
    3. There are constraints related to the expression of real-time properties. There are needed to express delays or time-outs. For instance, in the library system, the constraint (7) uses an extension of the temporal $\Diamond$ operator subscripted by a time period. This time period is made precise by using predefined functions that can be used to model the usual time units: *Sec, Min, Hours* and *Days*.

- Finally, it should be noted the use of a '•••' notation in the library's specification. This symbol is used to model that the set of properties which have been modelled here is not complete, viz. that the specification document is in an intermediate stage of its elaboration. This means that the analyst needs to further discuss with the customer to elicitate additional requirements. But even when the '•••' occurs, the semantics of our language supports formal checks and analysis on the requirements document and the deduction of properties about the system's behavior.

3.2 Organizing the Specification

In the previous sub-section, we proposed a first elicitation of the library problem in terms of an ERA diagram. A next step in the requirements process is to achieve a better structured version of the original specification in order to promote its readability, maintenance and reusability. To this end, the language offers number of mechanisms for organizing complex requirements descriptions. Hereafter, in Fig. 3, we present a better structured version of the library's specification introduced in the previous sub-section.

| Type Cluster LIBRARY |

State inspection operations

> **Fixed**   *Books* : *BOOK*
>   *Users* : *USER*
>
> **Varying** *Borrowings* : *BOOKUSER*
>   *Requests* : *BOOKUSER*

Constraints

* * Constraints (1), (2), (3), (4) and (7) are similar to Fig. 2

* * (5) Books available on shelves and for which requests are pending are allocated without unecessary delay
$OnShelves(b) \land (\exists u : Requests(b, u)) \Rightarrow \bigcirc (\exists u' : Borrowings(b, u'))$

* * (6) A book can only be allocated to a waiting user
$CheckingOuts(b, u) \Rightarrow \ominus (Requests(b, u))$

* * (8) A waiting user is waiting until he/she borrows the book he/she is waiting for
$\neg CheckingOut(b, u) \land \ominus (Requests(b, u)) \Rightarrow Requests(b, u)$

   ●●●

Auxiliary operations

> **Varying** *OnShelves* : *BOOK* → *BOOLEAN*
>   **asserts**
> $OnShelves(b) \Leftrightarrow \neg In(b, Borrowings)$
>   * A book is on-shelf if it is not borrowed
>
>   *CheckingOut* : *BOOK* × *USER* → *BOOLEAN*
>   **asserts**
> $CheckingOut(b, u)$
> $\Leftrightarrow Borrowings(b, u) \land \ominus (\neg Borrowings(b, u))$
>   * A user is checking out a book if he/she is borrowing a book that was not borrowed in the previous state

Data Type BOOK

Data Type USER

is $CP[Name : STRING, Surname : STRING]$

Data Type BOOKUSER

is $CP[BOOK, USER]$

Operations

> $In : BOOK \times SET[BOOKUSER] \rightarrow BOOLEAN$
> > **asserts**
> > $In(b, bu) \Leftrightarrow (\exists u : < b, u > \in bu)$
> > * Test the membership of a book to the relationship between books and users
>
> $In : USER \times SET[BOOKUSER] \rightarrow BOOLEAN$
> > **asserts**
> > $In(u, bu) \Leftrightarrow (\exists b : < b, u > \in bu)$
> > * Test the membership of a user to the relationship between books and users

---

Fig. 3

This new organization has been achieved by using two mechanisms.

- The first mechanism is based on the introduction of *auxiliary intermediate operations* inside the type cluster. These new operations help to better structure and clarify the set of constraints. Each operation is defined in terms of an assertion specifying the relationship that must hold between arguments in the domain and results in the range.
- The second mechanism proposes an organization of the new introduced operations following the O-O paradigm. To this end, the language offers the possibility to define additional *auxiliary types* on top of already existing ones by using the predefined types constructors. In our example, a new intermediate data type cluster (called BOOKUSER) has been introduced. This cluster associates two new intermediate operations with a new intermediate type defined as a set of tuples.

4 Specifying Composite Systems

In some recent work, we are investigating an incremental elaboration *process* starting with the specification of a problem considered as a monolithic one and gradually moving towards the description of a more complex composite system [Dub88b] [Dub91c]. More precisely, we propose:

1. to express specifications about the **goals** assigned to the system to be installed and to its environment (considered as a whole – black-box approach –) to be developed;
2. to express specifications about **finer requirements** that are assigned to the different components (e.g. a software component, a hardware piece, or a manual procedure) and to verify that the set of all requirements attached to individual components meet the goals originally introduced.

To support this approach, we need a language where, at some stage of the process, it is possible to capture descriptions of composite systems rather than to consider the system as a monolithic one. Thereby, we have extended our language so that it offers mechanisms for combining several single components together and for specifying properties characterizing the individual behavior of each separate component as well as the interactions taking place between the different components.

Let us refer to the library problem again. Up to now (see Fig. 2), we have considered this system as a monolithic one. At a more finer level, one could imagine a more detailed organization making the distinction between:

- The environment of the library system composed of users issuing requests and having books in their possession.
- The system itself where a librarian is in charge of managing the set of books on shelves in the library as well as the allocation of these available books according to the requests issued.
- The introduction of the system and its environment goes with the identification of the nature of the communications that should take place between them. A priori, each component only has access to the informations that it manages. Clearly some *communication medium* (i.e. *interface* [Doe91]) has to be installed between the different components so that a component may offer some services to another one.

In Fig. 4, we introduce a graphical ERA representation of the new situation where the system (LIBRARY-S) and its environment (LIBRARY-E) are made distinct. It should be noted that:

1. the library system is embedded in its environment. This is due to the fact that we want to indicate that changes occurring in the environment (i.e. requests and returns made by users) should not be constrained by the system behaviour.
2. we introduce events (graphically depicted with ovals) to describe the nature of the *interface* between the system and its environment. A *visibility* relationship (graphically depicted with arrows) makes precise the perception of a component with respect to events happening in the other component.

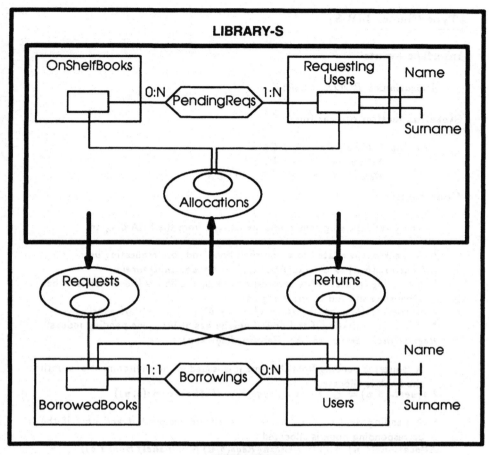

LIBRARY-E

Figure 4

In Fig. 5, we present the formal specification associated with the graphical representation presented above.

Type Cluster LIBRARY

Composed of

LIB-S is SYSTEM
LIB-E is ENVIRONMENT

Type Cluster LIB-S

Interface events

$Allocations: BOOK \times USER$

State inspection operations

Varying $OnShelfBooks: BOOK$
$RequestingUsers: USER$
$PendingReqs: BOOK \times USER$

Constraints

* The three following constraints are derived from the ERA diagram

* A check-out is related to an on-shelf book and to a requesting user
$Allocations(b, u) \Rightarrow OnShelfBooks(b) \land RequestingUsers(u)$
* A pending request exists between a book of the library (i.e. which is or has been on-shelf) and a requesting user
$PendingReqs(b, u) \Rightarrow \Diamond(OnShelfBooks(b)) \land RequestingUsers(u)$
* A user is requesting if and only if he/she has at least one pending request
$RequestingUsers(u) \Leftrightarrow \exists b: PendingReqs(b, u)$

* A request is pending from the time it is issued in the environment and until the book is allocated
$Requests(b, u) \Rightarrow \bigcirc (PendingReqs(b, u) \; U \; Allocations(b, u))$

* A pending request and a book on shelf are removed if and only if the corresponding book is allocated
$Allocations(b, u) \Rightarrow \bigcirc (\neg PendingReqs(b, u) \land \neg OnshelfBooks(b))$

* A book can only be allocated to a waiting user
$Allocations(b, u) \Rightarrow \ominus (PendingReqs(b, u))$

* Books available on shelves and for which requests are pending are allocated without unecessary delay
$(\exists b: OnShelfBooks(b)) \land (\exists u: PendingReqs(b, u))$
$\Rightarrow \bigcirc (\exists u': Allocations(b, u'))$

Type Cluster LIB-E

Interface events

$Requests : BOOK \times USER$
$Returns : BOOK \times USER$

State inspection operations

Fixed $Users : USER$

Varying $BorrowedBooks : BOOK$
   $Borrowings : BOOK \times USER$

Constraints

* The five following constraints are derived from the ERA diagram

* A request is issued by a user of the library
$Requests(b, u) \Rightarrow Users(u)$

* A return happens for a borrowed book of the library and is performed by a user of the library
$Returns(b, u) \Rightarrow BorrowedBooks(b) \wedge Users(u)$

* A borrowing links a borrowed book of the library to a user of the library
$Borrowings(b, u) \Rightarrow BorrowedBooks(b) \wedge Users(u)$

* A book is borrowed if and only if it is linked by a borrowing
$BorrowedBooks(b) \Leftrightarrow \exists u : Borrowings(b, u)$

* A book may be borrowed by at most one user
$Borrowings(b, u1) \wedge Borrowings(b, u2) \Rightarrow u1 = u2$

* A book is borrowed from its allocation to a user until it is returned to the library
$Allocations(b, u) \Rightarrow \bigcirc (Borrowings(b, u) \,\mathcal{U}\, Returns(b, u))$

* A borrowing and a borrowed book are removed if and only if the corresponding book is returned
$Returns(b, u) \Rightarrow \bigcirc (\neg Borrowings(b, u) \wedge \neg BorrowedBooks(b))$
$\ominus (Borrowings(b, u)) \wedge Returns(b, u) \Rightarrow Borrowings(b, u)$
$\ominus (BorrowedBooks(b)) \wedge (\not\exists u : Returns(b, u)) \Rightarrow BorrowedBooks(b)$

* A book can be returned only if it was borrowed
$Returns(b, u) \Rightarrow \ominus (Borrowings(b, u))$

* Borrowed books are returned within 30 days
$Allocations(b, u) \Rightarrow \diamondsuit_{\leq 30days}(Returns(b, u))$

* In the initial state, the set of borrowed books is empty
$\neg Empty?(BorrowedBooks) \Rightarrow \diamondsuit Empty?(BorrowedBooks)$

Data Type USER

is $CP[Name : STRING, Surname : STRING]$

Data Type BOOK

Fig. 5

Finally, due to the formality of our language, it would be possible to give a formal proof that the joint behavior of the two components meet the behavior of the original system. For example, in our first specification (Fig. 2), the set of books was declared fixed in time. This property is preserved by the combination of the behaviors of the two components of Fig. 5 from which it results that:

$$Books = BorrowedBooks \cup OnShelfBooks$$

(i.e. the set of books of the library is the union of both sets of borrowed and on-shelf books).

5 Capturing Problem Domain Knowledge

In Sect. 3, we have suggested how the use of *types* may provide help in the organization of a large requirements document. However, we have experimented that these mechanisms are not yet sufficient for promoting the use of a formal specification language. A major drawback relies on the number of formal statements that should be written so that the requirements be completely and consistently expressed. In particular, when we consider two applications belonging to the same application domain, it is definitively tedious to have to encode similar specifications twice. Those are conclusions which are shared for example by [Die89] and [Reu91] and which have led to the introduction of libraries of reusable cliches for some application domain. Analogously to the paradigm considered in the Esprit Project Ithaca [Pro89] [Per90], we feel essential to be able to distinguish between two roles for the analyst, namely the "application engineer" and the "application developer". The application engineer is responsible for providing generic concepts for a given application domain while the application developer is in charge of reusing and tailoring these generic concepts to the needs of the requirements expressed for a particular application.

In our language, the introduction of structuring mechanisms (in particular, the *parameterization* mechanism associated with the *syntactical inheritance* mechanism) follows the same objective, i.e. to make distinct the modelling of requirements typical of some application domain from the modelling of requirements specific to a particular application. In Fig. 6, we have illustrated the use of this mechanism by making distinct the part of the requirements related to a general allocation of resources problem from the specific requirements associated with the borrowing of books in the library. These specific requirements are obtained by instantiating the parameterized RESOURCE-ALLOCATION specification (Fig. 6a) with substitution of BOOK and USER for RESOURCE and CONSUMER respectively. In the resulting instantiation (Fig. 6b), it should be noted the renaming of the operations inherited from the parameterized cluster.

Doing so, it should be noted how the specification of the LIBRARY-S has been considerably simplified with respect to its previous specification presented in Fig. 5. Moreover, we have experimenting the usefulness of the RESOURCE-ALLOCATION parameterized type by considering it in a completely different case study related to a telephone switching network system.

Type Cluster RESOURCE-ALLOCATION[RESOURCE,CONSUMER]

Interface events

$Grants : RESOURCE \times CONSUMER$

State inspection operations

Varying $Resources : RESOURCE$
$WaitingConsumers : CONSUMER$
$PendingRequests : RESOURCE \times CONSUMER$

Constraints

* The three following constraints are derived from the ERA diagram

* A grant occurs to an available resource and for a waiting consumer
$Grants(b, u) \Rightarrow Resources(r) \wedge WaitingConsumers(c)$
* A pending request links a resource of the system (i.e. which is or has been available) and a waiting consumer
$PendingRequests(r, c) \Rightarrow \diamondsuit (Resources(r)) \wedge WaitingConsumers(c)$
* A consumer is waiting if and only if he/she has at least one pending request
$WaitingConsumers(c) \Leftrightarrow \exists r : PendingRequests(r, c)$

* A request is pending until the resource is granted
$PendingRequests(r, c) \Rightarrow \bigcirc (PendingRequests(r, c) \, U \, Grants(r, c))$

* A pending request and an available resource are removed if and only if corresponding resource has been granted
$Grants(r, c) \Rightarrow \bigcirc (\neg PendingRequests(r, c) \wedge \neg Resources(r)$
$\ominus (PendingRequests(r, c)) \wedge \neg Grants(r, c) \Rightarrow PendingRequests(r, c)$
$\ominus (Resources(r)) \wedge (\not\exists c : Grants(r, c)) \Rightarrow Resources(r)$

* A resource can only be granted to a waiting consumer
$$Grants(r,c) \Rightarrow \ominus (PendingRequests(r,c))$$

* Available resources for which requests are pending are granted without unnecessary delay
$$(\exists r : Resources(r) \wedge (\exists c : PendingRequests(r,c)) \Rightarrow \bigcirc (\exists c' : Grants(r,c'))$$

Data Type RESOURCE

Data Type CONSUMER

Fig. 6a

Type Cluster LIBRARY-S is RESOURCE-ALLOCATION[BOOK,USER]

Interface events

   CheckOuts for *Grants*

State inspection operations

   Varying *OnShelf Books* for *Resources*
   RequestingUsers for *WaitingConsumers*
   PendingReqs for *PendingRequests*

Constraints

   * Link with the requests coming from the environment
   $$Requests(b,u) \Rightarrow \bigcirc (PendingReqs(b,u))$$

Fig. 6b

6 Conclusion

For more than fifteen years, a number of requirements specification languages have been proven useful in industrial environments. These include, e.g., PSL/PSA [Tei77], SADT [Ros77], SREM [Alf77] or REMORA [Rol82]. We feel however that such languages present limitations of several natures. First, they lack a sound theoretical basis and the semantics of the various language constructs is in some cases ill-defined. Thereby, the accompanying tools provide limited support (essentially editing, storage and manipulation facilities) and analysis capabilities are restricted to syntactic checks. Second, they also have a limited expressiveness because only some aspects of the requirements can be formulated, like data-structures, data flows, and limited additional properties. In particular, it should be noted that, in most case, the dynamic aspects of the system evolution can only be captured with algorithmic descriptions, i.e. with the risk of introducing over-specifications.

By contrast, new emerging requirements languages (e.g. LARCH [Gut85], RML [Gre86], Z [Suf86] GIST [Fea87], MAL [Fin87], OBLOG [Ser89], ERAE [Dub88, Dub91a] or TELOS [Myl90]) are based on logical/mathematical semantics (e.g. initial algebras, first order logic) and exhibit two essential features, i.e. *expressiveness* and *structuring mechanisms*.

- At the expressiveness level, we have drawn the following conclusions:
  - the use of a first-order *logic* framework seems to be a reasonable basis because of the variety and the naturalness of constraints that can be expressed;
  - things of interest have not only to be expressed in terms of *data* but also in terms of *clusters* when we want to model real-world persistent entities;
  - dynamic aspects of the system can be modelled using a *state-based* view (with transitions explaining state changes) or an *event-based* view (with events supporting the description of interactions). We feel that the latter supports the description of interactive systems whereas the former is more suited for the description of sequential systems;
  - the description of a system can be *snapshot* or *history* oriented. The snapshot view only supports descriptions expressed in terms of two successive states of an history. By contrast, an historical perspective allows to refer to the whole history of states. The historical view supports a more declarative view than the snapshot view;
  - only a few approaches permit the reference to (i) real-time aspects without the introduction and the management of somewhat artificial clocks and to (ii) organizational aspects related to the responsibility and the cooperation of different agents within the system.
- At the structuring mechanisms level, it appears that many approaches only offer a *syntactical* scoping mechanism to deal with name's clashes in large specification. By contrast, within the *algebraic* framework, a number of more *semantic* relationships are envisaged (e.g. parameterization, inheritance, etc). However, in most cases, these mechanisms have been investigated within the framework of an 'equational' logic (i.e. a subset of first order logic), not sufficiently expressive for our requirements modelling purposes.

In the *Icarus* project, the conclusion of these experiences have led to the development of the GLIDER language (a General Language for an Incremental Definition and Elaboration of Requirements) [Dub91b] supporting the expression of the different kinds of requirements presented above and offering powerful semantic and syntactic structuring mechanisms (e.g. parameterization and inheritance). The language we have introduced in this paper is a dialect of this GLIDER language also inspired by some recent experiences of two of the authors with the ERAE language.

Our research plans are in four directions:

- the enhancement of the language with the expression of *organizational* requirements (like "this department is responsible for producing data to be processed by the computer system"). Preliminary experiences [Dub91c] consider the introduction of the notion of agent and action in order to model and to reason on a responsibility relationship as well as to be able to express requirements on performances, reliability and security aspects;
- the validation of the methodology proposed for composite systems through the study of the conclusions resulting from large experiments currently done in different industrial environments;
- the development of an integrated environment of tools made of textual and graphical syntactic editors, an object-oriented repository for managing intermediate specifications fragments and semantic analyzers for verifying consistency and completeness of requirements fragments and also for deriving some new relevant properties about them;
- the development of a *requirements assistant* supporting the *process* followed by the analysts during the elaboration of the requirements document, as well as the study of the *rationale* that have led to the choice of a particular process.

Acknowledgment: This work was partially supported by the European Community under Project 2537 (ICARUS) of the European Strategic Program for Research and Development Technology (ESPRIT). We are indebted to J.P. Finance, A. van Lamsweerde, F. Orejas, J. Souquières and P. Wodon who participated in the design of the GLIDER language. We are also grateful to J. Hagelstein for his basic contribution in the design of the ERAE language.

References

[Alf77]   M.W. Alford, "A Requirements Engineering Methodology for Real-time Processing Requirements," *IEEE Trans. Soft. Eng.*, SE-3(1), pp. 60-69, 1977.

[Die89]   N.W.P. van Diepen and H.A. Partsch, "Some Aspects of Formalizing Informal Requirements," Department of Computer Science, University of Nijmegen, The Netherlands, 1989.

[Doe91]   E. Doerry, S. Fickas, R. Helm and M. Feather, "A Model for Composite System Design," in *6th Int. Workshop on Software Specification and Design*, Milano, October 1991.

[Dub88]   E. Dubois, J. Hagelstein and A. Rifaut, "Formal Requirements Engineering with ERAE," *Philips Journal of Research*, 43, nos. 3/4, 1988.

[Dub88b] E. Dubois, "Logical Support for Reasoning about the Specification and the Elaboration of Requirements," in *The Role of Artificial Intelligence in Databases and Information Systems*, WG2.6/WG8.1 Conference, Guangzhou, China, pp. 29-48, July 1988.

[Dub90] E. Dubois, "Supporting an Incremental Elaboration of Requirements for Multi-agent Systems," in Draft Proceedings of *International Working Conference on Cooperating Knowledge Based Systems*, University of Keele (England), October 3-5, pp. 130-134, 1990.

[Dub91a] E. Dubois, J. Hagelstein and A. Rifaut, "From Natural Language Processing to Logic for Expert Systems. Chapter 6: a Formal Language for the Requirements Engineering of Composite Systems," A. Thayse (Editor), Wiley, 1991, 535 pages.

[Dub91b] E. Dubois, Ph. Du Bois, A. Rifaut, P. Wodon, "GLIDER User Manual," Spec-Func Deliverable, ESPRIT Project Icarus 2537, June 1991.

[Dub91c] E. Dubois, "Use of Deontic Logic in the Requirements Engineering of Composite Systems," *First International Workshop on Deontic Logic in Computer Science*, Amsterdam, The Netherlands, 11-13 december, 1991.

[Ehr90] H. Ehrig and B. Mahr, "Fundamentals of Algebraic Specifications : Module Specifications and Constraints," *EATCS Monographs on Theoretical Computer Science*, W. Brauer, G. Rozenberg, A. Salomaa (Eds), Springer-Verlag, 1990.

[Fia91] J. Fiadeiro and T. Maibaum, "Describing, Structuring and Implementing Objects," in *Proc. Foundations of Object-Oriented Languages*, Noordwijkerhoud (The Netherlands), LNCS 489, Springer Verlag, pp. 275-310, 1991.

[Fin89] A. Finkelstein and H. Fucks, "Multiparty Specification," in *Proc. Fifth International Workshop on Software Specification and Design*, pp. 185-195, 1989.

[Fea87] M.S. Feather. "Language Support for the Specification and Development of Composite Systems," in *ACM TOPLAS*, vol. 9, 2, pp. 198-234, April 87.

[Fea89] M.S. Feather. "Constructing Specifications by Combining Parallel Elaborations," in *IEEE Trans. Soft. Eng.*, vol. 15 (2), February 1989.

[Fin87] A. Finkelstein, C. Potts. "Building Formal Specifications Using 'Structured Common Sense'," in *Proc. Fourth International Workshop on Software Specification and Design*, pp. 108-113, 1987.

[Gre86] S.J. Greenspan, A. Borgida and J. Mylopoulos, "A Requirements Modeling Language and its Logic," *Information Systems*, vol 11(1), pp. 9-23, 1986.

[Gut85] J. Guttag, J. Horning and J. Wing, "Larch in Five Esasy Pieces," Research Report 5, Digital Systems Research Center, 1985,

[Joh88] W. L. Johnson, "Deriving Specifications from Requirements," in *Proc. 10th Int. Conf. on Software Engineering*, Singapore, pp. 428-438, 1988.

[Jun91] R. Junglaus, G. Saake and C. Sernadas, "Formal Specification of Object Systems," in *Proc. TAPSOFT'91*, Brighton (UK), LNCS 494, Springer-Verlag, pp. 60-82, 1991.

[Myl90] J. Mylopoulos, A. Borgida, M. Jarke and M. Koubarakis, "Telos : A Language for Representing Knowledge about Information Systems," *ACM Trans. Information Systems*, 1990.

[Ore89] F. Orejas, V. Sacristan and S. Clerici, "Development of Algebraic Specifications with Constraints," in *Categorical Methods in Computer Science*, Springer LNCS, 1989.

[Per90] B. Pernici, "Class Design and Metadesign," in *Object Management*, D. Tsichritzis (ed), Geneva University, p. 117-132, 1990.

[Pro89] A. Profrock, D. Tsichritzis, G. Muller and M. Ader, "ITHACA: an integrated toolkit for highly advanced computer application," in *Object Oriented Development*, D. Tsichritzis (ed), Geneva University, pp. 321-344, 1989.

[Reu89]   H.B. Reubenstein and R. C. Waters, "The Requirements Apprentice : An Initial Scenario," in *Proc. Fifth International Workshop on Software Specification and Design*, pp. 211-218, 1989.

[Reu91]   H.B. Reubenstein and R. C. Waters, "The Requirements Apprentice : Automated assistance for requirements acquisition," in *IEEE Trans. Soft. Eng.*, 17(3), March 1991.

[Rol82]   C. Rolland and C. Richard, "The Remora Methodology for Information Systems Design and Management," in *Information Systems Design Methodologies: A Comparative Review*, T.W. Olle, H.G. Sol, A.A. Verrijn-Stuart (eds), North-Holland, pp. 369-426, 1982.

[Ros77]   D.T. Ross and K.G. Schoman, "Structured Analysis for Requirements Definition," *IEEE Trans. Soft. Eng.*, SE 3(1), pp. 1-65, 1977.

[Ser80]   A. Sernadas, "Temporal Aspects of Logic Procedure Definition," *Information Systems*, vol. 5, pp. 167-187, 1980.

[Ser89]   A. Sernadas, C. Sernadas and H.-D. Ehrich, "Abstract Object Types: a Temporal Perspective," *Colloquium on Temporal Logic and Specification*, B. Banieqbal, H. Barringer and A. Pnueli (eds), LNCS 398, Springer-Verlag, pp. 324-350, 1989.

[Suf86]   B. Sufrin (ed), "Z Handbook," Oxford Programming Research Group, 1986.

[Tei77]   D. Teichroew and E.A. Hershey, "A Computer Aided Technique for Structured Documentation and Analysis of Information Processing Systems," *IEEE Trans. Soft. Eng.*, SE-3(1), pp. 41-48, 1977.

This article was processed using the LaTeX macro package with LMAMULT-LNCS style

OASIS: An Object-oriented Specification Language

Oscar Pastor Lopez[1]
Fiona Hayes[2]
Stephen Bear[2]

[1] Departamento de Sistemas Informaticos y Computacion (DSIC)
Universidad Politecnica de Valencia
Camino de Vera S/N
Apartado 22012
46071 Valencia.- Spain
phone: +34 6 3877350
fax: +34 6 3877359
email: plo@dsic.upv.es

[2] Hewlett Packard Labs.- Bristol
Filton Road, Sotke Gifford
Bristol UK
BS12 6QZ
email: fmh@hplb.hpl.hp.com
email: sb@hplb.hpl.hp.com

Abstract

This paper introduces Oasis, a language for specifying object-oriented information systems using a deductive (temporal) approach ([3]). Oasis extends first versions of OBLOG ([17]) and MOL([12]), a trace based specification languages, with:

1. *triggered relationships* which enable specification of active objects
2. supporting rapid prototyping by generating the First Order Theory formally equivalent to a specification.
3. introducing class operators within an algebraic formal environment to deal with object reification.

1 Introduction

Object-oriented approaches are increasingly popular as a useful paradigm covering the classical software development steps of analysis, design and programming. Several notations and methods are provided for object-oriented analysis and design[4],[2],[12],[15] in addition to a well-known collection of object-oriented programming languages such as C++[18] and Smalltalk-80 [7].

The object-oriented specification language MOL[12] defines the object-oriented paradigm by combining general system theory adapted to information systems[8], abstract object types of OBLOG[16] and clausal or equational logics. The operational semantics of the underlying logics provides an environment in which specifications of passive Information Systems can be executed by generating the Logic Program that represents the First Order Theory equivalent to a Specification ([12]). However, MOL cannot deal with the specification of active objects.

This paper presents Oasis, a language for the specification of open and active information systems with the following most relevant properties:

- extends MOL by defining *triggered relationships*, a new kind of active relationship between objects.

- uses a declarative approach for specifying Information Systems.

- defines class operators in an formal algebraic environment to deal with object reification

- allows rapid prototyping by generating and manipulating the First Order Theory equivalent to an Oasis Specification, as shown in [14].

In this paper, we focus on the set of notations that Oasis provides for developing specifications of object-oriented information systems. It is intended as the basis of an automated object-oriented software production environment.

2 The Object-oriented Model

Our objective is to develop an environment for specifying **open active information systems**.

First we define our terms. According to IFIP WG 8.1 definitions[8], a system is a collection of elements called the **system domain** which has at least one systematic property in relation to the environment that is not possessed by any of the elements. A **system view** is the set of elements of the system domain, the domain of the environment and the relationships between these elements which are necessary to explain the system.

The task of the analyst in object-oriented system specification is to specify a system view of the object system in order to produce the **conceptual model specification**. This approach is useful as object-oriented concepts can closely model real-world phenomena. Using object-oriented approaches, the semantic gap between what the system is and how it is to be represented is narrowed.

An object is a self contained operational unit, which has properties called **attributes**. It has a state that is the state of the set of its attributes. Each object has a name that identifies it during its existence.

Change of state is a fundamental concept. Objects may change state. The creation and destruction of objects change the state of the system. Individual objects may also change their state i.e. the value of their attributes. A **process** causes changes of state in an object. It is limited in time. The elementary parts of a process responsible for a single unified change of state are called **events**. An event is an abstraction of a change of state in the object system. It is discrete, has no duration and occurs at a certain point in time.

An object may be active or passive. We say that an object is **active** if is seen as involved as necessary for a change of state to take place. A **passive** object is one that cannot be seen as active within a relevant period of time.

A **trigger** is a relationship between an event and one or more other events that on a certain level of abstraction expresses the cause for the proper agents to carry out the execution of such other events. Potentially, every condition on events and/or attributes may serve as a trigger.

Behaviour is the dynamic manner of an object. The object exists during a temporal period, its life, that has a limited duration. Events happen at a certain point of time.

Objects belong to **types**. A type is a set of objects composed by the universe of objects of a class. A **class** is a set of properties which characterises the structure and behaviour that a collection of objects share.

In this environment, the linguistic operator 'instance of' works on a class and yields a member of the corresponding type as the result. The operator 'population of' yields the type for a class. We may have classes and subclasses denoting types and subtypes. Subtype populations are subsets of the supertype populations. Subclasses are defined by adding more properties from the super-classes. We define generalisation/specialisation as relations between classes and subclasses at the same abstraction level.

In the following section, we describe the language (**OASIS**), intended for the executable specification of open and active information systems.

3 Object-oriented Representation of Information Systems

3.1 Introduction

An object has two aspects; structure and behaviour. The structural aspect defines the object composition. A simple object's structure is given by the corresponding typed attributes. In complex classes built using class operators, the structure is defined by the composition of component class structures. The behavioural aspect alludes to the object life represented by the set of events and admissible traces. An observation function relates both aspects. The structure of an object is expressed as a function of its behaviour.

3.2 Class definition

An object class may be formalised as a 4-tuple (X,A,T,ob) where:

- X is the event set, including private and shared events. *Private events* are declared in only one class and participate in the traces of objects of only this class. *Shared events* must be declared in more than one class. They will form part of the traces of objects of all the classes in which they are declared.

  Events have parameters. In particular private events have always as the first parameter a surrogate value which identifies the object to which the event belongs. The parameters of a shared event must include a surrogate value for each object which shares the event.

- A is the typed attributes set, including *constant attributes* (those whose values do not change during the object life) and *variable attributes* (those that change depending on event occurrence)

  Every object instance has to have its own and unique surrogate identifying it during its life. This surrogate will be assigned once the object is created, by means of the corresponding object class creation event occurrence. The surrogate or key is defined as a combination of constant attributes.

  Each attribute has a parameter representing the object owner class. The parameter is a value of the surrogate data space. Attributes are typed: every attribute takes its actual value from its type.

- $T \subset X^*$ is the lifecycle set, equivalent to the admissible event sequences. They will represent the possible object instances.

  Every object trace will be made up of events of the event set X of its corresponding class. The precise specification of the correct traces for a class characterises behaviour.

  Each trace representing an object instance will be composed by an initial creation event, assigning to the object its surrogate and constant attributes, an adequate sequence of object class event occurrences and finally, a (optional) deletion event finishing its existence. All the events composed in an object trace will have as one argument the corresponding object key surrogate. Moreover, each event of the trace has the same key surrogate.

  The statement of what we mean by adequate for traces will describe, as said before, the object behaviour.

- $ob : T \rightarrow obs(A)$ is the observation function. Using it we will obtain for a given trace representing an object its corresponding set of pairs attribute-value obs(A) giving us the object attribute values as a function of the event sequences.

Classes are built over domains. Domains contain a set of values and a set of operations on these values. The domain type is the carrier set of the corresponding abstract data type. Domains denote data subspecification for classes and are used for object surrogates and attribute types. Their instances always exist, they are neither created nor destroyed and they do not have a changing state. Examples include the class Nat and Bool with obvious types $\{0,1,2...\}$, $\{true,false\}$.

If a class has events and attributes, and it is not built using class operators, it is an elementary class. Complex classes are built by combining elementary classes using the given class operators.

A conceptual schema for an information system can be incrementally built by combining classes. It is defined as the resultant class given by parallel composition of all the objects in the system. Its corresponding 4-tuple definition will have as A the set of all attributes of all defined classes, as X the set of all events, as T the interleaving of the object traces representing all the system life and as ob the observation in a given instant of the state of the object society.

An object is represented by a set of observable attributes over a life made up of its event trace. We can describe its structure in terms of its set of events and attributes, and its behaviour by its trace. The trace can be expressed in process algebra[5],[10], using petri nets or by specifying preconditions of events.

The link between structure and behaviour is given by the **observation function**[1] ob which defines the set 'obs' of object attributes-value pairs in the observed state. An observation indicates values for some of the attributes. An attribute has an unique value, so it may appear at most once in an observation. If an attribute value is undefined, it does not appear. The empty observation thus expresses that all attributes are undefined. An empty trace e expresses that the object remains nonexistent. The observation of a nonexistent object is always empty.

For each attribute a_i, we assume a data type $type(a_i)$ which determines the values a_i can have. Since object universes are always represented by domain values (due to its corresponding data type key surrogate space), the case of object-valued attributes is included.

The observation function can be implemented in two ways. In a query-oriented system, the occurrence of an event triggers a change of state of the IS. The event occurrence triggers changes in a forward inference style. In an event-oriented system, event occurrences are stored and the observation function is evaluated by backward inference.

4 An Example: Alarm Clock System

Consider an alarm clock system composed by three object classes: an **alarm**, a **window** and a **clock** as our example. An alarm can open and close a window. When the alarm rings it opens a window. When the alarm is not ringing the window is closed (iconised). The alarm checks the clock for the actual time. When the alarm time is reached, the alarm causes the bell window to be opened. If the alarm is not stopped, the bell window is closed after a fixed duration.

Every change of the system state is due to an event occurrence. For example, in order for an alarm to move from quiet to ringing an **openwindow** event must be activated.

An alarm is initially off and can be set. Once set by means of a **set** event it may be cancelled with a **cancel** event occurrence. In the ringing state the window is closed after a fixed duration which causes a **closewindow** event occurrence. A user can stop the alarm by explicitly activating a **stop** event. An alarm must be in a quiet state before an alarm setting can be cancelled. Each

---

[1] We haven't studied the extension of our model to observation relations. This is an interesting issue to explore.

event occurrence has an associated precondition that must be satisfied in order to activate it.

Each clock instance is related to a set of alarm instances, giving them the actual time continously. This time is represented by a **time** variable attribute that gives us the 'now'. The passing of time is represented by **time_unit** event occurrences.

Window instances will be identified by a bell identifier value. They may contain text written by repeated **type** events. Their **openwindow** and **closewindow** events shared with alarm instances will respectively open and iconise the window.

Next, we present the provided interaction mechanisms between objects. We will use and develop this example in the rest of the paper.

5   Interaction between Objects

There are two interaction mechanisms between objects:

1. **event sharing**: Shared events are those belonging to more than one class event set. They participate in the life cycles of the classes sharing them. When a shared event happens, it is added to all the traces of the relevant class instances sharing it.

   In our example we will have two events **openwindow** and **closewindow** shared between the **alarm** and **window** classes. Each occurrence of them will appear in the traces of objects of both the alarm and window.

   Shared events will have as first arguments the identifiers of all the objects that are sharing the given event.

2. **triggered relations**: Objects in our object society can have active relationships between them. A typical case is when an event occurrence is the cause of others event occurrences. We state these *triggered events* by declaring the so-called triggered relationships, that will show us which events occur in an automatic way when another event (the trigger) is activated.

   Any event belonging to a class can trigger events of any other class if some optional stated preconditions holds. For example, in the alarm clock system, a **closewindow** shared event occurrence is triggered when the alarm is stopped by a **stop** event occurrence, As **closewindow** is a shared event between the alarm and window classes, triggering it adds it to both the relevant alarm and window traces.

   Triggering relationships are expressed by

$$e1/e2[\text{if } pc2]$$

   meaning that an event e1 occurrence will trigger an event e2 if the precondition pc2 (if present) is satisfied.

A similar notion of triggers is used (in a Data Base environment) in OZ+ ([19]), an Object-Oriented Database System that introduces the concept of self-triggering rules as parameterless rules that execute whenever all their statements are executable.

Also in a Data Base context, Ode ([6]) declares triggers in a class specification, by defining conditions and its related actions. In terms of Oasis, conditions are event's occurrences and the subsequent action is the triggered event.

In both cases, a main difference lies in the declarative and deductive specification style used by Oasis contrasting the dynamic approach used in OZ+ and Ode.

These two mechanisms of interaction between objects will give us the key for expressing the traces defining the active behaviour of a system.

6   Representation of the Observation Function

The last component of our object class definition is the observation function ob. Given a trace $t \in T$, $ob(t)$ will map the attribute names of the object represented by t into attribute values of their types.

The observation function defines the values of constant and variable attributes. The constant attributes take their values when the creation event happens. An object's variable attributes values depend on the events of the object.

The observation function can be represented using first-order Horn clause logic. In this case the semantic observation function will be represented in the logic as a set of functions[2](one for each attribute). The resulting language is called Relational-OASIS. The observation function can be defined using equational logic for Functional-OASIS. The two approachs can also be combined. These language versions will differ only in the variable attribute definition. The executability of the Oasis language is derived from the representation of the observation function.

7   Types of classes

The specification of a society of interacting objects is based on three main constructs; domains, elementary classes and complex classes.

Each construct is defined in this section and is illustrated in the Oasis language. The alarm clock system presented in section 4 and in [1] illustrates the ideas. Other examples are presented in [11].

---

[2]modelled by relations

7.1 Domains

Domains denote the data subspecification and are used as object surrogates and attributes classes. Our object society will be built taking them as the basic data types upon which elementary classes are declared. They give us the set of unchanging 'platonic' entities that will be used for object identification (via object surrogates), and attribute types in our class definition.

The domains used in the object society will be declared at the beginning of the specification. The syntactic form is as below;

domains nat,bool,time,string

7.2 Elementary classes

Elementary classes are primitive and built only from the data domains. Each one has

1. a set of constant and variable attributes. A subset of the constant attributes define the surrogate.

2. a set of private and shared events,

3. a set of traces, describing the object behaviour

4. and an observation function, defining every object state as a function of its relevant event occurrences.

The syntactic elementary class representation will follow the template:

```
class name
  attributes
    constant
        ...
    variables
        ...
  events
    private
        ...
    shared
        ...
  preconditions
    [event:pc]
  triggering
    event1/event2 [if condition]
end class.
```

The two first components of our formal class definition are given by the attribute and event declarations. The adequate set of traces is expressed by means of the preconditions paragraph which associates to each event the precondition that must hold for an event occurrence. The observation function is represented in the variable attribute definition, defining with a deductive style every variable attribute in terms of their relevant events.

The triggering paragraph will allow us to establish active relationships between objects.

For example, the clock specification is

```
elementary class clock
   attributes
      constant
        code: string key
      variable
      ** the 'now', giving us the actual time value **
        time?(clock):time
           clauses: c:clock, t:time, sa:alarmsets
           time?(c)=t :- time_unit(c,sa,t).
   events
      private  c:clock, t:time
         newclock(c,t).
         delclock(c,t).
         setclock(c,t).
      shared c:clock, sa:alarmsets, t:time
         time_unit(c,sa,t).
   preconditions
         newclock(c,t):- not clock(c,t).
         delclock(c,t):- clock(c,t).
         time_unit(c,sa,t):- clock(c,t).
   triggering c:clock, sa:alarmsets, a:alarm, t:time
         time_unit(c,sa,t)/time_of_alarm_clock(a,t) if a in sa.
end class clock
```

The clock class has one constant attribute **code** used as key surrogate, and one variable attribute **time?**. The **time?** definition in terms of its relevant event **time_unit** constitutes the observation function representation. Three events are declared: **newclock** and **delclock** are the private creation and deletion events. **time_unit** is a shared event between clock and a complex class alarmsets, which groups individual instances of alarm class[3]. Each **time_unit** occurrence is shared between an instance of class clock and an instance of the alarmsets complex class (representing a set of individual alarm instances).

The triggering paragraph states the active clock class behaviour. Each **time_unit** occurrence will activate a **time_of_alarmclock** occurrence in every alarm clock belonging to the alarmsets grouping object denoted by sa.

The event **time_of_alarmclock** is an alarm class event.

---

[3]Complex classes construction is explained later. In particular, we will formally define the grouping composition.

7.3 Complex classes

Complex classes are those defined by class operators. They provide a constructive way for specifying an information system. Complex classes are built by composing other classes using one of four operators;

- aggregation/projection
- generalisation/specialisation,
- grouping
- and parallel composition.

We now state how each of the class operators is defined in terms of our 4-tuple class representation.

7.3.1 Aggregration and Projection

The aggregation class operator combines component classes. The resultant complex class has a constant attribute corresponding to the cartesian product of the component class surrogates. It also has its own set of attributes and events. Aggregation is used to abstract the shared behaviour of components. The approach is similar to aggregation as presented in static General Semantic Models (in particular, the Extended Entity-Relationship Model).

Given two classes $C1=\{X_1,A_1,T_1,ob_1\}$ and $C2=\{X_2,A_2,T_2,ob_2\}$ the definition of the aggregated class $C=\{X,A,T,ob\}$ is as follows:

- the set X will be composed of:
  1. the set of shared events between the component classes, declared as private events in the complex class and identified by taking the intersection of the component class event sets
  2. its own set of declared private and shared events
- the set A of attributes declared in the complex class: one constant attribute of the aggregate class will be the cartesian product of the component class keys.
- the set T of traces is built over the class events, but with the following constraint. Given C an aggregated class and C1 one of its component classes, we have that

  $\forall t \in T, \exists t_1 \in T_1$ such that the projection of t_1 on those of its shared event that are private in C, is equal to the projection of t on these events. And also, the key of the object represented by t_1 is just the projection of the key of the object represented by t on its C1 component.

  and the corresponding converse condition:

  $\forall t_1 \in T_1, \exists t \in T$ such that the projection of t on its private events that are shared in C1, is equal to the projection of t_1 on these events. And the projection of the key of the object represented by t on its C1 component is just the key of the object represented by t_1

This two conditions state that you cannot have a situation in which an event e of class C that is also a shared event between classes C_1 and C_2 occurs without satisfying the preconditions stated for e in everyone of these classes. It also states that if the precondition for a shared event is satisfied in one component class, it must be satisfied in all components that share it in the aggregate.

- the observation function is given as usual. There is no relation between the observation function of the aggregate class and the observation function of the component classes as they have no common variable attributes.

An aggregated class C of two classes C1,C2 is declared as C=C1*C2. We can break it down by means of the projection operator, resp. C[1], C[2]. It will give us the class surrogates of the components (C1 and C2 class surrogates respectively).

In this example, the alarm and window classes can be aggregated into a complex class icon representing their shared behaviour. Icon is defined by

$$ICON=ALARM*WINDOW$$

Each icon class instance is an aggregation of the alarm instance activating an **openwindow** event and the window instance being opened. Once again, we will have a constant attribute composed by the aggregation of its component class keys. The icon class may have an independent set of attributes (such as the time of the window opening etc.). The **openwindow** and **closewindow** shared events between alarm and window classes are private events of icon.

7.3.2 Generalisation and Specialisation

A generalised class is one built over a set of classes by abstracting their common features. Its corresponding inverse operator, the specialisation, allows us to define specialised classes from a parent class, by adding new events and attributes, or by redefining any of the inherited from the parent class.

The generalisation/specialisation operators are used to represent inheritance in Oasis.

An specialised complex class from another 'parent' class is intended to have the following interpretation:

- the set of events will be composed of:
  1. the set of events of the parent class, now owned by the specialised class
  2. newly (private or shared) defined events.
- the set of attributes contains all the parent attributes. New attributes may be added. The key of the specialised class is composed of at least the parent key constant attributes.

- the set T of traces, built as usual but with one constraint. When an event is triggered in the parent it must also be triggered in the specialisation. This means that for P a parent class with a child class C, and t_p and t_c two traces of their respective set of traces having the same key surrogate value, if an event $e \in T_p$ occurs and is relevant to the trace t_p, then it will be also relevant for the child trace t_c.

- the observation function, represented as in elementary classes. No special restriction is required on the relationships between the involved observation functions, to allow for the free redefinition of any inherited variable attribute definition.

The 4-tuple definition of a generalised class can be obtained in a similar way. The generalisation C of two classes C1 and C2 is defined by the following 4-tuple:

- $A = A_1 \cap A_2$.
  The generalised class key is the non empty intersection of C1 and C2 key constant attributes.

- $X = X_1 \cap X_2$ respecting the change in surrogate keys.

- T built as usual over X, with the same constraint stated when dealing when specialisation: an occurrence of any event $\in X$ will be a member of both the generalised and the component class traces.

- $ob = ob1$ restricted to the attributes $\in A$ (the intersection attributes set). We are assuming that we have the same observation function definition for the common attributes.

Syntactically, a generalised class C is declared by C=C1+C2. The inverse operation (specialisation) is allowed by means of the 'using' clause. So, we define: *class C1 using C* defines a specialised class C1.

For example, a specialised round_window class can be defined by inheriting events and attributes from window.

class ROUND_WINDOW using WINDOW

Or inversely, assuming defined two classes **round_window** and **squared_windo** with the same surrogate keys, a generalised class window is defined by

WINDOW=ROUND_WINDOW+SQUARED_WINDOW

The surrogates of the generalisation are the common key attributes of the component classes. In this simple example, if we assume that the key attribute of round_window and squared_window is a bellid, the WINDOW generalised class would have as key the bellid constant attribute.

7.3.3 Grouping and Ownership

Complex classes can be defined using the grouping operator as in 'collection' classes. The complex classes instances comprise a collection of instances of the grouped class.

The component instances of a grouping class can be given an ordered structure, as *lists, queues or stacks* or an unordered structure such as *sets* or *bags*.

The complex grouping class has two special features;

- It has a variable attribute *members* which is a generic type such as set, list, queue, stack of X where X is the surrogate type of the component class. Oasis provides syntactic constructs for defining a grouped class as desired. The definition of this *members* attribute is given as a function of the corresponding events of element addition and deletion, commented below.

- they will always have two specific events:

  1. insertion of new components to the grouped class instance. This insertion event is equivalent to the classical *push* for stacks or *insert* for the rest.

  2. deletion of existent components. Deletion corresponds to *pop* for stacks and *delete* for the others.

This insertion and deletion events will change the *members* attribute value, including or removing a component from the grouped class instance. They are implicitly declared in the complex grouping class.

The corresponding 4-tuple definition has:

- the set X of events declared in the new complex class, plus the two of insertion and deletion of components in grouping instances.

- the set A of attributes declared in the complex class, plus a variable attribute *members* as stated earlier.

- the set T of traces, built as usual.

- the observation function, represented as usual.

Grouping classes can be defined using the following explanatory keywords; setof, bagof, listof, queueof and stackof. A grouping class may also be defined by a clause 'group by'+condition, where condition defines the criteria for the grouping operation. The condition has the general form

$$attribute \, [\, OP \; value]$$

, where OP is a comparison operator of the attribute type. The use of the comparison operators $(<, >)$ will be allowed only if we have a partially ordered attribute type.

Component classes may be grouped by attribute. In this case, the complex class defines instances as collections of the component class with the same value for the attribute. We can build more complex grouping conditions using the classical logical operators *and, or, not.*

As an example, alarms may be grouped by by the maximum duration they may ring, the **finish** attribute. A complex grouping class ringing_alarm is defined as

class **RINGING_ALARM**= SETOF(ALARM) grouped by finish.

Ringing_alarm is a class with potential instances setof(alarm) with finish=50, ..., setof(alarm) with finish=60 and so on if we assume finish is a natural number.

7.3.4 Parallel Composition

Finally, the parallel composition class operator allows us to define a whole Conceptual Schema as a composition of previously defined classes.

For $C1=\{X_1,A_1,T_1,ob_1\}$ and $C2=\{X_2,A_2,T_2,ob_2\}$ two classes, we define the parallel composed class $C=\{X,A,T,ob\}$ ($C=C1||C2$). An instance of such a class will denote an element of the set of all the possible subsets of the union of the surrogate spaces of its component classes. So, if C_1 has a key k_1 of type t_1, and C_2 has a key k_2 of type t_2, an instance of C can be made up of o_1 of type t_1, or $\{o_1:t_1,o_2:t_2\}$, or $\{o_1:t_1,o_1/:t_1,o_2/:t_2\}$, etc.

The 4-tuple definition for C will have:

- a set X of events, the union of event sets of the component classes , all of them viewed as private events, plus its own creation and deletion events. The new and destroy events of the component classes are interpreted as private events of the composed class. They have a new parameter which represents the surrogate of the parallel composed class.

  For example, if we build a parallel composed class **alarmsystem** from **alarm**, **window**, **clock** and a grouping class **alarmsets**, the alarm component class **newalarm** event, creator of alarm instances, is regarded as a private event **newalarm(s:alarmsystem,a:alarm)** of the alarmsystem.

- a set A of attributes, the union of those (constant and variables) of the component classes. The key attributes of the component classes are constant attributes of the composed class. Each attribute is tagged with the new complex class surrogate.

  For example, in our Alarm Clock System, the **bellid** string constant attribute of the **window** component class is a constant attribute **bellid** of the alarmsystem and is tagged by the alarmsystem surrogate.

  bellid(w:window,t:string) $\rightarrow$ bellid(s:alarmsystem,w:window,t:string)

- a set T of traces, composed by interleavings components traces, respecting the synchronisation constraints for shared events and triggered relationships.

A further requirement for a parallel composed class is that events of the composed class are activated if and only if their preconditions are satisfied in each relevant component class.

- an observation function which is the 'sum' of the components' observation functions.

The syntax for the parallel operator is ||. Our alarm clock system conceptual schema alarmclock is defined by the parallel composition of the elementary classes alarm, clock and window and the grouping class alarmsets.

ALARMCLOCK=ALARM||WINDOW||CLOCK||ALARMSETS.

An alarmclock trace will be composed of any correct sequence of events of the component classes as defined in [1].

8 Conclusion

This paper presents an object-oriented specification language Oasis which extends notions from OBLOG[17] and MOL[12] to enable the specification of active systems.

Oasis provides the basis for a complete object-oriented software production environment. The operational semantics is based on clausal or equational logic which support the validation of specifications by software prototyping. Specifications can be animated using logic programming or by algebraic rewriting techniques. The development of an environment consisting of graphical tools, validation and code generation tools is now in progress.

References

[1] S.Bear,P.Allen,D.Coleman,F.Hayes. 'Graphical Specification of Object Oriented Systems'. OOPSLA 90.

[2] G.Booch 'Object Oriented Design with applications' Benjamin/Cummings 1990

[3] Bubenko,J.A.:Olive,A. *Dynamic or Temporal Modelling? An Illustrative Comparison* SYSLAB Working Paper 117,Nov.1986

[4] Coad,P.,Yourdon, E. 'Object Oriented Analysis' Englewood Cliffs Prentice-Hall 1990

[5] C.A.R. Hoare. 'Communicating Sequential Processes, Prentice-Hall International, 1985.

[6] Gehani,N.:Jagadish,H.V. *Ode as an Active Database:Constraints and Triggers* Proceedings of the 17th International Conference on Very Large Data Bases,VLDB 1991, Barcelona.

[7] A.Goldberg, D.Robson 'Smalltalk:The language and its implementation' Addison Wesley 1983

[8] P.Lindgreen ed. 'A framework of Information System Concepts'.FRISCO Interim Report. IFIP WG8.TG.90.

[9] J.W.Lloyd 'Foundations of Logic Programming' Springer-Verlag 1987

[10] R.Milner. 'A Calculus of Communicating Systems' Lecture Notes in Computer Science, vol 92,Springer-Verlag, 1980

[11] O.Pastor 'OASIS:Open and Active Specification of Information Systems' Internal Technical Memo. HP-Labs.Bristol.

[12] I.Ramos. 'Logics and OO-Data Bases:a declarative approach.' DEXA 90

[13] I.Ramos et al. 'A Conceptual Scheme Specification for Rapid Prototyping' XII IASTED Conference on Applied Informatics. Insbruck 90.

[14] Ramos,I:,Pastor,O.:Casado,V. *OO and Active Formal Information System Specification* In Proc, of DEXA-91, Springer-Verlag,Berlin,1991

[15] Rumbaugh,J.:Blaha,M.:Premerlani,W.:Eddy,F.:Lorensen,W. *Object-Oriented Modelling and Design* Prentice Hall 1991.

[16] A.Sernadas et al. 'Abstract Object Types: a temporal perspective' Colloquium on Temporal Logic and Specification.

[17] Sernadas,A.:Sernadas,C:Ehrich,H.D. *Object Oriented Specification of Databases: An Algebraic Approach.* Proc. 13th Int.Conf. on Very Large Data Bases VLDB'87,Brighton,1987. Morgan-Kaufmann, Palo Alto, 1987, pp. 107-116.

[18] B.Stroustrup 'The C++ Programming Language' Addison-Wesley 1987

[19] Weiser,S.P.:Lochovsky,F. *OZ+:An Object Oriented Database System* Object Oriented Concepts, Databases and Applications, ACM-Press 1989

Data Modelling in Complex Application Domains

A.H.M. ter Hofstede [1] H.A. Proper [2] Th.P. van der Weide [3]

Abstract

In many non trivial application domains, object types with a complex structure occur. Data modelling techniques which only allow flat structures are not suitable for representing such complex object types. In this paper a general data modelling technique, the Predicator Set Model, is introduced, which is capable of representing complex structures in a natural way.

The expressiveness of the Predicator Set Model is illustrated by means of a number of examples. In those examples, the Predicator Set Model's expressiveness is related to the expressiveness of more traditional modelling techniques. Furthermore, some notational conventions are defined, which enable a more compact representation of complex structures.

1 Introduction

The conventional Relational Model and ER approach allow for a high-level description of data and relations, abstracting from representation and implementation details. Main disadvantage, however, is their incapability of representing complex structures in a natural way. In these techniques, complex structures have to be "flattened", i.e. represented non-hierarchically, which leads to overspecification. This in turn does not comply with the *conceptualisation principle* as it is formulated in [Gri82].

Various application domains indeed contain objects with complex structures. Documents (and Hypertexts) are an example in the field of office automation. In [Wig90] it is estimated that 1% of all recorded information is contained in so-called formatted databases (e.g. a relational database), 4% is recorded on microfiche, while the remaining 95% is contained in unformatted databases. Unformatted databases are capable

---

[1] This work has been partially supported by SERC project SOCRATES. Software Engineering Research Centre (SERC), P.O. Box 424, 3500 AK Utrecht, The Netherlands, E-mail: hofstede@serc.nl

[2] The investigations were partly supported by the Foundation for Computer Science in the Netherlands (SION) with financial support from the Netherlands Organization for Scientific Research (NWO), University of Nijmegen, E-mail: erikp@cs.kun.nl

[3] University of Nijmegen, Toernooiveld, 6525 ED Nijmegen, The Netherlands, E-mail: tvdw@cs.kun.nl

of containing objects with variable components and varying size (e.g. documents and graphics; typically grammar governed data).

Another domain in which complex objects are important is the field of method engineering or meta-modelling ([VHW91]). In this field, meta-models are constructed, capturing the structure of models that are expressed in some modelling technique. Many modelling techniques contain concepts that correspond to complex structures, e.g. whole diagrams have such a complex structure. It is not natural to represent these object types as flat structures (see e.g. [Wel88]). Computer Aided Design (CAD) and Computer Aided Manufacturing (CAM) are also areas in which such complex structures frequently occur.

Finally, in the development of so termed Evolving Information Systems ([FOP91], [MS90], [Ari91], [Rod91]) where the information structure itself is allowed to change over time as well, there is a need for a modelling technique which incorporates all basic modelling concepts. This implies the need for a modelling technique with an expressivity which is based on a set of powerful modelling concepts.

In this paper a general data modelling technique is introduced, which has been defined formally in [HW91] and [HPW92]. This modelling technique, the *Predicator Set Modelling technique* (*Predicator Set Model* for short), indeed is capable of representing complex structures in a natural way. In this paper a number of examples are given to make it plausible, from a practical point of view, that the Predicator Set Model allows for the elegant representation of complex object types. Notational conventions will be introduced that allow for compact representations of complex objects.

2 Basic Data Modelling Concepts

One of the key concepts in data modelling is the concept of relation type or fact type. In ER ([Che76]) and NIAM ([NH89]) a relation type is considered to be an association between object types. In figure 1 the graphical representation of a binary relation type R between object types X_1 and X_2 in the NIAM style is shown, while in figure 2 the corresponding ER diagram is depicted.

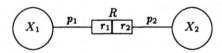

Fig. 1. A NIAM relation type

The basic building element of fact types is the connection between an object type and a role, the so-called *predicator*. In figure 1, p_1 is the predicator connecting X_1 to r_1, and p_2 the predicator that connects X_2 to r_2. In the Predicator Set Model, which is an extension of the Predicator Model ([BHW91], [HW92]), a fact type is considered to be a set of predicators. A relation type is therefore considered as an association between predicators, rather than between objects types. Fact types are regarded as object types. This is called objectification. In the sequel some examples of objectifications are shown. Sometimes, we will prefer to denote the predicators involved in a relation type seperately. In section 5 some examples of this are shown.

Fig. 2. The corresponding ER diagram

Two special kinds of object types are entity types and label types. The difference is that labels can, in contrast with entities, be represented (reproduced) on a communication medium. As a result, label types are also called *concrete* object types. All other object types are called *abstract*, they are not representable by themselves. As usual, a clear distinction is made between concrete object types and abstract object types. The gap between these concrete and abstract object types can only be crossed by special binary fact types. These fact types correspond to *bridge types* in NIAM ([NH89], [Win90]), and *attribute types* in ER ([Che76]). Each entity type must be identifiable in terms of label types.

Anothor basic concept of data modelling is specialisation, also referred to as subtyping. Specialisation is a mechanism for representing one or more (possibly overlapping) subtypes of a type. Intuitively a specialisation relation between a subtype and a supertype implies that the instances of the subtype are also instances of the supertype. For proper specialisation, it is required that subtypes be defined in terms of one or more of their supertypes. Such a decision criterion is referred to as the *Subtype Defining Rule* (see e.g. [BHW91]). Identification of subtypes is derived from their supertypes.

Specialisation relations are organised in so-called specialisation "hierarchies". A specialisation hierarchy is in fact not a hierarchy in the strict sense, but an acyclic directed graph with a unique top. A specialisation hierarchy can thus be considered a semi-lattice: for each pair of subtypes (in the same hierarchy), the least upper bound should exist. The least upper bound of two subtypes is that object type that is supertype of both subtypes, and that has no subtype with this property. The top of this semi-lattice, i.e. the top of a specialisation hierarchy, will be referred to as the *pater familias* (see [TMV88]). Consequently, the identification of every object type in the hierarchy is derived from the pater familias of the hierarchy.

As an example of a specialisation hierarchy, consider figure 3. There the following hierarchy is depicted:

Flesh-eater **Spec** Animal
Plant-eater **Spec** Animal
Carnivore **Spec** Flesh-eater
Omnivore **Spec** Flesh-eater
Omnivore **Spec** Plant-eater
Herbivore **Spec** Plant-eater

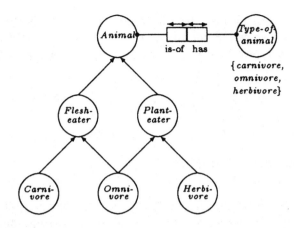

Fig. 3. Example of a specialisation hierarchy

Each specialisation relation is represented as an arrow in figure 3. As a consequence, the pater familias of object type *Carnivore* is *Animal*. The subtype defining rules are:

> Flesh-eater = Animal is-of Type-of-animal {carnivore, omnivore}
> Plant-eater = Animal is-of Type-of-animal {herbivore, omnivore}
> Carnivore = Animal is-of Type-of-animal {carnivore}
> Omnivore = Animal is-of Type-of-animal {omnivore}
> Herbivore = Animal is-of Type-of-animal {herbivore}

3 Generalisation

Generalisation is a mechanism that allows for the creation of a new object type as a generic type for other object types. The constituent object types in a generalisation are called the specifiers of the generalised object type. As a result, the generalised object type is covered by its constituent object types. This means that every instance of any specifier is also an instance of the generalised object type. Another consequence is that the identification of a generalised object type is determined by the identification of its specifiers.

As an example, for the motivation and use of generalisation, consider a pricelist for individually priced *Products*. A *Product* is either a *Car*, or a *House*. A *Car* is identified by a registration number, while a *House* is identified by the combination of its zip-code and house number. *Product* is thus considered to be a generic term for *House* and *Car*. *Products* have a price associated to them.

In traditional data modelling techniques, e.g. NIAM and ER, this Universe of Discourse is modelled by the schema in figure 4. Note that the uniqueness of the combination between a zip code and a house number is modelled by means of an encircled U, a so-called *uniqueness constraint*. For the semantics of complex uniqueness constraints, see [WHB92].

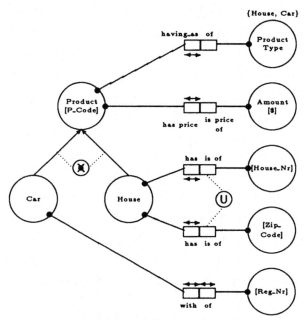

Subtype defining rules:

Car = Product having_as Product_Type 'Car'
House = Product having_as Product_Type 'House'

Fig. 4. Subtyping instead of Generalisation

We will point out that this schema suffers from overspecification. Firstly, a special label type (*P_code*) has to be introduced in order to identify *Products*. Secondly, a special fact type and a special type (*Product Type*) type are required to determine the type of the *Product*. This determination forms the *Subtype Defining Rule* for *Products* (see figure 4). However, these extra object types are not conceptually relevant. Their introduction should therefore be considered as a violation of the *Conceptualisation Principle* (see [Gri82], [NH89] or [Win90]).

Using the concept of generalisation, these overspecifications are avoided. In figure 4 a more appropriate schema for this Universe of Discourse is depicted. In this schema, the label type *P_code* is no longer needed, since products inherit their identification from *Cars* and *Houses*.

4 Power and Sequence Types

Another situation that invites a system analyst, using a conventional modelling technique as eg ER or NIAM, to a violation of the *Conceptualisation Principle*, is when groups of objects occur just as groups, without any other identification than their composition. The most primitive manifestations of this phenomenon are the power set mechanism in formal set theory, and the sequencing (lists) mechanism.

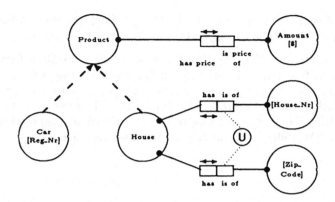

Fig. 5. Example of Generalisation

However, in its full glory, this phenomenon is a mechanism for *schema decomposition* (see also section 6).

In the Predicator Set Model the concept of *power type* is introduced as the equivalence of power sets in formal set theory. An instance of a power type is a set of instances of its *element type*. An instance of the power type is identified by corresponding instances of the element type, just as a set is identified by its elements in formal set theory (axiom of extensionality), see [HK87].

As an illustration of the expressive power of power object types the chemical reactions example from [Fal88] is discussed. The considered Universe of Discourse deals with simple chemical reactions. A chemical reaction takes a set of input substances with their associated quantities, and produces a set of output substances in corresponding quantities.

This Universe of Discourse could be modelled in an ER schema in terms of a quartenary relationship, as shown in figure 6. In this relation, the attribute CR_ID is used to identify chemical reactions. The entity type *Substance* describes wich substance is subject to the chemical reaction, and the entity type *Quantity* describes in what quantity. The *Input/Output indicator* makes the distinction between input and output substances to the chemical reaction. A first problem with this solution is the superfluous identification of a chemical reaction. Only some chemical reactions are sufficiently important, to have a name of their own. The others are just identified by their description in terms of what goes in and what comes out. The second problem is that this solution does not allow for the addition of a chemical reaction by one elementary update. This is caused by the fact that in the model of 6 several object instances are needed to denote one reaction.

The use of a power type offers a much better opportunity to model this Universe of Discourse (see figure 7). In this model, a chemical reaction is modelled as a relationship between a set of input reagents, and a set of output reagents. This schema is better understood by studying a sample population (see figure 7). This sample population is in the style of nested relations as, encountered in the NF^2 datamodel [SS86]. The main difference is that NF^2 uses a nested table heading (and

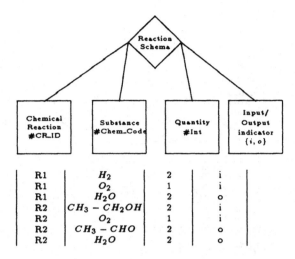

Fig. 6. Chemical Reactions in ER

thus nested tuples).

The solution of figure 7 also solves the update problem which was mentioned before. In this model a chemical reaction is denoted as a single object instance. Therefore, the above mentioned elementary update problem is solved. The consequence is that an update operation of a chemical reaction can be considered as a single operation in the Predicator Set Model.

Sequence types are ordered power types, their instances are tuples of arbitrary length. As an example, consider a freight train as depicted in figure 8. A train is identified by a train code, and consists of a locomotive followed by a sequence of freight cars. This Universe of Discourse is modelled in the information structure diagram of figure 9.

5 Relation with Context-Free Grammars

In this section the relation between context-free grammars and the Predicator Set Model is discussed. First we show how a context-free grammar is translated into a Predicator Set schema. In [HW91] a formalised translation mechanism is given.

Context-free grammars are generally employed for describing document structures (see for example [BW90], [SDBW91], [BW92]). The Predicator Set Model has sufficient expressive power to describe such structures elegantly. This is done by interpreting context free grammars in terms of the Predicator Set Model. The translation also shows the usefulness of the Predicator Set Model for describing hypertext information structures. In the translation, generalised object types will play a crucial role. In [HW91] the formalised translation mechanism is given. The reverse process, i.e translating a Predicator Set schema into a context free grammar, is discussed there as well.

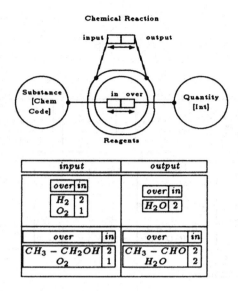

Fig. 7. Chemical Reactions

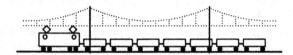

Fig. 8. An example Freight Train

In the world of documents a lot of effort has been put into the design of standards for the communication and denotation of document structures and contents ([ISO86]). In this example the following grammar, which is denoted in the style of SGML, is considered for describing the structure of a book.

$$\langle book \rangle \rightarrow \langle title \rangle \langle contents \rangle$$
$$\langle contents \rangle \rightarrow \langle chapter \rangle^+$$
$$\langle chapter \rangle \rightarrow \langle title \rangle \langle sections \rangle$$
$$\langle sections \rangle \rightarrow \langle section \rangle^+$$
$$\langle section \rangle \rightarrow \langle string \rangle$$

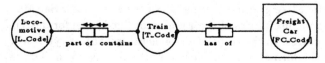

Fig. 9. The train composition administration

$$\langle \text{title} \rangle \rightarrow \langle \text{string} \rangle$$
$$\langle \text{string} \rangle \rightarrow \langle \text{char} \rangle^{+}$$

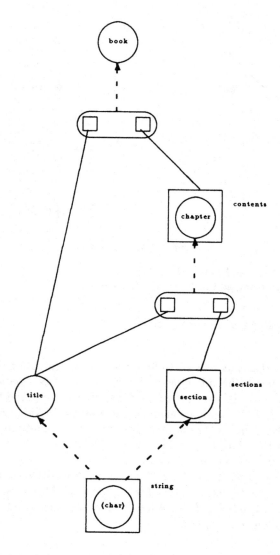

Fig. 10. Example of translation of SGML structure

This grammar can be translated to the Predicator Set Model schema of figure 10. In this figure, the predicators of fact types have been drawn seperately. The translation is directly derived from the grammar rules: each nonterminal symbol becomes an

entity type, and each terminal symbol a label type. Each production rule describes a specifier of the object type corresponding to the lefthand side.

It is important to note that the Predicator Set schema resulting from the translation of a context-free grammar does not exhibit explicitly the order of the symbols in the righthand side of production rules. This corresponds to a *mapping oriented* view to the righthand side of a production rule, rather than the usual tuple oriented view. The resulting Predicator Set schema can be viewed as a representation of the abstract syntax ([Mey90]) corresponding to the grammar at hand.

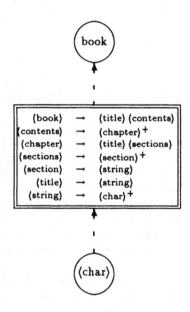

Fig. 11. The use of a grammar box

The grammar box is used as a notation to incorporate in this way context free grammars in the Predicator Set Model. The grammar box takes as inputs the object types that correspond to terminal symbols. The output of the grammar box is the start symbol.

With respect to this use of context-free grammars, a bad schema will result if the context-free grammar does not satisfy some aesthetical rules. Firstly, there can be useless symbols, i.e. symbols that do not occur in any derivation from the start symbol. In terms of the Predicator Set Model these symbols correspond to isolated object types. Secondly, the object types that correspond to the terminal symbols can be identified without making use of the grammar box, since they are interpreted as label types. The identification of the object type, corresponding with the start symbol of the grammar, then depends on the structure of the grammar.

6 Schema Decomposition

In this section a notational shorthand for schema objectification, which facilitates the specification of complex object types is introduced. This is done by discussing some examples, which make use of this shorthand, in order to demonstrate its elegance in modelling.

The need for decomposition in large systems has been generally recognised. A well known example is the decomposition mechanism for Activity Graphs ([Sch84]). In an Activity Graph, both processes and data may be subject to decomposition. However, data modelling techniques usually do not provide a decomposition mechanism. In the Predicator Set Model, schema objectification has been introduced for this purpose.

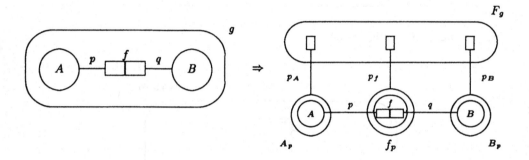

Fig. 12. Schema objectification

Schema objectification is a construction mechanism that allows us to define part of a schema as an object type. Instances of such object types are then populations of their corresponding schemas. As a result, these objectified schemas have to be valid information structures, i.e. Predicator Set Model. Furthermore, populations should satisfy the *decomposition rule*, meaning, that instances of an object type O should be valid populations of the objectified schema as well.

Schema objectification, however, is not an elementary concept, since it can be defined in terms of the concepts of power object type and fact type. The idea is to construct a power object type x_p for each object type x from the schema g to be objectified. Each of these power object types x_p is the base of a predicator p_x, that is part of a fact type F_g (see figure 12). This fact type is to relate sets of instances of the object types involved in the schema objectification, which are part of th same schema instance.

As an example of schema objectification, consider a meta-model for Activity Graphs. In figure 13 two sample activity graphs are depicted.

Activity Graphs are bipartite directed graphs consisting of activities and states. The direction of the arrow between an activity and a state indicates whether that state is input or output of that activity. Activities and states can be decompo-

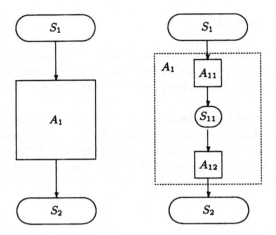

Fig. 13. Sample activity graphs

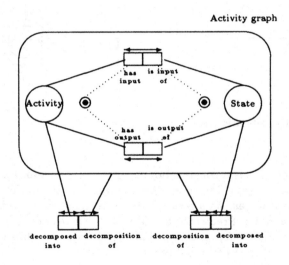

Fig. 14. Meta-model of activity graphs

sed in other Activity Graphs. In figure 13 the rightmost Activity Graph shows the decomposition of activity A1.

In figure 14, the meta-model of Activity Graphs is depicted. As can be seen there, an Activity Graph is an objectified schema consisting of activities, states and input and output relations. The binary relations between activity and Activity Graph and state and Activity Graph represent the decomposition relation.

7 Conclusions

The suitability of the Predicator Set Model for complex application domains has been illustrated by means of a number of examples. The theoretic background has been described in [HW91]. In that paper, the relation with contex free grammars and formal set theory has been established, thus giving evidence, from a formal point of view, for the completeness of the Predicator Set Model.

In the future a method will be developed to support the construction of schemata from informal descriptions. Heuristics and guidelines should be ingredients of this methods. A prototype implementation is considered.

References

[Ari91]   G. Ariav. Temporally oriented data definitions: Managing schema evolution in temporally oriented databases. *Data & Knowledge Engineering*, 6:451–467, 1991.

[BHW91]   P. van Bommel, A.H.M. ter Hofstede, and Th.P. van der Weide. Semantics and Verification of Object-Role Models. *Information Systems*, 16(5):471–495, October 1991.

[BW90]   P.D. Bruza and Th.P. van der Weide. Two Level Hypermedia - An Improved Architecture for Hypertext. In A.M.Tjoa and R.Wagner, editors, *Proceedings of the Data Base and Expert System Applications Conference (DEXA 90)*, pages 76–83. Springer Verlag, 1990.

[BW92]   P.D. Bruza and Th.P. van der Weide. Stratified Hypermedia Structures for Information Disclosure. *The Computer Journal*, 34(3), June 1992.

[Che76]   P.P. Chen. The entity-relationship model: towards a unified view of data. *ACM Transactions on Database Systems*, 1(1):9–36, 1976.

[Fal88]   E.D. Falkenberg. Deterministic Entity-Relationship Modelling. Technical Report 88-13, Department of Information Systems, University of Nijmegen, The Netherlands, 1988.

[FOP91]   E.D. Falkenberg, J.L.H. Oei, and H.A. Proper. A Conceptual Framework for Evolving Information Systems. In *Proceedings of the "Second International Working Conference on Dynamic Modelling of Information Systems"*, Washington DC, July 1991.

[Gri82]   J.J. van Griethuysen, editor. *Concepts and Terminology for the Conceptual Schema and the Information Base*. Publ. nr. ISO/TC97/SC5-N695, 1982.

[HK87]   R. Hull and R. King. Semantic Database Modelling: Survey, Applications and Research Issues. *Computing Surveys*, 19(3):201–260, Sept 1987.

[HPW92]   A.H.M. ter Hofstede, H.A. Proper, and Th.P. van der Weide. Formal Semantics of a Semi Natural Language for the Description and Manipulation of Information Systems. In Preparation, SERC, Software Engineering Research Centrum, Utrecht, The Netherlands, 1992.

[HW91]   A.H.M. ter Hofstede and Th.P. van der Weide. Expressiveness in Data Modelling. Report 91-07, SERC, Software Engineering Research Centrum, Utrecht, The Netherlands, July 1991. To be published.

[HW92]   A.H.M. ter Hofstede and Th.P. van der Weide. Formalisation of Techniques: Chopping down the Methodology Jungle. *Information and Software Technology*, 34(1):57–65, January 1992.

[ISO86] ISO. *Information Processing - Text and Office Systems - Standard General MarkUp Language (SGML)*. ISO8879, 1986.

[Mey90] B. Meyer. *Introduction to the Theory of Programming Languages*. Prentice Hall, 1990.

[MS90] E. McKenzie and R. Snodgrass. Schema Evolution and the Relational Algebra. *Information Systems*, 15(2):207–232, 1990.

[NH89] G.M. Nijssen and T.A. Halpin. *Conceptual Schema and Relational Database Design: A fact oriented approach*. Prentice Hall of Australia Pty Ltd, 1989.

[Rod91] J.F. Roddick. Dynamically changing schemas within database models. *The Australian Computer Journal*, 23(3):105–109, August 1991.

[Sch84] G. Scheschonk. *Eine auf Petri-Netzen basierende Konstruktions, Analyse und (Teil)Verificationsmethode zur Modellierungsunterstützung bei der Entwicklung von Informationssystemen*. PhD thesis, Berlin University of Technology, 1984.

[SDBW91] P.L. van der Spiegel, J.T.W. Driessen, P.D. Bruza, and Th.P. van der Weide. A Transaction Model for Hypertext. In *Proceedings of the Data Base and Expert System Applications Conference (DEXA 91)*. Springer Verlag, 1991.

[SS86] H.J. Schek and M.H. Scholl. The relational model with relation-valued attributes. *Information Systems*, 11(2):137–147, 1986.

[TMV88] O. de Troyer, R. Meersman, and P. Verlinden. RIDL* on the CRIS Case: A Workbench for NIAM. In T.W. Olle, A.A. Verrijn-Stuart, and L. Bhabuta, editors, *Proceedings of the IFIP WG 8.1 Working Conference on Computerized Assistence during the Information Systems Life Cycle*, pages 375 – 459, 1988.

[VHW91] T.F. Verhoef, A.H.M. ter Hofstede, and G.M. Wijers. Structuring Modelling Knowledge for CASE shells. In R. Andersen, J.A. Bubenko, and A. Sølvberg, editors, *Proceedings of the Third International Conference CAiSE'91 on Advanced Information Systems Engineering*, pages 502–524, Trondheim, Norway, May 1991. Lecture Notes in Computer Science 498.

[Wel88] R.J. Welke. The CASE Repository: More than another database application. In *Proceedings of 1988 INTEC Symposium Systems Analysis and Design: A Research Strategy*, Atlanta, Georgia, 1988.

[WHB92] Th.P. van der Weide, A.H.M. ter Hofstede, and P. van Bommel. Uniquest: Determining the Semantics of Complex Uniqueness Constraints. *The Computer Journal*, 34(2):148–156, April 1992.

[Wig90] R.E. Wiggins. Document Image Processing - New Light on an Old Problem. *International Journal of Information Management*, 10(4):297–318, 1990.

[Win90] J.J.V.R. Wintraecken. *The NIAM Information Analysis Method: Theory and Practice*. Kluwer Academic Publishers, 1990.

Augmenting the Design Process: Transformations from Abstract Design Representations

David Budgen and Grant Friel

Department of Computer Science

Keele University

Keele

Staffs. ST5 5BG

Abstract

Most of the software design practices that are in current use are based upon the use of graphical notations, and while providing a suitable vehicle for the designer's need to model abstract ideas about the structure of a solution and its expected behaviour, these forms lack any rigour in their syntax and semantics. This paper describes some of the work performed to transform abstract graphically-based design descriptions into a more formal notation that is capable of acting as a high-level prototype of the design. In particular, we describe the way in which these concepts have been encapsulated in an experimental "designer's workbench", and outline some possible future developments based upon using this as a framework for the development of further features and facilities.

1 Introduction

The development of a design for a large software-based system continues to form an area of difficulty for current software development technologies, both in terms of structuring the design process itself, and also of providing tools that can be used to support the design process. In this paper we explore some ideas about how the process of software design can be augmented and reinforced through the use of an experimental CASE tool, which assists both with developing a systematic graphical design representation, and also with transforming this into an executable prototype.

We can consider the process of software design as providing a 'how' stage in system development. Having determined, by means of some requirements analysis procedure, just 'what' is needed from a system in order to meet a customer's needs, the system developers then proceed to seek the means of achieving these aims. The planning process that results is generally considered to involve the design of a solution.

The current thinking about the nature of the design process in general is that this does not form an analytical process, as occurs in the domain of scientific research; but rather that it is one in which the designer postulates a model that represents their intentions, and then explores this to determine whether it can be developed to provide the required behaviour

[15, 10]. The Peters/Tripp model [16] is an example of how this view of design can be mapped on to the design procedures that are generally used for developing software. The design process is further complicated for the case of software design, since it involves the creation of an artifact which has both passive structure and dynamic behaviour, since software is represented by a *program* (with static qualities), which is then executed as a *process* (exhibiting dynamic behaviour).

The current widely-used software design practices make extensive use of graphical symbols, in conjunction with relatively unstructured text, in order to help the designer to handle highly abstract concepts in a relatively structured manner. The relatively abstract syntax and semantics of such forms are well suited to this initial stage in design, where the designer is building up their ideas about how a system might function (and then later considering how it might be structured). Experimental study of how designers work has indicated that they build 'mental models' of the intended system, and that during the process of development of a model, the designer will also 'mentally execute' the model in order to study its behaviour [3, 23].

More formal descriptive techniques that are based upon the use of mathematical notation, such as VDM and Z, provide a designer with a structure that can be used for reasoning about the behaviour of a system and about its other properties, in a more analytical manner than can be achieved through the use of systematic diagram-based forms. In particular, it is these features of formal notations that have made them of particular value for use in safety-critical systems, and in those systems where reliability of all kinds is of particular importance. However, the relatively intensive mathematics that is required for their use and understanding has so far limited the extent of their practical application.

A related field of work involves making use of formal mathematical descriptions in order to create executable prototypes of a system. Such a prototype then provides the designer with the means of 'executing' the description of a design at an early stage in its development. However, as is the case for almost all formal techniques, the skills that are required for developing such models are still relatively uncommon, and further, it is not evident that the more extensive syntax and semantics required to construct such models makes them particularly well suited to the initial exploration of the designer's ideas.

The general form of the design process that we have investigated can be summarised as follows:

1. Produce an initial design model using the MASCOT notation [1] to describe a network of cooperating parallel processes.

2. Extend the design model by providing behavioural descriptions for the MASCOT design objects, using State Transition Diagrams.

3. Transform the design model into the state-based CSP/*me too* form [11], and 'execute' this in order to explore the dynamic behaviour of the design.

(There are no specific 'method' assumptions to constrain this process.)

We have described elsewhere our work on design transformation that has helped towards putting the systematic description and 'formal' description techniques together in a manner that exploits the strength of each [11]. Using this approach, the more 'fuzzy' description forms based on diagrams are used for initial design modelling, and these are then transformed into a more rigorous form that can then be used as a prototype, as well as providing a basis for further refinement of the design (including the transformation to code). In many ways, this is the designer's equivalent of Pamela Zave's ideas about operational development versus lifecycle forms [24]. Her work has mainly concentrated on the prototyping of requirements specifications, but the general philosophy is very similar.

Our work in this area has identified a need for a degree of tool support if these ideas are to be explored further. In developing the architecture for a UNIX-based prototype of such a tool, termed the *Experimental Design Workbench* (EDW) we have also been able to integrate our ideas about design transformation with some other strands of our work. In this paper we report on:

- the work which has been done and is under way in the area of design transformation techniques;

- the way in which the framework of the EDW has enabled us to integrate this work with our previous experimental studies in design;

- our plans for future developments, both in terms of developing the technical ideas, and also in terms of widening their application;

and the rest of this paper is structured around the discussion of each of these three aspects.

2 Formalising the initial design model

The design of most software systems involves the development of a 'mental model' in the mind of the designer at an early stage in the design process. A large part of this model will be made up of fuzzy, or hazy notions about the intended system, and at this stage it contains little, if any detail and dwells primarily on gross system characteristics — the *formalism dimension* of the Peters-Tripp model [16]. During the initial stages of the software design process this 'mental model' has to be 'captured' and expressed in a form which can be used as a basis for evaluating the designer's ideas, and then for eventually developing the design. In the development of reactive, or real time systems these early stages in the design process are becoming of greater importance as the demand for high quality and increasingly complex software grows.

The more 'traditional' approach to recording the details of a design during software development has been to use natural language, usually with some imposed structure, and sometimes supplemented with diagrams, tables and formulae [13]. Clearly a more rigorous, or formalized approach that reflects the need of the designer is desirable.

More recently, a great deal of effort has been put into formalizing these more abstract aspects of the design process [21], the advantages of which are already well documented [18, 24]. The 'ideal' situation is therefore to have a formal representation of the initial design model from which the design can be developed. But, due to the mathematical nature of formal description languages and the lack of any well defined design procedure for using them, there is often great difficulty in expressing these initial design forms in this way.

Our recent work, described in [11], has shown how a formal design model can be generated through the use of informal design techniques. Using this approach the initial design structure is described by using the informal, but systematic design representation of MASCOT 3 [1], and then by using rule-based transformation techniques, we are able to generate a more formal CSP/*me too* description [9] for the design.

The transformation process involved carries out a change in form of description, and so can also be thought of as a transformation from one design viewpoint to another. Our original design form is described using MASCOT, which expresses the design from an architectural, or structural viewpoint (ie. the system is described in terms of both its internal and external components and the lines of communication, or connections between them). Using the automated design transformation process, this 'static' representation is then transformed into a state based description. That is, each of the identified design components is described in terms of a process and its *local state* and the operations which are carried out to effect a change in that state. These operations represent the *events* which take place within the system. What, in effect, we now have is an event driven, or behavioural viewpoint based upon an elaboration of the original design description — a 'dynamic' representation.

A CSP/*me too* specification is executable, therefore by using this technique the designer can effectively be provided with an experimental prototype at an early stage in the development of a design. Using this, it is then possible to model the *dynamic* behaviour of the system that corresponds to the design, and to compare this to the designer's intentions. In other words, it enables the designer to explore and refine the *mental model*, and thus provides a means of identifying and highlighting those areas where the original design description needs closer inspection and/or modification.

The *Experimental Designer's Workbench* was developed partly as a vehicle for exploring the ideas on design transformation. The need for such a support environment became apparent as a result of developing the design transformation tool described above.

3   The Experimental Designers Workbench

During the process of devising the transformation rules for generating CSP/*me too* structures from MASCOT, it became possible to identify the major limitations imposed by our use of the MASCOT representation. In particular, the dataflow-oriented MASCOT viewpoint provides no means of expressing the *behavioural* aspects of a design. To get around this problem, and therefore to enable the generation of a more complete and accurate CSP/*me too* specification, it became necessary to explore ways of supplementing the MASCOT representation with the required behavioural description (this is currently achieved by using State Transition Diagrams [22]). The workbench itself then provides the framework that is needed in order to integrate these components.

The *Experimental Designer's Workbench* (EDW) is an experimental platform on which a designer can develop and explore ideas during the various stages of the software design process. As discussed in the previous section, it was originally conceived as a means of testing out ideas about design tools and their roles in the design process, and especially those involving transformations between different design forms and viewpoints.

The workbench started off with the work described in [20], which included the design and implementation of the basic architecture of the MASCOT ACP diagram editor and devising the initial structure of the *Design Object Base* (*DOB*). The *DOB* is a form of *object-based* 'database' which holds all the information on each of the design objects, or components. It is discussed more fully in section 3.6.

A major influence in this work and in the early stages of developing the workbench was the MDSE [1] project [7, 5]. This was an Alvey project that investigated some ideas about the use of Knowledge Based Systems in design development. The EDW is in some ways a 'second go' at the MDSE, as we have made use of some of the ideas which it incorporated (as well as using MASCOT as the basic form of design description). A second major influence was the general development in design tool thinking that is reflected in Demo-CAEDE [19], which has similarly sought to support 'visual design' techniques.

We envisaged the workbench developing as a set of loosely coupled tools sharing access to a central 'Design Object Base' (the *DOB*), based on the UNIX philosophy of using separate processes to perform individual tasks. The workbench in its initial form (encompassing both design editor and object base as one monolithic process) had to be modified to conform to this, so the object base was modified to use the UNIX System V shared memory facilities, allowing it to maintain an existence as a separate entity. The design editor then became a separate process which could interrogate and update the *DOB* through its access procedures. Using this as a framework it then became a straightforward procedure to integrate further tools into the workbench.

3.1 The toolset

Currently, the workbench consists of a set of prototype tools, including two graphical design editors, the design transformation tool, and a static design assessment tool (the **Advisor**), each of which shares access to the *DOB*. The workbench architecture is illustrated by the schematic diagram shown in Figure 1. Originally, the workbench was developed on a Hewlett Packard UNIX (HP-UX)-based system using the HP-GKS graphics library. Current development is now being carried out on a Sun SPARC-Station platform, to which the workbench was successfully ported, and using the X-GKS library. This is an implementation of GKS which has been built around the X-Windows environment.

The toolset is intended to support the designer during the process of developing a formal representation of their *mental*, or conceptual model at an early stage in the design process, while placing the minimum degree of constraint upon how the designer organises this. (This is a similar philosophy to that used in the Designer's Notepad [12].) To achieve this, the model is first described using the MASCOT ACP diagram editor which results in a design form in terms of the identifiable objects within the system and its environment. Further elaboration of the design description can then be explored by using the State Transition Diagram (STD) editor, using a state machine form to describe the design's behavioural characteristics. This makes it possible for the designer to provide a behavioural description for each of the previously identified design components/objects (ie. each MASCOT system element can have an STD associated with it).

Using the design transformation tool this combined graphical design representation can then be used to generate the more formal description based upon CSP/*me too*. Note that is not necessary for all, or any, of the MASCOT system elements to have been further described using STD's for the transformation tool to be used, although clearly the quality and extent of the CSP/*me too* description will be improved if STDs are available.

The following is a brief description of each of the design tools and the *DOB*.

---

[1]MASCOT Design Support Environment

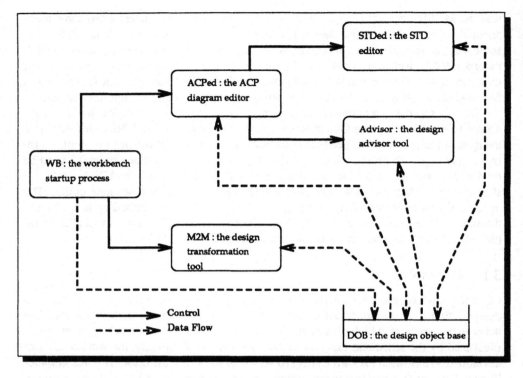

Figure 1: A schematic diagram of the EDW

3.2 The MASCOT ACP diagram editor

The MASCOT ACP diagram editor (ACPed) is a graphical design editing tool based on the MASCOT 3 design representation. MASCOT (an acronym for Modular Approach to Software Construction, Operation and Test) describes a model of a real-time system which contains distributed components and (potentially) many complex devices. This model is based on a network of cooperating parallel processes, using well defined interfaces.

Within the 'MASCOT machine' there are three principal components: a set of abstract concepts, represented by the system elements; a diagramatical representation of a network of system elements; and a runtime executive that supports realisation of the system elements and that provides support for their interactions.

There are three basic types of the above mentioned MASCOT system elements: the *Activity*, which is a single sequential process that performs the algorithmic functions of the system; the *Channel*, which acts as a 'pipeline' mechanism for the transmission of data (messages) between Activities; and the *Pool*, which provides a mechanism for giving Activities access to shared 'static' information. The only means provided for different Activities to communicate with one another, or to share data objects, are by using explicitly defined connections through Channels or Pools.

A MASCOT design is represented graphically by an ACP diagram (Activity,Channel,

Pool), which is a network diagram used to show the interconnections between the system elements.

The **ACPed** is an *object based* style of editor, with a menu and mouse driven interface. By *object based* we mean that the 'design objects' (in this case Ports, Windows, Activities, Data Flows etc) once created, can be manipulated either individually or collectively in groups, and are not fixed on initial placement, ie the editing space is treated as a set of building blocks and not as a drawing canvas. The user interface makes use of two main types of menu, namely *pull-down* menus and *context-sensitive pop-up* menus.

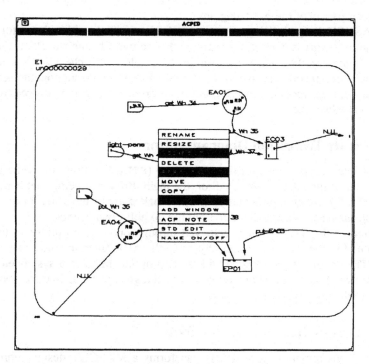

Figure 2: The ACP diagram editor (showing pop-up menu)

Pull-down menus are used for non-editing functions such as file handling, creating new design views, and invoking representation-specific applications (eg. the **Advisor**). They are continuously available via a set of pull-down menu 'buttons' positioned across the top of design editing window. An illustration showing the ACP editor in use is provided in Figure 2.

Pop-up menus facilitate the design editing functions and are *context sensitive* in the sense that the menu which appears depends on the particular type of object that has been selected, or where the mouse pointer is located when *clicked*. Selecting a particular design object will cause a menu to pop up that offers editing operations which are appropriate to that class of object. If appropriate, the options to invoke further design tools are included in these *pop-up* menus, as is for example the STD editor (see section 3.3). Other examples include provision for the future development of a *note editor* (to facilitate the attachment of notes to design objects) and a data dictionary description facility (to describe the forms of data used by design objects).

Alternatively, clicking on an area of empty space within the diagram will result in a pop-up menu which offers non-object-specific editing operations, such as the creation of a Channel, Activity or Pool.

It is worth noting at this point that one of the facilities provided within the ACP editor (as a pull-down menu option) is a pop-up static design display window, ie. without editing facilities. This can be used to display either the context of the subsystem currently being edited, or the top level of the ACP diagram.

As a MASCOT design is being constructed, checks are made within the editor to ensure that the diagram *syntax* is correct, for example that no two Channels or Pools are directly connected. At present, these checks are limited to simple syntax checking procedures and no attempt has been made to ensure more general consistency throughout the design. It is intended that separate tools for carrying out more extensive checking procedures will be incorporated at a later date.

3.3 The State Transition Diagram editor

The form of interface provided for the STD editor (**STDed**) follows the same basic philosophy as that of the ACP diagram editor, the main difference being that it is based on the graphical STD design representation [22]. It makes use of the same form of *context-sensitive pop-up menu* as the ACP editor, but has no pull-down menus.

Invocation of the STD editor is achieved through one of the options in the pop-up menus attached to the relevant design objects in the ACP diagram editor. By using this approach STDs are directly associated with the appropriate MASCOT system element and it also integrates of the two design editing tools in a logical manner. In effect, both editors will appear to the user to operate as a single tool.

3.4 The Design Transformation Tool

The Design Transformation Tool (**M2M**) transforms a MASCOT design representation into that of CSP/*me too* [9, 8]. This is an extension of the *me too* method of software design [4] and was developed by the DESCARTES Esprit Project, primarily for the design and development of embedded Ada systems. The *me too* method is concerned with the specification and development of sequential software systems and has been extended by the addition of CSP [14] to enable it to deal with concurrent systems.

Briefly, each MASCOT system element (ie Activity, Channel, Pool and Server) is translated into a CSP process and the data flows are translated into CSP events. For example, the Channel *Chan_1* in Figure 3 would be represented in CSP by:

```
Chan_1 = (    (sig_1_out  →  Chan_1)
          []  (sig_2_out  →  Chan_1)
          []  (new_sig  →  (Chan_1_reset  →  Chan_1))
```

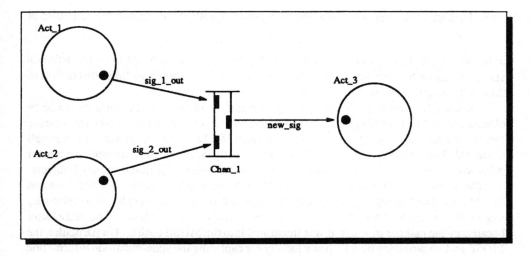

Figure 3: Section of a MASCOT ACP Diagram

Each of these CSP processes is represented by a *me too* module which has its own local
state, defined in terms of sets, sequences,maps relations, etc., and which exports operations
on that state. These operations are formally specified by the natural mathematical operations
allowed on the forementioned structures. In effect, *me too* describes each of these processes
in terms of its state and the operations on that state, while CSP constrains the ordering
of these operations. These processes are mapped on to physical processors and expected
execution times are allocated to the CSP events. The default processor/time configuration,
as generated by the **M2M** tool, can be easily modified manually if required.

Once a complete CSP/*me too* specification has been obtained, it is then used by the
CSP/*me too* interpreter to model the behaviour of the design using a 'state machine'
representation. This specification can be used to experiment with the effects of different
process to processor configurations and event execution times.

This process of design transformation and execution of the prototype is discussed more
extensively in [11], where there is an appendix providing a fuller worked example.

3.5 The Design Advisor

The Design **Advisor** is a rule-based design assessment tool which is used to comment on
the static structures of the design. It is currently invoked from one of the pull-down menu
options within the ACP diagram editor, and provides a report based on the current state of
the MASCOT design.

The role of a tool of this form was explored in the MDSE project. In this, we used a
Knowledge-Based 'Design Advisor' that incorporated three classes of rules:

1. Rules based upon the MASCOT syntax and semantics.

2. Rules based upon design theory and upon ideas about quality metrics.

3. Heuristic rules that were based upon experience with the use of MASCOT ('rules of thumb').

Since we view the third class as essentially being used to provide a bound upon the 'solution space' available to a designer, we prefer to term these *constraints*. A fuller discussion of these rules is given in [5].

The use of a general-purpose Expert System shell in the MDSE did not prove to be an efficient way of constructing such a tool. For the **Advisor** used in the workbench we have therefore used a more simple rule-based approach. So far, we have translated about half of the MDSE rule-set into this form, and it will shortly be extended to include assessment rules which can make use of the information provided in the STD descriptions of objects.

The inclusion of the **Advisor** provides a good example of the benefits that can be obtained from using the distributed architecture of the workbench. The relatively monolithic structure of the MDSE made it difficult to extend the rule-set of the **Advisor** because of the manner in which it was integrated into the MDSE toolset. (In particular, the MDSE had no provision by which any facility for capturing the state-transition information could easily be added to the design model.) By contrast, the workbench structure makes it relatively easy to add and integrate any further knowledge elicitation tools that might be needed for the development of the **Advisor**, and to add further structures to the *DOB* to support this if necessary.

3.6   The Design Object Base

The *DOB* is a database, in the loosest sense, which can be accessed by each of the workbench tools. It holds all of the information available for each of the design *objects*, or components, and it provides a set of access procedures which conceal the internal form of the *DOB* and act as the *object base* interface. The term *object base* is used in preference to the term 'database' as the latter carries with it many implicit implications of structure and characteristics which we are not concerned with at this point. Similarly, we have refrained from using the term 'Object Oriented' as it is increasingly being used, with varying interpretations, and hence is liable to lead to misunderstandings!

At present the *object base* is a simple text file which is divided up into four main sections, each of which contains its own type of data record. These sections are outlined below:

Access Interfaces   The intention was that there should be a record that would correspond to each *Access Interface* within the MASCOT ACP diagram. As yet, the *Access Interface* feature has not been fully implemented, and so this section of the object base is currently not used by the workbench tools. It was included as part of the initial object base implementation, because it forms part of the MASCOT standard and was implemented in the MDSE, and so has been included here for completeness.

Templates   A template record is normally associated with a MASCOT Subsystem and contains references to each of the Subsystem's components, including the *doors* which act as its external interface. The use of this feature differs somewhat from that specified by the MASCOT standard, where templates are used to facilitate the reuse of design components.

Objects Each record of this type corresponds to an individual component within the design. As well as the particular attributes of a given object, each object record also holds the information required to reconstruct the ACP and STD design forms. This includes information such as the data connections it is associated with, its parent object, and any subcomponents it might possess. Conceivably, an object record could contain any information (or a pointer to it) relating to that particular object, for example design notes or even outline implementation code. Tools to utilise this potential can easily be integrated into the workbench as has already been demonstrated in section 3.2.

Indexes The main purpose of the records in this section is to provide a means of referencing the various objects within the object base.

As the EDW toolset expands and the demands placed on the object base increase, it will probably become necessary to review its structure and form and to extend this to make use of more complete database management techniques.

3.7 Using the workbench

The EDW is started up as a single process which initialises the *DOB* and reads in a design, if one was specified on the command line (the *Workbench Start Up* process in Figure 1). Then, depending on the other command line arguments, either the ACP diagram editor or the Design Transformation tool is invoked. Ideally, the EDW start up process should provide a menu from which the required tool can be selected. Such a menu would be displayed continuously while the workbench was active, therefore enabling the user to invoke another tool while one is already being used, for example running the Design Transformation tool while the ACP diagram editor is being used.

4 Future Developments

In the preceding sections, we have described the general principles behind the use of the Design Transformation Technique, as well as the structure of the prototype design support environment (the EDW) that has been developed around this. In this section, we briefly discuss some of our ideas for further work, and in particular, we consider how these might be developed within the framework of the Experimental Designer's Workbench.

In terms of future developments in the use of Design Transformations, we have identified four fairly major themes that can usefully be investigated with the aid of the EDW. These are:

Verification of a design by evaluating it against the requirements specification.

Resource modelling in order to predict the processing requirements of the final system as it will be implemented.

Design Refinement by providing facilities that can be used to expand the *me too* structures in a controlled manner (including checking for consistency with the original design in systematic form).

Knowledge-Based Support can potentially be incorporated into the transformation process, making it possible to use transformation rules that are more context-sensitive in terms of the problem domain.

The next two sub-sections describe the first two of these ideas in a little more detail.

4.1 Design Verification

Verification is concerned with identifying whether the system as designed will meet the requirements originally specified by the customer ("are we building the system right"?). A major problem for verification lies in the very different viewpoints involved in the descriptive forms that are used to record requirements specifications and design specifications, since:

- the requirements documents are concerned with *problem*-centred issues;

- the design documents are concerned with *solution*-centred issues.

Not surprisingly, these often involve the use of rather different viewpoints. In particular, the requirements documents are concerned with describing required system *behaviour*, whereas design documentation is generally concerned with recording the *structure* of the intended system.

The distinctive feature of the design representation that is generated from our Design Transformation tool is that it is executable, and hence it can be used to model the behaviour of the system for particular scenarios. In matching the outputs from the modelling to the required behaviour specified in the requirements documents, the problem which needs to be resolved is how to match the information output from the *me too* interpreter to the forms used in requirements descriptions.

We are currently investigating this topic using a similar strategy to that used in testing code (although the context and form are very different). Our aim is to be able to use a requirements specification document to generate:

- the sequence of events;

- the predictions of behaviour;

for a number of scenarios, using some suitably prescribed format, and then to use the first of these to generate the inputs for the CSP/*me too* model. The outputs from executing the model will then be compared with the predicted results, in order to provide some basic degree of verification.

While the approach is not rigorous in any sense (at present), and inherits from testing techniques the problem of selecting suitable scenarios, we believe that it has considerable potential. In particular, it unifies the forms of description used for both specification and design, and hence makes some degree of comparison possible.

4.2 Resource Modelling

An important feature of the original MDSE system [7], was that it included a resource modelling facility that allowed a designer to produce predictions of likely cpu usage of the resulting system. This was considered to be particularly valuable for large systems and embedded systems, where such predictions are extremely desirable in terms of determining final configurations for systems. However, producing a model involved generating skeleton Ada code, which then had to be compiled and executed in order to generate the required predictions.

The availability of the high level prototype of the system means that by adding the facilities to attach resource usage estimates to the design objects, the 'execution' of a prototype can be used to predict the consumption of cpu and other resources in the final system. As with the original MDSE toolset, this can be parameterised to take account of a number of different models for the implementation form (for example, processor types, kernal characteristics and process to processor mappings). In particular, the model is easy to change, and can be refined in parallel with the development of the final design.

Adding this feature is likely to require the integration of a further form of editor (or making an extension to the ACP editor), together with some additions to the *me too* interpreter. There may also be some potential for including this performance information in the verification process described in the previous sub-section.

4.3   Refinements to the Designer's Workbench

The EDW itself is also undergoing continuing experiment and refinement, and in particular we are planning to:

- provide a *design animation* facility that will allow the execution of the *me too* design to be described in terms of the original systematic design forms;

- add checking mechanisms to provide consistency checking between the different viewpoints of an object and the expanded descriptions of objects;

- improve the user interface, so that the designer is not constrained by the tool in terms of how they manage the design process;

- adding a 'notes' facility that will allow the designer to append notes to design objects (the use of note-making is an observed practice of designers [3] and it is important to provide this to allow designers to develop the design in an opportunistic form [23]);

- provide a more refined means for saving and restoring designs.

Taken together, these will turn the workbench into a prototype that can be used for demonstrating our ideas on a reasonably large scale problem.

4.4   Related Developments

The EDW described in this paper is in many ways a prototype for use in exploring ideas about design support tools. However, even in this form it exhibits elements of many of the forms of tool integration defined by Wasserman [17]. (Platform Integration, Presentation Integration and Process Integration are certainly included, Data Integration is a lengthier objective, and only Control Integration is really lacking at this stage of development.) In this concluding section we briefly describe some related areas of work that are likely to lead to a more fully integrated system.

In the longer term, we are seeking to make use of our experiences with using the Workbench in order to identify the particular features of our present representation forms that make it possible to perform the various tasks required by the techniques that have been described in this paper. By associating 'methods' (or properties) with 'objects' in this manner, we can then seek to generalise the support for these techniques within the work of the GOOSE project (Generalised Object Oriented Support Environment) [2]. This is an externally funded project which will seek to take a more generalised view of design while trying to provide broadly similar facilities to those described here.

A related thread of work is connected with extending and developing our use of knowledge-based techniques in both the areas of static design analysis (as typified by the MDSE *Advisor* tool) and also of the Design Transformation Technique. Again, we hope to be able to generalise these ideas and to incorporate them into the GOOSE environment.

In that sense, the EDW is providing a valuable prototype that is operating within a specialised domain, which can then be used to help us construct a prototype for a more general design support environment.

We have argued elsewhere that the software design support environments of the next generation will need to contain tools that do more than just record a designer's ideas and check them for syntactic consistency [6]. A similar view is reflected in the work described in [19]. The work described in this paper is a further step in this direction, and it has already begun to demonstrate the potential benefits of using well-structured transformations for the development of a design.

Acknowledgements

Many people have contributed to the work that is described in this paper. Thanks are particularly due to Cor Yong Thed, who built the first prototype elements during his MSc project, and to Dr Mustafa Marashi and Mr Sam Nelson who provided ideas and contributions to the design and implementation of the workbench. Dr Robert Clark provided help with the development of the Design Transformation Tool. The support of SERC through the provision of a Research Studentship is also acknowledged.

References

[1] Special Issue on MASCOT. *Software Engineering Journal*, Vol. 1(No. 3), May 1986.

[2] Generalised object oriented support environment (goose), 1991. Three year research project.

[3] B Adelson and E Soloway. "The Role of Domain Experience in Software Design". *"IEEE Transactions on Software Engineering"*, SE-11(11):1351–1360, November 1985.

[4] H Alexander and Val Jones. *Software Design and Prototyping using me too*. Prentice-Hall, 1990.

[5] David Budgen and Mustafa Marashi. "MDSE Advisor: Knowledge based techniques applied to software design assessment.". *Knowledge Based Systems*, Vol 1(No. 4), September 1988.

[6] David Budgen and Mustafa Marashi. "Knowledge Use in Software Design". In Kathy Spurr and Paul Layzell, editors, *CASE on Trial*, pages 163–179. John Wiley, 1990.

[7] J A Chattam, R K James, H Patel, D Budgen, A G O'Brian, and M J Looney. MASCOT design support environment - final report. Technical Report MDSE/GEN/FR/1.1, Alvey Project SE/044, March 1989.

[8] Robert G Clark. The csp/me too method. Technical Report TR.61, Department of Computing Science, University of Stirling, May 1990.

[9] Robert G Clark. "The Design and Development of Embedded Ada Systems". *Software Engineering Journal*, Vol. 5(No. 3):175–184, 1990.

[10] N. Cross, editor. *Developments in Design Methodology*. John Wiley, 1984.

[11] Grant Friel and David Budgen. "Design Transformation and Abstract Design Prototyping". *Information and Software Technology*, November 1991.

[12] Neil Haddley and Ian Sommerville. Integrated support for systems design. *Software Engineering Journal*, pages 331–338, 1990.

[13] K.L. Heninger. "Software Requirements for Complex Systems: New Techniques and their Applications". *IEEE Transactions on Software Engineering*, SE-6:2–13, January 1980.

[14] C.A.R. Hoare. *Communicating Sequential Processes*. International Series in Computing Science. Prentice Hall, 1985.

[15] J. Christopher Jones. *Design Methods: seeds of human futures*. Wiley Interscience, 1970.

[16] Lawrence J.Peters. *Software Design : Methods and Techniques*. Yourdon Press, 1981.

[17] Anthony J.Wasserman. "Tool Integration in Software Engineering Environments". In Fred Long, editor, *Software Engineering Environments*. Springer Verlag : Lecture Notes in Computer Science No. 467, 1990.

[18] S. Patel, R.A. Orr, M.T. Norris, and D.W. Bustard. "Tools to Support Formal Methods". In *Proccedings of 11th International Conference on Software Engineering*. IEEE/ACM/CMU, May 1989.

[19] R.J.A.Buhr, Gerald M.Karam, C.J.Hayes, and C.M.Woodside. "Software CAD: A Revolutionary Approach". *IEEE Transactions on Software Engineering*, Vol. 15(No. 3):235–249, March 1989.

[20] Cor Yong Thed. An experimental designer's workbench. Master's thesis, Department of Computing Science, University of Stirling, Stirling, Scotland, 1991.

[21] K.J. Turner. "Towards better specifications". *ICL Technical Journal*, pages 33–49, May 1984.

[22] Paul T.Ward and Stephen J.Mellor. *Structured Development for Real-Time Systems*, volume 1 : Introduction & Tools. Yourdon Press, 1985.

[23] W Visser and J-M Hoc. *Expert Software Design Strategies*, pages 235–249. Academic Press, 1990.

[24] Pamela Zave. "The Operational Versus the Conventional Approach to Software Development". *Communications of the ACM*, Vol. 27(No. 2):104–118, February 1984.

A Methodology for Requirements Analysis and Evaluation of SDEs

Sanjay Dewal

University of Dortmund
Department of Computer Science
Chair for Software Technology
P.O.Box 500500
D-4600 Dortmund 50
Germany

Abstract

Nowadays software systems can be developed for nearly any purpose. For the development of such complex software systems appropriate software development environments (SDEs) are necessary as a "paper and pencil" development is intolerable. For a software producer the introduction of an SDE is part of the technology deployment process during which the staff must learn new methods, gain experience and knowledge by applying the SDE, etc. This paper focusses on a particular activity of the technology deployment process, namely the selection process (i.e. requirements analysis and evaluation of SDEs). The selection process must (1) produce selection results which are reproducible and comprehensive and (2) be repeatable and flexible in order to be applied for different software producers. We have developed a selection method which can be applied (1) for a thorough analysis of the requirements of the software producer, (2) for the evaluation of existing SDEs and (3) analyzing the evaluation results. For supporting the method we have developed the environment Requiem.

Keywords: Software Development Environments, CASE, Requirements Analysis, Evaluation, Selection, Reuse, Process Modelling

1 Introduction

Nowadays software systems of varying size and complexity are developed for nearly any purpose. **Software producers**[1] are aware of the fact that it is not sufficient to implement the software system, but also to perform a detailed requirements analysis and a design. As a development using "paper and pencil" only is intolerable, special software systems called **software development environments (or SDEs)** have been developed and marketed since many years.

For a software producer buying and introducing an SDE in his environment means that he has to introduce the methods supported by the SDE, train the staff for applying the methods and the SDE, etc. Such a **technology deployment process** takes a lot of time and increase in productivity and/or quality of the software systems produced cannot be expected for a short term. The success of the technology deployment is highly dependent on a "high quality" concept. For instance introducing a highly integrated SDE in an environment where tools such as editor, compiler and debugger are used currently will not be successful. A more convincing concept is to integrate the existing tools in the beginning and to add tools which support early development phases later on.

Thus the technology deployment process is performed repeatedly improving the current technology gradually. Within each cycle an SDE or parts of an SDE are selected (i.e. define requirements, evaluate SDEs, analyze evaluation results, compare software development processes (SDPs)), introduced and applied in the environment of the software producer and the deficiencies during the development are reported (see figure 1).

This paper focusses on a particular part of the technology deployment process, namely the **selection process**. Several high-level requirements on the selection process can be derived from the technology deployment process. The selection results[2] must be **comprehensive** and **software producer specific** which means that the environment and the needs of the particular software producer must be considered. The selection process can be applied **repeatedly** for the evolved requirements. In case a consulting company is performing the selection process it is highly important that the selection results are **reproducible** in order to exclude dependencies to the consulting company.

Existing techniques applied for the selection of SDEs are based on ad-hoc approaches like interviewing experts (see [5, 14, 18, 22, 23]) or evaluation of existing tools (see [12, 21, 2, 15]). The major disadvantage of these techniques are that (1)

---

[1] i.e. persons or institutions developing software systems

[2] the selection results are the requirements catalogue and the evaluation results of SDEs

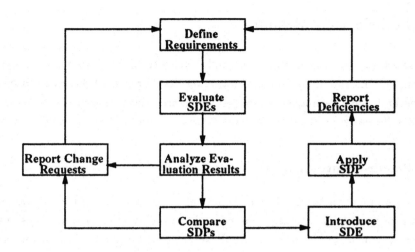

Fig. 1. The Technology Deployment Process

the techniques are applied once and can neither be applied for various software producers (i.e. not reproducible) nor repeatly for evolved requirements, and (3) it is difficult to guarantee comprehensive selection results.

We have developed a method (see [8, 10]) for the selection process which includes (1) the requirements analysis, (2) evaluation of existing SDEs, and (3) the analysis of the evaluation results for purchasing the most appropriate SDE. The definition of (1) a notation for the selection results and (2) a highly-incremental and flexible selection process based on the notation enables a consulting company to repeatedly apply the selection process and to reproduce selection results. Furthermore as various aspects of the environment of the software producer can be considered during the selection process the selection results produced by applying the selection method are comprehensive and software producer specific.

The rest of this paper is structured as follows. In section 2 we briefly describe the selection method. The description includes the key issues of the selection method as well as the particular process which can be applied. In order to provide appropriate support for applying the selection method, we have developed the environment **Requiem**. The architecture and some technical features of **Requiem** are presented in the sections 3 and 4, respectively. In section 5 we present some concluding remarks.

2 The Selection Method

The selection method consists of the high-level activities requirements analysis, evaluation of SDEs and analysis of evaluation results. For each of these activities particular methods have been defined (see [9]) which are briefly presented in the section 2.1, 2.2, 2.3. Some remarks on the complete selection method are given in section 2.4.

2.1 Requirements Analysis

The requirements analysis of SDEs is basically the definition of the software development process (SDP) currently applied and the improvements and extensions of this process planned for the near future. Several process models with various scope for describing such SDPs have been proposed. The process programming language (see [16]) or the graph grammar model (see [9]) can be applied for modelling and controlling the software development process. The formal process model FunSoft nets (see [13]) further allows to analyze and simulate the software development process.

The process models are not very useful for the definition of the SDP with the scope of evaluating SDEs, because elements such as pre- and post-conditions, firing behaviour, time constraints are necessary for the simulation, analysis and control of SDPs only and an evaluation of SDEs regarding such aspects is usually impossible. For the selection process a process model for defining the flow of documents is sufficient. Thus we introduce the **role model**. As process modellers usually connect with the term "activity" the pre- and postconditions as well as subactivities (see [6]), we preferably use the term "role" as a synonym. In the remainder of this section the role model is described briefly.

Role Model. The functionalities and/or tasks of the SDP are mapped onto **roles**[3]. A role is defined by a *rolename* and a *role description* which defines the functionality of the role, the necessary and produced documents, management decisions, non-functional aspects of the functionality, etc. The roles are the main vehicle to define subsets of requirements in the requirements catalogue. All requirements further called **role-based requirements** on the functionality of a role build a subset.[4]. The requirements may define various aspects of the functionality such as the particular functions, necessary and produced documents, management decisions, hardware and software platforms, integration and extension aspects, etc.

---

[3] Typical examples of roles are the Analyst, Designer, Implementor, Project Manager.

[4] For simplification reasons the definition of a role is extended such that a role consists of a rolename, a role description and the set of role-based requirements

The set of role-based requirements is further structured by defining subsets of role-based requirements called **requirements classes**. Role-based requirements of a requirements class define requirements on particular aspects such as necessary and produced documents, functions, integration aspects and non-functional aspects.

A role can be refined into **subroles** where a subrole covers part of the functionality of another role. The refinement of roles allows the identification of functionalities common in the software development process which are defined as **common subroles**. A typical common subrole is the version manager.

According to the definition of role-based requirements, the refinement of roles implies the refinement of the role-based requirements. Thus it is important to distinguish the importance of different role-based requirements. For instance the requirements on a particular software platform is usually much more important for a software producer than the 50th requirements on the functionality of a text editor. For each role-based requirement a rating which is a value within the interval $[1, 10]$ is defined for indicating the importance of the requested aspect. The rating 10 indicates that the role-based requirements is crucial, while 1 indicates a quite unimportant role-based requirement.

Checking the Requirements Catalogue. The role model allows particular checks within the requirements catalogue. The definition of the notation allows to check the syntactical correctness of the roles. The definition of relations between the requirements classes allows further to check the completeness of a role. For instance the definition of the **uses relation** defined between the role-based requirements on functions and necessary documents allows to check whether any role-based requirement on necessary documents have been defined and whether at least one function needs a necessary document defined. Otherwise such a document becomes obsolete.

For checking the redundancy and consistency of the requirements catalogue it is necessary to standardize and unify the terminology used. We introduce a term dictionary where terms (i.e. functions, documents, etc.) are defined using the method of conceptual structures (see [19]). The term dictionary is used for identifying synonyms, inconsistent usage of terms, etc.

Acquisition of Requirements. With the role model the requirements catalogue can be defined and checked. However, a software producer may not provide the information appropriate for the role definition. It is necessary to define how to acquire the appropriate information from the software producer. The acquisition includes the elicitation of the information by using various types of interviews and observation techniques. The elicited information is interpreted for identifying the terms and for standardizing the terminology of the software producer using conceptual structures.

The interpreted terms are stored in the term dictionary and used as a basis for the definition of roles.

The acquisition process is not only used for the definition of new requirements, but also for validation of acquired requirements.

Reuse of Existing Roles. The role model as well as the standardization of the terminology enables the reuse of existing roles. Reuse of roles is very likely, because many requirements are not software producer specific, but are dependent on the methods applied.

For appropriate reuse the roles are stored in a **global role library** (R-library). The software producer may retrieve roles by defining particular retrieval criteria from a global term dictionary or by navigating through the role hierarchy. As retrieval is based on viewing parts of a role only, it is important that the retrieved roles must be adapted, i.e. role-based requirements may be added, deleted and/or modified.

For enhancing reuse the quality of the global R-library is essential. For improving the quality it is indispensable to update and extend the contents of the global R-library. We ommit the maintenance process in this paper due to space limitations. A detailed definition of the various activities and cases is in [10].

2.2 Evaluation of SDEs

During the evaluation process existing SDEs are evaluated regarding the role-based requirements defined by applying the role model. For a software producer it is usually not sufficient to know whether a particular functionality is provided by an SDE or not, but also to know how "good" the functionality is. More precisely the functional requirements are evaluated regarding different **evaluation aspects**. Each evaluation aspect defines a particular view on the functional requirement defined. Examples of evaluation aspects are *user-friendliness, functional completeness* or *integratedness*. The evaluation aspects are defined in a special requirements class. This approach allows one to define the evaluation aspects for a potential software producer during the requirements definition process.

For the different evaluation aspects it is necessary to define different evaluation techniques. For instance documentation is sufficient to evaluate whether a function exists or not. However, aspects such as user-friendliness can be evaluated after a practical use of an SDE only. We distinguish two different evaluation techniques, namely **analytical evaluation** and **experimental evaluation**.

Analytical Evaluation. The analytical evaluation is based on any documents such as marketing material or user documentation. The aim is to evaluate existing SDEs on the basis of the documents available by using a bivalent measure only. Typical evaluation aspects considered are *functional completeness* and *integratedness*.

Experimental Evaluation. In contrast to the analytical evaluation the experimental evaluation is based on defining and executing a software producer specific experiment. Typically a part of the software systems usually developed by the software producer is developed during the execution of the experiment. There the experiment is defined by precisely identifying the different experiment steps which are executed sequentially. Typical evaluation aspects considered are *user-friendliness* and *performance*. The evaluation results of an SDE regarding role-based requirements using experimental evaluation are presented informally.

Aggregation of Evaluation Results. As the functional requirements are ordered in a hierarchy, it is sufficient to evaluate SDEs regarding **atomic requirements** (i.e. functional requirements which are not further refined). The evaluation results of an SDE regarding non-atomic requirements are aggregated from the evaluation results of the SDE regarding the atomic requirements. As the evaluation results of the analytical evaluation are mapped on a bivalent measure, it is possible to define a straightforward linear additive function for the aggregation. In contrast the aggregation of the evaluation results of the experimental evaluation must be performed manually, as the evaluation results are represented by an informal text.

The evaluation results of the different evaluation aspects are not aggregated, as it cannot be guaranteed that the different evaluation aspects are independent. Thus the evaluation results on an SDE of each evaluation aspect are presented to the software producer.

Exclusion of "unlikely" SDEs. Although many SDEs should be evaluated regarding the requirements of the software producer, it is sufficient to evaluate only "most likely" SDEs to the very detail. The ratings defined for the role-based requirements are used for identifying "unlikely" SDEs. The idea is that crucial requirements must be fulfilled by a selected SDE. This means that any SDE which does not fulfill a crucial requirement is regarded as "unlikely" and is therefore excluded from the further evaluation. Such crucial requirements usually focus on particular functionalities, hardware and software platforms, budget restriction and SDEs can be usually evaluated regarding the crucial requirements very quickly.

2.3 Analysis of Evaluation Results

The evaluation results must be analyzed thoroughly. In particular it is necessary to compare the evaluation results of the different SDEs. Furthermore the SDP defined by the requirements catalogue must be compared with the one supported by an SDE. For this purpose the functionalities, produced and used documents and the sequence of the functionalities are compared. A report is produced for each SDE indicating the particular deficiencies detected during the comparison. On the basis of the report the most appropriate SDE is suggested.

2.4 Remarks on the Selection Method

The role model and the processes defined for the different activities of the selection process allow to reproduce the selection results, to apply the selection method repeatedly, and to produce selection results which are comprehensive and software producer specific. The selection process is very complex and complicated. Figure 2 shows the top-level diagram of the selection process defined using Funsoft-nets (see [13])[5]. The boxes in figure 2 denote the activites and the circles denote the documents. Shaded boxes are refined further by a Funsoft-net.

Thus it is highly recommended to interlink the activities of the selection process and not to perform them sequentially. For instance a result that none of the existing SDE fulfills the requirements of the software producer, can be identified much quicker by interlinking the different activities. After the most appropriate SDE has been identified, the selection results for this SDE are stored in an archive. As the selection results of the chosen SDE describes the environment of the software producer after introducing this SDE, the effort of a repeated selection process is reduced by restoring the selection results and adding the evolved requirements.

3 The Architecture of the Environment Requiem

In the previous section we have presented the major issues of the selection method. Selections made for potential software producers (see [1, 3, 20]) have shown that the method is applicable. However, many data must be maintained throughout the selection process. For instance in [20] 300 requirements have been defined for a tool for the method Structured Analysis (see [7]) only. Five SDEs have been evaluated using five evaluation aspects. Thus around 1500 evaluation results hd to be maintained for each SDE. The huge amount of data and the complexity of the requirements definition and evaluation make it necessary to develop an environment which provides appropriate functionalities for applying the selection method. In this section we describe the architecture of the environment **Requiem**.

All components of the environment are integrated regarding the user-interface. In addition to the integration of the user-interface, data-integration is supported via

---

[5] Funsoft-nets are high-level Petri-nets.

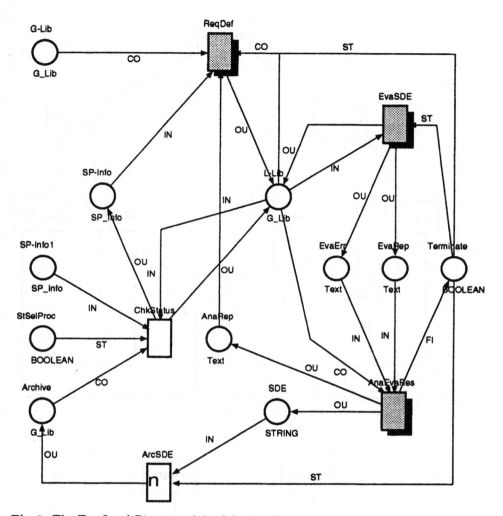

Fig. 2. The Top-Level Diagram of the Selection Process

a common database. All objects produced by the different components are stored in the common database. In figure 3 the complete architecture of the environment is shown. The boxes in figure 3 denote the different components of the environment (in the sense of modules), the arrows denote a use-relationship.

The common services are the user-interface (*X-Windows*) implemented using X-Windows and the database management system (*Oracle*) using a commercially

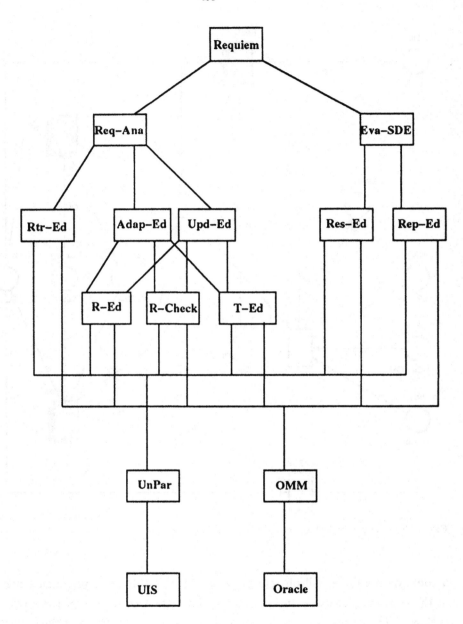

Fig. 3. Architecture of the Environment Requiem

marketed database management system Oracle. The user-interface is accessed by the different components of the environment via the unparser (*UnPar*) and the database management system is accessed via the object management module (*OMM*) which passes all requests of the components regarding objects stored in the database to the database management system.

On top of these components are the components providing the necessary functionalities for the requirements definition process and the evaluation process. A detailed description of the components is presented in [17]. In the following the functionalities provided by the different components are briefly described.

Role Editor (R-Ed). The role editor provides the functionalities for maintaining a role. Maintenance of a role means that it must be possible (1) to define a role "from scratch", (2) to modify a role, and (3) to delete a role. In particular it is possible (1) to maintain the role (i.e. the sets of superroles and subroles, as well as the rolename), (2) to view a role, (3) to maintain the role description of the role, (4) to maintain the role-based requirements of the different requirements classes, (5) to maintain the tuples which are elements of the relations defined between the requirements classes of the viewed role.

Term Dictionary Editor (T-Ed). The term dictionary editor provides the functionalities for maintaining terms in the term dictionary. In particular the functionalities provided must enable the requirements engineer (1) to maintain the terms, (2) to maintain the concept types, (3) to view terms, (4) to maintain the elements which are elements of the relations defined for terms and concept types.

Role Checker (R-Check). The role checker provides the functionalities for checking a single role or for checking a role hierarchy. The checking of the completeness of a single role as defined in section 2 is performed automatically.

In contrast to the checking of a single role, the checking of the role hierarchy cannot be automated. Therefore the functionalities provided by the component which support the requirements engineer must be appropriate and adequate for the checking task. For instance the component provides functionalities to navigate through the role hierarchy and to view each role. Furthermore the requirements engineer must be able to view terms defined in the local term dictionary in order to check the consistency of the terms used.

Retrieval Editor (Rtr-Ed). The retrieval editor provides the functionalities for retrieving roles from the global R-library. As described in the section 2 it is necessary to support the point retrieval as well as the guided retrieval. For the point retrieval the component provides functionalities for defining and executing queries. In particular it is possible (1) to view the global term dictionary to find the terms for the query, (2) to create a new query from already defined queries and (3) to view the roles retrieved. For the guided retrieval the component must provide functionalities for (1) navigating through the role hierarchy of the global R-library and (2) for viewing the role descriptions of a role.

Adaptation Editor (Adap-Ed). The adaptation editor provides the functionalities for adapting roles in the local R-library and the terms in the local term dictionary. The adaptation of a role means that retrieved roles can be modified or that a role can be defined "from scratch". Adaptation of a term means that retrieved terms can be modified or that terms can be defined "from scratch". The adaptation editor uses the components (1) *R-Ed* for maintaining a role, (2) *R-Check* for checking a role or the role hierarchy and (3) *T-Ed* for maintaining the terms in the local term dictionary.

Update Editor (Upd-Ed). The updating editor provides the functionalities for integrating the roles from the local R-library into the global R-library and for integrating the terms from the local term dictionary into the global term dictionary. There the integration of a role in the global R-library means that the requirements engineer must add the role from the local R-library to an existing role hierarchy into the global R-library. For this purpose the component provides functionalities (1) to navigate through the role hierarchy of both R-libraries (i.e. the global and the local R-library), (2) to view a role in the local R-library and (3) to maintain a role in the global R-library. Similar functionalities must be provided for integrating terms corresponding to integrated roles from the local term dictionary into the global term dictionary. The update editor uses the components (1) *R-Ed* for maintaining a role, (2) *R-Check* for checking a role or the role hierarchy and (3) *T-Ed* for maintaining the terms in the local term dictionary.

Evaluation Results Editor (Res-Ed). The evaluation results editor provides functionalities for maintaining the evaluation results for a given SDE. The component furthermore allows the maintenance of different evaluation aspects. In particular the component provides the functionalities for (1) viewing atomic requirements and assessable requirements of a role, (2) to maintain the evaluation results of the SDE regarding the atomic and assessable requirements and (3) to check whether the evaluation results of the SDE regarding all atomic requirements have been defined and whether all evaluation results of the SDE regarding all functional requirements refined from a non-atomic requirements have been defined.

In case an SDE is evaluated using the analytical evaluation, the component provides functionalities to define values (i.e. "0" for not fulfilled and "1" for fulfilled) as evaluation results. Furthermore the component provides the functionality for the aggregation of evaluation results in order to create the evaluation results for the SDE regarding the non-atomic requirements.

In case an SDE is evaluated using the experimental evaluation the component provides functionalities (1) to maintain experiments and to map each experiment step onto one or more atomic or assessable requirements, (2) to check the completeness of the experiment (i.e. are all atomic and assessable requirements covered by the experiment), (3) to maintain the evaluation results of an SDE regarding atomic and assessable requirements as well as (4) to maintain the evaluation results for non-atomic requirements.

Evaluation Report Editor. (Rep-Ed). The evaluation report editor provides the functionalities for maintaining the evaluation report presented to the software producer. Furthermore the component provides functionalities for viewing the totally aggregated evaluation results in order to produce and print the evaluation report.

Requiem Control. (Requiem). The Requiem control component control the complete environment **Requiem** and provides the functionalities for the invocation of the different components like the adaptation component, or the retrieval component.

Figures 4 and 5 give an idea about how the environment **Requiem** appears to the requirements engineer and the evaluation engineer, respectively. Figure 4 shows a snapshot of a session of the requirements engineer and figure 5 shows a snapshot of a session of the evaluation engineer.

4 Technical Details of the Environment Requiem

The environment **Requiem** has been implemented in C on Sun/Sparc workstations under the SUN OS 4.1.1. The current version of the environment consists of 70000 lines of code. As mentioned before we have used Oracle as the database management system in order to use a commercially distributed database management system which provides functionalities for parallel access as well as for security regarding system crash, etc. For increasing the user-friendliness of **Requiem** we have used the X-windows systems which is state-of-the-art and is widely accepted.

The current version of the environment **Requiem** has been already used to define several requirements catalogues. During the definition of these requirements catalogues we have detected several problems regarding the user-friendliness of the environment. A new version of **Requiem** which is currently developed will thus focus on the improvement of the user-friendliness by installing an improved help system

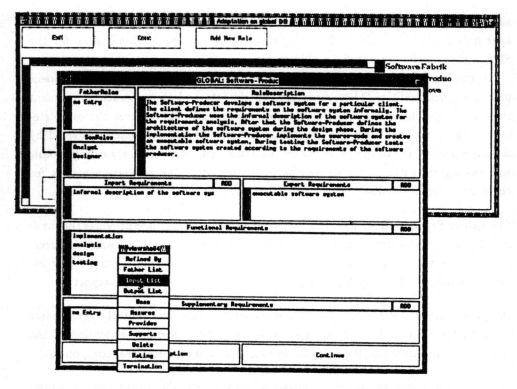

Fig. 4. A Snapshot from a Session with the Requirements Module Editor

and error handling as well as improvements of functionalities for the requirements definition and the evaluation of SDEs.

5 Conclusions and Summary

In this paper we have outlined the selection method and we have presented the environment **Requiem** which provides functionalities for applying the selection method adequately. The selection method has practically been applied for selecting SDEs for various software producers (see [1, 20], etc.). The practical experiments have pointed out that the selection method is appropriate for the selection of SDEs. Especially the possibility of reusing the roles from the global R-library enables the requirements engineer to support and especially guide the software producer during the definition of the requirements. The archiving of the requirements catalogue of a software producer allows the requirements engineer to consider the evolution of requirements of the software producer over a long period of time.

The development of the environment **Requiem** has increased the practicabil-

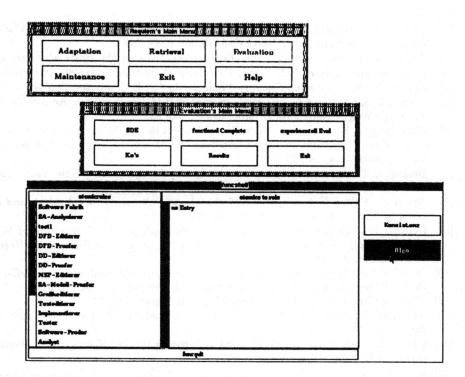

Fig. 5. Evaluation Editor

ity of the selection method, as the "paper and pencil" technique for applying the selection method prevented the use of all advanced features of the method. The first version of **Requiem** has been developed so far and shown that most of the functionalities necessary for supporting the selection method appropriately are already implemented and tested. The second version which is currently developed will focus on the improvement of **Requiem** regarding the missing functionalities and user-friendliness.

Acknowledgements Thanks to the members of the students group, Dirk Altenhoff, Christian Bunse, Hatice Carman, Mirco Gröger, Manfred Hübner, Martin Kampmann, Dirk Ohrndorf, Guido Quelle, Sabine Sachweh, Michael Schmidt and Paolo Secci, for their engagement in the development of the environment Requiem. Thanks also to my guides Prof. Herbert Weber and Udo Kelter for their valuable comments on the thesis.

References

[1] Albrecht, T.: *Evaluation and Comparison of several Tools supporting the Design*, M.S. thesis, University of Dortmund, to appear (in German)

[2] Baram, G., Steinberg, G.: *Selection Criteria for Analysis and Design of CASE Tools*, ACM Software Engineering Notes, Vol. 14, no. 6, Oct'89

[3] Becker, S.: *Evaluation of Software-Engineering-Tools on the Basis of a user-specific Requirements Analysis*, M.S. thesis, University of Dortmund, Jan'89 (in German)

[4] Boehm, B. W.: *Improving Software Productivity*, IEEE Computer, Sep'87

[5] Castor, V. L.: *Criteria for the Evaluation of ROLM*, Corporation's Ada Work Center, Air Force Wright Aeronautical Laboratories, Jan'83

[6] Cheatham, T. E.: *Emerging Issues*, Proceedings of the 4th International Process Workshop, editor C.J. Tully, Moretonhampstead, ACM SigSoft Software Engineer Notes, Vol. 14, Number 4, Jun'89

[7] DeMarco, T.: *Structured Analysis and System Specifica- tion*, New York, Yourdon Press, 1978

[8] Dewal, S., Kelter, U.,Stock, M.: *A Methodology for Requirements Analysis and Evaluation of SDEs*, ESF Seminar, Berlin, Nov'90

[9] Deiters, W., Schäfer, W., Vagts, J.: *Formal Methods for the Description of Software Development Processes*, Internal Memo of the Chair of Software Technology, University of Dortmund, Apr'88

[10] Dewal, S.: *A Methodology for Requirements Analysis and Evaluation of SDEs*, Ph.D. thesis, University of Dortmund, Department of Computer Science, Jan'92

[11] Working Group 8: *ESF Requirements*, Internal Report, Oct'87

[12] Glickman, S., Becker, M.: *A Methodology for Evaluating Software Tools*, Trans. on SE, Jan'85, p.190

[13] Gruhn, V.: *Validation and Verification of Software Process Models*, Ph.D. thesis, University of Dortmund, Jun'91

[14] Houghton, R. C.: *A Taxonomy of Tool Features for the Ada Programming Support Environment (ASPE)*, U.S. Department of Commerce, National Bureau of Standards, Dec'82

[15] Houghton, R. C., Wallace, D. R.: *Characteristics and Functions of Software Engineering Environments: An Overview*, ACM Software Engineering Notes, Vol. 12, no. 1, Jan'87

[16] Osterweil, L.: *Software Processes are Software too*, Proc. of the 9th Int. Conf. on Software Engineering, Monterey, California, Apr'87

[17] Projektgruppe Requiem: *Development of the Environment Requiem*, Final Report, University of Dortmund, to appear (in German)

[18] Schulz, A.: *Ein Klassifizierungs- und Bewertungsschema für Software-Engineering-Werkzeuge, insbesondere CAS- Systeme*, Angewandte Informatik, Vol.28, No.5, Mai'86, p191-197

[19] Sowa, J. F.: *Conceptual Structures: Information Processing in Mind and Machine*, Addison-Wesley, 1983

[20] Stock, M.: *Evaluation and Comparison of several Tools for the Method Structured Analysis*, M.S. thesis, University of Dortmund, to appear (in German)

[21] Troy, D. A.: *An Evaluation of CASE Tools*, CompSac'87, 1987, p124ff

[22] Weiderman, N. H., Habermann, A. N., Borger, M. W., Klein, M. H.: *A Methodology for Evaluating Environments*, SigPlan Notices, Jan'87, p199-207

[23] Zucconi, L.: *Selecting a CASE Tool*, ACM Software Engineering Notes, vol 14, no 2, Apr'89

This article was processed using the LaTeX macro package with LMAMULT style

Organizational Integration of the Information System Design Process[*]

Friedemann Reim
Fraunhofer-Institut für Arbeitswirtschaft und Organisation,
Nobelstr. 12c, D-7000 Stuttgart 80
Phone: +49-711-9702339

Subject Area: Information Systems Planning

Abstract: Design and operation of a distributed information system have to consider a dynamic environment of requirements and opportunities. Full usage of the power of an information system can only be achieved through its integration into the various interrelated design and management activities in an enterprise. Simultaneously engineering the entire design process is recommended. ESPRIT project COMANDOS takes an adaptive approach for the design and management of distributed information systems that allows the original design of the infrastructure to be modified as experience is gained and as user requirements towards the operating environment change. One tool out of a set of required tools is described in detail: DISDES - a tool for organizational design.

1   The Challenge for the Competitive Enterprise

Many enterprises consider information systems as a critical success factor. The advent of distributed information systems even increases opportunities for an improved support of business activities. However, it certainly also increases risks for the enterprise since the design and the operation of such systems are rather complex tasks which involve important new issues.

The design of the information system has to provide for continuous adaptation of the system to the task supported, to the business processes and to the organizational structure as a whole. This clearly calls for a well-defined coupling between the organizational design tasks, driven for example by a business analyst, and the engineering of the information system itself.

In the field of industrial product development this coupling of interrelated, parallel design processes is called *simultaneous engineering*. For the information system design and its integration within an enterprise this simultaneous engineering paradigm needs to be adopted. Sequential, more or less independently performed design tasks will not be successful.

---

[*] This work has been partly supported by ESPRIT Project 2071 Construction and Management of Distributed Open Systems (COMANDOS)

Simultaneous engineering leads to changes in the various tasks involved:

Configuration instead of new program development: Developing new applications will consist primarily of configuration, and only marginally of programming (cf. Tsichritzis, Nierstrasz (1988)).

Integration instead of isolation: The integration of the organizational and the technical design processes will be crucial.

Cooperation instead of self-sufficiency: The simultaneous engineering paradigm will lead to new ways of cooperation between the various departments and also change the role of the department responsible for electronic data processing.

2   The Distributed Information System Scenario

The emergence of medium and large computer installations throughout the enterprise will lead to an increasing demand for distributed applications. Increasing decentralization through powerful workstations, however, will be accompanied by an organizational integration into business processes spanning the whole enterprise. Available technology will decrease the cost for carrying out operations remotely. This opens new opportunities for the integration among organizational units.

Distribution transparency of the underlying information system and of the application neither will be the solution to the challenge of distribution nor will it be an independent goal. Most difficulties associated with distribution would not vanish even given full distribution transparency. Problems are in fact present even in centralized, sequential information systems. They become more serious in a distributed system (cf. Mühlhäuser (1991)).

Frequently knowledge about the application structure and behaviour can help to provide an optimized distribution service or can help to determine the location of users relative to application entities. This knowledge needs to be used for the design and the configuration of the distributed information system.

Approaches to organizational design and to technical design of information systems often are oriented towards a life-cycle model putting most emphasis on the early stages. These approaches tend to neglect the use and operation of an information system after implementation. This is certainly inappropriate when one is concerned with its continuing performance over a long period of operation. Distribution makes this problem more serious since the design of a distributed system is more complex. In addition, the dynamics of such a distributed environment tend to increase.

A distributed information system must be structurally responsive to changes in its environment and allow for a selective degree of distribution transparency.

3 The Design Tasks

Information system design often is viewed as a set of individual design processes. These processes differ in focus. They may take an organizational or a technical view. In distributed information systems also a specific view on security is recommended. Within each such process issues of an overall information processing strategy which, for instance, determines the desired degree of decentralization, have to be addressed. Based on this IP strategy issues of organizational structure, technology selection and its economy, installation and implementation have to be dealt with. The number of design alternatives is reduced when proceeding from IP strategy selection to operation of the system (cf. Figure 1).

Three types of design tasks are distinguished here: organizational management, configuration management and security management.

Organizational management is responsible for the appropriate design of the organizational structure, i.e. its engineering, which in turn determines the required functionality of the distributed information system.

The *configuration management* consists of hardware configuration and system administration which is more oriented to logical concepts than physical components. A system administration model comprises persons, users, groups, accounts, hosts, and home directories.

Security management has to achieve and enforce integrity, availability and confidentiality of information. For distributed information systems availability of information is a crucial point. Risks due to failure of system components have to be analyzed and evaluated.

All these design processes are strongly interrelated. A *simultaneous engineering approach to information systems design* requires a conceptual and technical integration among these processes.

Several methods and tools exist that support the design tasks for distributed information systems. However, no tool or set of tools covering the range from organizational design to configuration management exists that is integrated into the distributed information system itself, thus capable of fully exploiting its power (cf. Ness, Reim, Meitner and Niemeier (1986)).

Strategy of the company

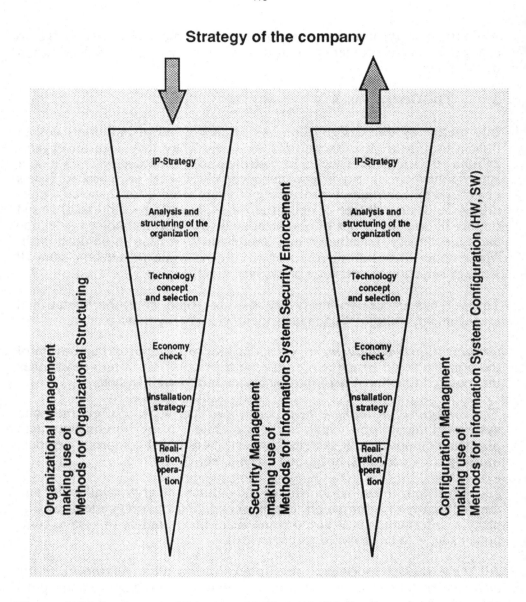

Figure 1: Major Issues of Integrated Information System Management

ESPRIT Project 2071 (Construction and Management of Distributed Open Systems, COMANDOS) provides an infrastructure and tools to construct and manage distributed information systems. It comprises a set of tools supporting management decisions on the general design as well as administration activities that transform these decisions into an operational distributed system (cf. Balter (1989)). The tools are coupled, thus integrating the various design processes. The basic management tasks supported by computer based tools are depicted in Figure 2.

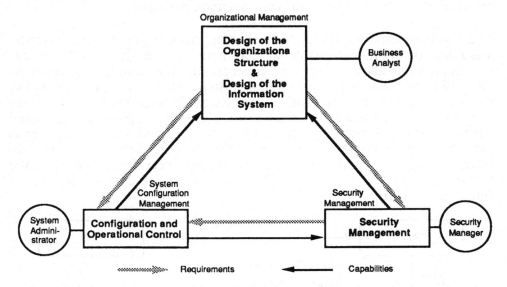

Figure 2: Basic Management Tasks Addressed in the COMANDOS Project

Two types of relationships exist between the management tasks: requirements and capabilities. The posing of the requirements sets the goals to be achieved by the other basic task and determines the major dependency direction in the hierarchy of the basic tasks. However, dependency is bidirectional because the basic management task posing a requirement must be informed about the capabilities of the other basic tasks in order to pose realistic requirements and to fully use the potential.

The organizational engineering approach of COMANDOS is described here. It refines the upper box of Figure 2. Other tools developed in the project are described in Reim, Meitner (1991).

4   Example: The Organizational Engineering Tool

The organizational design is based on a process-oriented view on office activities (cf. Bracchi, Pernici (1984)). Activities and processes are the basic elements for modelling the flow of office tasks. Actor-oriented features also are represented, thus allowing the modeling of capacity aspects. Figure 3 shows the model entities and their relations.

Activities are atomic tasks carried out by a position without interruption. *Processes* are sequences of a number of possibly parallel activities or (sub-) processes with a unique start and a unique end activity. *Positions* are the only organizational units capable of carrying out activities; they are held by humans. Relationships may exist between the entities. The *Control* relation represents the control flow between activities. *Supervise* poses responsibilities for carrying out activities upon positions.

The organizational model furthermore comprises *Organizational Groups* and *Persons*. In order to enable the configuration of a distributed information system, the above entities are conceptually related to the concepts for describing the distributed information system. This is achieved by typing the activities. The *Activity Types* - they also could be called activity classes - represent a classification of office work. Modelling at present is restricted software. Every activity type poses requirements (*Requires* relation) upon the software to be installed. Since this software provides a specific functionality, it is called *Function Software*. Every *User* known to the information system *Has A User Environment* which consists of a set of function software.

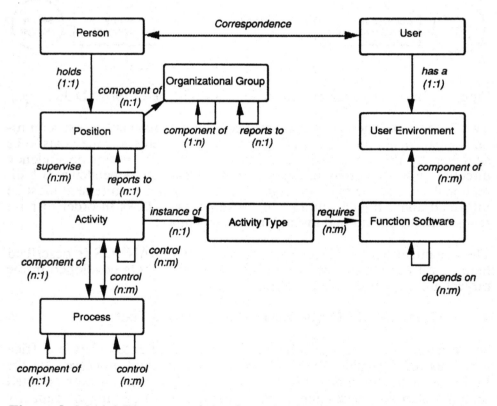

Figure 3: Model Elements of the Organizational and Information System Model

The modell represents the conceptual core of DISDES. *Distributed Information Systems DESigner (DISDES)* is a decision support system for the organizational designer / business analyst. His responsibilities include the selection of the information system components appropriate to support the office tasks.

DISDES has been implemented on a workstation. Figure 4 shows the logical structure of the tool.

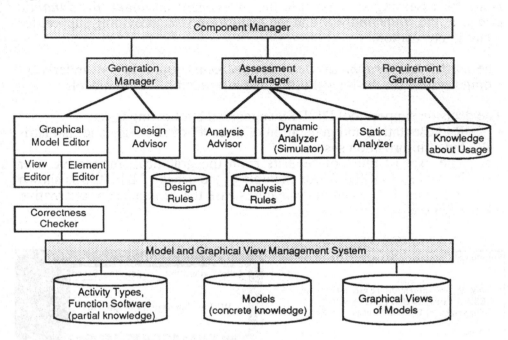

Figure 4: Architecture of the DISDES Tool

On the top level the organizational designer / business analyst interacts with the *component manager*. It allows to switch between generating solutions, assessing solutions, and automatically deriving requirements for the distributed infromation system.

The generation components support the organizational designer in understanding the problem, modeling, inventing and developing a better office and information system design. Representation and manipulation of an office model is supported, and active advise is given on how to carry out the design. The tool components for generating design solutions are the *generation manager* comprising a *graphical model editor* and an *element editor*, a *correctness checker*, and a *design advisor* which possesses a set of rules representing general design knowledge.

The assessment components support the organizational designer in testing and evaluating the solutions generated with respect to the goals of the design. They provide information about the quality of the design of the office and its information system by analyzing the model. Several ways of analyzing the model support a variety of possible assessment goals. Depending on the kind of analysis, different features of the model or different effects of its simulation are accounted for. The organizational designer then is supported in interpreting these results. The tool components for assessing solutions are the *assessment manager*, the *dynamic analyzer*, the *static analyzer* and the *analysis advisor* providing support for result interpretation.

The *model and graphical view management system* is the underlying storage system for the logical office and information system models.

The decision support tool DISDES supports the following tasks:
- Representation and generation of a model of an office and its distributed information system:
  The user of the tool benefits from the graphical, interactive user interface of DISDES. An example of the usage of DISDES is shown in Figure 5. Cut and paste features ease the generation of alternative solutions.

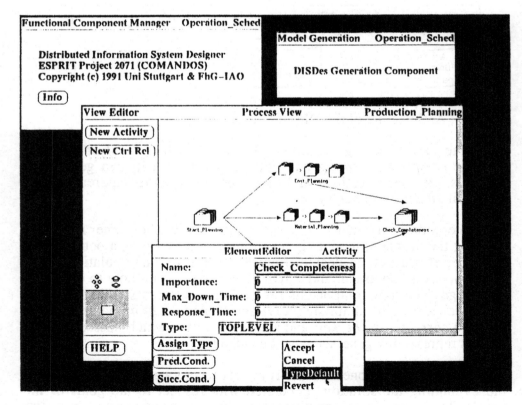

Figure 5: Screen dump showing usage of DISDES.

Figure 5 shows the generation of the model for the organizational design of the "production planning" *Process* in an enterprise. For the enterprise "production planning" is a generic procedure that has to be carried out frequently. It consists of various sub-processes, among them "cost planning" and "material planning". "Start planning" and "check completness" are atomic *Activities*. Arrows represent *Control* relations. Every element including the relations can be further described by attributes. The element editor is used to assign values. In Figure 5 the importance of the newly generated "check completeness"" activity is rated. Requirements for its maximally acceptable time of unavailability (down time) and requirements for response time can be stated. At creation time all values are set to "0".

The decision support tool DISDES furthermore supports:
- Assessment of alternative design solutions: The assessment components of DISDES allow the evaluation of the performance of proposed alternative solutions to a distributed information system design problem. The dynamic analysis is based upon a discrete simulation on the office model.

The design of the organizational structure and of the distributed information system has no direct coupling to the operational system. Coupling to the operational information system is achieved through the *Requirement Generator*. This component generates a specification of the required functionalities and gives hints on how to configure the distributed information system, i.e. by identifying the location of primary usage of software and data. Thus knowledge available during the organizational design process is made available directly to configuration management. The underlying model (Figure 3) allows for a selective level of detail - with respect to organizational as well as information system aspects.

In order to achieve this coupling the decision support tool DISDES supports the following task:
- Derivation of the required information system functionality including hints about expected usage patterns: To obtain requirements, DISDES needs tayloring to the specific enterprise. The function software components available within the enterprise need to be loaded into the the model and graphical view management system of DISDES (cf. Figure 4). This activity has to be carried out only once. When additional software is purchased this software component has to be added.
  In a similar way, a set of activities types has to be loaded into the the model and graphical view management system. The activity types represent a classification which is used to reduce the otherwise huge number of individual activities in an enterprise. It eases the assignment of software to activities. In principle, these activity types are

not necessary. However, without the types assigning function software to activities would be a prohibitively costly task.

In accordance with the CIM-OSA reference model this kind of information is called partial knowledge (cf. Stotko (1989)).

Figure 6 depicts the steps necessary to obtain requirements derived from the organization modell (cf. Reim (1992)).

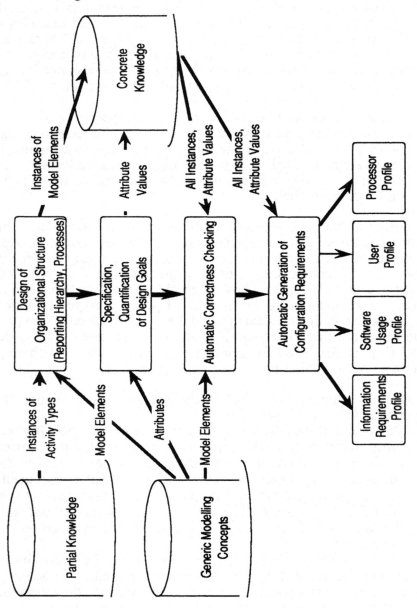

Figure 6: Necessary steps to generate requirements by using DISDES

Figure 7 summarizes the content of the various profiles generated by the requirement generator.

Information Requirements Profile	How frequently and at which location are the data accessed / updated?
Software Usage Profile	What is the intensity and the location of software usage?
User Profile	What users have to be installed? What access rights do they need?
Processor Profile	What proceesing power is needed in order to guarantee response times?

Figure 7: Requirements generated by DISDES

Requirements for security management are passed in a similar way.

5   First Experiences

First practical experiences with DISDES have been gained. In the following section the expert evaluation of one major application is described.

The tool has been applied for the organizational and technical design of the distributed information system of the service organization of a car manufacturer. Along with cost and quality, customer service more and more becomes a critical factor for their market success. The "computer aided service" supported by the *service network* will be part of an overall network that integrates suppliers and dealers with the manufacturer. The *supplier network* ensures just-in-time delivery of components and material. An *internal network* closely links research and development staff. Shorter product life cicles force a much closer integration with research and development of the suppliers. The sales organization offering several additional services such as insurance and financing needs direct communication with the manufacturer. The *distribution network* also is expected to improve the training capabilities. Figure 8 shows the envisaged network.

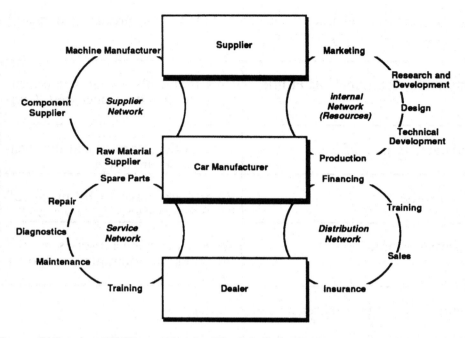

Figure 8: Integrated Network of a Car Manufacturer

A major German car manufacturer explores new ways for providing an improved service quality. The communication infrastructure for the emerging computer aided service relies on the wide area broadband network which currently is in a field test by the German PTT. It allows the local car dealer to use applications such as "online diagnostics supported by the central product development staff" or "online transmission of teaching material to the local mechanic".

Due to the capabilities of the communication system an entirely modified configuration of the distributed information system has been designed. Experts who manually, i.e. without computer supported tools, did accomplish this complex design task have been asked to "re-design" the service organization and its information system using the DISDES tool. They were then asked to compare the two design procedures and the results produced.

This comparative evaluation requires an in-depth knowledge of the service organization and of the information system. The number of experts available was very small. The results obtained represent a qualitative evaluation of DISDES. It was not possible to carry out a statistical survey.

Figure 9 summarizes the expert opinions upon the *effort required for applying DISDES*.

Criteria	Comparative Evaluation: DISDES tool vs. manual design			Comments
	Expert 1	Expert 2	Expert 3	
Turnaround time for entire design process	O	+	+	• No or minor improvements
Number of design alternatives considered	+	+	+	• Significant increase
Clearness of design documentation	+	+	O	• Significant improvement • Simple verification of relationships
Effort required to keep model up to date	+	-	+	• Improvement

Changes observed by the experts after using DISDES:
+ Improvement   O unchanged   - Deterioration

Figure 9: Evaluation of the Effort Required for Applying the Computer Aided Tool DISDES Compared to the Traditional, Manual Design

According to the experts, the turnaround time for the entire design process only showed minor, insignificant improvements. However, the number of design alternatives that have been considered during this time considerably increased. Also the tool clearly led to a better documentation. Modifications and adaptations of a design are more simple. Expert 2 in this case assumed that updates and, in particular, their documentation only occur in longer time intervalls. Availability of a tool might lead to more frequent modifications and consequently to an increased effort. In subsequent discussions he - as all the other experts - agreed that this results in a more appropriate, better design for the enterprise.

Figure 10 summarizes the expert opinions on the *quality of the results*.

Expert judgements for the quality of results achieved when using the DISDES tool show strong coherence. The level of detail has been increased for the organizational as well as for the technical aspects. Organizational aspects refer to the organizational structure which had to be modified to make optimal usage of the technical capabilities available. Technical aspects represent the requirements passed to the system administrator who has to configure the information system accordingly.

Criteria	Comparative Evaluation DISDES tool vs. manual design			Comments
	Expert 1	Expert 2	Expert 3	
Level of detail - for representation of organizational structure	+	+	+	• Higher level of detail
- of requirements derived for information system configuration	+	+	+	
Comleteness - for representation of organizational structure	O	O	+	• Improvement possible, depending on rule formulated by users
- of requirements derived for information system configuration	+	O	+	
Errors occuring in - for representation of organizational structure	O	+	+	• Significant improvement in particular for requirements generated
- of requirements derived for information system configuration	+	+	+	

Changes observed by the experts after using DISDES:

+ Improvement/ Increase   O no change   − Deterioration/ Decrease

Figure 10: Evaluation of the Results Produced with the Computer Aided Tool DISDES Compared to the Results of the Traditional, Manual Design Process

DISDES enforces the completeness. It also helps to detect and eliminate errors in the design. In summary, first practical experiences with DISDES are promising.

6 Status of Tool Implementation

Prototypes of several tools - not only of DISDES itself - and for services for system observation and control have been implemented on top of UNIX machines connected via Ethernet (Sun 3/50, Sun 3/60, Sun SPARCstation, Vax station II) and on IBM PC under MS/DOS (cf. Reim and Meitner (1991)). C++ has been chosen as the implementation language. For the graphical interface of the tools X-Windows and InterViews have been selected. A general and reusable structure of classes for the maintenance of object has been developed.

Research and development efforts currently address the conceptual and functional integration of available CASE tools. A major focus also deals with ways of supporting the design and operational control of business procedures.

7   References

Balter, R. (1989), Construction and Management of Distributed Office Systems - Achievements and Future Trends, in: ESPRIT´89, Proceedings of the 6th Annual ESPRIT Conference, Commission of the European Communities (Ed.), pp. 47-58

Bracchi, G.; Pernici, B. (1984), The Design Requirements of Office Systems, in: ACM Transactions on Office Information Systems 2 (1984) Nr. 2, pp. 151-170.

Mühlhäuser, M. (1991), Software Engineering in Distributed Systems - Approaches and Issues, in: The DOCASE Project - Part 2: Selection of Publications- Version 1.0, 1991, Digital - Campusbased Engineering Center, Karlsruhe.

Ness, A., F. Reim, H. Meitner and J. Niemeier (1986), Decision Support System for Planning and Design of Distributed Office Systems, Deliverable FHG-D1-T1.1-860829 of ESPRIT Project 834 (COMANDOS), Universität Stuttgart and Fraunhofer-Institut für Arbeitswirtschaft und Organisation, Stuttgart, August 1986

Reim, F. und H. Meitner (1991): A Toolset for Administration and Management of Distributed Information Systems, in: Human Aspects in Computing: Design and Use of Interactive Systems and Work with Terminals/ Ed. by H.-J. Bullinger, Elsevier Science Publishers, Amsterdam, 1991, pp 374-378.

Reim, F. (1992): Entwicklung eines Verfahrens zur rechnerunterstützten Gestaltung verteilter Informationssysteme, PhD Dissertation, Universität Stuttgart, 1992.

Stotko, E. C. (1989), CIM-OSA, in: CIM Management 5 (1989) No. 1, pp. 9-15.

Tsichritzis, D.C.; Nierstrasz, O., Application Development Using Objects, in: Information Technology for Organisational Systems/ Ed. by H.-J. Bullinger; E.N. Protonotarius; D. Bouwhuis; F. Reim. Amsterdam, North-Holland, 1988, pp. 15-23

A method for validating a conceptual model by natural language discourse generation

Hercules Dalianis

SYSLAB
Department of Computer and Systems Sciences
The Royal Institute of Technology and
Stockholm University
Electrum 230
S-164 40 Kista
SWEDEN
ph. (+46) 8 16 16 79
E-mail: hercules@dsv.su.se

Abstract. The support systems for conceptual modeling of today lack natural language feedback. The paper argues for the need of natural language discourse for the validation of a conceptual model. Based on this conclusion a suggestion is made on a natural language discourse generation system as a validation tool and also as a support tool in simulating a conceptual model. Various appropriate natural language discourses are then proposed in the paper. To conclude the paper a support system based on the natural language generation techniques of today and on previous working systems constructed by the author is suggested.

1. Introduction

During the construction of a large scale computer system, one should decide on the functionality of the system before starting its implementation. Constructing large computer systems is costly and when errors occur it becomes increasingly more difficult to correct them in later stages. Therefore a technique for modeling an information system has been developed, the so called conceptual modeling technique. This paper concerns the validation of a conceptual model.

Conceptual modeling is according to [ISO82] both a method for representing the user's view of the information and connect this view to the physical storage of the information that results from a system analysis. Since the conceptual model is described in a formal language the information can be difficult to understand for an inexperienced user. Therefore it is sometimes advisable to adapt the presentation of this information.

Most individuals are not well trained to understand formal descriptions, but every one understands at least one natural language, (NL). The advantage of using natural language is that a novice user does not have to learn a complicated language or formalism to understand the conceptual model.

Natural language is also justified to use because it will give the end users a direct feedback of the semantics of the formal representation, actually we will lower the conceptual barrier of the end user by using NL. Furthermore another advantage of natural language generation, (NLG), from a computer is that people who can help the novice user with explanations in NL very often are occupied with more important tasks. This is, for example, a well known scenario in large companies, so a self instructing computer system would help the novice user to utilize the system.

This paper shows why it is important to do a natural language generation from a conceptual schema and why the NLG should be in discourse form. A discourse is a piece of text or a set of logical interconnected sentences. The reason for the need of discourses and not single sentences aroused from the previous approaches of creating natural language descriptions of a conceptual model in [Dali89], where the constructed natural language generation system was critiqued for generating a set of unordered sentences. A discourse is also necessary to use to explain the overall semantics of the conceptual model, while each part of the conceptual model is related to one or many other parts of the model.

A number of appropriate discourses is proposed to answer the questions which are supposed to be posed by the users of a natural language generation system. The proposed discourses are analyzed with Hobbs' coherence relations [Hobbs85, 90] and a discourse grammar will be generalized from the discourses.

The discourse grammar and the methodologies of previous constructed NLG-systems, will be used to propose a natural language discourse generation system for a conceptual model. The generation in the NLG-system will be carried out at deep level and not a surface level, (To be explained later). The discourse is created using a subset of Hobbs' coherence relations, [Hobbs85, 90]. The discourse grammar is written in a Definite Clause Grammar, (DCG), grammar formalism [Pereir80, Clock84] in a Prolog-style syntax, where the formalism is extended with various Prolog predicates and features which controls the execution of the grammar.

Paper outline
Section 2. is a short introduction to the field of conceptual modeling and an overview of some support tools for conceptual modeling. Arguments for why these tools are not powerful enough to fulfill their tasks will be presented, then follows examples on appropriate natural language discourse generation for validation. Section 3. discusses discourse structure and text generation technology. Section 4. makes a proposal on a system for text generation which uses the technology in section 3 and a discourse grammar for describing the proposed texts of section 2.

2. Support systems for information and data modeling

2.1. The information system development process
The purpose of an information system is to store and retrieve information about a real world domain. During the construction of an information system various small problem can emerge. To avoid flaws in later stages of the information system development process, an information system has to be described at a higher level abstraction than at the programming level. For this purpose various high level and abstraction languages have been developed. One of them is the so called Conceptual MOdeling Language, (CMOL) [Buben84, 86].

A conceptual model, (CM), describes a piece of the real world, a domain, in an un-ambiguous and non-redundant way. A conceptual model is built and revised during a comparatively long period of time. Building a conceptual model of a system or an organisation is by necessity an iterative process ranging from a vague idea of what it will do to a full fledged system. But even when the computer system is fully developed new extensions of the system will be needed in order to cope with changes is the domain (real world).

2.1.1. Validation

The validation process checks if the constructed conceptual model is correct according to the real world. The validation process shall detect flaws and give suggestions for correction. This can be achieved by analyzing the conceptual model with expert systems, by doing consistency checking, to simulate the information system from the conceptual model or by paraphrasing the conceptual model back to the user for validation. The graphic representation of the domain is also a part of the validation tool.

Validation is one of the most important tasks in the requirements engineering, since the validation will reveal if something has gone wrong in the conceptual modeling phase. In this phase the domain expert will make his judgement if the conceptual model is the one he intended and that in respect to real world or domain.

A method of validation is to paraphrase the model into natural language, (NL). NL is a reference for all people involved in the development of the system. The paraphrasing is usually performed by the system engineer, but it would be convenient if it could be carried out automatic, so the domain expert himself could validate the conceptual model without having deeper knowledge in the conceptual modeling formalism.

2.2. A Conceptual model

According to [Boman91] and [Buben84,86], an information system contains a *conceptual model* and *an information processor*. A conceptual model, (CM), contains a conceptual schema, (CS) and *an information base* or a fact base. The conceptual schema describes the language used for reasoning about the object system and decides which statements are allowed to be included in the information base. The conceptual schema can be considered to be a *skeleton* description of the real world or domain, i.e. which entities possible can exist. The information base contains statements describing an object system i.e. the domain or real world. The purpose of the information processor is to enable users to query and update the conceptual schema and the information base.

A conceptual model consists of a static and a dynamic part. Certain rules concern the static properties of an object system, whereas other rules describe its dynamics. By a *static rule* is meant an expression, which takes into account only a single state. By a *dynamic rule* is meant an expression, which takes into account several states.

A conceptual schema consists of entity types, (objects) , relations, attributes, ISA-links, events, Static- and Dynamic integrity constraint rules and Derivation rules, (SDD-rules), and finally the information base contains instances, (facts). The SDD-rules are also mentioned in [Lloyd87].

2.3. Different support tools

A large number of support tools for conceptual modeling have been constructed. Some of them are called explicitly CASE, (Computer Aided Software Engineering), tools. What these tools have in common is that they are support systems for conceptual modeling. Examples on some of them are ALECSI, [Cauv91], RIDL*, [DeTro88], AMADEUS,

[Black87], MOLOC, [Johan90], etc. To carry out the tasks of requirements and design engineering, with the subtask of knowledge acquisition and validation respectively design and verification they use a broad spectrum of techniques as for example: natural language input, graphics, expert system techniques, simulating, concistency checking etc. [Kuntz89, Tauzo89, Wohed88].

2.3.1. Natural language input

Natural language, (NL), makes a system user friendly because NL lowers the conceptual barrier such that the user easier can approach the system. Systems working with natural language input and sometimes in combination with graphics are for example:AMADEUS, [Black87], a support tool which uses a combination of graphic and natural language input. Another system is ALECSI, [Cauv91], with its predecessor OICSI, [Cauv88], which supports both knowledge engineering and knowledge acquisition, modeling and validation and process engineering as guidance and explanation. But none of the NL-interfaces mentioned above has any natural language generation component.

2.3.2. Prototyping

MOLOC stands for MOdeling in LOgiC [Johan90], which is a prototype semantic database management system. MOLOC is a support system for conceptual modeling, where you can design and execute a conceptual model of a database. MOLOC shows how to do a fast prototype and testing without having to construct the real system. MOLOC has a graphical interface called MGI, MOLOC-Graphical Interface, You can design your conceptual schema in MGI, but the SDD-rules have to be stated directly in the MOLOC formalism.

2.4. Reasons for having natural language generation in conceptual modeling

To understand something requires a reference point. Without background knowledge it is difficult to understand. People are not tutored and do not gain understanding of a conceptual model, (CM), just by changing the model, there must also be examples and references, but of the systems discussed systems above, only the MOLOC system provides this. Further none of the above discussed systems has any natural language generation component.

Natural language is used by man both for communication and for reasoning. NL is for the brain, what the hand is for handcraft. NL is a tool which without there would not be communication between humans. We are using NL during a great part of the conceptual modeling process, and therefore it would be convenient with automatic NL input and output.

Many of the support systems are developed by different manufacturers and do not use a standard notation neither in the input nor in the output, therefore the validation would be easier carried out using a natural language generation system, since natural language is rather standardized.

The different users
Three groups of individuals which are using conceptual models and consequently could use a natural language generation system can be distinguished, namely: the domain expert, the system engineer and the end user. They have different needs and knowledge.

1) The *domain expert* , (DE), will need the model paraphrased to check if everything is correct represented, if all facts are present, if the concepts have correct names and if the model is logical.

2) The *system engineer*, (SE), is interested in the function of the conceptual model . The function for building a computer system. If the purpose of the model is correct.

3) The *end user*, (EU), wants to get a quick overview of the model to know how the knowledge is stored and how to navigate in the system.

Here we have separated three users of the conceptual model and three various types of information which need to be paraphrased into natural language.

2.5. Dictionary writing and knowledge acquisition
Domain experts maybe think they know everything in their area, but they have not structured all their knowledge. The process of knowledge acquisition and construction of the conceptual model, (CM) and validation of the CM will help them to structure their knowledge. Sometimes concepts can be merged together and sometimes they have to be separated. This is a typical conceptual modeling situation.

When the NLG-system generates a NL-description of a part of the CM for a domain expert, then s/he will discover that wrong words or concepts has been used. This explains why also the dictionary writing part is important. Another reason for the dictionary writing is important is the different users of the conceptual modeling tool will need to have concordance about the meaning of the different concepts. After this process the defined dictionary can be used for paraphrasing the conceptual model.

The system design must be transportable i.e. easy to adapt to different users and domains and there must be possibilities to define new words easily, [Grosz87].

There are various reasons for paraphrasing a CM to NL.
- To lower the conceptual barrier of the user.
- To ease the understanding of the CM-formalism for a DE.
- To give possibility for a DE to validate the model to himself.
- To ease the understanding of the domain for a SA.
- A method for detecting errors and traps in the CM.
- To focus on certain aspects of a CM.
- To have a reference language (NL) which the DE, SE and EU understands.
- To teach the conceptual model formalism for a DE or a SE.
- To introduce a newly assigned person to the domain.
- To give a quick overview in the beginning of the conceptual modeling phase where the persons involved in the modeling phase need to know what has been modeled until now.
- To inform an end user of a natural language interface to a database how the database is organized and which questions s/he can ask to obtain information from the database.
- The dictionary writing for the NLG-system will enhance the validation of the CM.

The generation will be divided and combined between generated information from both the CS, which describes the type of information and how it is stored in the database, and corresponding instances from the database. This combination will help both the design engineer to validate the CM and the end users to navigate in the computer system.

The natural language generation can do a sorting, selection or enumerating of e.g. subclasses, which will help the DE to remember if he has forgotten anything.

The generation from a CM can be performed at two levels one at a general conceptual schema level and the other on a conceptual model level where also instances of objects are used for explaining.

The questions which the system should handle
Here follows a set of questions and commands:
  • What do you know ?
  • Describe an entity type !
  • Describe instances of entity types !
  • What is the relationship between different entity types ?
  • What is the relationship between different instances ?
  • What events are there ?
  • What SDD-rules constraint the CM ?
  • Which entities types are affected by which event ?
  • List all entity types, (events, SDD-rules, instances) !

2.6. Various proposed discourses
Here follows examples on proposed discourses from both the author and from the users of the conceptual modeling tool MOLOC and MGI. These text examples should help the system engineer, (SE), the domain engineer, (DE) and the end user, (EU) in their various tasks. The proposed texts are written in *italics*.

These following proposed ideas are partly implemented on sentence level in AAIS-Prolog on a Macintosh. [Dali89,90] the sentence level translation has also been discussed in [Chen83].

The question types could for example by selected from menus, and the objects by pointing with a mouse on a graphical conceptual schema. The input to the question types could be extended with some limited text input.

Car schema

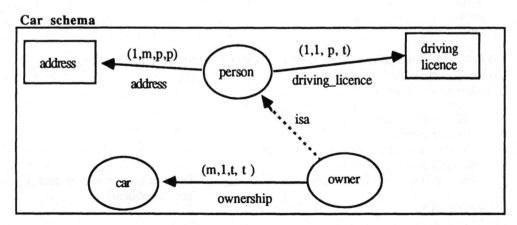

Car information base or fact base

```
person(carl).
driving_licence(carl,121).

person(lisa).
address(lisa,211).

owner(robert).
address(robert,311).
driving_licence(robert,321).

car(volvo).
ownership(robert,volvo).
```

What do you know ? (A sort of help function)
<u>What do you know ?</u>
*list all ***   (* stands for parts of the CM)
entity types
attributes
events
relationships between different entity types
relationships between different instances
relationships between entities types and events
SDD-rules
  Static integrity constraint rules
  Dynamic integrity constraint rules
  Derivation rules.
facts:
instances of entity types

List all [A] questions (The user will get an overview of the CM contain)
<u>List all entity types !</u>
person
owner
car

What-is-[A] ? questions (The user asks about an entity type or instance)
<u>What is a person ?</u>
1) *Some persons are owners*
    A person can have exactly one address
    and exactly one driving licence
    Carl is a person.
    He has a driving licence 121 and <u>no address</u>
    Lisa is a person
    She has an address 211 <u>and no driving licence</u>   (Informing about no existence of
                                                           facts is optional)

<u>What is Carl ?</u>
2) *Carl is a person.*   Facts
    He has a driving licence 121 and <u>no address</u>

A person can have exactly one address
and exactly one driving licence

Schema (This part is optional)

What does following SDD-rule mean ?
The Static rule expressed in MOLOC
inconsistent :-
     ownership(P,C),
     not(address(P,A)).

In Logic
IF P owns C AND
   NOT P has_address A
THEN inconsistent

The inconsistency is equivalent with that the static integrity constraint rule is false

3) *Every owner (person) who owns a car must have an address.*

What is an owner ?
4) *An owner is a person,*   Schema
  An owner has at least one car.
  Every owner who owns a car must have an address.
  Robert is an owner and
  has a address 311 and a car Volvo   Facts

What is Robert ?
5) *Robert is an owner and has a car Volvo,*   Facts
  he has an address 311 and a driving licence no 321
  An owner is a person and
  can have exactly one address   Schema (This part is optional)
  and exactly one driving licence

What-is-the-relation-between [A] and [B] and [C....] questions
What is the relation between a person and a car ?
6) Some persons are owners, who must *own one or more cars (at least one car)*

What is the relation between a car and a person ?
7) *A car can be owned by exactly one person, who must be an owner*

What is the relation between a owner and a car ?
8) *Every owner is a person,who must own one or more cars and*
                             every owner must have an address
          Schema   S-rule

What is the relation between a car and a owner ?
9) *A car is owned by exactly one owner.*

What is the relation between a person and an owner ?
10) *Every person is an owner*   Error in the ISA-relation
   (A person is an owner)
   Robert is a person and an owner
If the ISA-relation was in the wrong direction, then the NL-sentence above would be
generated otherwise the NL-sentence below would be generated.

11) *Some persons are owners*   OK in the ISA-relation
    (A person can be an owner)
    Robert is a person and an owner

<u>What is the relation between an owner and a person ?</u>
12) *Every owner is a person*
    Robert is an owner and a person

<u>What is the relation between Robert and car ?</u>
13) *Robert is an owner of a car Volvo*

<u>What is the relation between a car and a Volvo ?</u>
14) *A car can be a Volvo*
    A Volvo is a car

<u>What is the relation between a driving licence and a car ?</u>
15) *A driving licence belongs to a person who can be an owner who has a car.*

<u>What is the relation between a car and a driving licence ?</u>
16) *A car is owned by an owner who is an person who can have a driving licence.*

<u>What is the relation between a car and an address ?</u>
17) *A car is owned by an owner who is a person who can have an address.*

<u>What is the relation between a person and an address ?</u>
18) *A person can have exactly one (and only one) address*

<u>What is the relation between an address and a person ?</u>
19) *An address can have at least one person (living there)*

Events
Here follows questions which concern the dynamic part of the model.
<u>What events are there on cars ?</u>
   buy_car   Enumerating

<u>What are affected by the event buy_car ?</u>
buy_car affects:
      car
      person
      owner
      address
       and
      a static integrity constraint rule

<u>What are the relations between the event buy_car and car, person, owner, address ?</u>
20) *If a person buys a car*
    then he must became an owner
    Every person who owns a car must have an address.

Here follows an execution with MOLOC [Johan90] enhanced with a proposed NLG-system which gives explanation of what is carried out during an event.

The user executes an event.

<u>Which event to perform ?</u>
Let Carl buy a car VOLVO !
21) *If you let Carl buy the car VOLVO*
then the totality between attributes will be violated
A car must be owned by exactly one owner
Carl owns the car VOLVO
Robert owns the same car VOLVO

The user executes an event.

<u>Which event to perform ?</u>
Let Carl buy a car SAAB !
22) *If you let Carl buy a car*
then the static integrity constraint rule will not hold which says
For a person to became an owner of a car s/he must have an address
Carl has no address

3. Text generation

3.1. Discourse structure and analysis

Syntax and semantics of sentences have been well-studied and the syntax of a sentence is well defined. Previous constructed systems which generated natural language sentences from conceptual models are described in [Dali89,90], however, given that the information contained in a conceptual model is context dependent there has been a demand to describe the relationships between natural language sentences. i.e. a discourse which is a set of related and interconnected natural language sentences.

If we look at a discourse we know that the sentences there are more loosely kept together, than the parts of the sentences themselves. For example: if we mix a set of sentences in a discourse we would probably still understand the message but this would require a large effort and some information would of course be lost. A discourse which is easy to understand with less effort is called *coherent*.

There exists a large amount of methods for analyzing discourses and understand how sentences are connected. The main principle is to find so called key words or rhetorical primitives which are described in Rhetorical Structure Theory, (RST), [Mann84, Mann88] or the coherence relations of Hobbs, [Hobbs85,90]. The coherence relations, for example, relates two or more sentences to one unit, and this unit in turn is ordered in a higher hierarchical structure, which describes the entire discourse.

The assumption made is: A discourse is coherent if its sentences can be fit into one overreaching relation.

Here follows Hobbs' coherence relations:

Occasion relations	
occasion	a weak causal relation, a coherence between events in the world.
cause	special case of the occasion relation, the normal causal relation (keyword *if ..... then..*).
enablement	special case of the occasion relation, the first assertion enables the second assertion.
Evaluation relations	
evaluation	a meta comment, (keyword e.g. *Do you understand so far... This is good news*)
Ground-figure and explanation relations	
ground-figure	also called background, it is old information, background information, often time related and related to new information.
explanation	is an inverted cause, i.e. a proposition is caused by something. (keyword *because*)
Expansion relations	
elaboration	describes an object or event more in detail, (keyword *i.e. that is*)
exemplification	gives an exemplification of an type of event or object (key word *for example*).
generalization	a proposition is generalized, (keyword *it is well known that...*) it is the same as exemplification, but the order is switched.
parallel	two or more sequential propositions at the same level describing the same object or event level.
violated-	two different assertions gives two different results
expectation	a proposition is true but... (keyword *but*).
contrast	two similar assertions gives two completely different results.

3.2. Text generation technology

We will take a look at the state of art in the text generation technology to investigate what is possible to achieve:

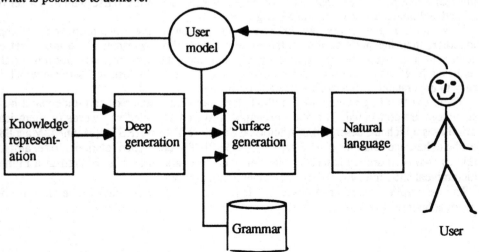

Fig 1. An "average" text generation system

3.2.1. Deep and surface generation

Many researchers consider the task of natural language generation from a computer to consist of two sub tasks, namely:

1) Deep generation
2) Surface generation

In the first sub task, the deep generation, it is decided what to say from the abundant knowledge base. The planning and organization of the information content is determined. Next it is concluded in what form it should be presented according to a specific user model. In which order should the sentences be generated to make the text coherent. The deep generation in a computer must make similar steps as when a human generates text. During the second sub task, the surface generation, it has to be decided how to say it, i.e. the realization of the syntactic structures. Moreover a selection of the lexical items appropriate to express the content has to be made. This paper concerns the first subtask the deep generation component of the natural language generation system.

3.2.2. Deep generation

No one has yet enumerated the kind of tasks a text planner should be able to do, but some of the problems are known. One problem is the content determination, i.e. to select what to say of the abundant information in a knowledge base. A partial solution to this problem is dependent on the question and the knowledge level of the user.

There is various approaches for solving these problems, for example **discourse strategies**. They are usually schema based or have a ready text plan to be used for generation. An example on this in the system **TEXT** by McKeown, [McKeo85a,85b].

To build the system TEXT McKeown had to analyze great deal of text written for the three purposes of *defining, comparing* and *describing* different objects. In the texts she found four rhetorical predicates and with these four rhetorical primitives McKeown defined four different schemas. These schemas can be used for answering three types of meta-questions about the contents in a data base.These three types of questions or commands are:

1) How is an object defined ?
2) What is the difference between two objects ?
3) Describe available information !

A second approach to constrain the knowledge base is **planning and reasoning**, which is concerned with manipulating a knowledge representation with a set of rules to achieve a goal. A possibility is to have a cooperative dialogue with a user which adds knowledge to the system and constrains the knowledge base, an example on this is the system KAMP, Knowledge And Modality Planner, by Appelt, [Appelt85].

The third approach in constraining the knowledge base is by utilizing a **user model**. One problem in natural language generation is to know on what level the user is and what type and organization of the text is needed for understanding the text message. One method is to have different user models of different users and generate a text which is adapted to that model. Paris has in [Paris85,88] described different strategies of generation depending on the knowledge level of the user. Paris studied two different types of encyclopedias written for adults and for children. She discovered that texts made for the adults describe all the parts of the objects, while in the texts written for the children the function, i.e procedural information, of the objects is explained. Moreover in the children encyclopedias the complete chain of inferences is described and there is more redundancies than in the text for the adults. Many times an expert can be a novice in one part of the domain, or vice versa, a novice can be expert in some other part of the domain. Therefore it is necessary to adapt to this type of users. Various methods for acquiring a user model and applying it to a text generation system for conceptual modeling are described in [Dali91].

3.3. Problem and hypothesis

A conceptual model is a passive and non-redundant and non-ambiguous representation of the real world which can partly be drawn in graphics, but there are parts like the SDD-rules and the fact base which can not be drawn. There is also a set of complicated dependencies between different parts of the conceptual model. The problem for many users of the conceptual models is to have an overview and understanding the represented concepts, therefore it seems obvious to translate the model into natural language. Since the conceptual model is heavily dependent on all its parts it seems appropriate to have a natural language discourse generation. This can be achieved by connecting each part of the conceptual model with the coherence relations of Hobbs [Hobbs85,90]. This will make the natural language generation produced from the system coherent and easily read.

A technique for natural language generation is available and the problem is to find what parts of the conceptual model corresponds to which coherence relations. The sentence level generation has already been carried out by the author and described in [Dali89,90].

4. System overview

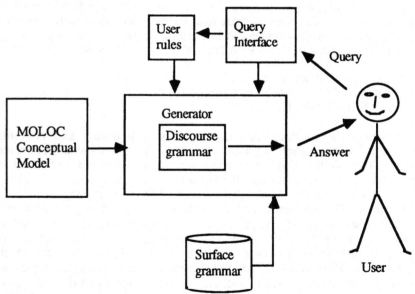

Fig 2. Overview of the proposed natural language generation system

The system is built around three modules: *the user rules, discourse* and *surface grammar*, with a query interface which processes the question input from the user. The query interface passes the processed input both to the user module and to the generator. The user module will find the intentional goals of the user and at what level the user is by the way

module will find the intentional goals of the user and at what level the user is by the way s/he is asking questions, this is described in [Dali91]. This information together with the query from the user will also answer to the user's first intention: to reply to the user's question by making a selection of information from the knowledge base.

The generation is carried out in three steps:
1) The user rules: Find out what the user knows and builds a dynamic user model which helps to select the correct information from the conceptual model.
2) The discourse grammar: Builds a discourse structure from the selected information. The discourse structure should fulfil the intentions and goals of the user.
3) The surface grammar is not described here. It is at a syntactic level and belongs to the surface generation.

4.1. Extracting discourse grammar rules.
An example on how the discourse grammar rules are defined from one of the previous proposed examples.

> What is a person ?
> 1) Some persons are owners
> 2) A person can have exactly one address and
> 3) (A person can have) exactly one driving licence
> 4) Carl is a person.
> 5) He has a driving licence 121
> (6) and (he has) no address)
> 7) Lisa is a person
> 8) She has an address 211
> (9) and (She has)no driving licence)

Gives following discourse tree:

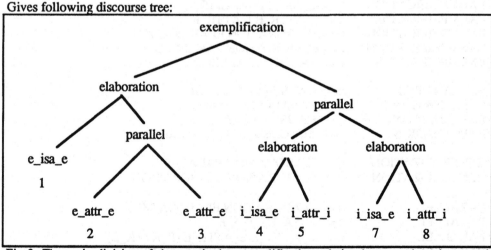

Fig 3. The main division of the text is the exemplification relation between the schema and instance level. The schema leaf is divided by the elaboration relation which elaborates the ISA relation into two equivalent attribute statements related by a parallel relation. In the instance leaf we find a parallel relation which describes two pieces of a discourse at the same level. Each discourse is described by an elaboration relation which elaborates an ISA-statement into an

attribute statement at instance level. (The numbers in the discourse tree corresponds to each sentence above).

Discourse grammar
The following discourse grammar will transform a piece of a conceptual model to a discourse structure which then easily can be transformed to a text by a surface generator. The discourse grammar below is defined according to the example and method above, from the previous proposed examples and from some other examples as well.

The representation below in Backus-Naur form or a Context Free Grammar.

{} means that something is optional. I means or ( )* means none, one or many times.

Top level

DISCOURSE	::== EXEMPLIFICATION	
DISCOURSE	::== {GENERALIZATION}	(optional)
DISCOURSE	::== ELABORATION {GENERALIZATION}	
DISCOURSE	::== CAUSE	
DISCOURSE	::== EXPLANATION	

Rest

ELABORATION	::== E_ISA_E PARALLEL
ELABORATION	::== I_ISA_E PARALLEL
ELABORATION	::== I_ISA_E I_ATTR_I
ELABORATION	::== E_ISA_E E_ATTR_E
ELABORATION	::== E_ATTR_E ELABORATION
ELABORATION	::== EVENT_NAME CAUSE
ELABORATION	::== PARALLEL EXPLANATION
ELABORATION	::== PARALLEL PARALLEL

EXEMPLIFICATION	::== E_ISA_E PARALLEL
EXEMPLIFICATION	::== E_ATTR_E I_ATTR_E
EXEMPLIFICATION	::== ELABORATION ELABORATION
EXEMPLIFICATION	::== ELABORATION PARALLEL
EXEMPLIFICATION	::== CAUSE PARALLEL

EXPLANATION	::== CAUSE ELABORATION
EXPLANATION	::== PARALLEL E_ISA_E
EXPLANATION	::== CAUSE I_ATTR_I
EXPLANATION	::== SUCCEED_FAIL S_RULE

GENERALIZATION	::== ELABORATION PARALLEL
GENERALIZATION	::== ELABORATION ELABORATION

PARALLEL	::== ELABORATION ELABORATION
PARALLEL	::== I_ISA_E I_ISA_E
PARALLEL	::== E_ATTR_E E_ATTR_E (E_ATTR_E)*
PARALLEL	::== E_ATTR_E E_ATTR_E (CAUSE)*
PARALLEL	::== I_ATTR_I I_ATTR_I (I_ATTR_I)*
PARALLEL	::== S_RULE S_RULE
PARALLEL	::== PRECONDITION PRECONDITION

CAUSE	::== E_ISA_E S_RULE

CAUSE	::== E_ATTR_E S_RULE
CAUSE	::== E_ATTR_E E_ISA_E
CAUSE	::== EVENT EXPLANATION
CAUSE	::== PARALLEL S_RULE
CAUSE	::== ELABORATION S_RULE

Terminals are sentences or parts of the CM

E_ISA_E	::== ENTITY TYPE1 ISA ENTITY TYPE2 (schema)
I_ISA_E	::== INSTANCE ISA ENTITY TYPE (mixed)
E_ATTR_E	::== ENTITY TYPE1 ATTR ENTITY TYPE2
I_ATTR_E	::== INSTANCE ATTR ENTITY TYPE
I_ATTR_I	::== INSTANCE ATTR ENTITY TYPE
EVENT	::== event name or type of event
PRECONDITION	::== precondition in an event
(SUCCEED_FAIL)	::== (the rule will succeed)l(the rule will not hold)
(SUCCEED_FAIL)	::== (the attributes will hold)l(the attributes will not hold)
S_RULE	::== (STATIC l DYNAMIC) rule
D-RULE	::== DEDUCTION rule

The above discourse grammar describes the connection between a conceptual model and a discourse form. This means that a question of the user together with the available conceptual model will create a discourse according to Hobbs classification of discourse structure.

The discourse grammar is almost executable as it stands in Prolog, only some minor syntactic changes are needed. The problem is then that the grammar will overgenerate and that it does not have a control mechanism. This control mechanism will be created by using the same method which was used for analysing the discourses and by implementing features and control predicates.

4.2. The implementation language is Prolog
The implementation language for the different already programmed parts is Prolog, which is well-suited both for parsing and for generation of natural language. The reason for this is that Prolog was developed for doing natural language research. Prolog is also well suited for fast prototyping specially for natural language processing due to its modularity. Today a large number of compatible Edinburgh syntax Prologs are available, e.g. SICStus, Quintus, Arity and AAIS Prolog for UNIX, MS-DOS, OS/2 and for the Macintosh operating system. Prologs which can be both interpreted and compiled and are fast and efficient and which can call or be called from other programming languages such as C or Pascal.

4.3. The discourse grammar and the control of the generation
A draft implementation using a subset of the discourse grammar has been carried out. The discourse grammar is a so called Definite Clause Grammar, DCG, grammar, [Pereir80, Clock84], and is executed and controlled by the Prolog interpreter. The execution of the grammar is performed backwards. The terminals consists of the selected information for each question. Each terminal consists of a single sentence at either schema, instance or mixed level. Further more various *features* and *predicates* of the grammar are implemented for controlling the generation.
The *features* with the values i,e,r,_ for describing entity types and instances of them.
     i stands for instance level

e for entity type or schema level

r for rule

_ for the anonymous variable or irrelevant.

The coherence relation *exemplification* extended with features is an example of the above control of the grammar. Exemplification is a divider between explanation at the schema level, and explanation at the instance level i.e.features entity type e or instance i. An other example is the *elaboration* relation which can be performed both at schema and instance level, but it has to be kept either of the ways. This both cases can be seen in the extract of the discourse grammar below.

Predicates

The predicate, *not_occur/2*, checks whether any part of the terminals are used more than once for generation, i.e. none of the terminals occur more than once in the discourse tree. The predicate *same/2*. is used to check if two clauses has any connection to each other at all, for example in elaboration. For example: to talk about same entities.

When a piece of discourse tree is generated it is checked for not violating the generation rules.

Extract from the discourse grammar which generates the discourse below

```
discourse(exemplification(E))
        --> exemplification(_,E).
exemplification(_,(elaboration(E) & parallel(P)))
        --> elaboration(e,E), parallel(i,P),{not_occur(E,P),!}
elaboration(i,i_isa_e(I1) & i_attr_i(I2))
        --> [I1,I2],{i_isa_e(I1), i_attr_i(I2),not_occur(I1,I2),same(I1,I2)}.
elaboration(i,i_isa_e(I) & parallel(P))
        --> [I],{i_isa_e(I) , parallel(i,P),not_occur(I,P)} .
parallel(e,(e_attr_e(E1) & e_attr_e(E2)))
        --> [E1,E2],{e_attr_e(E1), e_attr_e(E2),not_occur(E1,E2),same(E1,E2)}.
parallel(i,elaboration(I1) & elaboration(I2))
        --> elaboration(i,I1), elaboration(i,I2),{not_occur(I1,I2),!}.
```

Example on a generation

```
Question: What is a person ?

?- list_db.                              selected sentences
[some,persons,are,owners]
[carl,is,a,person]
[lisa,is,a,person]
[carl,has,an,driving_licence,121]
[lisa,has,an,address,211]
[a,person,can,have,exactly,one,address]
[a,person,can,have,exactly,one,driving_licence]
   yes

?- discourse(TREE,NL).
   TREE = exemplification(elaboration(e_isa_e(
                          [some,persons,are,owners])
                          &
                          parallel(
```

```
                                    [a,person,can,have,
                                     exactly,one,address])
                                &
                                e_attr_e(
                                    [a,person,can,have,
                                     exactly,one,
                                     driving_licence])))
                        &
                    parallel(elaboration(
                            i_isa_e([carl, (is),a,
                                    person]) &
                            i_attr_i(
                                [carl,has,a,
                                 driving_licence,121]))
                            &
                            elaboration(
                                i_isa_e([lisa, (is),a,
                                        person]) &
                                i_attr_i(
                                [lisa,has,an,address,
                                 211])))),
    discourse 1)
        NL =    [[some,persons,are,owners],
                [a,person,can,have,exactly,one,address],
                [a,person,can,have,exactly,one,driving_licence],
                [carl, (is),a,person],[carl,has,a,driving_licence,121],
                [lisa, (is),a,person],[lisa,has,an,address,211]]
```

The example above gives an idea how it would technically be possible to achieve the above proposal and how the discourse tree would look like.

5.Conclusions

Support tools for conceptual modeling lack natural language generation functions. In this paper we have argued for the need of natural language generation as a support tool for conceptual modeling.

   The paper proposes a set of appropriate questions which could be posed by the user and a set of suitable natural language discourses to answer these questions. From the proposed discourses a discourse grammar is generalized. The discourse grammar connects a conceptual model to a discourse structure. A natural language generation system built on this grammar is suggested. The goal of the system is to improve the validation of a conceptual model.

   The purpose of a natural language discourse is to answer a question to a user in a more satisfying and contextual sensitive way than a single sentence or a set of unordered sentences would. We know that natural language lowers the conceptual barrier for the user and that a natural language discourse gives a better comprehension, since the receiver of the discourse when reading the linear text will try to identify the higher order structure of the text, according to [Ander85], and consequently the conceptual model.

Future research will be to implement the proposed system and to extend the grammar for more cases and then test the system to determine which discourse structures the users require.

I would conclude with: Interpreted data gives information, reasoning about information gives knowledge and knowledge expressed in natural language gives understanding !

Acknowledgements

I would like to thank my advisor Carl Gustaf Jansson and my thesis committee: Janis Bubenko, Carl Brown and Östen Dahl for generously contributing of their knowledge in their fields and for their valuable comments. I would also like to thank Paul Johannesson and Rolf Wohed and others in the SYSLAB research group for interesting discussions which contributed to this paper and also, thank you, Stewart Kowalski for commenting on the English.

References

Ander85	J.R. Anderson: Cognitive Psychology and Its Implications, Carnegie-Mellon University, W.H. Freeman and Company 1985.
Appelt85	D.E. Appelt: Planning English Sentences, Cambridge University Press 1985.
Black87	W.J.Black: Acquisition of Conceptual Data Models from Natural Language Descriptions, In The Proceedings of The Third Conference of the European Chapter of Computational Linguistics , Copenhagen, Denmark 1987.
Boman91	M. Boman et al: Conceptual Modeling, Department of Computer and Systems Sciences, Stockholm University Oct 1991.
Buben84	J. Bubenko et al: Konceptuell modelering - Informationsanalys, Studentlitteratur, Lund 1984, (in Swedish)
Buben86	J. Bubenko: Information System Methodologies - A Research View, SYSLAB Report no 40, Department of Computer and Systems Sciences, Stockholm University, Sweden 1986.
Cauv88	C. Cauvet et al: Information Systems Design: An expert system approach, Proceedings of IFIP, Guangzhou China, 1988.
Cauv91	C.Cauvet et al: ALECSI: An expert system for requirements engineering, in Proceedings of Computer Aided Information System Engineering, CAISE-91, Eds. R. Andersen et al,Trondheim , 1991.
Chen83	P. P-S. Chen: English Sentence Structure and Entity Relationship Diagrams, Information Sciences 29, p.p. 127-149.
Clock84	W.F. Clocksin et al: Programming in Prolog, Springer Verlag 1984.
Dali89	H. Dalianis: Generating a Natural Language Description and Deduction from a Conceptual Schema, SYSLAB Working Paper no. 160, Royal Institute of Technology, Nov 1989.
Dali90	H. Dalianis: Deep generation strategies and their application for creating alternative descriptions form conceptual schemas, SYSLAB Working paper no. 177, Royal Institute of Technology, Nov 1990.
Dali91	H.Dalianis: Generating a Deep Structure from a Conceptual Schema with consideration of a User Model, SYSLAB Working paper no. 184, Royal Institute of Technology, Aug 1991.

DeTro88   O. De Troyer et al: RIDL* on the CRIS case: A workbench for NIAM,
             Computerized Assistance During the Information Systems Life Cycle.T.W
             Olle, et al. (eds).Elsevier Science Publishers B.V North Holland, 1988.
Grosz87   B.J. Grosz et al: TEAM: An experiment on the design of Transportable
             Natural Language Interfaces, J. of Artificial Intelligence, pp 173-243,
             no 32 1987.
Hobbs85   J.R Hobbs: On the Coherence and Structure of Discourse, Report No.
             CSLI-85-37, October 1985.
Hobbs90   J Hobbs: Literature and Cognition, CSLI Lecture Notes Number 21,
             Center for the Study of Language and Information, 1990.
ISO82   ISO Technical Report, Concepts and Terminology for the Conceptual
             Schema and the Information Base, ed J.J. van Griethuysen, ISO/TC97/SC5
             - N 695, 1982.
Johan90   P. Johannesson: MOLOC: Using Prolog for conceptual Modeling,
             Proceedings of the International Conference on Entity-Relationship
             Approach, North Holland 1991.
Kuntz89   M. Kuntz et al.: Ergonomic Schema Design and Browsing with More
             Semantics in the Pasta-3 Interface for E-E DBMSs, Proceedings of the 8th
             International Conference on Entity-Relationship Approach, Ed F.H.
             Lochovsky, Toronto, Canada, 1989.
Lloyd87   J.W.Lloyd: Foundations of Logic Programming, Springer-Verlag 1987.
Mann84   W. C. Mann: Discourse Structures for Text Generation, Proceedings of the
             22nd annual meeting of the Association of Computational Linguistic,
             Stanford, CA, June 1984.
Mann88   W.C Mann et al: Rhetorical Structure Theory: Towards a Functional
             Theory of Text Organization, In TEXT Vol 8:3, 1988.
McKeo85a   K.R. McKeown: Textgeneration: Using discourse Strategies and focus
             constraints to generate natural language text, Cambridge University Press
             1985.
McKeo85b   K.R. McKeown: Discourse Strategies for Generating Natural Language
             Text, Artificial Intelligence, vol 27 no 1, Sept 1985.
Paris85   C. Paris: Description Strategies for naive and expert users, Proc. of the
             23rd Annual Meeting of the Association of Computational Linguistics
             1985.
Paris88   C. Paris: Tailoring Object's descriptions to a User´s Level of Expertise,
             J. of Computational Linguistics, Vol 14, No 3, Sept 1988.
Pereir80   F.C.N Pereira et al: Definite Clause Grammars for Language Analysis - A
             Survey of the Formalism and a Comparison with Augmented Transition
             Networks. J. of Artificial Intelligence 13, 1980, pp 231-278.
Tauzo89   B. Tauzovich: An Expert System for Conceptual Data Modeling,
             Proceeding of the Entity Relationship Approach Toronto, Canada, 1989.
Woh88   R. Wohed: Diagnosis of Conceptual Schemas, SYSLAB report no 56,
             Department of Computer and Systems Sciences, Royal Institute of
             Technology and Stockholm University 1988.

Automated Validation of Conceptual Schema Constraints

T.A. Halpin and J.I. McCormack

Key Centre for Software Technology
Department of Computer Science
University of Queensland. Australia 4072
email: halpin@cs.uq.oz.au

Abstract. For a database application, conceptual design methods such as fact-oriented modelling and entity-relationship modelling are commonly used to specify a conceptual schema, which may then be mapped to a structure in a chosen data model (e.g. a relational database schema). Since conceptual data models support a rich variety of constraints, and these constraints may impact on one another, the task of ensuring that the constraints expressed in a conceptual schema are consistent is non-trivial. Moreover, because different constraint patterns may be equivalent, some optimization may be needed to select the best constraint pattern for explicit assertion. With reference to conceptual schemas expressed in FOrML (an enhanced version of NIAM) this paper discusses meta-rules for strong satisfiability and constraint preference, and outlines an efficient algorithm for validating four main types of constraints. Complexity analyses and benchmarks of the implemented algorithm are included.

1 Introduction

The use of workbenches to provide automated support for the development of database applications is becoming widespread. For the modelling phase, it is becoming increasingly common for the data-perspective to be first specified in a human-oriented conceptual notation, which is then mapped to the appropriate logical data model (typically relational). Although most workbenches support a variant of EER (Enhanced Entity Relationship modelling), fact-oriented modelling arguably has several advantages (stronger linguistic basis, more constraint types, and its conceptual schema diagrams are more stable and easier to populate). Fact-oriented modelling (FOrM) comes in various flavours, under various names (e.g. NIAM, Binary-Relationship Modelling), and is supported by various CASE tools; some of these tools are well known (e.g. RIDL* from IntelliBase) while others are due for release this year (e.g. ITI's Conceptual Designer, and ServerWare's InfoViews).

Research at the University of Queensland is extending the fact-oriented modelling method, including automated support via a prototype known as WISE (Workbench for Information System Engineering). A detailed overview of WISE is given in Halpin (1991b). To place the topic of this paper (constraint validation) in perspective, a brief sketch of this project is now given. Conceptual schema editors are used to enter or modify conceptual schemas in graphical or textual form (with automatic layout).

Most syntax errors in the schema are detected at the entry stage since the editors incorporate most of the knowledge in the meta-conceptual schema. The output from this stage is fed to the Quality Checker: this performs further constraint validation, then checks for derivability and splittability of fact types (Zhang & Orlowska 1991).

The checked schema is then passed to the conceptual schema optimizer, which transforms it to an optimal version using formal equivalence and implication theorems, and heuristic guidelines (Halpin 1989, 1991a, 1991c, 1992). The designer may interact with this module to over-ride defaults, provide better identifiers and allow information loss or gain. The optimized schema is then mapped to the appropriate data model (e.g. relational), generated, tested and tuned for a given DBMS. Other aspects under investigation include extending the schema languages and mapping algorithms, facilitating schema evolution and incorporating other object-oriented features. Only some of the phases just described have been implemented. This paper focusses on constraint validation.

Since conceptual data models support a rich variety of constraints, and these constraints may impact on one another, the task of ensuring that the constraints expressed in a conceptual schema are consistent is non-trivial. Moreover, because different constraint patterns may be equivalent, some optimization may be needed to select the best constraint pattern for explicit assertion. Section 2 defines the notion of strong satisfiability used for constraint consistency, and lists a number of results following from this definition. In section 3, various constraint implication theorems are cited, which indicate how some constraints may be implied by others, and guidelines are set out for explicit display of constraints. Section 4 specifies an algorithm for validating four kinds of constraint on lists of single roles. A similar algorithm is cited for lists of role-sequences. Complexity analyses and prototype benchmarks for these algorithms are included in section 5. The final section identifies some related problems for further research.

2   Strong Satisfiability of Conceptual Schemas

It is assumed that the reader has a basic grounding in logic and database theory. While much of our discussion can be translated into popular EER notions, we use fact-oriented modelling here since it facilitates work with constraints. For the reader who is unfamiliar with this method, we briefly discuss an example conceptual schema (see Figure 1). Entity types are denoted by named ellipses (e.g. Country). Value types (e.g. Number or CharString types) are shown as named broken ellipses (e.g. CountryName). Simple reference schemes for entity types are parentheisized (e.g. each Country is identified by its country code); a "+" on a reference mode indicates numeric reference (e.g. nr). Predicates are shown as named box-sequences (one box for each role); for example, the binary predicate plays_for has two roles. Predicates are ordered, with their name written in or beside their first role-box.

A bar across a sequence of one or more roles specifies a uniqueness constraint (instantiating object sequences may not be duplicated); arrow tips may be added to the bar (and must be if the roles are non-contiguous). For example, each team plays for only one country but a country may field many teams; the shirt relationship between Playing Country and Colour is many:many but the pants relationship is 1:1.

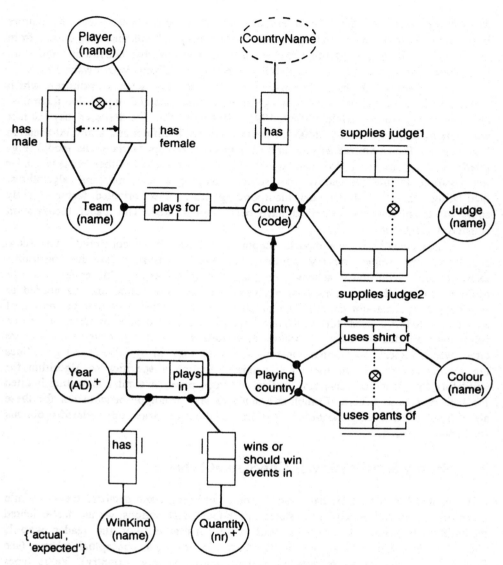

Playing_country =$_{df}$ Country **where exists** Team playing for Country

Fig. 1 An example of a fact-oriented conceptual schema diagram

Predicates which are completely spanned by a uniqueness constraint may be objectified; this nesting is shown as a frame (e.g. plays_in). A dot where *n* role-arcs connect to an object type indicates the disjunction of the *n* roles is *mandatory* or *total* (each object in the population of that type must play at least one of those roles). For example, each country must have a name, and supplies either one or two judges. An ⊗ symbol connecting role-sequences indicates mutual *exclusion* between the populations of these role-sequences. For example, a player cannot be both a male and female member of a team, and a country may not have a shirt colour which is the same as its pants colour. A dotted arrow from one role-sequence to another denotes a *subset* constraint (i.e. the population of the source is a subset of the target). A subset contraint in both directions is an equality constraint, and is shown as a dotted line with arrow-heads at both ends (e.g. a team has a male player if and only if it has a female player). A solid arrow from one object type to another indicates the former is a proper subtype of the latter; subtype definitions are specified at the bottom of the diagram (e.g. Playing_Country). Value-list constraints are shown in braces beside the relavent object type (e.g. WinKind). For a detailed background on fact-oriented modelling, see Nijssen & Halpin (1989); a recent overview is provided in Halpin & Orlowska (1992).

A conceptual schema diagram is mappable to a set of sentences in first order logic (Halpin 1989). An interpretation of a conceptual schema is then defined in the usual first-order way. An interpretation I of a conceptual schema CS is a *model* of CS iff each sentence of CS is true for I. A conceptual schema is *satisfiable* iff it has a model. In practice this notion of satisfiability is too weak, since it permits schemas with constraint patterns that are satisfiable only because these patterns are not populated. For example, a role with a uniqueness constraint and a frequency constraint of 2 generates a contradiction only if the role is populated: such constraint patterns are only *trivially satisfiable*.

The unsatisfactory nature of trivial models in relation to constraints has been noted in the literature. For example, Meyer, Weigand and Wieringa (1988, p. 13) attempt to avoid the problem by demanding that all models are non-empty. However, this is still too weak since it allows non-empty models with some empty predicates that are only trivially satisfiable. To demand that a CS must have a model in which all its predicates are non-empty is too strong, since legitimate exclusion and cardinality constraint patterns are rejected (Halpin 1989 pp. 6-3,4). We propose the following definition:

A conceptual schema CS is *strongly satisfiable* (or *population-consistent*) if and only if: (a) for *each* of its predicates, there is a model of CS in which *that* predicate is instantiated; and (b) for *each* inter-predicate role-sequence which is an argument to an explicit constraint, there is a model in which *that* role-sequence is instantiated.

An inter-predicate role-sequence is an ordered list of roles, at least two of which occur in different predicates. Halpin (1989) proved various metarules using part (a) of this definition to avoid various cases of trivial satisfiability. We extend this work by considering some new cases which underpin the constraint validation algorithms discussed later.

The first rule is *NXS* (*N*o e*X*clusion with a *S*ubset constraint). In the diagram, rs1 and rs2 are each sequences of n roles ($n \geq 1$). The constraint arguments are rs1 and rs2 (not just subsequences). The exclusion constraint (denoted by $\otimes$) means there is no model in which both rs1 and rs2 are populated. On the left, a subset constraint from rs2 to rs1 is shown as a broken arrow from rs2 to rs1: in all models, each instance in the population of rs2 is also an instance in the population of rs1. Similarly, a subset constraint from rs1 to rs2 is shown on the right.

NXS Any schema with both an exclusion constraint and a subset constraint between the same two role-sequences is population-inconsistent (i.e. not strongly satisfiable).

Illegal combinations (constraints apply between whole role-sequences)

The proof of NXS is trivial. Consider the left-hand version. Assume strong satisfiability and both constraints hold. By strong satisfiability there is a model in which rs2 is populated. Let an instance in its population be a. The subset constraint implies that a occurs in the population of rs1. So a populates both rs1 and rs2, which contradicts the exclusion constraint. So the original assumption is wrong, i.e. the constraints are not strongly satisfiable. By swapping rs1 and rs2 the right-hand version follows. The constraint pattern is trivially satisfiable (there in a model where both rs1 and rs2 are empty, both constraints do hold), i.e. although the pattern is consistent it is population-inconsistent.

In the unlikely event that a designer explicitly enters both exclusion and subset constraints between the same role-sequences, this will be rejected by the editor. However, as discussed later, it is still necessary to check whether such a constraint combination is implied by other constraints on the schema.

As a related issue, the editor should be provided with knowledge as to where constraints may be meaningfully asserted on the schema. Apart from the obvious restrictions captured by graphic constraints on the meta-conceptual schema, further textual constraints at the meta-level must be specified and enforced. In this paper we restrict our attention essentially to *MSEX* constraints: *M*andatory roles, *S*ubset constraints, *E*quality constraints and e*X*clusion constraints. Recall that a role is mandatory (or total) for an object type if and only if each population instance of that type must play that role. Our approach bears some similarities to the "set constraint consistency analysis" performed by RIDL* (De Troyer et al. 1988, p. 398), but there are some significant differences.

To begin with, the "total union" and exclusion constraints commonly asserted between subtypes in RIDL* are unlikely to be ever used explicitly in our approach, since they are typically implied by the subtype definitions in conjunction with constraints on the fact types used in these definitions. For example, if Person has a mandatory functional association with Sexcode {'m','f'}, and Man and Woman are defined as having Sexcode 'm', 'f' respectively then exhaustion (total union) and exclusion constraints for Man and Woman are implied.

Our treatment of subtypes is somewhat stricter than that of RIDL*. We demand that subtypes be definable in terms of roles played by their supertype(s), and give these definitions formal significance. If the designer ever tried to explicitly assert an exclusion or exhaustion constraint between subtypes this would be checked for consistency with the definitions and relevant constraints (see Halpin 1989 pp. 6-14,15 for relevant theroems), and typically allowed only as an implied constraint. In addition, subtypes are introduced only if they have a specific role to play. We feel this is a safer approach, as well as leading to less cluttered diagrams.

In some cases one might vacillate over whether to introduce a subtype or not (e.g. see Nijssen & Halpin 1989, p. 178). We resolve such cases by the following recursive *subtype introduction procedure* (SIP):

- If an optional role is played only by a well-defined subtype, then specify the subtype definition.
- If the subtype definition is stronger than "[not] playing a role directly attached to [one of its] supertype[s]" then introduce the subtype (and apply SIP to it).
- If the subtype definition can be expressed instead as a subset or exclusion constraint then do so, unless there are several roles which bear equality or subset constriants to the candidate subtype role (in which case introduce the subtype and apply SIP to it).

It is clear that subset, equality and exclusion constraints are allowed between role-sequences only if these are compatible (same corresponding host object types). Also exclusion constraints between exclusive subtypes, as well as subset constraints from subtype roles to mandatory supertype roles, are implied and hence omitted. Mainly as a consequence of the SIP procedure, other meta-rules follow which further restrict the explicit depiction of such constraints. In particular:

Consider two different object types B and C, with the same host supertype, and let r and s be roles attached to B and C.
- An explicit subset constraint from r to s is allowed only if r and s are optional and B is (directly or indirectly) a subtype of C.
- An explicit exclusion constraint between r and s is allowed only if r and s are optional and either B is a subtype of C or C is a subtype of B.

The significance of such rules is twofold: they allow such rule violations to be rejected at the schema entry stage; knowing these rules are now obeyed simplifies the working of the constraint validation checking applied later.

3   Constraint Implication and Display

Let *CS* be any well formed conceptual schema, and *C* be any well formed static constraint to be added to *CS*. Then *CS implies C* iff *C* is true in all models of *CS*. Using formal logic, Halpin (1989) proved several constraint implication theorems for fact-oriented schemas. We cite without proof the following results:

- If roles *r* and *s* are mandatory and optional for the same object type, then a subset constraint is implied from *s* to *r*.

  Let *rs1* and *rs2* be compatible role-sequences (of 1 or more roles). Then:
- A subset constraint from *rs2* to *rs1* implies a subset constraint from each subsequence in *rs2* to the corresponding subsequence of *rs1*.
- An exclusion constraint between *rs1* and *rs2* implies an exclusion constraint between all compatible supersequences of *rs1* and *rs2*.

- Let *rs1*, *rs2* and *rs3* be compatible role-sequences. A subset constraint from *rs1* to *rs2* combined with a subset constraint from *rs2* to *rs3* (transitively) implies a subset constraint from *rs1* to *rs3*.

- An exclusion constraint between *n* role-sequences is equivalent to the exhaustive conjunction of *n(n-1)/2* binary exclusion constraints between all possible pairs of these role-sequences.

- An equality constraint between two role-sequences is equivalent to subset constraints in both directions.

- If a single equality constraint between *n* role-sequences is allowed, it is equivalent to equivalent to the *n-1* binary equality constraints between adjacent role-sequences.

- If the disjunction of roles *r* and *s* is mandatory, and a subset constraint exists from *s* to *r*, then *r* is mandatory. In this case *r* should be displayed separately as mandatory.

Many other examples of constraint implication and display preferences are given in Halpin (1989), dealing with uniqueness, frequency, cardinality, subtype, asymmetry etc. constraints. However those results cited here provide sufficient background for the constraint validation algorithms which follow. We restrict ourselves to the following problem:

> Given a conceptual schema output from the CS editor, is the pattern of its MSEX constraints strongly satisfiable? If not, specify the violation(s) (and ideally interact with the designer to correct the schema). If it is strongly satisfiable, then optimize the display by hiding implied constraints except that mandatory roles are always to be depicted as mandatory.

For example, consider the constraint pattern of Figure 2. Each box denotes a single role. The exclusion constraint applies between the left-hand roles, but the subset constraint (by connecting the role-junction points) applies between the role-pairs. The pair-subset constraint implies subset constraints between the left-hand roles (and between the right-hand roles). From theorem NXS, this conflicts with the exclusion constraint and the schema is not strongly satisfiable. Note that because subset contraints are implied through all subsequences, we merely had to look for an implied subset constraint on the explicit exclusion constraint: we did not have to derive the supersequence exclusion constraints.

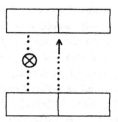

Fig. 2 This constraint pattern is not strongly satisfiable

As a simple example of optimizing constraint display, consider the left-hand diagram in Figure 3. Object types are depicted by ellipses. A dot connected to one or more roles means the disjunction of these roles is mandatory for the dotted object type. The pair-subset constraint implies subset constraints from the lower roles to the roles directly above them, which combined with the disjunctive mandatory role constraints imply that the top roles are mandatory and hence must be displayed as shown on the right.

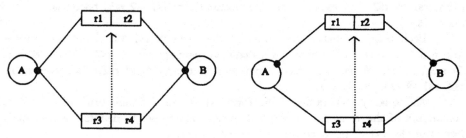

Fig. 3 The left-hand version should be converted to the right-hand version

The basic ideas underlying *MSEX constraint validation (checking for constraint satisfiability, and optimizing the constraint display)* have now been covered, so that an intelligent designer would normally be able to carry out this procedure manually. However, with large schemas this is both tedious and open to error (because of the large numbers of implied constraints). Hence it is desirable to have this validation performed automatically. The rest of the paper specifies algorithms for doing this efficiently.

4   MSEX Constraint Validation

We believe the algorithms presented here for validating MSEX constraints offer advantages such as efficiency and completeness compared with those used by other systems. For portability the algorithms have been coded in C. Basically, we perform a "populability check" of conceptual schemas, which focusses on potential schema populations, indicating any predicates which cannot be populated as well as any redundant subset constraints.

The basic principle of the algorithm is to build a series of graphs such that each graph represents a "population scenario" (possible world). A directed arc between two vertices u, v in a graph is equivalent to the subset constraint: every instance of an object-type which plays role u in this scenario also plays role v.

The population graphs are a series of directed graphs which represent possible populations of the schema, and are defined as either unary (compare single roles) or n-ary (compare sequences of at least 2 roles). Although, the unary case is just a special case of the n-ary, the algorithms are treated differently as they typically have to be implemented separately.

For simplicity, the main algorithms assume that exclusion and subset constraints span only two role-sequences. All constraints not of this form are pre-processed to give a series of binary constraints. All equality constraints are then pre-processed to form two subset constraints. The details of the pre-processing are as follows.

Pre-processing:

If n-ary equality constraints are allowed, each equality constraint of the form =(rs1,...,rsn) is transformed into (n-1) binary equality constraints between adjacent pairs: rs1 = rs2, .. , rsn-1 = rsn. For example, =(rs1,rs2,rs3) becomes: rs1 = rs2, rs2 = rs3.

Each n-ary exclusion constraint of the form $\otimes$(rs1,rs2,...,rsn) is transformed into n(n-1)/2 binary constraints by exhaustive pairing: rs1 $\otimes$ rs2,..., rs1 $\otimes$ rsn, rs2 $\otimes$ rs3,... , rs2 $\otimes$ rsn, ... , rsn-1 x rsn. For example, $\otimes$(rs1,rs2,rs3) becomes: rs1 $\otimes$ rs2, rs1 $\otimes$ rs3, rs2 $\otimes$ rs3.

All equality constraints of the form rs1 = rs2 are transformed into two subset constraints of the form rs1 → rs2, rs2 → rs1 (using "→" to denote "is a subset of"). For example, rs1 = rs2 becomes: rs1 → rs2, rs2 → rs1.

Finally, all subset constraints between sequences of n roles ($n > 1$) have the implied subset constraints generated for each of their subsequences. Thus a single such constraint is expanded to $2^n - 1$ subset constraints. For example, (rs11, rs12,rs13) → (rs21,rs22,rs23) is expanded to the 7 constraints:

unary:	rs11 → rs21; rs12 → rs22; rs13 → rs23
binary:	(rs11,rs12) → (rs21,rs22); (rs11,rs13) → (rs21,rs23);
	(rs12,rs13) → (rs22,rs23)
ternary:	(rs11,rs12,rs13) → (rs21,rs22,rs23)

This final expansion is used to optimize constraint display. If only a consistency check is needed, subset constraint generation can be limited by existing exclusion constraints.

Unary validation *(constraints which compare single roles):*

We construct a directed graph $G = (V,E)$, where V is a set of vertices and E is a set of edges. All $v \in V$ are roles whose connecting object-types have the same root in their subtype-graph, i.e. a population graph around some object-type O (with no super-types) has as its vertices all of the roles played by O (directly connected to O) or any subtypes of O. All $e \in E$ are edges of the form $(u \in V \rightarrow v \in V)$ where it can be shown that any instance of O playing role u must play role v.

The algorithm must be run for each subtype graph (possibly trivial) in the schema. A sub-type graph is identified by its root. From this point onwards, a role refers not only to the role within the schema but also to that role's corresponding vertex in the graph. An overview of the algorithm is now given.

Step 1:

The initial step in the algorithm is to add the vertices to the graph. Each vertex in the graph corresponds to a role which is directly connected to an object-type in the subtype graph of interest. All such roles are represented in the graph.

All edges in the graph are directed and have an extra attribute which records the constraint from which the edge was derived. This is useful for reporting redundant subset and exclusion constraints.

Step 2:

The next step adds to the graph the edges which are derived from non-disjunctive mandatory role constraints. Put simply this is: "For all such constraints which span a role r in the graph where r is connected to some object-type O, add directed edges to r from all other roles connected to either O or subtypes of O. Mark these edges as being derived from the relevant mandatory role constraint." At this point, the base-graph has been formed. Before any checking can be done, edges produced by subset and disjunctive mandatory role constraints are added to the graph.

Next a sequence of possible non-empty populations is built up from the disjunctive mandatory role constraints which span roles in the graph. Basically, we form the power-set and subtract the null set.

For example, suppose there are two disjunctive mandatory role constraints c1 and c2 which impact on the graph, where c1 spans roles r1, r2 and c2 spans roles r3, r4. The possible (non-empty) populations of roles 1 and 2 are $p1 = \{\{1\},\{2\},\{1,2\}\}$, i.e. either role 1 may be populated and not role 2, role 2 may be populated and not role 1, or both may be populated (there are 2^n-1 of these "population scenarios").

Similarly, the possible populations of roles 3 and 4 are $p2 = \{\{3\},\{4\}, \{3,4\}\}$. The total possible set of schema populations around the roles influenced by c1 and c2 is $M = \{ \{1,3\}, \{1,4\}, \{1,3,4\}, \{2,3\}, \{2,4\}, \{2,3,4\}, \{1,2,3\}, \{1,2,4\}, \{1,2,3,4\} \}$. The size of this set is #p1 * #p2, the product of the cardinalities of p1 and p2.

Step 3.

Using the base-graph as a starting point, apply the following algorithm to each $m \in M$.

Step 3.1 (add disjunctive-mandatory role constraints):

For all roles $r \in$ m, add edges to the graph using the same procedure as that used for non-disjunctive mandatory roles, i.e. if r is connected to some object-type O, add directed edges from all other roles connected to either O or subtypes of O to r. Mark these edges as being derived from the relevant mandatory role constraint.

Step 3.2 (add the subset constraints):

For each subset constraint $r \twoheadrightarrow s$ such that $r \in$ V and $s \in$ V, if no path from r to s exists in the graph, add an edge from r to s to the graph and mark it as being derived from the relevant subset constraint.

Step 3.3 (check the exclusion constraints):

For each exclusion constraint of the form $r \otimes s$ such that $r \in$ V and $s \in$ V if a path exists from r to s in the graph, the constraint is invalid since role r cannot be populated; if a path exists from s to r in the graph, the constraint is invalid since role s cannot be populated.

Step 3.4 (check the subset constraints):

For each subset constraint $r \twoheadrightarrow s$ such that $r \in$ V and $s \in$ V, if the path from r to s in the graph is not a single edge which has been derived from the subset constraint currently being checked, the constraint is redundant in this population scenario. If a subset constraint is redundant in all population scenarios (for all m in M) the constraint is redundant in the schema.

Step 3.5 (check for implied mandatory role constraints)

For each role r in the graph where it is possible to get from all other roles in the graph to r, r is mandatory for this population scenario. If a role is mandatory in all population scenarios, the role is mandatory in the schema. Note that the information needed for this check can be built up while adding the subset and mandatory role constraints.

As an example of the unary check, consider the incomplete schema fragment depicted in Figure 4. In this graph there are 13 roles labelled "r1".."r13" connected directly (or indirectly via subtypes) to the object type named "Target OT".

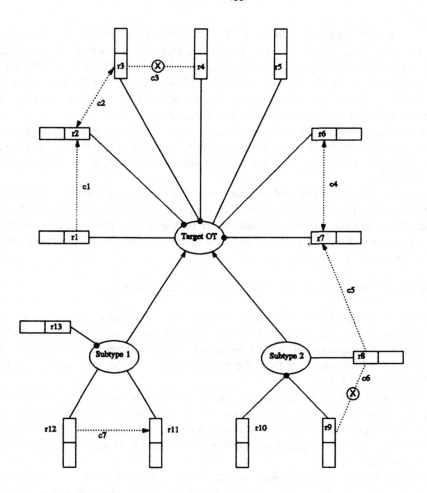

Fig. 4 A schema fragment used to illustrate unary validation

For this example, the algorithm is executed thus. The vertices V = {r1 .. r13}. Add directed edges added for non-disjunctive mandatory roles: r1 → r2, r3 → r2, r4 → r2, r5 → r2, r6 → r2, r7 → r2, r8 → r2, r9 → r2, r10 → r2, r11 → r2, r12 → r2, r13 → r2, r1 → r7, r2 → r7, r3 → r7, r4 → r7, r5 → r7, r6 → r7, r8 → r7, r9 → r7, r10 → r7, r11 → r7, r12 → r7, r13 → r7, r12 → r13, r11 → r13. Hence in the base graph G, all vertices have edges to r2 and r7, and there are edges from r12 to r13 and r11 to r13.

M = { {r3, r9}, {r3, r10}, {r3, r9, r10 }, {r4, r9},
      {r4, r10}, {r4, r9, r10 }, {r3, r4, r9}, {r3, r4, r10},
      {r3, r4, r9, r10 } }

Now consider iteration 1 of step 3. Add disjunctive mandatory roles. All vertices now have edges to r2, r3, r7, and r9. Adding subset constraints causes the following edges to be added: r2 → r3, r3 → r2, r6 → r7, r7 → r6, r1 → r2, r8 → r7, r12 → r11, r2 → r3, r3 → r2, r6 → r7, r7 → r6, r12 → r13, r11 → r13. The results of iteration 1 are: c1 marked as redundant; c2 can be replaced by a subset constraint to R2; c4 can be replaced by a subset constraint; c5 is redundant

The results of the complete execution of the algorithm are: c1 tagged as redundant; c2 can be replaced by a subset constraint to R2; c3 tagged as invalid since R4 cannot be populated; c4 can be replaced by a subset constraint; c5 is redundant; c6 is valid; c7 is valid.

Note that the algorithm detects all errors but makes a default assumption regarding the best way to remove the error. An improvement would be to interact with the designer to determine which error correction option is best (for example, another possible error correction with the current example is that r3 should have been mandatory, leaving c2 as implied.

N-ary validation *(constraints comparing sequences of 2 or more roles):*

An n-ary check checks all n-ary subset, equality and exclusion constraints in the schema (see Figure 4). Again G = (V,E) is a directed graph. A "population node" is derived from a role-sequence of two or more roles in a constraint. For example, in Figure 5 the pair-subset constraint from the role-pair (r1,r2) to the role-pair (r3,r4) has the population nodes r1#r2 and r3#r4.

A population node *n* is "population equivalent" to role-sequence *rs* iff all roles occurring in *n* occur in the same order in *rs*. A population node *n* is the "corresponding" population node to population node *m* within constraint *c* iff *c* is made up of *rs1* and *rs2*, and *n* is population equivalent to *rs1* and *m* is population equivalent to *rs2*, or vice-versa.

Given a binary constraint made up of rs1 = (r1,r2) and rs2 = (r4,r5) the population node n = r1#r2 is population equivalent to rs1, and the corresponding population node in rs2 of r1#r2 in the constraint is r4#r5.

Having described the n-ary form of the population graph, we now give an overview of the n-ary validation algorithm. This is similar in principle to the unary algorithm. Vertices in the graph used in the n-ary case represent sequences of n roles. For a given N, the algorithm must be run on every n-ary constraint in the schema.

For each n-ary constraint cc of the form p1 subset p2 or p1 exclude p2, where p1 and p2 are the n-ary population nodes which represent the n-length role-sequences in cc, add the vertices p1 and p2 to the graph (V = { p1,p2}) and proceed as follows:

```
Changed  = true;
C  =  {};  ( C is the set of constraints which have been processed )

while changed do
        for all subset constraints c where c spans some v ∈ V and c is not in C
                c is of the form pa subset pb
                C = C + c
                if pa is not in V
                        V = V + pa;
                        Changed  = true
                if pb is not in V
                        V = V + pb;
                        Changed  = true
                If no path form pa to pb exists in the graph
                        Add an edge from pa to pb
                        Mark the edge as being derived from c
```

if cc is a subset constraint and the path from p1 to p2 in the graph is not a single edge which is derived from cc, cc is redundant.

if cc is an exclusion constraint and there is a path from p1 to p2 in the graph, cc is invalid since p1 cannot be populated.

if cc is an exclusion constraint and there is a path from p2 to p1 in the graph, cc is invalid since p2 cannot be populated

As an example, consider the schema fragment shown in Figure 5. Intuitively, there is a problem since a pair-subset constraint is implied from (r1,r2) to (r3,r4), which is population-inconsistent with the exclusion constraint c1.

The algorithm checks the exclusion constraint c1 as follows. Initially V = {r1#r2,r3#r4} and E = {}. Adding c2 adds the vertex r5#r6 and the edge r5#r6 → r3#r4. Adding c3 adds the vertex r7#r9 and the edge r7#r9 → r5#r6. Adding c4 adds the edges r1#r2 → r7#r9 and r7#r9 → r1#r2. The final graph for the check of the exclusion constraint is as shown. Since there is a path from r1#r2 to r3#r4, the exclusion constraint is invalid because r1#r2 cannot be populated (by theorem NXS).

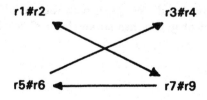

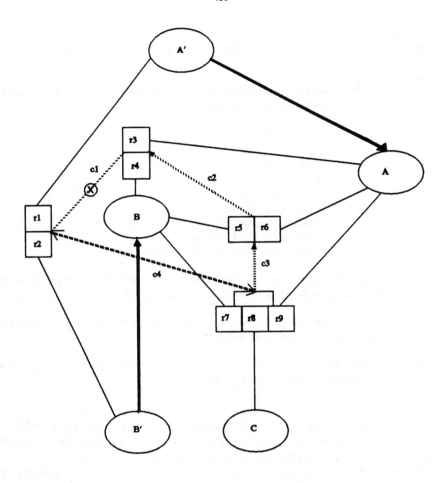

Fig. 5 A schema fragment used to illustrate n-ary validation

As a final example consider the first schema shown in Figure 3. The set of population scenarios for the (trivial) subtype graph with root A is M = { {r1}, {r3}, {r1, r3} }. Each of the 3 resultant graphs has an arc from r3 to r1 added due to the subset constraint.

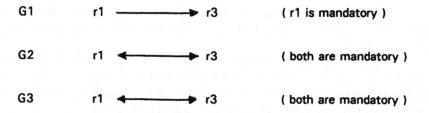

Since r1 is mandatory in all 3 population scenarios, r1 is mandatory in the schema and the disjunctive mandatory role constraint over roles r1 and r3 can be replaced by a single mandatory role conatraint over r1.

Similarly the disjunctive mandatory role constraint over r2 and r4 can be replaced by a single mandatory role constraint over r2.

The n-ary case has two nodes - r1#r2 and r3#r4 and one edge from r3#r4 to r1#r2. There are no redundancies or errors.

When the schema is re-assembled with the new mandatory role constraints the schema takes the more correct form of the second schema shown in Figure 3.

5   Complexity Analysis

The complexity analysis ignores the pre-processing step. Complexity of a *unary* check on a single subtype graph is determined as follows. Let R be the number of roles in the subtype graph. Let C be the number of subset, equality, exclusion and non-disjunctive mandatory role constraints constraints which impact on the subtype graph. Let NM be the number of non-disjunctive mandatory role constraints which impact on the subtype graph. Let P be the number of elements of the set M (the set of possible schema populations). P is exponential in the arity of the largest disjunctive mandatory role constraint which impacts on the subtype graph.

Step 1 is clearly O(R). Step 2 has a worst case complexity of O(R * NM). Step 3 is performed P times. Step 3.1 takes O(R * the number of elements in m). Step 3.2 takes O(R * R * the number of subset constraints involved in the graph) if an algorithm such as Dijkstra's is used to check for the path. Step 3.3 takes O (R * R * the number of subset constraints involved in the graph) if an algorithm such as Dijkstra's is used to check for paths. Step 3.4 also takes O(R * R * the number of subset constraints involved in the graph). Since the number of elements in m is never greater than the number of vertices in the graph, Steps 3.1 - 3.4 are O(#constraints * R * R). Hence the complexity of checking one subtype graph is O(R * R * P * C).

Let OTS = the number of object-types in the schema. Let RS = the number of roles in the schema. Let CS = the number of subset, equaliity, exclusion and non-disjunctive mandatory role constraints in the schema. Let DMS = the number of disjunctive mandatory role constraints in the schema.
Let SLDM = the size (arity) of the largest disjunctive mandatory role constraint in the schema. Let PS = the number of elements involved in the largest "possible world set " (M). This is $O(DMS * 2^{SLDM})$.

Each object-type may only occur in one subtype graph. Each role may only occur in one subtype-graph. Hence the complexity of the entire schema is O(RS * RS * CS * PS).

We now analyse the complexity of the n-ary case. Let C = the number of n-ary subset and exclusion constraints involved in the current graph. The complexity of checking a single n-ary constraint is is $O(C^3)$ since testing for an existing path between nodes is is $O(C^2)$. Hence, for a complete schema the complexity is: $O(CS^4)$ where CS = the number of n-ary subset, and exclusion constraints in the schema.

Although the complexity analysis for the unary algorithm yeilds a result which is exponential in the size of the disjunctive mandatory roles within the schema, the number of large disjunctive mandatory roles constraints is typically small. As a result of this the performance of the algorithm is not adverseley affected by the exponential complexity.

Furthermore, if the schema is only to be checked for strong-satisfiability, only those subtype graphs containing exclusion constraints need be checked for the n-ary case and only exclusion constraints need be checked for the nary case.

The preceding algorithms have been implemented, and produced the following results when run on a schema containing in excess of 250 object-types, 300 predicates, 400 mandatory role constraints, 6 non-trivial subtype graphs, 30 subtype & equality constraints and 10 exclusion constraints. On a SUN SparcStation 2 the full check (unary and n-ary) completed in 3 seconds. On an IBM compatable 16 MHz 80386-SX the same check completed in 68 seconds.

6   Conclusion

This paper has examined the notions of constraint satisfiability and implication for four important classes of constraints in fact-oriented modelling, and specified efficient algorithms for their checking and display optimization. Since these constraints are at least partially supported by various versions of EER modelling, the work has wider implications. While validation procedures have been developed for other classes of constraints (e.g. uniqueness), there are several other constraints in fact-oriented modelling which require a similar set of validation algorithms (e.g. frequency, asymmetry). The development and implementation of efficient validation algorithms for such constraints is a topic for future research.

References

Bry, F. & Manthey, R. 1986, 'Checking Consistency of Database Constraints: a Logical Basic', *Proc. Twelfth Int. Conf. on Very Large Data Bases*, VLDB, Kyoto, pp. 13-20.

De Troyer, O., Meersman, R. & Verlinden, P. 1988, 'RIDL* on the CRIS Case: a Workbench for NIAM', *Computerized Assistance during the Information Systems Life Cycle: Proc. CRIS88*, eds T.W.Olle, A.A. Verrijn-Stuart & L. Bhabuta, North-Holland, Amsterdam.

De Troyer, O. 1989, 'RIDL*: A Tool for the Computer-Assisted Engineering of Large Databases in the Presence of Integrity Constraints', *Proc. ACM-SIGMOD Int. Conf. on Management of Data*, Oregon.

De Troyer, O. 1991, 'The OO-Binary Relationship Model: a truly object-oriented conceptual model', *Advanced Information Systems Engineering: Proc. CAiSE-91*, Springer-Verlag Lecture Notes in Computer Science, no. 498, Trondheim.

Halpin, T.A. 1989, 'A Logical Analysis of Information Systems: static aspects of the data-oriented perspective', PhD thesis, University of Queensland.

Halpin, T.A. 1991a, 'Optimizing Global Conceptual Schemas', *Databases in the 1990s: 2*, eds B. Srinivasan & J. Zeleznikov, World Scientific, Singapore.

Halpin, T.A. 1991b, 'WISE: a Workbench for Information Systems Engineering', *Proc. 2nd Workshop on Next Generation of CASE Tools*, Trondheim.

Halpin, T.A. 1991c, 'A Fact-Oriented Approach to Schema Transformation', *Proc. MFDBS-91*, Springer-Verlag Lec. Notes in Computer Science, no. 495, Rostock.

Halpin, T.A. 1992, 'Fact-oriented schema optimization', to appear in *Proc. CISMOD-92*, India, July 1992.

Halpin, T.A. & Orlowska, M. E. 1992, 'Fact-Oriented Modelling for Data Analysis', *Journal of Information Systems*, vol. 2, no. 2, Blackwell Scientific, Oxford.

Halpin, T.A. & Ritson, P.R. 1992, 'Fact-Oriented Modelling and Null Values', *Research and Practical Issues in Databases: Proc. 3rd Australian Database Conf.*, eds B. Srinivasan & J. Zeleznikov, World Scientific, Singapore.

Lundberg, B. 1983, 'On Correctness of Information Models', *Information Systems*, vol. 8, no. 2, pp. 87-93, Pergamon Press.

Meyer, J., Weigand, H. & Wieringa, R. 1988, 'Specifying Dynamic and Deontic Integrity Constraints', Rapport IR-175, Vrije Universiteit, Amsterdam.

Nijssen, G.M. & Halpin, T.A. 1989, *Conceptual Schema and Relational Database Design: a fact-oriented approach*, Prentice Hall, Sydney.

Qian, X. & Wiederhold, G. 1986, 'Knowledge-based Integrity Constraint Validation', *Proc. Twelfth Int. Conf. on Very Large Data Bases*, Kyoto, pp. 3-12.

Rajagopalan, P. & Ling, T.W. 1987, 'A method for semantic validation of a class of integrity constraints', *Tech. Report*, Uni. of Singapore.

Zhang, Y. & Orlowska, M.E. 1991, 'Synthesizer+: an automatic tool for relational database design', *Proc. 14th Australian Computer Science Conf.*, Sydney.

An Approach to Eliciting the Semantics of Relational Databases

M.M.Fonkam   W.A.Gray

Dept. of Computing Maths, University of Wales College of Cardiff,
Cardiff CF2 4AG, email : mmf@uk.ac.cf.cm.

Abstract.   Relational database systems are currently the most dominant in both centralised and distributed database environments inspite of the many limitations of these systems. A fundamental weakness of these systems is that the logical structure of the data of their DBs which must be exploited by their users is usually buried in the DB schemas, application programs and in the minds of designers and programmers. The vast number of casual and inexperienced users currently employing these DBs for their day to day applications makes it imperative for their logical structure to be made explicit and readily available in some easily assimilated form.

A number of algorithms have been proposed for this reverse modelling activity which essentially generate a conceptual model from a given relational DB schema. In this paper we make a comparative study of three representative previous algorithms and then present a new improved and more general algorithm based on these previous attempts.

1 Introduction

The current dominance of the relational model in the commercial scene coupled with its lack of facilities by which users can easily display and understand the semantics of its databases has led to research into ways of converting the schemas (intension) of these databases into conceptual schemas using one of the semantic data models, usually the Entity-Relationship (ER) model or a semantically richer variant of it. The result of this research has been a number of algorithms, each prescribing a set of rules by which the implied semantics of a relational schema can be extracted and re-expressed using a semantic data model (SDM) where such semantics are made explicit, [DAV88, JOH89, KAL91, NAV88]. The input to these algorithms is the relational schema of a database possibly enhanced with extra information. The ER-models are heavily used as conceptual models since one of their attractive features is their ability to express the contents of a DB in a form quite close to a user's perception. Conceptual models such as the ER-model, explicitly maintain the relationships of the database and some of these models make provisions for querying such relationships in much the same way as one would query the data.

There are four main sources of the semantics of a given relational DB, namely; the *database schema;* the *application programs* written for specialised purposes; the *explicit integrity constraints* and *users of the designer and application programmer* categories. All four sources may be relevant for producing the conceptual schema of a relational DB that captures its complete semantics. This paper is concerned with the *inherent or structural semantics* of a relational DB and as such only those explicit integrity constraints that are also structural constraints will be considered. Our own work, like previous works in this area does not make use of the semantics embedded in application programs.

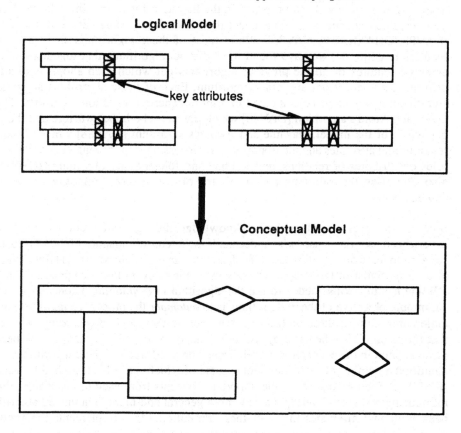

Fig. 1.   Reverse Modelling of A Relational Schema into a Conceptual Model

A notable problem of relational systems is that they represent relationships only implicitly through matching field values in relations and the majority of systems make no provision for allowing users to discover such relationships. The vast range and number of users now currently employing relational DBs justifies then the need for a reverse modelling process whereby the intension of the database can be mapped into a conceptual schema which shows its relationships and structure explicitly. This process of reverse modelling is graphically illustrated in Fig.1, where the logical model shows the tables of a relational schema being mapped into a more powerful pictorial representation. The need for such reverse modelling or reverse engineering is even greater in a Multidatabase System (MBS) [LIT88] environment where users do not only have access to their own local DBs but can also access remote independent DBs in a network of interconnected databases. Without such a tool in these environments, most users would find it practically impossible to exploit the wealth of data available to them.

Many algorithms have been proposed in the literature for converting relational database schemas into conceptual schemas under the ER model or some variant of the ER model [DAV88,JOH89,KAL91,NAV88]. While most of these algorithms share a number of features in common, we have found three distinct algorithms that together embody the essential features of all the previous algorithms but which each adopts a significantly different approach from any other algorithm. Each of these algorithms suggests some significant concepts to be embodied in a more generic translation algorithm. These are Davis and Arora's algorithm [DAV88] which translates both the structure and the explicit behaviour of the model, Navathe and Awong's algorithm [NAV88] which classifies the relations and attributes and incorporates a preprocessing step for renaming or changing the roles of attributes of relations, and Kalman and Johanneson's algorithm [JOH89] which also classifies the relations and attributes of the schema but only uses inclusion dependencies.

Most of the previous algorithms acknowledge the tight interaction needed with an experienced user (i.e. a user who understands the intended semantics of the DB) to alleviate certain semantic ambiguities about the data. Such an experienced user is typically assumed to be a specialist in DB design who possesses the relevant knowledge about the present DB and has the skills needed to use the algorithm in developing a conceptual model. A paramount objective of these algorithms is to *automate* the process as far as possible. The major limitation of these algorithms, however, is their *lack of generality* which means that for certain DB schemas they will miss out some very vital semantics that need to be made explicit in the conceptual model. From a detailed study of these algorithms, we have identified a number of their limitations, some of which have been studied by Kalman in [KAL91]. Then by extracting the important concepts from each of these algorithms and introducing some new concepts a new more general and highly automated algorithm has been built that alleviates many of these limitations. Our implementation produces a graphical output of the conceptual model which shows the relationship between the conceptual model obtained and the underlying relational model, thus enabling the user to directly frame DB queries from knowledge of the conceptual model alone. This linkage is an innovation of this algorithm which assists users by improving their perception of the DB semantics and its realisation in the relational model.

In the next section of this paper, we make a detailed comparison of the three main algorithms mentioned above highlighting their relevant contributions as well as their major limitations. This comparison is based on a number of criteria which we considered relevant for such translation algorithms. In Section 3, we briefly introduce the Entity-

Category-Relationship(ECR) model which we use to represent the semantic data model at the conceptual level. Section 4 considers modelling within the relational context. Sections 3 and 4 serve to give the reader a better understanding of the reasoning behind the new algorithm. Section 5 presents our new algorithm, first through examining the general rules that have been extracted from the previous algorithms, then by presenting new relevant rules. Section 6 is concerned with its implementation and explores the types of interactions needed with the user to extract further semantics. We also discuss the graphical output that represents the conceptual model produced by the new algorithm and then illustrate the technique adopted in this graphical output to assist the user gain an understanding of the connection between this conceptual model and the underlying relational schema. In the conclusions, Section 7, we examine the generality of our new algorithm, its contribution and present some directions for future work.

2 A Comparative Study of Existing Algorithms

Six main criteria have been used as a basis for our comparison. These are briefly introduced in this section. In this comparison process we will denote by Algorithm 1 Davis and Arora's algorithm, by Algorithm 2 Navathe and Awong's algorithm and by Algorithm 3 Kalman and Johanneson's algorithm.

a). the equivalence of the models - to what extent is the conceptual model a reflection of its relational model? As pointed out in Tsichristis and Lochovsky [TSI82], this equivalence can be shown if an inverse mapping can be found for converting the conceptual model back to the original relational model. The authors of Algorithm 1 actually showed in their work, [DAV88], how an inverse mapping could be found for mapping from the conceptual model back to the original relational model. An inverse mapping can also be easily found for Algorithms 2 and 3. In fact, this equivalence derives from the easy mapping of ER models to relational models, thus once a good ER model has been derived then the equivalence of these models is ensured[ELM89].

b). the inclusion and handling of subtype/supertype semantics - One main weakness of the relational model is its lack of an explicit means to model semantics of the generalisation/specialisation type. There is no generally agreed way of modelling such semantics implicitly in relational systems; some designers may choose to simply create separate base relations sharing common key attributes for the subtype and supertype, while others may employ views to model these semantics. The view approach [RAM89, RAM91] seems more attractive since to some albeit, limited extent, it incorporates the concept of inheritance which is the essence of subtype/supertype and it limits the degree of redundancy. The view approach also helps prevent the familiar 'update anomaly' problems [DAT84] which arise when the DB contains duplicates. Algorithm 1 simply ignores the possibility of this type of semantics existing in the relational model while algorithms 2 and 3 introduce steps to extract such semantics from the *user*. However, they only handle the case where such relationships are modelled by having separate base relations with common key attributes.

c). **attribute naming** - this is one of the most problematic areas in the translation process; the same attribute may be named differently in different relations (synonyms). However, a common name may be used to denote entirely different properties(homonyms). This is particularly relevant when the attributes are identifiers such as keys (primary, candidate or foreign keys). Algorithm 1 assumes unique naming of the attributes as no step is introduced to handle synonyms and homonyms. Algorithms 2 introduces a pre-processing step for renaming of attributes through querying the user. This can however, be a very tedious process. Algorithm 3, by assuming that all inclusion dependencies of the schema are given automatically rids itself of any attribute naming problems since inclusion dependencies clearly identify the synonyms. This incidentally also caters for problems with homonyms since we can simply assume that attributes in different relations are different, even if they have the same name, unless explicitly linked through inclusion dependencies. The extraction of inclusion dependencies could however, be a very tedious task requiring a lot of expertise on the part of the user.

d). **the role of candidate keys** - apart from the fact that there can be more than one candidate key for a single relation whereas only a single primary key is allowed, candidate keys can be, and often are, employed in place of primary keys. Vital schema semantics can be borne through candidate keys which could easily be ignored if the translation algorithm only used primary keys. Only Algorithms 2 and 3 consider the role of candidate keys but as will be shown later, their approach of simply swapping candidate keys with primary keys wherever they are used to denote relationdships normally represented with primary keys can lead to serious semantic difficulties and to some relationships not being shown. Such candidate keys ought to be treated independently of primary keys.

e). **the linkage between the conceptual model and the underlying relational model** - Where the conceptual model is merely used as an aid to understanding the semantics of the underlying relational model, it is important to show this connection as users still need to understand the structure of the latter before they can frame relevant queries of the DB using its query language. No algorithm to date has considered this linkage. Through this linkage, much information can be passed to the users about the semantics and the behaviour of the DB model.

f). **the extent to which the behaviour of the relational model is captured and made explicit at the conceptual level** - this criterion is cited in Davis and Arora's algorithm and is concerned with the insertion and update semantics of the conceptual model. This is a very significant contribution of Algorithm 1 which attempts to turn certain implicit constraints in the logical structure into explicit ones at the conceptual level, thus offering the designer, as the authors put it, "an ability to modify its behaviour". Their algorithm however, ignores cardinality semantics which constitute a significant part of that behaviour. Algorithms 2 and 3 introduce steps to capture cardinality constraints from the user but do not attempt to turn implicit constraints into explicit ones at the conceptual level.

3   The Entity Category relationship model (ECR)

The Entity-Relationship (ER) model is usually the favoured model for use at the conceptual level for the following reasons :-
- as a semantic data model, it supports rich semantics;
- it is easy to describe and understand the conceptual schema of a DB expressed as an ER-model.
- it allows for both structural and behavioural semantics to be described;
- it provides for easy mapping to traditional models;
- it embodies very few concepts, thus it is easy for the user to learn;
- it is widely employed for conceptual design being the basis of many CASE tools.

However, the original ER-model of Chen [CHE76] does not support abstractions of the generalisation/specialisation type and as such a variant of it supporting these additional semantics is usually adopted. One variant of this model supporting such additional semantics is the Entity-Category-Relationship (ECR) model [ELM85]. A category in the ECR model is defined as a subset of the union of one or more defining entity sets. If it is the subset of one defining entity set then it is a subclass category otherwise it is a superclass category.

Fig. 2 is a picturial representation of an Entity-Category-Relationship model. The ECR model like the ER model shows the maximum cardinality (degree) of each relationship; the one on the DEPARTMENT entity side of the Employs relationship means that an employee can belong to at most one department while the N on the EMPLOYEE entity side of the relationship means that a department can have any number of employees up to the maximum of N. Existence Dependency constraints are shown by enclosing the weak entity set (as it is called) in a double-rectangle on the Entity-Relationship Diagram (ERD), with an arrow pointing to this weak entity and a label of either E or ID in the associated relationship (which also becomes a weak relationship). An E is placed in the relationship box if the weak entity can be identified by the value (s) of its own attributes while an ID is used if the weak entity can only be identified by its relationship with the entity on which it is dependent. An ID dependency is automatically an existence constraint but an existence constraint is not necessarily an ID dependency. It is through existence dependencies and cardinality information that the ER and ECR models capture some of the behaviour of the DB.

4   Modelling in Relational Systems

The single modelling concept of the relational model is the *relation* which is defined as a subset of the cartesian product of its underlying domains. The relation is used to model both entities and relationships, though some relationships may also be modelled using foreign keys. The choice of whether to use a separate relation for a relationship (known as a relationship relation) or to introduce a foreign key in the related relation is usually dependent on the degree (cardinality) of the relationship; one-to-many relationships are usually supported by foreign keys while many-to-many relationships are supported through *relationship relations*. Thus to a limited extent, cardinality constraints are captured

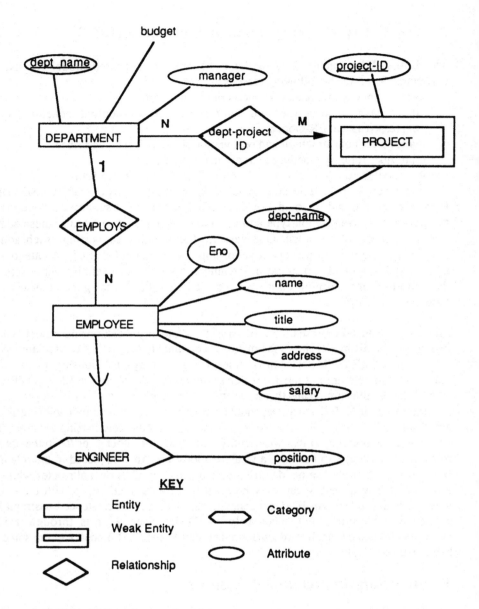

Fig. 2. An ECR Model For A Departmental DB

in the relational model. No generally agreed approach seems to exist for modelling subtypes and generalisation hierarchies in a relational model. Separate relations with common key attributes may simply be created for both the generic and subtype entities, or views could be adopted. The view approach [RAM89,RAM91] seems more intuitive since it encourages some amount of *inheritance* and also adheres to one modelling goal of the relational model, namely that of *removing redundancies*. To ascertain that each relation describes either a single entity or a single relationship rather than multiple entities or mixtures of entities and relationships, and to remove redundancies, the relations of the relational model are usually modelled as *third normal form (3NF)* relations.

5 A New Composite Algorithm For Mapping existing Relational Schemas to ECR Models

No classification of the relations and attributes of the relational schema is needed in our algorithm. Consideration of each relation's role is automated. Like previous approaches it is assumed that the relational schema is normalised up to 3NF. We will use the sample relational schema, in Fig.3, to illustrate the different steps of this algorithm. In this schema, relation keys are shown *underlined*, candidate keys are shown in *italics* and subtype/super-type relationships are represented by using common key attributes.

> person(<u>ssn</u>,name,address)
> student(<u>stud_id</u>,*ssn*,sname,address)
> undergrad(<u>undergrad_id</u>,*ssn*,year_of_study,sname,address).
> course(<u>number</u>,name,hour)
> Enrollment(<u>cou_number,undergrad_id</u>,date)
> Employee(<u>number</u>,*ssn*,name,salary,building_num,room)
> Employee_project(<u>empnum,proj_num</u>,hours_spent)
> Department_project(<u>deptnum,projnum</u>,buget).
> Job(<u>job#</u>,description,salary_range)
> Employee_job(<u>empnum,jobnum</u>)
> Location(<u>building#,room</u>,Description,Capacity)

Fig. 3. Sample Relational Schema

Steps of the Algorithm

Step 1. The Preprocessing Step - Renaming of attributes - identifying attributes such as keys and candidate keys must be uniquely named throughout the relational schema. To achieve this uniqueness of naming all synonyms must be identified and changed to a common name while all homonyms are given new names. Attribute names carry some limited semantics which however, is at too high a level to be interpretted by a computer. Knowledge of synonyms and homonyms must be supplied by the user. Relation names are used to achieve uniqueness in attribute naming throughout the schema by prefixing attribute names with relation names. If a relation does not exist for the particular attributes in question, as for relations only sharing common parts of their key attributes (not the whole key), then the user must be queried to supply a name; for example, the relations Employee_project and Department_project of Fig.3, share a common attribute represented by the synonyms *proj_num* in Employee_project and *projnum* in Department_project. After this step the schema of Fig. 3 is converted to Fig. 3.1 below.

```
person(ssn,name,address)
student(student_stud_id,ssn,sname,address)
undergrad(student_stud_id,ssn,year_of_study,sname,address).
course(course_number,name,hour)
Enrollment(course_number,student_stud_id,date)
Employee(employee_number,ssn,name,address,salary,
            location_building#,location_room)
Employee_project(employee_number,project#,hours_spent)
Department_project(dept#,project#,buget).
Job(job#,description,salary_range)
Employee_job(employee_number,job#)
Location(location_building#,location_room,Description,Capacity)
```

Fig. 3.1. Sample Relational Schema After Step 1.

Step 2. Subtype/Supertype relationship establishment.

This step is necessary at this early stage of the algorithm so that inferrable relationships need not be computed and represented. Where views are employed to capture semantics of the subtype/supertype nature, the establishment of the subtype/supertype relationship is trivial as this is implicit in the view definitions. An example will make the process more apparent. Consider a portion of a DB schema described by the following Prolog facts:

```
R1 : student(stud_id,sname,address)
R2 : undergrad(undergrad_id,year_of_study)
V  : undergrad_view([[undergrad_id,undergrad],[year_of_study,undergrad]
        [sname,student],[address,student]],[[undergrad_id,stud_id]]])
```

Where the R s stand for relation schemes and the V represents a view with each attribute of the view shown together with the relation from which it is derived and the *'where'* part of the view definition shown as the second argument. We assume suitable routines exist to extract the view definitions for subtype to supertype relationships and present them in the above format. Our algorithm simply stores information about the subtype/supertype relationship from R2 to R1. The process of identifying subtype/supertype relationships is more demanding when these relationships are simply captured through common keys and duplicated attributes. In this case, any two or more relations having the same key attribute(s) or where the primary key of one matches the candidate key of the other are presented to the user for confirmation of any subtypes/supertype relationships. Those attributes of the subtype relation that can be inherited from the supertype are deleted. During this step the relations Person, Student, Undergrad and Employee of Fig. 3.1 will be isolated and presented to the user. These relations will be modified as described above and subtype/supertype information stored as shown in Fig 3.2. Notice that candidate key attributes are maintained in the subtype entity since the relationship can be represented using candidate keys.

472

```
person(ssn,name,address)
student(student stud id,ssn)
undergrad(student stud id,ssn,year_of_study)
Employee(employee number,ssn,salary,location_building#,
         location_room)
subtype(person,student)
subtype(person,employee)
subtype(student,undergrad)
```

Fig. 3.2. Schema after Step 2 showing subtype/ supertype relationships and modified relations

Step 3   Isolation of regular entities

Algorithm 1 gives two rules for isolating regular entities out of relations of the schema. No user interaction is needed in this case. The rules are:

   a). relations with a single attribute as their primary key are converted into entities.

   b). relations with more than one attribute making up their key are examined and if this key is always used as a whole in other relations, and never used as disjoint parts separately in the keys of other relations, or if its attributes are never used again (i.e. as a whole or partially) then the corresponding relations are also converted to entities. During this step, the relations Person, Student, Undergrad, Course, Employee, Job and Location are converted into entities having the same attributes and keys as the converted relation.

In the following steps of the Algorithm we make reference to relation ID to stand for either the primary key of a relation or its candidate key. Relationships between entities can be represented using primary keys or candidate keys. Apart from the subtype/supertype relationship already described above, three other cases exist when candidate keys could play the normal role of a primary key :

   i) the candidate key of some relation R1 can occur as part of the primary key of another relation R2, where R2 is either a weak entity (see Step 4 below) or a relationship relation (step 5).

   ii) the candidate key of a relation, if formed by concatenation of primary keys of other relations, would denote a relationship relation between these entities.

   iii) the candidate key of a relation can also occur as a non-key attribute of another relation to denote the one-to-many relationship between the former entity relation and the latter.

Algorithms 2 and 3 while ignoring case iii) above suggest that for case i) above, the primary key of R1 replaces its candidate key in R2 while for case ii) the candidate key should become the new primary key of its relationship. The general problem with both suggestions is that the resulting conceptual model could mislead the user into making incorrect logical level joins. The specific problem with the second suggestion is that making the candidate key the new primary key can lead to certain relationships, represented through the old primary key not being found by the algorithm. For example, consider the sample of part of a typical relational schema given in Fig.4.

```
person(ssn,name).
employee(ssn,salary).
student(collegeno,ssn).
course(courseno,coursename).
enrollment(collegeno,courseno,date)
```
Fig 4. Part of a typical relational schema

Following the suggestion of algorithms 2 and 3, the primary key of student becomes *'ssn'* since a subtype/supertype relationship would naturally be confirmed by the user between the *student* and *person* entity relations. This change will mean that the relationship relation *'enrollment'* will be wrongly treated as a weak entity dependent on the course entity rather than a many-to-many relationship between students and courses. In our algorithm, candidate keys are considered independently but in much the same way as keys for possible hidden relationships. This means that in the ECRD diagram, the relationship key is not restricted to being a concatenation of the Primary keys of its entities but rather to being a concatenation of identifiers of its participating entities. We will consequently use the name ID to refer to either the Primary key or the Candidate key of a relation.

Step 4   Isolation of Weak Entities
This step also derives from algorithm 1 but with some modification to take the subtype/supertype relationships created so far and candidate keys into consideration. The approach is to compare the ID of the remaining relations of the relational schema with the ID of the entities derived so far. If one or more attributes of a non-relationship relation ID are left over, then this relation becomes a weak entity. The attribute(s) left over when the relation ID is compared to the entity ID is known as a *dangling key* and forms the only attribute(s) of the weak entity. A relationship is created between the new weak entity and the regular entity. The key of this relationship is made up of all the attributes of the original relation from which the weak entity derives. Where the entity used for comparison is involved in a generalisation hierarchy, then the user must be queried to see at which level of the hierarchy the relationship should be introduced and any other entities in the hierarchy could be ignored in this comparison. Information about the type of dependence of the weak entity on the regular entity as well as on the cardinality of the relationship has to be extracted from the user. In Algorithm 1, the cardinality of the relationship is simply made to be many-to-many. We argue that this may be too general to convey the specific semantics of the relationship.

From the remaining relations after Step 3 above, the Employee-project relation becomes a weak entity since the key of the Employee entity-set is employee_number and the key of the Employee_poject relation is (employee_number,project#). The project# is the dangling key attribute. A new entity-set Project will be created (after consulation with the user for its name) with its only attribute also forming its key. A relationship is created between the new weak entity and the entity on which it is dependent. The new Project entity-set will give rise to another weak entity from the Department_project relation, named Department with its only attributes being the dangling key (dept#,budget). This weak entity will be treated in like manner to the previous weak entity-set.

Step 5: The Many-to-Many Relationships
As explained in Section 4 above, many-to-many relations are normally modelled in relational systems by creating new relations and concatenating the IDs of the involved entities to form the ID of the new relation. Thus in the reverse process, any relation whose ID is made up of a concatenation of the IDs of entities that have been derived so far is turned into a many-to-many relationship between the involved entities. Again subtype/supertype relationships of the entities must be taken into consideration and the user queried if necessary to see at which level of the hierarchy the relationship should be introduced. The Employee_job relation and the Enrollment relation meet these criteria. Thus a many-to-many relationship will be created between their participant entities. In the case of the Enrollment relation, the user will need to say whether the relationship is between the Entity-sets Student and Course or Undergrad and Course. Owing to the possibility of a many-to-one relationship (see step 6) being modelled using a relationship relation, the user would have to be queried as to the exact cardinality of the relationship; i.e. whether the cardinality is many-to-many or many-to-one.

Step 6: The Many-to-one Relationships
By this stage, all the relations of the relational schema would have either been converted into regular entities, weak entities and their relationships, or many-to-many relationships. Many-to-One relationships are usually modelled in the relational model by including the ID of the entity on the One side of the relationship in the set of attributes of the entity on the Many side of the relationship. Thus if the ID of an entity that has been derived occurs as a non-key attribute in another entity, then a one-to-many relationship is created from the former entity to the latter. The exact cardinality of the relationship (i.e. one-to-one or one-to-many) can be found by querying the user. Entities involved in a generalisation hierarchy must be treated in like manner to the previous two steps. The user must also be queried to provide a suitable name for the relationship as well as any possible existence dependencies between the entities. A many-to-one relationship will be created, using this step, between the entity-sets, Employee and Location. This step completes the algorithm. The ECR Diagram derived in this way from the relational schema of Fig 3 is shown in Fig. 5.

6 Implementation of the Algorithm

All 6 steps of the algorithm described above have been implemented in the Arity/Prolog implementation of Prolog on an IBM PC machine [MAR86,ARI87]. This implementation of Prolog extends the standard Prolog version with very useful extralogical features to improve its performance and to cater for more algorithmic tasks. Amongst these features are *virtual memory management* capabilities and *text screen management* functions useful for implementing graphics. The graphics function was very useful in implementing the Entity-Category-Relationship Diagram (ECRD) of the conceptual model.

Step 1 of the algorithm described above requires that knowledge of synonyms and homonyms be supplied by the *user*. To facilitate this process, the system displays pairs of relations from the relational schema at a time and then asks the user to identify any possible synonyms and homonyms. As relation names are unique within a single database schema, uniqueness in attribute names is achieved by prefixing the individual attributes with the name of the parent relation. This approach appears more practical and easier to apply than previous ones which either require unique naming (Algorithm 1) or that all inclusion dependencies be stated and the relations and attributes classified. Algorithm 2, while recommending such renaming does not show how this can be achieved.

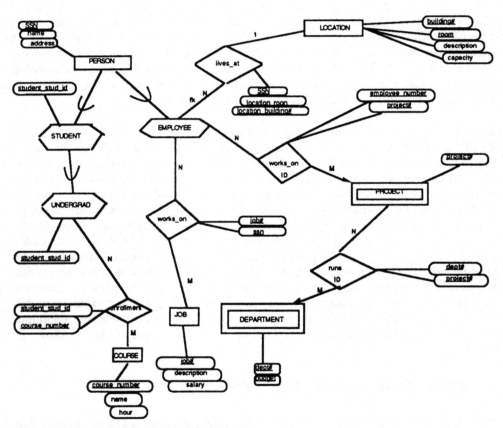

Fig. 5. An Entity-Category Relationship Diagram of the Sample Relational Schema.

Whenever input is required to test if a certain rule can 'fire', the system gives the user the choice of asking 'why' such input is needed; in which case the system would display the rule for which input is sought and then repeat the question. The rules have been structured in an easy-to-read manner and should assist the user gain a better understanding of the algorithm's reasoning process as well as the semantics of the DB. Example rules of this nature that may require input from the user include :

      - rules that capture cardinality constraints of relationships;
      - rules for capturing dependency constraints of weak entities;

- rules for determining at what level of a generalisation hierarchy a relationship should be introduced.
- rules that capture new relationship names.

The last set of rules involve relationships represented by foreign keys (i.e. keys, or more appropriately IDs, of some relations occuring as non-keys of other relations). Queries for rules, such as the last set, that capture relationship names, normally present the user with some conclusion that the system has drawn, for example, that a many-to-one relationship exists between some two entities. The *user* is given the option in this case to ask for an explanation of how this conclusion was arrived at; in which case the domain knowledge embodied in the rule for establishing many-to-one relationships from foreign keys is shown. The condition parts of this rule would have been instantiated. The system thus, exhibits some expert system capabilities. However, as some steps of the algorithm are fully automated and do not require input from the user, complete knowledge of how all steps of the algorithm are carried out cannot and need not be shown to the *user*.

A sub-module of our system is concerned with the graphical output. An Entity- Category Relationship Diagram (ECRD) of the model is automatically generated from the structures generated by the various steps, of the algorithm. These structures represent entities, relationships and relationship constraints. Some labels have been introduced in this ECRD to show the user how certain relationships of the conceptual model are represented at the logical level, thus assisting the user to make extensional database queries from a knowledge of this conceptual model. Where the relationship is represented by a foreign key in the relational schema, the label *"fk"* is placed on the line connecting the relationship diamond and the entity rectangle (or hexagon) in which the foreign key is placed; otherwise it is to be understood that the relationship and its participating entities are modelled at the logical level in the same way as at the conceptual level, i.e. by separate relations with the same attributes and the same keys. For subtype/supertypes captured at the logical level through views, a label V is placed on the line connecting the supertype entity to its subtype.

7 Conclusions

In this paper, we examined three existing representative algorithms for converting relational schemas to conceptual models. Through this comparative study, we identified the important contributions of each algorithm as well as its limitations. It became apparent that some of the limitations of one algorithm were addressed by another algorithm while some still remained to be solved. Thus a new algorithm was developed that integrated the important concepts of these algorithms and introduced new concepts to rectify their limitations. This new algorithm is more general and easier to apply than any of its predecessors. Its implementation also shows a high degree of automation. While certain steps of the algorithm are made transparent to the user in the implementation, users are given the choice to see some of the rules that implement other steps in an attempt to give them a better understanding of that part of the algorithm and as such make it easier for them to provide the algorithm with the correct input. Thus our approach adopts some

Expert System techniques useful in explaining parts of the algorithm to the user employing it. This should make the algorithm easier to use and available to a wider group of DB users.

Due to designer decisions, the exact approach used for modelling particular relationships at the logical level can be different. At the conceptual level however, relationships are modelled in the same fashion. Thus we found it necessary to augment the conceptual model represented by the ERD with new features (labels on arcs) that show how such relationships are modelled at the logical level. These new features should make the correspondence between the conceptual model and the underlying logical model more apparent. Thus, users querying the data of the database are assisted by the conceptual model which helps them see relationships and how they are modelled in the relational model.

One major contribution of our algorithm is in its treatment of subtype/supertype relationships and candidate keys. Subtype/supertype relationships are created at an early stage in the algorithm and any generalisation hierarchies built and maintained for use in later stages. As the entities in a subtype/supertype hierarchy have common IDs, when this ID is found as an attribute of some other relation(s) (i.e. as a foreign key), the system first presents the most generic entity in the hierarchy together with the other entity (the one with the foreign key) and asks the user if the relationship exists. If the response to this is 'yes', then no further entities in the hierarchy will be considered. If the answer is 'no', then the entities at the next level of the hierarchy will be considered. In this way redundant relationships are not be created. By treating candidate keys in the same way as primary keys when creating the relationships of the conceptual model, it became possible to identify the relationships embodied by these candidate keys without compromising those embodied by primary keys. This leads to a semantically richer conceptual model and one from which the logical model can be easily understood by its users; which should lead to correct utilisation of its semantics.

In [KAL91], an implementation followed by a critique of Algorithm 2 was carried out. One criticism pointed out in this work is that the algorithm cannot handle multi-level dependencies properly, e.g. if a weak entity A depends on another weak entity B which depends on a regular entity C, then the algorithm does not show the dependency of A on B since an entity can only be ID dependent on a regular entity. As pointed out in Step 4 of our algorithm, multilevel dependencies are automatically catered for. However, in the current implementation the concept of inheritance is not used; thus for the example above, A and B will be shown dependent on C as well as A being dependent on B. The fact that A is dependent on C is implicit in its being dependent on B which in turn is dependent on C. The modification needed for this is however, not difficult to implement. A's dependency on C could simply be deleted.

A useful future extension of this system would be to investigate how the semantics of the DB that are coded in its application programs can be used to aid the mapping process. The semantics captured in application programs are typically of two types; namely state constraints, e.g. to enforce a subrange constraint on an attribute of a relation defined in the schema as one of the basic types of the DBMS, and transition (behavioural) constraints which monitor changes made on the database. Another extension would be to introduce steps that can be used to first derive a global schema for a Multidatabase System(MBS) in relational form, and then employ the algorithm described in this paper to produce a global conceptual schema of the entire information of interest to the user.

A fundamental limitation of the whole approach to eliciting the semantics of a relational database as presented in this paper and previous similar works, is a general lack of consideration of the explicit constraints of the database, examples of which are cardinality constraints and dependency constraints. Explicit constraints are those constraints that are tangential to the data model and serve to augment the structure specification of the database. Constraints captured with the structure of the data model are called inherent constraints. The relational model is well known for being weak on capturing inherent constraints and as such a great deal of the semantics of the database is captured through the explicit constraints. No known diagrammatic approach exists for completely capturing all types of these explicit constraints. Thus, some other way must be found for making their semantics apparent to users. Some of these constraints actually refer to particular instances of the database. A simple approach may be to simply output the logic specification of these constraints together with the conceptual model and leave it to the user to interpret the output. The problem with this is that a significant part of the logical schema (up to 80 percent) could be made up of the explicit constraints, [DAT84].

A further extension of our work is to investigate how these explicit constraints can be employed in the Multidatabase environment, (where most difficulties arise regarding the semantics of a database; usually the semantics of remote databases), to enhance the user's knowledge of the semantics of these databases. These explicit constraints could be used to provide intensional answers to certain data related queries whenever the system, from knowledge of the explicit constraints, deems that such semantics need to be made clear to the user. This idea borrows from the recent research interest in intensional query processing in deductive databases [CHO87,IMI87,PIR30,SON90]. Thus a complete conceptual model of a database must embody its inherent and explicit constraints as well as other structural aspects.

Reference

[ABR74]   J.R,Abrial, *"Data Semantics"*, in Data Base Management Etd by J.W. Klimbie & K.L Koffeman, North-Holland, pp1-59, 1974

[ALL82]   F.W.Allen,M.E.S.Loomis & M.V.Mannino, *"The Integrated Dictionary/ Directory System"*, - Computing Surveys 1982.

[ARI87]   Arity Corporation, *"Arity/Prolog Programming Manual"* - Arity Corporation - 1987.

[BAT86]   C.Batini et al; *"A comparative analysis of database schema integration"*, ACM comp. surveys, Dec. 1986.

[BRA76]   G. Bracchi, P. Paolini & G. Pelagatti, *"Binary Logical Associations in Data Modelling"*, in Modelling in Data Base Management Systems edited by G.M.

Nijssen, pp. 125-148, North Holland, 1976

[CER84] S.Ceri & G.Pelagatti, *"Distributed Databases : Principles and systems"*, McGraw-Hill Int., 1984.

[CHE76] P.P. Chen, *"The Entity Relationship Model -- Towards a Unified View of Data"*, ACM TODS Vol. 1, No. 1, pp 9-36, March 1976.

[CHO87] L. Cholvy & R. Demolombe,*"Querying a Rule Base"*. In Procs. of the 1st International Conf. on Expert Database Systems, Pp365-371, S. Carolina - 1987. L. Kerschberg (Etd).

[COD70] E.F. Codd, *"A relational Model of data for large shared databanks"*, Communications of the ACM 1970.

[COD79] E.F.Codd, *"Extending the Database Relational Model to Capture more meaning"* ACM Trans. on Database Systems - 1979.

[DAT84] C.J. Date, *"Database Systems"*, Vols.1 & 2 , (4th Edition) - Addison-Wesley Pub -1984.

[DAT87] C.J.Date *"What is a Distributed Database System?"* , InfoDB, Vol 2, No 2,1987.

[DAV88] K.H. Davis & A.K. Arora, *"Converting a Relational Database Model into an Entity-Relationship Model"*, Seventh International Conference on Entity-relationship Approach", 1988.

[DOL87] D.R.Dolk & R.A.Kirsch, *"A Relational Information Resource Dictionary System"*, Comm. of the ACM - 1987.

[ELM85] R.Elmasri, J.Weeldreyer & A.Hevner, *"The Category Concept : An Extension to the Entity-Relationship model"*, In Data and Knowledge Engineering, Vol. 1, No. 1, June, 1985.

[ELM89] R.Elmasri & S.B.Navathe, *"Fundamentals of Database Systems"*, Addison-Wesley Pub. - 1989.

[GAR85] G.Gardarin & M.Jarke; *"Database Design Tools: An Expert Systems Approach"*; VLDB 1985.

[GAR90]. G.Gardarin & P. Valduriez, *"Relational Databases and Knowledge Bases"*, Adison-Wesley Pub-Co -1990.

[GRA88] P.M.D. Gray,G.E.Storrs & J.B.H. du Boulay, *"Knowledge Representations for database meta-data"*, - AI review 2,3-29 1988.

[GOT90] G.Gottlob, L.Tancia & S.Ceri,*"Surveys in Computer Science"*,Springer -Verlag - 1990.

[HAM81] M.Hammer & D.McLeod, *"Database Description with the SDM"*, ACM Trans. on DBSs, Sept 1981.

[IMI87] L. Imielinski, *"Intelligent Query Answering in Rule Based Systems"*, Journal of Logic Programming, 4(3):229-258, Sept, 1987.

[JAR84] M.Jarke & Y.Vassiliou, *"Databases and Expert systems: Opportunitiesand architectures for integration"*, - from New applications of DBs Eds. G.Gardarin & E. Gelembe - 1984.

[JOH89] P.Johannesson & K.Kalman, *"A Method for Translating Relational Schemas Into Conceptual Schemas"*, 8th International Conference On Entity-Relationship Approach, 1989.

[JOH84] R,G.Johnson; *"Integrating Data and Meta-data to enhance the user inteface"*,

BNCOD-4 1984.

[KAL91] K.Kalman, *"Implementation and Critique of an algorithm which maps a Relational Database to a Conceptual Model"*, CAiSE 1991.

[KEN79] W.Kent, *"Limitations of Record-Based Information Models"*, ACM TODS 1979.

[LIT88] W.Litwin, *"From Database Systems to Multidatabase Systems:Why and How"*; BNCOD-6 1988.

[MAR86] C. Marcus, "Prolog Programming- Applications for DBSs,Expert Systems and Natural Language Systems",- Arity Corporation - 1986.

[NAV88] S.B. Navathe & A.M. Awong, *"Abstracting Relational and /Hierarchical DataWith a Semantic Data Model"*, 7th International Conference on Entity-Relationship Approach- 1988.

[OMO89] A.O.Omololu,N.J.Fiddian & W.A.Gray, *"Confederated Database Management Systems"* - 7th British National Conference on Databases Etd. by M.H.Williams 1989.

[OXO87] E. Oxborrow, *"Databases and Database Systems"* - 1987

[PEC88] J. Peckham & F. Maryanski, *"Semantic Data Models"*, - ACM Computing Surveys,Vol.20,No.3,Sept.,1988.

[PIR89] A. Pirotte & D.Roelants, *"Constraints for Improving the Generation of Intensional Answers in a Deductive Answer"*, In the Procs. of the International Conf. on Data Engineering, Los Angeles, California - 1989.

[RAM89] A. Ramfos,N.J.Fiddian & W.A.Gray, *"Object-Oriented to Relational Inter-Schema Meta-Translation"*, 1989 WorkshopOn Heterogeneous Databases, Dec. 11- 13, 1989, Chicago.

[RAM91] A. Ramfos,N.J.Fiddian & W.A.Gray, *"Relational to Object-Oriented Schema Meta-Translation"*, Procs. of the 9th British National Conference On the management of Data, Wolverhampton 1991.

[ROU87] N.Roussopoulos & L.Mark *"Information Interchange between self-describing Databases"*, IEEE Trans. on Data Engineering 1987.

[SMI77] J.M.Smith & D.C.P.Smith, *"Database Abstractions: Aggregation and Generalisation"*, ACM TODS-1977

[SMI81] J.M Smith et al; *"Multibase - Integrating Heterogeneous Distributed Databases"*, Proc. AFIPS Nat. Comp. Conf. 1981.

[SON90] I-Y.Song,H-J.Kim & P. Geutner, *"Intensional Query Processing: A Three-Step Approach"*, Procs. 1st International Conf. on Databases and Expert Systems Applications, Vienna 1990.

[TSI82] D.C Tsichritzis & F.H. Lochovsky, *"Data Models"*, Published by Prentice Hall Inc. - New Jersey - 1982.

[VAS83] Y.Vassiliou & M.Jarke; *"How does an Expert Syustem get its data?"*, VLDB, 1983.

[VAS84] Y. Vassiliou & M. Jarke; *"Databases and Expert Systems: Opportunities and Architectures"*, New applications of Expert Systems and Databases, Edited by G.Gardarin, 1984.

Model Integration in Information Planning Tools

Alex A. Verrijn-Stuart & Guus J. Ramackers

Department of Computer Science
University of Leiden
The Netherlands

e-mail: verrynstuart@rulcri.LeidenUniv.nl

Abstract. Information Planning requires integration in two senses, (1) linking the information requirements identified in the business system into further application detail ['vertical integration'] and (2) comprehensive modelling of relevant aspects, such that consistency is maintained at all levels ['horizontal integration']. These requirements may be satisfied by a framework that recognizes both the organizational information usage and the formalized (computerizable) systems that will serve it. Metamodels are discussed that provide a formal basis for such an all-embracing approach. They are illustrated by a prototype tool for capturing an organizational description, from which a broad specification of application systems may be derived by semi-automated means.

Keywords: Information Planning, Information Systems Design, CASE-tools

1 INTRODUCTION

The term "Information System" (IS) is used in two senses. On the one hand, it may refer to the over-all organizational usage of information (including communication), on the other, it may concern a computerized application. In previous publications [13, 8, 7], we distinguished these under the names *ISB* ('*IS* in the *B*roader sense') and *ISN* ('*IS* in the *N*arrower sense'), respectively. The ISB covers all informational aspects of the 'Business System' (BS), irrespective of the availability of computerized support as such. An ISN may be the conceptual model or the specification of a computerized (sub)system. At the pragmatic level, the ISB consists of a number of interacting agents (person, departments, their interactions and so on), whereas an ISN is a computer program (package or module) allowing storage, updating, manipulation and retrieval of representations of information.

ISB and ISN belong to different organizational cultures and failure to distinguish between the two leads to difficulties in creating and maintaining of information resources and to under-utilization of the information resources that are available. This paper is concerned with the creation-and-maintenance problem.

The need to continuously monitor an organization's information requirements ('Information Planning') is generally recognized, although one rarely practices it as an on-going activity [9]. We shall present an integrated approach that not only will allow identification and formulation of such requirements, but actually may form the basis for linking the Information Plan to formal descriptions of potential or actual computer applications. This linking is referred to as 'vertical integration', as opposed to the 'horizontal integration' of views at one particular level of abstraction, say, interrelating the data model and functional specification in a conceptual IS description [10].

Note that vertical integration (also) should cover the expression of how the IP fits in the organization, in other words how a "technically" formulated ISN is "embedded" in the "organizationally" formulated ISB.

Building on our ISB\ISN Framework [8], the problem addressed here is best stated with reference to the following diagram.

> # ORGANIZATION : (1) BS ↔ (2) ISB ↔ (3) ISN

Information Planning (IP) implies information-oriented modelling of one's BS, such that the ISB is highlighted. Ideally, that model allows various (potential or existing) ISN to be identified in the subsequent "Information *Systems* Planning" (ISP) activity.

Step (1)→(2), in fact, is no more than a shading of physical reality, but does not per se require a statement of what ISN might be desired. However, in this stage, one normally does question the BS's information requirements in general. The possiblity of adapting one's way of working (e.g. by a reorganization) may well come up. Borrowing Lundeberg's terminology [5], we call the totality of such *information-affecting organizational modifications* "Change Analysis I".

Step (2)→(3), on the other hand, means that one considers what computerized systems one should install (or modify, if already existing). In other words, here one addresses the potentials of new forms of support. Hence, we refer to these *computer-related modifications* as "Change Analysis II".

In the next section we shall present metamodels that may serve as a formal basis for IP tools. These would be capable of interfacing with CASE tools for detailed analysis and design of any ISN to be embedded in the ISB.

2 INFORMATION PLANNING METAMODELS

An IP tool - in our view - must possess the following qualities:

1 Convenient interfacing for the information planning staff[1], such that all concepts and relationships are expressed in "organizational" terminology;
2 The underlying meta-model is rooted in the organizational semantics, but, at the same time, formalized on the basis of a well-founded, coherent theory.

---

[1] An organizational setup is assumed where IP is practised in a staff function reporting to the CEO, working jointly with divisional and/or departmental staff responsible for IS development and maintenance, although a different allocation of responsibilities might apply.

Formalization - apart from scientific soundness and elegance - provides means for consistency enforcement and completeness checking in a practical way. It also should enable further analysis of a model described when using the tool, e.g. in simulations or performance studies. Finally, a formalization-based IP tool should be capable of extension into tools for designing and (ideally) constructing/modifying the application systems (in fact, ISNs in our definition).

As an initial meta-model, we consider an organization as consisting of departments (named *Organization units*, or "OrgUnits"), who have organizational *Tasks*, for which they may employ *Resource Units* ("ResUnits", active resources: either persons or devices, and passive resources: either material of informational), by involvement in *Actions*; these Actions form part of the aforementioned Tasks (see Figure 1). Note that further sub-characterization of ResUnits and Actions may be considered so as to reflect real world roles (e.g. device: machine or computer; primary actions: production, investment, maintenance, and secondary actions: office, computation, information, etc.). Such detailing is important in applications, but need be mentioned here only in passing [9].

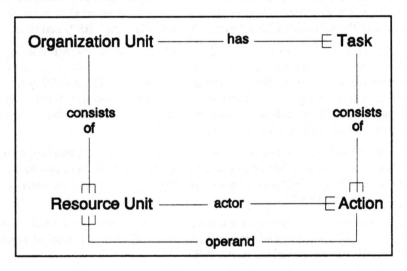

Figure 1: Initial Information Planning Meta-model.

To demonstrate the usefulness of these meta-models, a prototype IP tool, called **UNIS** (UNiversal Information System description tool) was built [14]. It allowed a two-phase homing in on one or more ISN, by the following steps:

- *Organizational Description*: If the system description is empty, the user is able to populate it with OrgUnits, Tasks, ResUnits and Actions - if it is not empty, the population may be modified and extended.
- *Change Analysis I*: A given description may be subjected to a 'projection', by which any non-informational element (ResUnit, Task and/or Action) is pushed into the background; while engaged in this (otherwise automated) action, the user is asked whether fully physical elements (e.g. material streams or processes) need to be reflec-

The **TransCorp** case [14] concerns a haulage company, whose primary business is transporting parcel and bulk goods; among other things modelling is required of a temporary "Freight Storage" (the storage facilities). In one sample of the BS description this led to:

Task	* [task-id 7]	Freight Storage	(a "primary" action in the real world)
Actions	[act-id 44]	Store Freight	(a "primary" action in the real world)
	[act-id 45]	Unstore Freight	(a "primary" action in the real world)
	[act-id 46]	Clean Store	(a "primary" action in the real world)
	* [act-id 47]	Fill-in Storage Form	(a "support" action in the real world)
	* [act-id 48]	Send Storage Form	(a "support" action in the real world)
	[act-id 51]	'Dummy/Empty'	(a [sofar] "undefined" action)

These actions are sequenced ('life cycle') : (46+51);44;47;48;45;47;48
where "+" stands for alternative action ("or"), and ";" for chaining

ResUnits	* [unit-id 15]	Depot worker	(actor for act-id 44)
	[unit-id 20]	Truck	(operand for act-id 44)
	[unit-id 29]	Freight	(operand for act-id 44)
	……….	…………….	………………………

No ResUnits had been associated with act-id 47-48; since the ISB highlights the "support" actions, while pushing into the background the real world activity, Change Analysis I might result in making the Storage Form handling explicit, as follows:

* [unit-id 15]	Depot worker	(actor for act-id 47)
* [unit-id 17]	Storage Form	(operand for act-id 47)
* [unit-id 15]	Depot worker	(actor for act-id 48)
* [unit-id 17]	Storage Form	(operand for act-id 48)

The items marked with an asterisk "*" would then appear in the *ISB* foreground.

Figure 2: Small portion of an ISB derivation and description.

ted in informational description terms (e.g. size of a stock, activity level of process, etc.); by reacting to these prompts, the user actially performs what amounts to "Change Analysis I", viz. introducing information flows and usage events, corresponding to decisions of new ways of (informational) working; the result is a description of the ISB, in which the various Actions may be chained as sequences and/or in parallel (see Figure 2).

- *Change Analysis II*: Given a "projected" system description of the ISB (i.e. where the informational elements have been indicated as such), the user is prompted to indicate whether any informational Actions should be computer-supported; deciding to do so constitutes Change Analysis II; if necessary, an informational device (computer) is "created"; the result is aan ISN description (see Figure 3).

The prototype (UNIS vs 1.0) was tested on a number of simple, yet non-trivial cases. This study revealed that the meta-model was quite satisfactory, but showed shortcomings in two respects. Firstly, descriptions took insufficient cognizance of data modelling and process modelling aspects (in fact, of the data, process and behaviour "perspectives", as a whole). These problems were referred to before under the generic name 'horizontal integration'. Secondly, the role of the ISNs was expressed such that each actor's involve-

In [14] a model had been given for the **TransCorp** case up to and including Change Analysis II. Whilst the explicit form of the resulting computerization is not relevant to this discussion, some of the choices are. They were as follows.

BS description:

Task	3	Global Planning	(a "support" task in the real world)
Action	17	Receive Order	(a "support" action in the real world)
	18	Cancel Order	(a "support" action in the real world)
	19	Confirm Order	(a "support" action in the real world)
	20	Send Order [adm]	(a "support" action in the real world)
	21	Send Cancel [client]	(a "support" action in the real world)
	36	Order Entry + Planning	(a "support" action in the real world)
	57	Receive Order [planner]	(a "support" action in the real world)

Action Sequencing $(17|57);(18;(21|20))+(19;36)$

["|" = independent action (concurrency), ";" = chaining, "+" = alternatives ("or")]

ResUnit	4	Order	("informational" operand: input)
	5	Planner	(actor: person)
	8	Global Plan	("informational" operand: output)
	10	Global Maintenance Plan	("informational" operand: output)

All actions and resunits in this example are associated with "support", hence are "informational"; when prompted to consider computer support (Change Analysis II), the choice was made to do so on behalf of the Planner, for action 36 (Order Entry for Planning, which leads to updated Global and Global Maintenance Plans, respectively).

Since, initially, the *ISB* did not have a computer facility embedded for use by the Planner (ResUnit 5), it is now introduced (**ResUnit 32: "I-ACTOR for ResUnit 5"**); upon selecting which operands are subjected to computerized support, the answer (in the treament of the case) is that the Order (ResUnit 4) is to serve as input and the two plans (ResUnits 8 and 10) will be output. Since (in the case) the latter two are only involved as output in connection with Entry (manual Action 36), Change Analysis II here leads to replacement of the original manual action by a computerized one (**New Action 58**).

Hence the **ISN description** will contain, among other things:

Task	3	Global Planning	(a "support" task in the real world)
Action	**58**	**Computerized Planning**	(resulting from **Change Analysis II**)
ResUnit	5	Planner	(User-Actor involved with **New Action 58**)
	32	**I-ACTOR for ResUnit 5**	(Computer made available for **New Action 58**)
	4	Order	(Input Operand for **New Action 58**)
	8	Global Plan	(Output Operand for **New Action 58**)
	10	Global Maintenance Plan	(Output Operand for **New Action 58**)

Figure 3: Small portion of an ISN derivation and description.

ment with computerized support would give rise to an independent Human-Computer Interaction situation ("HCI"); such a description is somewhat cumbersome, in that it implies that a large number of unrelated computerized systems might be constructed.

The data, process and behaviour models are, in fact, three different views on the same system. In the traditional design process, they are formulated separately, so that consistency enforcement becomes an external requirement. This is the aforementioned problem of 'horizontal integration'. Elsewhere, an object-based event-oriented model has been shown to provide a suitable approach for dealing with it [10]. We will now demonstrate how the meta-model may be expanded accordingly. Subsequently, the remaining 'vertical integration' problems (linking the BS, ISB and ISN descriptions) will be tackled.

The essence of the first meta-model was the way in which ResUnits may be "involved-in" Actions, viz. as Actors (one-to-many) or as Operands (many-to-one). That allowed formulating 'life-cycle' nets, describing such things as the handling of an order or the updating of a plan, i.e. *information flow*, as part of the Task description. Processing (in the sense of *data processing*) is implied in the concept of an "informational" Action. Whilst simple views of the behaviour models may be derived, the basis for the data model need to be extended, and some sophistication is required regarding the expression of information flows between OrgUnits, in order to specify the process model. The latter is achieved by introducing the concept Transaction (Figure 4).

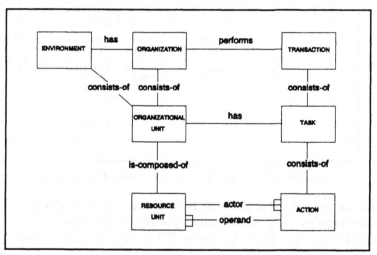

Figure 4: Meta-Model extension [1] (introducing Transactions).

The extensions required of the meta-model are, in fact, limited. They consist of making the "actor" and "operand" relationships of Figure 1 explicit and introducing suitable sub-typing. This modification is illustrated in Figure 5.

There is, however, a further need for extension, viz. an explicit meta-modelling of the 'life-cycle' involvement of Transactions, Tasks and Informational Objects. A nominal way of doing this is shown in Figure 6, which should be read as extending Figure 5 on the right hand side.

Finally, we need to make provisions for 'vertical integration'. As said before, that means (1) linking BS into ISB and (2) linking ISB into ISN. Requirement (1) has been met in the foregoing. Requirement (2) involves being more explicit as regards the role of computer support. This may be taken care of as follows.

Instead of a symmetrical position of Person-actors and Device-actors (both being "subject-of" some Action), one relates the Action directly, and asymmetrically, with the "primary"

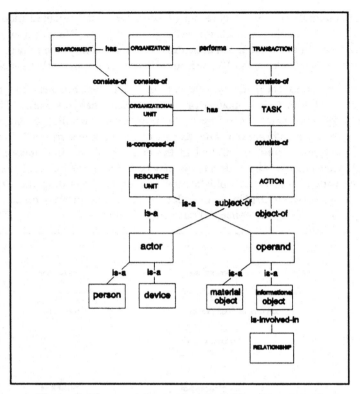

Figure 5: Meta-model extension -2- (adding data aspects)

Person-actor, on the one hand, and with the "co-actor" Device-informational (i.e. the computer), on the other. The latter is only necessary when an ISN is to be defined, but may be omitted when an implementation-free ISB is considered (see Figure 7).

Having formulated a BS in the foregoing terms and subsequently restricting onself to the informational aspects and specifying which actions require computerized support, i.e. expressing the model in the form of an ISB with embedded ISNs, the scene is set for more detailed system analysis. The ISN model described provides (1) an IS system architecture (consisting of initial analysis objects) and (2) a general organizational interaction context as input for systems analysis activity.

(1) A distributed *data model* is implied in the various allocated information operands. It is distributed in the sense that separate collections are associated with each OrgUnit, consisting of "local" entities, but possibly "shared" forms, with relationships defined for all. The ISN action *functionalities* - which may be defined in one's application as, e.g. "planning", "decision", "knowledge", "group", "transaction", etc. - can then be mapped to application objects. Again, these are distributed by OrgUnit.

Together, the sets of information and application objects constitute the *information system architecture*. Adding common objects, such as "archive" and "mailbox", and associating this structure with the hardware and generic software structure available, an initial model for full system analysis and subsequent design is specified.

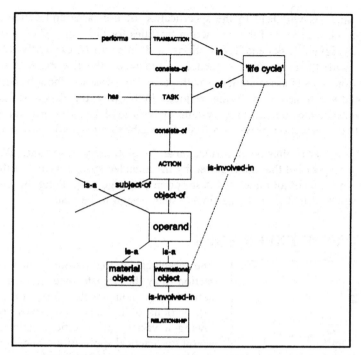

Figure 6: Meta-model extension -3- ('life cycle' added).

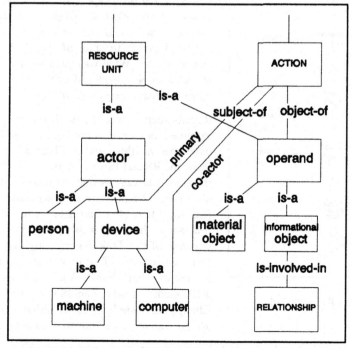

Figure 7: Meta-model extension -4- ("asymmetrical" ISN basis)

(2) Further analysis will lead to the specification of use-cases and office procedures, serving as descriptions of the interaction facilities for the user. The use-cases derive from the original Tasks and Transactions, and thus will be explicitly related to ISN actions, with their specified sequences. Likewise, the life cycle descriptions of information objects associate these with general use-cases, although their behaviour undoubtedly will have to be further refined. In this way, the Tasks, Transactions and Life Cycles relate the resulting system analysis model to the original Information Plan. This connection provides a basis for establishing specification control.

System analysis may be thus be performed on an "evolutionary" basis until all objects and interactions are specified that are required by the intended system users. If the specification is made in terms of an integrated description language (e.g. along the lines of [10]), a model is achieved that permits the final system design to be made.

3 PROTOTYPE EXPERIENCE

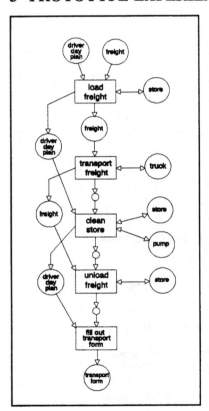

Figure 8a: BS Task

The graphical representations of the preceding section may be transformed into more specific definitions without much effort. For instance, in [9], various definitions were stated in BNF, allowing a variety of specific terminals that were useful for practical application. Such precise formal statements, in turn, facilitated programming the UNIS vs 1.0 prototype. Actual usage for *Organizational Description, Change Analysis I* and *Change Analysis II* turned out to be remarkably easy and rapid, in spite of the shortcomings discussed above. What was most missed - and what is intended to be introduced in the next version - is a more extensive graphical interface.

Results such as would have been achievable by the extended tool were worked out manually and would have been as illustrated in Figures 8 and 9. These show the BS and ISB views of a task (Fig. 8a-c) for the same test case as that from which the examples of Figures 2 and 3 were drawn, and an ISN task (i.e. the life cycle of an actor: Fig. 9). Figures 8 b-c show how (possibly automatic) "shading" portions of the Task diagram highlights the informational aspects. That demonstrates, for instance, a view of what Change-Analysis-I-options exist in a BS model or where an ISN my be introduced in Change Analysis II. Actors (humans or computers) are not shown, so as not to clutter up the diagram.

Our prototype study has demonstrated that integrated information planning is feasible, in principle. In particular, it is concluded that

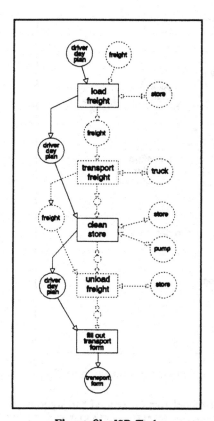 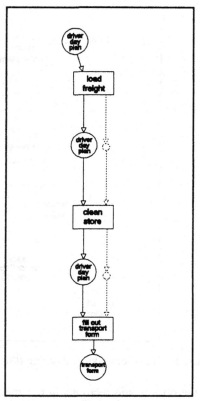

Figure 8b: ISB Task   **Figure 8c:** ISB view

The models illustrated in Figures 8 a-c are part of the **TransCorp** case task "Garage: Transport Freight". The BS includes all physical elements. The ISB shows how the "Driver Day Plan" and "Freight" (to be transported) trigger subsequent activity, with physical aspects shaded into the background. If cleaning of the store is not required for a particular freight, that action is empty. The "pure" ISB view displays informational activity only, with physical element summarized.

1. *Organizational embedding* of the ISN may be strongly supported; based on the underlying integrated BS\ISB\ISN meta-model, both the ISB and ISN are describable in *integrated views* (BS\ISB and ISB\ISN, respectively);

2. *Evolution* of an overall model is strongly supported at both the ISB and ISN levels; modification of the BS\ISB view corresponds to *Change Analysis I* (logical business model), evolution of the ISB\ISN view by introducing or modifying the computer support activity constitutes *Change Analysis II*;

3. The integrated model is *more effective* in support of system development because (i) a semantically richer information planning may be formulated, in *user terms* (i.e. the organization and its information function are modelled in terms that are not influenced by database or processing aspects as such) and (ii) a richer interface is provided to systems analysis, consisting of a *system architecture* and a *system behaviour context*.

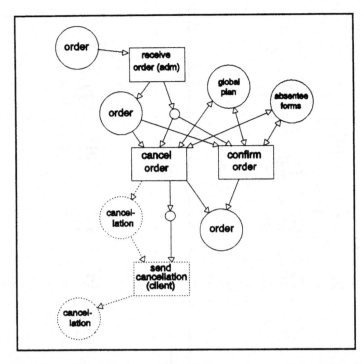

Figure 9: TransCorp Global Planning (ISN: full lines, non-computerized ISB: dotted lines)

Since the objects and relations in our meta-model remain related throughout, an IP tool as described conforms - in priciple - to the concept of "Hyper-CASE" [12, 2]. However, it is felt that the detailed system analysis and design required better be handled by separate CASE tools, that merely interface with the main IP tool [9]. In order to maintain consistency (and control), descriptions under the higher and lower tools should be "time-stamped" across the interface.

4 DISCUSSION

On the basis of the aforementioned experience, it seems highly feasible that a fully fledged Information Planning tool of the kind envisaged may be developed. The following points will then be considered.

The interface to (possibly automated) ISN system analysis (SA) tools will provide (1) an information architecture consisting of a distributed set of information objects and application objects (based on action functionalities), together with additional architecture objects (if any) and (2) a global context for adding system behaviour, applicable to use-cases to be associated with actions embedded in tasks and transactions, and forming a basis for further refinement of information object life cycles.

In order to be comprehensive, the SA tool should be "object-based" (e.g. as formulated in [10]). Then, it will be capable of adding "integrated" objects, that is to say, objects allowing each user point of view. Any such objects will be endowed with attributes, as required (e.g. order: client, freight, distribution date, etc.). Additionally, specialization and other relationships may be established. Finally, the dynamics will have to be introduced by describing 'use-cases' and 'life-cycles', involving the objects. These must be connected to actions at the ISN level.

A great advantage of an IP tool of this nature is that it allows a basic form of simulation of Place-Transition (P/T) nets (with multi-set places), since the task and transaction descriptions both use such nets. It should be noted that P/T nets [11] have less descriptive power than high level nets [4]. In particular, arc and transition inscriptions cannot be made, nor do tokens have explicit identity here. However, once these qualities are built into the formal model and the appropriate interface is installed, extensive animation studies may be envisaged (as e.g. in DESIGN/CPN [1] and ExSpect [3]). Thus, evolutionary analysis and continuous planning control will become possible that goes well beyond the ambitions of todays integrated tools (such as IEF [6]).

The manually worked extension of the UNIS vs 1.0 TransCorp case discussed and illustrated above, shows the kind of results that will be achieved. The detail of the specific modifications is under study and development of the next version will commence shortly.

References

1. K. Albrechts, K. Jensen and R. Shapiro, DESIGN/CPN, *A tool package suppporting the use of coloured Petri nets*, Meta Software Corp., Cambridge, Mass., U.S.A., 1988.
2. J.N. (Sjaak) Brinkkemper, *Formalisation of Information Systems Modelling*, Ph.D. Thesis, Catholic University, Nijmegen, Netherlands, 1990.
3. K.M. van Hee, L. Somers, M. Voorhoeve, *Executable Specifications for Distributed Information Systems*, in "Information Systems Concepts: An in-depth analysis", E.Falkenberg and P. Lindgreen, eds., North-Holland 1990.
4. K. Jensen, *Coloured Petri nets*, in "Petri Nets: Central models and their properties, W. Brauer, W. Reisig and G. Rozenberg, eds., LNCS nrs 254 & 255, Springer Verlag, 1986.
5. M. Lundeberg, G. Goldkuhl, A. Nilsson, *A Systematic Approach to Information Systems Development*, Inform. Systems 4 (1979) 1-12.
6. Ian G. Macdonald, *Automating the Information Engineering Methodology*[TM] *with the Information Engineering Facility*[TM], in "Computerized Assistance During the Information Systems Life Cycle", T.W. Olle, A.A. Verrijn-Stuart and L. Bhabuta, eds., North-Holland, 1988.
7. G.J. Ramackers & A.A. Verrijn-Stuart, *First and secord order dynamics in information systems*, Proceedings of the First International Working Conference on Dynamic Modelling of Information Systems, Noordwijkerhout, Netherlands, April 9-10, 1990 (also published by Elsevier Science Publishers, 1991).
8. G.J. Ramackers & A.A. Verrijn-Stuart, *The ISB-ISN framework of information systems* (Dept Comp.Sci., Univ. Leiden, Report 90-12).
9. G.J. Ramackers, K. Anzenhofer and A.A. Verrijn-Stuart, *Information Planning in the Office Environment* (Dept Comp.Sci., Univ. Leiden, Report 91-06).
10. G.J. Ramackers & A.A. Verrijn-Stuart, *Integrating information system perspectives with objects*, in "Object Oriented Approach in Information Systems", F. van Assche, B. Moulin and C. Rolland, eds., North-Holland 1991.
11. W. Reisig, *Petri Nets: An introduction*, EATCS Monographs on Theoretical Computer Science, Springer Verlag, 1985.
12. J.B. Smith, S.F. Weiss, *Hypertext*, Comm. ACM 31 (Nr 7, July 1988), 816-819 (Special issue on Hypertext).
13. A.A. Verrijn-Stuart, *The information system in the broader sense* (Dept Comp.Sci., Univ. Leiden, Report 89-13).
14. A.A. Verrijn-Stuart, UNIS: Prototype of a *UNiversal Information Systems description tool* (Dept Comp.Sci., Univ. Leiden, Report 91-05).

IDRIS : Interactive Design of Reactive Information Systems

Peter Osmon and Philip Sleat[*]

Systems Architecture Research Centre
Computer Science Department
City University
London EC1V 0HB

Abstract. The IDRIS project is developing a model, a methodology, a notation, and a CASE tool for the interactive design of real-time, or reactive, systems. Increasingly such designs are implemented on parallel hardware, for performance and reliability reasons. The work described here addresses performance, but not reliability, issues.

The model describes a real time system in terms of a database and a set of asynchronous tasks. Each task is the system's response to an external stimulus event. A task decomposes into atomic transactions, acting on entities in the database, connected by a control structure which is determined by entity access constraints.

Based on a static analysis of these data dependencies, the methodology is able to rely on scheduling rather than conventional locking to control access to the database. The model describes real time systems generally. The methodology concentrates on the class of hard real time systems designs - those which must guarantee to meet the response latency and throughput constraints specified by the requirements. The methodology uses scheduling and allocation heuristics to map tasks and their transactions onto physical processors.

The methodology has a number of stages and the designer is assisted by four graphical notations: event context diagrams; data dependency rings for capturing both intra task and inter task data dependencies; precedence graphs for expressing the intra task control structure implied by the data dependencies; Gantt charts for expressing worst case schedules. The methodology assumes a run time environment with a hierarchy of schedulers to control processing and access to data entities. An interactive CASE tool helps the designer capture and manipulate the design information, display partial designs, and perform allocation and scheduling trials against the specification. An example real time system design, for a ship control system, generated using the methodology and the CASE tool, is briefly described.

[*] present address: Marex Technology Ltd., Marex House, 88 The High Street, Cowes, I.O.W., U.K.

1.   Introduction

The paper introduces a real time systems model and then describes, a CASE tool and the associated methodology for designing hard real time systems, and the run time environment assumed by the methodology. These are described in more detail in [Sle 91].

Hard real time systems are reactive systems where the specification includes "non functional" performance criteria, for at least some of the stimuli, to the effect that- the responses must be guaranteed to occur within particular time intervals and minimum throughput rates must be supported. Evidently the design of hard real time systems must include analysis of worst case behaviour in order to verify conformance with the specification. (An alternative approach to real time system design involves a statistical analysis and probabilistic statements about conformance. This approach can indeed deliver real time system designs, but not "hard" real time system designs. Statistical designs, where the probability of failure to meet the stimulus-response latency and throughput constraints is below certain limits, may be called "firm" real time designs.)

For performance reasons many hard real time systems must be implemented on parallel hardware. The allocation of data and processing across the system and scheduling of the processing are then major design problems. These problems are generally too complex to be solved dynamically, while guaranteeing to meet the hard real time constraints, and so a static analysis must be performed off line. Capture of specification, optimisation, information and subsequent worst case analysis of designs containing many interacting parts is extremely tedious and prone to error and so mechanisation using a CASE tool is very desirable.

2.   The Model

2.1   Introduction

The model is consistent with the current practice of basing real time designs on a database. The model is, however, unusual in making two strong assertions about the behaviour of systems so as to simplify the design problem. The first is that systems can generally be partitioned into a set of highly decoupled subsystems ("tasks") where each task is associated with a distinct stimulus, or stream of stimuli. I.e. tasks have different stimuli and so there is no control coupling between them- they are asynchronous with respect to one another. The second assertion is an extension of the first: although there is no control coupling between tasks, they may share data, subject only to the constraints that writes are serialised and each task has a consistent view of the data. The only problem these assertions seem to cause is how to handle "freshness" which is treated as a constraint and introduced into the design at an iteration stage. As an example to illustrate these two asumptions consider a control system for a chemical plant. A particular chemical vat may respond to changes in temperature and pressure. A task could be activated in response to critical temperature conditions. A separate task could be activated to handle critical pressure conditions. Although decoupled by independent triggering events, these two tasks may share system data; for example each task may consult the same data set describing the operating condition for the chemical vat.

The model provides two levels of system decomposition (task and transaction) and two viewpoints at each level (control and data entity).

2.2 Decomposition

The criterion for decomposition of the specified system into tasks has been given above. Tasks are composed of transactions: each one is a function applied to stored data entities. Consider the "temperature task" controlling the chemical vat. This may be decomposed into transactions to examine the current temperature; check the desired temperature; generate changes to heaters; issue warnings to operators etc.

2.3 Control Viewpoint (Intra Task)

A control flow graph, or precedence graph, in which the nodes are the transactions and called the Transaction Precedence Graph (TPG), describes the order in which transactions respond to an external stimulus incident on the task. This ordering is based on constraints imposed by the system specification (for example: the temperature control task must strive to stabilise the temperature before informing the operator of critical conditions) as well as constraints necessary to protect the integrity of the database (for example, where two transactions both update the same entity, there must be "write serialisation").

2.4 Data Entity Viewpoint (Intra Task)

Transactions occur concurrently except where requirements specifies a partial ordering or serialisation of writes imposes a partial ordering. This ordering information, of transactions within a task, defines the precedence graph for each task referred to above.

Determinism requires that the value of a data entity accessed by a task instance (see next section) should only be changed by the transactions within that task instance.

For the purposes of the next section it is generally convenient to overlay the precedence graph with "regions" associated with each data entity. An *entity region* encloses all transactions accessing the entity. A *critical region* encloses transactions accessing the entity up to the one making the last write access.

2.5 Control Viewpoint (Task Level)

A definition of each task (effectively definitions of the constituent transactions plus the precedence graph) is stored in the machine. The effect of a stimulus event arriving is to "peel off" an instance of the task which then executes independently of other instances. This execution is guided by some static representation of the precedence graph.

2.6   Data Entity Viewpoint (Inter Task)

During its lifetime an entity has a succession of values or *versions* (identified by *version numbers* N).   To ensure determinism, critical regions on an entity occurring in different instances (of the same or different tasks) must be serialised.   To achieve this, versions must be "write once" and, after an instance has left the critical region, the version number should be one greater than on entry i.e. should change to N+1.

In the case of read-only access it may be desirable that the task instance is given access to the "latest" version of an entity, in the same way that writes are.   However, in general, this will constrain performance unnecessarily and it is preferable to satisfy explicit "freshness" constraints which should be specified in the requirements.

3.   The Methodology

3.1   Introduction

The design methodology, which rests on the model, relies on scheduling to implement write serialisation- both intra task and inter task.   Further, writes to an entity are only committed when a task instance leaves its critical region on the entity, allowing the scheduler to abort all transactions within the critical region up to this moment.

The methodology makes an assumption about the streams of stimuli incident on the system, without which a worst case analysis is impossible: the shortest interval between consecutive stimuli in a stream is finite and its value (called the minimum repetition time- MRT) is included in the specification. Consider the temperature control task for the chemical vat. The MRT for this task is guided by the physical behaviour of the devices that read the temperature; each device has a minimum time after being used before it can be used again. Consequently, there is a minimum time after "triggering" before the temperature task can trigger again.

In order to generate schedules by static analysis, when the analysis is performed it is necessary to know the trigger times for tasks.   Since aperiodic tasks are likely to be included in the task set, as well as periodic ones, this is not generally possible.   However, for purposes of worst case static analysis, which is what is required for hard real time systems, aperiodic tasks can be treated as though they are periodic with a period of their MRT.

For purposes of static analysis, the temporal properties of a task are encapsulated in the triple Task ID (execution time, deadline, MRT) the three components of the tuple being measured in the time units (TU's) of the design (eg microseconds).   Execution time (ET) is the elapsed time to complete the task. Deadline is the worst case latency (stimulus-response delay) and MRT (minimum repetition time) is the worst case throughput of this task specified by the requirements. (Note that the execution time must be less than the deadline.   Note also that MRT may be less than the deadline, implying that a sequence of instances of the same task, at different stages of processing, may be present concurrently in the system.)

The static analysis must be based on some scheduling heuristic. The scheduling policy used in IDRIS is earliest deadline first (EDF), but this choice is not fundamental and another could be substituted. IDRIS offers the designer a choice of EDF with, or without, preemption. (Preemptive designs involve tasks backing off to the beginning of critical regions and hence are more complex. However, they are sometimes necessary.)

The static analysis must also assume some heuristic for allocation of tasks and transactions to processors. The heuristic presently being used has two parts. First, each task is divided into subtasks, with sub tasks being allocated to different processors within a "cluster". Graphically, a sub task is a vertical slice of the task's TPG. This division into sub tasks, and allocation to different procesors, maximises the potential for concurrency, and may indeed be necessary in order to achieve an execution time less than the deadline. Second, the set of clusters of logical procesors is mapped onto the number of physical processors allowed by the requirements. In this mapping, transactions, from different tasks which share the same data entity, are, as far as possible, placed on the same processor, so as to minimise the traffic in data entities. This allocation scheme has similarities to [MA84] and [MLT82].

The worst case static analysis, making use of transaction ET's, is performed to determine whether all tasks can complete within their deadlines, without preemption. In the case of failure, preemption can be tried or attempts can be made to improve the allocation. Continued failure means the design is not feasible without a relaxation of the specified hard real time constraints.

3.2   Procedure

The methodology contains the following sequence of steps:

1 Identification of triggers (stimuli)
2 Decomposition of system into tasks
3a Identification of data entities, and
3b Decomposition of tasks into transactions
4 Representation of database interactions using DDR's
5 Representaion of tasks using TPG's
6 Conversion of aperiodic tasks to periodic
7 Allocation of tasks and data entities to processors
8 Static analysis of schedulability.

The content of some of these steps has been outlined already. In the first step, as the triggers are identified in the statement of requirements they are given unique names and sorted into periodic and none periodic sets. At the second step, independent tasks are named and identified one-to-one with the triggers. Each task is then decomposed into transactions (of some granularity appropriate to the implementation platform) which manipulate a set of data entities. This is the third step. The designer is expected to derive definitions of the transactions and the data entities within each task from the specification.

The definition of each task is not completed until the fifth step: derivation of the control structure, expressed as a Transaction Precedence Graph (TPG) for each task, linking the transactions in the task, followed by identification of the critical regions within the task.

But before this, the designer is required to make the fourth step- drawing data dependency rings (DDR's) for each entity. A DDR displays all the interactions with that entity by identifying the transactions in all tasks that access it. The DDR shows up the conflicting accesses by transactions within a task. These conflicts will be resolved by serialisation, thereby imposing a partial ordering on the transactions within a task. (There may be additional constraints on transaction order specified in the requirements.) The DDR also shows up data entity access conflicts at the task level. These too are resolved by serialisation, but not at the task level since this is unduly cautious: it is critical regions not whole tasks that set limits on sharing.

The sixth and seventh and eighth steps were discussed in the previous sub-section. If the procedure fails to generate a feasible design, then steps seven and eight are iterated. Continued failure means that it is not possible to meet the requirements, and these must be relaxed. Relaxation might allow more processors, or more powerful processors, to be used.

4.   Run Time Environment

The methodology assumes the existence of a run time environment on the implementation hardware, consisting of a hierarchy of three schedulers, to support the design. The highest level creates a task instance in response to a trigger. The middle level manages access to critical regions. the lowest level manages the individual transactions. Figure 1 shows the scheduler hierarchy and a system fragment consisting of three processors and two tasks.

The Task Scheduler is distributed across all processors. It is invoked by triggers (stimuli) and by "task finished" events. It maintains a table of task instances and ensures that successive instances of a task stay in sequence. The Critical Region Scheduler is invoked when a task enters a critical region and when it leaves. It maintains a lock table and a queue of waiting tasks and makes access and pre-emption (including back-off) decisions. The Transaction Scheduler (one for each task instance) is invoked by the Task Scheduler but subject to control by the Critical Region Scheduler. It includes a representation of the TPG for the task instance. The three levels of scheduling are arranged to cooperate to manage the processing in accordance with the EDF policy, while ensuring serialised writes and the atomicity of critical regions.

5.   Graphical Notations

5.1 Introduction

A number of graphical notations are used by the IDRIS methodology and CASE tool. They

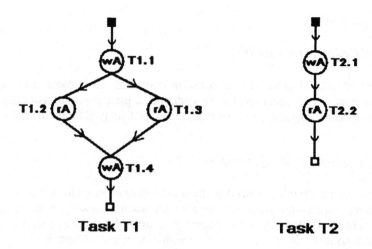

Fig. 1(a): Transaction Procedure Graphs for tasks T1 and T2

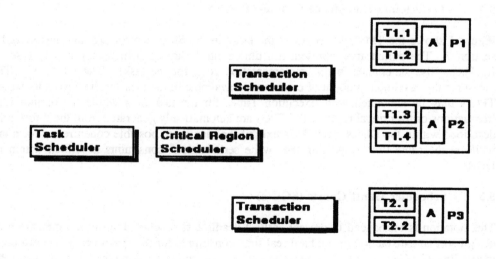

Fig. 1(b): Scheduler Hierarchy and Allocation to Processors

are summarised below.

5.2 Event Context Diagram (ECD)

This is a graphical notation adapted from dataflow diagrams. Its purpose is to capture all the stimuli and response events specified for the system as a preliminary to associating a distinct task with each stimulus-response pair. An example ECD displayed by the IDRIS tool is shown in Figure 2.

5.3 Data Dependency Rings (DDR's)

This is a graphical notation introduced to help the designer grapple with the complexities, referred to above, of the competition between transactions and between tasks for access to data entities. An example DDR is shown in Figure 3. Notice the tasks arranged round the ring, and the transactions involving the entity shown within each task. There is a separate DDR for every data entity in the system. When they have all been drawn the information content of all the precedence diagams for the system has been captured and these may then be drawn automatically. Ordering constraints imposed on transactions within a task may alse be described with an annotation around the edge of the DDR. For example in the first constraint described in section 2.3 we could indicate on the transaction which informs the operator of ciritcal temperature conditions that it must "wait for" the transaction that stabilises the temperature to finish.

5.4 Transaction Precedence Graphs (TPG's)

Figure 4 shows the TPG's for some of the tasks in the Ship Control example introduced in section 7. The dotted arcs represent run time control choices (which may be expressed as If...Then...Else statements in the implementation code for the task). The width of a TPG measures the maximum amount of concurrency available in the task for the design to exploit. TPG's may be annotated with Execution Times for the task as a whole or for individual transactions or for critical regions. the TPGs are automatically generated from the information described within the DDRs. The TPGs exhibit the maximum possible concurrency for a task while at the same time respecting the "write serialisation" constraints described within the DDRs.

5.5 Scheduler Gantt Charts (SGC's)

This notation is introduced to present earliest deadline first scheduling information from the design so that satisfaction of the hard real time constraints for the system may be verified by inspection. The Gantt chart has time along the "x-axis" and tasks along the "y-axis". The TPGs determine the maximum execution time for a task. The Gantt chart has a line for each task. On this line, those regions of time where the task is active are marked off, assuming the task is initially triggered at T_0 and each task is continuously retriggered at its MRT. An example of this is shown in figure 5. The Gantt chart can then be used to verify the feasibility of scheduling decisions.

502

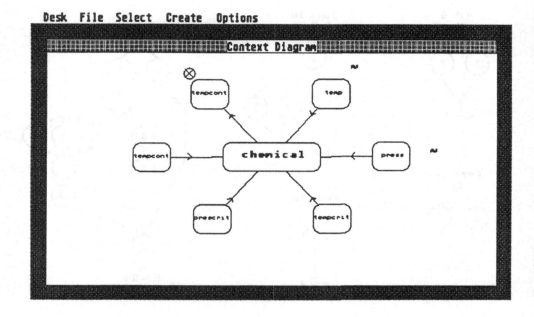

Fig. 2: An example Event Context Diagram

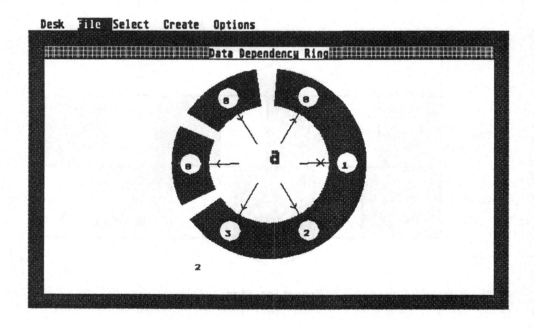

Fig. 3: An example Data Dependency Ring

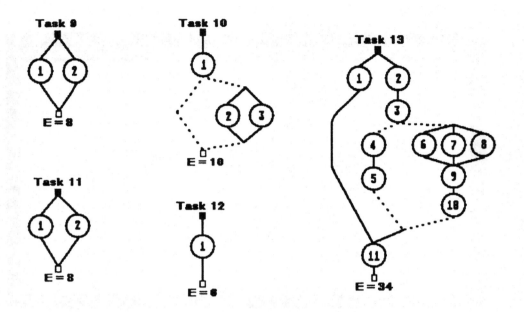

Fig. 4: Transaction Precedence Graphs, Tasks 9 to 13, Ship Control System

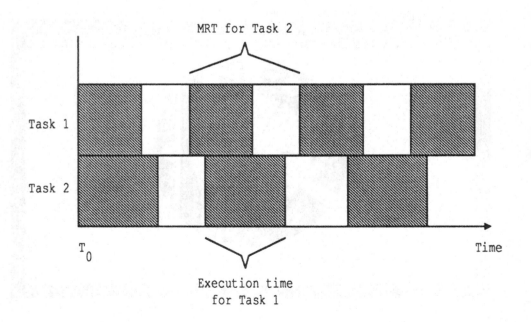

Fig. 5: An example Scheduler Gantt Chart

6.   The CASE tool

An interactive CASE tool has been written to assist designers using the IDRIS methodology. The user is prompted by the tool to input information in the order needed by the methodology and the tool presents partial designs using the various IDRIS graphical notations.

The tool has been written in C under a GEM environment to provide a user friendly "WIMP" (Windows, Icons, Menus, and Pointers) interface consisting of
- Drop Down Menus for selecting actions
- Forms for entering data
- Windows in which information and results are displayed.

Besides capturing design information, the tool relieves the designer of two tedious and error prone stages in the design process. The first is extraction of TPG's for the system once the set of DDR's has been defined. This involves scanning the DDR's and use of a concurrency optimising heuristic. The second is a detailed static analysis of the three levels of scheduling with reporting on the feasibility of the design.

7.   An Example System Design

IDRIS has been used in the design of a ship control system. This example is larger than many design examples described in the literature. The system is an embedded computer control system, for a fleet of commercial ships, which is responsible for automatically monitoring and controlling the state of a ship's engines, guiding the ship between destinations, accepting new courses and commands from the operator, monitoring and sending communications between ships of the fleet.

The method and CASE tool have been used to generate
- context diagram,
- DDR's,
- TPG's,
- allocation and schedule,

for a design for this system. The tool was then used to help the designer verify that with this allocation and schedule the system would satisfy the hard real time deadlines.

Analysis revealed 23 asynchronous tasks and hence 23 TPG's. Worst case task retrigger times specified in the requirements were entered. Critical regions were identified and worst case execution times calculated by summing transaction times on logical processors. 13 database tables +5 sub tables + 15 peripheral devices treated as database entities were identified and hence 33 DDR's were elicited from the requirements and scanned by the tool to determine the TPG's.

Allocation turned out to require 54 logical processors. Requirements had specified 6 physical processors. The logical to physical mapping was performed using the allocation heuristics outlined in this paper. Scheduler Gantt Charts for the physical processors, using worst case retrigger times for all the tasks, were generated to confirm that the requirements were met.

8.   Conclusions and Future Development

8.1 Conclusions

IDRIS emphasises an important property of reactive systems that appears to be undervalued in other design methods (for example [WM86] and [YC78]). This is the role of the shared data entity and its effect on both latency and throughput deadlines. The implicit control flow imposed on otherwise independent real time tasks is taken into account from the early stages of the design.

Essentially, the design method depends on a static analysis of the implicit control flows so that scheduling can take the place of conventional locking. The static analysis of the scheduling problem doesn't generate a schedule directly, as in other static scheduling techniques; the analysis simply determines the effectiveness of the dynamic heuristic (Earliest Deadline First). If the analysis shows that the heuristic is successful, then at run time the heuristic will correctly decide what to do with newly triggered tasks such that all deadlines are met. This approach is similar to [LL73].

8.2 The Future

The model implies a hierarchical run time environment for real time systems, involving three levels of scheduling, which appears to provide a good platform for addressing reliability issues in the next stage of development of the model.

At present the methodology stands alone and lacks a definite interface to the requirements specification stage of a project. We intend to investigate the possibility of tying the methodology to a particular model of requirements. [NS90] might provide a suitable starting point.

The first version of the IDRIS CASE tool is written in C and runs under GEM. It is currently being ported, and partially rewritten, to run on Unix platforms under X-Windows. The new version will provide better support for allocation and simulation of the run time environment.

References

[KN84] H. Kasahara and S. Narita. Practical Multiprocessor Scheduling Algorithms for Efficient Parallel Processing. *IEEE Transactions on Computers*, C-33(11), Nov. 1984.

[LL73] C.L. Liu and J.W. Layland. Scheduling Algorithms for Multiprogramming in a Hard Real-Time Environment. *Journal of the ACM*, 20(1), Jan. 1973.

[Ma84] R.P.Y. Ma. A Model to Solve Timing Critical Application Problems in Distributed Computer Systems. *IEEE Computer*, 1984.

[MLT82] R. Ma E.Y.S. Lee and M. Tsuchiya. A Task Allocation Model For Distributed Computing Systems. *IEEE Transactions on Computers*, C-31(1), Jan. 1982.

[NS90] M. Nejad-Sattary. An Extended Data Flow Diagram Notation for Specification of Real-Time Systems. *PhD Thesis, City University, 1990*.

[Sle91] P.M. Sleat. A Static, Transaction Based, Design Methodology, for Hard Real-Time Systems. *PhD thesis, City University*, 1991.

[SO91] P.M. Sleat and P.E. Osmon. A Methodology for Real-Time Database System Construction. *In Proceedings of the Third International Conference on Software Engineering for Real-Time Systems.IEE* Sept. 1991.

[WM86] P.T. Ward and S.J. Mellor. Structured Development for Real-Time Systems, volume 1,2 and 3. *Yourdon Press, New Jersey*, 1986.

[YC78] E. Yourdon and L. Constantine. Structured Design. *Yourdon Press*, 1978.

Constraint Confrontation : An Important Step In View Integration

I. Comyn-Wattiau *, M. Bouzeghoub**

* ESSEC, Ecole Supérieure des Sciences Economiques et Commerciales,
  av B Hirsch, BP 105, 95021 Cergy-Pontoise Cedex, France
  Tel : (33) 1 34 43 30 00 Fax : (33) 1 34 43 30 01 email : WATTIAU@FRESEC51
** Laboratoire MASI, Université Paris VI, Centre de Versailles, 45 av des Etats-Unis
   78000 Versailles France

Abstract. This paper addresses the problem of constraint integration in database design. The approach is inserted in an incremental database design methodology supported by the design environment KHEOPS. The view integration step using semantic unification is followed by the initial constraint confrontation. The detection phase is a deductive process in which the contradictions and redundancies between constraints are exhibited. The following conflict resolution depends on the strategy initially chosen by the designer. Four strategies are presented and discussed. An example of use is given to illustrate the application of those strategies. This approach could be enlarged in an object oriented context where schemata would have not only constraints but also methods to compare.

Key-words. database design, view integration, integrity constraint, forward chaining, conflict resolution, deductive process.

1 Introduction

Initial views considered for integration generally contain a set of integrity constraints. Those constraints complete the description of objects and relationships between objects. The atomic objects, that is attributes, are characterized by a set of possible values, called domain. The link between a molecular object and each of its components can be described by cardinalities. The relations between the different constituents of a molecular object may be defined in terms of functional and multivalued dependencies. The relationships between different molecular objects are also submitted to cardinality constraints. Finally, other semantic constraints can be described in specific situations.

Most of papers about view integration address the problem of generating a global schema starting from views. Such a process needs the comparison of view constituents. Roughly, for each pair of objects, this comparison can lead to the generation of (i) one object by merging of the constituents if they are found identical or equivalent, (ii) two objects connected by an inclusion link if one is found as a subset of the other, (iii) two disjoint objects if they are found different. In that comparison, the constraints can be considered as one criterion, but this step must be followed by the confrontation of initial view constraints with the global schema constituents in order to complete the global schema.

When dealing with the constraints, the view integration literature talks more generally about the conflict resolution. Indeed, constraint integration assumes the resolution of conflicts consisting of contradictions and redundancies between the different constraints. The authors suggest several strategies for conflict resolution but they don't proceed to an automatic constraint integration [El-Masri & Wiederhold 79, Navathe & Gadgil 82, Batini & Lenzerini 84, Navathe & al 84, Mannino & Effelsberg 84, Spaccapietra & Parent 90, see Batini & al 86 for a survey]. None of these strategies is the best one but each one can be applied in a specific context, that is for instance database integration.

The main contributions to constraint integration are the algorithms producing third normal form relations from sets of functional dependencies [Beeri & Bernstein 79, Bernstein 76]. Such procedures are able to produce a minimal set of functional dependencies, thus pointing at the contradictions and eliminating the redundancies. But functional dependencies are not sufficient to represent all the constraints between data.

From a theoretical point of view, Convent has proved that conflictfreeness is undecidable [Convent 86]. More precisely, the problem of deciding whether a given set of integrity constraints logically implies a single constraint is undecidable. So computer-aided integration needs heuristics to support designers in detecting conflicts for restricted cases in which logical implication is easily provable.

This paper describes an investigation in such a direction. The approach is inserted in an incremental object-oriented database methodology [Bouzeghoub & Métais 91]. The constraint integration comes after the global schema generation using a semantic unification of initial views [Bouzeghoub & Comyn 90]. Its main originality is to use deductive techniques to provide a better formalization of integrity constraint knowledge.

The paper is organized as follows. In Section 2, the view integration process is described. Section 3 describes the constraint integration, dividing the problem into (i) the detection of conflicts and (ii) the resolution. Section 4 concludes this paper and gives directions for further research.

2 View Integration by Semantic Unification

Abstractly, the unification problem is the following [Knight 89] : given two descriptions x and y, can we find an object z that fits both descriptions ? The logical unification of two expressions, as that used in Prolog, consists in successive variable substitutions of one expression by corresponding constants of the other expression. For example, the unification of the two following terms: $P(X,L(a,b),(Z,Y))$ and $P(a,f(Y,Z),(b,a))$ leads to the following result: $P(a,f(a,b),(b,a))$ and $P(a,f(a,b),(b,a))$ using the following substitutions : replace X by a, L by f, Z by b and Y by a in the first expression and replace Y by a, Z by b in the second expression.

A view is a structure composed of complex objects. View integration consists in the comparison of their structures in order to build a schema including the two initial structures. This process can be formalized as a semantic unification of the view structures. The unification of two views consists in comparing element by element, with respect to their types (atomic or molecular objects), the components of the two views. However, the expected result is not necessarily the strict equality of the two structures but the detection of the overlapping parts and the disjoint parts. More precisely, given two concepts from two different views, we expect the view integration process to report whether these two concepts are equivalent, similar or dissimilar. To reach one of these results, instead of making substitution of variables as done in the traditional unification, we apply particular restructuring rules which permit in a finite set of transformations to decide whether the two compared concepts are equivalent or not. If the two terms are equivalent, they are merged into a single fact and represented only once in the resulting schema. If the two terms are dissimilar, they are both included in the resulting schema. If the two terms are neither equivalent nor dissimilar but present some similarity, if possible, we backtrack again to the unification process which will enhance the similarity or the dissimilarity by applying other restructuring rules or by interacting with the human designer.

The general principle of view integration is similar to that of the logical unification but the substitution rules of the latter one are replaced by restructuring rules in the former one. Indeed, as view structures have no variable, the unification proceeds by analogy or by deduction process. Matching two symbols mainly consists in comparing their natures (atoms, molecules, constraints, etc), their structures (lists of components), their constraints (domains, keys, dependencies, cardinalities, etc) and the represented populations (instances). The logical unification is inserted into the resolution principle whose objective is to prove or to refute a hypothesis. At each resolution step i, if the unification succeeds the step i+1 is proceeded, if the unification fails there is a backtrack to the step i-1 to choose another rule or to match against another expression.

The view unification is inserted into a methodological process whose objective is to reach a unified representation (called a conceptual schema) of different perceptions of the same universe of discourse. At each integration step, if the semantics of the conceptual schema is enhanced, the integration is validated and the following step is initiated. Otherwise the view to be integrated is considered either as redundant with respect to the referent schema or as badly defined with respect to the common understanding of the universe of discourse. Figure 1 shows the different steps of integration. The syntactic comparison tool examines the two view components using deduction by inheritance if necessary. If the first unification does not succeed, a view restructuring is operated. The second unification step is validated by interaction with the human designer. The result of this unification, i.e. the global schema, is completed by the constraint integration.

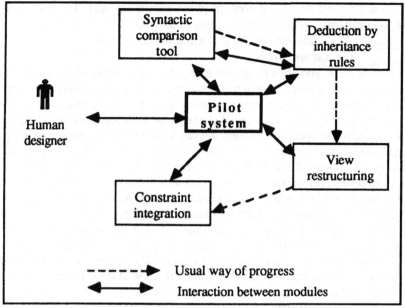

Fig 1. The view integration tool

The structural unification is based on three notions : the equivalence, the similarity and the dissimilarity.

(1) *Semantic equivalence between two concepts* : This notion depends on the nature of the two concepts to compare. Roughly, if we distinguish two levels of concepts, the basic level (atomic objects) and the structured level (molecular objects), we can intuitively define this semantic equivalence as follows :
* two atomic objects are equivalent if they have the same name and the same domain,
* two molecular objects are equivalent if they are composed of equivalent objects.

(2) *Semantic similarity between two concepts* : two given concepts (atomic or molecular) are similar if they have a same name, or a same domain, or a similar structure, or if they represent the same population. The similarity is not represented by a unique characteristic but by a set of properties which define a similarity degree whose value depends on the nature and the number of common properties. Then we consider the equivalence between two concepts as a similarity with its high degree, say value 1 if the similarity range is defined between 0 and 1.

(3) *Semantic dissimilarity between two concepts* : two concepts are dissimilar if they are neither equivalent nor similar. The dissimilarity between two concepts corresponds to a similarity with a lower degree, say 0 if the similarity range is defined between 0 and 1.

Consequently, we can represent the result of the unification of two concepts by a multiple information called similarity vector whose interpretation of the different components will vary from the equivalence to the dissimilarity. This vector is defined according to each type of concept. The differents types of concepts constitute a hierarchy starting from the most structured concept to the atomic concept. Then we distinguish two types of similarity vectors, corresponding to the two levels of objects :

$Sim_{structured\_object}(name, structure, constraints, population)$

$Sim_{atomic\_object}(name, domain)$

The *name* component specifies if the two names that are compared are identical or not. The *structure* component specifies whether the two compared concepts have same types or not. The type of an object consists in its list of components. The *constraint* component specifies if the two compared concepts have the same constraints or not. The *population* component specifies whether the two compared concepts represent the same set of instances or not. It concerns the intentional population. This component is only provided by the human designer who interacts with the view integration tool. The *domain* component specifies if two compared atomic objects have the same domain, included domains or different domains. Each of these components is a value ranging from 0 to +1. This value is assigned by the unification procedure. If this value is less than 1, the unification procedure generates a hypothesis (equivalence or dissimilarity depending on the value). If this hypothesis, say equivalence, is validated by the human designer, the component value becomes 1, otherwise (case of dissimilarity), the component takes the 0 value. Consequently, we have the following interpretation of the different components of the similarity vector :

- equivalence iff component = 1,
- similarity iff 0 < component < 1,
- dissimilarity iff component = 0,
- not considered iff component = '_ '.

The '_' symbol is used by analogy with the anonymous variable in Prolog.

Remark 1. Internally, when the designer is requested, we add 1 to the component (case of equivalence) or we subtract 1 from the component (case of dissimilarity). Hence at any time we know if the degree of similarity or dissimilarity is enhanced by the unification procedure or by the interaction with the human designer. At the end of the integration, the process may report the contribution of the human designer compared to the algorithmic decisions of the unification procedure.

Remark 2. This view integration process relies on one main heuristic, say 'if two objects have identical structures, they represent the same population'. Such a hypothesis is necessary to make the process more automatic.

A more detailed description of the unification procedure and mainly the evaluation of the similarity between views is given in [Bouzeghoub & Comyn 90].

3 Constraint Integration

We have defined earlier the role of constraints in the comparison of objects. These comparisons permit to enhance the similarity of the objects but they are not sufficient to infer the constraints associated to the global schema. The final step of integration consists in the constraint integration. The constraints which are considered are domains, keys, cardinalities and functional dependencies.

The domain constraints are considered at the time of the atomic constituent integration. So we consider here the integration of cardinalities, key and functional dependencies. It is relatively simple to detect a contradiction between two similar constraints, for example a contradiction between keys. If the subset A is a key for the object O in one view and the subset A is not a key for the same object in another view, the contradiction is explicit. However, it is necessary to detect contradictions between different constraints, that is for example between functional dependencies and keys. More generally, the conflict does not exist between only two constraints C and ¬C but inside a set of several constraints. For example, let E, A and B be objects belonging to both initial views, the set :

A is a key of E,
B is a monovalued constituent of E,
The functional dependency A->B is not valid.

contains a contradiction, but each pair of sentences is consistent.

To facilitate the expression of detection rules, we first describe the data model used. Then, the conflict detection process is described. The detection is followed by the resolution presented later.

3.1 The Data Model

The internal representation is the semantic model inspired by the different commonly used models (entity-relationship, extended entity-relationship, object models). Its content is easy to understand and allows a good representation of constraint interaction rules. We just describe the concepts used hereafter.

The atomic and molecular objects of views, namely attributes, entities and relationships, are the nodes of the semantic network. The arcs describe the semantic links between those objects. These arcs are labeled to express the constraints.

An arc 'p' goes from a molecular object to each atomic constituent. Its label contains minimum and maximum cardinalities of the link. The inverse arc is called 'a'. For example, $p(E,A,[1,1])$ means that each instance of the object E has exactly one value for its constituent A. $a(A,E,[1,1])$ means that each value of A corresponds to a unique instance of E.

The key constraint is expressed by the arc *key* : $key(E,A)$ means that the set of atomic constituents A is a key of the object E. The functional dependencies are represented by 'fd' arcs.

The constraint integration needs the representation of negative informations, for example it can be important to save the information about the fact that there is no functional dependency between two constituents. We use two arcs to express such negative information : $notkey(E,A)$ means that A is not a key of the object E. $notfd(E,A,B)$ means that, for the object E, the atomic constituent B is not functionally dependent on the subset A.

3.2 The Conflict Detection

The objective of view integration is to produce a minimal and consistent global schema. The minimality condition means that no redundancy may remain. The consistency condition means that any contradiction must be removed. The constraint integration operates as a deductive process aiming at the detection of contradictions and redundancies. The principle of this detection is described here.

The constraints contained in the initial views are added one by one to the global schema. They constitute the fact base. If the tool detects a contradiction between the fact base and the new constraint to be added, the conflict resolution step begins, leading to a possible fact base modification.

The rule base contains several types of rules. The first ones are Armstrong's axioms [Armstrong 74]. They formalize the interactions between functional dependencies. Let X, Y and Z be subsets of the set of atomic objects constituting the molecular object E :

RARM1 : If $X \supseteq Y$ Then fd(E,X,Y)

RARM2 : If fd(E,X,Y) Then fd(E, $X \cup Z$, $Y \cup Z$)

RARM3 : If fd(E,X,Y) and fd(E,Y,Z) Then fd(E,X,Z)

Another set of rules contribute to define the *notfd* and *notkey* predicates :

RNP1 : If not(fd(E,X,Y)) Then notfd(E,X,Y)

RNP2 : If not(key(E,X)) Then notkey(E,X)

A third set of rules formalize the interactions between all types of constraints. For example, let A and B be atomic constituents of E, RICC1 and RICC2 are two examples of interactions between keys and cardinality constraints :

RICC1 : If key(E,A) Then p(E,A,[1,1])

RICC2 : If key(E,A) Then a(A,E,[1,1])

The following RICD1 to RICD4 rules formalize part of the interaction between functional dependencies and cardinality constraints :

RICD1: If p(E,A,[_,1]) and fd(E,A,B) Then p(E,B,[_,1])

RICD2: If p(E,A,[_,1]) and $X \supseteq A$ and fd(E,X,B) Then p(E,B,[_,1])

RICD3: If p(E,B,[1,n]) and fd(E,A,B) Then p(E,A,[_,n])

RICD4: If fd(E,B,A) and a(A,E,[1,1]) Then a(B,E,[1,1]).

Others can be found in [Bouzeghoub 86]. Note that '_' is used to denote the 'unknown' value.

The inference mechanism uses a forward chaining technique. Before introducing the constraint C, the inference mechanism is applied to the set of consistent constraints. If C is deduced, then C is redundant and must not be inserted. If ¬C is deduced, then C is contradictory. Otherwise C can be added. The process ends when all the constraints have been considered.

3.3 The Resolution Strategies

The resolution of conflicts depends on the strategy chosen by the designer. We have defined four different strategies. In this section, we describe each one, giving in each case the possible use. Then the next sections will give an example and define the meta-rule which governs the use of those strategies.

The first three strategies have been found in the literature. The references and the suggested domains of application are given. The fourth one is original and can be seen as a step forward in the integration by generalization as defined by Dayal [Dayal & Hwang 84] and used in [Larson & al 89] to integrate attributes.

3.3.1 Predominant View Strategy

The first strategy consists in defining a preferred view. In case of conflicts, the preferred view is chosen. This strategy was suggested in [Navathe & Gadgil 82, Batini & Lenzerini 84]. In that case, the resolution process is made automatic by assigning preferences to views. Practically, the initial base fact contains the constraints associated to the preferred view. The other constraints are added one by one. If a contradiction or redundancy occurs, the constraint is not inserted.

This strategy has two main advantages : it makes the resolution an automatic process and it is very easy to implement. Such a strategy is applicable if both following conditions are valid. First, the preferred view is consistent. Secondly, the other views come as suggestions for improvement and thus can be partially rejected. Our opinion is that an incremental methodology database design meets these two conditions.

3.3.2 Interaction with the Designer

This strategy is completely opposite. It is based upon the idea that such a tool can be used to help the designer in the database schema generation. This help implies the detection of inconsistencies between the different designer declarations. These inconsistencies can be explained by the big size of the application or by the long lapse separating the beginning and the end of the process.

This strategy considers that contradictions are the results of wrong specifications. In case of such contradictions, the designer must be asked. So the conflict resolution is an interactive process in which the set of facts (including C) leading to a contradiction is presented to the designer who points at the wrong fact. If C is the wrong fact, C is rejected. If the wrong fact is already in the fact base, it is retracted and C is inserted.

An example of such dialog is given now. Suppose that the set of controlled constraint is defined by the four following constraints :

(1) $p(E,A,[1,1])$ (A is a monovalued constituent of E)
(2) $fd(E,A,B)$ (functional dependency from A to B inside E)
(3) $fd(E,BC,D)$ (functional dependency from BC to D inside E)
(4) $p(E,C,[1,n])$ (C is a multivalued constituent of E).

The constraint C now introduced is $p(E,D,[1,n])$. The forward chaining inference engine permits to deduce :

(5) $p(E,B,[\_,1])$ (deduced from 1 and 2 and RICD1)
(6) $p(E,D,[\_,1])$ (deduced from 3 and 5 and RICD2).

And C and (6) are inconsistent.

Practically, our tool paraphrases each constraint including C and proposes this list of

515

sentences to the designer. The screen is displayed Figure 2. The designer points at the wrong sentence. The corresponding constraint is retracted from the fact base.

You told me that :

(1) each E has one and only one A

(2) for each A of E, there is a unique B

(3) for each pair (B,C) of E, there is a unique D

(4) at least some E have several D.

This set of assertions is inconsistent,

which one is erroneous ?

Fig. 2. Interaction with the designer

This solution can be used for database design to help the designer in exhibiting the conflicts between views. The tool is responsible for the consistency of the result, but the choices are made by the designer. It can be very useful when all the initial specifications are available but have been generated without control of an expert. Such a tool can also be used for computer assisted instruction.

3.3.3 Loose Constraining

Another strategy was suggested in several papers [Motro 87, Spaccapietra & Parent 90]. These authors propose to build a global schema meeting all the initial specifications. So, in each case of conflict, the less restrictive solution is chosen. Then, to take into account each initial view, the mappings between the global schema and the initial view express the possible restrictions. A few situations and the less restrictive choice in each situation are presented Figure 3.

Two main advantages can be presented to defend such a strategy. First, it makes an automatic resolution. Secondly, it does not alter the initial views. So it can be used in database integration where data already exist and where the global schema must reflect as best as possible the different local representations of data.

VIEW 1	VIEW 2	GLOBAL SCHEMA
Domain D1	Domain D2	Domain $D1 \cup D2$
Minimal cardinality 0	Minimal cardinality 1	Minimal cardinality 0
Maximal cardinality 1	Maximal cardinality N	Maximal cardinality N
Key(E,A)	Notkey(E,A)	Notkey(E,A)
Functional dependency A -> B	Wrong functional dependency A -> B	Wrong functional dependency A -> B
Key(E,A)	Wrong functional dependency A -> B	Wrong functional dependency A -> B

Fig. 3. Contradictory specifications and resolution

3.3.4 Resolution by Specialization

The last strategy presented here is in keeping with the semantic modelling using generalizations and specializations [Smith & Smith 77]. The principle is to resolve the constraint conflict by specializing the object on which the contradiction takes place. This approach consists in declaring the contradictions between constraints as revealing overlapping class problems. In such a situation, the integration step must lead to a global schema where the different sub-classes with their own constraint sets coexist. Thus the resolution contributes to increase the automatic processing of class definition.

Practically, suppose that, for example, the object O1 in the first view, denoted View1(O1) and the object O2 in the second view, View2(O2) have been integrated in one unique object O in the resulting view. Suppose that two constraints C1 and C2 are respectively associated to O1 and O2 in the initial views. Four cases have to be considered :

1st case : *the constraints C1 and C2 are identical or equivalent*
formally C1=C2
In this case, C1 is added to the resulting view and associated to the object O.

2nd case : *the constraints C1 and C2 are contradictory*
formally $C1 = \neg C2$
The object O in the resulting view is specialized into two sub-classes O1 and O2. The constraints C1 and C2 are added to the resulting view and respectively associated to O1 and O2.

3rd case : *the constraints C1 and C2 are independant*
formally $C1 \neq C2$ and $C1 \neq \neg C2$
They are neither redundant (that is neither identical nor equivalent) nor contradictory. In

this case, the constraints C1 and C2 are added to the resulting view and both associated to O.

4th case : *the constraints C1 and C2 are compatible*
By compatible, we mean that one constraint is stronger than the other. For example in one view, one constituent of O is mandatory, in the other view it is optional. To express this compatibility, we have defined an order. This order is total inside a set of compatible constraints. It is defined as follows :

C1 > C2 if C1 is stronger than C2.

In this case, the object O in the resulting view is specialized in one sub-class O1. The constraints C1 and C2 are added to the resulting view. The stronger constraint, say C1, is associated to the sub-class O1. The other constraint, say C2, is associated to O. To illustrate our definition of order, Figure 4 enumerates a few cases of what we call constraint compatibility.

CONSTRAINT C1	CONSTRAINT C2
The domain of A is D1	The domain of A is $D2 \supset D1$
The set of attributes E1 is a key	The set of attributes $E2 \supset E1$ is a key
The set of attributes E is a key	The set of attributes E is not a key
There is a functional dependency from A to B	There is no functional dependency from A to B
The set of attributes E is a key	There is no functional dependency from E to any other constituent F
The attribute A is monovalued	The attribute A is multivalued
The attribute A is mandatory	The attribute A is optional
The minimum cardinality of entity E in relationship R is 1	The minimum cardinality of entity E in relationship R is 0
The maximum cardinality of entity E in relationship R is 1	The maximum cardinality of entity E in relationship R is n

Fig. 4. Compatible constraints where C1 > C2

The previous discussion was about the comparison of two constraints. But the integration process consist in adding one by one the constraints to a controlled set. So we give now the algorithm used for the introduction of a constraint C coming from the initial view Viewi and associated to the object which led to the integrated object O. The algorithm called CONSTRAINTINTEGRATION(Viewi, C, O) looks for possible constraints already inserted and contradictory or compatible with C. If such a constraint exists, the constraint C is associated to the object O or to one of its sub-classes. Figure 5 gives the algorithm. Figure 6 describes the subroutine BIND(C, O, Viewi) which associates the constraint C to the sub-class of O corresponding to the view Viewi.

```
CONSTRAINTINTEGRATION(Viewi,  C,  O)
BEGIN

IF Resultingview(O,C',Viewj) and C=C'
/* in the resulting view, a constraint C' identical or
   equivalent to C is associated to O */
  THEN
    REJECT C
  ELSE
   IF Resultingview(O,C',Viewj) and C'<C
     /* in the resulting view, a constraint C' compatible with C
     but less strong than C is associated to O */
   THEN
     BIND(C,O,Viewi)
   ELSE
    IF Resultingview(O,C',Viewj) and C'>C
     /* in the resulting view, a constraint C' compatible with C
     but stronger than C is associated to O */
    THEN
    /* associate C' to the sub-class of O corresponding the view Viewj */
     BIND(C',O,Viewj);
     RETRACT Resultingview(O,C',Viewj);
     /* associate C to O in the resulting view */
     INSERT Resultingview(O,C,Viewi)
    ELSE
     IF Resultingview(O,C',Viewj) and C' ¬= C
    /* in the resulting view, a constraint C' inconsistent
     with C is associated to O */
     THEN
       BIND(C,O,Viewi);
       BIND(C',O,Viewj);
       RETRACT Resultingview(O,C',Viewj)
     ELSE
      /* all the constraints already associated to O
      are independent of C */
      INSERT Resultingview(O,C,Viewi)
     ENDIF
    ENDIF
   ENDIF
ENDIF
END
```

Fig. 5. The algorithm

```
BIND(C,  O,  Viewi)

/* associates the constraint C to the sub-class of O
     coming from the view Viewi
     and creates this sub-class if not done */
BEGIN
IF Resultingview(s(O,Viewi,Oi))
  /* in the resulting view, the object O has a sub-class Oi matching
     with the correspondant object in Viewi */
THEN
     /* inserts the constraint C in the resulting view,
     associated to the object Oi */
 INSERT Resultingview(Oi,C,Viewi)
ELSE
     /* creates the sub-class of O corresponding to Viewi */
     INSERT Resultingview(s(O,Viewi,Oi));
     /* inserts the constraint C in the resulting view,
     associated to the object Oi */
     INSERT Resultingview(Oi,C,Viewi)
ENDIF
END
```

Fig. 6. A procedure to associate a constraint to an object in the resulting view

3.4 Example

This sections gives a very simple example of two views with different constraints. We show how each previous strategy applies in this case. The example describes the involvement of employees in projects. In the first view, each employee is involved in one and only one project. In the second view, an employe may participate in several projects. The two views are graphically described Figure 7. Suppose that the first view is the preferred view. The integration will lead to forbid employes several involvements. If the strategy is loose constraining, the second view is chosen. In case of resolution by specialization, the employees are allowed to participate in several projects, except a sub-class of them who are bordered on a unique project. By interaction with the designer, the two options are suggested. The four possible results of integration are summmed up Figure 8.

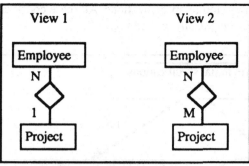

Fig. 7. The two initial views

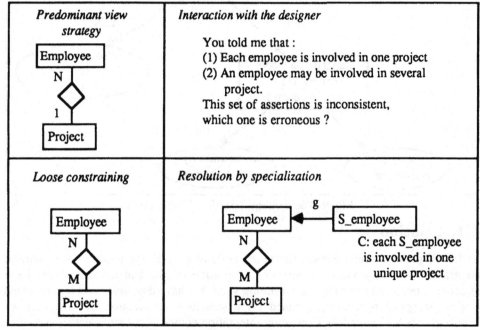

Fig. 8. Application of four strategies

3.5 Strategy Selection

For each strategy, we have defined above the different conditions of application and the advantages. This analysis allows us to describe now the decision support module which helps the designer in the choice of the best strategy.

The first and most important criterion to take into account is the initial specification reliability. Without this condition, no automatic resolution can be considered. The detection is made by the tool and the resolution emerges from a dialog with the designer. If the initial specifications are reliable, it is important to know if they are modifiable or not. In database integration for example, initial specifications represent real local databases and thus cannot be altered. Finally, the fourth strategy can be used if the data model allows the expression of specializations. All these considerations are summed up in the decision process graphically drafted Figure 9.

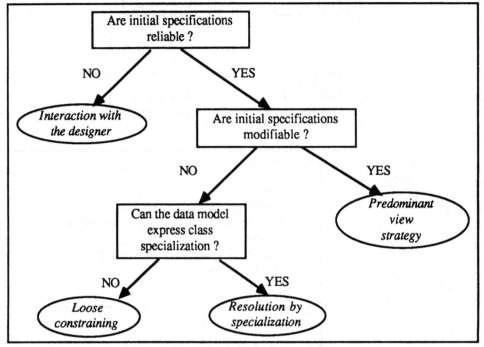

Fig. 9. The strategy selection decision tree

4 Conclusion

In this paper we have presented the principle of a deductive process for constraint integration. Our approach of constraint integration is added at the end of the view integration process to complete the resulting view. We have developed and implemented a view integration technique based on a structural unification of initial views [Bouzeghoub & Comyn 90]. Constraint integration comes after that to detect and solve the contradictions and redundancies between initial specifications. This constraint integration, as the view integration process, is to be considered as a decision support system which helps the designer in giving him information about similarities or contradictions. The final integration relies on the designer's decision.

The detection is a deductive process using a set of interaction rules modelling the relations between constraints. Key, functional dependencies, cardinalities and domains are considered. Some negative information is treated, thus making the technique applicable to incremental database design in which the global schema is obtained by successive refinements of an initial specification.

The conflict resolution depends on the strategy chosen by the designer. Four strategies have been defined and discussed. The last one, called resolution by specialization, is original. In case of conflict, it suggests to specialize the object into sub-classes in which constraints are no more contradictory.

We feel that this approach could also be enlarged to take into account integration problems in an object oriented context. That is an important issue which still remains to be investigated. Another interesting extension is to consider general integrity constraints and to confront our constraint integration methodology with such constraints.

References

[Armstrong 74] "Dependency Structures of Database Relationships", Armstrong W, Proceed. 1974 IFIP Congress, North-Holland, Amsterdam, 1974.

[Batini & Lenzerini 84] "A Methodology for Data Schema Integration in the E-R Model", Batini C, Lenzerini M, IEEE Transactions on Software Engineering, Nov 84.

[Batini & al 86] "A Comparative Analysis of Methodologies for Database Schema Integration", Batini C, Lenzerini M, Navathe SB, ACM Computing Surveys, Dec 86.

[Beeri & Bernstein 79] "Computational Problems Related to the Design of Normal Form Relational Schemas", Beeri C, Bernstein P, ACM Transactions on Database Systems, March 79.

[Bernstein 76] "Synthesizing third normal form relations from functional dependencies", Bernstein P, ACM Transactions on Database Systems, 1976.

[Bouzeghoub 86] "SECSI : Un Système Expert en Conception de Systèmes d'Information", Bouzeghoub M, Thèse de doctorat de l'université Paris VI, March 1986.

[Bouzeghoub & Comyn 90] "View Integration by Semantic Unification and Transformation of Data Structures", Bouzeghoub M, Comyn I, Proceed of the ER conf, Lausanne, 1990.

[Bouzeghoub & Métais 91] "Semantic Approach For Object Oriented Database Design", Bouzeghoub M, Métais E, Proceed of the VLDB conf, Barcelone, 1991.

[Convent 86] "Unsolvable Problems Related to the View Integration Approadch", Convent B, ICDT Conf, Roma, Sept 1986.

[Dayal & Hwang 84] "View Definition and Generalization for Database Integration in a Multidatabase System" Dayal U, Hwang H, IEEE Transactions on Software Engineering, Nov 1984.

[Elmasri & Wiederhold 79] "Data Model Integration Using the Structural Model" Elmasri R & Wiederhold G, Proceed. ACM-SIGMOD internat. conf., Boston 1979.

[Knight 89] "Unification : A Multidisciplinary Survey" Knight K, ACM Computing Surveys, 1989.

[Larson & al 89] "A Theory of Attribute Equivalence in Databases with Application to Schema Integration", Larson JA, Navathe SB, El-Masri R, IEEE Transactions on Software Engineering, Vol 15(4), 1989.

[Mannino & Effelsberg 84] "Matching Techniques in Global Schema Design", Mannino MV, Effelsberg W, Proceed. IEEE COMPDEC conf., Los Angeles, CA, 1984.

[Motro 87] "Constructing Superviews", Motro A, IEEE Transactions on Software Engineering, July 1987.

[Navathe & Gadgil 82] "A Methodology for View Integration in Logical Database Design", Navathe SB, Gadgil S, Proceed. 8th VLDB Conference, 1982.

[Navathe & al 84] "Relationship Merging in Schema Integration", Navathe S, El-Masri R, Sashidar T, Proceedings 10th VLDB Conference, 1984.

[Smith & Smith 77] "Database Abstractions : Aggregation and Generalization", Smith JM, Smith DCP, ACM Transactions on Database Systems Vol 2, N° 2, June 1977.

[de Souza 86] "SIS- A Schema Integration System", de Souza JM, Proc. BNCOD 5 conference, 1986.

[Spaccapietra & Parent 90] "View integration : A step forward in solving structural conflicts", Spaccapietra S, Parent C, Proc. of VIes Journées Bases de Données Avancées, Montpellier, Sept 1990.

[Tucherman & al 86] "A Software Tool for Modular Database Design", Tucherman L, Furtado AL, Casanova MA, Proceed. of 11th VLDB Conf, Stockholm, Aug 1985.

Methods for CASE: a Generic Framework

Mike Brough

Department of Computer Science, Keele University,
Staffs., ST5 5BG

This paper examines some of the method-related issues for CASE. In particular, it discusses the need to move away from the 'pencil and paper' mind-set to a more 'multi-dimensional' approach; a modelling framework, both conceptual and for design; and considers related problems of standards, portability and openness. It is intended that this framework can be used for CASE developers to incorporate generic system modelling techniques, rather than build tools for a single proprietary method.

1 Introduction: why is there a problem?

It might be thought by some that things are getting better for systems engineers in a nice smooth and monotonic fashion. We used to have no methods, then we had methods, better methods, computer-aided software engineering (CASE) tools, better CASE tools ... Is this not a continuing evolutionary improvement in our system engineering method? Unfortunately not. As elsewhere, things do not always get better, sometimes they get worse (and there are often evolutionary dead-ends). The process of evolution is not as gradual as one might think. In biological evolution, the fashionable approach is 'punctuated equilibrium', where long periods of gradual change are broken by sudden changes.

1.1 What are system development methods?

A method is a set of well-defined procedures that can be followed in a systematic way to achieve a goal. A system development method is a framework within which a system developer can work having some confidence that the delivered system will be: the one required; the 'best' way of meeting these requirements; and delivered in the most cost-effective and controlled manner.

This paper discusses methods for identifying system requirements and for designing and constructing systems to meet these requirements (system modelling). It will not be concerned with how to allocate resources, meet deadlines, control and motivate staff (project management). Some system development methods attempt to address both of these concern areas, but they are probably better separated. (Software tools for these two disciplines are usually described as CASE and project management tools, respectively.)

1.2 Why is a method needed?

In order to deal with any complex problem, the human mind requires that we abstract the more important features of the problem and suppress the specific detail. We do this by mapping the problem onto more abstract concepts. These concepts are organised into a framework for our thinking. For example, when writing procedural code, we have concepts such as 'statement', 'iteration', 'block', 'procedure', 'parameter' etc. These are the constructs provided by the framework of structured and modular programming. (Another good example of a conceptual framework is that provided by the ISO Open Systems Interconnection Model for communications.)

For large systems, we need to think about concepts related to the conceptual (policy) requirements, the run-time units used, interfaces, communications protocols, timing problems, file structures, etc.

Even if a CASE tool allowed very complex systems to be built, it would not be usable without a conceptual framework for using it. This framework is needed to understand what the tool does. Navigation around the models that the CASE tool supports requires a mental view of the 'where we are'. This conceptual framework is provided by a method. Without such a method the tool is unusable.

1.3 What is wrong with existing methods?

Why not use the 'old and tried' methods? Answer: we continue to find new ways of doing things that are: more cost-effective, easier, or more likely to produced a well-engineered system meeting the real requirements. The methods get better.

Additionally, the methods in use at present are those that were invented for pencil and paper. Now that we have finally admitted (!) that it would be a good idea to use computers to help us design and construct systems, surely there are some improvements that we could make. In fact, as yet, most CASE tools have only 'dabbled' with methods. Mostly, they just take the diagrams and supporting specifications that were used manually and allow the designer to store them (this is sometimes referred to as 'upper CASE'). Other tools are concerned with more efficient generation of code etc. (sometimes referred to as 'lower CASE'). CASE manufacturers claim to have 'integrated CASE' (iCASE), but even its name reveals its origin as a miscellany of manual and automated techniques.

Shifting target Methods must therefore evolve. However, this brings its own problems. The whole point about a method is that it should provide a standard framework within which we are confident we know what we are doing. If the framework is everchanging, then we are building on quicksand.

On a personal note, when I worked for Yourdon, I often went round to companies that used the 'Yourdon method' (naturally). We had what we thought was the best way of doing things (!). It was what we taught in seminars and used in consultancy (as documented by [1] and [2]). Most of the project teams that we trained used these methods and were converted to them. However, their management had often encountered 'the Yourdon approach' some years before and liked it (which is why we were working with them). What the managers had encountered was a different version of the method ([3], [4]). As a consequence, the managers did not always appreciate all of what their project team were doing. This confusion led Yourdon Inc. to name the method 'Yourdon Structured Method' (YSM), to distinguish it from the earlier structured analysis/structured design.

Eventually, to gain any degree of stability, methods have to be put under change control and properly documented. Historically, one of the most significant things about Structured Systems Analysis and Design Method (SSADM) was that there was version 2 (and then 3 and then 4 and ...). Yourdon also did the same thing (though rather later), designating the two previous versions of the method as YSM_1 and YSM_2, with the current method as YSM_3 [5]. For both CASE and successful project management, the version of the method in use must be well-defined. We will discuss these standardisation issues in §4.1.

Pencil and paper 'mindset' The most serious problem with existing methods is that they regard the model as *consisting of* a set of diagrams, possibly with supporting text. Each diagram is two-dimensional, but, of course the system space is multi-dimensional. Different aspects of the system appear on different diagrams, seen from different points of view. To be sure that a consistent, integrated model of the requirements has been formulated, the diagrams and other specifications have to be 'cross-checked'.

CASE vendors talk about this as if it is fundamental to the process of understanding the system requirements. It is not. It reflects a way of thinking tied up with the communication medium. In many cases, what they have provided is an 'electronic pencil and paper' system. Concepts such as 'vertical balancing' and 'horizontal balancing' reflect a way of thinking that is still conditioned by sheets of paper. To get the full benefit from the possibilities of CASE we must modify methods to get full benefit from CASE. Not only will the methods be supported by CASE, but also CASE should drive the methods. Once the break from 'model = diagram set' is made, there are many interesting new possiblities for methods and CASE.

Lack of semantic differentiation One technical problem flaw in some CASE tools is that there is a single 'name space' for all components seen on diagrams. Each item is named and and its specification held in a single data dictionary, identified by the name of the item. This causes: 1. problems in scoping names in large systems, 2. difficulty in distinguishing between items with different semantics. This problem is also a hangover from the restricted technology available in the past.

Ill-defined semantics As methods developed, the semantics of the modelling tools used were not always well-defined. Modellers could perceive the issues of syntax: "Is the box round, or is it a circle ... what do we call this shape on the diagram ... ?". Differing semantics that could be implicit (rarely explicit) in the tool are less obvious.

For example, consider the semantics of an entity relationship diagram. Some methods only allow binary relationships (some even disallow M:N relationships); others allow higher-order relationships. Even then, there may be more subtle differences. For example, both Ward/Mellor and YSM3 allow higher-order relationships [2], [5]. However, there are differences between these two versions of the ERD. Ward/Mellor define a relationship as a 'linked list' (so that a 1:N relationship is a single unit, consisting of one entity, with a list of occurrences of the other linked to it). On the other hand, YSM3 regards a relationship to be a set of relationship occurrences; each occurrence of the relationship is the same as any other; one relationship occurrence refers to specific occurrences of each of the entities that participate in the relationship. This difference is not visible in the ERD notations (they are the same), but the underlying semantics are very different. The cardinality of the relationship is a structural constraint in Ward/Mellor, but in YSM3 it is a specific type of participation constraint. (Participation constraints define rules about which occurrences of relationships are allowed.)

This example is typical of the ambiguity that can arise in interpreting diagrams. Because of these ambiguities, there have been many moves to place diagrammatic modelling techniques on a more formal basis. It is no longer acceptable to draw ERDs (for example) with sloppy ambiguity during analysis and defend the practice by saying that we will 'firm up' on what we really mean in design.

Of course, when a lower CASE tool is used, the semantics of the modelling tools provided are defined operationally (in terms of what happens). This may not always correspond to the way the system modeller thinks it operates!

The realisation that better defined semantics is needed to 'run' models has caused gradual changes in methods. For example, in the 'Yourdon' methods, there has been a gradual shift from functional decomposition (SA/SD, as described in [3]) through event-partitioning (YSM, as described in [2]) to a complete virtual machine [5] (see §2.4).

2 Moving away from pencil and paper

The main requirement is to move away from the pencil and paper 'mind-set'. This is achieved by a shift in the interpretation of the term 'model'. Rather than interpreting it as 'a set of diagrams, with supporting text', we will interpret it as 'a complete representation of the system'. In other words, it will include all issues of system behaviour and performance that we need to discuss.

The way the model is stored and organised can now break away from the 'page' unit. Of course, we still expect to be able to visualise specific areas of concern using diagrams (and text). These should be regarded as 'views into the model', rather the component parts of the model itself. For example, Figure 1 shows three views into a specific model.

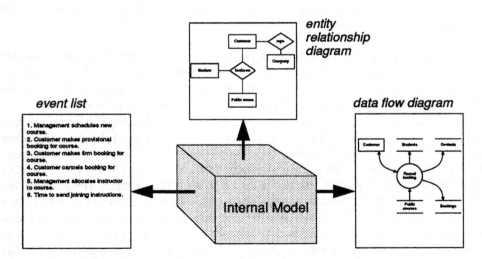

Figure 1: Three views into the internal model.

2.1 The internal model

In Figure 1, the model is labelled 'internal model'. This is because the way it is represented internally is of no interest to the system modeller. Of course, the CASE tool developer will be concerned with the way the internal model is stored. (See also §5.1.) It is a 'black box';

only by means of the views can its contents be defined or examined. The grammars of the internal model and external views are chosen with different aims. For the external views, the choice is to give 'user-friendliness' without confusing the user. For the internal model, the grammar is chosen to give rigour and aid emulation, checking for completeness etc.

2.2 An end to cross-checking

It is meaningless to talk about 'cross-checking' the views. There is only one internal model, so if there is an overlap between two views, two views into it *must* be consistent. In fact, this is a slight simplification because of the need to support way information is gathered.

A CASE tool must allow users to leave views incomplete (e.g. 'dangling' relationships) or inconsistent with other views ("I know I have two views showing the same relationship, but referring to different entities — I'll go away and think about it"). To deal with this, the CASE tool must implement a 'play' or 'pending' area. The possible states of different parts of the model are therefore: agreed (a baseline model), consistent (a working model) and incomplete (pending model fragments).

2.3 Many overlapping views

When a CASE tool supports the internal model and external views approach, the many overlapping views are a plus point (rather than a source of potential inconsistencies). As long as enough overlapping views have been used to capture all required aspects of the model, extra views do not give problems. The way is also open to views being generated automatically from the internal model. This can increase insight into the proposed system.

A view is a 'filter' and a 'translation' at the same time. By filter, we mean it shows some of the internal components only. This filtering may be by type, or subject area, or (more usually) both. An ERD, for example, shows a selection of entities and relationships — it does not show all entities and relationships, nor does it show functions. By a translation we mean it shows then in some user-friendly format. The same components can appear on different types of view. For example, figures 2 and 3 show some model components for a system in a company that runs training courses on a public basis.

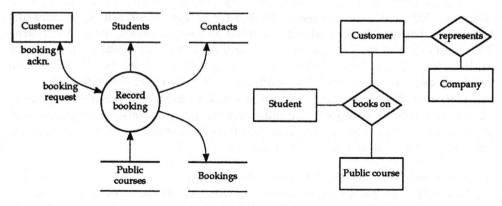

Figure 2: A data flow diagram.   **Figure 3:** An entity relationship diagram.

Identification of common components How do we know that the store 'Students' is the same as the entity 'Student'; or 'Contacts', the same as 'Customer', '<Customer> represents <Company>' and 'Company'? The 'pencil and paper' approach would have a data dictionary containing something like:

 Students = {Student}

and, more awkwardly:

 Contacts = {Customer} + {represents} + {Company}

In a CASE tool that supported the identification of stores and ERA components, we might have a 'frame specification' like that shown in figure 4.

```
STORE: Customers

ENTITIES: Customer, Company

RELATIONSHIPS: <Customer> represents <Company>
```

Figure 4: A 'frame' specification.

Of course, this is still really in the 'pencil and paper mind-set' approach. There are many better ways of declaring that a store icon on a DFD corresponds to a given area of an ERD. For example, we could show an ERD and DFD view in two windows on the screen at the same time. Association of ERD fragments with a store could then be achieved by 'pointing' at a store and then the corresponding ERD components. Once this association had been set up, an ERD store could be 'popped open' at any time to reveal an mini-ERD showing the same model components from a different point of view. (The way this association is maintained should be hidden within the CASE tool and not visible to the user.)

2.4 Virtual machine for conceptual model

Most methods distinguish between conceptual and implementation modelling. Conceptual modelling identifies the required policy for the system, without any implementation details; implementation modelling identifies a choice of technology for the system. The specification of the required policy is called the conceptual model (or the essential model, following [1]). The specification (or 'blueprint') of how the system will be constructed is called the implementation model (many other names are in use for this).

What kind of things form the minimal conceptual model? This depends on the method. The main criterion for what goes in the minimal model is that it should be complete enough to run in some virtual machine. The characteristics of this virtual machine are method-dependent. For example, we might use a virtual machine with:

- data transformations carried out by data processes;
- information organised around entities, relationships, attributes and abstract data types (*all* information, not just stored information);
- data manipulation operations that operate on ERA components;

- a set of primitive operations (together with the data manipulation operations, these are used to construct data processes, using a well-defined grammar;
- state machines to synchronise and control.

To avoid distorting the requirements, the performance of this virtual machine should be 'perfect', with: infinite, non-volatile memory; zero instruction time; zero cost, weight, power consumption and size; an infinite mean time between failures; all i-o carried out in zero time using 'extra-sensory perception'; ability to run many processes simultaneously.

There is no technology with these characteristics, of course! It is a convenient mental fiction to visualise the conceptual requirements. However, a CASE tool could emulate it to some degree, as long as the finite processing speed is accepted. The model would not (and could not) run in real time. However, it is an important requirement for CASE tools. 'Running' the models will be an expected feature. To allow this, the semantics of each model component type must be sufficiently well-defined.

2.5 Virtual machines for implementation model

For implementation models, we need to model technical issues such as: processor performance, execution units, data structures and access mechanisms, library routines, etc. The model must allow us to check that they are used to achieve the policy stated in the conceptual model.

It is important to decide what needs to be modelled and make sure these issues are covered by the minimal model. This should be done *before* deciding which views are to be provided. Fixing on a set of modelling tools (particularly diagram types) and then deciding how to cross-check them is not acceptable. That would be a pencil and paper approach.

We can again use the concept of virtual machines. For example, a run-time model uses an architecture that is the same as the one chosen in the actual run-time environment. This model acknowledges the effect of the architecture: the operating system, communications software, packages, DBMS, etc. In other words, we run the model in an virtual machine that has the same architecture as the final system.

More than one type of virtual machine could be used in design. A 'logically perfect' virtual machine can be used to run the model in given processors, with given performance (but suppressing the software architecture). A virtual machine that interpreted source code could be used to 'run' the model at the source code level.

These implementation virtual machines has an important characteristic that the conceptual processor does not have — they correspond to real technology (we shall return to this in §3.3).

2.6 Semantics and syntax

For a given view, we will allow different ways in which it can be presented. For example, a state machine can be modelled using a state transition diagram, or it can be modelled using the tabular equivalent. These are just different presentations of the same information. More formally, we use a modelling tool that prescribes how each model component type is presented. The presentation is derived from the model components shown in the view (acting as a 'filter') using the modelling tool syntax to carry out the translation. This distinction between view and presentation covers such concepts as different graphic icons (trivial), different procedural text grammars and different types of tool (e.g. the STD or tabular equivalents). Translating a view from one presentation to another using a different tool can be automated (default placement information would need to be generated for graphic modelling tools). Figure 5 shows three different presentations of inheritance, for example.

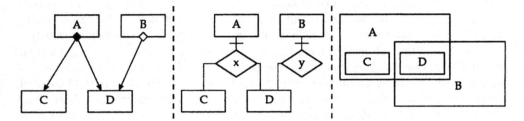

Figure 5: Three ways of showing 'inheritance'.

There is no semantic difference between them, only the graphic modelling tool has been changed for the same view. (Note: although the third diagram is perhaps, the more intuitive, there is nowhere for a CASE tool to provide a navigation path to the model concern over whether the subtyping is complete or partial. The other versions are better in this respect.) This separation of syntax from semantics is now well recognised [6].

Textual modelling tools and dialects The presentation concept extends considerably beyond graphic notation. A function defined internally in terms of its input and output parameters could be referenced in different ways in different presentations. The same program source code (or minispec) could be presented in different presentations of the same view in different ways for different audiences. For example, 'A := B;', 'LET A = B', 'assign (a b)', 'MOVE A TO B', 'Give A the same value as B' are equivalent to the same internal function with different presentation grammars (Modula, BASIC, LISP, COBOL, and 'minispec'). In fact, these are so similar that they might not merit the importance of being called different modelling tools. We might define a single procedural, block-structured language and refer to these as being different dialects of the same tool. A graphic tool (e.g. a Nassi-Schneiderman chart etc.), on the other hand, would be a different modelling tool, and thus give different presentations of the same view.

Different semantics is non-trivial Different methods do not just prescribe different syntax for modelling tools. They often have different semantics too. For example, different methods might use entity-relationship-attribute modelling in analysis. One might allow higher-order relationships, but not the other. An information model built in the more general framework can be translated to one in the less general, but not vice-versa [7]. Extra semantic input is required.

2.7 Generic tools

In the past, methods have used generic modelling tools. For example, DFDs have been used to model conceptual functions, processors, execution units and even source code modules and their interfaces. Each of these is slightly different in terms what the units on the diagram mean and how they would 'execute'. To resolve this ambiguity, the data flow diagram can be defined as being available in several 'flavours'. Each inherits some general properties (for example processes always represent active units and data flow represent transient interfaces), but there is additional semantic content. For example, on a module diagram (showing source code modules), it is illegal to show 'enables' between two units in the same execution unit (i.e. thread).

One specific area where the generic tool concept is useful is in distinguishing between conceptual and implementation models. Thus a generic DFD can be subtyped into conceptual data flow, processor, run–time unit, and module diagrams. Each shows different layers of technology. This is further discussed in §3.3. (Note: at present, many object-oriented approaches use generic tools and fail to distinguish between conceptual and implementation objects.)

Generic DFDs, STDs, etc. may inherit characteristics from even more generic types of tool, such as graphic tools, frame specifications, production grammars, and tables [5].

3 Framework for methods

We will assume that the method will be based around the idea of models, each consisting of a number of components. Each component is one of a number of pre-determined types; these types are specified by the method (e.g. entity, abstract data type). These components may be modelled using a range of modelling tools. The method will prescribe activities such as model construction and verification, with traceability built in.

3.1 The F^{I}T triangle

One very important framework concept is the idea of perspective [2], [8], [9]. The system can be modelled from different points of view: a functional, data or some other perspective. These are often overlapping to some extent, but an 'orthogonal' set of axes would be function, information and time[1] — the F^{I}T triangle. See figure 6.

These are chosen because a function can be defined, irrespective of when it is used (the function perspective); an event defined irrespective of what is done when it occurs (the time perspective); information modelled irrespective of what it is used for or when. Of course, we do need to model when information is used (the information–time plane); changes of system behaviour caused by events (the time–function plane); the information accessed by functions (the function–information plane).

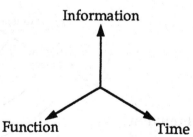

Figure 6: The Function-Information-Time triangle.

---

1 [2] and [8] chose different perspectives that were not orthogonal.

This framework is not only useful in conceptual modelling; it also persists into implementation. For example: system functions are implemented as 'functional' units (code); events become interrupts, program completion events, etc.; information becomes data structures.[2] In addition, the links between the perspectives are maintained. Conceptual information usage (in the function–information plane) becomes accesses to data structures. Activations (in the time–function plane can be modelled as 'enables', 'triggers' etc. in conceptual models; in an implementation they become the use of activation mechanisms (O-S and procedure calls) in a delivered system. The F^IT triangle acts as a useful organisation concept in checking allocations have been carried out (traceability) [9].

As described in [10], the existing system modelling tools can also be related to the F^IT triangle. See figure 7.

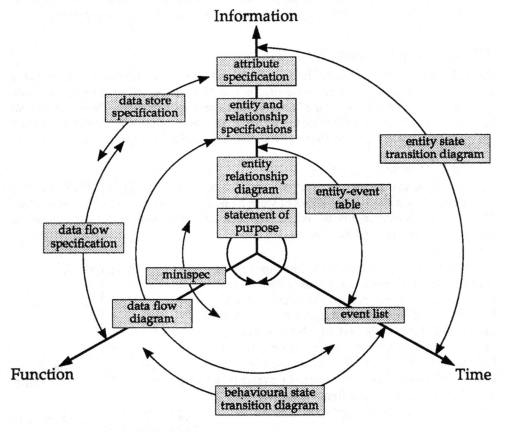

Figure 7: Modelling tools and the F^IT triangle.

---

2 Not absolutely true, because functions can be represented as rules (data) with interpreters, but it is more common for units not to cross perspective boundaries when they are mapped onto the technology.

3.2 Conceptual and implementation models

Conceptual modelling — complete or not? The conceptual model can be partial or complete. Some methods do not cover all parts of the F^IT triangle. They may also suggest that the conceptual model is deliberately high-level and incomplete. However, the author thinks that this is a dangerous stance and prefers the model to be complete. In any case, emulation requires that all policy is covered by the model. This wish to run models is one of the main reasons for moving away from the 'set of diagrams' approach.

One problem that needs to be addressed is what to do about 'fuzzy' decisions. Most system modelling methods require deterministic logic. YSM3, for example, requires that all processes are completely specified by state machines or minispecs [5]. The minispecs must unambiguously prescribe how the inputs are transformed to the outputs each time the process is activated. Minispecs are written using a well-defined grammar, that could in principle, allow them to be 'run'. In some systems, however, there are decisions that would be impossible to model in this way (this is often true when the intended processors include people). In these cases, a CASE tool could not emulate the policy, except by 'breaking out' of the model to ask the system modeller what the actions should be, each time the function is activated.

3.3 The relationship between system implementation models and the architecture

The implementation model shows allocation to technology. This includes allocating system policy to implementation units such as processors, execution units, files, data structures, modules, etc. As mentioned in §3.1, this generally maintains the position in the F^IT triangle.

Architecture structures and units A design cannot just be generic — it is always a design for a specific architecture. The run-time model must be organised to take account of the architectures of each intended processor type. Source code models must take account of the architecture of the programming language.

This is an important type of constraint that has been long realised. Experienced designers implicitly design for a specific architecture. However, methods have not usually dealt with this very satisfactorily[3]. There are two concepts that are useful in this area: the distinction between conceptual, technology and allocation views; strong typing of the implementation model.

Conceptual views Figure 2 is a conceptual view, showing a system function "Reserve place". All components on this diagram must correspond to an instance (or aggregate of instances) of one of the model components that can be seen in this type of view. For example:

- the process is view of a function (which also has a required internal view — a minispec);

---

3 Note: some CASE tools are specifically intended for design for a single architecture. They are not subject to this criticism. However, they are of less general application and we therefore ignore them.

- the data store is a view of a collection of stored data items, which are organised as occurrences of entities and/or relationships, together with their stored attributes;
- data accesses (between process and store) are a view of the access to stored information by the function (this can also be 'filtered' out of the corresponding minispec);
- the terminator is something outside the model scope that the model interacts with;
- data flows are a view of temporary data items (at the elemental level, each component is an attribute — possibly temporary, and not retained);

The fact that each component on the diagram represents an instance of a specific minimal component types is referred to as the 'strong typing of the conceptual model'. It provides semantic security, rather than just a 'pretty picture'. For the typing to be complete, we require (for example):

- All data accesses must use an allowed data access operation provided for a conceptual data model (probably an ERA model);
- All data items must be typed as an abstract data type (in rare cases, we might allow 'anonymous' ADTs, where comparisons do not need to be carried out).

Technology views In a run-time model, a particular execution unit might need to access several data structures. (By this stage in the design process both of these issues will have been addressed.) Figure 8 shows such an execution unit.

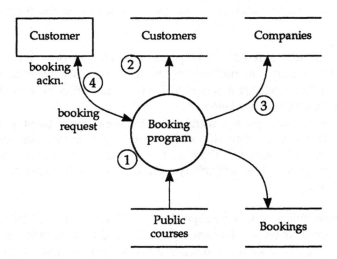

Figure 8: Strongly typed implementation view.

This is again a view into the minimal model (this time the implementation model), but the filter shows technology units. Each of these must correspond to technology provided by the run-time architecture. For example:

- The 'Booking program' must be identified with a type of execution unit allowed in this architecture.

- The 'Customers' store must correspond to an allowed run-time data structure (for example, an SQL table).
- Access to a data structure must be via the data manipulation operations provided by the architecture (e.g. 'select', 'project', etc. for a relational DBMS).
- User input-output must be associated with available technology, both hardware and software (including screen 'look and feel' standards).

This diagram is therefore a technology diagram, showing technology units. It is strongly typed by requiring that all units shown must be an instance of a type of unit provided by the run-time architecture. The $F^{I}T$ concept is useful here — for example, functions are usually implemented by 'processing type' units, as previously discussed.

Allocation views We can also show the conceptual 'fragments' allocated to a specific implementation unit. This is an allocation view. Allocation views can be used both for: functions allocated to an implementation unit (i.e. DFDs); information allocated to data structures (i.e. ERDs); functions, information and dynamics allocated to an implementation unit (i.e. object diagrams). In the example, we could show the ERD fragments allocated to the data structure Bookings (the entity Student and the relationship <Customer> reserves place for <Student> on <Public course>).

Resources and strong typing The link between systems models and reusable resources (which should be regarded as enterprise resources) is a particularly important one. Very few systems are built in isolation. The relationship between system models and resources such as the O-S and DBMS are particularly important. Only by checking that these interfaces are correct can the design be verified. One convenient way of thinking of an implementation model is shown in figure 9. This shows a system implementation model (the Code model, see [2]) as a conventionally levelled set of generic DFDs (of different subtypes). In addition, we see that each component of these technology diagrams is associated or 'tied' to a resource provided by the architecture. In this diagram, four resources are shown. Each provides a set of component types and services to a 'higher' layer. Each of these resources can be modelled using the same strategy. For example, a model of a communications service would interact with a client application; it would also use lower-layer resources such as 'hardware'.

Note: it is particularly attractive to model each of these resources as providing a set of objects that can be used by other (client) resources, including the application layer.

Resource libraries All available resources, whether execution unit types, functions, subroutines, abstract data types or communications protocols (for example) are enterprise resources. A CASE tool should hold a representation of the facilities they provide in a central repository. This repository is separate from the system models. This allows various desirable features to be provided by a CASE tool. One of these is the ability to 'browse' through a set of available resources when carrying out design. Conceptual units can be allocated to these resources on an interactive basis and this association retained by the CASE tool (internally) [11]. Technology and allocation views could then be automatically provided.

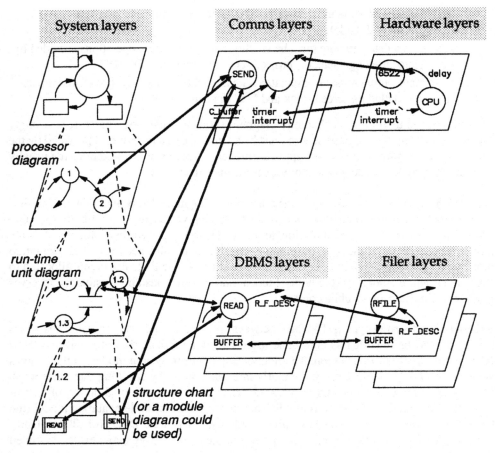

Figure 9: The links between technology layers.

Another benefit would be that individual resource types can be 'parameterised'. For example, an execution unit type might have a certain storage and activation overhead. We might allocate a certain function to a process of this type to provide part of a system's functionality. The function would have a complexity, which would require storage and processing resources for each instantiation of that function. In a sophisticated CASE environment, putative allocations could be carried out and a calculation of whether system performance constraints are met.

Parameterisation of this type would be a very large undertaking if all architectures were tackled, but a gradual 'capturing' of this data is feasible, once a framework is agreed. It is likely that the F^{I}T framework will be useful in this parameterisation. Additionally, the parameterisation needs to be at both the type and instantiation level. Sometimes there may be multiple instantiation level overheads. We might have a component for implementing an object on an execution unit and processor level, as well as the instance level.

In the P+D paradigm, data and functions are allocated in parallel. In the object paradigm, they are encapsulated (possibly even in analysis) and then allocated together.

3.4 Process+Data versus Object paradigms

The above framework is very general. The concept of technology layers of technology is still valid, whether the system is thought of as processes + data (information, data structures → execution units + data structures) or objects (conceptual objects → implementation objects).

Of course, the organisation of the models would be different. In the P+D approach, functions are allocated to processors, then execution units, then source code units. This progressively pushes down a 'technology line' towards the final organisation, as shown on the left of figure 9. On the other hand, if a conceptual object is distributed across processors, then the processors will appear 'within' the objects (in fact, hidden in transducer objects). 'Inter-task' transducer logic appears within an object when it is distributed to different run-time units (the 'inter-process' transducer logic disappears within these). None the less, we can still think about technology views (showing implementation objects and structures) and allocation diagrams (showing conceptual units allocated to them).

In either approach, strong typing of the implementation model requires that all services used in one resource must be typed to be an instance of a service type exported by another resource.

3.5 System scope

One of the more important characteristics of mature methods is the way in which they integrate multiple systems. Most methods now recognise the existence of both enterprise and system models [5]. The enterprise model is the summation of all system models within some larger scope (often the whole business enterprise). (Note: the enterprise model is different from the resource library. The enterprise model is a 'super-model', used to check access to shared items, such as information; the library is a collection of re-usable components.)

This scope distinction can be generalised so that all areas of activity can be considered to be 'chunks', consisting of information, activity and dynamics (they could also be described as 'conceptual objects'). In the middle range, we have system-size chunks; larger chunks correspond to enterprises; smaller chunks to objects.

The interfaces between the chunks are: shared information, messages, functions within one chunk used by another chunk, and events (actions in one chunk that cause responses in other chunks). Even interfaces to systems that are external to the enterprise can be described in the same way. This rationalisation allows another simplification in the traditional system-oriented, process+data approach. What was regarded as a terminator in a DFD can now be seen to be a chunk. If it is truly a black box, it can be thought of as a source or sink (terminator); if more insight is available, it can be modelled as an object, with visible external interface functions (or methods).

4 Method definition

4.1 Who owns methods?

The ownership of methods is an important issue. There are effectively four possibilities:

1 international standards body or government 'quango';

2   individual person, who develops method and advocates it via books and papers;

3   commercial company that specialises in consultancy, training and/or CASE;

4   open market-place standards set by common practice;

Each has some advantages and disadvantages:

Sponsor	Advantages	Disadvantages
Standard	Available, permanent, good support	Inertia, not best current practice
Individual	Often well-thought out and intuitive	Little support or permanence
Commercial	Good support	Expensive, inflexible. Often driven by commercial factors, leading to inertia. Best practitioners find this environment unattractive to work in.
Market-place	Available, dynamic	Ill-defined, dynamic. May lead to choosing a tool and method pair that is a good tool, supporting out of date method.

Probably the best compromise would be the development of 'method forums'. Individuals and companies who are interested in method enhancement would contribute to technical debate and development. They might also sponsor the development of software tools and training seminars. These groups might be organised on a regional or industry-type basis. This will give the flexibility of fairly rapid incorporation of new concepts, with the advantages of wide review and sufficient financial leverage for development of delivery vehicles and tools. Syndicates of this type have been used in some areas of software engineering (for example, expert systems), but it is not clear whether an similar initiative for method development would be successful.

4.2 Requirements for methods

What kind of thing should we be looking for in a method? Rather than getting trapped in the specific details, there are certain characteristics that we would expect to see in such a method.

Flexible It should be possible to use the same method in different ways for different ends. A method which is only applicable to a very small range of problems will not gain wide acceptance. There will be few tools available to support it and training will not be cost-effective. There will be problems with obtaining people who understand the method.

The method should also cater for individual tastes in approaches. A method that prescribed a single way of doing things is:

□   boring: and hence not conducive to quality work;

□   not cost-effective: different problems may allow different 'short cuts' to be taken to achieve the desired goal; always requiring the same approach ignores this;

- not realistic: a single 'cookbook' approach will not always work, in spite of its advocates trying to sell 'new clothes';

Two extreme approaches to system development might be to:

- Completely specify the system using 'structured techniques' before building any of it;
- Build a little, test a little, ... (the prototyping approach).

Neither of these approaches should be followed in too blinkered a way. Specifying without some prototyping is difficult and laid about by many pitfalls; prototyping without some modelling discipline becomes 'hacking', leading to very poor systems. We would therefore reject the advice of anyone who said "You only need to prototype", or "Prototyping should not be used".

The method may have features that are not applicable to all kinds of system. For example, it is often stated that state machines are not needed for business systems. The justification would be that adequate models can be built without them[4]. We would certainly allow this sort of thing (though not, perhaps, this specific example). We require that the same framework is used for a wide range of systems, even if all the facilities within the framework are not used on a specific project.

Adjustable rigour Not all users of a method will want to use the same level of rigour. Greater rigour may give increased confidence in quality of delivered systems, but at a cost. Not all projects justify this. The freedom to be more or less formal should be fundamental to the method. Similarly, building models with different degrees of completeness should also be allowed . In both cases, this should be a continuous spectrum.

Regarding a minispec in structured text as an informal modelling tool and the equivalent, written in Z is *not* the way to take advantages that software support can provide. In this specific case, the internal model/view/presentation approach works well. The internal model is a complete specification of the function. It can then be presented in different views using modelling grammars aimed at different audiences. The 'grammar' of the internal model is rigorous; the external views are derived.

Extensibility Methods should not be monolithic. As new modelling tools, models, heuristics etc. are developed, it should be possible to integrate them into the existing method to extend it. The approach proposed here should allow this extensibility, within the F^IT triangle. For example a new method heuristic (function) might be defined; a new model integrity rule (information) have their place in this framework.

Modelling concepts A method should provide conceptual building blocks of the same type (but not necessarily identical to) the ones presented in this paper: models, modelling tools, views, presentations, heuristics, rules, guidelines.

---

4 In fact, there are few systems that always operate to the same policy at all times. State logic is therefore probably required.

Scoping Any method must be allow modelling at several scope levels. Preferably, these levels would not be hard-coded into the method, but as a minimum, object, system and enterprise scopes must be recognised. Re-use of units (functions; objects; abstract data types; and implementation units such as packages, subroutines etc.) must be allowed for by providing a resource library modelling concept.

Models There should be a range of models, each addressing specific issues. Not all models need to be used in any one project, but the method should allow them if required. Each model should be defined as consisting of components that run in a virtual architecture of some type. If such a virtual machine cannot be defined, then the model is incomplete or ill-defined.

Modelling tools The method should provide a range of tools to provide views into the models. Each of these should have well-defined semantics in terms of which internal components are visible (filtering) and how they are shown in the view (translation). It should be possible to relate the modelling tools to some abstract framework, such as the $F^I T$ triangle. For example, a behavioural state transition diagram 'lies in' the time–function plane. See figure 7.

Notations For each modelling tool, there should be one (or more) well-documented notation. This is a syntax, rather than a semantic issue. For a DFD, we could allow different icons; for a procedural minispec, we might allow different presentations (e.g. in COBOL, Fortran, Z, structured text). (See §2.6.)

Heuristics, rules and guidelines There should be a set of rules and guidelines for completing and reviewing the models. Guidelines should also cover the definition of suitable views ('coherence' concept), layout of diagrams, naming of components, etc.

There should be techniques for construction of the models. These should range from heuristics, through open rules to closed rules. (A closed rule is one that is sufficiently well-defined to carry out without any human input, for example, as implemented by a compiler; an open rule is one that requires some ad-hoc human input [9].)

Management framework Although this paper suggests that system modelling should be distinguished from project management, the correct 'hooks' in system development methods are required. For example, the method must provide concepts such as deliverables, models, views, review sessions. Resource and construction cost requirements can also be related to the internal components (although probably only described as seen in views). As a management framework, building any system can be regarded as a construction problem in the $F^I T$ domain (a function).

5 The way forward

How shall we improve our systems engineering techniques? We assume that CASE and methods will develop hand in hand to increase our ability to construct quality systems for complex requirements.

One important issue is avoiding 'lock-in'. Being forced to use a single tool or method indefinitely, even when it is no longer the best, is clearly not a good idea, even apart from the commercial advantages of 'shopping around'. Monolithic CASE tools (typical of most currently available) have this disadvantage.

5.1 IRDS facilities

One of the important initiative in this area is the development of Information Resource Dictionary System (IRDS) frameworks, and hopefully, products. These separate the storage of models from the CASE tools, allowing some freedom to change tools. In the longer term, these will also incorporate the ability to accommodate different methods in the same IRDS and possibly event 'tailor' the methods.

There are several standards bodies working on this (ANSI, CDIF, ISO, and PCTE are the main groups), but there is a gradual convergence towards the initiative carried out under the auspices of the ISO standards committee [12], [13].

5.2 Framework for methods

To allow an IRDS to have the freedom to deal with different semantics and methods, several layers of abstraction are required. Figure 10 shows some of the concepts mentioned in this paper, organised according to the ISO framework.

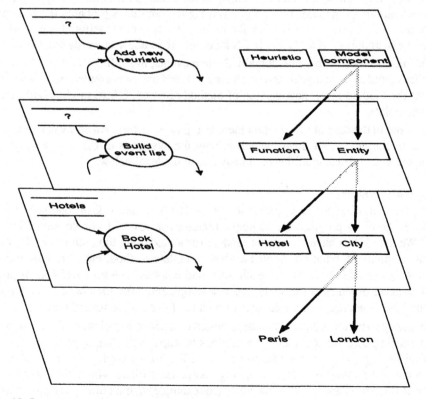

Figure 10: Layers of abstraction in system modelling

There are four layers of abstraction.

1 Application level. This level corresponds to the delivered system. Instance data corresponds to the actual real-world things that the system deals with.
2 Model level. This is where most people tend to think of methods and CASE. Instance data corresponds to information about which entities, processes, state machines etc. are required for the delivered system.
3 Method level. At this level the instance data corresponds to the modelling components used. For example, most methods use components such as entities, relationships, ...
4 Method definition level. At this level the instance data corresponds to concepts used in the method. For example, we might have models, views, presentations, modelling tools, heuristics, etc.

The semantics of any building block is always defined at a higher level. Discussion on whether relationships in YSM_3 ([5]) are the same as in YSM_2 ([2]) — they aren't — are discussions at the method definition level.

We can have functional type things too, shown as processes in figure 10. At the application. level, there are functions as seen on a typical system DFD. At the model level, they are activities like build model, cancel project, check event list. At an even higher level they are activities such as add new model, identify implementation for essential system component, add heuristic to method. We can go even higher, but this is probably too philosophically vague. We do not want activities like define new system modelling framework. This is particularly important if tools and IRDS facilities are to allow upwards-extension.

We can also look at the time domain. System events, modelling events such as essential model completed, customer agrees change to interface, management sets new project goals. At the method level, new version of method released, CASE module built, etc. are valid time points.

Note that in the case of information there is a 'pair' structure. An entity at one level has instances in the next level down, which is why the system is at the lowest level. Each function creates (deletes, modifies etc.) instances at the level below.

5.3 Contents modules
It would be ill-advised to try to define all of the IRDS framework in 'one go'. The ISO framework therefore provides for contents modules for standard system modelling techniques. We could thus have a contents module for a modelling tool, structure of a model, heuristic, a grammar, what constitutes a view, complete method, etc. It is important that these modules are able to reference each other and this has been provided for. At present, several contents modules are actively under development. After they have been delivered, it is hoped that guidelines for production of such modules will be formulated.

Generally speaking, contents modules cannot be defined in isolation. They will need to refer to existing contents modules. Less obvious perhaps, is the requirement that they tend to depend on higher-layers (in the ISO sense [12]). For example, we might attempt to define a content module for ERA modelling components (there would need to be several variants of this, of course). In this, an entity (for example) could either be regarded as:

- a component of an ERD, which is an instance of diagram type; each model consists of multiple instances of each diagram; each component has a corresponding specification ...;
- an instance of model component; it can be seen in various views; each view can be represented with different modelling tools ...

In other words, meta-modelling (discussion of what an entity is) requires meta^2-modelling to define model component, view, etc.

5.4 Implementation of this strategy

There are certain considerations of a political nature. Not all methods are openly available and documented (although one would be ill-advised to use a closed, proprietary method anyway). The support, adoption and promulgation of suitable standards will also be important. One trap that is not always recognised is trying to impose methods that do not work. Often, companies claim they use methods, when, in reality, the methods are talked about by the managers and politicians, but not actually used in the way they are described (the Emperor's new clothes problem).

Standards should cover: the modelling framework, lifecycle model, IRDS, modelling tools. Standards should be extensible, in the sense that there should be freedom to customise by: changing names, notation or syntax; adding or deleting method components and so on.

Education Books, consulting and education should promote the concepts, not notation or proprietary methods and tools. There should be a generic approach, with evolution within a framework to provide stability. This will require end-users to be aware of the issues and avoid getting 'locked into' specific commercial approaches.

Psychology There are also psychological factors that need to be considered. One is that people hide behind (and defend) a named method or CASE product, rather than the concepts behind it. For example, some people would get into very heated arguments about how important DFDs are in the system life cycle. Truth to tell, they are good at showing interfaces between functions, no more and no less. Is this all we are concerned about? No. Then we need other tools. They are not more or less important, they are other tools.

People can also get very aggressive about notation for no good reason. What research has been done indicates that notation should be sparse (but well-defined), rather than rich. Yet many still want to invent (and enrich) notations for all sorts of things.

The framework of the method used by a CASE tools should always be intuitive [14]. Arcane and esoteric ways of doing things should be seen for what they are — inefficient and outmoded. Most people accept the revolution of the GUI. On the other hand, we all cling to the word-processor that we first learnt. I have been through three word-processors now (and numerous text editors) and I still get into heated (sometimes aggressive) debates about which is the best!

Technology The CASE technology should support the generic approach that we have proposed in this paper. As IRDS concepts will never quite work as we mean them to (open availability to several CASE tools), it is important that standard import/export interfaces are defined too.

The semantic definitions should not be hard-coded into the CASE tool, but modelled as information and rules in the IRDS. This is some way off at present, and we may have to do with a range of generic techniques provided by the CASE tool.

The technology should win on adherence to standards, price, performance, user-friendliness etc. and not on 'our method is best'. It is in the customers interest to apply pressure to ensure this happens.

6 Conclusion

The above ideas are presented as an evolution of the ideas of other system engineers, particularly those who have used 'Yourdon-like' approaches. Few ideas are revolutionary, yet hopefully they will provide a framework for thinking about system modelling techniques using CASE.

Minimal models, views and presentations should provide a common philosophy for interacting with CASE products to produce models; association of implementation units with architecture features (strong typing), will enhance productivity and confidence in the design stages.

7 References

1. S. McMenamin and J. Palmer, Essential Systems Analysis. Yourdon Press, 1984
2. P. Ward and S. Mellor, Structured Development for Real-Time Systems. Yourdon Press, 1985
3. T. DeMarco, Structured Analysis and System Specification. Yourdon Press, 1978
4. E. Yourdon and L. Constantine, Structured Design: Fundamentals of a Discipline of Computer Program and Systems Design. Yourdon Press, 1978
5. J. Baker, M. Brough and N. Matzke, Yourdon Reference Manual. (obtainable from CGI Systems), 1990
6. D. Redmond-Pyle, Can formal methods be user-friendly? American Programmer, May 1991
7. M. Brough, Standards for CASE. European CASE II, Blenheim-Online, 1990
8. T. DeMarco, Controlling Software Projects. Yourdon Press, 1982
9. M. Brough, A Framework for Relating System Development Methods. Structured Development Forum X, San Francisco, 1988
10. M. Brough, Methods First, then Tools. DECUS (Methods, Languages and Tools special interest group), 1990
11. D. Budgen and G. Friel, Augmenting the Design Process: Transformations from Abstract Design Representations, CAiSE-92, Springer-Verlag, 1992
12. ISO/IEC 10027, Information Resource Dictionary Systems - Framework, 1990
13. Information Resource Dictionary System (IRDS) Services Interface, ISO/IEC draft standard 10728, 1991
14. R. Holmes, private communication, 1990

Metamodeling Editor as a Front End Tool for a CASE Shell

Matti Rossi[*1]

Mats Gustafsson[2]

Kari Smolander[*1]

Lars-Åke Johansson[2]

Kalle Lyytinen[1]

Abstract. Customizable Computer Aided Software Engineering (CASE) tools, often called CASE shells, are penetrating in the market. CASE shells provide a flexible environment to support a variety of information systems development methods. CASE shells are often cumbersome to use and in practice few people can model and implement methods in them. To overcome these problems we have developed a graphical metamodeling environment called MetaEdit and a method modeling interface to the CASE shell RAMATIC. Using this interface the methodology engineer can develop graphical models in RAMATIC's model definition language and then easily generate the resource files that control the operations of RAMATIC. MetaEdit is used as a graphical front end tool to develop, fast and in user-friendly manner, method models that can then be supported using RAMATIC. In this paper we shortly present the MetaEdit tool and then describe how the interface operates by illustrating how a new method for RAMATIC is defined using MetaEdit's interface tool. The defined method is called TEMPORA-ER.

[*] This research was in part funded by the Technology Development Center of Finland and Academy of Finland

[1] Department of Computer Science and Information Systems, University of Jyväskylä P.O. Box 35, SF-40351 Jyväskylä, Finland.

[2] Swedish Institute for Systems Development, Box 14225, SW-40020 Göteborg, Sweden

1. Introduction

Computer Aided Systems/Software Engineering (CASE) has been taken into extensive use in several companies. Most companies do not choose, however, a strategy to incorporate existing methods into tools, more likely the methods are determined by the chosen tool. This is the most obvious, but not in all situations, the most successful tool adaptation strategy. Therefore, one important research area is to examine how to develop CASE environments which can cover a variety of methods, and thus can satisfy the differing needs of various organizations. One solution is to use CASE shells - tools, by which one can tailor new functionality (ie. new method support) into a CASE environment. With a CASE shell, an organization can more easily build computer supported methods for a given task or project. A *method engineer* (an expert that defines the new methods) is usually needed to do this work, however.

One problem in this method adaptation process is that most CASE shells are quite cumbersome to use for method definition because they provide only low level and primitive mechanisms for this task. Therefore a limited number of people can actually model methods using CASE shells. To overcome this problem, one solution as proposed by Smolander et al. [10] is to use graphical tools for methodology modeling, i.e. graphical front-end tools for metamodeling, which we call metamodeling editors. These tools can be interfaced with different CASE shells and provide higher level mechanisms to accomplish the metamodeling task. The motivation to use a graphical model of method is to provide an abstraction layer that hides the peculiarities of a textual specification of the method.

We have developed a prototype metamodeling editor called MetaEdit [10]. In this study we discuss the general principles and architectures of metamodeling tools and demonstrate how we applied MetaEdit to specify methods into the CASE shell RAMATIC using its own specification language CML [1]. Our goal was to build an interface – a "bridge" – between MetaEdit and RAMATIC. This "bridge2 provides the sufficient functionality that allows a method engineer to graphically model a method in MetaEdit and then to create a text file which can be loaded into RAMATIC. The method engineer can concentrate on the critical tasks of method development such as method structure and content and let the tool handle the cumbersome production of a formal method specification that RAMATIC requires.

The paper is organized in six sections. The next section gives an overview of research that attempts to combine the CASE tools and provides motivation for our work. In the third section we shortly describe RAMATIC´s architecture. In the fourth section an overview of MetaEdit is presented with a more detailed description of the ReportGenerator that was used to implement the transformation system. The fifth section describes the functionality and structure of the bridge developed between

MetaEdit and RAMATIC. We also demonstrate how the modeling method TEMPORA-ER can be defined using this bridge. The final section suggests some future research issues and summarizes our results.

2. Connecting a Metamodeling Editor and a CASE Shell

2.1. Basic Preliminaries

Our interest in developing a metamodeling editor lies in our aim to model the methods used by the IS development groups to describe IS and it's environment. IS modelling is carried out by using a certain language, often referred to as a "description language". By a *method* we mean a set of steps and a set of rules that define how a representation of an IS is derived/transformed using a description language [9]. The "users" that define new description languages (*method engineers*) need corresponding languages (*meta languages*) to derive representations of the methods under development. These representations form a (IS) *metamodel* and the process of creating the meta model is called *metamodeling*.

The most obvious benefits of metamodeling are achieved[1] if we have a platform or a tool where the modeled method can be implemented. Such tools are called *CASE shells* and they offer mechanisms to specify a CASE tool for an arbitrary method or a chain of methods [4]. The concept of a CASE shell means that the shell can "learn" about methods which it did not "know" before. This learning will result in a tool that gives support for the use of the specified new method. To achieve this, one has to describe the method to the tool by defining the "method concepts" or design the object types of a specific description language (metalanguage). Meta concepts of a specific method may, for example, be objects, attributes, relationships, business functions, organizational units, information flows or whatever the methodology assumes to be useful in modeling the IS.

The meta languages vary from one CASE shell to another which makes their use difficult. Another problem is that often they use rigid and complicated textual languages which can be difficult to learn and apply. Therefore there is a need for more advanced method specification languages and associated support environments, which we call metamodeling tools or editors. A *metamodeling editor* is a special kind of CASE shell (meta tool), with which a method engineer can define methods for other (target) CASE shells graphically. In other words it can be "populated" by a set of meta languages used in different CASE shells.

---

[1]What are benefits if such an environment is not available are discussed in [3]. They are for example the concise description of methods, assesment of techniques and comparison of methods

The three main motivations in carrying out this study were: 1) there is a growing need for graphical (meta) modeling environments, 2) the best use of the graphical metamodels could be achieved if they can be transformed into the textual metalanguage of a given CASE shell by the metamodeling editor, and 3) the "programmability" of the metamodeling editor (meta CASE tool) gives us a chance to develop bridges into a number of CASE shells. The first item is obvious (see [10]) and also supported by the growing number of CASE shells in the market. The other two issues form the topic of the research reported in this paper.

2.2. The Motivation for Using Metamodeling Editors

The rationale behind using metamodeling editors is to provide a graphical environment for the methodology modeling. They are aimed to be general metamodeling environments which can be interfaced to different types of CASE shells with the appropriate "bridges".

One advantage of using graphical editors in metamodeling is that most of the meta models are easier to understand and maintain in a graphical form. Complex relationships between the concepts are easier to understand in pictorial form, than as lines of a textual definition. The maintenance, manipulation and modification of methods will also become easier when the meta models are kept in a graphical form. This allows for rapid modification of versions of meta models for different development situations and helps to improve their consistency and integrity. The possibility for versioning is essential in developing new methods, because method development tends to be cyclical and driven by method of trial and error [9,11]. This can be more easily achieved in computer environment where supported mechanisms are readily available (cf. version control systems). Finally, a benefit of graphical metamodeling is that it enhances the visibility of method development and gives the tool users a better understanding of the methods they use.

2.3. The Motivation for Using RAMATIC as a Target CASE Shell

The tool RAMATIC was chosen to act as the pilot CASE shell for interfacing because it has a large set of modeling constructs which form a "representative" example of those applied in other CASE shells. Hence, if we can "construct a bridge" for RAMATIC, we can probably implement it for other CASE shells as well.

In another study we have made a comparison between three CASE shells [7]. Results of the comparison of CASE shells show that RAMATIC has a powerful metamodeling language, but the method definition is rather difficult when compared to for example Excelerator´s Customizer [7]. The difficulties arise from CML´s rich set of concepts and their complex interdependencies. By using MetaEdit as a graphical interface we hope to achieve the best of both worlds: a powerful modeling language and the ease of using the graphical modeling. The functionality of bridge is also needed as there is not much sense in modeling the methods in RAMATIC's graphical language without being able to automatically transform them for the RAMATIC's native schema language.

2.4. Modeling the Connection Between Metamodeling Editors and CASE Shells

In order to model methods in a metamodeling editor for a given CASE shell the metamodeling editor has to provide support for the native description language contained in the CASE shell. This requires that the definition of the CASE shell's language (called the meta-metamodel of the CASE shell) has to be defined in the description language of the metamodeling editor (it's metalanguage). To make the bridge operational, the method engineer also has to define an output specification of how the metamodeling editor's graphical model will be translated into the CASE shell's native textual language. This output (report) specification and the metamodel specification together form the "bridge" between the two tools. The benefit of a two sided connection between tools is that it allows for both the use of a graphical specification method in the metamodeling tool and the seamless transportation of the resulting specification into the CASE shell. The mappings between the tools are illustrated in figure 1.

On the right hand side of the figure we represent the three levels of languages that are needed in delivering the functionality of a CASE shell. The IS specification level is the end user level where methods are used to develop IS representations. The syntax and the "semantics" of these models are defined on the metamodel level.

These metamodels limit and guide the usage of the tool. The metamodels themselves are in turn based on a modeling language and its presentation form (syntax and semantics). This language level is called the meta-metamodel of the CASE shell. This level is important as it is instrumental in offering the flexibility of the CASE shell environment. Therefore the expressive power and usability are important goals in developing these meta-meta languages. One example of a language developed for this level is RAMATIC's CML language which will be discussed in section 3.

The same three levels are also present in the metamodeling editor and they form the left hand side of figure 1. Analogously, in a metamodeling editor we have the meta-metamodel, the metamodel and the model. These operate, however, on one abstraction lever higher than in the CASE shell. Thus, the model level in a metamodeling editor defines the structure and the functionality of the IS modeling language i.e. the metamodel of the CASE shell. The metamodel in a metamodeling editor is the model that is used for specifying the methods in CASE shell i.e. the meta-metamodel of the CASE shell.

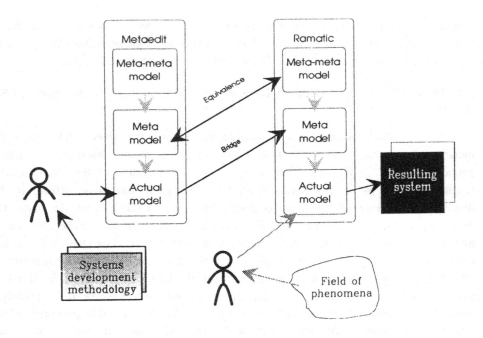

Fig 1. Mappings between MetaEdit and the target CASE shell

The third level defines the syntax and semantics of the metamodels used in the editor. The metamodels are used in specifying the method specifications for CASE shells. This highest level data model leverages the flexibility for the metamodeling editor. It allows users to define the CASE shell's metamodels in its "own metalanguage". This is achieved by defining the meta-metamodel of the CASE shell using the meta-metamodel of the metamodeling editor.

The connections between the tools are depicted by the two arrows in the figure 1. The upper arrow pointing from a CASE shell to the metamodeling editor represents a mapping of a CASE shell's meta-metalanguage into the metamodeling editor's language. The upper arrow from the viewpoint of the metamodeling editor represents a mapping of the metamodeling editor's language into the CASE shell's language. It involves functions defining the transformation between representation forms. The lower arrow represents the functional part of the bridge and it shows how the models derived using the metamodeling editor are then transformed into a CASE shell's metamodel. To demonstrate the viability of this approach, we will demonstrate how the metamodeling editor MetaEdit is used to translate graphical specifications into RAMATIC's textual metamodels. This is discussed in the section 5. Before this we shall shortly describe the functions and architecture of both MetaEdit and the CASE shell RAMATIC. This is done in sections 3 and 4, respectively.

3. The Architecture of the Ramatic CASE Shell

3.1. An Overview of RAMATIC

RAMATIC is a CASE shell - a "meta-tool" developed by the Swedish Institute for Systems Development (SISU). The development of RAMATIC started in 1985 with the objective to create a flexible environment for prototyping CASE tools for a large number of different methods employed by the different organizations supporting SISU.

3.2. The Architecture of RAMATIC

The architecture and functions of RAMATIC are shown in figure 2. The core of RAMATIC is the design object database (*DODB*). *DODB* consists of two parts: the conceptual database (*CDB*) and the spatial database (*SDB*). *CDB* stores information about the developed methods for example their objects, the relationships between the objects and their attributes. *SDB* contains information of how and where on the screen the conceptual objects are graphically represented.

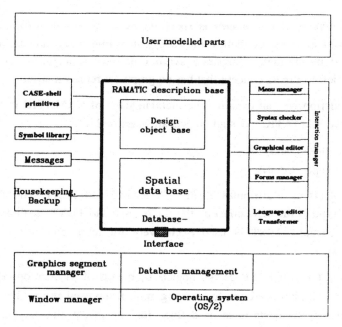

Fig 2. Architecture of RAMATIC

3.3. The Meta-metalevel of RAMATIC

RAMATIC uses a small set of meta-meta objects. These objects can have attributes which can be given values. The defined meta concepts and other definitions are stored in the "method knowledge base". As noticed above this base controls the uses of the tool in creating and manipulating design objects, according to the followed method.

In RAMATIC also graphical symbols can be defined on the metalevel by means of a symbol description language. This can be thought of as modifying the attributes of a "meta-meta symbol object". Design object types having graphical representation are then associated to one, or several symbol types.

3.4. Representation of Design Objects in RAMATIC

In RAMATIC certain design objects can exist independently of other objects, such as an entity type can exist as a "free" node in the ER-modeling. Other design objects, binary "relationships", can only exist if they are "connected" to two other object types. Such a relationship is defined as a "connection" design object. Accordingly, in a metamodel describing a business modeling technique we can recognize an information flow between two functions. This will be defined as a connection design object in RAMATIC. Attribute types for design object types can be defined as free nodes in RAMATIC. Alternatively they can be defined also as "subnodes" to the FREE object node. If we define these as FREE nodes, we can add more (meta)attributes to the attribute types.

The graphical representation of the objects is specified by a symbol definition. The symbols can be defined in terms of their form, size, color, line width and so on in RAMATIC. This is done through a separate symbol definition language. Notice, however, that we can define a meta concept that has no graphical representation.

After this short introduction we can examine the metalanguage of RAMATIC in more detail. As noticed above RAMATIC´s design objects are classified into:

- free meta concepts (FREE), and
- connecting meta concepts (CONN).

FREE- and CONN objects have attributes TYPE, ID, NAME and TEXT. The TYPE attribute indicates the type of the meta concept, the ID, NAME and TEXT attributes are used for names of concepts. TEXT is used exclusively for meta concepts having graphical representation.

CONN concepts connect pairs of FREE design objects by means of associations FROM and TO. CONN objects can, but need not, to have a graphical representation. The types of every valid pair of FREE objects must be defined for any CONN object type. The existence of any CONN object is dependent on the existence of those objects it connects. FREE and CONN objects can be defined also to possess attribute associations through an ASSOC statement.

For both FREE and CONN object types a SYMBOL TYPE can be attached. Moreover FREE- and CONN type objects can be grouped together by means of group (SET) objects.

Finally the metaconcepts of a specific modeling technique (these are usually handled in a separate session of the tool) are grouped together in one MODELTYPE. Meta concepts that appear in more than one model type are declared by INTER concepts. FREE and CONN objects of the same type may have IDENT associations. Furthermore, it is possible to define a set of integrity constraints for the design objects within one model type group. These constraints specify mostly the minimum and/or maximum cardinalities for the TO- and FROM associations. The constraints are formulated as FAULT expressions.

As an example of RAMATIC specification consider the following part of a definition of the meta concepts in an ER modeling technique developed by the ESPRIT project Tempora [12]. The Tempora ER model type constitutes an extended entity-relationship modeling technique with composite objects and time modeling.

```
MODELTYPE TEMPORA-ER
FREE ET    TPETRC   ID=NA NAME=MANDATORY NAME=UPPER
FREE ETT   TPETTRC  ID=MANDATORY NAME=MANDATORY NAME=UPPER
FREE DET   TPDETRC  ID=NA NAME=MANDATORY NAME=UPPER
FREE AVT   TPAVTRC  ID=NA NAME=MANDATORY NAME=UPPER
FREE RS    TPRSSQ   ID=NA NAME=NA
......
```

Examples of FREE design object types are here: Entity Type (ET), Timestamped Entity Type (ETT), Derived Entity Type (DET), Aggregate Value Type (AVT),Relationship (RS).

```
IDENT AVT
IDENT SVT
INTER ET
```

Aggregate value types and simple value types may have IDENT associations, which suggests a way of making multiple instances within one diagram possible. The INTER permits the connection of entities in one model type with for example data stores in another model type.

```
CONN BA  TPBAA  ET  RS   ID=OPTIONAL NAME=MANDATORY NAME=LOWER
CONN BA  TPBAA  ET  RST  ID=OPTIONAL NAME=MANDATORY NAME=LOWER
CONN BA  TPBAA  ET  DRS  ID=OPTIONAL NAME=MANDATORY NAME=LOWER
CONN BA  TPBAA  ET  DRST ID=OPTIONAL NAME=MANDATORY NAME=LOWER
......
```

The Binary Association (BA) CONN object type can connect an entity type to a relationship, to a timestamped relationship, to a derived relationship or to a timestamped derived relationship, etc. The line symbol (symbol type TPBAA) must, according to this example definition, be drawn from the entity type symbol to the relationship symbol i.e in the direction that the name attached to it suggests.

```
ASSOC ET DEFDATE
ASSOC ET CARDLTY
```

In addition to the TYPE, ID, NAME and TEXT attributes, an entity type may have additional attributes, such as definition date (DEFDATE) and cardinality (CARDLTY).

3.5. Specification of Methods Symbols, Menus and Forms in RAMATIC

The symbol types connected to the metaconcepts are defined in a separate part of the method specification base. This is accomplished through the symbol definition language. As a part of RAMATIC, a symbol library is available.

Any menu in RAMATIC is made up of several menu items, which can be texts or symbols. For each menu item, the following is defined:

- the text (TEXT) to appear in the menu, or if it is a symbol
- the symbol type (SYMBOL) and
- the shell function to be executed (MENUNR)

For the manipulation of non-graphical expressions RAMATIC provides forms in which one can modify and manipulate specific values of design objects. On the form definition level of RAMATIC one can define forms, how they should look like, how the field values are derived (from design objects), and how the tool should check the entered data values, etc.

4. The Architecture and Functions of MetaEdit

MetaEdit is a graphical metamodeling editor, a flexible methodology modeling environment. It can be interfaced with several CASE shells and thereby it can be populated with several metamodeling approaches. Moreover, it offers a graphical interface to carry out methodology modeling, and thereby it offers some advantages over the earlier environments. [10]

4.1. Functions

MetaEdit consists of three major functional components (see fig. 3):

1. **Main Window** offers the file and specification management functions. The selection of the modeling methodology and the maintenance of specifications in the methodology specification base (MSB) are done here. Other utilities of MetaEdit are also controlled from here.

2. **Draw Window** provides drawing functions to draw and edit specifications. It is generic and its behavior varies depending on the metamodel it uses.

3. **Output Generator** provides a programmable utility that helps to create reports, generate code or retrieve data from the methodology specification base. The tool

manager specifies the output specifications in the output specification base. The output specification base is a set of text files containing output generator code.

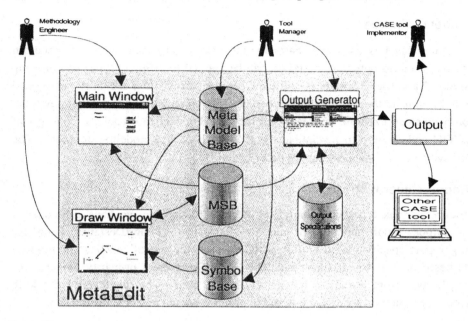

Fig 3. The Functional structure of MetaEdit

4.2. Datamodel

In MetaEdit the meta level datamodel is a fixed data structure based on the OPRR[2] data model [13]. The following defines the basic OPRR model :

Object is a "thing" which exists on its own. It is represented by its associated properties.

Property is a describing/qualifying characteristic associated with other object types (object, relationship, or role).

Role is a link between an object and a relationship. A role may have properties that clarify the way in which "things" participate in a certain part of a relationship. The role defines what "part" an object plays in a relationship.

Relationship is an association between two or more objects. It cannot exist without its associated objects. Relationships can also have properties.

The objects are always presented by graphical symbols in MetaEdit. The objects participate in relationships in certain roles. The roles are represented by symbols too. These symbols form the ends of relationship lines (for example arrow heads).

---

[2]OPRR stands for Object, Property, Role, Relationship model

Relationships are always represented by lines between two objects. Properties are represented by data fields. A field and it´s acceptable values are defined by a data type.

4.3. Model Definition

The meta-metalevel is used as a basis for all metamodel specification in MetaEdit. Depending on its instantiation, MetaEdit can be applied to different types of modeling approaches. Target level instances and their possible associations are fully determined by the definitions in the metamodel that can be changed on a user´s request at any time. Section 5 gives an example how we used the OPRR model to model the concepts of RAMATIC and thereby to instantiate the RAMATIC´s metamodeling approach. The detailed syntax of the metalanguage is described in [11].

4.4. Report Generation

To produce various types of output from MetaEdit´s models we have developed a general purpose report generator. It consists of two parts: ReportDesigner (a tool for building report specifications) and ReportGenerator, the actual machine to produce reports based on the stored definitions. The ReportDesigner is primarily intended for defining bridges from MetaEdit, but it can also be used to create integrity checking mechanisms for method specifications and to produce human readable documents.

The concept of a programmable transformation generator is similar to ideas in some other CASE shells. For example the Metaview environment has a transformation system for modelling transformations between model types [2] and Chen [4 pp. 130-136] has proposed a very similar environment to the ReportDesigner for a transformation language definition.

The ReportDesigner features an object-oriented query language, based on the syntax of Actor[3] language. The language has predefined functions for selecting objects from MetaEdit´s methodology specification base and for retrieving properties, roles and relationships of selected objects. The queries are constructed from these predefined functions by combining them into query methods. Each report specification contains one or more query methods that are joined together within a main function.

The ReportDesigner offers a Smalltalk[tm] style query browser. The user interface of the ReportDesigner is shown in Figure 4. It consists of four window portions within a main window. A report class window offers a list of defined reports. It is located in the upper left corner of the main window. When one of the report names is selected, the queries defined for that report are shown in the upper right-hand window, the query window. Again, when one of the queries is selected from the query window, its code is shown in

---

[3] Actor is a trademark of the Whitewater group

the edit window below. Between the report and query windows there is a model window where the constructs of the current metamodel are presented.

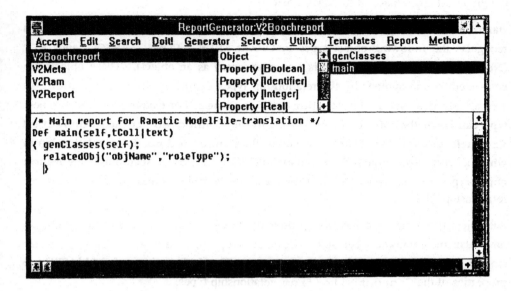

Fig. 4. The Interface of ReportDesigner

When the report specification is defined and compiled, it can be run in the ReportGenerator against the methodology specification base. The report generator can direct the generated reports to requested output devices while performing the requested query. The user can modify the behavior of the ReportGenerator by changing the report generator primitives in the ReportDesigner.

5. The Bridge Between MetaEdit and RAMATIC

This section presents the implementation of a graphical metamodeling editor for RAMATIC using MetaEdit. As the first step we defined RAMATIC´s meta-metamodel within MetaEdit using it´s OPRR metamodel. The mappings of RAMATIC´s design objects to MetaEdit´s OPRR constructs is presented in the next subsection. As the second step we define the report functions that represent the transformations from OPRR to RAMATIC´s CML.

5.1. Implementing RAMATIC´s Model Definition Language Within MetaEdit

We defined RAMATIC´s meta-metamodel in terms of MetaEdit´s OPRR meta-metamodel (the upper arrow pointing left in Figure 1). This step was accomplished by examining the design objects of RAMATIC and their properties and expressing them with OPRR constructs. All the roles and relationships embedded in RAMATIC´s CML had also to be defined. For all object types we defined the representation that specifies the graphical appearance of the CML object.

Based on the description of RAMATIC´s modeling language (see section 3) we can recognise the following object types in OPRR: FREE, CONN, ASSOC and SET (Note that the relationship CONN is also represented as an object). These objects are connected to one another by the relationship types Connected to, Connected from, Has assoc, is Member and is Owner. For example, a FREE object type can be in the roles of Free part in the Connected to and Connected from relationships. This defines one end of the Connected to/from relationship in which a CONN object type is always in the role of Conn part. Accordingly the Assoc object-types can be connected to CONN and FREE object types in a has assoc relationship type.

All object types have the identifying property Type name. FREE and CONN objects have also the properties Symbol identifier, Set auto, Ident, Inter model name and ID and Name options. The fault options of RAMATIC are properties of the Connected to/from relationship types.

To be able to present the method graphically we also defined the symbols for object types and line types for relationships (see fig. 5). The properties are handled in a property dialog which is generated automatically to fit with the properties of an object-, role- or relationship type (see fig. 6).

Note that this is only a partial definition of the whole metamodel. A more thorough definition can be found in [8] and a part of it is in Appendix 1. The resulting meta model was tested and verified and used as a basis to specify the graphical interface with which all modeling information associated with RAMATIC´s modeling language could be fed during the specification session. This formed the basis for the subsequent step to implement the transformation component of the bridge. In [10] we provide a more detailed description of the model definition in MetaEdit.

5.2. Mapping the MetaEdit's Design Objects to RAMATIC Model Definition Language

After specifying the modeling language and its representation forms in MetaEdit´s OPRR constructs, the transformation problem could be expressed in MetaEdit´s query language (The upper arrow in Figure 1 pointing to RAMATIC). The transformation task (method in object oriented vocabulary) could now be written as a series of query language commands by which the fixed expressions (reserved words used in RAMATIC´s method specification) could be attached to the object instances derived from a query to the specification base MSB. Hence this step produces the actual output for RAMATIC (bridge arrow in Figure 1).

In implementing this problem we had to define a translation method for each object type defined in the metamodel of MetaEdit. The principle of a translation method is as follows: first select the object instances for each object type and then specify how their properties (and relationships) are translated into the target language sentences. For example a method for transforming all FREE objects in MetaEdit into the corresponding FREE -lines in RAMATIC´s specification does roughly the following:

```
For all FREE-objs
   do
      getproperties(Type name, Symbol identifier, Set auto, ID options,
Name options)
      getrelatedobject(Assoc)
      print("FREE")
      print(Type name, Symbol identifier, Set auto)
      print(Assoc name)
      print(ID options, Name options)
   enddo
```

The method first retrieves all FREE objects (first line) from the specification base, and then a set of named properties (third line) and relationships (fourth line) for each FREE object are retrieved. Next a fixed expression (fifth line) is printed to the output stream and the retrieved properties (sixth and eight line), and finally names of the related objects (seventh line) are added in a specific order.

The Ident, Inter and Fault command lines are derived from properties of the FREE- and CONN object types and therefore the methods for producing them are of a slightly different form:

```
For all FREE-objs or CONN-objs with property(Ident)=TRUE
   do
      getproperty(Type name)
      print("IDENT")
      print(Type name)
   enddo
```

The difference is that now only a subset of FREE- and CONN objects with a certain value of a certain property are retrieved.

As most of the transformations are very straightforward the method engineer needs only to define the appropriate properties of the objects types and add some "syntactic sugar" to build a model definition clause in RAMATIC.

These examples shed some light on the main characterictics and the current status of the metamodeling editor and how it´s query definition facilities can be used to build effective bridges between MetaEdit and different CASE shells. The query formulation for producing FREE clauses in the CML language is shown in appendix 2. It points out that the current version of the query language uses rather complex syntax (if you do not like Smalltalk) and suits mostly for an experienced user. We believe, however, that the learning threshold is not a serious problem as long as MetaEdit is used mainly as a metamodeling editor, because on this level there are no "non-professional" users. The transformation task is for the first time quite tedious, but it has to be done only once and after that the query methods need only to be altered when the metamodel is restructured. Also the available query methods can be reused in creating new report specifications.

5.3. Using the Interface to Define the Tempora-ER Model

To demonstrate the usefulness of the metamodeling editor we used the editor to build a graphical model of the Tempora-ER model in RAMATIC´s modeling language. Note that now the model of the Tempora-ER method is build graphically in RAMATIC´s modeling language using the functionality of MetaEdit.

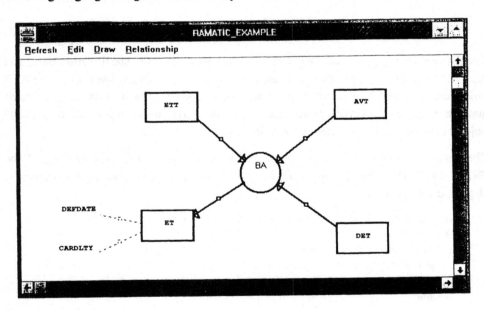

Fig 5. Tempora-ER in RAMATIC´s graphical modeling language using the metamodeling editor

The DrawWindow of MetaEdit with the Tempora-ER model is presented in figure 5. The FREE design objects of Tempora-ER are ETT, AVT, ET and DET (See subsection 3.3 for details) and are represented by rectangles in Figure 5. There is one CONN object (the circle in the picture), BA, which has relationships with all the FREE objects. The ET object has two associations CARDLTY and DEFDATE (labels in Figure 5).

Figure 6 presents a property dialog for the ET -free object which is generated by using the OPRR specification of the FREE object. It represents properties of object types using different data fields. For example a FREE type has a text field, whereas a boolean type Ident property is represented by a check box, and the ID options by a list with predefined values (see appendix 1 for property definitions).

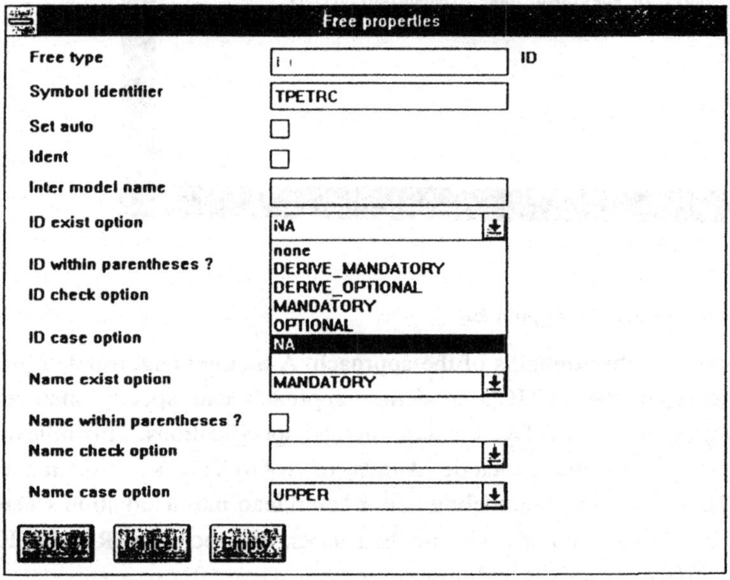

Fig 6. Property dialog for ET -object

Notice that this interface is generated automatically after we have specified the RAMATIC's modeling language in the OPRR notation and loaded it as metamodeling method into MetaEdit.

When the method engineer decides to produce a prototype of a report, in this example the TEMPORA-ER definition, s/he can run the report generator with the report specification for generating RAMATIC's modeling language constructs. For the user the ReportGenerator appears as a dialog that presents the user with a list of available reports and output devices. After selecting the RAMATIC report the user gets a method definition like that shown in Figure 7. This output is produced from the TEMPORA-ER model. The figure shows that all properties of the ER method have been successfully translated into the report output.

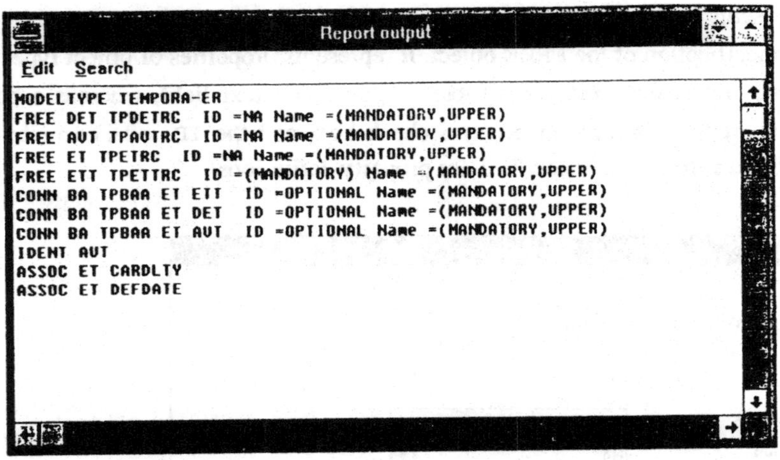

Fig 7. The generated report output of Tempora-ER

The example shows some of the strengths of the approach. A method engineer familiar with the basic concepts of RAMATIC´s modeling approach can specify methods graphically, and then generate RAMATIC´s textual method specifications. This relieves him/her from worrying about the syntactic details of RAMATIC´s CML model definition language. The use of a metamodeling editor could lead into a situation where the method engineer builds the methods with method users, and technical RAMATIC specialists build the interfaces (symbols and forms) for them. Thereafter new versions of the method could be developed by changing parts of the method specification in MetaEdit, and producing then the output for RAMATIC.

6. CONCLUSIONS

In this paper we have presented how an interface between a graphical meta modeling editor and a CASE shell can be developed. Currently, the bridge is a research prototype and cannot produce all the files needed to define a method for the RAMATIC CASE shell. The bridge is, however, capable of producing complete conceptual base model definitions of RAMATIC. These can be used as a basis for defining other necessary parts of the CASE environment. This part of the method definition forms also the most crucial part in the specification of the method. The menu and symbol definition parts of RAMATIC are currently being redefined by SISU, and for that reason they were not included into the prototype. When they have been frozen we intend to cover them in a future version of the "bridge".

A full method development for RAMATIC using the metamodeling editor needs also the ability to model the interdependencies between models. These interdependencies can be handled by the transformation system or using links between models.

The most urgent research task in the future is to define a full-scale metamodeling editor that covers the remaining parts of the RAMATIC method definition. The benefit of such an extension will be that the time to build a CASE tool to support a particular method using RAMATIC will be a matter of days, as opposed to the approximation that it takes a few weeks to develop a tool by hand [1]. Another benefit from this is that the method developer needs only to know the concepts of RAMATIC's modeling language and s/he does not have to worry about the "syntactic sugar" and the specific technical aspects of the language. Thus, a less experienced user can define methods for his/her own purposes and the learning curve will be steeper. In an optimal situation, one could make a model of a method with MetaEdit, produce some reports, load the new method definition into RAMATIC and try it out on the fly.

This graphical method modeling approach could be as well used for other CASE shell environments and in fact we have developed a similar bridge to develop graphically methods for MetaEdit itself. We claim that this approach would be desirable for commercial CASE shells as well.

MetaEdit's current report generation facility is still a prototype environment. In the future we hope to develop a less awkward language for the query formulation. One promising possibility is to use the developed graphical model (such as RAMATIC's graphical modeling language) in formulating queries. Despite its current limitations, the "bridge" demonstrates that graphical methodology specifications can be developed and automatically translated for use in a CASE shell. Hence, the modifiability of the metamodeling environment and its report generation facility gives method developers the possibility to deliver methods for specific CASE shell environments fast and effectively.

Acknowledgments

We would like to thank the referees and co-workers whose valuable comments greatly helped to improve the paper.

References

1. Bergsten, P., Bubenko, J., Dahl, R., Gustafsson, M., Johansson, L.-Å., RAMATIC - a CASE shell for implementation of specific CASE tools. TEMPORA T6.1, SISU, Stockholm, 1989. Draft of TEMPORA- report section 4.4.

2. Boloix, G., Sorenson, P., Tremblay, J., On transformations using a metasystem approach to software development, Dept of Computing Science, The University of Alberta, November 1991.

3. Brinkkemper, S., Formalization of Information Systems Modelling. PhD thesis, Thesis Publishers, University of Nijmegen, Nijmegen, Holland, 1990.

4. Bubenko, J., Selecting a strategy for Computer-Aided Software Engineering (CASE). SYSLAB-report n:o 59, University of Stockholm, Stockholm, Sweden, 1988.

5. Chen, M., The integration of Organization and Information Systems Modeling: A Metasystem Approach to the Generation of Group Decision Support Systems and Computer-Aided Software Engineering, University of Arizona, dissertation, 1988.

6. Dahl, R., RAMATIC description language, SISU, Sweden, 1990.

7. Marttiin, P., Rossi, M., Tahvanainen, V-P, Lyytinen, K., A Comparative Review of CASE shells, in Proceedings of the First Software Engineering Research Forum, Tampa, Florida, November 7 - 9, 1991, (ed. R. Rodriguez), University of West Florida, 1991.

8. MetaEdit user's guide, RAMATIC model manual, Rossi, M. Smolander, K. Marttiin, P., Jyväskylä, 1991

9. Lyytinen, K., Smolander, K., Tahvanainen, V.-P., Modeling CASE environments in systems development. in Proceedings of CASE89 The First Nordic Conference on Advanced Systems Engineering, Stockholm, 1989.

10. Smolander, K., Lyytinen, K., Tahvanainen, V.-P., Marttiin P., MetaEdit - A flexible graphical environment for methodology modelling, in Advanced Information Systems Engineering, (eds. R. Andersen, J. Bubenko, A. Sølvberg), Springer-Verlag, 1991, pp. 168-193.

11. Smolander, K. OPRR - A model for modeling systems development methods, In Proceedings of the Second Workshop on The Next Generation of CASE Tools, Trondheim, Norway, May 11 - 12, 1990, (eds. V-P. Tahvanainen and K. Lyytinen), University of Jyväskylä, Jyväskylä, 1991

12. TEMPORA, Concepts Manual, Tempora ESPRIT project, E2469, September, 1990.

13. Welke, R., Metabase - A Platform for the next generation of meta systems products. In Proceedings of CASE Studies 1988, Meta Systems, Ann Arbor, May 23-27, 1988, Meta Systems, Meta Ref. #C8824, 1988.

Appendix 1. FREE-object Definition in OPRR Metalanguage

```
shape "Rectangle"
    {shape (0@40, 0@160, 200@160, 200@40, 0@40);
    line type "Solid";
    line width 3;
    connection points (100@160,0@160,0@100,0@40,100@40,200@40);}


symbol "FreeNode"
    {shapes ("Rectangle");
    scale 0.4;
    labels { "Free type" at (10 60 190 140) centered;}}


property type "Free type"
    {datatype String;
    values unique;}
property type "ID options"
    { datatype list("NA","OPTIONAL","MANDATORY","none");
    number of values 1;}
property type "Name options"
    { datatype list("DUPLICATE","UNIQUE","IDENTIFY","none");
    number of values 1;}
property type "Symbol identifier"
    {datatype String;
    number of values 1;}
property type "Set auto"
    {datatype Boolean;
    number of values 1;}


object type "Free"
{ symbol "FreeNode";
    duplicates not allowed;
    properties ("Free type", "Symbol identifier", "Set auto",
"Ident", "Inter model name","ID options","Name options" );}
```

Appendix 2. Code Example of FREE-Definition in MetaEdit´s Query Language

```
/* This is a report method for RAMATIC FREE-object generation */
Def genFrees(self|freeColl,rol,txt)
{ freeColl:=selObj(mme,"meta","Free",nil,nil,nil);
  do(freeColl,
  {using(elem)
    add(reportFile,"FREE "+getPropVal(elem,"Free type"));
    add(reportFile,getPropVal(elem,"Symbol identifier"));
    if getPropVal(elem,"Set auto")
        then add(reportFile,"SETAUTO ");
    endif;
    rol:=findRelRoles(elem,"add type","has Assoc");
    do(rol,
    {using(e)
      if getPropVal(theRelationship(e), "Add on create ?")
        then add(reportFile,"ADD"
getPropVal(relatedObj(e),"Assoc name"));
      endif;
    });
    endif;
    if getPropVal(elem,"ID qualifiers")
    then add(reportFile," ID=(",getPropVal(self,elem,"ID")),")");
    endif;
    if getPropVal(elem,"Name qualifiers")
        then add(reportFile,"
NAME=("+getPropVal(self,elem,"Name",',')+,")");
    endif;
    separator(self);
  });
```

A Meta-CASE Environment for Software Process-centred CASE Environments

Flávio Oquendo[†], Jean-Daniel Zucker[‡] and Philip Griffiths*
[†]CRISS - Pierre Mendès France University
BP 47, 38040 Grenoble Cedex 9, FRANCE
[‡]GIE EMERAUDE
C/o BULL, BP 3, 78430 Louveciennes, FRANCE
*ICL Defence Systems
Eskdale Road Winnersh, Wokingham Berkshire RG11 5TT, UK

Abstract. There has been a recent explosion of interest concerning the construction of computer-aided software engineering environments assisting users during the software development process. Such environments, called process-centred, are characterised by their ability to provide some assistance or automatisation of the software process being carried out. This paper describes the ALF Meta-CASE environment developed in the framework of the ALF ESPRIT project. It consists of a formalism for modelling computer-assisted software processes and mechanisms for supporting the generation of process-centred CASE environments. These environments are able to enact formal software processes models and to assist developers during their enaction.

1 Introduction

The software crisis has been with us for some time and will continue to worsen, at least for the next few years. Two important reasons for this are that there is an ever increasing demand for software, and there are demographic problems, i.e. there are fewer and fewer people available to write this software. This latter reason will be alleviated to some extent as the third world enters the market; but this still leaves us with a severe productivity problem.

The field of software process modelling is one of several that have developed to address the software crisis. Examples of other important areas are in programming technology, design methods, and to some extent in hardware. The last of these has allowed the software community to free itself to a large degree from the shackles of hardware related constraints.

Much has been written elsewhere on the importance of software process modelling [Dowson 1991, Osterweil 1987, Stenning 1987]. But software process modelling also has the great advantage that it brings the other advances in software technology together in a way that allows them to complement each other.

We call *software process* the total set of software engineering activities needed to transform user's requirements into software. A *software process model* is a software process definition that can be instantiated for a specific project or organisation. Different software processes can be driven by the same software process model. The formal notation for describing software process models is called *the software process formalism*. *Software process enaction* is the action of enacting software process models. *Enacting* means executing by an agent that may be a human or a machine.

In the ALF[1] project [Benali et al. 1989, Griffiths et al. 1989], our approach to support software process modelling has been to develop a *meta* computer-aided software engineering environment: a meta-CASE environment for generating software process-centred CASE environments. A process-centred CASE environment is a knowledge based CASE environment that is able to take initiatives and assist software developers according to the knowledge it has of software process models to be carried out. An important aspect is that the meta-CASE environment will be able to generate environments to support many software life-cycle models, e.g. the "waterfall model" [Royce 1970] or "the spiral model" [Boehm 1986], and many design and development methods, e.g. HOOD or SADT. More information on how our approach compares to related work can be found in [Arbaoui and Oquendo 1991].

The main objectives of ALF generated CASE environments are:

* *to support process modelling and enaction,*

* *to provide user assistance.*

Other aims are:
* to support the whole software production process,
* to support process decomposition to the level of tools,
* to model the whole organisation to the level of roles,
* to be multi-project, multi-team, and multi-user,
* to support user communication and cooperation.

The technique for software process modelling that has been developed in ALF is generic. Furthermore the approach taken is not restricted to one paradigm; there is enough functional richness to be object oriented, to be rule based or to be constructive. Genericity is achieved by instantiation, that is where an object or operation is described in a model, the object instance or actual tool to be used does not have to be identified, i.e. instantiated, until it is needed. The "tool" might not be an actual tool but another sub-process, which, of course, can be modelled.

---

1. The ALF "Accueil de Logiciel Futur" project is partially funded by the Commission of the European Communities under the ESPRIT programme, Project Ref. No. 1520.

The following section of this paper looks at the formalism for describing software processes that has been developed in ALF. Later on the instantiation and enaction of process models are discussed. There follows a brief description of the ALF meta-environment architecture. Finally the ALF System is presented from the user's point of view, with its main contributions to increase productivity and software quality.

2 The MASP Process Modelling Formalism

An important thread of the work in the ALF project has been to design a formalism for software process modelling [Oquendo 1990]. The formalism we have developed, called *the MASP* (meta-*Model for Assisted Software Processes*), provides the means to describe rigorously computer-assisted software process models. These descriptions are *enactable* and can be used to provide better *understanding* of software processes and *communicating* software process models to people such as developers and managers involved in their enaction.

The MASP concept provides mechanisms that support the description of generic software process models which can be incrementally and repeatedly instantiated in order to produce particular software process models specific to projects or organisations. In this way software process models can be easily *reused*.

The *evolution* of software process models is supported by the MASP concept through mechanisms for interleaving instantiation and enaction. This allows changes to be made "on the fly", to software process models. These may be a consequence of changes in the organisation structure, project policies, changing deadlines, and so on; also these may be as a consequence of the feedback mechanisms provided by the underlying environment in order to tune the software process models being enacted.

The facilitating of the *management* of software processes is supported in the MASP concept by means of mechanisms for scheduling the software process activities, controlling their enaction, and monitoring their progress.

An assisted software process model is described by a MASP in terms of object types, semantic constraints to be enforced on the objects of these types, operator types defined on these object types, and control on the execution of the operators of these types.

A MASP description [Derniame et al. 1991] is composed of six models (see figure 1):

- an object model,
- an operator model,
- an expression model,
- an ordering model,
- a rule model,
- a characteristic model.

```
masp =                          domain_and_range =
    MASP specification              '(' ( parameter { ';' parameter } )
    description                     ')'
    END MASP ';'
                                parameter =
specification =                     par_access par_list ':' par_type
    identifier HAS TYPE operator_type
    ':' (domain_and_range ';' )  par_access =
                                    IN I OUT I INOUT I READ I
description =                        READWRITE
    object_model_definition ';'
                                par_list =
    ( expression_model_definition ';' )
                                    parameter_name { ','
    operator_model_definition ';'   parameter_name}

    ( ordering_model_definition ';' )  par_type =

    ( rule_model_definition ';' )       object_type_name

    ( characteristic_model_definition   I relationship_type_name
    ';' )
                                        I attribute_type_name
```

Fig. 1. MASP specification (i.e. operator's signature) and description

The first two of the MASP components are the object and operator models, the expression model is only a means of defining conditions to be reused on the other models, the other three models (i.e. rule, ordering, and characteristic) compose the control model.

The first component of a MASP is the object model (see figure 2). The chosen formalism for expressing the object model is based on the PCTE+'s OMS [Oquendo et al. 1991].

The MASP object model, which is structurally object-oriented, enhances the PCTE+'s OMS data model with new mechanisms including structured and multi-valued attributes, triggers and semantic constraints [Oquendo et al. 1990]. It provides a distributed object base and includes features for managing single and composite objects and their versions [Oquendo et al. 1989a, Oquendo et al. 1989b].

A MASP object model defines an object base schema by means of a list of schema definition sets (SDS) (figure 2). Each SDS gathers a set of related object, relationship and attribute type definitions and extensions. An important feature of the SDSs is the sharing of type definitions amongst SDSs. This is provided by the importation facility. The importation of a type definition from an SDS into another makes this definition visible in both SDSs. In this way, type definitions can be shared amongst several SDSs. The view of the object base defined by the MASP object model is given by the set of type definitions which is the union of all of the type definitions in the SDSs of the list. A new object type is always defined as a subtype of (i.e. a specialisation of) one or more other types. In addition to its applied attribute and relationship types, the new defined type inherits all of the applied attribute and relationship types of its supertypes. A predefined object type, called **object**, is the common ancestor type of all object types. The structure formed by these subtypes constitute a connected direct acyclic graph having only one root, the type object. Multiple inheritance is therefore provided.

```
object_model_definition =

    OBJECT MODEL IS

    list_of_schema_definition_sets ';'

    END OBJECT MODEL

list_of_schema_definition_sets = sds {
';' sds}

sds = sds_name I sds_definition I
sds_extension

sds_definition =

    NEW SDS sds_name IS type_list ';'

    END sds_name

sds_extension =

    EXTEND SDS sds_name WITH
    type_list ';'

    END sds_name
```

```
type_list = type { ';' type }

type =

    object_type_definition

    I object_type_extension

    I relationship_type_definition

    I attribute_type_definition

    I type_importation

object_type_definition =

    ot_name ':' SUBTYPE OF
    object_type_names ( WITH

    ( ATTRIBUTE attribute_type_ d_list
    ';' )

    ( LINK relationship_type_d_list ';' )

    END ot_name )
```

Fig. 2. MASP object model

The second component of a MASP is a set of expressions (see figure 3). They are logical expressions which describe particular states of software processes. The chosen formalism for specifying expressions is based on first-order predicate calculus.

Expressions, like assertions in IPSE 2.5 [Warboys 1989], are only a means of defining a set of conditions which are then used in many places within a software process model, without the need to re-define them on each occasion. The basic terms in the description of expressions are events (on objects or operators) and logical expressions. In MASPs, expressions are used in pre- and post-conditions of operator types, in rules and characteristics.

The third component of a MASP is the operator model (see figure 4). It is defined by a set of operator type definitions and importations. An operator type describes a class of operators. The chosen formalism for expressing operator types is similar to, but an extension of, the ones adopted by Marvel [Kaiser and Feiler 1987] and Inscape [Perry 1987]. In these, pre- and post-conditions are only used for describing the semantics of the software process activities that are performed by software tools. We extend this approach by relaxing that restriction of applying pre- and post-conditions only to activities performed by tools, and thus allowing also to describe the semantics of complex activities described by MASPs. As in Marvel, pre- and post-conditions are the basis for backward and forward reasoning.

```
expression_model_definition =
    EXPRESSION MODEL IS
    list_of_expressions ';'
    END EXPRESSION MODEL


list_of_expressions = expression { ';'
    expression }

expression =
    event_definition
    I logical_exp_definition
    I expression_definition


expression_definition =
    ex_name ':'
    ON event_d { ';' event_d }
    EVALUATE logical_expression_d
```

```
event_d = event_name I
    event_description

event_definition =
    event_name ':' EVENT
    event_description

event_description =
    user_defined_event_situation
    I read _event_situation
    I update_event_situation
    I create_event_situation
    I delete_event_situation
    I move_event_situation
    I convert_event_situation
    I expression_event_situation
    I invoke_operator_event_situation
    I exit_operator_event_situation
    I time_event_situation
```

Fig. 3. MASP expression model

A software process model is described by a hierarchy of MASPs. Indeed, a MASP has a specification (i.e. an operator's signature) and contains a set of operator types which in turn can be described by MASPs, and so on (see figure 5). So each MASP describes a part of the software process model at an appropriate level of abstraction. The binding between an operator type and a MASP or a software tool and the MASP instantiation are done at enaction time. New MASPs can also be created.

The fourth component of a MASP is a set of orderings (see figure 6). Orderings express restrictions on the execution of operators. They are used to describe whether two specified operators must be executed sequentially, alternatively or concurrently. They are also used to describe whether an operator can be executed repeatedly, arbitrarily often, or if it can be executed simultaneously with other occurrences of itself.

---

operator_model_definition =

   OPERATOR MODEL IS

   list_of_operator_types ';'

   END OPERATOR MODEL

list_of_operator_types =

   operator_type { ';' operator_type }

operator_type =

   operator_type_definition

   I operator_type_importation

operator_type_definition =

   op_name ':' (domain_and_range)

   PRECONDITION ':'
   logical_expression_d

   POSTCONDITION ':'
   logical_expression_d

   KIND ':' '-' I INTERACTIVE I NON
INTERACTIVE

---

logical_expression_d =

   log_exp_name I
   log_exp_description

logical_exp_definition =

   log_exp_name ':'
   log_exp_description

log_exp_description = ...

   "It is a logical expression built using the logical connectors AND, OR, NEGATION, and IMPLICATION, where variables may be typed and universally or existentially quantified..."

Fig. 4. MASP operator model

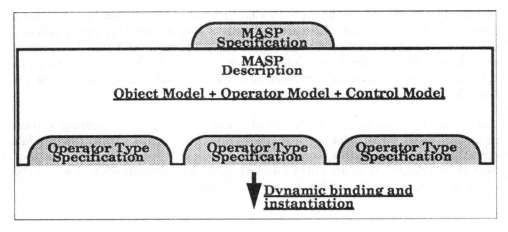

Fig. 5. Binding of operator types and MASP instantiation are done at enaction time

```
ordering_model_definition =

    ORDERING MODEL IS

    list_of_orderings ';'

    END ORDERING MODEL

list_of_orderings =

    ordering { ';' ordering }

ordering =

    ( or_name ':' ) path_expression

connection =

    FOR ALL variable ':'
    object_type_name

    ( IN ( variable I constant ) ':'
    object_type_name )
```

```
path_expression =

    ( connection DO ) operator_exp

    I ( connection DO ) br_path_exp

    I ( connection DO ) bi_path_exp

br_path_exp =

    '{' path_expression '}'

    I '(' path_expression ')'

    I '(*' path_expression '*)'

    I '(' path_expression ')'

    I '(' path_expression ')' counter

bi_path_exp =

    path_expression 'I I'
    path_expression

    I path_expression 'I'
    path_expression

    I path_expression ';'
    path_expression
```

Fig. 6. MASP ordering model

The chosen formalism for expressing orderings is based on indexed path expressions [Campbell and Habermann 1974]. In a path expression (figure 6) ';' means sequential execution, '{' '}' simultaneous execution, 'I I' concurrent execution, 'I' alternative execution, '("' '")' optional execution, '(' ')' repeated execution, and '(' ')' grouping of operators. An ordering does not define a unique sequence of operator executions. It does define the set of all possible sequences of operator executions. In other approaches such as in Marvel and HFSP [Katayama 1989] the scheduling of operator executions is deduced implicitly from the data dependencies amongst operators.

The fifth component of a MASP is a set of rules (see figure 7). The chosen formalism for expressing rules is based on production rules. They define explicitly the possible automatic reactions to specific situations arising during the software process. In approaches such as in Marvel a user request may produce a chain of reactions which dies down eventually. In these approaches only a user request can cause this chain of reactions. This differs from our approach where this chain of reactions can be caused by a user request or by a specific situation that triggers rules (i.e. system initiative).

```
rule_model_definition =

    RULE MODEL IS

    list_of_rules ';'

    END RULE MODEL

list_of_rules =

    rule { ';' rule }

rule =

    ( ru_name ':' )

    IF expression_d

    THEN operator_name '(' (
    parameter_list ) ')'
```

```
expression_d =

    event_d

    | logical_expression_d

    | expression_name

    | expression_description

parameter_list =

    par { ',' par }

par =

    variable | constant
```

Fig. 7. MASP rule model

The sixth, and last, component of a MASP is a set of characteristics (see figure 8). The chosen formalism for expressing characteristics are MASP expressions. They describe constraints on the software processes' states that should be enforced during their enaction. In other approaches these are generally limited to constraints on the software product states. Backward and forward reasoning on the pre- and post-condition of operator types can be used in order to deduce a sequence of operator executions to react to characteristic violations. Another possible reaction is to abort the operator execution.

characteristic_model_definition =

    CHARACTERISTIC MODEL IS

    list_of_characteristics ';'

    END CHARACTERISTIC MODEL

list_of_characteristics =

    characteristic { ';' characteristic }

characteristic =

    (ch_name ':')

    logical_expression_d

    I expression_name

    I expression_definition

Fig. 8. MASP characteristic model

A very simple example of a MASP description is presented in figure 9. This MASP describes a process model for editing, compiling, and linking C programmes.

MASP c_prog_pm HAS TYPE c_prog_develop:
    (IN _program : c_program ;
    OUT _exec : exec_module) ;

OBJECT MODEL IS c_prog ;
END OBJECT MODEL ;

OPERATOR MODEL IS

    edit :
    (INOUT _m : c_module);

    compile :
    (IN _m : c_module ; OUT _o : object_module)
    PRECONDITION: edited (_m, TRUE)
    POSTCONDITION : o (_m, _o)
    KIND : NON INTERACTIVE ;

    link :
    (IN _p : c_program ; OUT _e : exec_module)

PRECONDITION : FOR ALL _m : c_module SUCH THAT c (_p, _m, _) AND compiled (_m, TRUE)
POSTCONDITION : exec (_p, _e)
KIND : NON INTERACTIVE ;

END OPERATOR MODEL ;

RULE MODEL IS

    module_linked : IF CREATE LINK exec (_p, _e) THEN set (linked, _p, TRUE) ;

END RULE MODEL ;

ORDERING MODEL

    order : DO (link(_program, _exec)) ; exit(_exec)

END ORDERING MODEL ;

CHARACTERISTIC MODEL IS

    exec(_program, _exec) ;

END CHARACTERISTIC MODEL ;

END MASP ;

Fig. 9. A very simple example of a MASP description

3 The Software Process Instantiation Mechanism

A MASP description defines a generic process model that can be incrementally instantiated in order to produce project-specific software process models. When a MASP has been designed there is usually not only one MASP, but a hierarchy of MASPs (figure 10). A MASP describing a complex development method or a complex software process model usually includes a lot of complex operator types which are again described by using the concept of MASP.

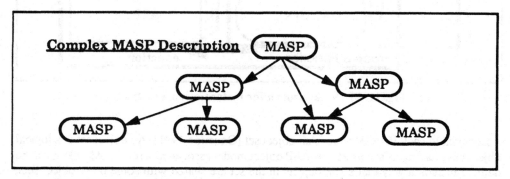

Fig. 10. A complex software process model is described by a MASP hierarchy

An approach one can think of for *instantiation of MASPs* is that the complete MASP hierarchy is instantiated and then the enaction of the resulting instantiated MASP hierarchy can begin. [Lehman 1987] points out that such a way of working (i.e. "static" instantiation) is not flexible enough. A software process may last for a long time (weeks, months, and even years) so it is not reasonable to demand that a complete instantiation must be done before the start of the enaction. Another disadvantage of static instantiation is that there is no chance to tune the behaviour of the software process to special situations; everything is fixed at the beginning and it is impossible to react to deviations of the current software process model from what was expected. Since the aim is to be able to evolve the software process model "on the fly", static instantiation is unacceptable, "dynamic" instantiation is therefore needed.

The overall approach for MASP instantiation and enaction is depicted in figure 11. Our approach is to interleave instantiation and enaction. This approach provides the possibility to consider the part of the development that has been executed before instantiating a further part. It takes into account the dynamism of process models. An *instantiated MASP* is called an *IMASP*.

The instantiation mechanism consists of instantiating the object and operator models by defining object instances and actual operators. The instantiation process is supported by a dialogue between the instantiation environment service and the MASP instantiator. There is the possibility of re-using an instantiated MASP to instantiate an operator type. The flexibility of this approach lies in the fact that a given MASP can be instantiated many times and that different instantiated MASPs can share objects.

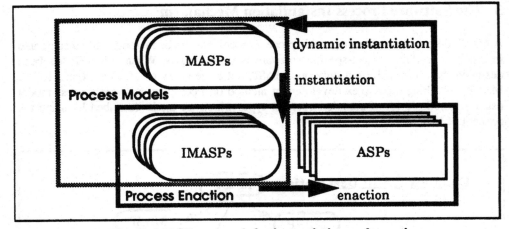

Fig. 11. MASP approach for instantiation and enaction

Associated to each IMASP there is an object set [Oquendo 1991]. An object set is a logical object base having as schema the MASP object model associated with the IMASP. It can be defined in such a way that some objects in the set are shared with some other object sets. Each software process enacting an IMASP accesses these shared objects through its MASP object model view point. A shared object then becomes the synthesis of several different software process activities, where each one contributes to build the object in function of the software process model view point it enacts. Concurrent access to shared objects is controlled by a nested transaction mechanism [Oquendo et al. 1991].

We distinguish two cases for instantiating object types:

- Object sharing. If an object exists in the object set of an existing IMASP and if its object type is compatible with the object type to be instantiated, then the object can be inserted in the object set of the MASP under instantiation. Cooperation between IMASPs is achieved by means of object sharing.

- Creation of new objects. Object sharing is not the only way of instantiating an object type. The other way is to insert new objects of that type explicitly during the instantiation dialogue.

During the instantiation of the operator model of a MASP it is necessary either to identify CASE tools (or any other kind of executable software) that can be linked to operator types or to identify MASPs that are of the corresponding types. Here we face the problem that instantiation is based on assumptions about tools and MASPs. Each available tool and each MASP is typed. A tool is typed by the person who brings that tool into the ALF meta-environment. For instance, let us take the operator type `compile` in the MASP `c_prog_pm` (figure 9). All tools that can potentially be used for instantiating that operator type are classified as of type *compile*. During instantiation the process relies on the specifications given by the typing of tools and MASPs.

We distinguish three cases for instantiating operator types:

- To link an operator type to a tool. In general it is necessary to build an envelope around that tool [Gisi and Kaiser 1991].

- To share an operator type's instantiation. This is analogous to the sharing of objects. A prerequisite for sharing the instantiation of an operator type is that the operator types used in the different MASPs are compatible. This is the case if operator type descriptions are exactly the same, or if the operator type is defined in one MASP and imported by the other. To share an instantiation can either mean linking the operator type to a tool (if the operator type, whose instantiation is shared, is instantiated by a tool) or linking the operator type to an already existing IMASP (if the operator type, whose instantiation is shared, is instantiated by an IMASP).

- To link an operator type to a MASP of the corresponding type. This possibility for instantiating an operator type is the most sophisticated one. It consists of linking an operator type to a MASP of that type. If the linked MASP is not instantiated the instantiation is continued by instantiating the linked MASP.

4 Software Process Enaction and the MASP Interpreter

When a MASP is instantiated, which gives an instantiated MASP (IMASP), enough information has been gathered to *enact* software processes. The information related to the control is already present at the level of the MASP, the information about the context of execution is given by the IMASP. In the MASP approach, enaction is an *interpretation* of the MASP using the IMASP as a knowledge base in a context local to an *assisted software process* (ASP). The interpreter of a MASP is a process that can be thought of as an "expert server":

- *expert* because this process will perform some forward and backward reasoning upon the activity of other processes being under its control,

- *server* because it will interpret many assisted software processes (ASPs) that are connected to the IMASP.

The overall architecture of MASP interpretation is depicted in figure 12.

The ASPs, where the real work is done, are "clients" to these servers, i.e the MASP interpreters. Each different ASP which is a client of a particular MASP interpreter will be a different *dynamic context* of execution from the same *static context* defined by the instantiated MASP. As a client, an ASP will hence have a list of possible actions to execute. Its actions will be controlled by pre- and post-conditions of operators, orderings, rules, and characteristics. Some of its actions might also trigger system initiatives.

The MASP interpreter also coordinates the flow of dynamic information between the ASPs so that one ASP can take an action as a result of a different ASP activity. For example, if some objects are shared between different MASP interpreters, they all will be informed of a change in the status of these objects.

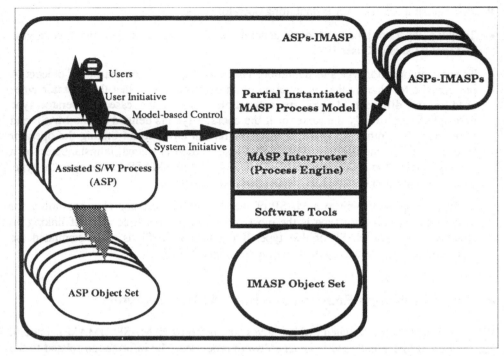

Fig. 12. Interpretation of an IMASP (static context) by ASPs (dynamic contexts)

Obviously, in the life of a MASP interpretation, the interpreter might need to instantiate an operator type by a MASP that was not needed and therefore not defined at the beginning of the interpretation. Therefore a cascade of MASP instantiations may occur.

At a given time, there are several ASPs being enacted. Each ASP carries out a software process step. Some of these are sub-processes created by expansion (i.e. binding and instantiation of an operator by a MASP) from a higher level software process (figure 13).

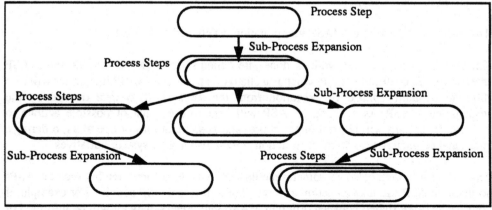

Fig. 13. ASP hierarchy of software process steps under enaction

5 The ALF Meta-Environment Architecture

In the previous sections we have described the formalism and the conceptual approach for defining, instantiating and enacting software process models in the ALF meta-CASE environment. This meta-environment, called *the ALF System*, provides the set of tools and services for generating process-centred software environments that can support the enaction of software process models in live projects. In this section the architecture of the ALF System is outlined.

Figure 14 sketches the architecture of the ALF System. Its main architectural component, the MASP Interpreter, will be briefly described hereafter.

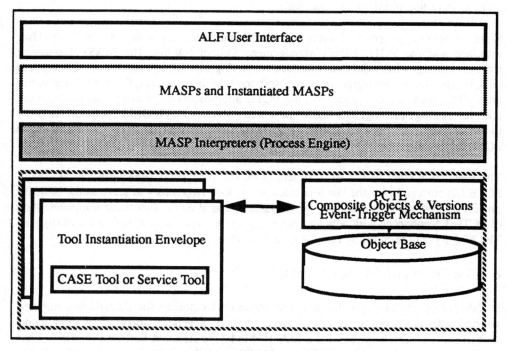

Fig. 14. The ALF System architecture

The MASP interpreter operates as a system that monitors the work done by the software developers and that takes initiatives whenever necessary. It provides assistance and guidance to software developers. The MASP Interpreter provides the most characteristic functionalities of the ALF System. These functionalities are obtained, amongst other thinks, through interpretation of software process models described by MASPs.

The MASP Interpreter has been implemented using the ALF-Rete Expert System Generator, a production system based on the Rete matching algorithm. It supports the integration of knowledge represented by rules with existing applications algorithmicly programmed, providing data sharing between the procedural and the heuristic parts of an application. ALF-Rete works together with the PCTE Object Management System using an integration mechanism that has been designed to fulfil this function and that is based on the PCTE trigger mechanism [Oquendo et al. 1990]. ALF-Rete supports production rules in the form of *if condition then action* with forward chaining. These rules can be grouped into packets. Enhancements such as backward chaining, composite structures, quantifiers, and a mechanism for dynamic activation of rule packets with shared memory have also been introduced in order to support the MASP interpretation features. All these features together with the PCTE concurrence, synchronization and communication mechanisms have been used extensively.

The conjunction of the MASP Interpreter together with guidance and explanation, observation, history generation and feedback provides the basis for piloting the software process according to the MASP concept.

From an operational point of view, the MASP Interpreter communicates with the User Interface and the PCTE Object Management System (OMS). The MASP Interpreter receives messages from the User Interface containing user requests and sends messages to the User Interface with display requests. Both the User Interface and the MASP Interpreter are PCTE processes and, therefore, the PCTE interprocess communication facilities are used for message passing. The MASP Interpreter invokes PCTE OMS operations in order to request services from PCTE and to invoke CASE tools (that are stored as objects in the PCTE OMS' object base).

The foundation layer of the ALF System is PCTE[1] [Campbell 1988, Minot et al. 1988]. PCTE has emerged over the last few years as an Open Repository to serve as the basis for project support environments. The ALF System is based on the Emeraude implementation of PCTE 1.5 enhanced with new features such as composite objects, versions and triggers. The ALF System is currently running on a network of SUN workstations.

6 Conclusion and Future Work

In this paper, we have presented a representation formalism for describing computer-assisted software process models. A description of a generic software process model written in this formalism is called a MASP (Model for Assisted Software Process). Then we have presented the instantiation of MASPs and the enaction of assisted software processes. Finally we have sketched the architecture of the ALF meta-CASE environment that has been implemented to support the MASP concept.

In summary, a MASP (i.e. a generic process model) describes a class of IMASPs (i.e. project-specific software process models derived by instantiation) and each IMASP represents a class of run-time behaviours of software processes (ASPs). The ALF System provides a set of tools and services for editing, analysing, instantiating and enacting MASPs. The generation of process-centred CASE environments is supported by the instantiation of MASPs by MASPs or CASE tools in the ALF System.

---

1. European Computer Manufacturers Association (ECMA) Standard 149.

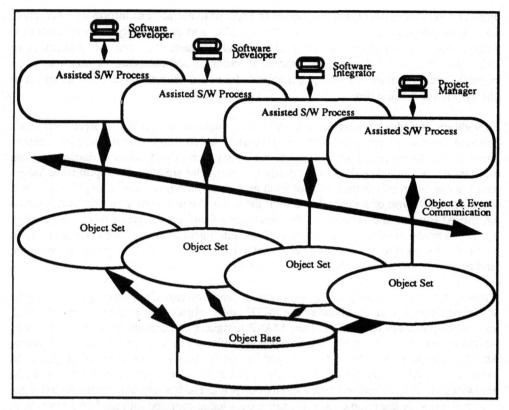

Fig. 15. The ALF System from the user's point of view

Using the ALF System, software house or large organisation's methods group can generate its specific project support environments in an Open CASE Environment Framework basis.

Figure 15 shows how does the ALF System look like to software engineers. What ALF means to software developers is a much more helpful development environment. Some of this help comes from the application of rules that constrain the developer to follow the procedures and methods of his organisation and to use the techniques chosen by that organisation for the different tasks he has to carry out. Although this may seem to some people like too much control, it will ease the developer's work by helping him to avoid forgetting the right way to do certain things and ignoring which technique (tool) to use for a particular stage of the development.

Yet more help comes from being able to get guidance on how best to proceed, explanation on what has been happening and why, and access to the ever-increasing historical information that can be used to make improved forecasts of what is likely to occur in the future. Just being able to use those tools which are appropriate to his work will be a great help to the normal software developer who is becoming snowed under by the variety of tools he can find on his workstation.

Formal descriptions of software processes as opposed to narrative or informal descriptions, have been adopted in ALF first, to improve quality and productivity through automatic interpretation of processes and data and second, to raise the level of abstraction in describing and manipulating such process in order to accommodate as many users as possible with minimum of training, particularly for new users who have to use a method or the system for the first time.

In addition, the idea of integrating such formal notations with expert system techniques whereby knowledge about the software process is stored into a knowledge base, renders the ALF System an expert advisor on a continuously increasing number of domains and on such issues as method or data applicability to a particular situation (i.e. optimising usage) and interpretation of the outcomes of such an activity; the provision of explanations and guidance on the use of a method or a tool; the use and interpretation of performance data on the ALF users, the process, or the system itself and on the reuse of components or systems already available in the system. Thus, intelligent "trainers" are embedded in the software processes themselves and can be activated by the user or at the system's initiative and as required within a particular working session.

Finally, a further contribution to productivity and increased software quality may be achieved through ALF by allowing the PCTE OMS' object base to act as a repository of models of processes or MASPs. Thus MASP designers can capture the characteristics of processes which are desirable and as these are reflected in an organisation's experience, and store them in ALF to be further used by individual users for different purposes. In other words, ALF provides the means for a possible wider acceptance of the standards, knowledge or data developed over a number of years. The benefits derived through this are that end users are the recipients of the same knowledge captured into the MASP but, also, the same users are guided by the system on the proper use/reuse and interpretation of the required knowledge or facts. Certainly, this is more advantageous to new users of a method or tool who not only need to learn how to apply it but also be aware of the consequences, of their actions.

Different aspects of existing design and development methods and life-cycle models have been modelled using MASPs, including technical as well managerial ones. Examples of models that have been described are VDM, JSD, HOOD, C Programming, and Configuration Management. Up to now the MASP concept seems to provide a powerful and flexible formalism for describing a wide range of process models.

Future work is mainly concerned with experimentation of the ALF meta-CASE environment for generating large-scale process-centred CASE environments for modelling and enacting real large-scale software processes and with experimentation of these environments in real work contexts to give feedback on how this novel technology works in practice. Psychological and sociological aspects are also important issues to be studied in order to assess the ALF System.

Acknowledgements

The authors acknowledge the contribution to the work presented in this paper from all of the members of the ALF project. The partners involved in the ALF project are: GIE Emeraude (Bull, Eurosoft, Syseca) (France), CSC NV/SA (Belgium), Computer Technologies Co.-CTC (Greece), Grupo de Mecánica del Vuelo, S.A. (Spain), International Computers Limited (United Kingdom), University of Nancy-CRIN (France), University of Dortmund-Informatik X (Germany), Cerilor (France), Catholic University of Louvain (Belgium) and University of Dijon-CRID (France). This work is partially sponsored by the Commission of the European Communities under the ESPRIT programme (Project Ref. No. 1520).

References

[Arbaoui and Oquendo 1991] Arbaoui, S. and Oquendo, F., "Où en est la modélisation du processus de production du logiciel?", *Proceedings of the 4th International Conference on Software Engineering and its Applications*, Toulouse, France, December 1991 (in French).

[Benali et al. 1989] Benali, K., Boudjlida, N., Charoy, F., Derniame, J-C., Godart, C., Griffiths, Ph., Gruhn, V., Jamart, Ph., Legait, A., Oldfield, D. E., Oquendo, F., "Presentation of the ALF Project", *Proceedings of the International Conference on System Development Environments and Factories*, Berlin, May 1989.

[Boehm 1986] Boehm, B., "A Spiral Model of Software Development and Enhancement", *ACM Software Engineering Notes*, Vol. 11, August 1986.

[Campbell 1988] Campbell, I.,"Portable Common Tool Environment", *Computer Standards and Interfaces*, No. 8, North-Holland, 1988.

[Campbell and Habermann 1974] Campbell, R. and Habermann, A., "The Specification of Process Synchronisation by Path Expressions", *Lecture Notes in Computer Science*, Springer, Vol. 16, 1974.

[Derniame et al. 1991] Derniame, J-C. et al., "Reference Manual for the MASP Definition Language", *Technical Report*, ALF Project, CEC ESPRIT Research Programme, July 1991.

[Dowson 1991] Dowson, M., "Why is Process Important?", *Proceedings of the 1st International Conference on the Software Process*, Redondo Beach, USA, October 1991.

[Gisi and Kaiser 1991] Gisi, M. A. and Kaiser, G. E., "Extending a Tool Integration Language", *Proceedings of the 1st International Conference on the Software Process*, Redondo Beach, USA, October 1991.

[Griffiths et al. 1989] Griffiths, Ph., Legait, A., Menes, M., Oldfield, D., Oquendo, F., "ALF: Its Process Model and its Implementation on PCTE", *Proceedings of the International Software Engineering Environment Conference*, Durham, England, April 1989. Published as *Software Engineering Environments -- Research and Practice*, K. H. Bennett (ed.), Ellis Horwood Books in Information Technology, England, 1989.

[Kaiser and Feiler 1987] Kaiser, G. E. and Feiler, P. H., "An Architecture for Intelligent Assistance in Software Development", *Proceedings of 9th International Conference on Software Engineering*, Monterey, April 1987.

[Katayama 1989] Katayama, T., "A Hierarchical and Functional Software Process Description and its Enaction", *Proceedings of the 11th International Conference on Software Engineering*, Pittsburgh, May 1989.

[Lehman 1987] Lehman, M. M., "Process Models, Process Programs, Programming Support", *Proceedings of 9th International Conference on Software Engineering*, Monterey, April 1987.

[Minot et al. 1988] Minot, R., Gallo, F., Boudier, G., Oquendo, F., Thomas, I., "The Object Management System of PCTE and PCTE+", *Proceedings of the IEE Colloquium on Standard Interfaces for Software Tools*, London, September 1988.

[Oquendo et al. 1989a] Oquendo, F., Gallo, F., Minot, R., Thomas, I., "Modeling Composite Objects in a Software Engineering Object Management System", *Proceedings of the 3rd International Workshop on Computer-Aided Software Engineering*, London, July 1989.

[Oquendo et al. 1989b] Oquendo, F., Berrada, K., Gallo, F., Minot, R., Thomas, I., "Version Management in the PACT Integrated Software Engineering Environment", *Proceedings of the 2nd European Software Engineering Conference*, Warwick, September 1989.

[Oquendo 1990] Oquendo, F., "Building Object and Process-centered Software Environments on the PCTE Public Tool Interface", *Proceedings of the 6th International Software Process Workshop*, Hokkaido, Japan, October 1990.

[Oquendo et al. 1990] Oquendo, F., Tassart, G., Zucker, J-D., "Support for Software Tool Integration and Process-centered Software Engineering Environments", *Proceedings of the 3rd International Conference on Software Engineering and its Applications*, Toulouse, France, December 1990.

[Oquendo 1991] Oquendo, F., "Supporting Software Process Communication and Cooperation Through Object Sets", *Proceedings of the 7th International Software Process Workshop*, Yountville, USA, October 1991.

[Oquendo et al. 1991] Oquendo, F., Boudier, G., Gallo, F., Minot, R., Thomas, I., "The PCTE+'s OMS: A Distributed Software Engineering Database System for supporting Large-Scale Software Development Environments", *Proceedings of the 2nd International Symposium on Database Systems for Advanced Applications*, Tokyo, Japan, April 1991.

[Osterweil 1987] Osterweil, L., "Software Processes are Software Too", *Proceedings of the 9th International Conference on Software Engineering*, Monterey, March 1987.

[Perry 1987] Perry, D. E., "Software Interconnection Models", *Proceedings of the 9th International Conference on Software Engineering*, Monterey, March 1987.

[Royce 1970] Royce, W., "Managing the Development of Large Software Systems", *Proceedings of IEEE WESCON*, August 1970.

[Stenning 1987] Stenning, V., "On the Role of an Environment", *Proceedings of the 9th International Conference on Software Engineering*, Monterey, March 1987.

[Warboys 1989] Warboys, B., "The IPSE 2.5 Project: Process Modelling as the basis for a Support Environment", *Proceedings of the International Conference on System Development Environments and Factories*, Berlin, May 1989.

A Declarative Conceptual Modelling Language:
Description and Example Applications

Marco A. Casanova[1], Andrea S. Hemerly[1] and Antonio L. Furtado[1,2]

[1]Centro Científico Rio
IBM Brasil
Caixa Postal 4624
20.001, Rio de Janeiro, RJ - Brasil

[2]Departamento de Informática
Pontifícia Universidade Católica do RJ
R. Marquês de S. Vicente, 225
22.453, Rio de Janeiro, RJ - Brasil

ABSTRACT. A declarative conceptual modelling language, implemented as an extension to Prolog, is described. The language is based on an extended version of the entity-relationship (ER) model for the declaration of the information classes and the formulation of queries, and adopts an abstract data type (ADT) approach to define and execute application-oriented update operations.

The language is an integral part of a workbench that provides rapid prototyping at the conceptual level and that supports expert level features. Simple examples to illustrate the direct use of the workbench over a database / knowledge base application and the addition of expert level features are also included.

1. Introduction

This paper first describes a declarative conceptual modelling language that is part of a workbench to support the direct use of knowledge base/database applications, as well as to serve as a foundation for expert level features to be developed over these applications. Then it illustrates the direct use of the workbench over a database / knowledge base application and the addition of expert level features.

The language follows an extended version of the entity-relationship (ER) model for the declaration of the information classes and the formulation of queries, and adopts an abstract data type (ADT) approach to define and execute application-oriented update operations. The language is implemented as an extension to Prolog, following a declarative style, in the sense that every aspect of an application is declared with the help of facts and clauses, including the update operations.

In this ER/ADT information/operation model, individual entity instances retain their identity across the different classes to which they may belong (via the is_a hierarchy), with respect to their existence, attributes and participation in relationship instances. Also, in the spirit of abstract data types, update requests are limited to the utilization of application-oriented operations.

The workbench permits rapid prototyping of the ER design, that is, the workbench does not treat the ER design as a mere documentation of the application, but as an executable specification. The workbench provides a better basis for expert level features, because their specification can take advantage of the richer ER/ADT semantics. The workbench also contains a transparent SQL interface and a query-the-user facility, described in [Fu2].

The direct use of the workbench is demonstrated over an example database. After presenting its specification, we describe the execution of queries and update operations. Next, it is shown how to add rules, as needed when extending databases to knowledge bases. Over the example thus expanded, we show how queries can be handled by expert level features, running under the workbench, so as to avoid *misconstruals*. Features like these are being experimented in prototypes developed as part of project **NICE** [CF,HCF], whose purpose is to investigate *cooperative* query processing methods to reduce the cost of developing "help desks" and similar advanced database interfaces. Cooperative query processing has been explored, for example, in [BJ,CCL,CD], through the use of richer conceptual models, and in [Mo], via the generalization of failed queries. A natural language database query system, which recognizes users' presuppositions about the application domain, is also described in [Ka]. The problem of detecting and responding to plan-generation misconstruals is investigated in [Qu]. A good survey of user model techniques can be found in [KW].

The paper is organized as follows. Section 2 presents the syntax for the structural aspects of the languages and discusses queries and updates. Section 3 illustrates the direct use of the workbench over an example, which is taken again in section 4 where expert level features that contribute to avoid misconstruals are examined. Section 5 contains the conclusion. Finally, Appendix A lists the complete specification of the example in section 3 and Appendix B gives a Prolog implementation of the algorithm to block misconstruals, described in section 4.

2. Description of the Language

2.1. Facts and Fact Frames

A *fact* denotes the existence of either an entity or a relationship instance, or captures that one such instance has a certain value for a given attribute. In the prototype, whenever the same attribute name is used in the definition of more than one entity or relationship class, it implies that the attribute will have the same domain. A *key* is an identifying attribute, in the sense that entity or relationship instances that have the same value for the key are indeed the same instance, regardless of the class to which such instances belong. In the current prototype, entity instances cannot have compound keys, i.e. keys consisting of more than one attribute. The key of a relationship instance, on the contrary, is in general compound, since it consists of the keys of the participating entity instances; an exception is the case of binary one-to-n relationship instances, whose key is that of the determining participant (i.e. the participating entity depicted on the "n side" in the ER diagram).

A *database* for a conceptual schema is a set of facts. The syntax for facts is:

```
<entity class>¢<key>
<entity class>¢<key>\<attribute>(<value>)
<relationship class>#<participants list>
<relationship class>#<participants list>\<attribute>(<value>)
```

where `<participants list>` is a list of pairs of the form `<entity class>¢<key>`.

To refer to more than one attribute of an entity or relationship instance, a frame construct can be used:

```
<entity class>¢<key> has <attribute frame>
<relationship class>#<participants list> has <attribute frame>
```

where `<attribute frame>` is a list of `<attribute>:<value>` pairs. If `<attribute>` is multivalued, then `<value>` will unify with one of the values the attribute currently has, and with the other values upon backtracking.

If this is not the appropriate behavior, a different construct can be used:

```
<entity class>¢<key> has_gr <attribute frame>
<relationship class>#<participants list> has_gr <attribute frame>
```

where `<attribute frame>` contains a pair, `<attribute>:<value>`, if the attribute is single valued, or a pair `<attribute>:<list of values>`, if the attribute is multivalued. In the latter case, `<list of values>` naturally is the list of values `<attribute>` currently has.

2.2. Classes of Facts

The conceptual schema of a database at the ER/ADT level is specified through clauses that define the entity and relationship classes that exist and the structure of the is_a hierarchy. Relationships of arbitrary arity are allowed and binary one-to-n relationships are singled out. The syntax of the clauses to declare the conceptual schema is:

```
entity(<entity class>,<key>)
is_a(<entity class>,<entity class>)
relationship(<relationship class>,<participant classes>)
one_to_n(<relationship class>,<determining participant class>)
attribute(<entity class>,<attribute>)
attribute(<relationship class>,<attribute>)
domain(<attribute>,<value variable>,<validity check>,<cardinality>)
```

where `<participant classes>` is a list of `<entity class>` elements, `<validity check>` is an expression involving `<value variable>` to define the possible values that can be associated with `<attribute>`, and `<cardinality>` is either "single" or "multi", to distinguish between single and multivalued attributes.

Attributes and participation in relationships are inherited along the is_a hierarchy. The current prototype does not provide mechanisms to avoid ambiguities in case of inheritance from more than one parent class, or when a class inherits an attribute also defined in the class.

2.3. Data Structure Declaration and Mapping

Facts are stored in relational data structures, which can take the form of ground unit clauses of Prolog predicates or tuples of SQL tables. In both cases, the relational schema is declared by clauses of the form:

```
structure(<structure name>, <attribute list>)
```

where `<structure name>` is either a predicate symbol or the name of an SQL table. The names of the structures to be handled as SQL tables should be indicated in a clause:

```
sql_structures(<list of structure names>)
```

To ease the mapping between ER/ADT and relational schemas, the current prototype requires that the names of the columns of SQL tables be the same as the names of the corresponding attributes. On the other hand, the names of the data structures (predicates or tables) are arbitrary. The mapping between the two schemas is established by clauses with the following format:

```
ent_structure(<entity class>, <name of data structure>)
rep_ent_structure(<entity class>, <name of data structure>)
rel_structure(<relationship class>, <name of data structure>)
rep_rel_structure(<relationship class>, <name of data structure>)
ext_ent_structure(<entity class>, <relationships>, <name of data structure>)
```

where `<relationships>` is a list of `<relationship class>`.

The motivation for these different clauses comes from the way we design relational structures to accommodate the entity-relationship facts. Exactly one data structure, designated respectively by an "ent_structure" or "rel_structure" clause, must correspond to each entity or relationship class, storing the key attributes together with all the single-valued attributes. For each multivalued attribute, there must be a data structure, indicated in a "rep_ent_structure" or "rep_rel_structure", containing only the key and the attribute involved. Finally, whenever an entity class E participates in one or more one-to-n relationship classes, the data structure of E is extended to also represent the relationships. In such cases, an "ext_ent_structure" clause (instead of an "ent_structure" clause) is used to designate the data structure. A detailed description of the design method is found in [TCF].

2.4. Operations over Facts

In the spirit of abstract data types, the only way to update facts is through predefined application-oriented operations. Following a convenient STRIPS-like scheme [FN,LA], each operation 0 is specified by a set of clauses, which indicate the facts that are added and deleted by 0 (i.e., the effects of 0) and the preconditions for the execution of 0, in terms of logical expressions involving facts that should or should not hold. The syntax of the clauses to specify operations is:

```
<operation>(<name of operation>, <parameter list>)
added(<fact>,<operation>) <- <antecedent>
deleted(<fact>,<operation>) <- <antecedent>
precond(<operation>,<expression involving facts>) <- <antecedent>
```

where <parameter list> consists of the names of the domains to which the parameter values must belong. An "operation" clause provides the *signature* of an operation, and the designer must ensure its consistency with the other clauses referring to the operation. In the "added", "deleted" and "precond" clauses, the <antecedent>, which is a Prolog expression, is often omitted. When present, it provides additional criteria to check whether the clause is applicable and contributes to the instantiation of variables appearing in the head of the clause. Notice that the Prolog expression may in particular refer to other such clauses and to database facts. Of special interest is the case of the antecedent expression of a "precond" clause of an operation 0 referring to "added" and "deleted" clauses of 0; in such cases, the "precond" clause may indeed express a post-condition rather than a precondition, since it is allowed to look at the effects that the execution of 0 would have.

Preconditions are used to enforce integrity constraints dynamically, in the sense that they restrict the application of the defined operations to guarantee that they can only lead to valid states.

In adherence to the original ADT principles, operations do not "belong" to classes, as happens with strict object-oriented systems. Instances of several classes may be affected by an operation that refers to them through its parameters. As a consequence, inheritance of operations along the is_a hierarchy is provided in a trivial way. To see why this is true, assume the existence of an instance i of an entity class E, such that E is_a F. Assume further that an operation 0 includes as one of its parameters a reference to an instance of class F. Then, since we require that instances of an entity class must also exist as instances of all classes located above it in the is_a hierarchy, we conclude that 0 is applicable to i simply because i is also an instance of F.

As a related point that can be illustrated by further elaborating the above example, consider the specification of an operation 0' this time referring to instances of E. Suppose that we want the effects of 0' to subsume the effects of 0, in the sense that 0' has all the effects of 0 plus some others. The indication of subsumed effects can be succinctly done by including either or both of the following clauses in the definition of 0':

```
added(F, 0') <- added(F, 0)
deleted(F, 0') <- deleted(F, 0)
```

the same provision being possible for preconditions, through the inclusion of "precond" clauses of an analogous format.

In addition to the precond, added and deleted clauses belonging to a specific application, there may be present a number of general (i.e. application-independent) clauses of these types distinguished by the prefix "sys". The current version of the prototype contains "sys:precond" clauses establishing that:

P1. an instance of an entity-class E such that E is_a F can be added only if the instance exists in class F

P2. a value of an attribute of an entity or relationship instance can only be added if the instance exists

P3. a relationship instance can be added only if all participating entity instances exist

Clauses of type "sys:deleted" are also included, establishing that:

D1. if an instance of an entity-class E is deleted, then it is also deleted from all entity-classes F such that F is_a_ E (letting "is_a_" be the transitive closure of "is_a")

D2. if an instance of an entity or relationship class is deleted then all its attributes are also deleted

D3. if an instance of an entity-class is deleted then all relationship instances where it participates are deleted

These general clauses are based on assumptions that are often adopted with the entity-relationship model. Broadly speaking, they preserve integrity constraints inherent in the model. The "sys:precond" clauses *restrict* additions, whereas the "sys:deleted" clauses *propagate* deletions. The presence of these "sys" clauses reduces the number of clauses that an application designer has to introduce for each operation. On the other hand, the designer can make a "sys:precond" clause vacuous for a specific operation 0 by simply providing an appropriate "precond", "added" or "deleted" clause in the definition of 0. For example, pre-condition P2 becomes vacuous, if an operation 0 that is allowed to add a value for an attribute of an instance, also adds the instance itself. Similarly, the propagation of deletions can be changed into blocking for an operation 0 by attaching a "precond" clause to 0 that enforces the blocking of the operation. For example, the designer may include a "precond" clause preventing the deletion of an entity instance, if a certain attribute of the entity is still defined, or if the instance still participates in some instance of a specified relationship class.

A few "sys:added" and "sys:deleted" clauses were included to handle certain situations where null values are involved. Although these clauses are meaningful at the conceptual level, since nulls are used here to express undefined values, we must point out that their presence is mainly justified to ensure the correct mapping of the ER facts into the relational structures. In our STRIPS-based method to define operations, a "deleted" clause is the way to indicate that an operation 0 causes, as one of its effects, a single-valued attribute A of an entity or relationship instance to become undefined. A "sys:added" clause complements the deletion of the current value of A, by assigning to it the null value. Conversely, the addition of a value to a currently undefined attribute is complemented by the removal of its null value, through a "sys:deleted" clause. Note that, in the present prototype, to replace a non-null value of a single-valued attribute by another non-null value, both a "deleted" and an "added" clause must be provided. One-to-n relationships are treated in about the same way as single-valued attributes. The removal of an one-to-n relationship instance, which of course entails the removal of all its attributes, is complemented through "sys:added" clauses to indicate (by inserting nulls) that the participant on the "one side" and the single-valued relationship attributes have become undefined. Notice that, if this participant is replaced by another one, rather than removed, the current relationship attributes are equally removed. Finally, a "sys:deleted" clause provides the deletion of a null denoting an undefined participant when a valid participant is added.

We have still two more "sys:precond" clauses to mention. They implement our strategy (proposed in [VF]) to handle operations in case some of its effects already hold. These clauses prevent the execution if one or more facts that the operation should add are already present in the database or if facts to be deleted are absent. We find that this "all or nothing" strategy is compatible with the notion of *database transactions*, where several commands are involved and there is no commitment with respect to database updates if any failure occurs.

2.5. Query and Update Requests

Over an ER/ADT database, a user can formulate *query requests* and *update requests* as Prolog goals. For queries, a goal would consist of a Prolog expression involving one or more facts with the syntax described in section 2.1.

If a query refers to an attribute of an entity or relationship instance and, although the instance exists, the value of the attribute is currently undefined, the query fails as would be expected. However, we decided that the prototype should allow queries on undefined attributes declared as single-valued to succeed in the special case where the query mentions the "null" value explicitly.

The frame construct is convenient in the formulation of queries if more than one attribute is mentioned in connection to the same entity or relationship instance. Frames can be used in flexible ways. If a term corresponding to a frame is indicated by a variable, the execution of the goal will instantiate the variable to a list involving all attributes of the given entity or relationship instance which have non-null values in the database. If the user is only interested in a few specific attributes, he may indicate the frame explicitly as a list containing the desired attributes in any order he chooses, paired with variables to be instantiated with the corresponding values; in this case, for attributes whose value is not defined the respective variables will remain uninstantiated. Powerful operations have been introduced for frames, especially unification and generalization [Fu1]. Moreover, a query with frames has a better performance than a conceptually equivalent query where attributes of the same instance are indicated separately, since by working on entire frames the prototype is able to collapse database accesses so that each access retrieves all values requested that happen to be kept in the same underlying data structure.

Query requests can also involve schema information. All types of declarative clauses described in sections 2.2 and 2.4 (and even section 2.3, if one needs to reach a lower level) can appear in goal expressions.

Update requests are effected by goal expressions containing calls to the defined operations. Although, syntactically, these calls are direct, they are actually intercepted by a meta-predicate "exec_op" which checks the values of the parameters that are not variables or "null"s, tests the preconditions and, in case of success, applies additions and deletions to the appropriate data structures to reflect what the added and deleted clauses specify.

At the beginning of a session, where query and update requests will be posed, two preparatory goals must be executed:

```
<- enable_structures().
<- enable_operations().
```

the effect of the former being that the "sql_fact" predicate of the PSQL tool is applied (as described in [Fu2]) to all structures in the "sql_structures" clause, whereas the effect of the latter is to add to the workspace clauses of the form:

```
<operation template> <- exec_op(<operation template>)
```

where <operation template> consists of the operation name followed by a parenthesized sequence of variables denoting the formal parameters of the operation. The ability to enter calls to operations directly, that we mentioned earlier in this section, results from the presence of these clauses.

3. An Example of Direct Utilization of the Workbench

This section briefly describes an application and illustrates the power of the query language. Appendix A contains the complete description of the example as it runs under the Prolog prototype.

3.1. Conceptual Level Specification of the Application

The conceptual level specification defines entity classes that correspond to employees, trainees, departments, projects and clients, where trainees are a subclass of employees. It also defines relationship classes capturing that employees work in departments and participate in projects, and that clients sponsor departments in view of specific projects. Furthermore, the specification contains integrity constraints requiring that an employee can work in only one department and that he can only participate in sponsored projects of his department.

The mapping between the conceptual level specification and the relational data structure level specification has the following properties: it keeps the data on employees and on departments in SQL tables; it embeds the "works" one-to-n relationship in the "emp" table, together with the attributes of employees; and it maintains the attribute "task" of relationship "participates", which is multivalued, in a separate table.

The application has operations to install a department indicating the city where its headquarters will be, to hire employees to work in a department, to hire trainees, to separately designate the job that an employee will have in his department, to raise an employee's salary, to fire an employee, to propose a project, to associate in a sponsorship contract a client and a department with respect to a project, to assign employees to projects, to add more tasks to assigned employees, to give final approval to a project, and a few others.

Some features in the definition of operations deserve comments (we refer the reader to Appendix A). The assign operation has a precondition saying that an employee E can be assigned to a project P only if E works in a department that sponsors P. The salary raise operation affects only the salary of an employee, by adding the indicated amount (to reflect this update, only one field of the appropriate "emp" tuple is changed). When a project is initially proposed, it is marked as pending, a condition that can be later removed by an execution of the approve operation issued by the Projects Control Department, say (this removal is implemented by setting to "null" the second field of the corresponding "pr" clause. The definition of operation to hire trainees includes an "added" clause concisely declaring that the operation adds all facts added by the operation that hires employees.

3.2. Sample Executions of the Operations

Suppose that the database is initially empty and that the following operations are executed:

```
G1.  <- install('D1','NY').
G2.  <- hire('McCoy',100,'D1').
G3.  <- designate('McCoy','chair').
G4.  <- propose('Alpha').
G5.  <- associate('Spock Ltd.','D1','Alpha',1991,'c123').
G6.  <- hire_tr('Savik',80,'D1','graduate').
G7.  <- assign('Savik','Alpha','record-keeping').
G8.  <- add_task('Savik','Alpha','communications').
```

From the definition of the operations in Appendix A, the reader may find what facts will start to hold or cease to hold when these goals are executed, and how the data structures will be updated. In particular, the reader may appreciate the consequences of the application-independent clauses (prefixed with "sys") that establish general preconditions and effects of operations. For instance, if the goal "<-fire('Savik')" is executed, the direct effect is that Savik ceases to exist as an employee, but the "sys" clauses will also make her cease to exist as a trainee, and all facts related to attributes of this entity instance in both entity classes, as well as of its participation in relationships, will be also removed.

By way of an example, we follow the execution of G6. Recall from Appendix A the definition of "hire" and "hire-tr":

```
H1.  operation(hire, [name,sal,dname]).
H2.  added(emp¢N, hire(N,S,D)).
H3.  added(emp¢N\sal(S), hire(N,S,D)).
H4.  added(works#[emp¢N,dept¢D], hire(N,S,D)).

H5.  operation(hire_tr,[name,sal,dname,level]).
H6.  added(F, hire_tr(N,S,D,L)) <- added(F, hire(N,S,D)).
H7.  added(trainee¢N, hire_tr(N,S,D,L)).
H8.  added(trainee¢N\level(L), hire_tr(N,S,D,L)).
```

The execution of goal G6, "<- hire_tr('Savik',80,'D1','graduate')", directly creates the following new facts, via H7 and H8:

```
F1.  added(trainee¢'Savik', hire_tr('Savik',80,'D1','graduate')).
F2.  added(trainee¢'Savik'\level('graduate'),
           hire_tr('Savik',80,'D1','graduate')).
```

and, indirectly, the following new facts, via H6 and H2, H3 and H4:

```
F3.  added(emp¢'Savik', hire('Savik',80,'D1')).
F4.  added(emp¢'Savik'\sal(80), hire('Savik',80,'D1')).
F5.  added(works#[emp¢'Savik',dept¢'D1'], hire('Savik',80,'D1')).
```

The conceptual information expressed by F1 through F5 is in fact stored, via the mapping clauses, as the following two ground unit clauses (but recall that it is in part physically stored as SQL tuples):

```
R1.  emp('Savik',80,'D1',null).
R2.  tr('Savik','graduate').
```

The complete database at the end of the execution of the operations in G1 through G8 also contains the clauses:

```
R3.  dept('D1','NY').
R4.  emp('McCoy',100,'D1','chair').
R5.  pr('Alpha',true).
R6.  cln('Spock Ltd.','new').
R7.  spon('Spock Ltd.','D1','Alpha',1991,'c123').
R8.  part('Savik','Alpha').
R9.  tsk('Savik','Alpha','record-keeping').
R10. tsk('Savik','Alpha','communications').
```

3.3. Sample Queries

Considering the database state reached through the executions of operations given in the preceding section, it is easy to see that the sample queries below will produce the result indicated (notice that queries (3) and (5) use the frame construct):

```
(1) query:    who works in department D1?
```

```
      in Prolog:  <- forall(works#[emp¢N,dept¢'D1'], write(N)).
      answer:     'McCoy', 'Savik'
```

```
(2) query:      to what entity classes does Savik belong?
    in Prolog:  <- forall(E:'Savik', write(E)).
    answer:     emp, trainee
```

```
(3) query:      give all attributes available on Savik, as trainee.
    in Prolog:  <- trainee¢'Savik' has F & write(F).
    answer:     [level:graduate, sal:80]
```

```
(4) query:      is there some employee whose job is still undefined?
    in Prolog:  <- works#[emp¢N,dept¢D]\job(null) & write(N-D).
    answer:     'Savik' - 'D1'
```

```
(5) query:      which tasks have been assigned to Savik in project Alpha?
    in Prolog:  <- participates#[emp¢'Savik',proj¢'Alpha'] has_gr F
                   & write(F).
    answer:     [task: ['communications','record-keeping']]
```

```
(6) query:      is it true that project Alpha is sponsored for 1991?
    in Prolog:  <- sponsors¢[client¢*,dept¢*,proj¢'Alpha']\year(1991)
                   & write(yes).
    answer:     yes
```

```
(7) query:      has project Alpha been approved already?
    in Prolog:  <- (¬ proj¢'Alpha'\pending(*) & write(yes)
                   | prst('still pending') & nl).
    answer:     still pending
```

3.4. Adding a Knowledge Base Rule

Until now we have only considered a factual database in the present example.
Knowledge bases would, in addition, include *rules*. To provide an example, to be
further explored in connection with the expert level features of the next section,
we introduce a rule establishing that a project is "ongoing", in the sense that its
execution is under way, if it is being sponsored for the current year and it is no
longer pending. Besides the rule, we assume some way to indicate the current
year, which could be an access to the system's internal clock or a unit clause. The
Prolog declarations follow. As a step towards a pseudo-natural language notation,
"ongoing" is introduced as a prefix operator, obviating the need for the special
symbols used at the ER/ADT level:

```
op("ongoing",prefix,50).
```

```
current(1991).
```

```
ongoing P <-
  current(Y) &
  sponsors#[client¢*,dept¢*,proj¢P]\year(Y) &
  ¬proj¢P\pending(true).
```

Given the state of the database captured in clauses R1 through R10, the query request

```
<- ongoing 'Alpha'.
```

will fail, since the project is indeed currently sponsored but it is still pending.

4. An Example of Expert Level Features: Avoiding Misconstruals

In this section we illustrate how the user interface provided by the workbench can be enhanced by the superimposition of expert level features.

The purpose of the features to be presented is to intercept query requests and provide more than literal answers to what is asked. More specifically, answers will in some situations be expanded in order to avoid invalid user inferences, or *misconstruals* [We], as explained in section 4.1. To detect that an answer can lead a particular user to a misconstrual, one must have available *models* of the individual users (or classes of users).

In [HCF] we have outlined a formal approach to user modelling that is fully compatible with the logic programming paradigm. Based on this approach, we propose an algorithm to prevent a broad class of misconstruals, in the context of queries only, described in section 4.2. Section 4.3 traces two queries that may induce misconstruals, over the example introduced in section 3.4.

4.1. Misconstruals and User Modelling

When interacting with a database, a user is typically tempted to infer further information from that explicitly obtained from previous queries. However, his inferences are not necessarily valid, because his model of the world is often incomplete or even faulty. For example, after consulting the database, an auditor may find that a project, P, has gained the support of a client for the current year, and unadvisedly infer that its execution will start at once, when the actual beginning of the activities still depends on the approval of the Projects Control Department. A more **cooperative** database system would have informed the auditor that the client's sponsorship has indeed been granted, assumed as the original question, and would have added that the beginning of activities has been delayed. To achieve cooperativeness, the system would naturally have some model of typical auditors.

To address the problem of invalid user inferences, we consider a *cooperative interface* that passes additional information to the user when it discovers that he has gathered enough data to infer information that contradicts the database. The interface essentially simulates user's inferences and compares the result with what can be derived from the database.

We assume that, in the context of a given session, the user remembers his past interactions with the deductive database and that he can use the information thus obtained in his (real world) inferences. The results of past interactions in the current session are kept in a *log*, which will indicate that certain facts hold and that certain other facts do not hold in the database.

For simplicity, we consider that the interface knows exactly the class of users accessing the database at a given time, which isolates our problem from that of classifying users. Thus, from now on, when we refer to the user, we mean any user in this class. The *user model* is a theory, designed together with the database, that abstracts out the rules that the user adopts to reason about the domain of discourse in question. We stress that we use the term "user model" to mean a model of how the user reasons, which is somewhat different from the use of the term in the literature.

We model the user's inferences during a session by the deductions from the user model and the positive facts that the current log indicates to hold. In particular, we assume that the user reasons about negated facts only through *negation as finite failure* [Ll]. This intuitively means that, in a given session, we model the inference of a negated fact $\neg A$, by the failure, in a finite number of steps, to find a proof for A from the user model and the facts that the log indicates to hold.

For a detailed discussion of the theoretical aspects involved, see [HCF].

4.2. Algorithm to Avoid Misconstruals

The cooperative interface we propose uses an algorithm to process users' queries so as to avoid misconstruals. It does not take into account update operations, however. This section informally outlines the algorithm for the propositional case only, whereas Appendix B contains the Prolog implementation for the full first-order case.

The algorithm consists of two mutually recursive parts, that we call *"query"* and *"propagate"*. In the *"query"* part, given a query request A formulated by a user U, the algorithm first checks if A follows from what the user already knows, i.e. from the model of U extended with the knowledge placed in the user log during the process. If this fails, query A is posed to the database (provided that the authorization requirements are fulfilled). If this also fails, the process stops. If A follows from the database, A is added to the log, and the *"propagate"* part is entered to look at possible misconstruals induced by A.

More specifically, *"propagate"* takes in turn each conditional clause Y <- B in the model of U such that A is one of the facts conjoined in B and processes the clause as follows. If Y follows from what the user already knows and also from the database, then Y is not by itself a misconstrual, but it may indirectly cause one, which is checked by calling "propagate" recursively to examine the consequences of Y. If Y follows from what the user already knows, but it does not follow from the database, then Y is a misconstrual. To avoid that the user infer Y, the algorithm first looks for some negated fact Z in the body B of the clause in question such that Z follows from the database. To check Z against the database, "query" is called recursively. If one such negated fact is found, it is added to the log, effectively inhibiting henceforward the erroneous deduction of Y. Otherwise, on returning to the execution of "propagate", a clause is added to the log to explicitly block the deduction of Y.

If the algorithm is executed again for the same query A, the query will be answered from the user's model plus log and no further action is needed. Also, queries involving the misconstruals thus identified will correctly end in failure.

The Prolog implementation of the algorithm was designed for the full first-order case and it is prepared to handle the propagation of variable bindings, as suggested in [HCF]. It also distinguishes the clauses belonging to the user's model (and to his log) from the system's clauses by adding to the former a prefix which is typically the user's identification (*userid*).

4.3. Informal Description of two Examples

We give in this section two examples, both related to the rule introduced in section 3.4, to indicate how the interface operates. The examples are introduced informally, with the pertinent Prolog expressions shown in figures 1, 2 and 3. The first example illustrates how to avoid misconstruals that arise when the user incorrectly invokes negation as finite failure for the lack of information, whereas the second example has to do with a type of misconstrual that arises when the user has inadequate rules.

Consider that the deductive database has a rule saying that a project is ongoing if duly sponsored by a client and if it is not pending. Suppose that project alpha is sponsored for the current year and that it is still pending (i.e. the Projects Control Department has not yet issued its approval). That is, let D be the following deductive database (see Figure 1 for the formal definition):

D.1. Project p is ongoing, if p is sponsored and it is not pending
D.2. Project Alpha is sponsored
D.3. Project Alpha is pending

```
/* rules */

op("ongoing",prefix,50).

ongoing P <-
  current(Y) &
  sponsors#[client¢*,dept¢*,proj¢P]\year(Y) &
  ¬proj¢P\pending(true).

/* facts */

current(1991).

dept('D1','NY').
pr('Alpha',true).
cln('Spock Ltd.','new').
spon('Spock Ltd.','D1','Alpha',1991,'c123').
```

Figure 1: Deductive Database

Suppose that the user believes in the same rule as the database, that is, that a project is ongoing if duly sponsored by a client and if it is not pending. This is equivalent to assuming a user model U that contains only one rule (see Figure 2 for the formal definitions):

U.1.   Project p is ongoing, if p is sponsored and it is not pending

Suppose now that the user starts the dialog with the query:

Q.   Is project Alpha sponsored?

The answer to Q therefore is YES. That is, at this point the user knows:

A_1.   Project Alpha is sponsored

If no extra information is passed to the user in the log, after the first query he will know fact A_1, from which he would wrongly infer fact A_2:

A_2.   Project Alpha is ongoing

However, the interface will anticipate and avoid this misconstrual as follows. By applying the algorithm of the preceding section to simulate a deduction R of A_2 from the user model U and A_1, it will detect that R cannot be accepted because it is possible to infer the negation of fact A_3:

A_3.   Project p is pending

from U and A_1, by negation as finite failure, whereas it is not possible to infer the negation of A_3 from the database (since the database in fact includes A_3). Hence, the interface will include A_3 in the log to avoid the user's misconstrual. Indeed, the user can no longer infer A_2 using the complete information he obtained from the database (that is, A_1 and A_3).

The answer combined with the extra information in the log is roughly equivalent to the following English sentence:

Project Alpha is sponsored, but it is not ongoing because it is pending

---

```
/* knowledge when session starts */

u: (ongoing P) <-
   current(Y) &
   u: (sponsors#[client¢*,dept¢*,proj¢P]\year(Y))  &
   ¬ u: (proj¢P\pending(true)) .

/* query posed */

<- query(sponsors#[client¢*,dept¢*,proj¢'Alpha']\year(1991), a).

/* knowledge added to log */

u:(sponsors#[client¢'Spock Ltd.', dept¢'D1', proj¢'Alpha']\year(1991)).
u:(proj¢'Alpha'\pending(true)).
```

Figure 2: User U

We stress that the misconstrual we just illustrated was caused by an incorrect use of negation as finite failure and that it could be blocked by including an additional fact in the log. Our next example illustrates a second type of misconstrual that arises when the user has inadequate rules.

Suppose now that the user believes that a project is always ongoing, if it is sponsored. That is, let the user model now be V (see Figure 3 for the formal definitions):

V.1.   Project p is ongoing, if p is sponsored

Assume the same deductive database D (including rule D.1 exactly as before). Then, the answer to Q remains unchanged, from which the user can again wrongly infer fact A_2. The interface will again detect that A_2 does not follow from the database. The interface cannot block this misconstrual, however, by inserting additional facts in the log because the user's perception of the domain of discourse differs from that captured by the rules of the database. The interface will then act differently and include in the log an indication that A_2 is not deductible from the database.

The user can still infer A_2 from the answer to his query. However, his inference will not be consistent with the current log, since the log indicates that A_2 does not hold.

The final answer will then be equivalent to the sentence:

Project Alpha is sponsored but it is not ongoing.

```
/* knowledge when session starts */

v: (ongoing P) <-
   current(Y) &
   v: (sponsors#[client¢*,dept¢*,proj¢P]\year(Y)).

/* query posed */

<- query(sponsors#[client¢*,dept¢*,proj¢'Beta']\year(1991), b).

/* knowledge added to log */

v:(sponsors#[client¢'Spock Ltd.', dept¢'D1', proj¢'Alpha']\year(1991)).
v:failed(ongoing 'Alpha').
```

Figure 3: User V

5. Conclusion

We described a declarative conceptual modelling language that is an integral part of a workbench that provides rapid prototyping at the conceptual level and that supports expert level features. We also provided simple examples to illustrate the direct use of the workbench over a database / knowledge base application, as well as the exploration of its use in connection with expert level features aiming at providing cooperative interfaces to information systems.

The prototype of the workbench is at an early stage of development, but it already implements all features of the language here described. It can be extended in several ways, either as a consequence of enriching the ER/ADT model, or to focus on the optimization of the algorithms and their implementation, among other points.

References

[AP] J. F. Allen and C. R. Perrault, "Analyzing intentions in utterances", *Artificial Intelligence* 15:3 (1980), 143-178.

[BJ] L. Bolc and M. Jarke (eds.), *Cooperative Interfaces to Information Systems*, Springer-Verlag (1986).

[CCL] W. Chu, Q. Chen and R-C. Lee, "Cooperative Query Answering via Type Abstraction Hierarchy", Proc. Int. Working Conference on Cooperating Knowledge based Systems, Univ. Keele, UK (1990).

[CD]   F. Cuppens and R. Demolombe, "Cooperative answering: a methodology to provide intelligent access to databases", Proc. of the Second International Conference on Expert Database Systems, L. Kerschberg (ed.), Benjamin/Cummings (1989), 621-643.

[CF]   M. A. Casanova and A. L. Furtado, "An Information System Environment based on Plan Generation", Proc. Int. Working Conference on Cooperating Knowledge based Systems, Keele, UK (1990).

[FN]   R. E. Fikes and N. J. Nilsson - "STRIPS: a new approach to the application of theorem proving to problem solving" - Artificial Intelligence 2 (1971) 189-208.

[Fu1]   A. L. Furtado - "Exploring the extensibility of IBM Prolog" - technical report CCR-124 - Rio Scientific Center of IBM Brasil (1991).

[Fu2]   A. L. Furtado - "Two integrated tools for IBM Prolog: query-the-user & transparent use of SQL" - technical report CCR-126 - Rio Scientific Center of IBM Brasil (1991).

[HCF]   A. S. Hemerly, M. A. Casanova and A. L. Furtado, "Cooperative behaviour through request modification", Proc. 10th Int'l. Conf. on the Entity-Relationship Approach, San Mateo, CA, USA (1991) 607-621.

[Ka]   S. J. Kaplan, "Cooperative Responses from a Portable Natural Language Query System", *Artificial Intelligence* 19:2 (1982), 165-187.

[KW]   A. Kobsa and W. Wahlster (eds.), *User Models in Dialog Systems*, Springer-Verlag (1989).

[LA]   D. J. Litman and J. F. Allen - "A plan recognition model for subdialogues in conversations" - Cognitive Science 11 (1987) 163-200.

[Ll]   J.W. Lloyd, *Foundations of Logic Programming*, Springer-Verlag (1987).

[Mo]   A. Motro, "Query generalization: a technique for handling query failure", Proc. First International Workshop on Expert Database Systems (1984), 314-325.

[Qu]   A. Quilici, "Detecting and Responding to Plan-Oriented Misconceptions", in *User Models in Dialog Systems*, A. Kobsa and W. Wahlster (eds.), Springer-Verlag (1989).

[TCF]   L. Tucherman, M. A. Casanova and A. L. Furtado - "The CHRIS consultant - a tool for database design and rapid prototyping" - Information Systems 15:2 (1990).

[VF]   P. A. S. Veloso and A. L. Furtado - "Towards simpler and yet complete formal specifications" - in "Information systems: theoretical and formal aspects" - A. Sernadas, J. Bubenko and A. Olive (eds.) - North-Holland Pub. Co. (1985) 175-189.

[We]   B. L. Webber, "Questions, answers and responses: interacting with knowledge base systems", in *On knowledge base management systems*, M.L. Brodie and J. Mylopoulos (eds.) - Springer (1986).

APPENDIX A

% EXAMPLE DATABASE / KNOWLEDGE BASE

% declaring entity classes and attributes

```
entity(emp,name).
entity(trainee,name).
entity(dept,dname).
entity(proj,pname).
entity(client,cname).

trainee is_a emp.

attribute(emp,sal).
attribute(trainee,level).
attribute(dept,city).
attribute(proj,pending).
attribute(client,status).

relationship(works, [emp,dept]).
relationship(participates, [emp,proj]).
relationship(sponsors, [client,dept,proj]).

one_to_n(works, emp).

attribute(works,job).
attribute(sponsors,contract).
attribute(sponsors,year).
attribute(participates,task).

domain(name,V,is_string(V),single).
domain(dname,V,is_string(V),single).
domain(pname,V,is_string(V),single).
domain(cname,V,is_string(V),single).
domain(sal,V,is_numb(V),single).
domain(level,V,
        V == 'graduate' | V == 'undergraduate',single).
domain(city,V,is_string(V),single).
domain(pending,V,V == true,single).
domain(status,V,is_string(V),single).
domain(job,V,is_string(V),single).
domain(contract,V,
        stconc('c',N,V) & st_to_at(N,M) & is_int(M),single).
domain(year,V,in_range(V,1900,2000),single).
domain(task,V,is_string(V),multi).
```

```
% declaring data structures

structure(emp, [name,sal,dname,job]).
structure(dept, [dname,city]).
structure(pr, [pname,pending]).
structure(tr, [name,level]).
structure(acc, [name,account]).
structure(part, [name,pname]).
structure(tsk, [name,pname,task]).
structure(cln, [cname,status]).
structure(spon, [cname,dname,pname,year,contract]).

sql_structures([emp,dept]).


% mapping between classes and data structures

ext_ent_structure(emp, [works], emp).
ent_structure(trainee, tr).
ent_structure(dept, dept).
ent_structure(proj, pr).
ent_structure(client, cln).

rel_structure(participates, part).
rel_structure(sponsors, spon).

rep_rel_structure(participates, tsk).


% defining operations

operation(install, [dname,city]).
added(dept¢D, install(D,C)).
added(dept¢D\city(C), install(D,C)).

operation(propose, [pname]).
added(proj¢P, propose(P)).
added(proj¢P\pending(true), propose(P)).

operation(approve, [pname]).
deleted(proj¢P\pending(true), approve(P)).

operation(hire, [name,sal,dname]).
added(emp¢N, hire(N,S,D)).
added(emp¢N\sal(S), hire(N,S,D)).
added(works#[emp¢N,dept¢D], hire(N,S,D)).
```

```
operation(hire_tr,[name,sal,dname,level]).
added(F, hire_tr(N,S,D,L)) <- added(F, hire(N,S,D)).
added(trainee¢N, hire_tr(N,S,D,L)).
added(trainee¢N\level(L), hire_tr(N,S,D,L)).


operation(raise,[name,increment]).
added(emp¢N\sal(S), raise(N,I)) <-
  emp¢N\sal(S0) & S := S0 + I .
deleted(emp¢N\sal(S0), raise(N,I)) <-
  emp¢N\sal(S0).


operation(designate, [name,job]).
added(works#[emp¢N,dept¢*]\job(J), designate(N,J)).
deleted(works#[emp¢N,dept¢*]\job(J), designate(N,K)) <-
  works#[emp¢N,dept¢*]\job(J).


operation(fire, [name]).
deleted(emp¢X, fire(X)).


operation(assign, [name,pname,task]).
precond(assign(N,P,T),
  works#[emp¢N,dept¢D] &
  sponsors#[client¢*,dept¢D,proj¢P]).
added(participates#[emp¢N,proj¢P], assign(N,P,T)).
added(participates#[emp¢N,proj¢P]\task(T), assign(N,P,T)).


operation(add_task, [name,pname,task]).
added(participates#[emp¢N,proj¢P]\task(T), add_task(N,P,T)).


operation(associate, [cname,dname,pname,year,contract]).
added(client¢C,associate(C,D,P,Y,Cn)) <- ¬client¢C.
added(client¢C\status('new'),associate(C,D,P,Y,Cn)) <-
  ¬client¢C\status(*).
added(sponsors#[client¢C,dept¢D,proj¢P],
      associate(C,D,P,Y,Cn)).
added(sponsors#[client¢C,dept¢D,proj¢P]\year(Y),
      associate(C,D,P,Y,Cn)).
added(sponsors#[client¢C,dept¢D,proj¢P]\contract(Cn),
      associate(C,D,P,Y,Cn)).



% example of a knowledge-base rule

op("ongoing",prefix,50).


current(1991).
```

```
ongoing P <-
  current(Y) &
  sponsors#[client¢*,dept¢*,proj¢P]\year(Y) &
  ¬proj¢P\pending(true).
```

APPENDIX B

```
/* ALGORITHM TO AVOID MISCONSTRUALS */

query(X,U) <-
  U : X & /.

query(X,U) <-
  authorized(X) &
  X &
  nl &
  write(sys : X - succeeds) &
  log(U : X) &
  propagate(X,U).

propagate(X,U) <-
  forall( conditional_clause(U : Y <- B) &
          in_conjunction(U : X,B) &
          (delax(gb(*)) | true) & addax(gb(nil)) & U : Y,
          (gb(C) & inv(C,C1) & certU(C1,U) &
              (certD(C1,Z)   -> ( write(sys : Z - fails) &
                                  log_mis(Z,U));
                              propagate(Y,U)) & fail )).

/* certification test for the deductive database */

certD([],X)      <- / & fail.
certD([¬V!C],X) <- ¬V-> (/ & certD(C,X)); X=¬V .
certD([ V!C],X) <-  V-> (/ & certD(C,X)); X=V .

/* certification test for the log - an optimization */

certU([],U)      <- /.
certU([¬V!C],U) <- / & certU(C,U).
certU([V!C],U)   <- / & (U:failed(V)-> (/ & fail); certU(C,U)).

log_mis(¬X,U) <- addax(U:X,log,1) & write (¬X - blocked).
log_mis( X,U) <- addax(U:failed(X),log,1) & write (X - blocked).

log(X) <- addax(X,log) & write (X - added).
```

```
y_(X) <- gb(C) & delax(gb(C)) & addax(gb([X!C])).
n_(X) <- gb(C) & delax(gb(C)) & addax(gb([¬X!C])).

authorized(X).

/* utilities */

conditional_clause(X) <-
  ax(*,X).

in_conjunction(X,X) <- ¬X =.. ["&"!*] & /().
in_conjunction(X,X & *).
in_conjunction(X,* & R) <- in_conjunction(X,R).

inv(L,L1)<-inv(L,[],L1).
inv([],L,L)<-cut().
inv([H!L],LL,L1)<- cut() & inv(L,[H!LL],L1).
```

A Method for Reasoning about Deductive Conceptual Models of Information Systems

Dolors Costal
Antoni Olivé

Universitat Politècnica de Catalunya
Facultat d'Informàtica
Pau Gargallo 5
08028 Barcelona - Catalonia

Abstract. We describe a new method for reasoning about conceptual models of information systems developed in the deductive approach. The method allows checking the effect of external events on the Information Base and generating plans able to perform a transition between two states of the Information Base. Our method has the full power of the methods developed so far for the traditional, operational approach to conceptual modelling. The reasoning capabilities provided by our method are helpful and improve the validation task of conceptual models of information systems.
Keywords. Deductive Conceptual Models, Requirements Validation, Plan Formation

1 Introduction

Modern conceptual models of information systems provide a complete specification of both the static and dynamic aspects of those systems. Many different languages for conceptual modelling of information systems have been proposed. However, despite their differences, there are only two basic approaches to the modelling of the dynamic aspect. We call them the "operational" and the "deductive" approaches.

In the operational approach, changes to the Information Base (IB), corresponding to changes in the Universe of Discourse (UoD), are defined by means of operations. The occurrence of a real-world, external event triggers the execution of an operation (transaction), which reflects the effect of the event on the IB. These effects consist usually of insertions, updates or deletions to the IB. On the other hand, operations, as well as queries and integrity constraints usually can only access to the current state of the IB.

In the deductive approach, the IB is defined only in terms of the external events, by means of deductive rules, and queries and integrity constraints are defined as if the complete history of the IB were available. A deductive conceptual model (DCM) is a specification of an IS in the deductive approach. A detailed comparison of the operational and deductive approaches can be found in [BuO86, Oli86].

In this paper, we are interested in the validation of DCMs. By validation we mean the determination of the correctness of a conceptual model with respect to the user needs and requirements [ABC82]. This is one of the most important and crucial problems in information systems engineering.

Classical ways for dealing with validation are based on "user-friendly" specifications and rapid prototyping techniques, but it is obvious that much more research is needed [Bub86]. In this respect, a promising research direction suggests the use of some kind of reasoning method about the specifications. Sometimes, these methods are described as "infological simulation" [Bub86] or "semantic prototyping" [LTP91]. The aim is to provide the designer with a set of automated reasoning capabilities that allows him to check the validity of the conceptual model.

In this paper, we present a method for reasoning about DCMs. The method uses SLDNF resolution as proof procedure and plan generation techniques developed in the Artificial Intelligence field. The basic reasoning capabilities offered by the method are:

a) Given an initial and a target state, together with a sequence of external events, check whether the sequence is able to perform the transition between both states.
b) Given an initial and a target state, obtain one or more sequences of external events (plans) able to perform the transition between both states.

The work most similar to ours, in the field of conceptual modelling using the operational approach, is that done by Furtado et al., described in [FuM84,VeF85,FuC90,CFT91]. They have developed a set of software tools, called "Expert helpers", to aid in the specification, usage and maintenance of IS. We include some comments on this work in Sections 3 and 5.

In the "deductive" approach, Lundberg [Lun82a, Lun82b] developed the IMT (Information Modelling Tool), which checks the satisfiability of a model in a given state of the UoD. Our method extends this work by considering not only the static aspect but also the dynamic aspect of an IS.

In the medium term, we would like to have, and we need, analytical tools such as those developed in Petri nets modelling. In fact, there is a strong similarity between the problems described above and the reachability problem in Petri nets [Pet77].

The paper is organized as follows. Next section defines basic concepts of DCMs and introduces a simple example that will be used throughout the paper. Section 3 describes our method for checking the effect of events on the IB. The method uses the DCM. Section 4 describes the Internal Events Model (IEM) of an IS. This model, which is derived from a DCM, defines the relationship between two consecutive IB states, and plays a major role in our method for plan generation. The method is described in section 5. Finally, section 6 gives the conclusion and points out future work.

2 Deductive Conceptual Models

A deductive conceptual model (DCM) of an IS consists of:

- A set B of base predicates
- A set DR of deductive rules defining derived predicates
- A set IC of integrity constraints

- A set Q of predefined queries

In the following, we briefly describe each of these sets. However, in order to focus on our objective, we omit in this paper query definition and handling. Figure 1 shows a simple example that will be used throughout the paper. The example is taken from [VeF85].

Base predicates correspond to the external event types. Each fact of a base predicate, called base fact, is an occurrence of an external event. Base facts are the inputs to the IS. We assume, by convention, that the last term of a base fact gives the time when the event occurred and was communicated to the IS. If $p(a_1,..., a_n,t_i)$ is a base fact we say that $p(a_1,..., a_n)$ is true or holds at t_i.

All times are expressed in a unique time unit (such as second, day, etc.) small enough to avoid ambiguities. The life span L of an IS is the time interval in which the system operates. It is defined as a set of consecutive time points, expressed in the given time unit, $L = \{t_0,...,t_{end}\}$, where t_0 and t_{end} are the initial and final times, respectively. We use sometimes the standard predicate time(T). A fact time(t) holds if t belongs to the life span.

In the example of figure 1 we have four base predicates: offer, enroll, transfer and cancel. A base fact offer(c,t) means that course c is offered as a new course at time t. A base fact enroll(s,c,t) reports that student s enrolls in course c at time t. A base fact transfer(s,fc,tc,t) means that at time t student s is tranferred from course fc to course tc. A base fact cancel(c,t) means that course c is cancelled at time t. We take as time unit a second.

Derived predicates model the relevant types of knowledge about the Universe of Discourse. Each fact of a derived predicate, called derived fact, represents an information about the state of the UoD at a particular time point. We also assume that the last term gives the time when the information holds.

Each derived predicate is defined by means of one or more deduction rules. A deduction rule of predicate p has the form $p(X_1,...,X_n,T) \leftarrow L_1,...,L_m$, where $p(X_1,...,X_n,T)$ is an atom denoting the conclusion and $L_1,...,L_m$ are literals representing conditions. Each L_j is either an atom or a negated atom. Variables in the conclusion or in the conditions are assumed to be universally quantified over the whole formula. The terms in the conclusion must be distinct variables, and the terms in the conditions must be variables or constants.

Condition predicates may be ordinary or evaluable ("built-in"). The former are base or derived predicates, while the latter are predicates, such as the comparison or arithmetic predicates, that can be evaluated without accessing a database.

We assume every rule to be allowed [GMN84], i.e. any variable that occurs in the rule has an occurrence in a positive condition of an ordinary predicate. We also require every rule to be time-restricted. This means that for every positive literal $q(...,T1)$ of a base or derived predicate q occurring in the body, the condition $L_1,...,L_m \rightarrow T1 \leq T$ must hold. This ensures that $p(X_1,...,X_n,T)$ is defined in terms of q-facts holding at time T or before.

In the example, there are five derived predicates, with their corresponding (and hopefully self-explanatory) rules. Note that predicate enrolled is defined by two deductive rules, since a student is enrolled in a course either by a enroll or by a transfer base fact.

Integrity constraints are closed first-order formulas that base and/or derived facts are required to satisfy. We deal with constraints that have the form of a denial $\leftarrow L_1,...,L_m$, with $m \geq 1$, where the L_j are literals and variables are assumed to be universally quantified over the whole formula. More general constraints can be transformed into this form as described in [LIT84]. For the sake of uniformity, we associate to each integrity constraint an inconsistency predicate icn with at least a time term, and thus it has the same form as the deductive rules. We call them integrity rules.

In the example of figure 1 we show six inconsistency predicates, with their rules. To see how an inconsistency may arise, assume that base facts offer(db,1) and enroll(mary,db,3) were received at times 1 and 3, respectively. Now, if at time 6 the IS receives transfer(mary,db,is,6), inconsistency ic2(6) is violated, because offered(is,6) does not hold. Therefore, the base fact transfer(mary,db,is,6) must be rejected.

We note in passing the declarative nature of the deductive approach. Enforcement of the single integrity constraint ic2 in the operational approach requires three preconditions: for cancel, that no students are taking the course cancelled; for transfer, that the course to which the student is tranferred is being offered; and for enroll, that the course to which the student is enrolled is being offered.

The standard predicate ic(T) is defined by the set of rules ic(T) $\leftarrow$ icj (T), for $j = 1...n$, where n is the number of integrity constraints in the DCM. A fact ic(t) holds if at time t some integrity constraint is violated.

base predicates
offer(Course,Time)
enroll(Student,Course,Time)
transfer(Student,From_course,To_course,Time)
cancel(Course,Time)
derived predicates
DR.1 offered(C,T) $\leftarrow$ offer(C,T1), T1 $\leq$ T, not(cancelled(C,T1,T)).
DR.2 cancelled(C,T1,T) $\leftarrow$ offer(C,T1), cancel(C,T2), T2 $\geq$ T1, T2 $\leq$ T.
DR.3 takes(S,C,T) $\leftarrow$ enrolled(S,C,T1), T1 $\leq$ T, not(transferred(S,C,T1,T)).
DR.4 enrolled(S,C,T) $\leftarrow$ enroll(S,C,T).
DR.5 enrolled(S,C,T) $\leftarrow$ transfer(S,Fc,C,T).
DR.6 transferred(S,C,T1,T) $\leftarrow$ enrolled(S,C,T1), transfer(S,C,Tc,T2), T2 $\geq$ T1, T2 $\leq$ T.
integrity constraints
ic1(T) $\leftarrow$ offer(C,T), offered(C,T-1).
ic2(T) $\leftarrow$ takes(S,C,T), not(offered(C,T)).
ic3(T) $\leftarrow$ enroll(S,C,T), takes(S,C,T-1).
ic4(T) $\leftarrow$ transfer(S,Fc,Tc,T), takes(S,Tc,T-1).
ic5(T) $\leftarrow$ transfer(S,Fc,Tc,T), not(takes(S,Fc,T-1)).
ic6(T) $\leftarrow$ cancel(C,T), not(offered(C,T-1)).

Fig.1. Example of Deductive Conceptual Model

3 Checking the Effect of Events

The deductive approach to conceptual modelling of IS allows a simple solution to the problem of checking the effect of a given sequence of external events (base facts) on the Information Base. The equivalent problem in the operational approach is checking the effect of a sequence of operations on the IB.

This problem appears in several, related contexts during the validation of a conceptual model. For example, the designer might want to check whether or not a sequence of events is acceptable with respect to the set of integrity constraints defined in the model. If the result is not as expected, it might suggest the need for refinements of the integrity constraints [VeF85]. As another example, the designer might want to check whether or not a sequence of events leaves the IB in a given state. Again, if the result is not as expected, it might suggest the need for refinements of the deductive rules.

Stated more precisely, the problem is: Given an initial state of the IB, a sequence U of base facts and a final state of the IB, check whether the sequence performs the transition between both states. The initial state is defined by an initial time t_i and a set IBF of base facts, and the final state is defined by a final time t_f and a goal G.

For example, $t_i = 3$, $t_f = 7$,

IBF = {offer(c1,1), enroll(john,c1,3)}
U = {offer(c2,5), transfer(john,c1,c2,6), cancel(c1,7)}
G ← not(offered(c1,7))

defines an initial state, corresponding to time 3, where both offered(c1,3) and takes(john,c1,3) hold, and we want to check that U produces a final state, corresponding to time 7, where offered(c1,7) does not hold.

Our method for checking the effect of events on the IB is entirely based on the use of standard SLDNF resolution. Let IBF and U be sets of base facts, and G a conjunction of literals. Ignoring for the moment the integrity constraints, G holds in the final state if {←G} succeeds from input set DCM ∪ IBF ∪ U.

However, we have to ensure that the IB is consistent at any time between the initial and final states. We take this into account by defining a standard auxiliary predicate:

ic_violated ← time(T), T ≥ t_i, T ≤ t_f, ic(T)

and then G holds in the final state if { ←G, not(ic_violated)} succeeds from input set DCM ∪ IBF ∪ U.

Figure 2 shows (part of) the refutation of the goal {←G, not(ic_violated)} in our example.

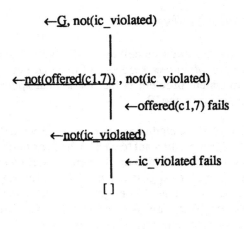

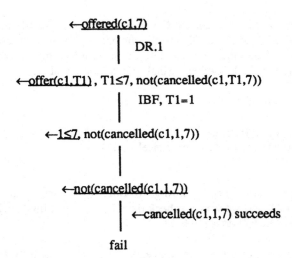

Fig.2. Refutation of G

Application of our method requires the initial state be defined as a set IBF of base facts. However, we could also start with an initial state defined by an initial goal, consisting of a conjunction of literals.

The method proposed by Furtado et al. [FuM84,VeF85], which deals with the operational approach, solves this problem by executing the operations in the order given, and comparing the resulting final state against the expected one. The most significant difference that we see between this method and ours, is that an analysis of the derivations that we obtain in the refutation may show which base facts have been used, and which ones are irrelevant for reaching the final state. In some cases, such analysis might be helpful in the validation.

4 The Internal Events Model

In the previous section, we have shown a method for checking the effect of a set of base facts on the IB. Now, we would like to have a similar method for generating a set of base facts (a plan) able to perform a transition between two given initial and final states.

In our deductive approach, this problem is similar to the view updating problem in deductive databases. In that context, the problem is: given a deductive database D, consisting of a set of base facts and a set of deductive rules, and a view update (insertion or deletion of a derived fact), find a set of updates on the base facts such that leaves the updated database D' in a state where the required derived fact holds (if insertion) or does not hold (if deletion).

In a previous work [TeO92], we have developed a new method for view updating in deductive databases, which gives a complete set of correct solutions to a view update request. The method is based on an events model of a deductive database, which is formally derived from the deductive rules.

We extend in this paper the above work to develop a method for plan generation in DCMs. The method will use an Internal Events Model (IEM), which is a generalization of the events model of deductive databases. The IEM was defined in [Oli89,San90], where a formal procedure to derive it from a given DCM was also given. Before describing our method in the next section, we need to introduce here the main concepts of an IEM.

4.1 Classification of Predicates

Predicates defined in a DCM can be classified according to their temporal behaviour. For our purposes, the most important classification is the following. Let p be a predicate. Assume that fact $p(k)$ holds at time T-1, where k is a vector of constants, and assume that no external events happen at time T, that is, no base facts are received at T. What can we say about the truth of $p(k)$ at time T?. There are three cases:

a) If we can say that $p(k)$ will be false at time T, then we classify p as P-transient.
b) If we can say that $p(k)$ will be true at time T, then we classify p as P-state.
c) If the truth of $p(k)$ depends on the truth of some condition that must be evaluated at time T, we classify p as P-spontaneous.

In our DCM example of figure 1, predicates offered, cancelled, takes and transferred are P-state; while predicate enrolled is P-transient. Base predicates are always assumed to be P-transient.

4.2 Internal Events

The concept of internal event tries to capture in a natural way the notion of change in the extension of a predicate. We associate to each P-state or P-spontaneous predicate p an insertion internal events predicate ιp and a deletion internal events predicate δp defined as follows:

(1) $\forall X,T$ $(\iota p(X,T) \leftrightarrow p(X,T) \wedge \neg p(X,T-1))$
(2) $\forall X,T$ $(\delta\, p(X,T) \leftrightarrow p(X,T-1) \wedge \neg p(X,T))$

where X is a vector of variables, and then:

(3) $\forall X,T$ $(p(X,T) \leftrightarrow (p(X,T-1) \wedge \neg\, \delta p(X,T)) \vee \iota p(X,T))$
(4) $\forall X,T$ $(\neg p(X,T) \leftrightarrow (\neg p(X,T-1) \wedge \neg\, \iota p(X,T)) \vee \delta\, p(X,T))$

To P-transient predicates we only associate an insertion internal events predicate ιp defined as:

(5) $\forall X,T$ $(\iota p(X,T) \leftrightarrow p(X,T))$

If p is a derived predicate, then ιp facts and δp facts represent induced insertions and deletions of derived facts, respectively. If p is an inconsistency predicate, then ιp facts that occur at time T will correspond to violations of its integrity constraint. Note that, for inconsistency predicates, δp facts cannot happen in any transition, since we assume that the IB is consistent at time T-1 and, thus, $p(X,T-1)$ is always false.

We also use the internal events concept for base predicates. In this case, ιp facts represent the external events (given by the environment) corresponding to insertions of base facts. We use sometimes the term "event" to denote either an internal or external event.

4.3 Transition Rules

Let $p(X,T) \leftarrow L_1,...,L_m$ be a deductive or inconsistency rule. The rule defines the extension of p at time T in terms of the extensions at time T, or before, of the predicates appearing in the body of the rule. A transition rule for p is a rule that defines the extension of p at time T in terms of the extensions at time T-1, or before, of the predicates appearing in the body of the rule, and the internal events of these predicates that occur at time T. We obtain the transition rules substituting each L_j, j = 1...n, by its equivalent expression (see [Oli89,San90] for details).

Consider, for example, rule DR.1:

offered(C,T) $\leftarrow$ offer(C,T1), T1 $\leq$ T, not(cancelled(C,T1,T))

Literal offer(C,T1) can be replaced by $((\text{offer}(C,T1) \wedge T1 < T) \vee (\iota \text{offer}(C,T) \wedge T1 = T))$. Similarly, literal not(cancelled(C,T1,T)) can be replaced by $((\neg \text{cancelled}(C,T1,T-1) \wedge \neg \iota \text{cancelled}(C,T1,T)) \vee \delta \text{cancelled}(C,T1,T))$, as given by (4). After distributing $\wedge$ over $\vee$, we get:

offered(C,T) $\leftarrow$ offer(C,T1), T1 < T, not(cancelled(C,T1,T-1)), not(ιcancelled(C,T1,T))
offered(C,T) $\leftarrow$ offer(C,T1), T1 < T, δcancelled(C,T1,T)
offered(C,T) $\leftarrow$ ιoffer(C,T), not(cancelled(C,T,T-1)), not(ιcancelled(C,T,T))
offered(C,T) $\leftarrow$ ιoffer(C,T), δcancelled(C,T,T)

which are the transition rules for predicate offered. Note that these rules allow us to infer which courses are offered at time T in base to the offer and cancelled facts holding at time T-1 or before, and the events ιcancelled, δcancelled and ιoffer that occur at time T.

4.4 Internal Events Rules

An internal event rule is a rule that defines the conditions upon which an internal event happens. Thus, internal event rules allow us to deduce which internal events happen in a given transition. For example, the rules:

ιoffered(C,T) ← ιoffer(C,T)
δoffered(C,T) ← ιcancel(C,T)

are an insertion and a deletion internal event rule, respectively. The first rule states that the occurrence of an ιoffer fact (in this case, the insertion of an offer base fact) induces a corresponding ιoffered fact. The second rule states that the occurrence of a ιcancel fact (again, the insertion of a cancel base fact) induces a corresponding δoffered fact.

We get the internal events rules using a procedure (described in [Oli89,San90]) based on the definitions (1), (2) and (5), replacing $p(X,T)$ by its transition rules, and applying a set of standard simplifications, that may involve the integrity constraints. Application of this procedure to the DCM example gives the internal events rules shown in figure 3.

IDR.1	ιoffered(C,T) ← ιoffer(C,T)
IDR.2	δoffered(C,T) ← ιcancel(C,T)
IDR.3	ιcancelled(C,T1,T) ← offer(C,T1), ιcancel(C,T), T1 < T
IDR.4	ιtakes(S,C,T) ← ιenrolled(S,C,T)
IDR.5	δtakes(S,C,T) ← ιtransfer(S,C,Tc,T)
IDR.6	ιenrolled(S,C,T) ← ιenroll(S,C,T)
IDR.7	ιenrolled(S,C,T) ← ιtransfer(S,Fc,C,T)
IDR.8	ιtransferred(S,C,T1,T) ← enroll(S,C,T1), ιtransfer(S,C,Tc,T), T1 < T.
IDR.9	ιic1(T) ← ιoffer(C,T), offered(C,T-1).
IDR.10	ιic2(T) ← ιtakes(S,C,T), not(offered(C,T-1)), not(ιoffered(C,T)).
IDR.11	ιic2(T) ← takes(S,C,T-1), not(δtakes(S,C,T)), δoffered(C,T).
IDR.12	ιic2(T) ← ιtakes(S,C,T), δoffered(C,T).
IDR.13	ιic3(T) ← ιenroll(S,C,T), takes(S,C,T-1).
IDR.14	ιic4(T) ← ιtransfer(S,Fc,Tc,T), takes(S,Tc,T-1).
IDR.15	ιic5(T) ← ιtransfer(S,Fc,Tc,T), not(takes(S,Fc,T-1)).
IDR.16	ιic6(T) ← ιcancel(C,T), not(offered(C,T-1)).
IDR.17...22	ιic(T) ← ιic$j$(T) j=1..6

Fig.3. Internal events model of the DCM example.

5 Generating Plans

5.1 Our Approach

In this section we will apply the internal events model (IEM) for generating a set of base facts (a plan) able to perform a transition between two given initial and final states of the IB. The equivalent problem in the operational approach is generating a sequence of operations that change the IB from an initial state to a final state.

This problem is very important, because many questions about the correctness of a DCM can be translated into instances of this problem [Pet77]. For example, the designer can ask whether there exist some events sequences leading to an illegal state. If it is so, this might suggest the need for refinements in the integrity constraints. As another example, the designer could ask which are the different ways (plans) to reach some legal state. If some plan is not valid, it could suggest the need for refinements in the deductive rules and/or the integrity constraints [VeF85].

Stated more precisely, the problem is: Given an initial state, defined by an initial time t_i and a set IBF of base facts, and the final state defined by a final time t_f and a goal G, obtain one or more event sequences able to perform the transition between both states.

For example, if we have $t_i = 3$, $t_f = 5$,

IBF = {offer(c1,1), enroll(john,c1,3)}
G(5) ← takes(john,c2,5),takes(peter,c2,5)

a possible plan could be:

P_1 = {offer(c2,4),transfer(john,c1,c2,5),enroll(peter,c2,5)}
or also:
P_2 = {offer(c2,4),enroll(john,c2,5),enroll(peter,c2,5)}

Our approach to this problem consists in generating a subplan for each of the $t_f - t_i$ time points comprised in the interval [t_i, t_f], starting at time t_f and ending at time t_i. At the stage corresponding to time T, we have a goal G(T) that we want to reach and we obtain a subplan P(T) (events that must occur at time T) and a previous goal PG(T-1) that must be true at time T - 1. A plan is successful if PG(t_i) holds in the initial state.

Checking whether PG(t_i) holds in the initial state is a particular case of the problem of checking the effect of events, as described in section 3. Thus, standard SLDNF resolution can be used.

We now focus on the problem to solve at a stage T. We have a goal state G(T) and we want to obtain a subplan P(T) and a previous goal PG(T-1). We will first derive the transition rules of G(T), as explained in the previous section. In general, we obtain n ≥ 1 transition rules, corresponding to n different ways to achieve G(T) using facts holding at time T - 1 and events that occur at T. We denote by TR(G(T)) this set of transition rules.

A subplan P(T) and a previous goal PG(T-1) are sets of literals such that using SLDNF resolution, the goal {←G(T)} succeeds from input set IEM ∪ TR(G(T)) ∪ P(T) ∪ PG(T-1). A subplan P(T) and a previous goal PG(T-1) are obtained by having some failed derivation of IEM ∪ TR(G(T)) ∪ {←G(T)} succeed. This is effected by including in the input set P(T) a ground instance of each positive external event literal selected during the derivation, and by including in the input set PG(T-1) a ground instance of each non-event literal selected during the derivation.

All possible ways in which a failed derivation of IEM ∪ TR(G(T)) ∪ {←G(T)} can succeed lead to a different P(T) and PG(T-1). Each different P(T) and PG(T-1) may lead, in subsequent stages, to a different successful plan or to a contradictory state.

In order to ensure that a generated plan satisfies integrity constraints, the initial goal state $G(t_f)$ should include the literal not(ic(t_f)). Note that if ic does not hold at t_f, it can not hold at any previous time.

The following example illustrates our approach. We give the formal definition of the method in section 5.3.

5.2 An Example

Assume that the initial state is:

t_i=3, IBF={offer(c1,1), enroll(john,c1,3)}

and that we want to reach at time t_f=5 the final goal:

G(5)←takes(john,c2,5), takes(peter,c2,5), not(ic(5))

(Our method also allows to leave undefined the final time t_f but, for purposes of presentation, we will not consider this case here)

We have to obtain the plans (sets of external events) that lead to the final state from the initial state.

At first stage our current goal state is the final state, G(5). We have to determine the previous goal state at time 4, PG(4), and the subplan, P(5), that performs the transition from PG(4) to G(5).

The set of goal transition rules, TR(G(5)), for our current goal state G(5), is:

GTR.1   G(5) ← takes(john,c2,4), not(δ takes(john,c2,5)), takes(peter,c2,4),
              not(δ takes(peter,c2,5)), not(ic(4)), not(ιic(5))

GTR.2   G(5) ← takes(john,c2,4), not(δ takes(john,c2, 5)), ιtakes(peter,c2,5),
              not(ic(4)), not(ιic(5))

GTR.3   G(5) ← ιtakes(john,c2,5), takes(peter,c2,4), not(δtakes(peter,c2,5)),
              not(ic(4)), not(ιic(5))

GTR.4   G(5) ← ιtakes(john,c2,5), ιtakes(peter,c2,5), not(ic(4)), not(ιic(5))

623

Possible previous goals, PG(4), and subplans, P(5), can be obtained by making a failed SLDNF derivation of IEM ∪ TR(G(5)) ∪ {←G(5)} succeed. This is shown in figure 4, where the circled labels are references to the rules of the method, defined in section 5.3.

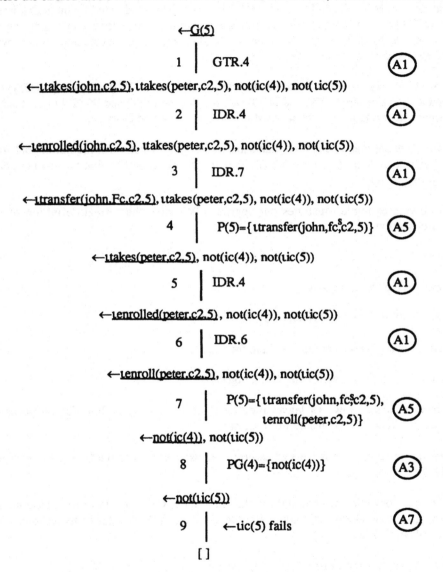

Fig.4. Example.

Steps 1, 2, 3, 5 and 6 are SLDNF resolution steps where rules of IEM and TR(G(5)) act as input clauses. We may have several alternative rules to resolve with. For example, at step 3, rule IDR.6 could have been used as input clause instead of IDR.7. Each alternative may lead to a different plan.

At steps 4 and 7, selected literals are ιtransfer(john,Fc,c2,5) and ιenroll(peter,c2,5), respectively. In order to get a successful derivation they should be included in the input set and used as input clauses. As they are external events literals, they are included in the subplan set, P(5). As literal ιtransfer(john,Fc,c2,5) is not ground we would have to add to P(5) an existentially quantified literal ∃Fc (ιtransfer(john,Fc,c2,5)), that cannot be directly used in a resolution based system. Thus, we have to replace existentially quantified variables in it with skolem constants: ιtransfer(john,fc^s,c2,5). In the following, symbols as $x^s,y^s,t^s,...,$will be skolem constants.

At step 8, the selected literal is not(ic(4)). As it is a non-event literal, it is included in the previous goal set PG(4).

At step 9, selected literal is not(ιic(5)). In order to get a successful derivation, SLDNF-search space must fail finitely for { ←ιic(5)} ∪ IEM ∪ TR(G(5)) ∪ P(5) ∪ PG(4). We show in figure 5 failure for ←ιic(5).

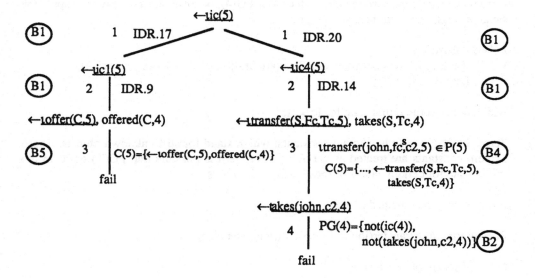

Fig.5. Example.

In the first step a branch in the SLDNF-search space appears for every integrity constraint of the example, although only two branches are shown here. In the left branch, steps 1 and 2 are SLDNF resolution steps where rules of the IEM act as input clauses. At step 3 the branch fails because there is no fact in the input set P(5) to resolve with the selected literal. This current goal is included in a condition set C(5) to check that later on, during the derivation process, new additions to P(5) do not make this branch succeed.

In the right branch, steps 1 and 2 are SLDNF resolution steps where rules of the IEM act as input clauses. At step 3 a fact from the subplan set P(5) is used as input clause. We include the current goal in the condition set C(5) to check that later on, during the derivation process, new additions to P(5) do not make this branch succeed. At step 4 the selected literal is non-event. The negation of it is included in the previous goal set PG(4) to ensure failure for it.

After completing the tree in figure 5, P(5) remains unchanged:

$P(5)=\{\iota transfer(john,fc^s,c2,5), \iota enroll(peter,c2,5)\}$

and PG(4) is:

$PG(4)=\{not(ic(4)), offered(c2,4), not(takes(peter,c2,4)), not(takes(john,c2,4)),$
$\qquad takes(john,fc^s,4)\}$

Then, in the initial derivation of figure 4, we obtain the empty clause and first stage is finished obtaining P(5) and PG(4) as mentioned above.

At second stage, new current goal state G(4) is PG(4), obtained at first stage. We apply the same process, just described, and we get:

$P(4)=\{\iota offer(c2,4)\}$
$PG(3)=\{not(ic(3)), not(takes(peter,c2,3)),not(takes(john,c2,3)), takes(john,fc^s,3),$
$\qquad not(offered(c2,3))\}$

which holds in the initial state for $fc^s=c1$.

Terms in PG(T) may be skolem constants, which stand for still unknown objects. These skolem constants are treated as variables, because it is possible that PG(T) holds in the initial state for certain values of those skolem constants.

From above, the obtained plan is:

$P=\{\iota offer(c2,4), \iota transfer(john,c1,c2,5), \iota enroll(peter,c2,5)\}$

Other plans are obtained similarly.

5.3 Our Method

In this section, we give a formal definition of the method illustrated in the above example.

The plan will be generated by obtaining a subplan for each of the time points comprised in the interval $[t_i,t_f]$. At the stage corresponding to time T, we have a goal G(T) that we want to reach and we obtain a subplan P(T) (events that must occur at time T) and a previous goal PG(T-1) that must be true at time T - 1. A plan is successful if $PG(t_i)$ holds in the initial state.

Let G(T) be the current goal state. P(T) will be the subplan that makes the transition from previous goal state PG(T-1) to G(T) if there exists a *constructive derivation* from $(\leftarrow G(T)$ {} {} {}) to ($\Box$ P(T) C(T) PG(T-1)). A constructive derivation, described below, derives a consistent subplan P(T) and previous goal PG(T-1). Consistency will be ensured by consistency derivations.

In order to define constructive and consistency derivations we will need the following conventions:

- Goal literal is a literal corresponding to the predicate associated to the current goal state (G(T)).
- Non-event literal is a literal correspondig to a base, derived or inconsistency predicate.
- s(L) is the result of skolemising literal L, that is, replacing all its existentially quantified variables in it with skolem constants. For example, $s(\iota transfer(john,Fc,c2,5)) = \iota transfer(john,fc^s,c2,5)$
- To homogenise a clause is to transform it into an equivalent one that has no constant symbols in its head atom and no variable symbol occurs more than once in its head atom. For example, the homogenised clause equivalent to $\iota transfer(john,fc^s,c2,5)$ is $\iota transfer(john,Y,c2,5) \leftarrow Y=fc^s$

Constructive Derivation Description

A constructive derivation from $(G_1(T)\ P_1(T)\ C_1(T)\ PG_1(T))$ to $(G_n(T)\ P_n(T)\ C_n(T)\ PG_n(T-1))$ via a safe selection rule R, that selects literals not corresponding to evaluable predicates with priority, is a sequence:
$(G_1(T)\ P_1(T)\ C_1(T)\ PG_1(t-1)), (G_2(T)\ P_2(T)\ C_2(T)\ PG_2(T-1)),..., (G_n(T)\ P_n(T)\ C_n(T)\ PG_n(T-1))$
such that for each i>1, $G_i(T)$ has the form $\leftarrow L_1,...,L_k$, $R(G_i(T))=L_j$ and $(G_{i+1}(T)\ P_{i+1}(T)\ C_{i+1}(T)\ PG_{i+1}(T-1))$ is obtained according to one of the following rules:

A1) If L_j is a positive internal event or goal literal then $G_{i+1}(T)=S$, $P_{i+1}(T)=P_i(T)$, $C_{i+1}(T)=C_i(T)$ and $PG_{i+1}(T-1)=PG_i(T-1)$, where S is the resolvent of some clause in IEM or TR(G(T)) with $G_i(T)$ on the selected literal L_j.

A2) If L_j is a positive, non-event literal then $G_{i+1}(T)=S$, $P_{i+1}(T)=P_i(T)$, $C_{i+1}(T)=C_i(T)$ and $PG_{i+1}(T-1)=PG_i(T-1) \cup \{s(L_j)\}$, where S is the resolvent of $s(L_j)$ with $G_i(T)$.

A3) If L_j is a negative, ground and non-event literal then $G_{i+1}(T)= \leftarrow L_1,... ,L_{j-1}, L_{j+1},..., L_k$, $P_{i+1}(T)=P_i(T)$, $C_{i+1}(T)=C_i(T)$ and $PG_{i+1}(T-1)=PG_i(T-1)\cup\{L_j\}$.

A4) If L_j is a ground and evaluable literal then $G_{i+1}(T)= \leftarrow L_1 ,..., L_{j-1}, L_{j+1},..., L_k$, $P_{i+1}(T)=P_i(T)$, $C_{i+1}(T)=C_i(T)$ and $PG_{i+1}(T-1)=PG_i(T-1)\cup\{L_j\}$.

A5) If L_j is a positive, external event literal and $C_i(T)=\varnothing$, then $G_{i+1}(T)=S$, $P_{i+1}(T)=P_i(T)\cup\{s(L_j)\}$, $C_{i+1}(T)=C_i(T)$ and $PG_{i+1}(T-1)=PG_i(T-1)$, where S is the resolvent of $s(L_j)$ with $G_i(T)$.

A6) If L_j is a positive, external event literal, $C_i(T)=\{\leftarrow Q_1,...,\leftarrow Q_k,..., \leftarrow Q_n\}$ and there exist *consistency derivations*
from $(\{\leftarrow Q_1\}\ P_i(T) \cup\{s(L_j)\}\ C_i(T)\ PG_i(T-1))$ to $(\{\ \}\ P^1(T)\ C^1(T)\ PG^1(T-1))$, ...,
from $(\{\leftarrow Q_k\}\ P^{k-1}(T)\ C^{k-1}(T)\ PG^{k-1}(T-1))$ to $(\{\ \}\ P^k(T)\ C^k(T)\ PG^k(T-1)))$, ... ,

from $(\{\leftarrow Q_n\} P^{n-1}(T) C^{n-1}(T) PG^{n-1}(T-1))$ to $(\{ \} P^n(T) C^n(T) PG^n(T-1))$,
then $G_{i+1}(T)=S$, $P_{i+1}(T)=P^n(T)$, $C_{i+1}(T)=C^n(T)$ and $PG_{i+1}(T-1)=PG^n(T-1)$, where S is
the resolvent of $s(L_j)$ with $G_i(T)$.

A7) If L_j is a negative internal or external event literal "not(Q)" and there exists a
consistency derivation from $(\{\leftarrow Q\} P_i(T) C_i(T) PG_i(T-1))$ to $(\{ \} P'(T) C'(T) PG'(T-1))$
then $G_{i+1}(T) = \leftarrow L_1,..., L_{j-1}, L_{j+1},..., L_k$, $P_{i+1}(T)=P'(T)$, $C_{i+1}(T)=C'(T)$ and $PG_{i+1}(T-1)=PG'(T-1)$.

The step corresponding to rule A1) is an SLDNF resolution step. At steps corresponding
to rules A2), A3) and A4), non-events literals are added to the previous goal set PG(T-1)
and used as input clauses. This is done in order to have a failed derivation of IEM $\cup$
TR(G(T)) $\cup$ $\{\leftarrow G(T)\}$ succeed. In case A5) external events are added to the subplan set
P(T) and used as input clauses if condition set C(T) is empty. This is also done in order to
have a failed derivation of IEM $\cup$ TR(G(T)) $\cup$ $\{\leftarrow G(T)\}$ succeed. In case A6) external
events are added to the subplan set P(T) and used as input clauses if consistency for each
condition in C(T) can be ensured having these events in P(T). This may require in some
cases the inclusion of new elements in P(T), C(T) and/or PG(T-1). This is also done in
order to have a failed derivation of IEM $\cup$ TR(G(T)) $\cup$ $\{\leftarrow G(T)\}$ succeed. In case A7)
consistency for negative events literals is ensured. Again, this may require additions to
P(T), C(T) and/or PG(T-1).

There are different ways in which a constructive derivation can succeed. Each one may lead
to different plans.

Consistency Derivation Description

A consistency derivation from $(F_1(T) P_1(T) C_1(T) PG_1(T))$ to $(F_n(T) P_n(T) C_n(T)$
$PG_n(T-1))$ via a safe selection rule R, that selects literals not corresponding to evaluable
predicates with priority, is a sequence:
$(F_1(T) P_1(T) C_1(T) PG_1(T-1)),(F_2(T) P_2(T) C_2(T) PG_2(T-1)),...., (F_n(T) P_n(T) C_n(T)$
$PG_n(T-1))$
such that for each i>1, $F_i(T)$ has the form $\{\leftarrow L_1,..., L_k\} \cup F'_i(T)$ and *for some* j=1...k,
$(F_{i+1}(T) P_{i+1}(T) C_{i+1}(T) PG_{i+1}(T-1))$ is obtained according to one of the following rules:

B1) If L_j is a positive and internal event literal then $F_{i+1}(T)=S' \cup F'_i(T)$ where S' is the
set of all resolvents of clauses in IEM with $\leftarrow L_1,..., L_k$ on the literal L_j, $P_{i+1}(T)=P_i(T)$,
$C_{i+1}(T)=C_i(T)$ and $PG_{i+1}(T-1)=PG_i(T-1)$.

B2) If L_j is a ground and non-event literal then $F_{i+1}(T)=F'_i(T)$, $P_{i+1}(T)=P_i(T)$,
$C_{i+1}(T)=C_i(T)$ and $PG_{i+1}(T-1)=PG_i(T-1)\cup\{not(L_j)\}$.

B3) If L_j is a ground and evaluable literal then $F_{i+1}(T) =F'_i(T)$, $P_{i+1}(T) =P_i(T)$,
$C_{i+1}(T)=C_i(T)$ and $PG_{i+1}(T-1) =PG_i(T-1) \cup\{not(L_j)\}$.

B4) If L_j is a positive and external event literal then $F_{i+1}(T) = S' \cup F'_i(T)$ where S' is the
set of all resolvents of homogenised facts in P(T) with $\leftarrow L_1,...,L_k$ on the literal L_j, and $[]$
$\notin S'$, $P_{i+1}(T)=P_i(T)$, $C_{i+1}(T)=C_i(T)\cup\{\leftarrow L_1,..., L_k\}$ and $PG_{i+1}(T-1)=PG_i(T-1)$.

B5) If L_j is a positive and external event literal and there are no homogenised facts in $P(T)$ that can be unified with L_j, then $F_{i+1}(T)=F'_i(T)$, $P_{i+1}(T)=P_i(T)$, $C_{i+1}(T)=C_i(T)\cup\{\leftarrow L_1,..., L_k\}$ and $PG_{i+1}(T\text{-}1)=PG_i(T\text{-}1)$.

B6) If L_j is a ground, negative and external event literal "not(Q)" and $Q\in P_i(T)$ then $F_{i+1}(T)=F'_i(T)$, $P_{i+1}(T)=P_i(T)$, $C_{i+1}(T)=C_i(T)$ and $PG_{i+1}(T\text{-}1)=PG_i(T\text{-}1)$.

B7) If L_j is a ground, negative and internal or external event literal "not(Q)" and there exists a *constructive derivation* from $(\{\leftarrow Q\}\ P_i(T)\ C_i(T)\ PG_i(T\text{-}1)\ )$ to $(\Box\ P'(T)\ C'(T)\ PG'(T\text{-}1)\ )$ then $F_{i+1}(T)=F'_i(T)$, $P_{i+1}(T)=P'(T)$, $C_{i+1}(T)=C'(T)$ and $PG_{i+1}(T\text{-}1)=PG'(T\text{-}1)$.

Step corresponding to rule B1) is a SLDNF resolution step. In cases B2) and B3) the negation of non-event literals is added to the previous goal set PG(T-1). This is done in order to make a successful SLDNF branch fail. The branch can be dropped because failure for it is ensured. In case B4) we resolve with a fact from current subplan set P(T). In case B5) current branch already fails and it can be dropped. In cases B4) and B5) we include the current goal to the condition set C(T) to ensure that later additions to P(T) do not make this branch succeed. In case B6) the current branch already fails and thus it can be dropped. In case B7) the selected literal is a negative event literal, the current branch will be dropped if there exists a constructive derivation for the negation of the selected literal. This ensures failure for it.

Consistency derivations do not rely on the particular order in which selection rule R selects literals, since in general, all the possible ways in which a conjunction $\leftarrow L_1,...,L_k$ can fail should be explored. Each one may lead to a different plan.

5.4 Comparison with other Work

To our knowledge, there is no similar work, in the deductive approach, to the one presented here. For this reason, we only give a brief comment on the work done in the operational approach.

The method proposed by Furtado et al. is based on an extension of Warren's algorithm [War74]. The most significant difference that we see between this method and ours, is that our method also allows to include in a plan two or more external events that occur at the same time. The equivalent solution in the operational approach would be to require the simultaneous execution of two or more operations, which is not allowed.

Thus, in the example given in section 5.2 we have obtained the plan P= { ιoffer(c2,4), ιtransfer(john,c1,c2,5), ιenroll(peter,c2,5)}, which means that two external events (ιtransfer, ιenroll) occur at time 5. This solution is not obtained in Furtado et al's method.

In [Cos91] we compare our method with Kowalski's method [Kow79], using the well-known "blocks world" model as example.

6 Conclusions

We have presented a new method for reasoning about deductive conceptual models of information systems. The method consists of two parts: checking the effects of events on the Information Base, and generating plans able to perform a transition between two states of the Information Base.

In our method, checking the effect of events is based on the use of standard SLDNF resolution and, thus, can be implemented directly in Prolog.

We have shown that the problem of generating a plan is strongly related to the view update problem in deductive databases. Our method is based on the use of the internal events model, and a simple extension of the SLDNF procedure allows us to obtain all valid plans.

Our method provides at least the same reasoning capabilities of the methods developed for the operational approach in the last years. Thus, we consider our method as a significant step in the development and acceptance of the deductive approach to conceptual modelling of information systems.

Use of our method may be very useful during conceptual models validation. We hope that, by exploiting the reasoning capabilities provided by our method, we can improve the important task of model validation in information systems engineering.

Our future plans will focus on development of heuristics that help to reduce the search spaces generated during plan generation.

Acknowledgements

We would like to thank Enric Mayol, Joan Antoni Pastor, Carme Quer, Maria Ribera Sancho, Jaume Sistac, Ernest Teniente, Carme Torras and Toni Urpí for many useful comments and discussions on an earlier draft of this paper.

This work has been supported by the CICYT PRONTIC program project TIC 680.

References

[ABC82] Adrion,W.R.;Branstad, M.A.;Cherniavsky,J.C. "Validation, verification and testing of computer software", ACM Computing Surveys, Vol. 14, No. 2, June 1982, pp. 159-192.

[BuO86] Bubenko,J.; Olivé,A. "Dynamic or temporal modelling?. An illustrative comparison", SYSLAB Working Paper No. 117, University of Stockholm, 1986.

[Bub86] Bubenko,J.A. "Information system methodologies - A research view". In Olle,T.W.; Sol,H.G.;Verrijn-Stuart,A.A. (Eds.) "Information systems design methodologies: improving the practice", North-Holland, 1986, pp. 289-318.

[CFT91] Casanova,M.A.;Furtado,A.L.;Tucherman,L. "A software tool for modular database design", ACM TODS, Vol. 16, No. 2, June 1991, pp. 209-235.

[Cos91] Costal,D. "An approach to validation of Deductive Conceptual Models", Proc. of the Second International Workshop on the Deductive Approach to Information Systems and Databases, Aiguablava (Catalonia), September 1991, pp. 50-72.

[FuC90] Furtado,A.L.; Casanova,M.A. "Plan and schedule generation over temporal databases", Proc. of the 9th International Conference on Entity-Relationship Approach, Lausanne, 1990, pp. 235-248.

[FuM84] Furtado,A.L.; Moura,C.M.O. "Expert helpers to data-based Information Systems", First International Workshop on Expert Database Systems, 1984.

[GMN84] Gallaire,H.; Minker,J.;Nicolas,J.M. "Logic and databases: A deductive approach". ACM Computing Surveys, Vol. 16, No. 2, June 1984, pp. 153-185.

[Kow79] Kowalski,R.A. "Logic for problem solving", North-Holland, 1979.

[LlT84] Lloyd, J.W.; Topor,R.W. "Making Prolog more expressive". J. Logic Programming, 1984, No.3, pp. 225-240.

[LTP91] Loucopoulos,P.;Theodoulidis,B.;Pantazis,D. "Business rules modelling: conceptual modelling and object-oriented specifications". In Van Assche, F.; Moulin,B.;Rolland,C. (Eds.) "Object oriented approach in information systems", North-Holland, 1991, pp. 323-342.

[Lun82a] Lundberg, B. "IMT- An information modelling tool", In Schneider,H.-J.; Wasserman, A.I. (Eds.) "Automated tools for information systems design", North Holland, 1982, pp. 21-30.

[Lun82b] Lundberg, B. "On correctness of information models", SYSLAB Report No. 11, Chalmers Univ. of Technology, June 1982.

[Oli86] Olivé,A. "A comparison of the operational and deductive approaches to conceptual information systems modelling", Proc. IFIP-86, Dublín, pp. 91-96.

[Oli89] Olivé,A. "On the design and implementation of information systems from deductive conceptual models", Proc. of the 15th VLDB, Amsterdam, 1989, pp. 3-11.

[Pet77] Peterson,J.L. "Petri nets", ACM Computing Surveys, Vol. 9, No.3, September 1977, pp. 223-252.

[San90] Sancho,M.R. "Deriving an internal events model from a deductive conceptual model", Proc. of the International Workshop on the Deductive Approach to Information Systems and Databases, S'Agaró (Catalonia), 1990, pp. 73-92.

[TeO92] Teniente, E; Olivé, A. "The Events Method for View Updating in Deductive Databases", Proc. of the International Conference EDBT'92, Vienna, 1992.

[VeF85] Veloso,P.A.S.; Furtado,A.L. "Towards simpler and yet complete formal specifications", Proc. of the IFIP Working Conference on Theoretical and Formal Aspects of Information Systems, 1985, pp. 175-189.

[War74] Warren,D.H.D. "WARPLAN: a system for generating plans" - Memo 76 - University of Edinburgh, 1974.

The Basic Query Machine of the KIWIS system‡

N. Leone, A. Mecchia, G. Rossi, P. Rullo

CRAI - Loc. S. Stefano, 87036 Rende (Italy)

Abstract. KIWIS is an advanced environment for large database systems which supports knowledge-based applications and provides a seamless integration of information coming from different external sources. The system relies on a new knowledge representation and manipulation language, called LOCO, that is based on a tight integration between the object-oriented and the logic programming paradigm. The implementation of LOCO is supported both by a top-down and a bottom-up executor, allowing great flexibility and suitability for large knowledge based applications. This paper describes the basic implementation principles as well as the integrated architecture of the Basic Query Machine (BQM) - the module of KIWIS in charge of implementing the bottom-up model of execution of a class of LOCO programs. The structure of such programs (called *stratified*), amenable of an efficient bottom-up evalutation even in case of data intensive applications, is discussed in details. The mechanism for a strict cooperation with the top-down evaluator, is also presented.

1. Introduction

KIWIS is an advanced environment for large database systems which supports knowledge-based applications and provides a seamless integration of information coming from different external sources ([KIWIS89,VL90,Ahl91]).

The system relies on a new knowledge representation and manipulation language, called LOCO [LVVS90], that is based on a tight integration between the object-oriented and the logic programming paradigm. In addition, the language supports features such as defeasible and default reasoning, making it suitable also for AI-flavored applications (e.g. expert systems).

The overall architecture of the system is shown in Figure 1.1.

The *Abstraction Layer* (AL) and the *Basic Query Machine* (BQM) [LMRR91] provides the necessary support for the native KIWIS language, LOCO, by implementing respectively backward (top-down) and forward (bottom-up) chaining. The rationale of having two different execution strategies is twofold: the bottom-up engine ensures the proper termination of fully declarative LOCO programs, granting an efficient execution also with large amount of data; on the other hand, the top-down evaluator supports the execution of general LOCO programs (even if termination is not granted), including updates, metaprogramming and extra-logical predicates. Thus, the coexistence of top-down and bottom-up engines becomes one of the relevant features of the KIWIS system, allowing great flexibility, suitability for large knowledge based

---

‡ Research partially supported by *EEC* in the framework of ESPRIT II project EP2424 "KIWIS".

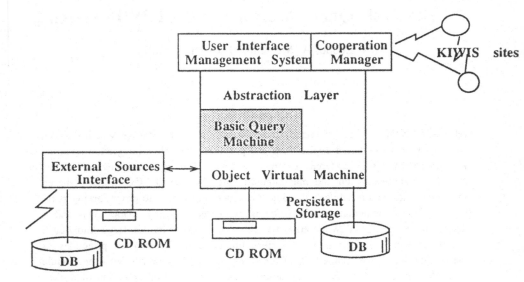

Figure 1.1: Overall KIWIS Architecture

applications.

Both AL and BQM can rely on the *Object Virtual Machine* (OVM) for the efficient management of complex objects both in main and secondary memory. On the other hand, based on the AL and BQM services, the *User Interface Development System* (UIDS) supports customizable views on the data together with several interaction paradigms of increasing complexity [SLT90,STVDT91].

Finally, two kinds of "hooks" to external information sources represent a valuable channel for the import, export, and (re-)usage of existing data.

In one case, the *External System Interface* (ESI) provides an extendible, read-only interface to a variety of external information sources (e.g. traditional, text or picture databases and applications, possibly residing on remote systems). Alternatively, the *Cooperation Manager* (CM) allows to define KIWIS as a federation [AJ90] of loosely coupled (KIWIS) knowledge bases, to form a network for information sharing and cooperation without a commitment to a centrally maintained global schema.

The aim of this paper is to describe the design of the BQM (as bottom-up machine) and its interaction with the AL (as top-down machine). We start, in the next Section, with an informal description of the query capabilities supported by LOCO. Then, Section 3 presents the BQM language, i.e. a class of LOCO programs (indicated as *stratified*) that are amenable of an efficient bottom-up evaluation. Finally, Section 4 illustrates the relevant aspects of the actual BQM architecture. For details on some basic implementation principles, the reader is referred to the Appendices.

2. Language Overview

This section gives an informal presentation of the main features of a (fully declarative) subset of the LOCO language.

As already pointed out, LOCO is a fresh attempt of enhancing the logic programming paradigm with some of the most relevant Object Oriented (OO) features [LVVS90]. From the deductive approach, LOCO maintains a clearly defined semantics along with declarative query capabilities. On the other hand, from the OO field, the notions of object identity, structured object, and (multiple) inheritance are formally accomodated into the language as first class features. On top of this, non-monotonic and default reasoning are introduced in the language following some recent proposals [GL90,GS90,KS90,LSV90] on negative logic programs (i.e. allowing negation in the head of rules).

The language presented here, that we call *Extended Ordered Logic (EOL)*, fully captures the query capabilities of the LOCO language and is a direct evolution of the *Ordered Logic (OL)* programming. The main extention of EOL with respect to OL boils down to a sort of message passing mechanism. More formal and detailed discussions about OL can be found in [LSV90,LV90,Lae90,LR91].

As a very basic starting point, an EOL program consists of a number of *objects*, each one identified by a (unique) name and composed of a set of rules possibly with negative head literals. We briefly recall that a rule is a statement of the form $L_0 \leftarrow L_1, \ldots, L_n$, where $L_0, L_1, \ldots, L_n$ are literals. L_0 is the *head literal* while the set of literals $L_1, \ldots, L_n$ constitutes the *body* of the rule. A rule with an empty body is also called *fact*. A positive (negative) literal has the format $p(X)$ $(\neg p(X))$ where X is a list of arguments and p $(\neg p)$ is a literal symbol. We will often denote simply by p a generic literal symbol, either positive or negative.

Example 2.1. *(objects)*
$$fred = \{ \ name(\text{"Fred"}).$$
$$married :- wife(X).$$
$$wife(sally). \ \}$$

fred, is the object identifier; the literal symbols *name*, *married*, and *wife* are used to define the properties of *fred*. In particular, the facts *name*("Fred"), and *wife*(*sally*) hold along with the property *married* which is inferred by the rule *married* :- *wife*(X). No negative literals appear in *fred*. □

In short, an object is a logical theory or, mainly according to personal taste and background, one might imagine facts and rules instead of, e.g., instance variables and methods, respectively. In the above example, *name* could be seen as an instance variable whose value is *Fred*, and *married* as a boolean instance variable. Further, the rule *married* :- *wife*(X) might represent a method for 'computing' the property *married*.

Inheritance is a central characteristic of the EOL language. The knowledge of an object is not confined exclusively to its own rules: a simple and general specificity relation (sub/super-object) is used to model how rules filter down from one object to another.

Example 2.2. *(inheritance)* Consider the following program, where *fred* is now a sub-object of *person*. (Note: each object is preceeded by the list of its immediate super-objects).

$$person \quad = \{ \quad married :- wife\,(Y).$$
$$(person) \quad fred \quad = \{ \quad wife\,(sally).$$
$$name\,("Fred").\ \}$$

It should be intuitively clear that the properties of *fred* have not changed from the previous example. The rule for *married* is inherited from *person* so that *married* can be inferred for *fred*. On the other hand, no property holds for *person* as it misses the necessary facts for any valid inference. □

Concluding, each object has its own perception of the knowledge base, given by its local rules plus some *global* rules, that is, those of the objects that are connected to it via the sub-object links. However, it is possible for an object, to refer explicitly to the properties of another object. This is achieved by allowing, within rules' bodies, *extended literals* of the form $X.p$, where X is either an object identifier or a variable and p is a literal. Intuitively, an extended literal $X.p$ should be read as "p is true at object X" or "the property p of the object X".

Example 2.3. *(extended literals)*

$$fred \ = \{ \quad wife\,(sally).$$
$$child\,(john).\ \}$$
$$sally \ = \{ \quad husband\,(fred).$$
$$child\,(X) :- husband\,(Y),Y.child\,(X).\ \}$$
$$john \ = \{\ \ \}$$

The program describes a married couple, *fred* and *sally*, with only one child, *john*. Instead of declaring explicitly *john* as *sally*'s child, we use a rule with an extended literal. The rule $child\,(X) :- husband\,(Y),Y.child\,(X).$ says that for each husband Y of *sally*, the child X of Y is also a child of *sally*. Thus, since $husband\,(fred)$ holds in *sally* and $child\,(john)$ is true at object *fred*, it is possible to infer $child\,(john)$ for *sally*. □

Notice how the extended literals mimic the message passing mechanism of object-oriented languages; indeed, $Y.child\,(X)$ can be seen as a message to all Y objects, asking for the value of the *child* property. Consistently, a query to an EOL program is an extended literal, e.g. $sally.child\,(X)$ asks for all X values of the *child* property for *sally*.

Let us now turn our attention to the treatement of contradictions. As we shall see, contradictions are mastered by two simple rules, namely *overruling* and *defeating*, driven by the relationships between the involved objects.

Example 2.4. *(overruling)*

$$person \quad = \{ \ taxPayer.\ \}$$
$$(person) \quad unemployed = \{ \ \neg taxPayer.\ \}$$
$$(unemployed) \quad tom \quad = \{\ \}$$
$$(person) \quad john \quad = \{\ \}$$

The property *taxPayer* acts as a "default": it is visible from all *person*'s sub-objects and it holds unless explicitly contradicted. In fact, *taxPayer* is true for *person* and for *john*. On the contrary, only the property ¬*taxPayer* holds for *tom* and *unemployed*, and the property *taxPayer* is rejected or, as we say, *overruled*. The rationale of such a preference rule is that more specific information is certainly more reliable than inherited, more general properties. □

Unlikely the situation above, where the ordering between the involved objects suggests an intuitive solution to contradiction handling, there are many real-world situations that are intrinsically ambiguous. The well known *Nixon Diamond* example [Tou86], shown next, illustrates a case of ambiguity coming from the multiple inheritance.

Example 2.5. *(defeating)*

$$quaker \quad = \{ \ pacifist. \ \}$$
$$republican = \{ \ \neg pacifist. \ \}$$
$$(quaker \ republican) \ nixon \quad = \{ \ \}$$

The program states: quakers are pacifist, republicans are not pacifist, nixon is both a quaker and a republican. Now, consider the question: is nixon a pacifist ? There is no correlation between *republican* and *quaker* and, actually, no indication of which point of view should be thrusted: the network is perfectly ambiguous and both conclusions are rejected or, as we say, *defeated*. □

The above examples can be exploited for a further comment on the sub/super-object relation. As a matter of fact, it turns out that such a relation is able to capture both classification and generalization hierarchies. For instance, in the Example 2.4 the objects *person* and *unemployed* could be viewed as a sort of class objects, whereas *john* and *tom* constitute the class population of resp. *person* and *unemployed*; hence, *tom* could be considered an *instance−of unemployed*, while *unemployed IS−A person*.

It is worth noting that the language actually supports true negation instead of negation by failure, i.e., a negative fact can be inferred only if explicitly derived by a rule of the program, so that any negative information is as much valuable as a positive one.

Example 2.4. *(true negation)*

$$person = \{ \ taxPayer. \ \}$$
$$(person) \quad tom \quad = \{ \ \neg taxPayer :- \neg rich. \ \}$$

The meaning of this program is that *tom* is a *taxPayer*. The reason is that the failure to prove *rich* is not sufficient to infer ¬*rich* and, consequently, ¬*taxPayer*. □

3. Stratified programs

For clarity's sake, in this section we restrict ourselves to EOL programs where no extended literal appears. Such programs are known in literature as Ordered Logic programs [LSV90,LV90,Lae90,LR91] (OL programs, for short). Then, we single out a meaninful class of OL programs, that we call *stratified programs*. The extension of the notion of stratified program to cope with the presence of extended literals is rather immediate and it is discussed in Appendix 1.

A formal semantics for OL, based on an extension of the well-founded semantics of traditional logic programming [VGRS88], has been defined in [LMRR91, LR91]. In particular, a bottom-up model of computation of such a semantics is given as a suitable adaptation of the algorithm presented in [Van89] for classical logic programs. Unfortunately, as in that case, it turns out that the computation of the well-founded model is quite demanding.

It is possible, however, to specialize the general method and make it very efficient for a meaningful class of programs, called stratified OL programs ([LMRR91,LR91]).

Typically, a stratified program shows a two-level structure: the definition of a property belongs to a certain object, while the exceptions (i.e. conflicting rules) belong only to its subobjects. In a sense, the notion of stratification can be intended as a way to detect when an OL program has a simple structure w.r.t. the treatment of contradiction so that its well-founded model can be computed in a monotonic fashion.

We illustrate the basic intuition by an example.

Example 3.1.

$$
\begin{array}{lll}
& person & = \{ \; taxPayer. \; \} \\
(person) & unemployed & = \{ \; \neg taxPayer :- \neg rich. \; \} \\
(unemployed) & tom & = \{ \; \neg rich. \; \} \\
(person) & john & = \{ \; \}
\end{array}
$$

The evaluation of *tom*'s properties could proceed as follows: first, we derive the fact $\neg rich$; then we infer $\neg taxPayer$ from the rule $\neg taxPayer :- \neg rich.$ defined in *unemployed*. Thereafter, *taxPayer* is derived through the rule in *person*, but, since $\neg taxPayer$ has already been inferred, *taxPayer* is discarded. Actually, $\neg taxPayer$, and $\neg rich.$ are the only facts holding for *tom* (they are the *well-founded* model for *tom*).
The reason why this approach works correctly in this case is that the above OL program has a syntactic structure ensuring the existence of a bottom-up rule evaluation ordering that preserves the "precedence" of more specific over more general rules (e.g. the precedence of the rule $\neg taxPayer :- \neg rich.$ w.r.t. *taxPayer.*). Thus, we say that the program for *tom* is stratified. $\square$

Now, let P_o denote the set of rules defined at o and all its superobjects: this corresponds to the program visible by the object o. Given two literal symbols q_1, and q_2 appearing in P_o, we say that q_1 *depends–on* q_2, denoted by $(q1,q2)$, if either:

1) q_2 appears in the body of a rule for q_1, or

2) q_1 and q_2 are complementary literal symbols [1], defined by rules r_1 and r_2 (resp.), and $o_{def}(r_1)$ is not a sub-object of $o_{def}(r_2)$.

where $o_{def}(r)$ denotes the object where r appears.

Example 3.2. The program P_{tom} of example 3.1 is composed by the following rules: *taxPayer. $\neg taxPayer :- \neg rich. \; \neg rich.*
The depends-on relation for such a program gives $(\neg taxPayer, \neg rich)$ by condition 1), and $(taxPayer, \neg taxPayer)$ by condition 2), as $o_{def}(taxPayer.) = person$ is not a sub-object of $o_{def}(\neg taxPayer :- \neg rich) = unemployed$.

---

[1] i.e., either $q_1 = \neg q_2$ or $q_2 = \neg q_1$.

Let us now consider the program P_{nixon} of example 2.5. The depends-on relation gives: ($\neg pacifist,pacifist$) and ($pacifist,\neg pacifist$) as *quaker* is not a sub-object of *republican* and viceversa. $\square$

At this point we can give the definition of *dependency graph* for an object o. Given the program P_o for o, the associated *dependency graph* DG_o is a directed graph such that: i) the nodes are the literal symbols appearing in P_o, and ii) there is an arc from node q_1 to q_2 iff q_1 depends-on q_2.

Figure 3.1 shows the dependency graphs for the objects *tom* of Example 3.1, and *nixon* of Example 2.5.

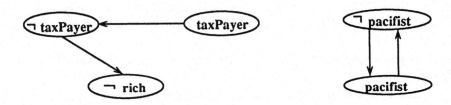

Figure 3.1: DG_{tom} *and* DG_{nixon}

Hence, the dependency graph associated to an object o is a compact representation of the KB, as it is perceived by o. Now, let us denote by $DG_{o.p}$ the subgraph of DG_o that consists of the node p and all nodes that are reachable from p (in DG_o). We denote by $P_{o.p}$ the program consisting of all rules (of P_o) whose head literals label the nodes of $DG_{o.p}$. Thus, a program $P_{o.p}$ is *stratified* if no cycle of $DG_{o.p}$ contains two complementary literal symbols.

Example 3.4 Consider the following program:

$$person \quad = \{ \; taxPayer.$$
$$citizen \; :- \; taxPayer.$$
$$\neg citizen \; :- \; alien. \; \}$$
$$(person) \quad unemployed = \{ \; \neg taxPayer \; :- \; \neg rich. \; \}$$
$$(unemployed) \quad tom \quad = \{ \; \neg rich. \; \}$$

The dependency graph DG_{tom} is shown in Figure 3.2. Notice that the program $P_{tom.taxPayer}$ is stratified, while $P_{tom.citizen}$ is not, as the graph $DG_{tom.citizen}$ (which is equal to DG_{tom}) contains a cycle with two complementary literal symbols, namely *citizen* and $\neg citizen$. $\square$

We are now ready to single out a convenient evaluation order of the rules of a stratified program, by devising a total ordering called *stratification*.

Given $DG_{o.p}$, let us build a new, cycle-free graph $\overline{DG}_{o.p}$ obtained by collapsing each strongly connected components of $DG_{o.p}$ into a single node of $\overline{DG}_{o.p}$ [2]. There exists a topological sort $<C_1, \ldots, C_n>$ of the nodes of $\overline{DG}_{o.p}$ (i.e., such that if there is

---

[2] accordingly, there is an arc (C_i, C_j) in $\overline{DG}_{o.p}$ if there exists at least an arc (n_i, n_j) in $DG_{o.p}$ where $n_i \in C_i$ and $n_j \in C_j$.

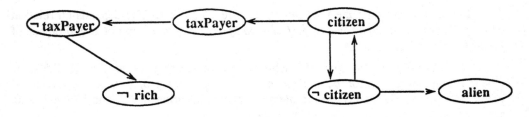

Figure 3.2: DG_{tom}

an arc from C_i to C_j in $\overline{DG}_{o.p}$, then $i < j$), that induces a totally ordered partition $S = <S_n, \ldots, S_1>$ of $P_{o.p}$, where S_i is the set of rules whose head literal symbols are in C_i.

Given a stratified program $P_{o.p}$, the partition S is called *stratification* and each S_i is a *stratum*.

The notion of stratification is crucial for the bottom-up evaluation of a program $P_{o.p}$. Indeed, as in traditional logic programming, the process proceeds (bottom-up) from the "lower" strata to the "upper" ones. The facts that are derived for a stratum S_i are used as input data for any stratum S_j such that $i < j$. In addition, contradictions can be easily solved taking into account that literals derived from "lower" strata are more reliable. In fact, since in a stratified program rules with complementary head literal symbols appear in different strata, we are guaranteed that while solving a rule for $o.p$, either (i) no rule for $\neg p$ appears in $P_{o.p}$, as $o.p$ does not depend on $o.\neg p$; or (ii) all rules for $o.\neg p$ have been already solved as they are in "lower" strata. Hence, contradictions can be solved by simple set difference.

The *stratified* naive algorithm for OL programs is shown in Figure 3.3

Example 3.5 A stratification for $P_{tom.taxPayer}$ is $<\{\neg rich.\}, \{\neg taxPayer :- \neg rich.\}, \{taxPayer.\}>$. Given such a stratification, the stratified algorithm follows the computation order intuitively shown in example 3.1. $\Box$

4. BQM Architecture

As mentioned in the introduction, the Abstraction Layer provides a top-down evaluation of general LOCO programs. However, the actual execution is supported by a dedicated Warren Abstract Machine. Hence, to this respect, the main task of the AL is to translate a LOCO program into a persistent description of the objects, generate WAM code realizing the application, and manage the WAM execution.

The BQM, in turn, is devoted to the bottom-up evaluation of a meaningful class of LOCO programs, that we called stratified. The general framework in which AL and BQM interact is shown in Figure 4.1: whenever a stratifed (sub)query is found during the top-down WAM evaluation of a query, the BQM is invoked for its bottom-up execution. The result of such a computation is then returned (one tuple at-a-time) to the WAM.

Two main distinct blocks constitute the BQM architecture: the *Static Compiler* and the *Run-Time Environment*, interfaced through the *BQM Metaschema*. Given that

---

The Stratified Naive Algorithm

INPUT: a query $o.p(\overline{X})$ and a stratification $<S_1, \ldots, S_n>$ for the program $P_{o.p}$
OUTPUT: the answer to the query
METHOD: the algorithm computes ordinately the fix-point of every stratum S_i by means of the functions $fixPoint$ and $evalRules$.

```
function fixPoint(S_i, I)
        begin
                repeat
                        I̅ := I;
                        I := evalRules (S_i I̅);
                until I = I̅;
                return(I);
        end;

function evalRules({r_1, . . . ,r_m}, I)
        begin
                for each rule r_i do
                        let o'.p'(t) be derived by r_i with the facts available in I
                                if I does not contain the complementary of o'.p'(t) then
                                        I := I∪{o'.p'(t)};
                end
                return(I);
        end;

begin {main}
        I := ∅;
        for i:=1 to n do
                I := fixPoint (S_i ,I);
        return({o.p(t)∈I s.t. unifies with o.p(X̅)} );
end.
```

Figure 3.3

---

most of the intensional information (clauses, classes, etc) is rather stable, the aim of the static analysis is to provide the run time environment with a suitably compact representation of such a knowledge. In particular — given the information gathered by the AL compiler into the *AL metaschema* (i.e. classes' hierarchy, clauses, rules, etc.) — the Static Compiler recognizes all stratified programs and stores in the BQM metaschema the result of its compilation.

The BQM Metaschema is the natural interface between the Static and the Run-Time Environment: it is constructed by the former and consulted by the latter. The main goal of the Metaschema design has been to allow a straightforward retrieval of

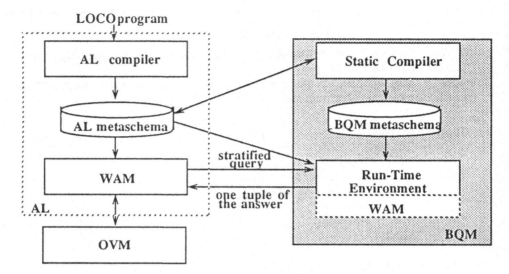

Figure 4.1: Architecture of the Basic Query Machine

programs and their stratifications.

The BQM Run-Time Environment is automatically and transparently activated by the WAM for each query on a stratified program. By using the BQM and AL Metaschema, it retrieves the LOCO program, produces an equivalent flat DATALOG program, and performs an optimized bottom-up evaluation. The crucial advantage of such a choice is that it allows the application of already consolidated optimization techniques for deductive databases. The mapping is rather straightforward and it is shown in Appendix 2.

As to the AL-BQM coupling, one of the main concerns is that the WAM, as top-down machine, consumes one tuple at a time, fetching new tuples on backtracking, while the BQM, as bottom-up machine, computes the whole answer at once. As we shall see, a simple mechanism will allow the BQM to save the computed answer and to return each tuple on WAM demand.

The remainder of this section gives more details about the BQM modules and the AL-BQM interaction.

4.1. The Static Compiler

The goal of the Static Compiler is threefold: i)for each literal symbol $o.p$, determine if the associated program $P_{o.p}$ is stratified, ii)for each stratified program, save the stratification along with enough information for a subsequent fast retrieval of the program itself, and iii)modify the AL metaschema by building up rules that allow the WAM to invoke the BQM only for stratified subprograms.

As a first task, the Static Compiler builds a compact symbolic representation of the whole KB based on the notion of dependency graph. Clearly, the analysis is restricted to the intentional part of the KB (a more precise distinction between classes and instances in the framework of LOCO implementation is reported in Appendix 2).

In order to determine the sets of mutually recursive literal symbols (called clusters), the strongly connected components of the dependency graph are singled out, by using the Tarjan algorithm [Tar72]. Then, the condition of stratification of a program $P_{o.p}$ is checked, by verifying the absence of complementary literal symbols in each cluster of $P_{o.p}$. The relevant information concerning the recognized stratified programs are saved in the BQM metaschema. It is composed by two relations, namely *bqmPred* and *dependsOn*. The first relation describes all stratified literal symbols while the second one represents, in a compact way, the depends-on relation.

At this point the Static Compiler sets up the activation of the Run-Time Environment through the mechanism of AL external predicates. Such a mechanism represents the standard interface between the AL and external modules, allowing to associate a non-AL function to a predicate. In our case, the external unary predicate *bqm* constitutes the interface between the AL and the Run-Time Environment. In particular, for each *o.p* such that $P_{o.p}$ is stratified, the Compiler replaces the result of the AL compilation for *p* at the object *o* with the simple *meta* rule:

$$p(\bar{X}) :- bqm(p(\bar{X})).$$

As a consequence, the subsequent WAM code generation will produce a call to the main entry of the Run-Time Environment, whenever this is appropriate.

4.2. The Run-Time Environment

The BQM Run-Time Environment is activated by the WAM and is composed by two main blocks under the overall control of the *BQM manager* (see Figure 4.2): the *Dynamic Compiler*, that produces a (optimized) flat DATALOG program with negation for the query resolution; the *Executor*, a fix-point machine currently implemented on the WAM;

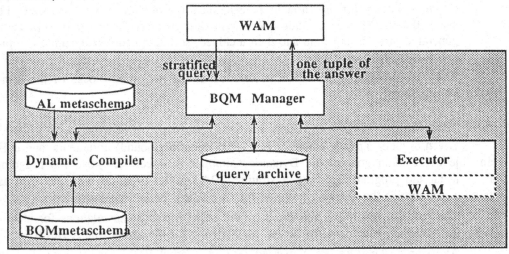

Figure 4.2: Architecture of the Run-Time Environment

The Run-Time Environment is invoked in three possible cases:

first call

a query on the literal symbol $o.p$ with binding pattern b is fired for the first time. In this case, the BQM manager activates the Dynamic Compiler for the dynamic compilation and optimization. Then, the Executor first produces WAM code for the implementation of the fix-point of the optimized program and the construction of the whole answer relation, and then invokes the WAM for the actual execution. Thereafter, a cursor on the answer relation is created and its first tuple is returned to the calling WAM environment. Additionally, the WAM code for the triple $<o,p,b>$ is saved in the Query Archive.

backtracking

a query on $o.p$ is still active, but the set of tuples of the (already computed) answer have not been all consumed. This case occurs during the top-down WAM execution of a conjunction like $...o1.p(X),X.q(Y)...$, where $o1.p(X)$ has been solved by the BQM. In fact, each time that $X.q(Y)$ backtracks, a new tuple of the answer to the query $o1.p(X)$ is required to the BQM. By means of a valid cursor associated to the query, the BQM is able either to return a new tuple from the answer relation, or to fail if no more tuples are available.

archived query

a query on $o.p$, with a given binding pattern, has been previously (dinamically) compiled, and then *archived*. Thus, the BQM manager immediately retrieves from the Query Archive (see Figure 4.2) the address of the corresponding WAM code, and requires its execution to the WAM with the actual query binding. As for a 'first call', the first tuple is returned. A typical situation is represented by a conjunction of the form $...o1.p(X,Y),o2.q(Y,Z)...$, where the subquery $o2.q(Y,Z)$ is repeatedly passed (from the WAM) to the BQM, each time with a different binding for the variable Y. But, since the binding pattern is always the same, the WAM code for this query (with the given binding pattern) has been generated just the first time and then archived, so that no further dynamic compilation is required.

The next subsections contain a description of the two main blocks of the Run-Time Environment.

4.2.1. Dynamic Compiler

Given a query $o.p(\bar{X})$, where $\bar{X}$ is a list of (possibly bound) arguments, and o is an object, the main goal of the Dynamic Compiler is threefold: i)load the program $P_{o,p}$; ii)flat the program $P_{o,p}$ into a stratified DATALOG program with negation as failure; iii)optimize the resulting program for an efficient bottom-up execution.

The program loading is supported by the BQM Metaschema relations for identifying the necessary rules, and by the AL Metaschema for the actual rule retrieval.

Afterwards, the rules are converted into an internal BQM format, according to the technique presented in Appendix 2.

At this point, existing techniques for efficient bottom-up implementation of stratified DATALOG programs can be applied. To this aim, some rewriting techniques, derived from deductive databases [SDMPDN87], based on the *magic* and the *counting* [BMSU86,BR87b,SZ87,SZ89] methods, are used. Such a rewriting produces two groups of rules: the first one exploits the binding propagation by computing sets (called *magic sets*) of facts that are relevant for the query evaluation; the second group contains the original rules opportunely modified so that their evaluation is restricted by such sets. Safety issues are also taken into account by a careful ordering of the goals in the rules. The same techniques have been succesfully employed in the previous ESPRIT project KIWI [KIWI88], as well as in the LDL [NT88] and NAIL! [MUV86] systems.

4.3. Executor

The Executor is based on a bottom-up evaluation technique which results from the combination of the semi-naive method [BR87a] with the query/subquery approach [Vie86]. The advantage of the semi-naive method w.r.t. a pure (naive) bottom-up computation is that of cutting off a number of duplicated computations that are performed by the naive strategy, where the same tuples may be recomputed over and over. On the other hand, the query/subquery strategy improves on the straight bottom-up computation by allowing binding propagation.

As it has been already pointed out, the WAM is, for the current prototype, the 'final' target (or executor) of the BQM programs. Hence, the main task of the Executor is to enforce, on a top-down evaluator (i.e. the WAM), a bottom-up execution. The technique is well known and it is based on a careful use of some procedural features of Prolog, eg. rule ordering, cut and fail, asserting and retracting facts and suitable flags. A detailed description of such a technique can be found in [SDMPDN87].

Clearly, besides of the generation of the appropriate WAM code, the module is also in charge of the final activation of the WAM interpreter.

References

[ABW88] Apt, K., Bair, H., and Walker, A., "Towards a Theory of Declarative Knowledge", *Foundations of Deductive Databases and Logic Programming*, Minker, J. (ed.), Morgan Kaufman, Los Altos, 1987, pp. 89-148.

[Ahl91] Ahlsen, M., Johannesson, P., Laenens, E., Leone, N., Rullo, P., Rossi, G., Staes, F., Tarantino, L., Van Beirendonck, L., Van Cadsand, F., Van Sant, W., Van Slembroeck, J., Verdonk, B., Vermeir, D. (ed.), "The KIWIS Knowledge Base Management System", in *Proceedings of the third Int. conference CAiSE'91*, Trondheim, Norway, may 1991.

[AJ90] Ahlsen, M., and Johannesson, P., "Contracts in Database Federations" in Int'l Working Conf. on Cooperating Knowledge Based Systems, Keele, Springer, 1990

[BMSU86]Bancilhon, F., Maier, D., Sagiv, Y., and Ullman, J. D., "Magic Sets and Other Strange Ways to Implement Logic Programs", *Proceedings of the 5th ACM SIGMOD-SIGACT Symp. on Principles of Database Systems*, 1986.

[BR87a] Balbin, I., and Ramamohanarao, K., "A Generalization of the Differential Approach to Recursive Query Evaluation", *Journal of Logic Programming*, 4(3), pp. 259-262, 1987.

[BR87b] Beeri, C. and Ramakrishnan, R., "On the Power of Magic", in *Proc. 6th ACM SIGMOD-SIGACT Symp. on Principles of Databases Systems, 1987, pp. 269-283.*

[GL90] Gelfond, M. and Lifschitz, V. "Logic Programs with Classical Negation", *Proc.of 7th ICLP*, Jerusalem, 1990, pp 579-597

[GS90] Greco, S. and Saccà, D. "Negative Logic Programs", *Proc. of North American Logic Programming Conference* , 1990.

[KIWI88] KIWI Team, *A System for Managing Data and Knowledge Bases*, ESPRIT Project 1117, in Proceedings of the ESPRIT Technical Week, North-Holland eds., 1988

[KIWIS89]The KIWIS team, "The KIWI(s) project: past and future", in Proc. of 6th ESPRIT Conf., 1989, pp. 594-603

[KS90] Kowalski, R.A. and Sadri,. F. "Logic Programs with Exceptions ", *Proc.of 7th ICLP*, Jerusalem, 1990, pp 598-616

[Lae90] Laenens, E., "Foundations of ordered logic", Ph.D. thesis, Univ. of Antwerp, 1990.

[LMRR91]Leone, N., Mecchia, A., Rossi, G. and Rullo, P., "Revised Design Documentation of the Basic Query Machine", *Tech. Report BQM5/91, ESPRIT project P2424 KIWIS, 1991.*

[LR91] Leone, N., and Rossi, G., "Well-founded Semantics and Stratification for Ordered Logic Programs", submitted for publication, 1991

[LSV90] Laenens, E., Saccà, D., and Vermeir, D., "Extending Logic Programming", *Proc. of ACM SIGMOD*, May 1990.

[LV90] Laenens, E., and Vermeir, D., "A Fixpoint Semantics for Ordered Logic", *Journal of Logic and Computation*, vol.1, N.2, december, 1990, pp. 159-185.

[LVVS90] Laenens, E., Verdonk, B., Vermeir, D., and Saccà, D., "The LOCO Language: Towards an Integration of Logic and Object Oriented Programming". in Proc. of the Workshop on Logic Programming and Non-Monotonic Logic, Austin, Texas, 1990, pp. 62-72

[MUV86] Morris, K.1, Ullman, J.D., and Van Gelder, A. "Design Overview of the Nail! system" Third Int'l Conf. on Logic Programming, pp. 554-568

[NT88] Naqvi, S. and Tsur, S. *A Logical Data Language for Data and Knowledge Bases*, Computer Science Press, New York, 1988.

[SDMPDN87]
Sacca' D., Dispinzeri M., Mecchia A., Pizzuti C., Del Gracco C., Naggar P. *The Advanced Database Environment of the KIWI System*, Database Engineering, Vol. 10, No. 4, Dec. 87

[SLT90] Staes, F., Laenens, E., and Tarantino, L., "Towards a Flexible Interaction Environment for Knowledge Bases", in Proc. of 1990 IEEE Workshop on Visual Languages and Computing, Skokie, IL, October, 3-6, 1990.

[STVDT91] Staes, F., Tiems, B., Van Cadsand, L., D'Atri, A., and Tarantino, L., "Revised Design Documentation of the User Interface Prototype", Tech. Report UI4/91, ESPRIT project P2424 KIWIS, 1991

[SZ87] Sacca, D. and Zaniolo, C., "Magic Counting Methods", Proceedings of the 1987 ACM SIGMOD conference, 1987, pp. 49-59

[SZ89] Sacca, D. and Zaniolo, C., "The Generalized Counting Method of Recursive Logic Queries for Databases", *Theoretical Computer Science*, no. 62, Nov. 1989, pp. 187-220.

[Tar72] R. Tarjan, Depth First Search and Linear Graph Algorithms, SIAM J. Comput., Vol. 1, No. 2, 1972

[Tou86] Touretzky, D.S., *The Mathematics of Inheritance Systems*, Pitman London, 1986.

[Van89] Van Gelder, A., "The Alternating Fixpoint of Logic Programs with Negation" *Proc. ACM Symp. on Principles of Database Systems, 1989*.

[VGRS88] van Gelder A., Ross, K. and Schlipf, J.S., "Unfounded Sets and Well-Founded Semantics for General Logic Programs", *Proc. ACM SIGMOD-SIGACT Symp. on Principles of Database Systems*, March 1988, pp 221-230.

[Vie86] Vieille, L., "Recursive Axioms in Deductive Databases: The Query/Subquery Approach", Proc. of the First Int. Conf. on Expert Database Systems, Charleston, 1986, pp. 253-268.

[VL90] Vermeir, D., and Laenens, E., "Advanced Knowledge-Base Environments for Large Database Systems", *Knowledge-Based Systems*, vol.3, n.4, 1990, pp. 215-220

Appendix 1: Stratified Programs with Extended Literals

Because of extended literals, the program P_o does not reduce to the rules coming from o and its super-objects, but has to include a number of rules coming from completely unrelated objects. In order to avoid the collection of totally useless rules, we try to foresee which objects of the KB can be involved in the computation.

To this aim, we first define the *range* of an extended literal symbol $X.q$ as the set of objects equals to: i) $\{o\}$, if X is equal to the object o; ii) the set of all objects that own or inherit a rule for q, otherwise.

Let us consider, as an example, the following EOL program.

$$
\begin{array}{lll}
& o' & = \{ \; p(X) :- q(Y), Y.r(X). \\
& & \quad \neg w(X) :- s(X). \\
& & \quad w(X) :- p(X). \; \} \\
(o') & o & = \{ \; \neg p(X) :- s(X). \; \} \\
(o) & o_1 & = \{ \; q(\bar{o}_1). \; s(a). \; s(b). \; \} \\
& \bar{o} & = \{ \; r(X) :- p(X). \; \} \\
(\bar{o}) & \bar{o}_1 & = \{ \; p(a). \; \} \\
& \hat{o} & = \{ \; r(X) :- p(X). \; \}
\end{array}
$$

According to the above definition, the range of the extended literal $Y.r(X)$, appearing in the rule for p at o', is equal to $\{\bar{o}, \hat{o}\}$ as they are the only objects with rules for r.

At this point, the program P_o associated to the object o can be identified as the set of rules that belong to: i)o and all its super-objects; ii)the programs $P_{o'}$ for each $o' \neq o$ in the range of each extended literal symbol $X.q$ appearing in P_o.

To remark the difference between literal symbols defined on different objects, a generic literal symbol p appearing in a rule of P_o will be denoted by a dot-notation like $t.p$ where $t=o$ if the rule is determined by condition i) above, or $t=o'$ when given by condition ii).

Let us consider again the objects defined in the previous example. In order to determine the program P_o, we first take all rules at o and o'. Thereafter, the same process is iterated for all objects in the range of $Y.r(X)$, yielding, after the inclusion of $P_{\bar{o}}$ and $P_{\hat{o}}$, the following program:

$$
\begin{array}{lll}
o.w(X) :- o.p(X). & o.\neg w(X) :- o.s(X). & \\
o.p(X) :- o.q(Y), \bar{o}.r(X). & o.p(X) :- o.q(Y), \hat{o}.r(X). & o.\neg p(X) :- o.s(X). \\
\bar{o}.r(X) :- \bar{o}.p(X). & \hat{o}.r(X) :- \hat{o}.p(X). &
\end{array}
$$

Notice that the instantiation of the extended literal $Y.r(X)$ has generated two rules for $o.p$, one for each object in its range.

Now, it is not difficult to see that the dot-notation introduced above for denoting a generic literal symbol extends the validity of all definitions given for the stratification, to the presence of extended literals. Thus, the depends-on relation for the program P_o is represented by $(o.w, o.p)$, $(o.\neg w, o.s)$, $(o.w, o.\neg w)$, $(o.\neg w, o.w)$, $(o.p, o.q)$, $(o.p, \bar{o}.r)$, $(o.p, \hat{o}.r)$, $(o.p, o.\neg p)$, $(o.\neg p, o.s)$, $(\bar{o}.r, \bar{o}.p)$, $(\hat{o}.r, \hat{o}.p)$. Consequently, the dependency graph looks like in Figure Notice that the dependency graph for o includes the dependency graphs for $\bar{o}$ and $\hat{o}$.

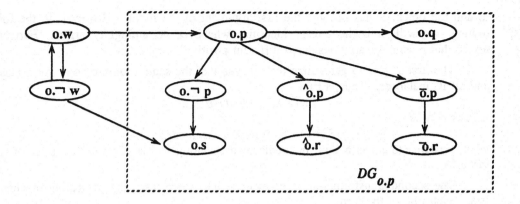

Now, just as shown in Section 3, the programs needed to solve any query on o can be still singled out from the graph, and the stratification can be checked against the dependency graph by taking into account that two complementary literal symbols are of the form $o.p$ and $\neg o.p$. In the example, the programs $P_{o.w}$ and $P_{o.\neg w}$ are not stratified. In fact, the dependency graphs $DG_{o.w}$ and $DG_{o.\neg w}$, which coincide with DG_o, contain a cycle with $o.w$ and $o.\neg w$. On the other hand, the program $P_{o.p}$ is stratified, as it is clear from the dependency graph $DG_{o.p}$ shown in figure.

Appendix 2: From EOL to DATALOG

It has already been shown in [LMRR91,LR91] that a stratified OL program can be constructively transformed into an equivalent (stratified) DATALOG program. In this Appendix, we present, in a step-by-step fashion, the transformation as it has been devised for an actual implementation of EOL programs.

As a preliminary consideration, we note that, for efficiency reasons, it is convenient to introduce a distinction between the *class* and *instance* objects. An instance is an object that i)has only facts in its definition, ii)has no sub-object, and iii)has only one super-object, which is its *class*. All other objects are *classes*. Hence, programs associated to instances are only slightly different from those of their classes. Notice that such a distinction follows the dualism between schemes and instances of the traditional database approach, with the main advantage of limiting the analysis of the KB only to classes.

Now, let us assume that we have identified the (stratified) program $P_{o.p}$ needed to solve a query onto $o.p$, that the program has been divided into cluster of mutually recursive predicates, and that the associated stratification is known. Further, for semplicity, we suppose that each cluster is associated to a unique identifier c.

To begin with, all rules of $P_{o.p}$ are adorned such that each literal $\hat{o}.q(\overline{X})$ appearing in $P_{o.p}$ is rewritten as $q^c(\hat{o},\overline{X})$, where c is the identifier of the cluster $\hat{o}.q$ belongs to and the object $\hat{o}$ has become the first argument of the literal. However, in the following, we will omit the cluster identifier whenever no ambiguity arises. Further, notice that p and $\neg p$ are considered different positive literal symbols.

The first step is to generalize the rules so that the same program holds for a class and all its instances. Thus, a rule

$$q(\hat{o},\bar{X}) :- body(\hat{o},\bar{X}).$$

is rewritten as

$$q(S,\bar{X}) :- body(S,\bar{X}), instance(S,\hat{o}).$$

where $instance(S,\hat{o})$ is a built-in predicate associating to the class $\hat{o}$ the set S of its instances.

The second transformation aims to code into the clauses the overruling mechanism. Each rule of the form

$$q(S,\bar{X}) :- body(S,\bar{X}), instance(S,\hat{o}).$$

such that $P_{o,p}$ contains a rule $\neg q(S,\bar{Y}) :- ..., instance(S,\bar{o})$. where $\hat{o}$ is a super-object of $\bar{o}$, and $\neg q$ denotes the complementary of q, is rewritten as

$$q(S,\bar{X}) :- body(S,\bar{X}), instance(S,\hat{o}), not(\neg q(S,\bar{X})).$$

where not is interpreted as negation as failure.

The above rewritten rule simply states that a fact $q(t)$ can be derived only if the complementary fact $\neg q(t)$ cannot be derived. Notice that such a transformation fully captures the idea of overruling for stratified EOL programs.

An analogous approach is used for dealing with simple cases of non-stratified programs, where the non-stratification is induced by facts defined on the instances. The idea is that, whenever a rule $q(S,X):-body(S,X),instance(S,o1)$ is contradicted by some facts for $\neg q$ declared at any instance of $o1$, then it is rewritten as

$$q(S,X):-body(S,X), instance(S,o1), not(\neg q_{base}(S,X)).$$

where $\neg q_{base}$ will match only the facts for $\neg q$ defined on the instances.

A further transformation involves the management of extended literals. Given a rule $q^c(S,X) :- \cdots, Y.t(Z), \cdots.$ let $o_1,\ldots,o_i$ be the objects in $range(Y.t(Z))$ and let $c_1,\ldots,c_i$ denote the clusters of respectively $o_1.t,\ldots,o_i.t$. Then the rule is rewritten as:

$$q^c(S,X) :- \cdots \bar{t}^k(Y,Z), \cdots.$$
$$\bar{t}^k(S,Z) :- t^{c_1}(S,Z).$$
$$\cdots \qquad \cdots$$
$$\bar{t}^k(S,Z) :- t^{c_i}(S,Z).$$

where $\bar{t}$ is a new literal symbol, added for avoiding a duplication of the original rule (i.e. a rewriting for each t^{c_i}). Moreover, if any t^{c_i} is mutually recursive with q^c (i.e. any $c_i=c$), then $\bar{t}$ gets the cluster identifier c (i.e. $c=k$) and becomes mutually recursive with q^c, otherwise $\bar{t}$ gets a new cluster identifier.

The transformation of the stratified EOL program $P_{o,p}$ into an equivalent DATALOG program is now complete. It is also possible to see that the resulting program is stratified (in classical sense [ABW88]) and that its stratification can be derived from that of the original EOL program.

As a matter of fact, from one hand, the insertion of literals defined only by facts (e.g. *instance*) cannot affect the stratification S of the EOL program; on the other hand, the usage of $not(q)$ in the rules for $\neg q$ implies that such rules belong to a stratum higher than the stratum containing the rules for q: because of overruling, this fact is already granted in S. Finally, the addition of rules for the new literal symbol $\bar{i}^k$ modifies S in a very simple way: the rules for $\bar{i}^k$ are either in the same stratum S_q of the rules for q^c if $k=c$, or in a new stratum that must immediately precede S_q.

Lecture Notes in Computer Science

For information about Vols. 1–504
please contact your bookseller or Springer-Verlag